THE CHINESE
CLASSICS VOLUME 4

THE CHINESE CLASSICS VOLUME 4:

The She King, or the Book of Poetry.

Part 1

By James Legge, D.D.,

In Seven Volumes

Volume 4.,

With

Translation, Critical and Exegetical Notes, Prolegomena, and Copious Indexes.

St. George Press

St. George Press

Edited by the St. George Press Editorial Team

Copyright 2023

ISBN: 9798374722888

This St. George Press edition, published in 2023 republication of first edition of 1871 Volume 4 "The Chinese Classics" Series

Editorial Introduction

The Odes of classic Chinese civilization has greatly fallen out of study in the East and West. It was the pillar of cultured understanding in the wider Far Eastern world for over a thousand years. Generations of Chinese, Koreans, Japanese, and Vietnamese were raised memorizing these works as a mark of education and refinement. With the fall of the traditional order in the 19th and 20th centuries, much of these works have gone out of popularity. They can now often be framed as part of the "old bad things" quoting either Mao or the Japanese Emperor Meiji's Charter oath. The goal of these series of books is to bring back the study of the tradition to give literacy to the modern student of Asia attempting to understand the world as it was known from the Han dynasty until the fall of the traditional order in the 20th century.

This version was selected by our editorial team because of its inclusion of the original text in Chinese, the full indexes, text in English, and copious explanations. James Legge was a famous translator of Chinese civilization into English and is still a key access point of that tradition for modern learners. He studied the tradition while it was still a living tradition with hundreds of millions of adherents. Having this context helps us better understand how it was viewed at its own height.

Our team has put extensive work into making this text legible, with special emphasis on legibility of the Chinese script. Many man hours were committed to make it as clear as possible. As this is a folio reproduction from several original copies, some of the text may still encounter issues. In this first edition, we have done what we can to make it as good as we can within our limitations. Future editions we will continue to improve the quality of the scans, and continue to increase the quality of the text. The text is split into 2 volumes to improve legibility. The first will have James Legge's original introduction, and the second volume will have the full index of Chinese characters. For those who are interested we recommend both volumes together.

St. George Press Editorial Team

stgeorgepress@proton.me

不以文
害辭不
以辭害
志以意
逆志是
爲得之。

MENCIUS, V. Pt. I. iv. 2.

PREFACE.

When the author published his third volume, containing the Book of Historical Documents, in 1865, he hoped to proceed in 1867 to print the Book of Poetry which is only now offered to the public. He was obliged, however, early in that year to return to England, from which he came back to Hongkong in the spring of the past year, prepared to go to press at once with the present volume; but the loss by shipwreck of his printing paper rendered it necessary to defer the commencement of the work till towards the end of the year. The one delay and the other have enabled him to give the translation repeated revisions.

The Book of Poetry was translated into Latin about the year 1733, by Father Lacharme, of the Society of Jesus, but remained in manuscript till 1830, when it was edited by M. Jules Mohl, one of the eminent sinologues of Paris. M. Callery, in the Introduction to his version of the Le Ke, p. xix., has characterized Lacharme's translation as '*la production la plus indigeste et la plus ennuyeuse dont la sinologie ait à rougir.*' The translation is, indeed, very defective, and the notes accompanying it are unsatisfactory and much too brief. The author hopes that the Work which he now offers will be deemed by competent scholars a reliable translation of the original poems. He has certainly spared no labour on the translation, or on the accompanying notes and the prolegomena, to make it as perfect as he could attain to.

One great difficulty which a translator of the Book of Poetry has to contend with is the names of the plants, birds, quadrupeds, fishes, and insects, with which it abounds. To have transferred these to his translation, as Lacharme did, would have greatly abridged the author's labour, but would have been, he conceived, disappointing to his readers. He endeavoured, therefore, to make out from the

descriptions of native writers what the plants, &c., really were;
and in this inquiry he derived great assistance from Dr. J. C.
Hepburn of Yokohama. Having sent to that gentleman a copy of
the Japanese plates to the Book of Poetry, described on p. 180 of
the prolegomena, he was kind enough to go over the whole, along
with Mr. Kramer, an English botanist; and in this way a great many
plants and animals at which there had been only guesses before have
been identified. Where the identification could not be made out, the
author has translated the names by some synonym, from the Pun-
ts'aou or other Work, which could conveniently be given in English.
There remain still a few names of plants and trees which he has been
obliged to transfer. It is to be hoped that sinologues penetrating
to their habitat in the interior of the country will shortly succeed
in identifying them.

The author has to acknowledge anew his obligations to the Rev.
Mr. Chalmers for the indexes of Subjects and Proper names. The
index of subjects is fuller than the corresponding indexes to the
previous volumes, and the author has been struck with its accuracy
and completeness in preparing the chapters of the prolegomena. He
has also made the index of Chinese characters and phrases, at the
request of several friends, more extensive, as regards the references,
than formerly.

Mr. Frederick Stewart, Head master of the Government schools,
has again given his efficient help in correcting the proofs; as also
the Rev. F. S. Turner of the London Missionary Society. Even
with their help and his own assiduous attention, it has not been
possible entirely to avoid typographical mistakes. They will be
found, however, to be few and unimportant.

Volume V., containing the Ch'un Ts'ëw, with the commentary
and narratives of Tso K'ëw-ming complete, has been for several
months in the printers' hands, and will be, it is hoped, ready for
publication, in the autumn of next year.

Hongkong, December 14th, 1871.

CONTENTS

I THE PROLEGOMENA.

CHAPTER I.

THE EARLY HISTORY, AND THE PRESENT TEXT OF THE SHE-KING,

CHAPTER II.

THE SOURCES OF THE ODES AS A COLLECTION. THEIR INTERPRETATION AND AUTHORS. THE PREFACES AND THEIR AUTHORITY............................ 23

CHAPTER III.

THE PROSODY OF THE SHE; THE ANCIENT PRONUNCIATION OF THE CHARACTERS; AND THE POETICAL VALUE OF THE ODES.

CHAPTER IV.

THE CHINA OF THE BOOK OF POETRY, CONSIDERED IN RELATION TO THE EXTENT OF ITS TERRITORY, AND ITS POLITICAL STATE, ITS RELIGION, AND SOCIAL CONDITION.......... 127

CHAPTER V.

LIST OF THE PRINCIPAL WORKS WHICH HAVE BEEN CONSULTED IN THE PREPARATION OF THIS VOLUME.

II. THE BODY OF THE VOLUME.

PART I.

LESSONS FROM THE STATES.

ERRATA.

I. IN THE CHINESE TEXT.

Page.	Column.				Page.	Column.			
35	5, et al.	for 姬 read 姬			196	2	after 中 dele ○.
60	8	after 2d 兮 add ○.			210	8	for 國人 read 歌以
63	8	for 兄弟父母 read			212	6	„ 窈 „ 慢受
		父母兄弟.			237	1	„ 不 „ 亦
79	5	„ 兮 read 桑			257	9	} „ 恆 „ 恆
133	9	„ 寁 „ 寁			470	5 and 7	}
159	5	„ 筍敝 „ 敝筍					

II. CHINESE CHARACTERS IN THE NOTES.

Page.	Column.	Line.			Page.	Column.	Line.		
7	2	5	for 2d 谷 read 木		177	2	4	for 愊 read 愉
80	2	17	„ 彊 „ 彊		191	2	24	„ 室 „ 瑟
115	2	23	„ 迅 „ 迅		307	2	7	„ 隋 „ 蹐
159	2	17	„ 惟 „ 唯		417	1	11	„ 卬 „ 卬

III. CHINESE CHARACTERS IN THE PROLEGOMENA.

Page.	Line.				Page.	Line.			
53	8	after 盧 insert 令			90	7	for 猷 read 鼓
66	11	for 菜 read 采			131	3	„ 昊 „ 旻
87	6	„ 矯 „ 短					

IV. CHINESE CHARACTERS IN INDEX III.

Page.	Column.	Line.			Page.	Column.	Line.		
692	1	4	for 子 read 于		760	1	22	for 荃 read 荏
715	2	8	„ 恆 „ 恆		764	2	31	} „ 裼 „ 裼
728	1	30	„ 梴 „ 梴		765	1	11	}
742	2	23	„ 獲 „ 蕕		777	172d Radical	„ 隹 „ 隹

V. IN THE TRANSLATION.

Page	Line				
170	11		for three	read	thirty.
197	9		„ rouged as	„	as if rouged.
203	1 and 5		„ nephew	„	uncle.
337	2		„ undressed	„	without undressing.
346	1		„ porcelain	„	earthen.
352	4		„ held	„	brought.
376	3		„ flesh	„	blood.
474	1		„ cheek	„	palate.
502	7		„ porcelain	„	earthen.
523	after line 8	insert			Alas! alas for the kingdom!
528	„ „ — 6	„			There is no Spirit I have not sacrificed to.
640	„ „ 7	„			He reverenced God.
144	„ 1		for XXVII read XVII.		
150	„ 1		„ XIII „ VIII.		
335 351	} running heading		„ SEOAU „ SEAOU.		
363	„		„ PIN „ PIH.		

Any mistakes in the Chinese titles of the odes as expressed in Italic letters may be corrected from the table of Contents.

ERRATA.

VI. IN THE NOTES.

Page.	Column.	Line.					Page.	Column.	Line.			
60	1	20	for chose	read close.			359	1	12	for {St. read St. 8. / iii. II. „ ii. III.		
214	1	21	„ callen	„ called.								
231	2	3	„ adjunets	„ adjuncts.			382	2	17	„ IV. „ V.		
243	2	13	„ Kwang	„ Kwan.			525	2	3	„ VIII. „ X.		
260	2	3	„ III.	„ IV.			466	1·	44	after Kuh insert a comma.		
295	1	10	„ xii.	„ xi.								

VII. IN THE INDEXES.

Page.	Column.	Line.			Page.	Column	Line.		
653	1	28	cheek should be palate.		715	2		咀 should be read tah.	
668	2	21	porcelain „ earthen.		728	1	31	for III. read IV.	

VIII. IN THE PROLEGOMENA.

From p. 96 to 101, in the running heading, change CH. II. APPENDIX III. to CH. III. SECTION I.
„ 102 to 104, „ „ CH. II. APPENDIX III. to CH. III. SECTION II.

PROLEGOMENA.

CHAPTER I.

THE EARLY HISTORY AND THE PRESENT TEXT
OF THE BOOK OF POETRY.
APPENDIX:—SPECIMEN OF ANCIENT POETICAL COMPOSITIONS
BESIDES THOSE IN THE SHE.

SECTION I.

THE BOOK BEFORE CONFUCIUS; AND WHAT, IF ANY,
WERE HIS LABOURS UPON IT.

1. Sze-ma Ts'ëen, in his memoir of Confucius, says:—'The old poems amounted to more than 3,000. Confucius removed those which were only repetitions of others, and selected those which Statements of Chinese scholars. would be serviceable for the inculcation of propriety and righteousness. Ascending as high as Sëeh and How-tseih, and descending through the prosperous eras of Yin and Chow to the times of decadence under kings Yëw and Le, he selected in all 305 pieces, which he sang over to his lute, to bring them into accordance with the musical style of the Shaou, the Woo, the Ya, and the Sung.' This is the first notice which we have of any compilation of the ancient poems by Confucius, and from it mainly are derived all the subsequent statements on the subject.

In the History of the Classical Books in the Records of the Suy dynasty (A.D. 589–618), it is said:—'When odes ceased to be made and collected, Che, the Grand music-master of Loo, arranged in order those

¹ 史記四十六孔子世家第十七:–古者,詩三千餘篇.
及至孔子,去其重,取可施於禮義,上采契后稷,中述殷
周之盛,至幽厲之缺,三百五篇孔子皆弦歌之,以求合
韶武雅頌之音

which were existing, and made a copy of them. Then Confucius expurgated them; and going up to the Shang dynasty, and coming down to the State of Loo, he compiled altogether 300 pieces.'[2]

Gow-yang Sëw (A. D. 1,006—1,071) endeavours to state particularly what the work of expurgation performed by Confucius was. 'Not only,' says he, 'did the sage reject whole poems, but from others he rejected one or more stanzas; from stanzas he rejected one or more lines; and from lines he rejected one or more characters.'[3]

Choo He (A.D. 1,130—1,200), whose own classical Work on the Book of Poetry appeared in A.D. 1,178, declined to express himself positively on the question of the expurgation of the odes, but summed up his view of what Confucius did for them in the following words:—'Poems had ceased to be made and collected, and those which were extant were full of errors and wanting in arrangement. When Confucius returned from Wei to Loo, he brought with him the odes which he had gotten in other States, and digested them, along with those which were to be found in Loo, into a collection of 300 pieces.'[4]

I have not been able to find evidence sustaining these representations, and propose now to submit to the reader the grounds which

These statements not supported by evidence. The view of the author.

prevent me from concurring in them, and have brought me to the conclusions that, before the birth of Confucius, the Book of Poetry existed substantially the same as it was at his death, and that, while he may have somewhat altered the arrangement of its Books and odes, the principal service which he rendered to it was not that of compilation, but the impulse to the study of it which he communicated to his disciples. The discrepancy in the number of the odes as given in the above statements will be touched on in a note.

2. If we place Ts'ëen's composition of the memoir of Confucius in B.C. 100,[5] nearly four hundred years will thus have elapsed be-

[2] 隋書卷三十二志第二十七經籍一：王澤竭而詩亡魯太師摯次而錄之孔子刪詩上采商下取魯凡三百篇   [3] 歐陽修曰刪詩云者非止全篇去也或篇刪其章或章刪其句或句刪其字. Quoted in Choo E-tsun's 經義考卷九十六詩一．   [4] 朱子曰王迹熄而詩亡其存者謬亂失次孔子自衛反魯復得之他國以歸定著為三百篇. Quoted in the 綱領 of the K'ang-he She.   [5] See the prolegomena to vol. III., p. 44, on the age of the Historical Records.

tween the death of the sage and any statement to the effect that he
The groundlessness of the above statements. expurgated a previous collection of poems, or
compiled that which we now have, consisting of
a few over 300 pieces; and no writer in the interval affirmed or implied any such facts.　But independently of this consideration, there
is ample evidence to prove, first, that the poems current before
Confucius were not by any means so numerous as Sze-ma Ts'ëen
says, and, secondly, that the collection of 300 pieces or thereabouts,
digested under the same divisions as in the present Classic, existed
before the sage's time.

3.　[i.] It would not be surprising, if, floating about and current
among the people of China, in the 6th century before Christ, there
The old poems were not numerous. had been even more than 3,000 pieces of poetry.
The marvel is that such was not the case.　But in
the 'Narratives of the States,'[6] a Work attributed by some to Tso
K'ëw-ming,[7] there occur quotations from 31 poems, made by statesmen and others, all anterior to Confucius; and of those poems it
cannot be pleaded that more than two are not in the present
Classic, while of those two one is an ode of it quoted under another
name.　Further, in the Tso Chuen,[8] certainly the work of Tso K'ëw-
ming, and a most valuable supplement to Confucius' own Work of
the Ch'un Ts'ëw, we have quotations from not fewer than 219
poems; and of these only thirteen are not found in the Classic.
Thus of 250 poems current in China before the supposed compilation of the Book of Poetry, 236 are found in it, and only 14 are
absent.　To use the words of Chaou Yih,[9] a scholar of the present
dynasty, of the period K'ëen-lung (A.D. 1,736—1,795), 'If the poems
existing in Confucius' time had been more than 3,000, the quotations found in these two Books of poems now lost should have been
ten times as numerous as the quotations from the 305 pieces said to
have been preserved by him, whereas they are only between a
twenty-first and twenty-second part of the existing pieces.　This is
sufficient to show that Ts'ëen's statement is not worthy of credit.'[10]
I have made the widest possible induction from all existing Records
in which there are quotations of poems made anterior to Confucius,
and the conclusion to which I have been brought is altogether confirmatory of that deduced from the Works of Tso K'ëw-ming.　If

---

6 國語.　　7 Wylie's Notes on Chinese Literature, p. 6.　　8 左傳　　9 趙翼.
10 See the 陔餘叢考, 卷二·一古詩三千之非·

Confucius did make any compilation of poems, he had no such work of rejection and expurgation to do as is commonly imagined.

[ii.]   But I believe myself that he did no work at all to which the name of compilation can properly be applied, but simply adopted an existing collection of poems consisting of 305, or at most of 311 pieces.   Of the existence of the Book of Poetry before Confucius, digested under four divisions, and much in the same order as at present, there may be advanced the following proofs:—

Proofs of the existence of the Book of Poetry before Confucius.

First, in the 'Official Book of Chow,' we are told that it belonged to the grand-master 'to teach the six classes of poems,—the *Fung*, with their descriptive, metaphorical, and allusive pieces, the *Ya*, and the *Sung*.'[11]   Mr Wylie says that the question of the genuineness of the Official Book may be considered as set at rest since the inquiry into it by Choo He, and that it is to be accepted as a work of the duke of Chow, or some other sage of the Chow dynasty.[12]   Without committing myself to any opinion on this point, as I find the passage just quoted in the Preface to the *She* (of which I shall treat in the next chapter), I cannot but accept it as having been current before Confucius; and thus we have a distinct reference to a collection of poems, earlier than his time, with the same division into Parts, and the same classification of the pieces in those Parts.

Second, in Part II. of the *She*, Book vi., ode IX.,—an ode assigned to the time of king Yëw, B.C. 780—770, we have the words,

> ' They sing the *Ya* and the *Nan*,
> Dancing to their flutes without error.'

So early then as the 8th century before our era, there was a collection of poems, of which some bore the name of the *Nan*, which there is nothing to forbid our supposing to have been the Chow-nan, and the Shaou-nan, forming the first two Books of the first Part of the present classic, often spoken of together as the *Nan;* and of which others bore the name of the *Ya*, being probably the earlier pieces which now compose a large portion of the second and third Parts.

11 See the Chow Le, 卷 二 十 三, par. 3:—教 六 詩, 曰 風, 曰 賦, 曰 比, 曰 興, 曰 雅, 曰 頌.   12 Notes on Chinese Literature, p. 4.

Third, in the narratives of Tso K'ëw-ming, under the 29th year of duke Sëang, B.C. 543, when Confucius was only 8 or 9 years old, we have an account of a visit to the court of Loo by an envoy from Woo, an eminent statesman of the time, and of great learning. We are told that, as he wished to hear the music of Chow, which he could do better in Loo than in any other State, they sang to him the odes of the Chow-nan and the Shaou-nan; those of P'ei, Yung, and Wei; of the Royal domain; of Ch'ing; of Ts'e; of Pin; of Ts'in; of Wei; of T'ang; of Ch'in; of Kwei; and of Ts'aou. They sang to him also the odes of the Minor Ya and the Greater Ya; and they sang finally the pieces of the Sung.[13] We have here existing in the boyhood of Confucius, before he had set his mind on learning,[14] what we may call the present Book of Poetry, with its Fung, its Ya, and its Sung. The odes of the Fung were in 15 Books as now, with merely some slight differences in the order of their arrangement;—the odes of Pin forming the 9th Book instead of the 15th, those of Ts'in the 10th instead of the 11th, those of Wei the 11th instead of the 9th, and those of T'ang the 12th instead of the 10th. In other respects the *She*, existing in Loo when Confucius was a mere boy, appears to have been the same as that of which the compilation has been ascribed to him.

Fourth, in this matter we may appeal to the words of Confucius himself. Twice in the Analects he speaks of the odes as a collection consisting of 300 pieces.[15] That Work not being made on any principle of chronological order, we cannot positively assign those sayings to any particular periods of Confucius' life; but it is I may say the unanimous opinion of the critics that they were spoken before the time to which Sze-ma Ts'ëen and Choo He refer his special labour on the Book of Poetry.[16] The reader may be left, with the evidence which has been set before him, to form his own opinion on the questions discussed. To my own mind that evidence is decisive on the points.—The Book of Poetry, arranged very much as we now have it, was current in China long before the sage; and its pieces were in the mouths of statesmen and scholars, constantly quoted by them on festive and other occasions. Poems not included in it there doubtless were, but they were comparatively few. Confucius may

13 See the 左傳,襄二十九年, par. 8.   14 Confucian Analects, II. iv. 1.   15 Confucian Analects, II. ii.; XIII. v.   16 See the 97th chapter of the 經義考, and especially the author's summing up of the evidence on the questions which I have discussed.

have made a copy for the use of himself and his disciples; but it does not appear that he rejected any pieces which had been previously received, or admitted any which had not previously found a place in the collection.

4 Having come to the above conclusions, it seems superfluous to make any further observations on the state-ments adduced in the first paragraph.   If Confucius expurgated no previous Book, it is vain to try and specify the nature of his expurgation as Gow-yang Sëw did.[17] From Sze-ma Ts'ëen we should suppose that there were no odes in the *She* later than the time of king Le, whereas there are 12 of the time of king Hwuy, 13 of that of king Sëang, and 2 of the time of king Ting. Even the Sung of Loo which are referred to by the Suy writer and Choo He are not the latest pieces in the Book. The statement of the former that the odes were arranged in order and copied by Che, the music-master of Loo,[18] rests on no authority but his own;—more than a thousand years after the supposed fact. I shall refer to it again, however, in the next chapter.

Further errors in the state-ments in the first paragraph

5 The question arises now of what Confucius really did for the Book of Poetry, if, indeed, he did anything at all. The only thing from which we can hazard the slightest opinion on the point we have from his own lips. In the Analects, IX. xiv., he tells us:—'I returned from Wei to Loo, and then the music was reformed, and the pieces in the Ya and the Sung all found their proper places.' The return from Wei to Loo took place when the sage was in his 69th year, only five years before his death. He ceased from that time to take an active part in political affairs, and solaced himself with music, the study of the Classics, the writing of the Ch'un Ts'ëw, and familiar intercourse with those of his disciples who still kept about him. He reformed the music,—that to which the poems were sung; but wherein the reformation consisted we cannot tell. And he gave to the pieces of the Ya and the Sung their proper places. The present order of the Books in the Fung, slightly differing, we have seen, from that which was common in his boyhood, may also have now been determined by him. As to the arrangement of the odes in the other Parts of the Work, we cannot say of what extent it was.

Did Confucius then do anything for the Book of Poetry?

17 Every instance pleaded by Sëw in support of his expurgation of stanzas, lines, and characters has been disposed of by various scholars;—particularly by Choo E-tsun, in the note just referred to.   18 When this Che lived is much disputed. From the references to him in Ana. VIII. xv., XVIII. ix., we naturally suppose him to have been a contemporary of Confucius.

6]

What are now called the *correct* Ya precede the pieces called the Ya *of a changed character* or of a degenerate age; but there is no chronological order in their following one another, and it will be seen, from the notes on the separate odes, that there are not a few of the latter class, which are illustrations of a good reign and of the observance of propriety as much as any of the former.　In the Books of the Sung again, the occurrence of the Praise-songs of Loo between the sacrificial odes of Chow and Shang is an anomaly for which we try in vain to discover a reasonable explanation.

6.　While we cannot discover, therefore, any peculiar labours of Confucius on the Book of Poetry, and we have it now, as will be shown in the next section, substantially as he found it already compiled to his hand, the subsequent preservation of it may reasonably

Confucius' service to the *She* was in the impulse which he gave to the study of it.

be attributed to the admiration which he expressed for it, and the enthusiasm for it with which he sought to inspire his disciples.　It was one of the themes on which he delighted to converse with them.[19]　He taught that it is from the odes that the mind receives its best stimulus.[20]　A man ignorant of them was, in his opinion, like one who stands with his face towards a wall, limited in his views, and unable to advance.[21]　Of the two things which his son could specify as particularly enjoined on him by the sage, the first was that he should learn the odes.[22]　In this way Confucius, probably, contributed largely to the subsequent preservation of the Book of Poetry;—the preservation of the tablets on which the odes were inscribed, and the preservation of it in the memories of all who venerated his authority, and looked up to him as their master.

19 Analects, VII. xvii.　　20 Ana., VIII. viii., xvii. IX.　　21 Ana., xvii. X.　　22
Ana. XVI. xiii.

SECTION. II.

The Book of Poetry from the time of Confucius till the general acknowledgement of the present text.

1.　Of the attention paid to the study of the Book of Poetry from the death of Confucius to the rise of the Ts'in dynasty, we

have abundant evidence in the writings of his grand-son Tsze-sze, of
From Confucius to
the dynasty of Ts'in. Mencius, and of Seun K'ing. One of the acknowledged distinctions of Mencius is his acquaintance
with the odes, of which his canon for the study of them prefixed to
my volumes is a proof; and Seun K'ing survived the extinction of
the Chow dynasty, and lived on into the times of Ts'in.[1]

2. The Poems shared in the calamity which all the other classical Works, excepting the Yih, suffered, when the tyrant of Ts'in
issued his edict for their destruction. But I have shown, in the
prolegomena to vol. I., that only a few years elapsed between the
The Poems were all recovered
after the fires of Ts'in. execution of his decree and the establishment of the Han dynasty, which distin-
guished itself by its labours to restore the monuments of ancient
literature. The odes were all, or very nearly all, recovered;[2] and
the reason assigned for this is, that their preservation depended on
the memory of scholars more than on their inscription upon tablets
and silk.[3] We shall find reason to accept this statement.

3 Three different texts of the odes made their appearance early
Three different texts. in the Han dynasty, known as the She of Loo, of
Ts'e, and of Han; that is, the Book of Poetry was recovered from
three different quarters.

[i.] Lëw Hin's catalogue[4] of the Works in the imperial library
of the earlier Han dynasty commences, on the She King, with a
Collection of the three Texts in 28 chapters,[5] which is followed by
two Works of commentary on the Text of Loo.[6] The former of
The Text of Loo. them was by a Shin P'ei,[7] of whom we have some
account in the Literary Biographies of Han.[8] He was a native of
Loo, and had received his own knowledge of the odes from a scholar
of Ts'e, called Fow K'ëw-pih.[9] He was resorted to by many disci-

1 Prolegomena to vol. II., p. 81.   2 In the last section reference was made to the number
of the odes, given by Confucius himself as 300. He might mention the round number, not thinking it worth while to say that they were 305 or 311. The Classic now contains the text of 305
pieces, and the titles of other 6. It is contended by Choo and many other scholars, that in Confucius' time the text of those six was already lost, or rather that the titles were names of tunes only.
More likely is the view that the text of the pieces was lost after Confucius' death. See in the
body of this volume, pp. 267,268.   3 凡三百五篇遭秦火而全者以
其諷誦不獨在竹帛故也;—see Pan Koo's note appended to the catalogue of
Lëw Hin, Section 詩.   4 Proleg. Vol. I. p. 5.   5 詩經二十八卷魯齊
韓三家一漢書三十藝文志.   6 魯故二十五卷;魯說
二十八卷.   7 申培.   8 儒林傳第五十八漢書八十
八   9 浮丘伯.

ples whom he taught to repeat the odes, but without entering into discussion with them on their interpretation. When the first emperor of the Han dynasty was passing through Loo, Shin followed him to the capital of that State, and had an interview with him. The emperor Woo,[10] in the beginning of his reign (B.C. 139), sent for him to court when he was more than 80 years old; and he appears to have survived a considerable number of years beyond that advanced age. The names of ten of his disciples are given, all men of eminence, and among them K'ung Gan-kwoh. A little later, the most noted adherent of the school of Loo was a Wei Hëen, who arrived at the dignity of prime minister, and published 'the She of Loo in Stanzas and Lines.'[11] Up and down in the Books of Han and Wei are to be found quotations of the odes, which must have been taken from the professors of the Loo recension; but neither the text nor the writings on it long survived. They are said to have perished during the Tsin dynasty (A.D. 265—419). When the catalogue of the Suy library was made, none of them were existing.

[ii.] The Han catalogue mentions five different works on the She of Ts'e.[12] This text was from a Yuen Koo,[13] a native of Ts'e, The Text of Ts'e. about whom we learn, from the same chapter of Literary Biographies, that he was one of the Great scholars of the court in the time of the emperor King (B.C. 155—142),[14] a favourite with him, and specially distinguished for his knowledge of the odes and his advocacy of orthodox Confucian doctrine. He died in the next reign of Woo, more than 90 years old; and we are told that all the scholars of Ts'e who got a name in those days for their acquaintance with the She sprang from his school. Among his disciples was the well known name of Hëa-how Ch'e-ch'ang,[15] who communicated his acquisitions to How Ts'ang,[16] a native of the present Shan-tung province, and author of two of the Works in the Han catalogue. How had three disciples of eminence,—Yih Fung, Sëaou Wang-che, and K'wang Häng.[17] From them the Text of Ts'e was transmitted to others, whose names, with quotations from their writings, are scattered through the Books of Han. Neither

[10] 武帝.   [11] 韋賢魯詩章句.   [12] 齊后氏故二十卷; 齊孫氏故二十七卷; 齊后氏傳三十九卷; 齊孫氏傳二十八卷; 齊雜記十八卷.   [13] 轅固.   [14] 景帝.   [15] 夏侯始昌.   [16] 后蒼字近君東海郯人   [17] 翼奉蕭望之匡衡.

text nor commentaries, however, had a better fate than the She of Loo. There is no mention of them in the catalogue of Suy. They are said to have perished even before the rise of the Tsin dynasty.

[iii.] The Text of Han was somewhat more fortunate. The Han catalogue contains the titles of four works, all by Han Ying,[18] whose The Text of Han Ying. surname is thus perpetuated in the text of the She which emanated from him. His biography follows that of How Ts'ang. He was a native, we are told, of the province of Yen, and a 'Great scholar' in the time of the emperor Wăn (B.C. 178—156),[19] and on into the reigns of King and Woo. 'He laboured,' it is said, 'to unfold the meaning of the odes, and published an "Explanation of the Text," and "Illustrations of the She," containing several myriads of characters. His text was somewhat different from the texts of the She of Loo and Ts'e, but substantially of the same meaning.'[19] Of course Han founded a school; but while almost all the writings of his followers soon perished, both the Works just mentioned continued on through the various dynasties to the time of Sung. The Suy catalogue contains the titles of his text and two Works on it;[20] the T'ang those of his text and his Illustrations;[21] but when we come to the catalogue of Sung, published in the time of the Yuen dynasty, we find only the Illustrations, in 10 Books or chapters; and Gow-yang Sëw tells us that in his time this was all of Han that remained. It continues, entire or nearly so, to the present day, and later on in these prolegomena there will be found passages of it sufficient to give the reader a correct idea of its nature.

4. But while these three different recensions of the She all disappeared with the exception of a single fragment, their unhappy fate was owing not more to the convulsions by which the empire was often rent, and the consequent destruction of literary monuments, such as we have witnessed in our own day in China, than to the appearance of a fourth Text which displaced them by its superior A fourth Text; that of Maou. correctness, and the ability with which it was advocated and commented on. This was what is called the Text of Maou. It came into the field later than the others; but the Han catalogue contains the She of Maou in 29 chapters, and a commen-

18 韓故,三十六卷; 韓內傳, 四卷; 韓外傳, 六卷; 韓說,
四十一卷   19 作內外傳, 數萬言, 其語頗與齊魯間
殊, 然歸一也.   20 韓詩二十二卷; 韓詩翼要, 十卷; 韓
詩外傳, 十卷.   21 韓詩二十卷; 韓詩外傳, 十卷.

tary on the text in 30.[22] According to Ch'ing K'ang-shing, the author of this commentary was a native of Loo, known as Maou Hăng or the Greater Maou,[23] who was a disciple, we are told by Luh Tih-ming, of Seun K'ing. The Work is lost.[24] He had communicated his knowledge of the She, however, to another Maou,—Maou Chang, or the Lesser Maou,[25]—who was a 'Great scholar' at the court of king Hëen of Ho-këen.[26] This king Hëen was one of the most diligent labourers in the recovery of the ancient Books, and present-ed Maou's text and the Work of Hăng at the court of the emperor King,—probably in B.C. 129. Chang himself published his 'Ex-planations of the She,'[27] in 29 chapters, which still remains; but it was not till the reign of the emperor P'ing (A.D. 1—5)[28] that Maou's recension was received into the imperial college, and took its place along with those of Loo, Ts'e, and Han.

The Chinese critics have carefully traced the line of scholars who had charge of Maou's text and explanations down to the reign of P'ing;—Kwan Ch'ang-k'ing, Hëae Yen-nëen, and Seu Gaou.[29] To Seu Gaou succeeded Ch'in Këah,[30] who was in office at the court of the usurper Wang Mang (A.D. 9—22). He transmitted his treasures to Sëay Man-k'ing,[31] who himself commented on the She; and from him they passed to the well-known Wei King-chung or Wei Hwang,[32] of whom I shall have to speak in the next chapter. From this time the most famous scholars addicted themselves to Maou's text. Këa Kwei (A.D. 25—101) published a Work on the 'Meaning and Diffi-culties of Maou's She,'[33] having previously compiled a digest of the differences between its text and those of the other three recensions, at the command of the emperor Ming (A.D. 58—75).[34] Ma Yung (A.D. 69—165) followed with another commentary[35];—and we arrive at Ch'ing Heuen, or Ch'ing K'ang-shing, who wrote his 'Sup-plementary Commentary to the She of Maou,' and his 'Chronological

---

[22] 毛詩二十九卷; 毛詩故訓傳三十九卷.   [23] 毛亨,
大毛公.   24 The work is mentioned in a catalogue of the Imperial Library, early in the Sung dynasty; and Choo E-tsun supposes that it was then extant. The editor of the catalogue, however, assigns another reason for the appearance of the title.   25 毛萇, 小毛公.
26 The petty kingdom of Ho-këen embraced three of the districts in the present department of the same name in Chih-le, and one of the two districts of Shin Chow. King Hëen's name was Tih (德).   27 毛氏詩傳二十九卷.   28 平帝.   29 貫長
卿; 解延年; 徐敖.   30 陳俠.   31 謝曼卿   32 衞敬仲,
衞宏.   33 貫逵, 毛詩雜義難.   34 明帝.   35 馬融毛
詩注.

Introduction to the She.'[36]   The former of these two Works complete, and portions of the latter, are still extant.   That the former has great defects as well as great merits, there can be no question; but it took possession of the literary world of China, and after the time of Ch'ing the other three texts were little heard of, while the name of the commentators on Maou's text and his explanations of it speedily becomes legion.   Maou's grave is still shown near the village of Tsun-fuh, in the departmental district of Ho-këen.[37]

5   Returning now to what I said in the 2d paragraph, it will be granted that the appearance of three different and independent texts, immediately after the rise of the Han dynasty, affords the

The different texts guarantee the integrity of the recovered She.   }

most satisfactory evidence of the recovery of the Book of Poetry, as it had continued from the time of Confucius.   Unfortunately only fragments of them remain now; but we have seen that they were diligently compared by competent scholars with one another, and with the fourth text of Maou, which subsequently got the field to itself.   In the body of this Work attention is called to many of their peculiar readings; and

The texts were all taken down at first from recitation.   }

it is clear to me that their variations from one another and from Maou's text arose from the alleged fact that the preservation of the odes was owing to their being transmitted by recitation.   The rhyme helped the memory to retain them, and while wood, bamboo, and silk were all consumed by the flames of Ts'in, when the time of repression ceased scholars would be eager to rehearse their stores.   It was inevitable that the same sounds, when taken down by different writers, should in many cases be represented by different characters.

Even in the existing text the careful reader of my notes will find not a few instances of characters which give the sound, without giving any indication, in their component parts, of the meaning. There are, e. g., 鼠 for 癙, in II. iv. X. 7; 齊 for 粢, in II. vi. VII. 2; 龍 for 寵, in II. ii. IX. 2, et al.; 魚 as the name of a horse, in IV. ii. I. 4; 麋 for 湄, in II. v. IV. 6; 靑 for 菁, in II. viii. IX. 2; et al.   Then again there are many places which even Choo He acknowledges that he does not understand, and out of which a consistent meaning has to be 'chiseled.'   It would not be difficult, I conceive, to produce a Chinese text superior to Maou's, and which

³⁶ 鄭玄· 鄭康成· 毛詩箋; 詩譜·   ³⁷ For many of the particulars in this paragraph, see the supplement to Twan-lin's Cyclopædia, Bk. 200, article 毛萇.

would remove many anomalous meanings out of the dictionary; but it would be interesting only to native scholars, and they would, for the present at least, scout the attempt as presumption on the part of a foreigner. Accepting the text as it exists, we have no reason to doubt that it is a near approximation to that which was current in the time of Confucius.

APPENDIX.

SPECIMEN OF ANCIENT POETICAL COMPOSITIONS BESIDES THOSE WHICH ARE CONTAINED IN THE BOOK OF POETRY.

I have thought it would be interesting to many of my readers to see a good proportion of the ditties, songs, and other versified compositions, which have as high an antiquity attributed to them as the odes of the She. Some of them, indeed, are referred to a much more remote age;—on, to my mind, quite insufficient evidence. Into that question it is not necessary to go. I have taken the pieces from 'The Fountain of old Poems (古詩源),' by Shin Tih-ts'ëen (沈德潛, al. 沈確士), a scholar of the present dynasty, who died in 1769 at the age of 95. His first book contains 100 pieces, all purporting to be anterior to the Han dynasty.

1. *Song of the peasants in the time of Yaou.* From the 帝王世紀.

> We rise at sunrise,
> We rest at sunset,
> Dig wells and drink,
> Till our fields and eat;—
> What is the strength of the emperor to us?

2. *Children's ditty, overheard by Yaou in the streets.* From Lëeh-tsze, (仲尼篇).

> We people are established,
> All by your perfect merit.
> Unconsciously,
> We follow our Emperor's pattern.

3. *A prayer at the winter thanksgiving.* From the Le Ke, XI. ii. 11.

> Clods, return to your place;
> Water, flow back to your ditches;
> Ye insects, appear not;
> Grass and trees, grow only in your marshes.

¹ 擊壤歌-日出而作, 日入而息, 鑿井而飲, 耕田
而食, 帝力于我何有哉.
² 康衢謠-立我蒸民, 莫匪爾極, 不識不知, 順帝
之則.
³ 伊耆氏蠟辭-土反其宅, 水歸其壑, 昆蟲毋作,
草木歸其澤.

4 *Yaou's warning.* From Hwae Nan (**人間訓**).

Be tremblingly fearful:
Be careful night and day.
Men trip not on mountains;
They trip on ant-hills.

5.—7. *Shun intimates his purpose to resign the throne to Yu.* From Fuh-săng's Introduction to the Shoo (**尚書大傳**).

Splendid are the clouds and bright,
All aglow with various light!
Grand the sun and moon move on;
Daily dawn succeeds to dawn.

6. *Response of his eight ministers*

Brilliant is the sky o'er-head,
Splendid there the stars are spread.
Grand the sun and moon move on,
All through you, one man alone.

7. *Rejoinder of Shun.*

The sun and moon move in their orbits;
The stars keep to their paths;
The four seasons observe their turns,
And all the people are truly good.
Oh! such music as I speak of
Corresponds to the power of Heaven,
Leading to worth and excellence;
And all listen to it.
Vigorously strike it up.
Dance high to it!
The splendour [of my work] is done;
I will lift up my robes and disappear.

8. *Shun's Song of the South Wind.* From the Family Sayings (**辯樂解**).

The fragrance of the south wind,
Can ease the angry feelings of my people.

4 堯戒-戰戰慄慄　日謹一日,　人莫躓于山,　而躓
　　于垤.

5 卿雲歌-卿雲爛兮,　糺縵縵兮,　日月光華,　旦復
　　旦兮.

6 八伯歌-明明上天,　爛然星陳,　日月光華,　弘于
　　一人.

7 帝載歌-日月有常,　星辰有行,　四時順經,　萬姓
允誠,　於予論樂,　配天之靈,　遷于賢善,　莫不咸
聽,　鼖乎鼓之,　軒乎舞之,　菁華已竭,　褰裳去之.

8 南風歌-南風之薰兮,　可以解吾民之慍兮.

14]

The seasonableness of the south wind,
Can make large the wealth of my people.

9. *On a jade tablet of Yu.* Source not given.

Chuh-yung presided over the region, and produced my beauty;
Bathed in the sun, washed in the moon, among the precious things I grew.

10. *Ditty of Yu on casting the nine Tripods.* From Mih Teih.

How brilliant the white clouds,
In the north and the south,
In the east and the west!
These nine tripods are made,
And will be transmitted through three dynasties.

11. *An Inscription of the Shang dynasty.* From the Narratives of the States (晉語, 一.)

Small virtue
Is not worth approaching.
It is not to be boasted of,
And will only bring sorrow.
Small amount of emolument,
Is not worth desiring
You cannot get fat on it,
And will only fall into trouble.

12. *Song of the Wheat in Flower.* By the viscount of Ke (Shoo, IV. x.). From the Historical Records (世家, 第八).

The flowers of the wheat turn to spikes;
The rice and millet look bright.
That crafty boy.
Will not be friendly with me!

13. *Song of the Fern-gathering.* By Pih-e and Shuh-ts'e (Ana. V. xxii.). From the Historical Records (列傳第一).

We ascend that western hill,
And gather the thorn-ferns.
They are changing oppression for oppression,

南風之時兮, 可以阜吾民之財兮.
9 禹玉牒辭-祝融司方發其英, 沐日浴月百寶生.
10 夏后鑄鼎綠-逢逢白雲, 一南一北, 一西一東,
九鼎既成, 遷于三國.
11 商銘-嗛嗛之德, 不足就也, 不可以矜, 而祇取
憂也, 嗛嗛之食, 不足狃也, 不能爲膏, 而祇離
咎也.
12 麥秀歌-麥秀漸漸兮, 禾黍油油, 彼狡童兮, 不
與我好兮.
13 采薇歌-登彼西山兮, 采其薇矣, 以暴易暴兮

And do not know their error.
Shin-nung, Yu, and Hëa,
Have suddenly lost their influence.
Whither shall we go?
Ah! we will depart!
Withered is the appointment [of Heaven].

14—19. *Inscription on a bathing vessel.* From the Le of the elder Tae (卷第六).

Than to sink among men,
It is better to sink in the deep.
He who sinks in the deep
May betake himself to swimming.
For him who sinks among men
There is no salvation.

Inscription on a girdle.

The fire being extinguished, adjust your person;
Be careful, be cautious, ever reverent.
Be reverent and your years will be long.

Inscription on a Staff.

Where are you in peril?
In giving way to anger,
Where do you lose the way?
In indulging your lusts.
Where do you forget your friends?
Amid riches and honours.

Inscription on a robe.

[Here is] the toil of silkworms,
And the labour of women's work,
If, having got the new, you cast away the old,
In the end you will be cold.

Inscription on a pencil.

[Look here at] the bushy hair.
If you fall into water, you may be rescued;
If you fall by your composition, there is no living for you.

不知其非矣, 神農虞夏, 忽焉沒分, 吾適安歸矣,
吁嗟徂分, 命之衰矣.

14 盥盤銘-與其溺于人也, 寧溺于淵, 溺于淵 猶
可游也, 溺于人, 不可救也.

15 帶銘-火滅修容, 慎戒必恭, 恭則壽.

16 杖銘-惡乎危, 於忿懥, 惡乎失道, 於嗜欲, 惡
乎相忘, 於富貴.

17 衣銘-桑蠶苦, 女工難, 得新捐故, 後必寒.

18 筆銘-豪毛茂茂, 陷水可脫, 陷文不活.

16]

Inscription on a spear.

You have made the spear, you have made the spear;
And by a moment's want of forbearance
You may disgrace your whole life [with it].
This is what I have heard,
And tell to warn my descendants.

20—26. From the 太平御覽, professing to be extracts from a book of
T'ae-kung Shang-foo, at the beginning of the Chow dynasty.

A writing on a chariot.

Seeking his own ends, one is urgent;
Conveying another, one is slow.
When one's desires are without measure,
Let him turn inwards and deal with himself.

A writing on a door.

Go out with awe;
Come in with fear.

A writing on a shoe.

In walking keep the correct path;
Be not looking out for good luck.

A writing on an ink-stone.

Where the stone and the ink meet, there is blackness.
Let not a perverse heart and slanderous words
Stain what is white.

A writing on a pointed weapon.

A moment's forbearance
Will preserve your person.

A writing on a staff.

Helping a man, be not rash;
Holding up a man, do not wrong.

A writing on a well.

The spring bubbles up,
But in the cold it ceases.

19 矛銘–造矛造矛, 少間弗忍, 終身之羞. 余一人
所聞, 以戒後世子孫

20 書車–自致者急, 載人者緩, 取欲無度. 自致
而反.

21 書戶–出畏之. 入懼之.

22 書履–行必履正, 無懷僥倖.

23 書硯–石墨相著, 而黑, 邪心讒言, 無得汙白.

24 書鋒–忍之須臾, 乃全汝軀.

25 書杖–輔人無苟, 扶人無咎.

26 書井–原泉滑滑, 連旱則絕.

17]

In taking, observe the regular course;
In your requisitions be guided by economy.

27. *The ditty of the white clouds.* From the 穆天子傳 卷三.

The white clouds are in the sky;
The mountain-masses push themselves forth.
The way between us is very long,
With hills and rivers intervening.
I pray you not to die;—
Perhaps you will come here again.

28. *The K'e-shaou.* From the Tso Chuen, X. xii. 9.

Mild was [the course of] the minister Shaou,
Well displaying his virtuous fame.
To him the measures of the king
Were as precious as gold or gems.
He would regulate them by the strength of the people,
And put from him drunkenness and gluttony.

29. *The oracle of E-she.* From the Tso Chuen, III. xxii. 3,

The phœnixes fly;
Harmoniously sound their gem-like notes.
The posterity of this scion of Kwei
Will be nourished among the Këang.
In five generations they will be prosperous,
The highest ministers of Ts'e;
After eight generations,
There will be none so great as they.

30. *Inscription on a tripod, belonging to one of Confucius' ancestors.* From the Tso Chuen, X. vii. 6.

In the first grade, he walked with head bowed down;
In the second, with shoulders bent;
In the third, with his body stooping.
So he hurried along the wall, [saying],
'Thus no one will dare to insult me.
I will have gruel in this boiler,
And congee in this boiler,
To satisfy my hunger!'

取事有常. 賦斂有節.

27 白雲謠-白雲在天. 丘陵自出. 道里悠遠. 山川
　間之. 將子無死. 尚復能來.

28 新招-新招之惜惜. 式昭德音. 思我王度. 式如
　玉式如金. 形民之力. 而無醉飽之心

29 懿氏綠-鳳凰于飛. 和鳴鏘鏘. 有嬀之後. 將育
于姜. 五世其昌. 並于正卿. 八世之後. 莫之與京

30 鼎銘――命而僂. 再命而傴. 三命而俯. 循牆而
走. 亦莫余敢侮. 饘于是. 粥于是. 以餬于口

18]

31. *The Forester's warning.*   From the Tso Chuen, IX. iv., after par. 7.

> Yu travelled wide and long about,
> When the nine regions he laid out,
> And through them led the ninefold route.
> Men then their temples safe possessed;
> Beasts ranged the grassy plains with zest.
> For man and beast sweet rest was found,
> And virtue reigned the kingdom round.
> Then took E E the emperor's place;
> His sole pursuit the wild beasts' chase.
> The people's care he quite forgot;
> Of does and stags alone he thought.
> War and such pastimes we should flee;
> The rule of Hëa soon passed from E.
> A forester, these lines I pen,
> And offer to my king's good men.

32. *The Cow-feeder's song.*   By a Worthy in disguise, seeking advancement. Said to be from Hwae Nan-tsze.   Found in the 太平御覽卷五百七十二.

> On the bare southern hill,
> The white rocks gleam.
> Born when no Yaou and Shun resign their thrones,
> With a short and single garment of cloth, reaching to my calf,
> From morning to midnight I feed my cattle.
> Long is the night;—when will it be dawn?
> Mid the waters of Ts'ang-lang, the white rocks shine;
> There is a carp, a foot and a half long.
> With a single garment of tattered cloth, reaching to my calf,
> From the clear morning to midnight, I feed my cattle.
> Ye yellow calves, go up the hill, and lie down;—
> I will be minister to the State of Ts'e.
> Going out at the east gate, they rub their horns on the stone slabs;
> Above are the pines and cypresses green and rare.

³¹虞箴-芒芒禹跡， 畫爲九州， 經啓九道， 民有寢
廟， 獸有茂草， 各有攸處， 德用不擾， 在帝夷羿，
冒于原獸， 忘其國恤， 而思其麀牡， 武不可重， 用
不恢于夏家， 獸臣司原， 敢告僕夫．
³²飯牛歌-南山矸， 白石爛， 生不逢堯與舜禪， 短
布單衣適至骭， 從昏飯牛薄夜半， 長夜漫漫何
時旦，
滄浪之水白石粲， 中有鯉魚長尺半， 弊布單衣
裁至骭， 清朝飯牛至夜半， 黃犢上坂且休息， 吾
將梣汝相齊國，
出東門兮厲石班， 上有松柏青且闌．

19]

My garment of coarse cloth is frayed and ragged;
In my time there are none like Yaou and Shun.
Do your best, ye cattle to eat the soft grass;
A great minister is by your side.
I will go with you to the State of Ts'oo.

33. *The Lute song.* Sung by the wandering wife of Peh-le He. From the 風俗通. Found in the 太平御覽, as above.

Pih-le He,
[Sold for] five sheep-skins,
Do you remember the time of our parting,
How we cooked our brooding hen,
With the bar of our door?
Now amid riches and honours,
You forget me!

34. *The Song Hea-yu.* From the Narratives of the States (晉語, 二).

Irresolute to please [his ruler],
He is not equal to a crow.
All collect on the umbrageous trees,
And only he on the withered trunk.

35—37. *Hwa Yuen of Sung, and the workmen.* From the Tso Chuen, VII. ii. 1.

The builders sing:—

With goggle eyes and belly vast,
The buff-coats left, he's back at last,
The whiskers long, the whiskers long
Are here, but not the buff-coats strong.

Hwa Yuen replies:—

On other bulls hides may be found,
Rhinoceroses still abound,
Those buff-coats lost was no great wound.

A builder rejoins:—

Granted that the hides you furnish,
Where, I pray, is the red varnish?

蟲布衣兮縕縷, 時不遇兮堯舜主, 牛兮努力食
細草 大臣在爾側 吾當與汝適楚國

33 琴歌-百里奚, 五羊皮, 憶別時. 烹伏雌,
炊扊扅, 今日富貴, 忘我爲.

34 眼鯠歌-眼鯠之吾吾, 不如烏烏, 人皆集于菀
己獨集于枯

35 宋城者謳-睅其目. 皤其腹, 棄甲而復, 于
思于思. 棄甲復來.

36 驂乘答歌-牛則有皮, 犀兕尚多, 棄甲則那.

37 役人又歌-從其有皮, 丹漆若何.

38. *Song of the grackles.* The Tso-chuen, X. xxv. 3.

Here are grackles apace;
The duke flies in disgrace.
Look at the grackles' wings;
To the wilds the duke flings;
A horse one to him brings.
Look how the grackles go!
In Kan-how he is low,
Wants coat and garment now.
Behold the grackles' nest;
Far off the duke does rest.
Chow-foo has lost his toil;
Sung-foo with pride does boil.
O the grackles so strange!
The songs to weeping change.

39. *Song of builders in Sung.* From the Tso Chuen, IX. xvii. after p. 7.

The White of the Taih gate
Laid on us this task
The Black in the city's midst
Would comfort our hearts.

40. *Song of the Noble Lament.* Said to be from the tombstone of Sun Shuh-gaou,
a minister of Ts'oo.

An officer should not be covetous, and yet he should;
An officer should be pure, and yet he should not.
Why should an officer not be covetous?
He gets in his time a vile name.
Why should he be so?
He leaves his descendants with a family built up.
Why should an officer be pure?
He gets in his time a bright name.
Why should he not be so?
He leaves his posterity in straits and poverty,
Wearing cloth of hair and carrying faggots.

38 鸜鵒歌-鸜之鵒之, 公出辱之, 鸜鵒之羽,
公在外野, 往饋之馬, 鸜鵒跦跦, 公在乾侯,
徵褰與襦, 鸜鵒之巢, 遠哉遙遙, 稠父喪勞,
宋父以驕, 鸜鵒鸜鵒, 往歌來哭.

39 澤門之晰謳-澤門之晰, 實與我役, 邑中之
黔, 實慰我心.

40 忱慷歌-貪吏而不可爲而可爲, 廉吏而可爲而
不可爲, 貪吏而不可爲者, 當時有汙名, 而可
爲者, 子孫以家成 廉吏而可爲者. 當時有清名,
而不可爲者, 子孫困窮, 被褐而負薪,

A covetous officer rolls in wealth;
A pure officer is poor.
Saw you not the premier of Ts'oo, Sun Shuh-gaou,
How thrifty and pure he was, not receiving a cash!

43. *Two songs on Tsze-ch'an by the people of Ch'ing.* From the Tso Ch'uen, IX. xxx., at the end.

We must take our robes and caps, and hide them all away;
We must count our fields by fives, and own a mutual sway;
We'll gladly join with him who this Tsze-ch'an will slay.

By and by their words were:—

'Tis Tsze-ch'an who our children trains;
Our fields to Tsze-ch'an owe their grains;
Did Tsze-ch'an die, who'd take the reins?

Tsze-ch'an was only a little anterior to Confucius, and the pieces which follow relate to the sage himself, to his times, and to subjects of a later date. The preceding pieces are different in style from the odes of the She, and hardly one of them is introduced with the formula 詩曰, which so frequently introduces quotations from the acknowledged Book of Poetry.

貪吏常苦富，　　廉吏常苦貧，　　獨不見楚相孫叔敖，
　　　　　　廉潔不受錢．

43 子產誦二章-取我衣冠而褚之，　　取我田疇而伍
　　之，　孰殺子產，　吾其與之．
我有子弟，　子產誨之，　我有田疇　　子產殖之，
　　子產而死，　誰其嗣之．

CHAPTER II.

THE SOURCES OF THE ODES AS A COLLECTION; THEIR INTER-
PRETATION AND AUTHORS; THE PREFACES
AND THEIR AUTHORITY.

APPENDIXES—THE GREAT AND LITTLE PREFACES;
A CHRONOLOGICAL TABLE OF THE ODES; SPECIMENS
OF HAN YING'S ILLUSTRATIONS OF THE ODES.

1. It has been shown in the first section of last chapter that the
Book of Poetry existed as a collection of odes before the time of
Confucius. It becomes a question of some interest whether we can
ascertain how the collection came to be formed, and account for the
gaps that now exist in it,—how there are no poetical memorials at
How were the odes collected in
the first place? How is the col-
lection now so incomplete? all of several of the reigns of the Chow
kings, and how the first Part embraces
only a portion of the States of which the kingdom was composed.

2. Sir Andrew Fletcher of Saltoun tells us the opinion of 'a very
wise man,' that 'if a man were permitted to make all the ballads of
of a nation, he need not care who should make its laws.'[1] The
theory of Chinese scholars is that it was the duty of the kings to
make themselves acquainted with all the odes and songs current in
the different States, and to judge from them of the character of
The theory of Chinese scholars
about a collection of the odes for
governmental purposes. the rule exercised by their several princes,
so that they might minister praise or blame,
reward or punishment accordingly.

3. The *one* classical passage which is referred to in support of
this theory is in the Le Ke, V. ii., parr. 13, 14:—'Every fifth year,
The classical passage which
supports the theory. the son of Heaven made a progress through
the kingdom, when the grand music-master
was commanded to lay before him the poems collected in the States

---

1. See Fletcher's account of a Conversation on Governments. Sir John Davis (The Poetry of the
Chinese, p. 35) adduces the remark of a writer in the Spectator (No. 502):— I have heard that
a minister of State in the reign of Queen Elizabeth had all manner of books and balladsobrought
to him, of what kind soever, and took great notice how much they took with the people; upon
which he would, and certainly might, very well judge of their present dispositions, and of the
most proper way of applying them according to his own purposes.'

23]

of the several quarters, as an exhibition of the manners of the people.'[2] Unfortunately, this Book of the Le Ke, the 'Royal Ordinances,' was only compiled in the reign of the emperor Wăn of the Han
dynasty (B.C. 179—155). The scholars entrusted with the work did
their best, we may suppose, with the materials at their command.
They made much use, it is evident, of Mencius, and of the E Le.
The Chow Le, or the 'Official Book of Chow,' had not then been
recovered. But neither in Mencius, nor in the E Le, do we meet with
any authority for the statement before us. The Shoo mentions
that Shun every fifth year made a tour of inspection through his
empire; but there were then no odes for him to examine, as to him
and his minister Kaou-yaou is attributed the first rudimentary
attempt at the poetic art.[3] Of the progresses of the sovereigns of
the Hëa and Yin dynasties we have no information;[4] and those of
the kings of Chow were made, we know, only once in twelve years.
The statement in the 'Royal Ordinances,' therefore, was probably
based only on tradition, and is erroneous in the frequency of the
royal progresses which it asserts.

Notwithstanding the difficulties which beset the text of the Le
Ke, however, I am not disposed to reject it altogether. It derives
a certain amount of confirmation from the passage quoted in the
last chapter, p. 4, from the 'Official Book of Chow,' showing that
in the Chow dynasty there was a collection of poems, under the divisions of the Fung, the Ya, and the Sung, which it was the business of the grand music-master to teach the musicians and the
elèves of the royal school. It may be granted then, that the duke
of Chow, in legislating for his dynasty, enacted that the poems produced in the different feudal States should be collected on the occasions of the royal progresses, and lodged thereafter among the
archives of the bureau of music at the royal court. The same
thing, we may presume a fortiori, would be done with those produced within the royal domain itself.

4. But the feudal States were modelled after the pattern of the
royal State. They also had their music-masters, their musicians,

---

[2] 禮記 王制:－天子五年一巡守……命大師陳詩以
觀民風.   [3] See the Shoo, II. i. 9; iv. 11.   [4] Ch'ing K'ang-shing says on the text:—
天子以海內爲家，時一巡省之，五年者虞夏之制也，周
則十二歲一巡守；on which the imperial editors observe, 夏殷巡守之
年，諸書無考，鄭氏不知何據，而孔氏又從而爲之辭.

and their historiographers. The kings in their progresses did not

The music-master of the king) visit each particular State, so that their mu-
would get the odes of each State>
from its music-master.   ) sic-masters could have an opportunity to
collect the odes in it for themselves. They met, at well-known
points, the marquises, earls, barons, &c., of the different quarters of
the kingdom; there gave them audience; adjudicated upon their
merits; and issued to them their orders. We are obliged to suppose
that the princes would be attended to the places of rendezvous by
their music-masters, carrying with them the poetical compositions
collected in their several regions, to present them to their superior
of the royal court.

5. By means of the above arrangement, we can understand how
the poems of the whole kingdom were accumulated and arranged
among the archives of the capital. Was there any provision for dis-
seminating thence the poems of one State among all the others?

How the collected poems) There is sufficient evidence that this dissemina-
were disseminated through->
out the States.   ) tion was in some way effected. Throughout
the 'Narratives of the States' and the details of Tso K'ëw-ming on
the history of the Ch'un Ts'ëw, the officers of the States generally are
presented to us as familiar not only with the odes of their particular
States, but with those of other States as well. They appear equally
well acquainted with all the Parts and Books of our present collection; and we saw in chapter I., p. 5, how the whole of the present
She was sung over to Ke-chah of Woo when he visited the court of
Loo. My opinion is that there was a regular communication from
the royal court to the courts of the various States of the poetical
pieces, which for one reason or another were thought worthy of
preservation. This is nowhere expressly stated; but it may be
argued by analogy from the account which we have in the 'Official
Book of Chow' of the duties of the historiographers, or recorders, of
the Exterior. 'They had charge of the Histories of all the States;
of the Books of the three August [rulers] and of the five emperors.
They communicated to all parts of the kingdom the writings [in
their charge].'⁵ For want of fuller information it is not easy to give a

⁵ 周官義疏卷二十六·春官宗伯第三之十一外史掌四
方之志 (Acc to 劉彝, these Che related to everything about the feudal States, and the
outlying barbarous tribes, the history of their princes and chiefs, their origin and boundaries,
their tributes, their ceremonies, music, customs, &c.); 掌三皇五帝之書 (We try in
vain to discover what the Books of those three August ones were); 掌達書名於四方·
(This sentence is the most important for my argument. I cannot accept the interpretation of

thoroughly satisfactory account of the Histories and the Books referred to in these brief sentences; but I quote them merely to establish the fact that, according to the constitution of the kingdom under the dynasty of Chow, not only were the literary monuments of the feudal States collected for the satisfaction of the kings, but they were again sent forth to the courts of the different princes, and became the common possession of the cultivated classes throughout the whole country.   The documentary evidence of the fact is scanty, owing to the imperfect condition in which the Books of Chow were recovered during the Han dynasty, and so we have no special mention made of the odes in the passages of the 'Official Book,' which I have adduced; but that they, as well as the other writings which are vaguely specified, were made known to Loo, Ts'e, Tsin, and all the other States seems to have the evidence of analogy in its favour, and to be necessary to account for the general familiarity with them which, we know, prevailed.

6.   But if the poems produced in the several States were thus collected in the capital, and thence again disseminated throughout the kingdom, we might conclude that the collection would have been far more extensive and complete than we have it now.   The smallness of it is to be accounted for by the disorder and confusion into which the kingdom fell after the lapse of a few reigns from king Woo.   Royal progresses ceased when royal government fell into decay, and then the odes were no longer collected.[6]   We have no account of any progress of the kings during the period of the Ch'un Ts'ëw.   But, before that period, there is a long gap of 143 years between kings Ch'ing and E, covering the reigns of K'ang, Ch'aou, Muh, and Kung, of which we have no poetic memorials, if we except two doubtful pieces among the sacrificial odes of Chow.   The reign of Hëaou who succeeded to E is similarly uncommemorated, and the latest odes are of the time of Ting, when a hundred years of the Ch'un Ts'ëw had still to run their course.   I cannot suppose but that many odes were made and collected during the 143 years after king Ch'ing.   The probability is that they perished during the feeble and disturbed reigns of E,[7] Hëaou, E,[8] and Le.   Of the reign of the first of these we have

How the collection is so small and incomplete.

書名, in which many acquiesce, as simply = the names of the written characters.   Biot gives for the whole:—'Ils sont chargés de propager les noms ecrits, ou les signes de l'ecriture, dans les quatre parties de l'empire.'   I believe that I have given the sense correctly.)   6 See Mencius, IV. ii. XXI.   7. 懿王.   8. 夷王.

only five pieces, of all of which Choo considers the date to be uncertain; of that of the second, as has been observed above, we have
no memorials at all; of that of the third we have only one piece,
which Choo, for apparently good reasons, would assign to a considerably later date.   Then follow four pieces, the date of which is
quite uncertain, and eleven, assigned to the reign of Le,—some of
them with evident error.   To Le's succeeded the long and vigorous
reign of Seuen (B.C. 828—781) when we may suppose that the ancient custom of collecting the poems was revived.   Subsequently to
him, all was in the main decadence and disorder.   It was probably
in the latter part of his reign that Ch'ing-k'aou-foo, an ancestor of
Confucius, obtained from the Grand music master of the court of
Chow twelve of the sacrificial odes of the previous dynasty, with
which he returned to Sung which was held by representatives of
the House of Shang.   They were used there in sacrificing to the old
kings of Shang, and were probably taken with them to Loo when
the K'ung family subsequently sought refuge in that State.   Yet
of the twelve odes seven were lost by the time of Confucius.

   The general conclusion to which we come is, that the existing
Book of Poetry is the fragment of various collections made during
the early reigns of the kings of Chow, and added to at intervals,
especially on the occurrence of a prosperous rule, in accordance with
the regulation which has been preserved in the Le Ke.   How it is
that we have in Part I. odes of not more than a dozen of the States
into which the kingdom was divided,[9] and that the odes of those
States extend only over a short period of their history:—for these
things we cannot account further than by saying that such were the
ravages of time and the results of disorder.   We can only accept the
collection as it is, and be thankful for it.   It was well that Confucius was a native of Loo, for such was the position of that State
among the others, and so close its relations with the royal court,
that the odes preserved in it were probably more numerous and
complete than anywhere else.   Yet we cannot accept the statement
of the editor of the Suy catalogue adduced on page 2, that the
existing pieces had been copied out and arranged by Che, the
music-master of Loo, unless, indeed, Che had been in office during
the boyhood of Confucius, when, as we have seen, the collection
was to be found there, substantially the same as it is now.

   9. I say not quite a dozen, for Books III., IV., and V., all belong to Wei, and Books X. and
probably also XIII., to Tsin.

7. The conclusions which I have sought to establish in the above paragraphs, concerning the sources of the She as a collection, have an important bearing on the interpretation of many of the odes. The Bearing of the above para- remark of Sze-ma Ts'ëen, that 'Confucius graphs on the interpretation of particular pieces. selected those pieces which would be serviceable for the illustration of propriety and righteousness,' is as erroneous as the other, that the sage selected 305 pieces out of 3000. Confucius merely studied and taught the pieces which he found existing, and the collection necessarily contained odes illustrative of bad government as well as of good, of licentiousness as well as of a pure morality. Nothing has been such a stumbling-block in the way of the reception of Choo He's interpretation of the pieces as the readiness with which he attributes a licentious meaning to those of Book VII., Part I. But the reason why the kings in their progresses had the odes of the different States collected and presented to them, was 'that they might judge from them of the manners of the people,' and so come to a decision regarding the government and morals of their rulers. A student and translator of the odes has simply to allow them to speak for themselves, and has no more reason to be surprised at the language of vice in some of them than at the language of virtue in many others. The enigmatic saying of Confucius himself, that the whole of 'the three hundred odes may be summed up in one sentence,—*Thought without depravity,*'[10] must be understood in the meaning which I have given to it in the translation of the Analects. It may very well be said, in harmony with all that I have here advanced, that the odes were collected and preserved for the promotion of good government and virtuous manners. The merit attaching to them is that they give us faithful pictures of what was good and what was bad in the political State of the country, and in the social habits of the people.

8. The pieces in the collection were of course made by individuals who possessed the gift, or thought that they possessed the gift, The writers of the odes. of poetical composition. Who they were we could tell only on the authority of the odes themselves, or of credible historical accounts, contemporaneous with them or nearly so. They would in general be individuals of some literary culture, for the arts of reading and writing even could not be widely diffused during the Chow dynasty. It is not worth our

10. See the Ana. II. ii.

while to question the opinion of the Chinese critics, who attribute
many pieces to the duke of Chow, though we have independent
testimony only to his composition of a single ode,—the second of
Book XV., Part. I.[11] We may assign to him also the 1st and 3d odes
of the same Book; the first 22 of Part II.; the first 18 of Part III.;
and with two doubtful exceptions, all the sacrificial Songs of Chow.

Of the 160 pieces in Pt. I. only the authorship of the 2d of Bk.
XV., which has just been referred to, can be assigned with certainty.
Some of the others, of which the historical interpretation may be
considered as sufficiently fixed, as the complaints of Chwang Këang,
in Bkk. III., IV., V., are written in the first person; but the author
may be personating his subject. In Pt. II., the 7th ode of Bk. IV.
was made by a Këa-foo, a noble of the royal State, but we know
nothing more about him; the 6th of Bk. VI., by a eunuch styled
Măng-tsze; and the 6th of Bk. VII., from a concurrence of external
testimonies, may be ascribed to duke Woo of Wei.

In Pt. III., Bk. III., the 2d piece was composed by the same duke
Woo; the 3d by an earl of Juy in the royal domain; the 4th must
have been made by one of Seuen's ministers, to express the king's
feelings under the drought which was exhausting the kingdom; and
the 5th and 6th claim to be the work of Yin Keih-foo, one of Seuen's
principal officers.

9. In the preface which appeared along with Maou's text of the
She, the occasion and authorship of many more of the odes are
given; but I am not inclined to allow much weight to its
testimony. It will be found in the first appendix to this
The Preface.
chapter, as it is published in every native edition of the Book of
Poetry of any pretensions, and is held by a great proportion of the
scholars as an authoritative document. In the body of this volume
I have shown in a multitude of cases the unsatisfactoriness of the
view which it would oblige us to take of particular odes. There are
few western Sinologues, I apprehend, who will not cordially concur
with me in the principle of Choo He, that we must find the meaning of the odes in the odes themselves, instead of accepting the
interpretation of them given by we know not whom, and to follow
which would reduce many of them to absurd enigmas.

From the large space which the discussion of the Preface occupies
in Chinese critical works, it is necessary that I should attempt a

11. See the Shoo, V. vi. 15.

summary of what is said upon it;—on no subject are the views of native scholars more divided.

According to Ch'ing K'ang-shing, what is now called 'the Great preface' was made by Confucius' disciple Tsze-hëa, and what is called 'the Little preface' was made also by Tsze-hëa, but afterwards supplemented by Maou.[12]   In Maou, however, there is no distinction made between a Great and a Little preface.   As the odes came down to him, the Preface was an additional document by itself, and when he published his commentary, he divided it into portions, prefixing to every ode the portion which gave an account of it.[13] In this way, however, the preface to the *Kwan ts'eu*, or the first ode of the collection, was of a disproportionate length; and very early, this portion was separated from the rest, and called *the Great Preface*.[14] But the division of the original preface thus made was evidently unnatural and inartistic; and Choo He showed his truer critical ability by detaching only certain portions of the preface to the *Kwan ts'eu*, and dignifying them with the same name of *the Great preface*. This gives us some account of the nature and origin of poetry in general, and of the different Parts which compose the She.   But Choo should have gone farther.   In what is left of the preface to the *Kwan ts'eu*, we have not only an account of that ode, but also what may be regarded as a second introduction to Part I, and especially to the first and second Books of it.   To maintain the symmetry of the prefaces there ought to be corresponding sentences at the commencement of the introductory notices to the first odes of the other Parts.   But there is nothing of the sort; and this want of symmetry in the preface as a whole is a sufficient proof to me that it did not all proceed from one hand.

In Section II. of last chapter I have traced the transmission of

How it is attempted to trace} Maou's text from its first appearance until it
the Preface to Tsze-hea   } got possession of the literary world of China.
Scholars try to trace it up to Tsze-hëa, and consequently through

[12] 沈重曰, 按鄭詩譜, 大序子夏作, 小序子夏毛公合作;—See the 經義考, 詩二, p. 1.   [13] On the preface to the *Nan Kue*, or II. i. X., Ch'ing says, 遭戰國及秦之世, 而亡南陔之文, 其義則與眾篇之義合編, 故存, 及至毛公為詁訓傳, 乃分眾篇之義各置於其篇端云.   [14] 李樗曰, 詩皆有序獨關雎為最詳, 先儒以謂關雎為大序, 葛覃以下為小序;—see the 經義考, as above, p. 7.

him to Confucius; but the evidence is not of an equally satisfactory character. The first witness is Seu Ching, an officer of the State or Kingdom of Woo in the period of 'the Three Kingdoms (A.D. 229—264),' who says, as reported by Luh Tih-ming:—'Tsze-hëa handed down the She, [which he had received from Confucius], to Kaou Hăng-tsze; Hăng-tsze to Sëeh Ts'ang-tsze; Ts'ang-tsze to Mëen Mëaou-tsze; and Mëaou-tsze to the elder Maou'.[15] Luh Tih-ming gives also another account of the connexion between Maou and Tsze-hëa:—'Tsze-hea handed down the She to Tsăng Shin; Tsăng Shin to Le K'ih; Le K'ih to Măng Chung-tsze; Măng Chung-tsze to Kin Mow-tsze; Kin Mow-tsze to Seun K'ing; and Seun K'ing to the elder Maou.'[16] There is no attempt made, so far as I know, on the part of Chinese critics, to reconcile these two genealogies of Maou's She; but there is no doubt that, during the Han dynasties, the school of Maou did trace their master's text up to Tsze-hëa. Yen Sze-koo states it positively in his note appended to Lëw Hin's catalogue of the copies of the She;[17] and hence, as the text and the preface came to Maou together, there arose the view that the latter was made by that disciple of the sage. It became current, indeed, under his name, and was published separately from the odes, so that, in the catalogue of the T'ang dynasty, we find 'The Preface to the She by Puh Shang, in two Books,' as a distinct Work.[18]

But there is another account of the origin of the Preface which seems to conflict with this. In par. 4 of the 2d section of last chap-

Different account of the
origin of the Preface. ter I have made mention of Wei King-chung or Wei Hwang, one of the great Han scholars who adopted the text of Maou. He serves as a connecting link between the western and eastern dynasties of Han; and in the account of him in the 'Literary Biographies' we are told that 'Hwang became the pupil of Sëay Man-k'ing, who was famous for his knowledge of Maou's She; and he afterwards made the Preface to it, remarkable for

15. 徐整云‧于夏授高行子；高行子授薛倉子‧薛倉子 授帛妙子；帛妙子授河間人大毛公；毛公爲詩詁傳 於家以授趙人小毛公‧ The Kaou Hăng-tsze here is identified by many with 'the stupid old Kaou,' whose view of one of the odes is adduced and condemned in Mencius, VI. ii. III. This seems to me very doubtful. 16 子夏傳曾申 (the son of Tsăng Sin, one of Confucius' principal disciples); 申傳魏人李克；克傳孟仲子 (acc. to Ch'ing, a disciple of Tsze-sze); 孟仲子傳根牟子；根牟子傳趙人孫 卿子 (the philosopher Seun); 孫卿子傳魯人大毛公   17 又有毛 公之學‧自謂子夏所傳‧   18 卜子商詩序二卷

the accuracy with which it gives the meaning of the pieces in the Fung and the Ya, and which is now current in the world.'[19]   A testimony like this cannot be gainsayed.   If we allow that, when Maou first made public his text, there were prefatory notes accompanying it, yet Hwang must have made large additions to these, as Maou himself, in the opinion of Ch'ing K'ang-shing, had previously done.

Since the time of Choo He, many eminent scholars, such as Yen Ts'an in the Sung dynasty, and Këang Ping-chang in the present, adopt the first sentence in the introduction to each ode as what constituted the original preface, and which they do not feel at liberty to dispute.   They think that so much was prefixed to the odes by the historiographers of the kingdom or of the States, when they were first collected, and they would maintain likewise, I suppose, that it bore the stamp of Tsze-hëa.   Këang calls these brief sentences 'the Old preface' and 'the Great preface,' and the fuller explanation which is often appended to them, and which he feels at liberty to question, he calls 'the Appended preface,' and 'the Little preface.'

After long and extensive investigation of the subject, I have no hesitation in adopting the freer views of Choo He, with a condensed account of which I conclude this chapter:—

Choo He's views on the Preface.

'Opinions of scholars are much divided as to the authorship of the Preface.   Some ascribe it to Confucius;[20] some to Tsze-hëa; and some to the historiographers of the States.   In the absence of clear testimony it is impossible to decide the point; but the notice about Wei Hwang, in the literary Biographies of the Han dynasties,[21] would seem to make it clear that the Preface was his work.   We must take into account, however, on the other hand, the statement of Ch'ing Heuen,[22] that the Preface existed as a separate document when

[19] 九江謝曼卿善毛詩乃爲其訓, 宏從受學因作毛詩序, 善得風雅之旨, 於今傳於世;—see the 後漢書, 七十九下, 儒林傳第六十九下   [20] This is too broadly stated. No one has affirmed that the Preface as a whole was from the hand of Confucius. Ch'ing E-ch'uen (A.D. 1,083—1,107) held that the Great preface was made by him. The style, he says, is like that of the appendixes to the Yih, and the ideas are beyond what Tsze-hëa could have enunciated (詩大序, 其文似繫辭 非子夏所能言也, 分明是聖人作此以教學者)! Wang Tih-shin (王得臣; later on in the Sung dynasty) ascribed to Confucius, the first sentence of all the introductory notices, and called them the Great preface.   [21] Adduced above.   [22] Also adduced above.

Maou appeared with his text, and that he broke it up, prefixing to each ode the portion belonging to it. The natural conclusion is that the Preface had come down from a remote period, and that Hwang merely added to it and rounded it off. In accordance with this, scholars generally hold that the first sentences in the introductory notices formed the original Preface which Maou distributed, and that the following portions were subsequently added.

'This view may appear reasonable; but when we examine those first sentences themselves, we find some of them which do not agree with the obvious meaning of the odes to which they are prefixed, and give merely the rash and baseless expositions of the writers. Evidently, from the first, the Preface was made up of private speculations and conjectures as to the subject-matter of the odes, and constituted a document by itself, separately appended to the text. Then on its first appearance there were current the explanations of the odes which were given in connexion with the texts of Ts'e, Loo, and Han, so that readers could know that it was the work of later hands, and not give entire credit to it.[28] But when Maou no longer published the Preface as a separate document, but each ode appeared with the introductory notice as a portion of the text, this seemed to give to it the authority of the text itself. Then after the other texts disappeared and Maou's had the field to itself, this means of testing the accuracy of its prefatory notices no longer existed. They appeared as if they were the production of the poets themselves, and the odes seemed to be made from them as so many themes. Scholars handed down a faith in them from one to another, and no one ventured to express a doubt of their authority. The text was twisted and chiseled to bring it into accordance with them, and nobody would undertake to say plainly that they were the work of the scholars of the Han dynasty.'

23 On the important fact that the other texts, as Maou's, all had their prefaces, often differing from the views of the odes given in that, see Choo E-tsun's note, concluding his chapter on the Preface to the She.

APPENDIX. I.

[i.] THE GREAT PREFACE.

1. Poetry is the product of earnest thought. Thought [cherished] in the mind becomes earnest: exhibited in words, it becomes poetry.

2. The feelings move inwardly, and are embodied in words. When words are insufficient for them, recourse is had to sighs and exclamations. When sighs and exclamations are insufficient for them, recourse is had to the prolonged utterances of song. When those prolonged utterances of song are insufficient for them, unconsciously the hands begin to move and the feet to dance.

3. The feelings go forth in sounds. When those sounds are artistically combined, we have what is called musical pieces. The style of such pieces in an age of good order is quiet, going on to be joyful;—the government is then a harmony. Their style in an age of disorder is resentful, going on to the expression of anger;—the government is then a discord. Their style, when a State is going to ruin, is mournful, with the expression of [retrospective] thought;—the people are then in distress.

4. Therefore, correctly to set forth the successes and failures [of government], to move Heaven and Earth, and to excite spiritual Beings to action, there is no readier instrument than poetry.

5. The former kings by this regulated the duties of husband and wife, effectually inculcated filial obedience and reverence, secured attention to all the relations of society, adorned the transforming influence of instruction, and transformed manners and customs.

6. Thus it is that in the [Book of] Poems there are six classes:—first, the Fung; second, descriptive pieces; third, metaphorical pieces; fourth, allusive pieces; fifth, the Ya; and sixth, the Sung.[1]

大序

1. 詩者志之所之也，在心爲志，發言爲詩。
2. 情動於中，而形於言，言之不足，故嗟歎之，嗟歎之不足，不知手之舞之足之蹈之也。
3. 故情發於聲，聲成文謂之音，治世之音安以樂，其政和，亂世之音怨以怒，其政乖，亡國之音哀以思，其民困。
4. 故正得失，動天地，感鬼神，莫近於詩。
5. 先王以是經夫婦，成孝敬，厚人倫，美教化，移風俗。
6. 故詩有六義焉，一曰風，二曰賦，三曰比，四曰興，五曰雅，六曰頌。

---

1 This paragraph has been referred to in Ch. I. more than once, as taken from the 'Official Book of Chow.' If we had not the Book of Poetry to help us in determining its meaning, we should never be able to make it out from the text itself. We should conclude that anciently there were six classes of poems, called the *Fung*, the *Foo*, the *Pe*, the *Hing*, the *Ya*, and the *Sung*.

So it appears in Biot's translation of the Official Book:—'Il enseigne aux musiciens les six sortes de chants notés, qui sont appelés *Fong, Fou, Pi, Hing, Ya, Sung.*' But the names Fung, Ya, and Sung are those of the three Parts into which the She-king is divided, intended to indicate a difference in the subject-matter of the pieces composing them; while Foo, Pe, and Hing are the names

7. Superiors, by the Fung, transformed their inferiors, and inferiors, by them, satirized their superiors. The principal thing in them was their style, and reproof was cunningly insinuated. They might be spoken without giving offence, and the hearing of them was sufficient to make men careful of their conduct;—hence they are called *Fung*, [or Lessons of manners].

8. When the administration of the kings fell into decay, the rules of propriety and righteousness were neglected, the instructions of government failed of effect, different methods of government obtained in different States, and the customs of the [great] Families in them had come to vary;—then the changed (or inferior) Fung, and the inferior Ya, were made.[2]

7. 上以風化下·下以風刺上·主文而譎諫·言之者無
罪·聞之者足以戒·故曰風·
8. 至於王道衰·禮義廢·政教失·國異政·家殊俗·而變
風變雅作矣·

applied to those pieces, intended to denote the form or style of their composition. They may, all of them, be found equally in all the Parts. As Këa Kung-yen (賈公彥; T'ang dyn.) says:—風·雅·頌·詩之名也·但
就三者之中有賦·比·興·故
總謂之六詩· The Fung, Ya, and Sung are, in Chinese phraseology, the warp of the Book of Poetry, and the Foo, Pe, and Hing are its woof.

I have entered sufficiently on the meaning of the terms Fung, Ya, and Sung in the notes on the titles of the different *Parts*; but it may be well to discuss here the significance of the terms Foo, Pe, and Hing more fully than I have elsewhere done.

The term *Foo* needs little explanation. It is descriptive of a narrative piece, in which the poet says what he has to say right out, writing it down in a simple straightforward manner, without any hidden object. There is no meaning intended beyond what the words express, excepting in so far as we may infer from *what is said* the state of mind or the circumstances of the writer or subject. Odes 2 and 3 of Pt. I., Bk. I., are of this class, according to the view of them taken by Choo He, which I have followed; and other instances of the *Foo*, about which there can be no doubt, are to be found everywhere.

I have called the *Pe* metaphorical pieces. They must be translated as we translate the *Foo;* but the writer has under the language a different meaning altogether from what it expresses, —a meaning which there should be nothing in the language to indicate. The metaphorical piece in the She may thus be compared to the *Æsopic fable;* but while it is the object of the fable to enforce the virtues of morality and prudence, an historical interpretation is to be sought for the *pe*. There is, *e. g.*, ode 5 of Part. I. Bk. I., in the letter of which we find only locusts and their wonderful increase; while we are taught that the poet had in his mind the wife of king Wǎn and the fruitfulness of his

harem. Ode 2 of Pt. I. Bk. XV. is another purely metaphorical piece, where we seem to hear only the plaint of a bird, whose young, reared by her with toil, have been destroyed by an owl, and who is afraid that her nest also will be destroyed; but we know from the Shoo that the duke of Chow intended himself by the bird, and that he wished in the piece to vindicate the stern course which he had adopted to put down rebellion. As Choo He says:—比是以一
物比一物·而所指之事·常
在言外· The *Hing*, or allusive piece, commences with a couple of lines, which are repeated often through all the stanzas, as a sort of refrain. They are generally descriptive of something in the animal or the vegetable world; and after them the writer proceeds to his proper subject. Often the allusive lines convey a meaning harmonizing with that of the lines which follow, as in I. i. IV.; where an English poet would begin the verses with a *Like* or *As*. They are in fact metaphorical. But the difference between an allusive and a metaphorical piece is, that in the lines following the allusive lines the author states directly the theme he is occupied with, whereas the lines of the metaphorical piece are all of the same character. After the sentence on the *Pe* which I quoted above from Choo He, he goes on to say on the *Hing*:—興是借彼一物以引
起此事·而其事常在下句· Often, however, we cannot discover any metaphorical element in the allusive lines, and can only deal with them as a refrain. Where there is a metaphorical element, the piece is described as 興之兼比者; where there is no such element, it is 興之不兼比者.—Occasionally the three styles all come together in one ode.

2 I do not know when the distinction of the odes of Parts I., II., and III., into *Correct* and *Changed*, or Pieces of an age of good government,

35]

9. The historiographers of the States, understanding the indications of success and failure, pained by the changes in the observance of the relations of society, and lamenting the severity of punishments and of [the general] government, gave expression in mournful song to their feelings, to condemn their superiors;—they were intelligent as to the changes of circumstances, and cherished [the recollection of] the ancient customs.[3]

10. Thus it is that the Fung of a state of change, though produced by the feelings, do not go beyond the rules of propriety and righteousness. That they should be produced by the feelings was in the nature of the people; that they should not go beyond those rules was from the beneficent influence of the former kings.

11. Therefore, the pieces in which the affairs of one State are connected with the person of one man, are called the Fung.

12. The pieces which speak of the matters of the kingdom, and represent the customs of its whole extent, are called the Ya. Ya means correct. They tell the causes why royal government decays or flourishes. In government there are great matters and small, and hence there are the small Ya and the great Ya.

13. The Sung are so called, because they praise the embodied forms of complete virtue, and announce to spiritual Beings its grand achievements.[4]

14. These are called the four primary [divisions of the Book of Poems]; [in them we have] the perfection of poetry.

9. 國史明乎得失之迹,傷人倫之變,哀刑政之苛,吟詠情性以風其上,達於事變而懷其舊俗者也.

10. 故變風,發乎情,止乎禮義,發乎情,民之性也,止乎禮義,先王之澤也.

11. 是以一國之事,繫一人之本,謂之風.

12. 言天下之事,形四方之風,謂之雅,雅者正也,言王政之所由廢興也,政有小大,故有小雅焉,有大雅焉.

13. 頌者,美盛德之形容,以其成功告於神明者也.

14. 是謂四始,詩之至也.

and Pieces of a degenerate age, took its rise. We find it here in the Preface; but the age of the Preface is uncertain. The distinction is misleading. There are both in the Fung and the Ya many odes of a changed character, which by their spirit and style are equal to any of those that are ranked in the better class.

3 This paragraph would seem to attribute the odes to the historiographers of the royal and other courts;—a view which is maintained nowhere else.

4 This is a very incomplete account of the Sung, and leaves the anomaly of the Sung of Loo, as placed along with those of Chow and Shang, unaccounted for. See on the title of Pt. IV., Bk. II.

[ii.] THE LITTLE PREFACE.

ODES OF CHOW AND THE SOUTH.

1. The *Kwan ts'eu* celebrates the virtue of the queen.

This is the first of the Lessons of manners. By means of it the manners of all under heaven were intended to be formed, and the relation of husband and wife to be regulated; and therefore it was used at meetings in villages, and at the assemblies of princes.

For Lessons of manners the term *wind* is used, denoting the influence of instruction. Wind moves [things], and instruction transforms the people.

Thus, then, the transforming power in the *Kwan ts'eu* and the *Lin che* exhibit the influence of the true king, and they are therefore attributed to the duke of Chow. The South [in the name of the Book] implies the north, showing that the influence went from the north to the south. The virtue in the *Ts'ëoh ch'aou* and the *Tsow yu* exhibit the manners of princes,—the effects of the instruction of the former king, and they are therefore attributed to the duke of Shaou. [These two Books], the Chow Nan and the Shaou Nan, show how the beginning was made correct, and the foundation of royal transformation.

Therefore in the *Kwan ts'eu* we have joy in obtaining virtuous ladies to be mates to her lord; anxiety to be introducing ladies of worth; no excessive desire to have her lord to herself; sorrow about modest retiring ladies [not being found for the harem], and thought about getting ladies of worth and ability,—all without any envy of their excellence :—this is what we have in the *Kwan ts'eu*.

2. The *Koh t'an* sets forth the natural disposition of the queen.

We see her in her parents' house, with her mind bent on woman's work; thrifty and economical, wearing her washed clothes, and honouring and reverencing her matron-teacher. Being such, she might well [in after time] pay her visits to her parents, and transform the kingdom on the subject of woman's ways.

3. The *Keuen urh* shows us the mind of the queen.

It shows also how she felt that she ought to assist her husband; to seek out men of talents and virtue, and carefully place them in office; to recognize the toilsome labours of officers. Though she had thus the mind to introduce men of talents and virtue, she never thought of using artful words or speaking for relatives of her own; but morning and evening she thought of the matter, till she was painfully anxious about it.

小 序
周 南

1. 關雎后妃之德也.
風之始也所以風天下而正夫婦也故用之鄉人焉用之邦國焉.
風風也教也風以動之教以化之.
然則關雎麟趾之化王者之風故繫之周公南言化自北而南也鵲巢騶虞之德諸侯之風也先王之所以教故繫之召公.
周南召南正始之道王化之基.
是以關雎樂得淑女以配君子憂在進賢不淫其色哀窈窕思賢才而無傷善之心焉是關雎之義也.
2. 葛覃后妃之本也.
后妃在父母家則志在於女功之事躬儉節用服澣濯之衣尊敬師傅則可以歸安父母化天下以婦道也.
3. 卷耳后妃之志也.

4.   The *Kĕw muh* shows the queen's condescension to the ladies below her.

It tells how she could so condescend without any feeling of jealousy.

5.   The subject of the *Chung-sze* is the numerousness of the queen's progeny.

It says they were like locusts; for having no jealousy, her progeny was so numerous.

6.   The *T'aou yaou* shows the effects produced by the queen.

Through her freedom from jealousy, the relation between males and females was made right; marriages were celebrated at the proper time; and there were no unmarried people in the kingdom.

7.   The *T'oo tseu* shows the transforming influence of the queen.

When that influence, as celebrated in the *Kwan ts'eu*, went abroad, all loved virtue, and men of talents and virtue were very numerous.

8.   The *Fow e* shows the admirable excellence of the queen.

All became harmony and peace, and then women delighted to have children.

9.   The *Han kwang* shows how widely the influence of virtue reached.

The ways of king Wăn affected the States of the South; his admirable transforming influence went forth over all the country about the Këang and the Han.   There was no thought of violating the rules of propriety; and young women would be solicited in vain for their favours.

10.   The *Joo fun* shows how the transforming influence of [the king's] ways went abroad.

It went through the States along the banks of the Joo, till wives could at once compassionate [the toils of] their lords, and at the same time exhort them to what was right.

11.   The *Lin che* is the proper sequel to the *Kwan ts'eu*.

又當輔佐君子,求賢審官,知臣下之勤勞,內有進賢之志,而無險詖私謁之心,朝夕思念,至於憂勤也.

4.樛木,后妃逮下也.

言能逮下,而無嫉妬之心焉.

5.螽斯,后妃子孫眾多也.

言若螽斯,不妬忌,則子孫眾多也.

6.桃夭,后妃之所致也.

不妬忌,則男女以正,昏姻以時,國無鰥民也.

7.兔罝,后妃之化也.

關雎之化行,則莫不好德,賢人眾多也.

8.芣苢,后妃之美也.

和平,則婦人樂有子矣.

9.漢廣,德廣所及也.

文王之道,被於南國,美化行乎江漢之域,無思犯禮,求而不可得也.

10.汝墳,道化行也.

文王之化行乎汝墳之國,婦人能閔其君子,猶勉之以正也.

11.麟之趾,關雎之應也.

The transforming influence indicated by that having gone abroad, then under heaven there was no such thing as any violation of propriety. Even in a degenerate age the sons of the duke were all sincere and good, as in the time when the *lin's* footsteps were seen.

ODES OF SHAOU AND THE SOUTH.

1. The *Ts'eoh ch'aou* sets forth the virtue of some prince's wife.

By the accumulation of meritorious deeds, the prince has reached his dignity, and the lady comes from her parents' home, and occupies it with him. Her virtue being like that of the dove, she is a mate for him.

2. The *Ts'ae fan* shows a prince's wife not failing in her duty.

Capable of assisting at his sacrifices, she does not fail in her duty.

3. The *Ts'aou ch'ung* shows how the wife of a great officer maintained the guard of propriety.

4. The *Ts'ae pin* shows how the wife of a great officer could observe the rules for her conduct.

Able to observe those rules, she could take part in the services to [her husband's] ancestors, and share in the sacrifices to them.

5. The *Kan t'ang* is in praise of the Chief of Shaou.

His instructions were brilliantly displayed in the States of the South.

6. In the *Hing loo* we have the Chief of Shaou listening to a litigation.

The manners of a period of decay and disorder were passing away, and the lessons of integrity and sincerity were rising to influence. Oppressive men could not do violence to well-principled women.

關雎之化行,則天下無犯非禮,雖衰世之公子,皆信厚,如麟趾之時也.

召南

1. 鵲巢,夫人之德也.
國君積行累功,以致爵位,夫人起家而居有之,德如鳲鳩,乃可以配焉.
2. 采蘩,夫人不失職也.
夫人可以奉祭祀,則不失職矣.
3. 草蟲,大夫妻能以禮自防也.
4. 采蘋,大夫妻能循法度也.
能循法度,則可以承先祖,共祭祀矣.
5. 甘棠,美召伯也.
召伯之教,明於南國.
6. 行露,召伯聽訟也.
衰亂之俗微,貞信之教興,强暴之男,不能侵陵貞女也.

7. The *Kauu yang* shows the consequences flowing from the merit celebrated in the *Ts'eoh ch'aou.*

The States to the south of Shaou were transformed by the government of king Wăn. Those who held office in them were all economical, correct, and straight-forward, their virtue like that emblemed by their lamb-skins and sheep-skins.

8. In the *Yin k'e luy* we have a great officer exhorted to righteousness.

Belonging to one of the States south of Shaou, he goes far away on the service of the govt., and has no leisure for the enjoyment of home. His wife is able at once to compassionate his toil and to exhort him to righteousness.

9. The *P'éaou yëw mei* is about marriages at the proper time.

9. In the States south of Shaou, under the transforming influence of king Wăn, young men and maidens were able to marry at the proper times for their doing so.

10. In the *Sëaou sing* we have the kindness of a princess descending to the ladies beneath her.

Abstaining from all courses of jealousy, her kindness reaches to the meanest con-cubines, who go in and share the favours of the prince. They acknowledge the dif-ference between the lot of the noble and mean, and can serve her with all their heart.

11. The *Këang yëw sze* is in praise of the cousins of some princess who should have accompanied her to the harem.

They endured their painful position without murmuring, and she repented of her fault. In the time of king Wăn, between the Këang and the T'o, there was a princess who would not have her cousins to complete the complement of the harem. They endured the bitterness without murmuring, and she also repented of her course.

12. The *Yay yëw sze keun* expresses disgust at the want of the observances of propriety.

All under heaven there had been great disorder, and oppressive men had offered insult to the women, so that lascivious manners were the consequence. Through the transforming influence of king Wăn, even in an age of such disorder, there came to be a dislike of the want of those observances.

7. 羔羊, 鵲巢之功致也.
召南之國, 化文王之政, 在位皆節儉正直, 德如羔羊也.
8. 殷其靁, 勸以義也.
召南之大夫, 遠行從政, 不遑寧處, 其室家能閔其勤勞, 勸以義也.
9. 摽有梅, 男女及時也.
召南之國, 被文王之化, 男女得以及時也.
10 小星, 惠及下也.
夫人無妒忌之行, 惠及賤妾, 進御於君, 知其命有貴賤, 能盡其心矣.
11. 江有汜, 美媵也.
勤而無怨, 嫡能悔過也, 文王之時, 江沱之閒, 有嫡不以其媵備數, 媵遇勞而無怨, 嫡亦自悔也.
12. 野有死麕, 惡無禮也.

13. The *Ho pe ming e* is in praise of some daughter of the royal House.

Though she was thus of royal birth, and in descending to marry one of the princes, she was not restricted in her carriages and robes by her husband's rank, and they were only one degree inferior to the queen's, yet she was firmly observant of wifely duty, and displayed the virtues of reverence and harmony.

14. *Tsow yu* is the proper sequel to the *Ts'ëoh ch'uou*.

The transforming influence indicated by that having gone abroad, the relations of society were rightly regulated, and the court well-ordered. The whole kingdom came under the influence of king Wän; vegetation was luxuriant; hunting was conducted at the proper seasons; princes' benevolence was like that of the *Tsow yu*; and royal government was fully realized.

ODES OF P'EI.

1. The *Pih chow* tells of a virtuous officer neglected by his ruler.

In the time of duke K'ing of Wei (B.C. 866—854), virtuous men did not meet with his confidence, and mean men were by his side.

2. The *Luh e* contains the plaint of Chwang Këang of Wei (B.C. 752—) over her lot.

The place of the wife was usurped by a concubine, and the wife herself was degraded:—these were the circumstances which gave occasion to this piece.

3. The *Yen-yen* has reference to Chwang Këang of Wei's escorting a concubine on her return to her native State.

4. In the *Jih yueh* Chwang Këang bemoans her lot.

天下大亂，強暴相陵遂成淫風，被文王之化雖當亂
世，猶惡無禮也．

13. 何彼穠矣，美王姬也．

雖則王姬，亦下嫁於諸侯，車服不繫其夫，下王后一
等，猶執婦道，以成肅雝之德也．

14. 騶虞，鵲巢之應也．

鵲巢之化行，人倫既正，朝廷既治，天下純被文王之
化，則庶類蕃殖，蒐田以時，仁如騶虞，則王道成也．

邶

1. 柏舟，言仁而不遇也．
衞頃公之時，仁人不遇，小人在側．
2. 綠衣，衞莊姜傷己也．
姜士僭夫人失位，而作是詩也．
3. 燕燕，衞莊姜送歸妾也．
4. 日月，衞莊姜傷己也．

It is a piece about the hard suffering she endured from Chow-yu, and deplores the want of responsive affection which she had experienced in her deceased husband, which brought her to such straits and destitution.

5. In the *Chung jung* we have Chwang Këang of Wei bemoaning herself.

She was cruelly treated by Chow-yu, and met with incessant contempt and insult.

6. The *Keih koo* is expressive of resentment against Chow-yu of Wei.

Calling out his troops in an oppressive and disorderly manner, he sent Kung-sun Wăn-chung with them as general, and made peace with Ch'in and Sung, [in order to secure his success]. The people murmured because of his warlike proclivities and disregard of all propriety.

7. The *K'ae fung* is in praise of filial sons.

Such were the dissolute manners of Wei, that even a mother of seven sons could not rest in her house. The piece therefore expresses admiration of the sons, who could exercise to the utmost their filial duty, so as to comfort the heart of their mother, and give full expression to their own desire.

8. The *Hëung che* is directed against duke Seuen of Wei (B.C. 717—699).

Dissolute and disorderly, he paid no attention to the business of the State. He frequently engaged in military expeditions. The great officers were employed on service for a length of time Husbands and wives murmured at their solitariness. The people, suffering from these things, made this ode.

9. *P'aou yёw k'oo yeh* is directed against duke Seuen of Wei.

Both he and his wife were guilty of licentious conduct.

10. The *Kuh fung* is directed against violation of duty, as between husband and wife.

The men of Wei, through the influence of their superiors, became devoted to indulgence with new matches, and abandoned their old wives. Husband and wife were thus estranged and separated; the manners of the State were injured and went to ruin.

遭州吁之難傷己不見答於先君以至困窮之詩也·

5. 終風衛莊姜傷己也

遭州吁之暴見侮慢而不能正也·

6. 擊鼓怨州吁也·

衛州吁用兵暴亂使公孫文仲將而平陳與宋國人怨其勇而無禮也·

7. 凱風美孝子也·

衛之淫風流行雖有七子之母猶不能安其室故美七子能盡其孝道以慰其母心而成其志爾·

8. 雄雉刺衛宣公也·

淫亂不恤國事軍旅數起大夫久役男女怨曠國人患之而作是詩·

9. 匏有苦葉刺衛宣公也,

公與夫人並爲淫亂·

10. 谷風刺夫婦失道也·

衛人化其上淫於新昏而棄其舊室夫婦離絕國俗傷敗焉·

11. In the *Shih we* we have the marquis of Le residing for a time in Wei, and his ministers exhorting him to return [to his own State].

12. The *Maou-k'ew* is a reproof of the prince of Wei.

The Teih had driven out the marquis of Le, who was living consequently for the time in Wei. But [the marquis of] Wei could not discharge his duty as the Chief of a region, banding together and leading on other States for common service; and the ministers of Le therefore thus reproved Wei.

13. The *Keen he* is directed against the neglect of men of worth in Wei.

Such men, employed as pantomimes, were all fit to be ministers to a king.

14. In the *T'euen shwuy* we have a daughter of the House of Wei wishing to make a visit to her native State.

She was married to the prince of another State, and her parents being dead, though she wished to visit her relatives, she could not do so. She therefore made this ode to show her feelings.

15. The *Pih mun* is directed against the fact that the officers of Wei did not get the opportunity to accomplish the objects which they had at heart.

It tells how loyal men were deprived of this.

16. The *Pih fung* is directed against the cruel oppression which prevailed in Wei.

All was awful oppression in Wei; the common people could not keep together in their relative circles, but took one another's hands, and went away.

17. The *Tsing neu* is directed against the times.

The marquis of Wei was without principle, and the marchioness without virtue.

18. The *Sin t'ae* is directed against duke Seuen of Wei.

When the duke was bringing to the State a wife for [his son] Keih, he built the new tower near the Ho, and there forced her. The people hated his conduct, and made this ode.

11. 式微、黎侯寓于衞、其臣勸以歸也.

12. 旄丘、責衞伯也.

狄人迫逐黎侯、黎侯寓于衞、衞不能修方伯連率之職、黎之臣子以責於衞也.

13. 簡兮、剌不用賢也.

衞之賢者、仕於伶官、皆可以承事王者也.

14. 泉水、衞女思歸也.

嫁於諸侯、父母終、思歸寧而不得、故作是詩以自見也.

15. 北門、剌士不得志也.

言衞之忠臣、不得其志爾.

16. 北風、剌虐也.

衞國並爲威虐、百姓不親、莫不相攜持而去焉.

17. 靜女、剌時也.

衞君無道、夫人無德.

18. 新臺、剌衞宣公也.

納伋之妻、作新臺于河上而要之、國人惡之而作是詩也.

19. The *Urh tsze shing chow* shows how the people thought of Keih and Show. Those two sons of duke Seuen contended which should die for the other. The people thought of them with sorrow, and made this ode.

ODES OF YUNG.

1. The *Pih chow* relates the solemn vow of Kung Këang.

Kung Pih, heir to the State of Wei, having died an early death, his wife was holding fast her righteousness, when her parents wished to force her to another marriage. She refused her consent with an oath, and made this ode to put an end to their design.

2. In the *Ts'ëang yen tsze*, the people of Wei censure their superiors.

The [former] marquis's son Hwan was living in intercourse with the [present] marquis's mother. The people hated the thing, but it could not be spoken of [directly].

3. The *Keun tsze këae laou* is directed against the marchioness-[dowager] of Wei.

She was living in a state of lascivious disorder, and failed in duty to her husband. The piece therefore sets forth the virtue of a prince's wife, with the rich array of her robes, and how she ought to grow old with her husband.

4. The *Sang chung* is directed against improper connexions.

Through the licentious disorder that prevailed in the ruling House, men and women came to run to one another's arms. Even men of hereditary families, sustaining high offices, stole one another's wives and concubines, arranging meetings in hidden and distant spots. Government was relaxed, the people became demoralized, and the [tide of] evil could not be stopped.

5. The *Shun che pun pun* is directed against Seuen Këang of Wei.

The people considered that she was not so good as a quail or a magpie.

19. 二子乘舟·思伋壽也·
衞宣公之二子·爭相爲死·國人傷而思之·作是詩也·

鄘

1. 柏舟·共姜自誓也·
衞世子共伯蚤死·其妻守義·父母欲奪而嫁之·誓而
弗許·故作是詩以絕之·
2. 牆有茨·衞人刺其上也·
公子頑通乎君母·國人疾之·而不可道也·
3. 君子偕老·刺衞夫人也·
夫人淫亂·失事君子之道·故陳人君之德·服飾之盛·
宜與君子偕老也·
4. 桑中·刺奔也·
衞之公室淫亂·男女相奔·至於世族在位·相竊妻妾·
期於幽遠·政散民流·而不可止·
5. 鶉之奔奔·刺衞宣姜也·
衞人以爲宣姜·鶉鵲之不若也·

6. The *Ting che fang chung*, is in praise of duke Wăn of Wei (B C. 659—634).

The State had been extinguished by the Teih, and [the people] removed eastwards across the Ho, residing in the open country of the tract of Ts'aou.   Duke Hwan of Ts'e smote the Teih, and re-established the State; when Wăn removed his residence to Ts'oo-k'ëw.   There he began by building the walls of a city and a market-place, after which he reared his palace, regulating things according to the exigency of the time.   The people were pleased with him, the population greatly increased, and the State became wealthy.

7. In the *To tung* we have the cessation of improper connexions.

Duke Wăn of Wei, by his right ways, transformed the people.   They became ashamed of licentious connexions, and would not be ranked with those guilty of them.

8. The *Sëang shoo* satirizes the want of propriety.

Duke Wăn of Wei corrected the manners of his ministers, and censured those in office, who, through the influence on them of former rulers, were without dignity of deportment.

9. The *Kan maou* is in praise of the love of what is good.

Many of the ministers of duke Wăn of Wei loved what was good, and men of talents and virtue rejoiced to set forth good ways to them.

10. The *Tsae ch'e* was made by the wife of Muh of Heu.

Pitying the overthrow of her native State, she was grieved that she could not save it.   Duke E of Wei had been killed by the Teih; the people were dispersed, and living in huts about Ts'aou.   The wife of duke Muh of Heu, pitying the ruin of Wei, and pained by the feebleness of Heu which was unable to save it, wished to return to Wei and condole with her brother.   And as correct propriety forbade that, she expressed her sentiments in this ode.

6. 定之方中·美衞文公也·
衞爲狄所滅·東徙渡河·野處漕邑·齊桓公攘戎狄而
封之·文公徙居楚邱·始建城市而營宮室·得其時制·
百姓說之·國家殷富焉·

7. 蝃蝀·止奔也·
衞文公能以道化其民·淫奔之恥·國人不齒也·

8. 相鼠·刺無禮也·
衞文公能正其羣臣·而刺在位·承先君之化無禮
儀也·

9. 干旄·美好善也·
衞文公臣子多好善·賢者樂告以善道也·

10. 載馳·許穆夫人作也·
閔其宗國顛覆·自傷不能救也·衞懿公爲狄人所滅·
國人分散·露於漕邑·許穆夫人閔衞之亡·傷許之小·
力不能救·思歸唁其兄·又義不得·故賦是詩也·

ODES OF WEI

1. The *Ke yuh* celebrates the virtue of duke Woo (B.C. 812—757).

He was accomplished, and could moreover listen to counsel and remonstrance, keeping himself under the restraints of propriety. In consequence of this he was received as its chief minister at the court of Chow, where they admired him, and made this ode.

2. The *K'aou pwan* was directed against duke Chwang (B.C. 756—734).

He could not continue the method of his predecessor, so that men of talents withdrew from public service and lived in obscurity.

3. The *Shih jin* is expressive of pity for Chwang Këang.

Duke Chwang, led away by his love for his favourite concubine, allowed her proudly to usurp the superior place. Worthy as Chwang Këang was, she received no responsive kindness from him, and all her life had no child. The people pitied her, and were sorry for her case.

4. The *Mang* was directed against the times.

In the time of duke Seuen (B.C. 718—699), propriety and righteousness disappeared, and licentious manners greatly prevailed. Males and females did not keep separate;—the one side seduced, and the other consented. But when the flower of beauty had faded, the man abandoned and turned his back on his paramour. A woman was brought by suffering to repentance [for having cohabited improperly]. The piece therefore relates the circumstances, as a condemnation of the times, praising her return to the right, and branding dissoluteness.

5. In the *Chuh kan* we have a daughter of the House of Wei wishing to return to that State.

Married in another State where her affection was not responded to, she wished [to return to Wei], but was able to submit to propriety.

衞

1. 淇澳,美武公之德也.
有文章又能聽其規諫,以禮自防,故能入相于周,
美而作是詩也.
2. 考槃,刺莊公也.
不能繼先公之業,使賢者退而窮處.
3. 碩人,閔莊姜也.
莊公惑於嬖妾,使驕土僭,莊姜賢而不答,終以無子,
國人閔而憂之.
4. 氓,刺時也.
宣公之時,禮義消亡,淫風大行,男女無別,遂相奔
誘,華落色衰,復相棄背,或乃困而自悔,喪其妃耦,故序
其事以風焉,美反正,刺淫泆也.
5. 竹竿,衞女思歸也.
適異國而不見答,思而能以禮者也

6. The *Hwan-lan* was directed against duke Hwuy (B.C. 698—668).

Proud and unobservant of propriety, the great officers made him the object of their satire.

7. The subject of the *Ho kwang* is the mother of duke Sëang of Sung (B.C. 649 —636).

She had returned for good to Wei, but could not cease from thinking of him, and therefore made this piece.

8 The *Pih ho* was directed against the times.

It tells how an officer, on public service, where he was in the van before the king's chariots, was detained beyond the proper time, unable to return.

9. The *Yëw hoo* was directed against the times.

The males and the females of Wei were losing the time for marriage without becoming husband and wife. Anciently, when a State was suffering from the misery of famine, the rules were relaxed so that there might be many marriages; and males and females who had no partners were brought together, in order to promote the increase of the people.

10. The *Muh kwa* is in praise of duke Hwan of Ts'e (B C. 683—642).

The State of Wei had been ruined by the Teih, and the people had fled and were living in Ts'aou. Duke Hwan came to their rescue, and re-instated Wei. sending gifts, moreover, of carriages, horses, utensils, and robes. When the people thought of his conduct, they wished to recompense him largely, and made this piece.

ODES OF WANG.

1. The *Shoo le* is expressive of pity for the old capital of Chow.

A great officer of Chow, travelling on the public service, came to it, and, as he passed by, found the places of the ancestral temple, palaces, and other public buildings, all overgrown with millet. He was moved with pity for the downfall of the

6. 芄蘭, 刺惠公也.
騎而無禮. 大夫刺之.

7. 河廣. 宋襄公母歸於衛. 思而不止. 故作是詩也.

8. 伯兮. 刺時也.
言君子行役. 爲王前驅過時而不反焉.

9. 有狐. 刺時也.
衛之男女失時. 喪其妃耦焉. 古者國有凶荒. 則殺禮而多昏. 會男女之無夫家者. 所以育人民也

10. 木瓜. 美齊桓公也.
衛國有狄人之敗. 出處于漕. 齊桓公救而封之. 遺之車馬器服焉. 衛人思之. 欲厚報之. 而作是詩也.

王

1. 黍離. 閔宗周也.
周大夫行役. 至于宗周. 過故宗廟宮室. 盡爲禾黍.

House of Chow, moved about the place in an undecided way, as if he could not bear to leave it, and made this piece.

2. The *Keun-tsze yu yih* was directed against king P'ing.

An officer being away on service, without any period fixed for his return, the great officers, thinking of his perils and hardships, were moved to this satire.

3. The *Keun-tsze yang-yang* is expressive of pity for Chow.

Officers, amid the disorders of the times, invited one another to serve for emolument, wishing simply to preserve their persons, and to keep away from harm.

4. The *Yang che shwuy* was directed against king P'ing.

Instead of seeking to promote the comfort of his people, he kept them stationed on guard far away in his mother's country. The people of Chow murmured, and longed for their homes.

5. The *Chung kuh yew t'uy* is expressive of pity for Chow.

The affection between husband and wife decayed daily and became less, till in a bad year, when famine prevailed, they abandoned each other.

6. The *T'oo yuen* is expressive of pity for Chow.

King Hwan having lost his faith to them, the States revolted from him. Animosities arose, and calamities followed one another, till the king's army was defeated and himself wounded. Superior men had no enjoyment of their life.

7. In the *Koh luy* we have king P'ing's own kindred finding fault with him.

In the House of Chow all right principles were decayed, and the king was casting away the nine classes of his kindred.

8. The *Ts'ae koh* indicates the fear of calumniators.

9. The *Ta keu* was directed against the great officers of Chow.

The rules of propriety and righteousness were violated and neglected; males seduced, and women hastened to their embraces. Hence the piece sets forth the ways of antiquity to brand the present. The great officers of the time were unable to listen properly to the cases of litigation between males and females.

閔周室之顚覆彷徨不忍去而作是詩也.
2. 君子于役刺平王也,
君子行役無期度大夫思其危難以風焉.
3. 君子陽陽閔周也,
君子遭亂相招爲祿仕全身遠害而已.
4. 揚之水刺平王也.
不撫其民而遠申戍于母家周人怨思焉.
5. 中谷有蓷閔周也.
夫婦日以衰薄凶年饑饉室家相棄爾.
6. 兎爰閔周也.
桓王失信諸侯背叛構怨連禍王師傷敗君子不
樂其生焉.
7. 葛藟王族刺平王也.
周室道衰棄其九族焉.
8. 采葛懼讒也.
9. 大車刺周大夫也.

10   The *K'ëw chung yëw ma* shows how the people longed for men of worth. King Chwang (B. C. 695—681) was devoid of intelligence, and drove men of worth away from the court. The people thought of them, and made this piece.

ODES OF CH'ING.

1.   The *Tsze e* is in praise of duke Woo (B. C. 770—743).

His father and he were both ministers of Instruction in the court of Chow, and well discharged the duties of that office, so that the people of the State approved of him; and therefore they here praised his virtue to illustrate how the holders of States should add one good quality to another.

2.   The *Tsëang Chung-tsze* was directed against duke Chwang (B. C. 742—700).

The duke could not manage his mother, and injured his younger brother. That brother, Shuh, was going on badly and the duke did not restrain him. Chung of Chae remonstrated, but the duke did not listen to him;—thus by his want of resolution, when little effort was needed, producing great disorder.

3.   The *Shuh yu t'ëen* was directed against duke Chwang.

Shuh resided in King, where he provided coats of mail and weapons of war, going out thereafter to hunt. The people of the State were pleased with him, and embraced his side.

4.   The *Ta shuh yu t'ëen* was directed against duke Chwang.

Shuh was distinguished for his ability, and fond of valour, so that, though he was unrighteous, he attracted the multitudes to himself.

5.   The *Ts'ing jin* was directed against duke Wăn (B.C. 671—627).

禮義陵遲, 男女淫奔, 故陳古以刺今, 大夫不能聽
男女之訟焉.

10. 丘中有麻, 思賢也.

莊王不明, 賢人放逐, 國人思之, 而作是詩也.

鄭

1. 緇衣, 美武公也.

父子並爲周司徒, 善於其職, 國人宜之, 故美其德,
以明有國善善之功焉.

2. 將仲子, 刺莊公也.

不勝其母以害其弟, 弟叔失道, 而公弗制, 祭仲諫,
而公弗聽, 小不忍以致大亂焉.

3. 叔于田, 刺莊公也.

叔處于京, 繕甲治兵, 以出于田, 國人說, 而歸之.

4. 大叔于田, 刺莊公也.

叔多才而好勇, 不義而得眾也.

5. 清人, 刺文公也.

Kaou K'ih being fond of gain, and paying no regard to his ruler, duke Wăn hated him, and wished to remove him to a distance. He was unable to do so, however, and sent him to the borders to oppose the hordes of the north. There he displayed his forces, and kept them moving about, near the Ho. So long a time elapsed without their being recalled, that the troops dispersed and returned to Ch'ing, Kaou K'ih himself fleeing to Ch'in. The Kung-tsze Soo made this piece to express his views, how the advancement of K'aou K'ih contrary to propriety, and duke Wăn's wrong method of procuring his retirement, led to the endangering of the State and the ruin of the army

6. The *Kaou k'ew* was directed against the court [of Ch'ing.]

It describes the courtiers of old as a satire on those of the time.

7. The *Tsun ta loo* shows how [the people] thought of their superior men.

Duke Chwang having abandoned the proper path, superior men were leaving him, and the people of the State thought longingly of them.

8. The *Neu yueh k: ming* was directed against the want of delight in virtue.

It sets forth the righteous ways of old times, to brand the character of the existing time which had no pleasure in virtue, and loved only sensual enjoyment.

9. The *Yew neu t'ung keu* was directed against Hwuh [the eldest son of duke Chwang, known as duke Ch'aou, (B.C. 701—694)].

The people of Ch'ing satirize in it his refusal to marry a princess of Ts'e. Before his accession he had done good service to that State, the marquis of which wanted to give him one of his daughters to wife. She was a lady of worth, but Hwuh declined the alliance; and the result was that for want of the help of a great State he was driven out of Ch'ing. On this account the people satirized him.

10. The *Shan yĕw foo-soo* was directed against Hwuh.

Hwuh gave his esteem to those who were not deserving of it.

11. The *T'oh he* was directed against Hwuh.

高克好利而不顧其君,文公惡而欲遠之,不能,使高
克將兵而禦敵于竟,陳其師旅,翶翔河上,久而不召,衆
散而歸,高克奔陳,公子素惡高克進之不以禮,文公退
之不以道,危國亡師之本,故作是詩也.

6. 羔裘,刺朝也.
言古之君子,以風其朝焉.

7. 遵大路,思君子也.
莊公失道,君子去之,國人思望焉

8. 女曰雞鳴,刺不說德也.
陳古義以刺今,不說德而好色也.

9. 有女同車,刺忽也.
鄭人刺忽之不昏于齊,太子忽嘗有功于齊,齊侯請
妻之,齊女賢而不取,卒以無大國之助,至於見逐,故
國人刺之.

10. 山有扶蘇,刺忽也.
所美非美然.

11. 蘀兮,刺忽也.

The ruler was weak and his ministers were strong, so that he could not give them the note, and make them follow him.

12. The *Kĕaou t'ung* was directed against Hwuh.

He was not able to take counsel on affairs with men of worth, and powerful ministers arrogated the right of making enactments.

13. The *K'ëen chang* expresses the desire of the people of Ch'ing to have the condition of the State rectified.

The 'artful boy' was pursuing his course of disorder, and they wished for a great State to rectify their affairs.

14. The *Fung* was directed against prevailing disorder.

The proper rule for marriages was not observed. The male gave the note, and the female did not respond; he led the way, and she did not follow.

15. The *Tung mun che shen* was directed against prevailing disorder.

There were men and women who flew to one another, without waiting for the proper ceremonies.

16. The *Fung yu* expresses the longing to see a superior man.

In an age of disorder, the writer longs for a superior man,—one who would not change his rules of life.

17. The *Tsze k'in* was directed against the neglect of schools.

In an age of disorder, these were not attended to.

18. The *Yang che shwuy* bewails that there were no [right] ministers.

Some superior man made this piece, pitying Hwuh who had been brought to exile and death through his want of faithful ministers and good officers.

19. The *Ch'uh k'e tung mun* bewails the prevailing disorder.

Five times was there a struggle among the sons of duke [Chwang] for the State; hostilities never ceased; husbands and wives were separated; and the people longed for some way to preserve their families.

君弱臣彊不倡而和也·

12. 狡童刺忽也·
不能與賢人圖事權臣擅命也·

13. 褰裳思見正也·
狂童恣行國人思大國之正己也·

14. 丰刺亂也·
昏姻之道缺陽倡而陰不和男行而女不隨·

15. 東門之墠刺亂也·
男女有不待禮而相奔者也·

16. 風雨思君子也·
亂世則思君子不改其度焉·

17. 子衿刺學校廢也·
亂世則學校不修焉·

18. 揚之水閔無臣也·
君子閔忽之無忠臣良士終以死亡而作是詩也·

19. 出其東門閔亂也·
公子五爭兵革不息男女相棄民人思保其室家焉·

20.   The *Yay yëw man ts'aou* expresses a desire for some time of marriage.

No favours from the ruler flowed down to the people, who were exhausted by the constant hostilities.   Males and females lost their proper time for marriage, and wished that they might come together without any previous arrangements.

21.   The *Tsin Wei* was directed against the prevailing disorder.

The weapons of strife never rested; husbands and wives were torn from one another, lewd manners went abroad, and there was no delivering the people from them.

Ts'e.

1.   The *Ke ming* expresses longing thoughts of a worthy consort of the ruler.

Duke Gae (B.C. 933—894) was wildly addicted to sensual pleasure, indolent, and careless of his duties, therefore the ode sets forth how a worthy consort [of an earlier ruler], a chaste lady, in the morning while it was yet night, admonished and warned her husband, showing how a consort should perfect the ruler.

2.   The *Seuen* is directed against wild addiction to hunting.

Duke Gae was fond of hunting, and insatiate in pursuing the chase.   The people were influenced by his example, so that this fondness for the chase became a general habit.   He who was practised in hunting was accounted worthy, and he who was skilful in charioteering was pronounced good.

3.   The *Choo* is directed against the times.

At that time the bridegroom did not go in person to meet his bride.

4.   The *Tung fang che jih* is directed against the decay [of the times].

The relation of ruler and minister was neglected.   Men and women sought each other in lewd fashion; and there was no ability to alter the customs by the rules of propriety.

20. 野有蔓草,思遇時也·

君之澤不下流,民窮於兵革,男女失時,思不期而會焉·

21. 溱洧,刺亂也·

兵革不息,男女相棄,淫風大行,莫之能救焉·

齊

1. 雞鳴,思賢妃也·

哀公荒淫怠慢,故陳賢妃貞女,夙夜警戒相成之道焉·

2. 還,刺荒也·

哀公好田獵,從禽獸而無厭,國人化之,遂成風俗,習於田獵謂之賢,閑於馳逐謂之好焉·

3. 著,刺時也·

時不親迎也·

4. 東方之日,刺衰也·

君臣失道,男女淫奔,不能以禮化也·

52]

5. The *Tung fang we ming* is directed against the neglect of the proper seasons for affairs.

The court disregarded the times for rising and sleeping; its commands came forth at improper times; the officer of the clepsydra was not able to discharge his duties.

6. The *Nan shan* is directed against duke Sëang (B.C. 696—685).

His conduct was like that of a beast, for he maintained an incestuous connection with his sister. [Some] great officer, in consequence of this wickedness, made the piece, and left the court.

7. In the *Foo t'ëen* a great officer speaks against duke Sëang.

Without propriety or righteousness he aimed at great achievements, and without cultivating virtue he sought to gain the chief place among the States. His great aims [only] toiled his mind, the way in which he sought them not being the proper one.

8. The *Loo ling* is directed against the wild addiction to hunting.

Duke Sëang was fond of the chase. He pursued it with hand-net and shooting-line, not attending to the business of the people. The people suffered from his course, and here set forth the ancient ways in condemnation of his.

9. The *Pe kow* is directed against Wăn Këang.

The people of Ts'e hated the weakness of duke Hwan of Loo, who was not able to restrain Wăn Këang, so that she proceeded to the lewd disorders which proved calamitous to the two States.

10. In the *Tsae k'ow* the people of Ts'e brand duke Sëang.

Devoid of all propriety and righteousness, he made a great display of his carriage and robes, drove rapidly on the public road, and in a great town was guilty of lewdness with Wăn Këang, publishing his wickedness to all the people.

11. The *E ts'ëay* is directed against duke Chwang (B.C. 692—661) of Loo.

5. 東方未明,剌無節也.
　朝廷興居無節,號令不時,挈壺氏不能掌其職焉.
6. 南山,剌襄公也.
　鳥獸之行,淫乎其妹,大夫遇是惡,作詩而去之.
7. 甫田,大夫剌襄公也.
　無禮義而求大功,不修德而求諸侯,志大心勞,所以求者非其道也.
8. 盧,剌荒也.
　襄公好田獵畢弋,而不修民事,百姓苦之,故陳古以風焉.
9. 敝笱,剌文姜也.
　齊人惡魯桓公微弱,不能防閑文姜,使至淫亂,為二國患焉.
10. 載驅,齊人剌襄公也.
　無禮義,故盛其車服,疾驅於通道大都,與文姜淫,播其惡於萬民焉.
11. 猗嗟,剌魯莊公也.

53]

The people of Ts'e were pained by duke Chwang, with dignified demeanour and skilled in arts, yet unable to restrain his mother, so that he failed in his duty as a son, and was accounted a son of the marquis of Ts'e.

ODES OF WEI.

1. The *Koh keu* was directed against narrowness of disposition.

The territory of Wei was narrow and confined; its people were ingenious, artful, and eager for gain; its rulers were stingy, narrow-minded, and without virtue to guide them.

2. The *Fun ts'eu joo* was directed against niggardliness.

The ruler was niggardly, and could be industrious; but the piece exposes his being so contrary to what was proper.

3. The *Yuen yëw t'aou* was directed against the times.

Some great officer made it, distressed about his ruler who, pressed hard in a small State, was yet parsimoniously stingy, unable to use his people, and giving them no lessons of virtue, so that the State was daily encroached upon and stript of territory.

4. In the *Chih hoo* we have a filial son abroad on the public service, and thinking of his parents.

The State was hard-pressed, and suffering frequent dismemberment. It was obliged to engage in service for greater States, so that parents [and children], elder and younger brother, were separated and dispersed. [In such a state of things], this piece was made.

5. The *Shih mow che këen* was directed against the times.

It tells how the State was dismembered and made small, so that the people had not space to dwell in it.

齊人傷魯莊公有威儀技藝然而不能以禮防閑其
母失于之道人以爲齊侯之子焉

魏

1. 葛屨刺褊也
魏地陿隘其民機巧趨利其君儉嗇褊急而無德以
將之
2. 汾沮洳刺儉也
其君儉以能勤刺不得禮也
3. 園有桃刺時也
大夫憂其君國小而廹而儉以嗇不能用其民而無
德教日以侵削故作是詩也
4. 陟岵孝子行役思念父母也
國廹而數侵削役乎大國父母兄弟離散而作是詩也
5. 十畝之間刺時也
言其國削小民無所居焉

6. The *Fah t'an* was directed against greediness.

Those in office were covetous and mean, taking their salaries, without doing service for them, so that superior men could not get employment.

7. The *Shih shoo* was directed against heavy exactions.

The people brand in it their ruler, levying heavy exactions, and silkworm-like eating them up, not attending well to the government, greedy and yet fearful, like a great rat.

T'ANG.

1. The *Sih-tsuh* was directed against duke He of Tsiu (B.C. 839—822).

He was economical, but in being so violated the rules of propriety; and the people made this piece in compassion for him, wishing him to take his pleasure when it was the time for it, and according to propriety. This Book contains the odes of Tsin, which is called T'ang, because the people in their deep anxieties with thought of the future, and their economy regulated by propriety, exemplified the manners which had come down to them from the example of Yaou.

2. The *Shan yëw ch'oo* was directed against duke Ch'aou of Tsin (B.C. 744—738).

Unable to cultivate the right method to order his State, with wealth and yet unable to use his people, possessed of bells and drums and yet incapable of taking pleasure from them, not sprinkling and sweeping his court-yards, the government was neglected, and the people dispersed. He was going on to ruin, and the States all around were plotting to take his territories, without his being aware of it. The people therefore made this piece to express their condemnation of him.

3. The *Yang che shwuy* was directed against duke Ch'aou of Tsin.

He divided his State, and invested [his uncle] with Yuh, which increased and became strong, while he grew small and weak. The people were about to revolt and go over to Yuh.

6 伐檀 刺貪也.

在位貪鄙 無功而受祿 君子不得進仕爾.

7. 碩鼠 刺重斂也.

國人刺其君重斂 蠶食於民 不修其政 貪而畏人,
若大鼠也.

唐

1. 蟋蟀 刺晉僖公也.

儉不中禮 故作是詩以閔之 欲其及時 以禮自虞
樂也 此晉也 而謂之唐 本其風俗憂深思遠 儉而用
禮 乃有堯之遺風焉.

2. 山有樞 刺晉昭公也.

不能修道以正其國 有財不能用 有鐘鼓不能以
自樂 有朝廷不能洒埽 政荒民散 將以危亡 四鄰謀
取其國家而不知 國人作詩以刺之也.

3. 揚之水 刺晉昭公也.

4. The *Tseäou lëaou* was directed against duke Ch'aou of Tsin.

Superior men, seeing the opu ence and strength of Yuh, and how [its chief] attended to his government, knew how it would increase in prosperity and size, and that his descendants would possess the State of Tsin.

5. The *Chow mow* was directed against the disorders of Tsin.

In consequence of the disorder marriages were not entered into at the proper time for them.

6. The *Te too* was directed against the times.

The ruler was unable to keep the affections of his relatives; his own flesh and blood were separated from him and dispersed; he dwelt alone and brotherless; and he would be swallowed up by Yuh.

7. The *Kaou k'ëw* was directed against the times.

The people of Tsin brand in it those who were in office, and did not compassionate their people.

8. The *Paou yu* was directed against the times.

After duke Ch'aou there was great confusion through five changes of ruler. Some man of position, obliged to descend and go forth on the public service, so that he was prevented from nourishing his parents, made the piece.

9. The *Woo e* expresses admiration of duke Woo of Tsin (B.C. 678—676).

Immediately on his absorption of that State, one of his great officers, requesting in his behalf the confirmation of his right in it from an envoy of the king, made the piece.

10. The *Yew te che too* was directed against duke Woo of Tsin.

The duke standing in his solitary distinction, though all the branches of his House were subject to him, did not seek for men of worth to help himself.

昭公分國以封沃·沃盛彊·昭公微弱·國人將叛而歸沃焉·

4. 椒聊·刺晉昭公也·
君子見沃之盛彊·能修其政·知其蕃衍盛大·子孫有晉國焉·

5. 綢繆·刺晉亂也·
國亂·則昏姻不得其時焉·

6. 杕杜·刺時也·
君不能親其宗族·骨肉離散·獨居而無兄弟將爲沃所幷爾·

7. 羔裘·刺時也·
晉人刺其在位·不恤其民也·

8. 鴇羽·刺時也·
昭公之後·大亂五世·君子下從征役·不得養其父母·而作是詩也·

9. 無衣·美晉武公也·
武公始幷晉國·其大夫爲之請命乎天子之使·而作是詩也·

10. 有杕之杜·刺晉武公也·
武公寡特·兼其宗族·而不求賢以自輔·焉·

11. The *Kuh săng* was directed against duke Hëen of Tsin (B.C. 675—650).
Fond of warfare, he occasioned the death of many of the people.

12. The *Ts'ae ling* was directed against duke Hëen of Tsin.
He was fond of listening to slanders.

Ts'ɪɴ.

1. The *Keu lin* was in praise of Chung of Ts'in (B.C. 843—821).
With him began the greatness of Ts'in, and he had what men prize,—chariots and horses, observances of ceremony, music, and attendants.

2. The *Sze t'ëeh* was in praise of duke Sëang (B.C. 776—765).
He first was constituted a prince of the kingdom, engaged in the chase, and had the pleasure of parks.

3. The *Sëaou jung* was in praise of duke Sëang.
He made complete preparation of arms to punish the western Jung, who were then in such strength that his expeditions against them never ceased. The people gloried in the chariots and mail, while wives were moved with pity for their husbands.

4. The *Këen këa* was directed against duke Sëang.
Incapable of using the proprieties of Chow, there was no way for him to strengthen his State.

5. The *Chung-nan* conveyed a warning to duke Sëang.
He was able to secure to himself the territory of Chow, took his place, the first in Ts'in, as a prince of the empire, and received the dress of that distinction. Some great officer, admiring him, made this piece, to warn and advise him.

11. 葛生,刺晉獻公也.
　好攻戰,則國人多喪矣.
12. 采苓,刺晉獻公也.
　獻公好聽讒焉.

秦

1. 車鄰,美秦仲也.
　秦仲始大有車馬禮樂侍御之好焉.
2. 駟驖,美襄公也.
　始命有田狩之事,園囿之樂焉.
3. 小戎,美襄公也.
　備其兵甲,以討西戎.西戎方彊,而征伐不休,國人則矜其車甲,婦人能閔其君子焉.
4. 蒹葭,刺襄公也.
　未能用周禮,將無以固其國焉.
5. 終南,戒襄公也.
　能取周地,始爲諸侯受顯服.大夫美之,故作是詩以戒勸之.

6. The *Hwang nëaou* bewails the fate of 'the three worthies.'

The people, condemning the act of duke Muh (B.C. 620) in having people buried with him, made this piece.

7. The *Shin fung* is directed against duke K'ang (B.C. 619—608).

He forgot all the achievements of duke Muh, and commenced with discountenancing his worthy ministers.

8. The *Woo e* is directed against the frequent hostilities that were carried on.

The people condemn in it their ruler's fondness for war, his excessive recourse to it, and his not sharing with the people the things which they wished.

9. In the *Wei yang* we have duke K'ang thinking of his mother.

His mother was a daughter of duke Hëen of Tsin. When duke Wăn was suffering from the evil brought on him by Le Ke, and before he returned [to Tsin], his aunt in Ts'in died. When duke Muh then restored him to Tsin, duke K'ang was the heir-apparent, made presents to Wăn, and escorted him to the north of the Wei. He thought how he could no longer see his mother, but the sight of his uncle seemed to bring her to his sight again. When he succeeded to his father, all this occurred to him, and he made this piece.

10. The *K'euen yu* is directed against duke K'ang.

He forgot the old ministers of his father, and though he began with treating men of worth well, he did not end so.

CH'IN.

1. The *Yuen k'ew* is directed against duke Yëw (B.C. 853—834).

He was wildly addicted to sensual pleasure, benighted and disorderly, indulging in dissipation beyond measure.

6. 黃鳥,哀三良也.
國人剌穆公以人從死,而作是詩也.

7. 晨風,剌康公也.
忘穆公之業,始棄其賢臣焉.

8. 無衣,剌用兵也.
秦人剌其君好攻戰,亟用兵,而不與民同欲焉.

9. 渭陽,康公念母也.
康公之母,晉獻公之女,文公遭麗姬之難,未反而秦姬卒,穆公納文公,康公時爲太子,贈送文公于渭之陽,念母之不見也,我見舅氏,如母存焉,及其卽位,思而作是詩也.

10. 權輿,剌康公也.
忘先君之舊臣與賢者,有始而無終也.

陳

1. 宛邱,剌幽公也.
淫荒昏亂,游蕩無度焉.

2. The *Tung mun che fun* expresses disgust at the disorder which prevailed.

Through the influence which went out from the wild addiction of duke Yëw to sensual pleasure, males and females abandoned their proper employments, hurried to meet one another on the roads, and danced and sang in the market places.

3. The *Hăng mun* is designed to stimulate duke He (B.C. 833—795).

He was well-meaning, but without strength of will, and some one therefore made this piece to encourage him.

4. The *Tung mun che ch'e* is directed against the times.

The writer was disgusted at the sensuality and blindness of his ruler, and longed for a worthy lady to be his mate.

5. The *Tung mun che yang* is directed against the times.

Marriages were not made at the proper season. Males and females often acted against one another. There were cases in which though the bridegroom went in person to meet the bride, she would not come to him.

6. The *Moo mun* was directed against T'o of Ch'in (B.C. 706).

Through having no good tutor or assistant, he proceeded to unrighteousness, of which the evil consequences fell upon the myriads of the people.

7. The *Fang yëw ts'eoh ch'aou* is expressive of sorrow on account of the injuries wrought by slanderers.

Duke Seuen (B.C. 691—647) gave much credence to such, which made superior men anxious and afraid.

8. The *Yuëh ch'uh* was directed against the love of sensual pleasure.

Those who were in office did not love virtue, but sought pleasure in beauty.

9. The *Choo lin* was directed against duke Ling (B.C. 612—598).

He carried on a criminal intercourse with Hëa Ke, and visited her morning and night without ceasing.

2. 東門之枌,疾亂也.
幽公淫荒風化之所行,男女棄其舊業,亟會於道路,歌舞於市井爾.

3. 衡門,誘僖公也.
愿而無立志,故作是詩以誘掖其君也.

4. 東門之池,刺時也.
疾其君之淫昏,而思賢女以配君子也.

5. 東門之楊,刺時也.
昏姻失時,男女多違,親迎,女猶有不至者也.

6. 墓門,刺陳佗也.
陳佗無良師傅,以至於不義惡加於萬民焉.

7. 防有鵲巢,憂讒賊也.
宣公多信讒,君子憂懼焉.

8. 月出,刺好色也.
在位不好德,而說美色焉.

9. 株林,刺靈公也.
淫乎夏姬,驅馳而往,朝夕不休息焉.

10. The *Tsih p'o* was directed against the times.

It tells how duke Ling and his ministers practised lewdness in the State, so that males and females, in their desire for one another, thought with anxious grief and had intense distress.

ODES OF KWEI.

1. In the *Kaou k'ëw* we have a great officer on a proper ground leaving [the service of] his ruler.

The State was small and hard-pressed [by other States], while the ruler, instead of taking the proper path, loved to have his robes clean and bright, and to saunter about and amuse himself, unable to show any energy in the business of government. Hence this piece.

2. The *Soo kwan* is directed against the neglect of the three years' [mourning].

3. The *Sih gëo ch'ang-ts'oo* is expressive of disgust at dissoluteness.

The people hated their ruler's lewd dissoluteness, and longed for one without his passions.

4. In the *Fei fung* we have a longing for the ways of Chow.

The State being small, and the government in disorder, the author was troubled about the coming of calamities, and longed for the ways of Chow.

ODES OF TS'AOU.

1. The *Fow-yëw* is directed against the extravagance of the ruler.

10. 澤陂, 刺時也.

言靈公君臣淫於其國男女相悅憂思感傷焉.

檜

1. 羔裘, 大夫以道去其君也.
國小而迫, 君不用道, 好潔其衣服, 逍遙游燕, 而不能自強於政治, 故作是詩也.
2. 素冠, 刺不能三年也.
3. 隰有萇楚, 疾恣也.
國人疾其君之淫恣, 而思無情慾者也.
4. 匪風, 思周道也.
國小政亂, 憂及禍難, 而思周道焉.

曹

1. 蜉蝣, 刺奢也.

Though the State was small and pressed upon by others, duke Ch'aou (B.C. 660—652) took no proper method to defend himself. He was extravagant, employed small men, and was going on to find himself without any to rely on.

2. The *How-jin* is directed against the ruler's intimacy with small men.

Duke Kung (B.C. 651—617) put away from him superior men, and kept small men about him.

3. The *She-kёw* is directed against the want of uniformity [in what is correct].

There were no superior men in office, through [the ruler's] not uniformly applying his heart to virtue.

4. The *Hёa ts'euen* expresses a longing for good order.

The people of Ts'aou disgusted with the encroachments and oppression of duke Kung, through which the lower people had no enjoyment of life, thought in their sorrow of the intelligent kings and worthy viceroys [of the past].

ODES OF PIN.

1. The *Ts'ih yueh* sets forth the beginnings of the royal House.

The duke of Chow, in consequence of the changes which were occurring, set forth the source of the transforming influence which proceeded from How-tseih and other early princes of their House,—the hard toils which led to the rise of its prosperity.

2. In the *Ch'e-hёaou* we have the duke of Chow saving the country from the disorder [which threatened].

King Ch'ing continued ignorant of the duke's object, who thereupon made this ode, and sent it to him, naming it the *Ch'e hёaou.*

3. The *Tung shan* relates to the duke of Chow's expedition to the east.

昭公國小而迫, 無法以自守, 好奢而任小人, 將無所依焉.

2. 候人, 刺近小人也.
共公遠君子而好近小人焉.

3. 鳲鳩, 刺不壹也.
在位無君子, 用心之不壹也.

4. 下泉, 思治也.
曹人疾共公侵刻下民, 不得其所, 憂而思明王賢伯也.

豳

1. 七月, 陳王業也.
周公遭變, 故陳后稷先公風化之所由, 致王業之艱難也.

2. 鴟鴞, 周公救亂也.
成王未知周公之志, 公乃爲詩以遺王, 名之曰鴟鴞焉.

3. 東山, 周公東征也.

61]

The duke having returned from this expedition at the end of three years, rewarded and commended his men, on which some great officer, in admiration of him, made this poem. The 1st stanza tells how the men had all been preserved; the 2d, their anxious thoughts; the 3d, how their families had been looking out for them; and the 4th expresses the delight which seasonable marriages occasion. The superior man, in his relations with other men, appreciates their feelings and pities their toils; —thus giving them satisfaction and pleasure. Then, when he employs them, thus satisfied, they will forget death in his service:—it is in the *Tung sha..* that we see this.

4. The *P'o foo* is in praise of the duke of Chow.

Some great officer of Chow gave expression in it to his detestation of the four [rebellious] States.

5. The *Fah ko* is in praise of the duke of Chow.

Some great officer of Chow condemned the court in it for its non-acknowledgment of the duke.

6. The *Këw yih* is in praise of the duke of Chow.

Some great officer of Chow condemned in it the court for its non-acknowledgment of the duke.

7. The *Lang poh* is in praise of the duke of Chow.

When he was acting as regent, there arose, at a distance, in the four States, calumnious rumours against him, and at hand, the king did not recognize [his worth and aim]. Some great officer of Chow expressed in it his admiration that in these circumstances the duke did not lose his sagely virtue.

周公東征三年而歸,勞歸士,大夫美之,故作是詩之其
也,一章言其完也,二章言其思也,三章言其室家序其
瑩女也,四章樂男女之得及時也,君子之於人,人唯東
情而閔其勞,所以說也,說以使民,民忘其死,其
山乎.

4. 破斧,美周公也.
　周大夫以惡四國焉.

5. 伐柯,美周公也.
　周大夫刺朝廷之不知也.

6. 九罭,美周公也.
　周大夫刺朝廷之不知也.

7. 狼跋,美周公也.
　周公攝政,遠則四國流言,近則王不知,周大夫美其
不失其聖也.

PART. II.

MINOR ODES OF THE KINGDOM.

BOOK I. DECADE OF LUH MING.

1. The *Luh ming* is a festal song, proper to the entertainment of the ministers,—admirable guests.

When the ruler had feasted them with food and drink, he also presented them with baskets of silken fabrics, to carry out his generous feeling, so that afterwards those loyal ministers, admirable guests, would do their utmost for him.

2. The *Sze mow* is congratulatory of an envoy on his return.

When one does good service and his merit is recognized, he feels pleased.

3. In the *Hwang-hwang chay hwa* we have a ruler sending off an officer on some commission.

It describes the sending him away with ceremonies and music, and shows how, when at a distance, he might make himself distinguished.

4. The *Chang-te* is a festal ode proper to the entertainment of brothers.

The piece was made in compassion for the way in which [the chiefs of] Kwan and Ts'ae had erred.

5. The *Fah muh* is appropriate to the feasting of friends and old acquaintances.

From the Son of Heaven down to the multitudes of the people, there is no one but needs friends in order to his perfection. When the ruler by his affection for his kindred makes them harmonious, when he makes friends of men of worth and does not forsake them, when he does not forget his old associates, then the people become truly virtuous.

6. In the *T'een paou* the ministers gratefully respond to their sovereign.

When the ruler condescends to those beneath him, and thereby gives the finish to his government, they are prepared to express their admiration in return to him.

小雅
鹿鳴之什,二之一

1. 鹿鳴,燕羣臣嘉賓也.
  既飲食之.又實幣帛筐篚以將其厚意.然後忠臣嘉賓得盡其心矣.
2. 四牡,勞使臣之來也.
  有功而見知則說矣.
3. 皇皇者華,君遣使臣也.
  送之以禮樂,言遠而有光華也.
4. 常棣,燕兄弟也.
  閔管蔡之失道.故作常棣焉.
5. 伐木,燕朋友故舊也.
  自天子至於庶人,未有不須友以成者.親親以睦.友賢不棄.不遺故舊.則民德歸厚矣.
6. 天保,下報上也.
  君能下下以成其政.臣能歸美以報其上焉.

7. The *Ts'ae we* celebrates the despatch of troops for guard-service.

In the time of king Wăn, there was trouble from the tribes of the Keun in the west, and from the Hëen-yun in the north, and by orders from the Son of Heaven he commissioned a general, and despatched troops to guard the Middle State. The *Ts'ae we* was sung on occasion of their despatch. The *Ch'uh keu* was to congratulate them on their return. The *Te too* celebrated their return from their toils.

8. The *Ch'uh keu* congratulates the general on his return.

9. The *Te too* congratulates the men on their return.

10. In the *Nan kae* filial sons admonish one another on the duty of nourishing parents.

BOOK II. DECADE OF PIH HWA.

1. The *Pih hwa* speaks of the spotless purity of filial sons.

2. The *Hwa shoo* speaks of the harmonious seasons, and abundant years, favourable to the millets.

[Of this and the two preceding pieces] the subjects have been preserved, but the words are lost.

3. The *Yu le* is expressive of admiration of the abundance in which all things were produced, enabling every ceremony to be fully performed.

In the *Ts'een paou* and previous pieces we see how Wăn and Woo regulated all within the kingdom, and in the *Ts'ae we* and those that follow, how they regulated the parts beyond. They began with anxiety and toil; they ended with ease and joy; therefore this piece celebrates the abundance of all things, through which announcement of their circumstances could be made to Spiritual Beings.

4. The *Yëw kăng* speaks of how all things were produced according to their proper nature.

7. 采薇. 遣戍役也.

文王之時. 西有昆夷之患. 北有玁狁之難. 以天子
之命. 命將帥. 遣戍役. 以守衞中國. 故歌采薇以遣之.
出車以勞還. 杕杜以勤歸也.

8. 出車. 勞還率也.

9. 杕杜. 勞還役也.

10. 南陔. 孝子相戒以養也.

白華之什. 二之二

1. 白華. 孝子之潔白也.

2. 華黍. 時和歲豐. 宜黍稷也.
有其義而亡其辭.

3. 魚麗. 美萬物盛多. 能備禮也.
文武以天保以上治內. 采薇以下治外. 始於憂勤. 終
於逸樂. 故美萬物盛多. 可以告於神明矣.

4. 由庚. 萬物得由其道也.

5. In the *Nan yёw kёa yu* we have the ruler sharing his joy with men of ability and virtue.

In a time of great peace the ruler rejoiced, with the utmost sincerity, to share his advantages with such men.

6. The *Sung k'ёw* speaks of how all things obtained the greatest and highest amount of production of which they were capable.

7. In the *Nan shan yёw t'ae* we have the ruler rejoicing in the finding of men of worth.

When he had found such men, he was able to lay the foundation of great peace for the State.

8. The *Yёw e* speaks of how all things were produced, every one as it ought to be.

[Of this piece, No. 4, and No. 6,] the subjects have been preserved, but the words are lost.

9. In the *Luh Sёaou* we have the royal favours extending to the four seas.

10. In the *Chan loo* we have the Son of Heaven entertaining the feudal princes.

BOOK III. DECADE OF T'UNG KUNG.

1. In the *T'ung kung* we have the Son of Heaven conferring [the red bow] on a prince who had achieved [some great] service.

2. The *Ts'ing-ts'ing chay go* expresses joy because of the nourishment of talent.

When the ruler developes and nourishes men of talent, then all under heaven rejoice and are glad thereat.

3. The *Luh yueh* celebrates king Seuen's punishment of the northern tribes.

When the state set forth in the *Luh ming* ceased, there was an end of such harmony of joy. When that in the *Sze mow* ceased, there were no more such

5. 南有嘉魚,樂與賢也.
太平之君子,至誠樂與賢者共之也.
6. 崇丘,萬物得極其高大也.
7. 南山有臺,樂得賢也.
得賢,則能爲邦家立太平之基矣.
8. 由儀,萬物之生,各得其宜也.
有其義而亡其辭.
9. 蓼蕭,澤及四海也.
10. 湛露,天子燕諸侯也.

彤弓之什,二之三

1. 彤弓,天子錫有功諸侯也.
2. 菁菁者莪,樂育材也.
君子能長育人材,則天下喜樂之矣.
3. 六月,宣王北伐也.
鹿鳴廢,則和樂缺矣,四牡廢,則君臣缺矣,皇皇者

65]

sovereigns and ministers. When that in the *Hwang-hwang chay hwa* ceased, there was an end to such loyalty and truth. When that in the *Chang-te* ceased, there were no more such brothers. When that in the *Fah muh* ceased, there were no more such friends. When that in the *T'een paou* ceased, the happiness and dignity there auspiced disappeared. When that in the *Ts'ae we* ceased, there was an end of such corrective and punitive expeditions. When that in the *Ch'uh keu* ceased, such service and energy disappeared. When that in the *Te too* ceased, such numerous hosts passed away. When that in the *Yu le* ceased, good laws and order failed. When that in the *Nan kae* ceased, there was an end of such filial piety and fraternal duty. When that in the *Pih hwa* ceased, purity and modesty disappeared. When that in the *Hwa shoo* ceased, there was no more such accumulation of stores. When that in the *Yëw kang* ceased, the active and passive powers of nature failed to act in their proper way. When that in the *Nan yëw kea yu* ceased, men of worth lost their repose, and inferior ministers their proper position. When that in the *Sung k'ëw* ceased, all things were disorganized. When that in the *Nan shan yëw t'ae* ceased, the foundations of the kingdom were destroyed. When that in the *Yëw e* ceased, all things were turned into disorder. When that in the *Luh sëaou* ceased, the out-goings of royal favour were perverted. When that in the *Chan loo* ceased, the States fell off from their allegiance. When that in the *T'ung kung* ceased, the kingdom fell into decay. When that in the *Ts'ing-ts'ing chay go* ceased, the observances of propriety disappeared. The conditions proper to the Minor odes of the court were no more found, and the wild tribes on every side made their incursions, each more fiercely than another, so that the Middle kingdom was exceedingly reduced.

4. In the *Ts'ae k'e* we have king Seuen sending a corrective expedition to the south.

5. In the *Keu kung* we have king Seuen bringing back the ancient prosperity. King Seuen, within the kingdom, reformed the government, and he punished the wild tribes beyond it. He restored the boundaries of Wǎn and Woo. His chariots and horses were in good repair and condition. All the weapons of war were abundantly provided. He again assembled the feudal princes in the eastern capital, and led them to the chase, to make proof of his chariots and footmen.

華友車度黍魚遂失矣雅
廢缺廢缺廢廢矣其廢
則矣則矣則則南形盡
忠天功南蓄賢道弓廢
信保力陔積者山廢則
缺廢缺廢缺不有理則四
矣則矣則矣安臺矣諸夷
常棣福祿林杜友庚由下不蒙夏交
廢缺廢缺廢廢則其則衰侵
則矣則矣則則為國恩菁中
兄弟采薇師衆華陰失其所矣隊乖者菁國
廢缺廢缺廢廢矣基矣矣微
則征伐魚麗廉恥道理崇丘則由露則無矣
伐木缺矣則矣則矣南有萬物萬國萬儀矣
廢缺廢廢則則儀廢則
朋出法華嘉不物離小

4. 采芑宣王南征也.
5. 車攻宣王復古也.

宣王能內修政事外攘夷狄復文武之竟土修車
馬備器械復會諸侯於東都因田獵而選車徒焉.

6. The *Keih jih* is in praise of king Seuen.

He paid careful attention to small matters, and kindly condescended to all beneath him, so that they did their utmost to honour and serve him, their superior.

7. The *Hung yen* is in praise of king Seuen.

The myriads of the people were dispersed abroad, and had no rest in their dwellings. He, however, was able to comfort and bring them back, to establish, tranquillize, and settle them; so that even those in the most pitiable condition and widowed found the comfort that they needed.

8. The *T'ing lëaou* is in praise of king Seuen.

At the same time opportunity was taken to admonish him.

9. The *Mëen shwuy* is intended to correct king Seuen.

10. The *Hoh ming* is intended to instruct king Seuen.

Book. IV. Decade of K'e-foo.

1. The *K'e-foo* is directed against king Seuen.
2. In the *Pih keu* a great officer writes against king Seuen.
3. The *Hwang nëaou* is directed against king Seuen.
4. The *Go hing k'e yay* is directed against king Seuen.
5. The *Sze kan* has for its subject the building of a palace by king Seuen.
6. The *Woo yang* has for its subject the flocks and herds collected by king Seuen.
7. In the *Tsëeh nan shan* Këa Foo writes against king Yëw.
8. In the *Ching yuch* a great officer writes against king Yëw.

6. 吉日, 美宣王田也.
能慎微接下, 無不自盡, 以奉其上焉.

7. 鴻鴈, 美宣王也.
萬民離散不安其居, 而能勞來還定安集之, 至于矜
寡無不得其所焉.

8. 庭燎美宣王也.
因以箴之.

9. 沔水, 規宣王也.

10. 鶴鳴, 誨宣王也.

祈父之什, 二之四

1. 祈父, 刺宣王也.
2. 白駒, 大夫刺宣王也.
3. 黃鳥, 刺宣王也.
4. 我行其野, 刺宣王也.
5. 斯干, 宣王考室也.
6. 無羊, 宣王考牧也.
7. 節南山, 家父刺幽王也.
8. 正月, 大夫刺幽王也.

9. In the *Shih yueh che këaou* a great officer writes against king Yëw.

10. In the *Yu woo ching* a great officer writes against king Yëw.

The rain is what comes down from above; but when ordinances are numerous as the drops of rain, this is not the way to administer government.

BOOK V. DECADE OF SEAOU MIN.

1. In the *Sëaou min*, a great officer expresses his condemnation of king Yëw.

2. In the *Sëaou yuen* a great officer expresses his condemnation of king Yëw.

3. The *Sëaou pwan* is directed against king Yëw.

It was made by the tutor of the king's eldest son.

4. The *K'ëaou yen* is directed against king Le.

Some great officer, suffering from slanders, made this piece.

5. In the *Ho jin sze* the duke of Soo writes against the duke of Paou.

The duke of Paou was a high minister of the court, and slandered the duke of Soo, who thereupon made this piece to disown his friendship.

6. The *Hëang pih* is directed against king Yëw.

A eunuch, suffering from slanderers, made it.

7. The *Kuh fung* is directed against king Yëw.

Throughout the kingdom manners were degenerated, and the principles of friendship cast aside.

8. The *Luh ngo* is directed against king Yëw.

People and officers were toiled and moiled, and unable to watch over their parents at their end.

9. 十月之交,大夫刺幽王也.

10. 雨無正,大夫刺幽王也.

雨,自上下者也.衆多如雨,而非所以爲政也.

小旻之什,二之五

1. 小旻,大夫刺幽王也.

2. 小宛,大夫刺幽王也.

3. 小弁,刺幽王也.

太子之傅作焉.

4. 巧言,刺厲王也.

大夫傷於讒,故作是詩也.

5. 何人斯,蘇公刺暴公也.

暴公爲卿士而譖蘇公焉,故蘇公作是詩以絶之.

6. 巷伯,刺幽王也.

寺人傷於讒,故作是詩也.

7. 谷風,刺幽王也.

天下俗薄,朋友道絶焉.

8. 蓼莪,刺幽王也.

民人勞苦,孝子不得終養爾.

9. The *Ta tung* is directed against the prevailing disorders.

The States of the east were distressed with the service required from them, and had their wealth taken away, so that a great officer of T'an made this piece to announce their distress.

10. In the *Sze yueh* a great officer expresses his condemnation of king Yëw

The men in office were covetous and rapacious; the States were ever producing [new] calamities: repinings and disorders arose on every side.

Book VI. Decade of Pih shan.

1. In the *Pih shan* we have a great officer expressing his condemnation of king Yëw.

Employment on distant services was not equally distributed. The writer was toiled in discharging the affairs entrusted to him, so that he could not nourish his parents.

2. In the *Woo tsëang ta keu* a great officer expresses his regret at having advanced mean men to employment.

3. In the *Sëaou ming* a great officer expresses his regret that he had taken service in an age of disorder.

4. The *Koo chung* is directed against king Yëw.

5. The *Ts'oo ts'ze* is directed against king Yëw.

The government was vexatious, and the exactions were heavy. Many of the fields and pastures were uncultivated, so that famine prevailed with its attendant misery and death, and the people were scattered about, sacrifices also ceasing to be offered. On account of these things superior men thought of ancient times.

6. The *Sin nan shan* is directed against king Yëw.

9. 大東，刺亂也．
東國困於役而傷於財，譚大夫作是詩以告病焉

10. 四月，大夫刺幽王也．
在位貪殘，下國構禍，怨亂竝興焉．

比山之什，二之六

1. 北山，大夫刺幽王也．
役使不均，己勞於從事，而不得養其父母焉．

2. 無將大車，大夫悔將小人也．

3. 小明，大夫悔仕於亂世也．

4. 鼓鐘，刺幽王也．

5. 楚茨，刺幽王也．
政煩賦重，田萊多荒，饑饉降喪，民卒流亡，祭祀不饗，故君子思古焉．

6. 信南山，刺幽王也．

69]

He was not able to administer his domain as king Ch'ing had done, marking out the smaller and larger divisions of the fields, thus carrying out the work of Yu. On account of this, superior men thought of ancient times.

7. The *Foo t'een* is directed against king Yëw.

Superior men, grieved by their present experience, thought of ancient times.

8. The *Ta t'éen* is directed against king Yëw.

It tells how the poor and widows could not preserve themselves.

9. The *Chen pe loh e* is directed against king Yëw.

The writer thought of the ancient wise kings, who could give dignities and charges to the princes, could reward the good and punish the evil.

10. The *Shang-shang chay hwa* is directed against king Yëw.

The emoluments of officers in ancient times descended to their posterity. Mean men were [now] in office, so that slanderers and flatterers advanced together. The race of the worthy were neglected, and the families of meritorious ministers were extinguished.

<hr>

BOOK VII.   DECADE OF SANG HOO.

1. The *Sang hoo* is directed against king Yëw.

The ruler and his ministers, superiors and inferiors [no longer] observed the elegance of propriety in their conduct.

2. The *Yuen yang* is directed against king Yëw.

The author was thinking of the ancient, intelligent kings, who deported themselves towards all creatures and things in the right way, and employed them for their own support with moderation.

3. In the *Kwei péen* we have all his ducal relatives censuring king Yëw.

不能修成王之業, 疆理天下, 以奉禹功, 故君子思古焉.

7. 甫田, 刺幽王也.
君子傷今而思古焉.

8. 大田, 刺幽王也.
言矜寡不能自存焉.

9. 瞻彼洛矣, 刺幽王也.
思古明王能爵命諸侯, 賞善罰惡焉.

10. 裳裳者華, 刺幽王也.
古之仕者世祿, 小人在位則讒諂竝進, 棄賢者之類, 絕功臣之世焉.

<hr>

桑扈之什, 二之七

1. 桑扈, 刺幽王也.
君臣上下, 動無禮文焉.

2. 鴛鴦, 刺幽王也.
思古明王, 交於萬物有道, 自奉養有節焉.

3. 頍弁諸公刺幽王也.

He was tyrannical and oppressive, showing no natural affection, not feasting nor rejoicing the princes of his surname. He effected no harmony by his kindly regard among the nine classes of his kindred, so that they were solitary, in peril, and going on to ruin; and with reference to this state of things this piece was made.

4. The *Keu hĕah* is directed against king Yĕw.

Paou Sze was jealous; men without principle were advanced to office; calumny and cunning were destroying the kingdom; no kindness nor favour descended on the people. The people of Chow longed to get a lady of worth to be a mate for the king; and therefore they made this piece.

5. In the *Ts'ing ying* a great officer censures king Yĕw.

6. In the *Pin che tsoo yen* duke Woo of Wei expresses his condemnation of the times.

King Yĕw was wildly indifferent to his duties, cultivated the intimacy of mean creatures, drank without measure; and the whole kingdom was influenced by him. Rulers and ministers, high and low, became sunk in drink and filthy lust. When duke Woo went to the court, he made this piece.

7. The *Yu ts'aou* is directed against king Yĕw.

It tells how creatures failed to get the nourishment their natures required, and how the king residing in Haou was unable to enjoy himself. On this account some superior man thought of the former king Woo.

8. The *Ts'ae shuh* was directed against king Yĕw.

He was insulting and disrespectful to the princes of the States, and when they came to court, he did not confer any tokens of favour on them, as the rules of propriety required. He would often assemble them, but had no faith nor righteousness. Some superior man, seeing those germs of evil, thought of the former times.

9. In the *Kĕoh kung* his uncles and cousins censure king Yĕw.

Showing no affection to the nine branches of his kindred, and loving calumniators and glib-tongued talkers, his own flesh and bones resented his conduct, and therefore made this piece

暴戾無親不能宴樂同姓親睦九族孤危將亡故作是詩也.

4. 車舝, 大夫剌幽王也.

褒姒嫉妒無道並進譖巧敗國德澤不加於民周人思得賢女以配君子故作是詩也.

5. 青蠅, 大夫剌幽王也.

6. 賓之初筵, 衛武公剌時也.

幽王荒廢媟近小人飲酒無度天下化之君臣上下沈湎淫液武公既入而作是詩也.

7. 魚藻剌幽王也.

言萬物失其性王居鎬京將不能以自樂故君子思古之武王焉.

8. 采菽剌幽王也.

侮慢諸侯諸侯來朝不能錫命以禮數徵會之而無信義君子見微而思古焉.

角弓, 父兄剌幽王也.

不親九族而好讒佞骨肉相怨故作是詩也.

10. The *Yuh lew* is directed against king Yëw.

Tyrannical, oppressive, and without natural affection, punishing where punishment was not due, the princes of the States did not wish to attend at court. The piece tells how such a king was not one whose court was to be frequented.

BOOK VIII. DECADE OF TOO JIN SZE.

1. In the *Too jin sze* the people of Chow censure the want of regularity in the dress [of the times].

Anciently, the leaders of the people never varied in their dress, but, easy and natural, maintained uniformity; and thus presided over the people, who became virtuous, all of them. The writer was grieved that in his day he could see none like the men of old.

2. The *Ts'ae luh* is directed against [the government which produced great] murmuring because of widowhood.

In the time of king Yëw, there were many who had to mourn at being left in a state of widowhood.

3. The *Shoo mèaou* is directed against king Yëw.

[The king] was not able to enrich the kingdom with his favours, and his high ministers were not able to discharge duties like those of the earl of Shaou.

4. The *Sih sang* is directed against king Yëw.

Mean men were in offices, and superior men were neglected. [The writer] longs to see superior men, whom he would serve with all his heart.

5. The *Pih hwa* is directed against the queen of Yëw.

King Yëw married a daughter of Shin, and made her his queen; but he afterwards degraded her on getting possession of Paou Sze. In consequence the inferior

10. 菀柳,刺幽王也.

暴虐無親,而刑罰不中,諸侯皆不欲朝,言王者之不可朝事也.

都人士之什,二之八

1. 都人士,周人刺衣服無常也.

古者長民衣服不貳,從容有常,以齊其民,則民德歸壹,傷今不復見古人也.

2. 采綠,刺怨曠也.

幽王之時,多怨曠者也.

3. 黍苗,刺幽王也.

不能膏潤天下,卿士不能行召伯之職焉.

4. 隰桑,刺幽王也.

小人在位,君子在野,思見君子,盡心以事之.

5. 白華,周人刺幽后也.

幽王取申女以爲后,又得褒姒而黜申后,故下國化

States were influenced by his example. Concubines and their sons took the place of wives and their sons, and the king did nothing to regulate [such a state of things], with reference to which the people of Chow made this ode.

6. In the *Mëen man* a small officer writes against the [prevailing] disorder.

The great ministers manifested no kindness of heart, but neglected and forgot the small and the mean, unwilling to supply them with food or drink, with teaching or the means of conveyance. With reference to this, this ode was made.

7. In the *Hoo yeh* a great officer censures king Yëw.

Superiors set the [ancient] rules aside, and would not observe them. Although they had cattle and stalled beasts, and meat cooked and raw, they would not employ them. This made the writer think of the men of antiquity, who would not in the smallest things neglect the [ancient] usages.

8. In the *Tsan-tsan che shih* we have the inferior States censuring king Yëw.

The Jung and the Teih had rebelled; King and Seu did not acknowledge his authority. On this he ordered a general to lead an expedition to the east. [The States], long distressed with service in the field, made this ode.

9. In the *T'ëaou che hwa* we have a great officer compassionating [the misery of] the times.

In the time of king Yëw, the Jung on the north and the E on the east made emulous inroads on the Middle kingdom. Armies were called out on every side, and the consequence was famine. Some superior man, compassionating the approaching ruin of the House of Chow, and grieved at being involved in it himself, made this piece.

10. In the *Ho ts'aou puh hwang* we have the inferior States censuring king Yëw.

The wild tribes on every side made emulous inroads; in the Middle kingdom there was rebellion; the use of weapons never ceased; the people were regarded as beasts. Some superior man, sad for such things, made this ode.

之，以妾為妻，以孽代宗，而王弗能治，周人為之作此
詩也.

6. 蓼莪，微臣刺亂也.
  大臣不用仁心，遺忘微賤，不肯飲食教載之，故作
是詩也.
7. 菰葉，大夫大刺幽王也.
  上棄禮而不能行，雖有牲牢饔餼，不肯用也，故思古
之人，不以微薄廢禮焉.
8. 漸漸之石，下國刺幽王也.
  戎狄叛之，荊舒不至，乃命將率東征，役久病於外，
故作是詩也.
9. 苕之華，大夫閔時也.
  幽王之時，西戎東夷，交侵中國，師旅並起，因之以
饑饉，君子閔周室之將亡，傷己逢之，故作是詩也.
10. 何草不黃，下國刺幽王也.
  四夷交侵，中國背叛，用兵不息，視民如禽獸，君子憂
之，故作是詩也.

PART III.

THE TA YA.

BOOK I. DECADE OF WAN WANG.

1. The *Wăn wang* tells how king Wăn received the appointment [of Heaven], and founded [the dynasty] of Chow.

2. The *Ta ming* tells how king Wăn possessed illustrious virtue, and Heaven repeated its appointment to king Woo.

3. The *Mëen* shows how the rise of king Wăn is to be traced to king T'ae.

4. The *Yih p'oh* shows how king Wăn was able to put [the right] men into office.

5. The *Han luh* shows how [the dignity of the House of Chow] was received from its ancestors.

The ancestors of Chow had for generations cultivated the exan.ple shown them by How-tseih and duke Lëw, and [then] king T'ae and king Ke had all kinds of blessings, and the dignity which they sought, extended anew to them.

6. The *Sze chae* shows how it was that king Wăn approved himself a sage.

7. The *Hwang e* is in praise of [the House of] Chow.

Heaven saw that to supersede Yin there was no [House] like Chow; and among its princes who had from age to age cultivated their virtue there was none like king Wăn.

8. The *Ling t'ae* refers to the first giving of their allegiance by the people to Chow.

King Wăn had received the appointment [of Heaven], and the people rejoiced in his possession of marvellous virtue, reaching even to birds, beasts, and all living creatures.

9. The *Hëa woo* refers to the successor of Wăn.

King Woo was possessed of sagely virtue, received the renewal of Heaven's appointment; and made more illustrious the merit of his father.

大雅
文王之什,三之一

1. 文王. 文王受命作周也.
2. 大明. 文王有明德. 故天復命武王也.
3. 綿. 文王之興. 本由大王也.
4. 棫樸. 文王能官人也.
5. 旱麓. 受祖也.
　周之先祖. 世修后稷公劉之業. 大王王季. 申以百福干祿焉.
6. 思齊. 文王所以聖也.
7. 皇矣. 美周也.
　天監代殷. 莫若周. 周世世修德. 莫若文王.
8. 靈臺. 民始附也.
　文王受命. 而民樂. 其有靈德. 以及鳥獸昆蟲焉.
9. 下武. 繼文也.
　武王有聖德. 復受天命. 能昭先人之功焉.

10. The *Wăn wang yëw shing* tells how [Wăn's] conquests were continued.
King Woo enlarged the fame of king Wăn, and finished his work of conquest.

BOOK II. DECADE OF SANG MIN.

1. The *Săng min* [is intended] to honour the [great] ancestor [of the House of Chow].
How-tseih was the son of Këang Yuen; the meritorious work of Wăn and Woo commenced from that of How-tseih, whom therefore [his descendants] ascended to, appointing him the assessor of Heaven.

2. The *Hăng wei* [celebrates] the magnanimity [of the House of Chow].
The House of Chow was animated by magnanimity; its benevolence extended even to vegetable life, and thus it was able to harmonize all within the nine grades of its own relationships, and beyond these to do honour and service to the old, nourishing their age, and asking their counsel; thus making complete its happiness and dignity.

3. The *Kè tsuy* [celebrates] the great peace [that prevailed].
Filled with [the king's] spirits, and satiated with his kindness, men displayed the bearing of officers of a superior character.

4. The *Hoo e* [celebrates] the maintenance of established [statutes].
The sovereign, in a time of great peace, was able to support his fulness and maintain the established statutes. The Spirits of Heaven and Earth, and of his ancestors, reposed and rejoiced in him.

5. The *Këa loh* is in praise of king Ch'ing.

6. The *Küng lëw* was made by duke K'ang of Shaou to caution king Ch'ing.
King Ch'ing being about to take the government in hand himself, [the duke] warned him about the business to be done for the people, and presented this ode in praise of duke Lëw's generous devotion to the people.

10. 文王有聲，繼伐也．
武王能廣文王之聲，卒其伐功也．

———

生民之什，三之二

1. 生民，尊祖也．
后稷生於姜嫄，文武之功，起於后稷，故推以配天焉．

2. 行葦，忠厚也．
周家忠厚，仁及草木，故能內睦九族，外尊事黃耇，養老乞言，以成其福祿焉．

3. 既醉，太平也．
醉酒飽德，人有士君子之行焉

4. 鳧鷖，守成也．
太平之君子，能持盈守成，神祇祖考安樂之也．

5. 假樂，嘉成王也．

6. 公劉，召康公戒成王也．
成王將涖政，戒以民事，美公劉之厚於民，而獻是詩也．

.75]

7. In the *Heung choh* duke K'ang of Shaou cautions king Ching.

It tells how great Heaven loves the virtuous, and favours those who go in the right way.

8. In the *K'euen o* duke K'ang of Shaou cautions king Ch'ing.

It tells him how he should seek for men of talents and virtue, and employ good officers.

9. In the *Min laou* duke Muh of Shaou reprehends king Le.

10. In the *Pan* the earl of Fan reprehends king Le.

BOOK III. DECADE OF TANG.

1. In the *Tang* duke Muh of Shaou gives expression to his grief-on account of the great decay of the House of Chow.

King Le was without any principle of right procedure, and throughout the kingdom the rules of government and the statutes were being utterly subverted. In consequence of this, [the duke] made this ode.

2. The *Yih* was directed by duke Woo of Wei against king Le, with the view also of admonishing himself.

3. In the *Sang yëw* the earl of Juy reprehends king Le.

4. The *Yun han* was made by Jing Shuh to show his admiration of king Seuen.

King Seuen succeeded to the remnant of power left by Le, and was bent on putting away the disorders that prevailed. When the calamity [of drought] occurred, he was afraid, and with bent body set himself to cultivate his conduct, if so he might succeed in securing its removal. The whole kingdom rejoiced at the revival of a true royal transformation, and entered with sympathy into the king's sorrow. With reference to this, [Jing Shuh] made this ode.

7. 泂酌召康公戒成王也.
　言皇天親有德饗有道也.
8. 卷阿召康公戒成王也.
　言求賢用吉士也.
9. 民勞召穆剌厲王也.
10. 板凡伯剌厲王也.

蕩之什三之三

1. 蕩召穆公傷周室大壞也.
　厲王無道天下蕩蕩無綱紀文章故作是詩也.
2. 抑衞武公剌厲王亦以自警也.
3. 桑柔芮伯剌厲土也.
4. 雲漢仍叔美宣王也.
　宣王承厲王之烈內有撥亂之志遇裁而懼側身修行欲銷去之天下喜於王化復行百姓見憂故作是詩也.

5. The *Sung kaou* was made by Yin Keih-foo to show his admiration of king Seuen.

The kingdom was again reduced to order, and [the king] was able to establish new States, and show his affection to the princes, [exemplified in] his rewarding the chief of Shin.

6. The *Keang han* was made by Yin Keih-foo to show his admiration of king Seuen.

Able now to raise up the decaying, and to put away disorder, [the king] gave charge to the duke of Shaou to reduce to order the wild tribes of the Hwae.

7. The *Ching min* was made by Yin Keih-foo to show his admiration of king Seuen.

Through the giving of office to men of worth, and the employment of men of ability, the House of Chow had again revived.

8. The *Han yih* was made by Yin Keih-foo to show his admiration of king Seuen.

[The king] was [now] able to issue his charges to the princes.

9. The *Chang woo* was made by duke Muh of Shaou to show his admiration of king Seuen.

[The king] possessed a constant virtue in which he accomplished his warlike undertakings. [The duke] took occasion from this to speak in the way of admonition.

10. In the *Chen jang*, the earl of Fan reprehends king Yëw for the great ruin [he was bringing on].

11. In the *Shaou min*, the earl of Fan reprehends king Yëw for the great ruin [he was bringing on].

Min means to pity. In pity for the kingdom there was no minister like the duke of Shaou.

5. 崧高,尹吉甫美宣王也.
天下復平,能建國親諸侯,褒賞申伯焉.

6. 烝民,尹吉甫美宣王也.
任賢使能,周室中興焉.

7. 韓奕,尹吉甫美宣王也.
能錫命諸侯

8. 江漢,尹吉甫美宣王也.
能興衰撥亂,命召公平淮夷.

9. 常武,召穆公美宣王也.
有常德以立武事,因以爲戒然.

10. 瞻卬,凡伯刺幽王大壞也.

11. 召旻,凡伯刺幽王大壞也.
旻閔也,閔天下無如召公之臣也.

PART IV.

SACRIFICIAL ODES AND PRAISE-SONGS.

BOOK I.   SACRIFICIAL ODES OF CHOW.

[i.]   DECADE OF TS'ING MEAOU.

1.   The *Ts'ing meaou* was used in sacrificing to king Wăn.

When the duke of Chow had finished the city of Loh, he gave audience to the feudal princes, and led them on to sacrifice to king Wăn.

2.   In *Wei t'een ch' ming*, we have an announcement to king Wăn of the universal peace [which was secured].

3.   The *Wei ts'ing* was an accompaniment of the *Sëang* dance.

4.   The *Lëeh wăn* was used at the accession of king Ch'ing to the government, when the princes assisted him in sacrifice.

5.   The *T'een tsoh* was used in sacrificing to the former kings and dukes [of Chow].

6.   The *Haou t'een yëw ch'ing ming* was used at the border sacrifice to Heaven and Earth.

7.   The *Go tsëang* was used in sacrificing to king Wăn in the Hall of light.

8.   The *She mae* was used in a royal progress, as an announcement when the burning pile was kindled to Heaven, and the king looked towards the hills and rivers.

9.   The *Chih king* was used in sacrificing to king Woo.

10.   In the *Sze wăn* How-tseih appears as the correlate of Heaven.

頌
周頌、四之一
清廟之什、四一之一

1. 清廟、祀文王也.
   周公既成洛邑、朝諸侯率以祀文王焉.
2. 維天之命、太平告文王也.
3. 維清、奏象舞也.
4. 烈文、成王即政、諸侯助祭也.
5. 天作、祀先王先公也.
6. 昊天有成命、郊祀天地也.
7. 我將、祀文王於明堂也.
8. 時邁、巡守告祭柴望也.
9. 執競、祀武王也.
10. 思文、后稷配天也.

78]

[ii.] DECADE OF SHIN KUNG.

1. The *Shin kung* was used when the princes had assisted in sacrifice, and [the king] was dismissing them in the ancestral temple.

2. The *E he* was used in spring and autumn, when praying for grain to God.

3. The *Chin loo* has reference to the visitors, who had come to assist in sacrifice.

4. The *Fung neën* was used in thanksgivings in autumn and winter.

5. The *Yëw koo* was used when the instruments of music had first been completed, and they were all employed in the ancestral temple.

6. The *Ts'ëen* was used in the first month of spring when a fish was presented, and in summer, when a sturgeon was presented.

7. The *Yung* was used at the grand sacrifice to the highest ancestor.

8. The *Tsae hëen* was used when the feudal princes were first introduced to the temple of king Woo.

9. In the *Yëw k'ih* we have the viscount of Wei, come to court and introduced in the ancestral temple.

10. The *Woo* was an accompaniment to the *woo* dance.

[iii.] DECADE OF MIN YU SEAOU-TSZE.

1. In the *Min yu sëaou-tsze* we have the heir-king giving audience in the ancestral temple.

2. In the *Fang loh* we have the heir-king in council in the ancestral temple.

3. In the *King che* we have all the ministers addressing admonition to the heir-king.

4. In the *Sëaou pe* we have the heir-king asking for assistance.

臣工之什、四一之二

1. 臣工、諸侯助祭遣於廟也·
2. 噫嘻、春夏祈穀于上帝也·
3. 振鷺、二王之後來助祭也·
4. 豐年、秋冬報也·
5. 有瞽、始作樂而合乎祖也·
6. 潛、季冬薦魚春獻鮪也·
7. 雝、禘大祖也·
8. 載見、諸侯始見乎武王廟也·
9. 有客、微子來見祖廟也·
10. 武、奏大武也·

閔予小子之什、四一之三

1. 閔予小子、嗣王朝於廟也·
2. 訪落、嗣王謀於廟也·
3. 敬之、羣臣進戒嗣王也·
4. 小毖、嗣王求助也·

5. The *Tsae shoo* was used in praying to the Spirits of the land and of the grain, when the king ploughed the royal field in spring.

6. The *Lëang sze* is a thanksgiving in the autumn to the Spirits of the land and of the grain.

7. The *Sze e* is about the feasting the personators of the dead on [the day of] the repetition of the sacrifice.

The scholar Kaou says, 'The personator was of the Ling star.

8. The *Choh* was used in announcing the completion of the Woo dance.

It tells how [Woo] observed the ways of his ancestors in nourishing the kingdom.

9. The *Hwan* was used in declarations of war in sacrificing to God and to the Father of war.

The *Hwan* shows the aim of Woo.

10. The *Lae* relates to the great investment with fiefs in the ancestral temple.

Lae means to give; referring to the gifts which were conferred on good men.

11. The *Pwan* or *Pan* relates to the sacrifices, in a royal progress, to the four mountains, the rivers, and the seas.

BOOK. II.   PRAISE-SONGS OF LOO.

1. The *Keung* celebrates the praise of duke He.

Duke He observed the rules of Pih-k'in, was economical so as to have sufficient for his expenditure, was generous in his love of the people, was attentive to husbandry and made much of the cultivation of grain, and pastured his horses near the remote borders of the State. On account of these things the people honoured him; and Ke-sun Häng-foo having requested permission from Chow, the historiographer K'ih made this *Sung*-piece.

5. 載芟春籍田而祈社稷也·
6. 良耜秋報社稷也·
7. 絲衣繹賓尸也·
　　高子曰靈星之尸也·
8. 酌告成大武也·
　　言能酌先祖之道以養天下也·
9. 桓講武類禡也·
　　桓武志也·
10. 賚大封於廟也·
　　賚予也言所以錫予善人也·
11. 般巡守而祀四岳河海也·

魯頌四之二

1. 駉頌僖公也·
僖公能遵伯禽之法儉以足用寬以愛民務農重
穀牧于坰野魯人尊之於是季孫行父請命於周而
史克作是頌·

2. The *Yëw peih* celebrates the praise of duke He, showing how well-ordered was the relation between the ruler and his ministers.

3. The *Pwan shwuy* celebrates the praise of duke He, showing how he repaired the college of the State.

4. The *Pei kung* celebrates the praise of duke He, showing how he recovered all the territory of the duke of Chow.

BOOK III.   SACRIFICIAL ODES OF SHANG.

1. The *Na* was used in sacrificing to T'ang the successful.

Between the viscount of Wei and duke Tae, the ceremonies and music [of Shang] had fallen into neglect and been lost. Then one Ching-k'aou-foo got twelve of the sacrificial odes of Shang from the grand music-master of Chow, at the head of which he placed the *Na*.

2. The *Lëeh tsoo* was used in sacrificing to Chung-tsung.

3. The *Heuen nëaou* was used in sacrificing to Kaou-tsung.

4. The *Ch'ang jah* was used in the great sacrifice to the remote ancestor of Shang.

5. The *Yin woo* was used in sacrificing to Kaou-tsung.

2. 有駜,頌僖公君臣之有道也.
3. 泮水,頌僖公能修泮宮也.
4. 閟宮,頌僖公能復周公之宇也.

商頌,四之三

1. 那,祀成湯也.
　微子至于戴公,其閒禮樂廢壞,有正考甫者,得商頌
十二篇於周之大師,以那為首.
2. 烈祖,祀中宗也.
3. 玄鳥,祀高宗也.
4. 長發,大禘也.
5. 殷武,祀高宗也.

APPENDIX II.

A TABLE

OF THE PIECES IN THE SHE CHRONOLOGICALLY ARRANGED.

I. BELONGING TO THE SHANG DYNASTY................ B.C. 1,765—1,122.
Five pieces:—the Sacrificial odes of Shang. Of the *Na* (I.), the *Leeh tsoo* (II.), and the *Ch'ang fuh* (IV.), the date of the composition is uncertain. I think that Ode IV. is the oldest, and may have been made any time after B.C. 1,719.

The *Heuen neaou* (III.) and the *Yin woo* (V.) were made after B.C. 1,264. Ode V. should be referred, probably, to the reign of Te-yih, B.C. 1,190—1,154.

II. BELONGING TO THE TIME OF KING WAN......... „ 1,184—1,134.
Thirty-four or thirty-five pieces. These are commonly included in the three hundred and six pieces of the Chow dynasty; but we can only date the commencement of that from the reign of Wăn's son, king Woo. The composition, or the collection at least, of most of the Odes relating to Wăn and his affairs, is attributed to his son Tan, the duke of Chow, and must be referred to the reigns of kings Woo and Ch'ing........................... „ 1,121—1,076.
These pieces embrace —

In Part I., all the 11 pieces of Book I.:—the *Kwan ts'eu*, the *Koh t'an*, the *Keuen urh*, the *Kew muh*, the *Chung-sze*, the *T'aou yaou*, the *Too tseu*, the *Fow e*, the *Han kwang*, the *Joo fun*, and the *Lin che che*; and 12, or perhaps 13 pieces, of Book II.:—the *Ts'eoh ch'aou*, the *Ts'ae fun*, the *Ts'aou ch'ung*, the *Ts'ae pin*, the *Hăng loo*, the *Kaou yang*, the *Yin k'e luy*, the *P'eaou yew mei*, the *Seaou sing*, the *Yay yew sze keun*, the *Keang yew sze* and the *Tsow yu*, with perhaps also the *Kan t'ang* (V.)

In Part II., 8 pieces of Book I.:—the *Luh ming*, the *Sze mow*, the *Hwang-hwang chay hwa*, the *Fah muh*, the *T'een paou*, the *Ts'ae we*, the *Ch'uh keu*, and the *Te too*.

In Part III., 3 pieces of Book I.:—the *Yih p'oh*, the *Han luh*, and the *Ling t'ae*.

III. BELONGING TO THE CHOW DYNASTY.

[i.] Of the time of King Woo.................................... „ 1,121—1,115.
In all 8 or 9 pieces, viz.—

In Part I., Book II., the *Ho pe nung e*, and perhaps the *Kan t'ang*; In Part II., the *Nan kae* of Book I.; the *Pih hwa*, the *Hwa shoo*, and the *Yu le*, of Book II., though the date of these pieces is not certain;

In Part III., the *Meen*, the *Sze chae*, and the *Hwang e*,—all in Book I.

[ii.] Of the time of King Ch'ing.................................... „ 1,114—1,076.
In all 60 pieces, viz.—

In Part I., all the seven pieces of Book XV., the *Ts'ih yueh*, the *Ch'e-heaou*, the *Tung shan*, the *P'o foo*, the *Fah ko*, the *Kew yih*, and the *Lang poh*. All these are assigned to the duke of Chow in the reign of Ch'ing.

In Part II., ten pieces :—the *Chang te*, of Book I. ; the *Yew käng*, the *Nan yew kea-yu*, the *Sung k'ew*, the *Nan shan yew t'ae*, the *Yew e*, the *Luh seaou*, and the *Chan loo*, of Book II. ; the *Tung kung*, and the *Ts'ing-ts'ing chay ngo*, of Book III. Of these ten pieces, however, Choo He thinks that the date of all but the first is uncertain.

In Part III., twelve pieces :—the *Wän wang*, the *Ta ming*, the *Hea woo* and the *Wän wang yew shing*, of Book I. ; the *Säng min*, the *Häng wei*, the *Ke tswy*, the *Hoo e*, the *Kea loh*, the *Kung Lew*, the *Heung choh*, and the *K'euen o*, of Book II.

In Part IV. thirty-one pieces, viz.—all the pieces of Book I. [i.] :— the *Ts'ing meaou*, the *Wei T'een che ming*, the *Wei ts'ing*, the *Leeh wän*, the *T'een tsoh*, the *Haou Teen yew ch'ing ming* (assigned by Choo He to the time of king K'ang), the *Go tseang*, the *She mae* (assigned by Choo to the time of king Woo), the *Chih king* (assigned by Choo to the time of king Ch'aou), and the *Sze wän;* all the pieces of Book I. [ii.] :—the *Shin kung*, the *E he* (assigned by Choo to the time of king K'ang), the *Chin loo*, the *Fung neen*, the *Yew koo*, the *Ts'een*, the *Yung* (assigned by Choo to the time of king Woo), the *Tsae heen*, the *Yew k'ih*, and the *Woo;* and all the pieces of Book I. [iii.] :— the *Min yu seaou tsze*, the *Tang loh*, the *King che*, the *Seaou pe*, the *Tsae shoo*, the *Leang sze*, the *Sze e*, the *Choh*, the *Hwan*, the *Lae*, and the *Pan*.

[iv.] Of the time of King E (懿 王)............................. B.C. 933—909.

Five pieces, all in Part I. Book VIII.:—the *Ke ming*, the *Seuen*, the *Choo*, the *Tung fang che jih*, and the *Tung fang we ming*. All these are supposed to belong to duke Gae of Ts'e or his times, but Choo He considers their date uncertain.

[v.] Of the time of king E (夷 王)............... .... „ 893—8 78.

One piece, the *Pih chow* of Part I., Book III., assigned to the time of duke K'ing of Wei; but Choo He would place it later in the time of king P'ing.

[vi.] Of the time of the above king E or of king Le............ „ 893—841.

Four pieces, all those of Part I., Book XIII , but Choo considers them to be of uncertain date :—the *Kaou k'ew*, the *Soo kwan*, the *Sih yew ch'ang ts'oo*, and the *Fei fung*.

[vii.] Of the time of king Le.................................... „ 877—841.

In all, eleven pieces, viz.—

Two in Part I., Book XII.:—the *Yuen k'ew*, and the *Tung mun che fun*. Choo considers both these as of uncertain date.

Four pieces in Part II.:—the *Shih ywh che keaou* (correctly assigned by Choo to the time of king Yew), and the *Yu woo ching* (Choo would also assign a later date to this), in Book IV.; the *Seaou min*, and the *Seaou yuen*, both considered by Choo to be of uncertain date.

Five pieces in Part III.:—the *Min laou,* and the *Pan,* of Book II.; the *Tang,* the *Yih* (correctly assigned by Choo to the time of king P'ing), and the *Sang yew* of Book III.

[viii.] Of the period Kung-ho.. B.C. 840—827.

One piece, the *Sih tsuh* of Part I., Book X., but Choo considers the date to be uncertain.

[ix] Of the time of king Seuen........................ .... „ 826—781.

Twenty-five pieces, viz.—

In Part I., five pieces :—the *Pih chow* of Book IV.; the *Keu lin* of Book XI. (according to Choo uncertain); and the *Hàng Mûn,* the *Tung mun che ch'e,* and the *Tung mun che yang,* of Book XII., all according to Choo uncertain.

In Part II., fourteen pieces, viz.—

In Book III., the *Luh yueh,* the *Ts'ae k'e,* the *Kou kung,* the *Keih jih,* the *Hung yen,* the *T'ing leaou* (according to Choo uncertain), the *Meen shwuy* (acc. to Choo uncertain), and the *Hoh ming* (acc. to Choo uncertain); in Book IV., the *K'e foo,* the *Pih keu,* the *Hwang neaou,* the *Go hàng k'e yay,* the *Sze kan,* and the *Woo yang,* all according to Choo of uncertain date.

In Part III., six pieces, viz.—

The *Yun han,* the *Sung kaou,* the *Chin] min,* the *Han yih,* the *Keang han,* and the *Chang woo,* all in Book III., and all admitted by Choo, but the *Han yih,* of which he considers the date uncertain.

[x.] Of the time of king Yew .... „ 780—770.

In all forty-two pieces, viz.—

Of Part II. 40 pieces :—in Book IV., the *Tseeh nan shan,* and the *Ching yueh* (Choo considers the date of this uncertain, but there is some internal evidence for its being of the time of king Yew); in Book V., the *Seaou pwan,* the *K'eaou yen,* the *Ho jin sze,* the *Heang pih,* the *Kuh fung,* the *Luh go,* the *Ta tung,* and the *Sze yueh,* the date of all of which is with Choo uncertain; in Book VI., the *Pih shan,* the *Woo tseang ta keu,* the *Seaou ming,* the *Koo chung,* the *Ts'oo ts'ze,* the *Sin nan shan,* the *Foo t'een,* the *Ta t'een,* the *Chen pe Luh e,* and the *Shang-shang chay hwa,* of all which Choo denies the assigned date, excepting in the case of the *Koo chung;* in Book VII., the *Sang hoo,* the *Yuen yang,* the *Kwei peen,* the *Keu heah,* the *Ts'ing ying,* the *Pin che tsoo yen,* the *Yu ts'aou,* the *Ts'ae shuh,* the *Keoh kung,* and the *Yuh lew,*—but of these Choo allows only the *Pin che tsoo yen* to be capable of determinate reference to the time of Yew; and in Book VIII., the *Too jin sze,* the *Ts'ae luh,* the *Shoo meaou* (referred by Choo to the time of king Seuen), the *Sih sang,* the *Pih hwa,* the *Meen man,* the *Hoo yeh,* the *Ts'een tseen che shih,* the *T'eaou che hwa,* and the *Ho ts'aou pah hwang,* but Choo only agrees in assigning the *Pih hwa* and the *Ho ts'aou puh hwang* to Yew's reign.

In Part III., Book III. two pieces;—the *Chen jang* and the *Shaou min.*

[xi.] Of the time of king P'ing....................................... „ 769—719.

In all 28 pieces, viz.—

In Part I., 1 in Book III.,—the *Luh e*; 3 in Book V.,—the *K'e yuh*, the *K'aou pwan*, and the *Shih jin*, but Choo considers the date of the *K'aou pwan* to be uncertain; 6 in Book VI.,—the *Shoo le*, the *Keun-tsze yu yih*, the *Keun-tsze yang-yang*, the *Yang che shwuy*, the *Chung kuh yew t'uy*, and the *Koh luy*, of which Choo agrees in the assignment of one only, the *Yang che shwuy*; 7 in Book VII.,—the *Tsze e*, the *Tseang chung-tsze*, the *Shuh yu t'een*, the *Ta shuh yu t'een*, the *Kaou k'ew*, the *Tsun ta loo*, and the *Neu yueh ke ming*, of which Choo allows the assignment of the *Tsze e*, the *Shuh yu t'een*, and the *Ta shuh yu t'een*; 7 in Book X.,—the *Shan yew ch'oo*, the *Yang che shwuy*, the *Tseaou leaou*, the *Chow mow*, the *Te too*, the *Kaou k'ew*, and the *Paou yu*, of which Choo agrees in the assignment only of the *Yang che shwuy* and the *Tseaou leaou*; 4 in Book XI.,—the *Sze t'eeh*, the *Seaou yung*, the *Keen kea*, and the *Chung nan*, Choo allowing only the *Seaou jung*.

[xii.] In the reign of king P'ing or king Hwan .... B.C. 769—696.
Seven pieces, all of Part I., Book IX., and all, according to Choo, of uncertain date;—the *Koh keu*, the *Hwun tseu joo*, the *Yuen yew t'aou*, the *Chih hoo*, the *Shih mow che keen*, the *Fah t'an*, and the *Shih shoo*.

[xiii.] In the reign of king Hwan............................ „ 718—696.
Thirty-two pieces, all of Part I., viz.—

17 in Book III.:—the *Yen yen*, the *Jih yueh*, the *Chung fung*, the *Keih koo*, the *K'ae fung*, the *Heung che*, the *P'aou yew k'oo yeh*, the *Kuh fung*, the *Shih we*, the *Maou k'ew*, the *Keen he*, the *Ts'euen shwuy*, the *Pih mun*, the *Pih fung*, the *Tsing neu*, the *Sin t'ae*, and the *Urh tsze shing chow*, of which Choo allows only the date assigned to the *Yen yen*. the *Jih yueh*, the *Chung fung*, and the *Keih koo*; 4 in Book IV.,—the *Ts'eang yew tsze*, the *Keun-tsze keae laou*, the *Sang chung*, and the *Shun che pun pun*, in regard to all of which but the *Sang chung* Choo coincides; 5 in Book V. the *Măng*, the *Chuh kan*, the *Hwan lan*, the *Pih he*, and the *Yew koo*, all acc. to Choo of uncertain date; 3 in Book VI.,—the *T'oo yuen*, the *Ts'ae koh*, and the *Ta keu*, also of uncertain date with Choo; 2 in Book VII.,—the *Yew neu t'ung keu*, and the *Keen shang*, with him uncertain; and 1 in Book XII.,—the *Moo mun*, whose date Choo in the same way does not think can be determined.

[xiv.] Of the time of king Chwang........................ .... „ 695—681.
Fifteen pieces, all in Part I., viz.—

1 in Book VI.,—the *K'ew chung yew ma*, with Choo uncertain; 8 in Book VII., all with Chow uncertain,—the *Shan yew foo soo*, the *T'oh he*, the *Keaou t'ung*, the *Fung*, the *Tung mun che shen*, the *Fung yu*, the *Tsze k'in*, and the *Yang che shwuy*; and 6 in Book VIII., the date and occasion of the 2d and 3d of which only are deemed uncertain by Chow,—the *Nan shan*, the *Foo teen*, the *Loo ling*, the *Pe kow*, the *Tsae k'eu*, and the *E tseay*.

[xv.] Of the time of king Le (釐王)............................. „ 680—676.
Five pieces, all in Part I., viz.—

3 in Book VII all with Choo uncertain,—the *Ch'uh k'e tung mun*, the *Yay yew man ts'aou*, and the *Tsin wei;* 2 in Book X., the date assigned to the former of which is admitted by Choo, the *Woo e*, and the *Yew te che too.*

[xvi.] Of the time of king Hwuy..................................... B.C. 675—651. Twelve pieces, all in Part I., viz.—

5 in Book IV., all admitted by Choo,—the *Ting che fang chung*, the *Te tung,* the *Seang shoo,* the *Kan maou,* and the *Tsae ch'e;* 1 in Book V., with Choo uncertain,—the *Muh kwa;* 1 in Book VII., admitted by Choo, the *Ts'ing jin;* 2 in Book X., with Choo uncertain,—the *Koh säng* and the *Ts'ae ling;* 2 in Book XII., with Choo uncertain,—the *Fang yew ts'eoh ch'aou,* and the *Yueh ch'uh;* and 1 in Book XIV., also with Choo uncertain,—the *Fow yew.*

[xvii.] Of the time of king Sëang.................................... „ 650—618. In all thirteen pieces, of which 9 are in Part I., viz.—

1 in Book V., admitted by Choo,—the *Ho kwang;* 5 in Book XI., of which Choo admits only the first and fourth,—the *Hwang n~aou*, the *Shin-fung,* the *Woo e,* the *Wei yang,* and the *K'euen yu;* 3 in Book XIV., of which Choo accepts only the first,—the *How-jin*, the *She-kew,* and the *Hea ts'euen.*

In Part IV., the 4 pieces of Book II., in the occasion assigned for the first and last of which Choo agrees,—the *Keung*, the *Yew peih*, the *Pwan-shwuy,* and the *Pei kung.*

[xviii.] Of the time of king Ting................................... „ 605—585. Two pieces in Part I., viz.—

the *Choo lin,* admitted by Choo, and the *Tsih p'o* in Book XII.

The K'ang-he editors say:—

'The dates of the composition of the odes it was found difficult to examine thoroughly after the fires of Ts'in, and so we find them variously assigned by the writers of the Han, T'ang, and other dynasties.

'But the old Preface made its appearance along with the text of the Poems, and Maou, Ch'ing, and K'ung Ying-tah maintained and defended the dates assigned in it, to which there belongs what authority may be derived from its antiquity.

'When Choo He took the She in hand, the text of the poems was considered by him to afford the only evidence of their occasion and date, and where there was nothing decisive in it, and no evidence afforded by other classical Books, he pronounced these points uncertain;—thus deciding according to the exercise of his own reason on the several pieces.

'Gow-yang Sew followed the introductory notices of Ch'ing, but disputed and reasoned on the subject at the same time. Heu K'een, and Lew Kin followed the authority of Choo, now and then slightly differing from him.

'In the Ming dynasty appeared the "Old meanings of the text of the She," chronologically arranged by Ho K'eae, adducing abundance of testimonies, but with many erroneous views. We have in this Work collected the old assignments of the Preface, supported by Maou, Ch'ing, and K'ung, and given due place to the decisions of Choo. The opinions of others we have preserved, but have not entered on any discussion of them.'

APPENDIX III.

SPECIMENS OF HAN YING'S ILLUSTRATIONS OF THE SHE.

1.   When Tsăng-tsze held office in Keu, he received [only] three *ping* of grain. At that time [any amount of] salary was of importance to him, and he thought but little of himself. After his parents were dead, Ts'e would have met him and made him its chief minister, and Ts'oo and Tsin would have given him their highest honours, [but he declined their proffers]. At that time he wished to maintain the dignity of his person, and cared but little for salary. With him who keeps his precious jewel in his bosom, and allows his State to be led astray, we cannot speak of benevolence. With him who is in distress himself, and allows his parents also to be in straits, we cannot speak of filial duty. He who has to travel far under a heavy load rests without careful selection of the place; and he whose family is poor, and whose parents are old, accepts service without selecting his office. Therefore a superior man may hurry forward, when an opportunity presents, in a short garment of haircloth, under the urgency of necessity. I have said that, when one takes office without meeting with the proper time for it, he will discharge its duties, while pressed in his mind by his own anxieties, and will fulfil any commission, though his counsels are not followed;—all and simply because of poverty. The ode (I. ii. XI. 1) says:—

> ' Day and night are we about the prince's [business];
> Our lot is not like theirs.'

2.   The lady in the *Hăng loo* was engaged to be married, but she had not yet gone [from her parents' house]. While she saw a single thing incomplete, a single rule of propriety uncomplied with, she would maintain her purity and the chastity of principle, and would rather die than go [to the gentleman's house]. The superior man considered that she possessed the right view of woman's duty, and therefore he exhibited her case and handed it down, and set forth her praise in song, to prevent [men] from urging requirements contrary to right, and [women] from walking in the way of defilement. The ode (I. ii. VI. 3) says:—

> ' Though you have forced me to trial,
> Still I will not follow you.'

曾其方者重君敦公傳一宜行具之
仕于身是不道于其寶曰一宜行
於沒時與者褐爲不行夫不舉詩禮故乎
莒之曾語不趨爲不同露守傳難
得後子仁擇時使之節之
粟齊重窘地擇時許嫁楊之速
三迎其其而當使人貞我
相而身而務不理楊不
方以輕約貧入嫁守歌而訟
是楚而而家急其矣死之不
之迎其親傳謀而往絕從
時以祿親云貧然不以爾從
于迎其親老不爲未君無
曾令懷者之逢故往于道
于尹其不不時也也以之
重晉寶可擇而詩見爲求
其迎而與官仕曰一得防
祿以迷語而任夙物婦汙
而上其仕事夜不道道

87]

3. Want of virtue proceeding to the neglecting of one's parents; want of loyalty proceeding to rebellion against one's rulers; want of truthfulness proceeding to the deceiving of one's friends :—these three extreme cases are visited by sage kings with death, and there is no forgiveness for them. The ode (I. iv. VIII. 1) says :—

'If a man have no proper demeanour,
What should he do but die ?'

4. King invaded Ch'in, the west gate of whose capital was injured. The conquerors employed some of the people who had surrendered to repair it, and Confucius passed by, [while they were engaged in the work], without bowing forward to the cross-bar of his carriage. Tsze-kung, who was holding the reins, said, 'The rules require that, when you pass three men, you should descend, and to two men you should bow forward to the cross-bar of the carriage. Here there is a multitude at work repairing the gate;—how is it that you, Sir, did not bow forward to them ?" Confucius replied, 'When one's State is perishing, not to know the danger shows a want of wisdom. To know the danger and not to struggle for the State shows a want of loyalty To allow it to perish without dying for it shows a want of valour. Numerous as the repairers of the gate are, they could not display one of these virtues, and therefore I did not bow to them.' The ode (I. iii. I. 4) says :—

'My anxious heart is full of trouble,
And I am hated by the crowd of mean creatures.'

A multitude of mean men are not worth showing politeness to!

5. King Chwang of Ts'oo returning late one day from his morning audience of his ministers, Fan Ke descended from the hall to meet him, and said, 'How late you are! Do you not feel hungry and tired?' The king replied, 'To-day I was listening to words of loyalty and worth, and did not think about being hungry or tired.' Fan Ke said, Who was this man of loyalty and worth whom you speak of? A visitor from one of the States? Or an officer of the Middle State?' 'It was my chief minister Shin,' said the king; upon which the lady put her hand upon her mouth and smiled. 'What are you smiling at?' asked the king; and she replied, 'It has been my privilege to wait on your majesty when bathing and washing your head,

3. 傳曰,不仁之至,忽其親,不忠之至,倍其君,不信之
至,欺其友,此三者,聖王之所殺而不赦也,詩曰,人而
無儀,不死何爲

4. 荆伐陳,陳西門壊,因其降民使脩之,孔子過而不式,
子貢執轡而問曰,禮過三人則下,二人則式,今陳之
脩門者衆矣,夫子不爲式何也,孔子曰,國亡而弗知不
智也,知而不爭,非忠也,亡而不死,非勇也,脩門者雖
衆,不能行一於此,吾故弗式也,詩曰,憂心悄悄,慍于
羣小,小人成羣,何足禮哉

5. 楚莊王驪朝罷晏,樊姬下堂而迎之曰,何罷之晏
也,得無饑倦乎,莊王曰,今日聽忠賢之言,不知饑倦也,
樊姬曰,王之所謂忠賢者,諸侯之客歟,中國之士歟,莊
王曰,則沈令尹也,樊姬揜口而笑,王曰,姬之所笑何

to hold your napkin and comb, and to arrange your coverlet and mat, for eleven years. Yet I have not neglected to send men all about to Lëang and Ch'ing, to search for beautiful ladies to present to you as companions. There are ten of the same rank as myself, and two who are more worthy than I. It was not that I did not wish to monopolize your favour; but I did not dare with a selfish desire to keep other beauties in the background, and I wished that you should have many of them about you and be happy. Now Shin has been chief minister of Ts'oo for several years, and I have not yet heard of his advancing any man of worth, or dismissing any of a different character;—how should he be regarded as loyal and worthy?'

Next morning the king related her words to the chief minister, who immediately left his place, and brought forward Sun Shuh-gaou. Shuh-gaou had the administration of Ts'oo for only three years, when that State obtained the presidency of all the others. The historiographer of it took his pencil, and wrote on his tablets that the presidency of Ts'oo was due to Fan Ke.

The words of the ode (I. iv. X. 4),

> 'The hundred plans you think of
> Are not equal to the course which I take,'

might have been used of Fan Ke.

6. Măng Shang-këun asked to become a pupil of Min-tsze, and sent a carriage to meet [and bring him to his house]. Min-tsze, however, said, 'In the Le, men are required to come to learn (Le Ke, I. i. 12). If one get a teacher to go and teach him, he will not be able to learn. According to the Le, if I go to teach you, I shall not be able to influence you. You may say that, [if I do not go], you cannot learn; but I say that, [if I do go], I cannot teach with effect.' Upon this Măng Shang-këun said, 'I respectfully receive your orders.' Next day he went without his robes and begged to receive instruction. The ode (IV. i. [iii.] III.) says :—

> 'Let there be daily progress and monthly advance.'

7. Although a sword be sharp, without [the frequent use of] the grindstone, it will not cut; though a man's natural abilities be excellent, without learning, he will

也矣也寵數楚莊敖楚姬之　姬然妾妾與敢矣且敖樊霸謂也　曰妾妾未同私未嘗以楚姬三年之力也　得未嘗列願見樊姬年　於不者十藏見姬進之而　王遣人人賢眾進賢言而　王者人賢於妾而告沈令尹　尚湯沐鄭之間求美人而進之於王之相乎　執巾櫛之二人妾豈不欲擅王之令尹　振祍席十有一年　美人妾娛今沈令尹忠賢　而進之於王之　進之於王之相乎　令尹避席而進孫叔曰　楚史援筆而書之於策曰　百爾所思不如我所之　樊

6. 孟嘗君請教致學者也明日袪衣請受業詩曰日就月將　往能教學者也　不能命矣　請學師而臣所謂　於閔子學不能　子使車往迎閔子曰禮有來　往教則不能化君也君所敬　迎不能化者也於是孟嘗君曰敬

7. 劍雖利不厲不斷材雖美不學不高雖有旨酒嘉

not rise high. The spirits may be good and the viands admirable, but, till you taste them, you do not know their flavour; principles may be good, but until you have learned them, you do not know their value. Hence it is by learning that a man knows his deficiencies, and by teaching that he knows his want of thoroughness. Let him be ashamed of his deficiencies and exert himself; let him use all helps to enlarge his knowledge till he is thorough in it. Looking at the thing in this way, we see that teaching and learning help, one the other, to distinction. Tsze-hëa having asked about one of the odes, when he was told one thing, he knew a second from it, on which Confucius said, 'It is Shang who can bring out my meaning. Now I can begin to talk about the odes with him (Ana. III. viii.).' Confucius distinguished that heroic disciple, and his sagely virtue was complete. The scholar enjoys the light of the master and his virtue is displayed. The ode says:—

'Let there be daily progress and monthly advance.'

8. Confucius was looking about in the ancestral temple of Chow, when he came upon a vessel [which was hanging] unevenly [in a frame]. He asked the keeper of the temple what it was, and was told that it was the vessel of the festive board. 'I have heard,' said he, 'that this vessel topples over when full, hangs unevenly when empty, and is perfectly straight when half full;—is it so?' 'It is so,' replied the keeper; and Confucius then made Tsze-loo bring water to try it. When filled, it toppled over: when half-filled, it hung straight; when emptied, it fell to one side. Confucius looked surprised, and sighed. 'Ah!' said he, 'when was there anything or anyone full that did not topple over?' Tsze-loo asked whether there was any way to deal with such fulness, and Confucius said, 'The way to deal with fulness is to repress and diminish it.' 'And is there any way to diminish it?' asked the other. Confucius said, 'When one's virtue is superabundant, let it be kept with reverence; when one's lands are extensive, let them be kept with economy; when one's place is honourable and his emoluments large, let them be kept with humility; when one's men are numerous and his weapons strong, let them be kept with apprehension; when one's natural abilities are extraordinarily great, let them be kept with stupidity; when one's acquirements are extensive and his memory great, let them be kept

殼不嘗不知其旨雖有善道不學不達其功故學然
後知不足教然後知不究不足故自愧而勉不究故
盡師而熟由此觀之則教學相長也子夏問詩學一而
知二孔子曰起子者商也始可與言詩已矣孔子賢
乎英傑而聖德備弟子被光景而德彰詩曰日就月
將

8. 孔子觀於周廟有欹器焉孔子問於守廟者曰此
謂何器也對曰此蓋爲宥座之器孔子曰聞宥座器
滿則覆虛則敧中則正有之乎對曰然孔子使子路取
水試之滿則覆中則正虛則敧孔子喟然而嘆曰嗚呼
惡有滿而不覆者哉子路曰敢問持滿有道乎孔子曰德盛
持滿之道抑而損之子路曰損之有道乎孔子曰德盛
行寬裕者守之以恭土地廣大者守之以儉祿位尊盛
者守之以卑人衆兵強者守之以畏聰明睿智者守之

with shallowness. This is what I mean by repressing and diminishing fulness. The ode (IV. iii. III. 3) says :—

> 'T'ang was not slow to descend,
> And his wisdom and virtue daily advanced.'.

9. Këeh made a lake of spirits in which he could sail a boat, while the dregs of the grain formed a mound from which one could see to a distance of ten *le*, and there were 3,000 men who came and drank like so many oxen. Kwan Lung-fung came to remonstrate with him, saying, 'The ancient sovereigns trod the paths of propriety and righteousness, loved the people and used their wealth with economy ; and so the kingdom was tranquil, and they themselves were long-lived. Now you use your wealth as if it were inexhaustible, and you put men to death as if you could not do it fast enough ;—if you do not change, the judgment of Heaven is sure to descend, and your ruin must [shortly] arrive. I pray your Majesty to change.' With this he stood up, and did not offer the usual homage. Këeh threw him into prison, and then put him to death. When superior men heard of it, they said that it was the decree of Heaven. The ode (II. v. IV. 1) says :—

> 'The terrors of Heaven are very excessive ;
> But indeed I have committed no offence.'

10. The four seasons under the sky, spring, summer, autumn, and winter, wind, rain, hoarfrost, and dew, all convey lessons of instruction. Where there is clear intelligence in the person, the influence and will are like those of a Spirit. When what is desirable is about to come, the indications of it are sure to precede ; [as when] heaven is sending down seasonable rain, the hills and streams send forth clouds. The ode (III. iii. V. 1) says :—

> 'Grandly lofty are the mountains,
> With their large masses reaching to the heavens.
> From these mountains was sent down a Spirit,
> Who gave birth to the princes of Foo and Shin.
> Foo and Shin,
> Are the support of Chow,
> Screens to all the States,
> Diffusing [their influence] over the four quarters of the kingdom.'

以愚博聞强記者守之以淺夫是之謂抑而損之詩
日湯降不遲聖敬日躋

9 桀爲酒池可以運舟糟丘足以望十里而牛飮者三
千人關龍逢進諫曰古之人君身行禮義愛民節財故
國安天殃必降而誅必至矣君其革之立而不及朝桀囚
革天殃之君子聞之曰天之命矣詩曰昊天大憮于慎
而殺之無辜

10. 天下四時春夏秋冬風雨霜露無非教也清明在
躬氣志如神嗜欲將至有開必先天降時雨山川出雲
詩曰崧高維嶽峻極于天維嶽降神生甫及申維申
及甫維周之翰四國于藩四方于宣此文武之德也

91]

This was the virtue of Wăn and Woo. The elevation of the kings who founded the three dynasties was preceded by their excellent fame. The ode (III. iii. VIII. 6) says:—

> 'Very intelligent is the son of Heaven;
> His good fame is without end.
> He shall display his civil virtues,
> Till they permeate all quarters of the kingdom.'

This was the virtue of king T'ae.

11. King Seuen of Ts'e said to T'ëen Kwo, 'I have heard that the learned enjoin mourning for a parent three years;—which is most important, the ruler or a parent? Kwo replied, 'The ruler, I apprehend, is not so important as a parent?' 'How then,' asked the king angrily, 'does a man leave his parents to serve his ruler?' 'If it were not for the ruler's land,' was the reply, 'he would have nowhere to place his parents; nor without the ruler's pay could he support them; nor without his rank could he honour and distinguish them. All that is received from the ruler is that it may be devoted to our parents' The king looked disquieted, and gave no reply. The ode (II. i. II. 3) says:—

> 'The king's business was not to be slackly performed,
> And I had not leisure to nourish my father.'

12. Formerly, when Tsze-han, the minister of Works, was acting as premier in Sung, he said to his ruler, 'The security or danger of a State, and the order or disorder of the people, depend on the doings of the ruler. Now rank, emolument, rewards, and gifts, are what all men love; do you take the management of them. Executions and punishments are what the people hate; let me undertake them.' 'Good,' said the king; 'I shall receive the praise of the one department, and you will incur the odium of the other. I know that I shall not be laughed at by the other princes.' But when it was known in the State that the power of death and punishment was entirely in the hands of Tsze-han, the great officers paid their court to him, and the people stood in awe of him. Before a round year had expired, Tsze-han proceeded to put away his ruler, and monopolize the whole of the government. Therefore

三代之王也必先其令名詩曰明明天子令聞不已矢
其文德洽此四國此犬王之德也 The whole of this passage is also found in the Le Ke, XXIX., 8, 9.

11. 齊宣王謂田過曰吾聞儒者親喪三年君與父孰重,
過對曰殆不如父重王忿然曰曷爲士去親而事君對
曰非君之土地無以處吾親非君之祿無以養吾親非
君之爵無以尊顯吾親受之於君致之於親凡事君以
爲親也宣王悒然無以應之詩曰王事靡盬不遑將父,
12. 昔者司城子罕相宋謂宋君曰夫國家之安危百姓
之治亂在君之行夫爵祿賞賜舉人之所好也君自行
之殺戮刑罰民之所惡也臣請當之君曰善寡人當
其美子受其惡寡人自知不爲諸侯笑矣國人知殺戮
之刑專在子罕也大臣親之百姓畏之居不期年子

Laou-tsze said, 'Fish ought not to be taken from the deep; the sharp instruments of a State should not be given to any one.' The ode (II. iv. IX. 5) says:—

> 'Why do you call us to action,
> Without coming and consulting with us?'

13. [A part of] mount Lëang having fallen down, the marquis of Tsin summoned the great officer Pih-tsung [to court]. On his way he met a man pushing a barrow along, who insisted on keeping the road fronting his inside horses. Pih-tsung made the spearman on his right get down to use his whip to the man, who said, 'Is it not a long journey on which you are hurrying? Is it right for you to proceed without knowing the business?' Pih-tsung with joy asked him where he was from; and when the man said he was from Këang, he further asked him what news he had. 'Mount Lëang has fallen, and the course of the Ho is stopped up. For three days its stream has not flowed; and it is on this account that you have been summoned.' 'What is to be done?' asked the officer, and the man replied, 'The hill is Heaven's, and Heaven has made it fall; the Ho is Heaven's, and Heaven has stopt its flow;— what can Pih-tsung do in the case?' Pih-tsung then privately questioned him, and he said, 'Let the marquis lead forth all his officers; let them weep over the calamity in mourning garments; and thereafter let him offer a sacrifice, and the river will resume its flow.' The man then declined to tell his surname and name; and when Pih-tsung arrived at the court, and the marquis asked him [what was to be done]. he replied in the man's words. On this the marquis in mourning robes led forth all his officers to weep over the calamity, and then offered a sacrifice, whereupon the river resumed its flow. When the marquis asked Pih-tsung how he knew what was to be done, he did not tell that he had learned it from the man with the barrow, but pretended that he knew it of himself. When Confucius heard of the affair, he said, 'Pih-tsung, we may believe, will have no posterity, stealing in such a way the credit that was due to another man.' The ode (III. iii. III. 7) says:—

> 'Heaven is sending down death and disorder,
> And has put an end to our king.'

Another ode (IV. [i.] VII.] says:—

> 'Revere the majesty of Heaven,
> And thus preserve its favour.'

罕遂去宋君而專其政·故老子曰·魚不可脫於淵·國之
利器不可以示人·詩曰·胡爲我作·不卽我謀·—Han must
have taken the words of the ode here in some peculiar meaning of his own; but I cannot make
any translation out of them to suit his illustrative story.

13. 梁山崩·晉君召大夫伯宗·道逢輦者·以其輦服共
道·伯宗使右下·欲鞭之·輦者曰·君超道登不遠矣·不知
事而行·可乎·伯宗喜·問其居·曰·絳人也·伯宗曰·于亦
有聞乎·曰·梁山崩·壅河·頔三日不流·是以召子·伯宗曰·
如之何·曰·天有山·天崩之·天有河·天壅之·伯宗將如
之何·伯宗私聞之·曰·君其率羣臣·素服而哭之·既
而祠焉·河斯流矣·伯宗問其姓名·弗告·伯宗到·君問·伯
宗以其音對·於是君素服率羣臣而哭之·既而祠焉·河
斯流矣·君問伯宗何以知之·伯宗不言受輦者·詐以

14. Tsze-loo said, 'If a man treat me well, I will also treat·him well; and if a man do not treat me well, I will not treat him well.' Tsze-kung said, 'If a man treat me well, I will also treat him well; and if a man do not treat me well, I will [try to] lead him [to do so], simply conducting him forward, or letting him fall back.' Yen Hwuy said, 'If a man treat me well, I will also treat him well, and if a man do not treat me well, I will still treat him well.' As each of the three had his own view on the subject, they asked the master about it, who said, 'Yew's words are those of a barbarian; Ts'ze's those of a friend; and Hwuy's those of a relative.' The ode (I. iv. V. 1.) says :—

'This man is all vicious,
And I regard him as my brother.'

15. Duke King of Ts'e went out to shoot birds with an arrow and string at the lake of Ch'aou-hwa. Yen Tăng-ts'eu had charge of the birds [which were caught], and let them all go, upon which the duke was angry, and wanted to put him to death. Gan-tsze said, 'Tăng-ts'eu is guilty of four capital offences; let me enumerate them' and then execute him.' The duke assented, and Gan-tsze said, 'Tăng-ts'eu had charge from you of the birds, and let them go :—this is his first offence. He is causing you for the sake of some birds to kill a man :—this is his second offence. He will cause the princes throughout the kingdom, when they hear of it, to think of your lordship as regarding your birds as of more value than your officers:—this is his third offence. When the son of Heaven hears of it, he will certainly degrade and dismiss your lordship, putting our altars in peril, and extinguishing the sacrifices of your ancestral temple :—this is his fourth offence. With these four offences, he ought to be put to death without forgiveness; allow me to execute the sentence.' The duke said, 'Stop. Here I also am in error. I wish you for me to make a respectful apology.' The ode (I. vii. VI. 2) says :—

'It is he in the country who ever holds to the right.'

自知, 孔子聞之曰, 伯宗其無後, 懷人之善, 詩曰, 天降
喪亂, 滅我立王, 又曰, 畏天之威, 于時保之.—In the Tso Chuen,
on VIII. v. 4, we have a considerably different version of this story.

14. 子路曰, 人善我, 我亦善之, 人不善我, 我不善之,
子貢曰, 人善我, 我亦善之, 人不善我, 我則引之, 進退
而已耳, 顏囘曰, 人善我, 我亦善之, 人不善我, 我亦善之,
三子所持各異, 間於夫子, 夫子曰, 由之所言, 蠻貊之言
也, 賜之所言, 朋友之言也, 囘之所言, 親屬之言也, 詩
曰, 人之無艮, 我以爲兄.

15. 齊景公出弋昭華之池, 顏鄧聚主鳥而亡之, 景公怒
而欲殺之, 晏子曰, 鄧聚有死罪四而數之, 景之也, 景公使以危敬
曰諸以鳥之故而輕士, 是罪三也, 天子聞之必將貶絀吾君,
君重社稷, 請加誅焉, 詩曰邦之司直.

94]

16. King Chwang of Ts'oo sent a messenger, with a hundred catties of gold, to invite Pih-kwoh to his court. Pih-kwoh said, 'I have one who attends to the basket and broom for me; let me go in and consult her.' He then [entered her apartment], and said to his wife, 'Ts'oo is wishing me to become its chief minister; if to-day I accept the office, I shall at once have my carriage and four with ranks of attendants, and my food will be spread before me over a space of ten cubits square;—what do you say to it?' His wife replied, 'You have hitherto made your living by weaving sandals. You live on congee and wear straw shoes, with none to make you afraid or anxious;—simply because you undertake no responsibilities of management. If now you had your carriage and four, with ranks of attendants, you could rest only in a space sufficient for your two knees; and if you had your food spread before you over ten cubits square, you could enjoy only one piece of meat. Will it be wise for that space for your knees, and the taste of that piece of flesh, to plunge yourself into all the anxieties of the kingdom of Ts'oo?' Upon this he declined the invitation, and along with his wife left Ts'oo. The ode (I. xii. IV. 3) says:—

> 'That admirable, virtuous lady
> Can respond to you in conversation.'

The above sixteen paragraphs, taken very much at random, are sufficient to give the reader an idea of Han Ying's method in his 'Illustrations of the She.' Whatever we may have lost through the perishing of his other works, we have not gained anything by the preservation of this, towards the understanding of the odes. The editors of the catalogue of the imperial library under the present dynasty, in the conclusion of their notice of it, quote with approval the judgment of Wang She-ching of the Ming dynasty, that 'Han quotes the odes to illustrate his narratives, and does not give his narratives to illustrate the meaning of the odes.'

16. 楚莊王使使齎金百斤聘北郭先生先生曰臣有箕
帚之使願入計之即謂婦人曰楚欲以我爲相今日相
即結駟列騎食方丈於前愀與憂者何哉與物無治也今如結
食食粥羹履所安一肉之味而殉楚國之憂其可乎於是遂不
願列騎所安一肉之味而殉楚國之憂其可乎於是遂不
容膝之安與婦去之詩曰彼美淑姬可與晤言
應聘

95]

CHAPTER III.

THE PROSODY OF THE SHE; THE ANCIENT PRONUNCIATION
OF THE CHARACTERS; AND THE POETICAL
VALUE OF THE ODES.

APPENDIX: ON THE VARIOUS MEASURES IN WHICH THE
CHINESE HAVE ATTEMPTED POETRY.

SECTION I.

THE PROSODY OF THE SHE.

1. The reader of the Book of Poetry is at once struck by the brevity of the lines, and by the fact that nearly all the pieces in the collection are composed in rhyme. Under these two heads of the metre and the rhyme may be comprehended nearly all that is necessary to be said on the prosody of the She.

Metre and rhyme

2. All the earliest attempts of the Chinese at poetical composition appear to have been of the same form,—in lines consisting of four words, forming, from the nature of the language, four syllables. In the Book of History, II. iv. 11, we have three brief snatches of song by Shun and his minister Kaou-yaou, which may afford an illustration of this measure; and some of the paragraphs in 'The Songs of the five Sons,' III. iii., are constructed after the same model.[2] The pieces of ancient songs and odes, appended to Chapter I. of these prolegomena, may also be referred to. Wherever there is any marked deviation in them from this type, the genuineness of the composition, as a relic of antiquity, becomes liable to suspicion.

The metre

---

[1] 股 肱 喜 哉, 元 首 起 哉. 百 工 熙 哉; with the two rejoinders of Kaou-yaou. The marquis D' Hervey-Saint-Denys, in his 'Poesies de l' Epoque des Thang,' Introduction, pp. 59, 60, falls into error in saying that it is the particle *tsae* (哉) which forms the rhyme in these triplets. The rhyme is on the penultimate characters. 明, in the first line of the second triplet, was anciently pronounced *mang*. So we find it throughout the She, with one exception where it is made to rhyme with 人. It is to be observed also that the first line of the third triplet consists of 5 characters.　　　　[2] See particularly parr. 6,7, and 9.

3. But though the line of four words is the normal measure of the She, it is by no means invariably adhered to. We have in one

Irregularities of the metre. ode, according to the judgment of several scholars, a line of only one word in each of its stanzas.[3] Lines of two, of three, of five, of six, of seven, and even of eight words, occasionally occur.[4] When the poet once violates the usual law of the metre, he often continues his innovation for two or three lines, and then relapses into the ordinary form. He is evidently aware of his deviations from that, and the stanzas where they occur will be found in general to be symmetrically constructed and balanced. So far as my own perception of melody in numbers is concerned, I could wish that the line of four characters were more frequently departed from.[5]

4. The pieces, as printed, appear divided into stanzas;—and

The division of the odes into stanzas; and its irregularities. properly so, though the Han scholars say that such division was first made by Maou Chang. He did his work well, guided mainly by the rhyme, and by the character of the piece as narrative, allusive, or metaphorical. The very few cases in which a different division from his is now followed have been pointed out in the body of the volume.

In most pieces the stanzas are of uniform length, and are very frequently quatrains; but the writers allowed themselves quite as much liberty in the length of the stanza as in that of the line. Stanzas of two lines are very rare, but I. viii. VIII. is an example of

3 I. vii. I. The second line in each stanza, as printed in the body of this volume, consists of six characters (敝予又改爲兮, &c.). Many scholars make the first word in each of the three lines (敝. 敝. 還) to stand as a line by itself, but it seems to me that one character can hardly sustain the place of a whole line. The ode in question, it may be observed, is generally irregular in its construction. The 1st and 3d lines in each quatrain consist of 5 characters; the second, as I have printed it, contains 6, and the 4th, 7.   4 Lines of two characters occur in the first three stanzas of II. ii. III., and iv. I.; and in IV. i. [i.] III. Lines of three characters occur in I. i. V., consisting of three quatrains, where all the lines are thus formed, but the third; in I. iii. XIII., and in IV. ii. II. Five characters occur in the 2d and 3d stanzas of I. ii. VI., and in both stanzas of I. iii. XI. Six characters occur in I. i. III., stt. 2, 3, l. 3, and in the last lines of all the stanzas of II. ii. V.; seven in I. ix. IV., stt. 1, 2, 3, l. 3; and eight in II. iv. IX. 8, l. 8.
5 Take for instance stanzas 1—3 of II. ii. III.:—

1	魚麗于罶,	鱨鯊,	君子有酒,	旨且多.
2	魚麗于罶,	魴鱧,	君子有酒,	多且旨.
3	魚麗于罶,	鰋鯉,	君子有酒,	旨且有.

or stanzas 1 and 2 of IV. ii. II.:—

1	有駜有駜,	駜彼乘黃,	夙夜在公,	在公明明,
	振振鷺,	鷺于下,	鼓咽咽,	醉言舞.	于胥樂兮.
2	有駜有駜,	駜彼乘牡,	夙夜在公,	在公飲酒,
	振振鷺,	鷺于飛,	鼓咽咽,	醉言歸.	于胥樂兮.

an ode made up of them; and in II. ii. III. there are three such
stanzas following three quatrains.   Triplets are also rare; but we
have odes made up of them, as I. i. XI.; ii. V. and XIV.; vi. VIII.;
and others where triplets are intermixed with stanzas of other
lengths, as I. ii. VI. and XII.; vii. XIV.; xv. VI.   Stanzas of five lines
are rare, but they do occur, forming the structure of whole odes, as
I. ii. X. and XI.; vii. III., and III. i. X.; and intermixed with others,
as in II. iv. V.   Stanzas of six lines, of eight, of ten, and of twelve
are frequently met with.   II vii. VI. is made up of stanzas of fourteen lines each, and in IV. ii. IV. we find stanzas of as many as
sixteen and seventeen.   Stanzas of seven lines, as in I. ii. III.; iv. I.,
IV. and VI.; of nine lines, as in I. ix. VI., and x. VI.; and of eleven
lines as I. xv. I., in all the stanzas but one, are all unusual.   Generally speaking, stanzas with an even number of lines greatly out-
number those with an odd.

As instances of odes where stanzas of different lengths are mixed
together, I may refer to II. iv. V., where we have one of 7 lines,
four of 5, then one of 7, one of 5, and two of 7; to the 7th ode of
the same Book, consisting of four stanzas of 8 lines and four of 4; and
to II. v. VI., where there are three stanzas of 4 lines, then one of 5,
one of 8, and one of 6.   In III. i. II. stanzas of 6 and 8 lines alternate,
and in III. ii. VIII. we have first six stanzas of 5 lines, and then
four of 6.   Other arrangements the reader can notice for himself.
No laws can be laid down upon the subject.—I have drawn no illustrations in this paragraph from the sacrificial odes, which are distinguished by various peculiarities of structure, both in regard to
rhyme and stanzaic arrangement.

5.   The manner in which the rhymes are disposed has received
much attention from the Chinese themselves.   Postponing to the
next section any discussion as to the number and
exactness of the rhymes, I will here content my-
self with a description of the principal rules observed in their
arrangement, drawing my materials mainly from Këang Yung's
' Adjustment of ancient Rhymes.'[6]

[i.]   The first case is that where lines rhyme in succession.[7]   We
have an instance of two lines so rhyming in I. i. I. 1, ll. 1, 2; of
three lines, in I. i. II. 3, ll. 2—4; of four lines, in I. i. II. 2, ll. 1—4;

6. 婺源·江永古韻標準. Këang Yung, styled Këang Shin sëw (慎修), died,
at the age of 82, in A.D. 1762. He was a native of Woo-yuen dis., dept. Hwuy-chow, Gan-hwuy.
7 Called 連句韻.

of five lines, in I. iv. VI. 1, ll. 3—7; of six lines, in I. v. III. 4, ll. 2 —7; of seven lines, in I. v. IV. 6, ll. 2—8; of eight lines, in I. v. IV. 1, ll. 1—8; of nine lines, in III. ii. VI. 1, ll. 2—10; of ten lines, in II. vi. V. 2, li. 1—10; of eleven lines, in IV. iii. II. ll. 12—22; and even of twelve lines, in IV. ii. IV. 4, ll. 1—12.

[ii.] Where the rhyming lines are interrupted by one or more lines intervening which do not rhyme with them.[8] Thus in I. i. I. 1, ll. 1, 2, and 4 rhyme, separated by l. 3, which does not; and in I. xv. I. 5, ll. 1—5 rhyme; l. 6, not rhyming, intervenes; and the rhyme is resumed in ll. 7—9. Then come two lines, not rhyming, and l. 13, which closes the stanza, resumes the rhyme again.

The rhymes are sometimes wide apart, the intervening lines not rhyming at all, or rhyming differently together.[9] E. g., in III. iii. II. 3, a stanza of eight lines, only ll. 2 and 8 can be said to rhyme, though Twan-she makes out an irregular rhyme between ll. 4 and 6. In III. ii. I. 3, ll. 2 and 6 rhyme, two of the intervening lines, 3 and 4 being assonances, and 5 not rhyming at all; and in st. 8, ll. 4 and 8 rhyme, with intervening lines all rhyming differently together.

[iii.] Where the stanza contains only one rhyme, as I. i. I. 1.[10] Sometimes two stanzas succeed each other, with the same rhyme in both, as stt. 7, 8 of II. iii. V., and 3, 4 of III. i. VIII.

[iv.] Where the stanza contains two or more rhymes,[11] as I. i. I. 2; II. vii. VI. 1.

[v.] Where the different rhymes alternate[12];—with more or less regularity or irregularity. In I. i. VII. the stanzas are quatrains proper, ll. 1 and 3 rhyming together in each, and also ll. 2 and 4. In I. ii. VI. 3, containing six lines, ll. 1 and 3 rhyme, and also ll. 2 and 4, whose rhyme is then continued in ll. 5, 6. So in I. ii. X., the stanzas of which are of five lines, ll. 1 and 3, rhyme, and then ll. 2, 4, 5. In I. i. II. 1, ll. 2 and 5 rhyme, and then ll. 3, 4, 6 In III. iii. VII. 1, ll. 2, 4, 6 rhyme; ll. 3 and 5; and then ll. 8, 9, 10, 12.

[vi.] Where one or more lines at the commencement of the different stanzas in a piece, or their concluding lines, rhyme with one another.[13] The former case occurs in I. xv. III.: II. vi. VIII.: III. iii. I. 2—8; the latter, in I. i. XI.; ii. XIV.; iv. IV.; vi. III.; vii. XIII.; xi. X.: III. i. X.: IV. ii. II. But in all these instances we

---

[8] 閒 句 韻·   [9] 隔 數 句 遙 韻· and 隔 韻 遙 韻·   [10] 一 章 一 韻·   [11] 一 章 易 韻·   [12] 隔 韻· and 三 句 隔 韻·   [13] 隔 章 章 首 遙 韻· and 隔 章 尾 句 遙 韻·

have the repetition of the whole lines, and not of the rhymes in them only.

[vii.]   What we call *medial* rhymes are found occasionally.[14] *E. g.*, I. iii. I. 5, 1. 1; IX. 2. 1. 2 (doubtful); XVI. 1, 2, 3, 1. 5; iv. III. 1, 1. 3; xiv. II. 4, ll. 1, 2: II. v. VI. 1, 2, 1. 1: IV. iii. I., l. 1.   Këang gives two instances under this case, where the members of different lines in the same stanza rhyme:—I. ii. X., 2, ll. 2, 4, and III. ii. VIII. 9, ll. 5, 6.

Without specifying any additional characteristics of the rhymes, which the minute research of native scholars has pointed out, it is to be observed that in all the Parts of the She, there are multitudes of lines, sometimes one, and sometimes more, which do not rhyme with any others, in the same stanza, while in Part IV., Book I., there are at least 8 pieces in which there is no attempt at rhyme at all.   Even in the 4th and 5th stanzas of III. i. VI., and the 4th stanza of iii. XI., it is only by a violent exercise of poetic license that we can make out any rhymes.   We may consider such disregard of rhyme as an approach in Chinese to the structure of blank verse; but while every other irregularity in the ancient odes has met with imitators, I am not aware that this has received any favour.   So far from the Chinese having any sympathy with Milton's contempt for rhyming as 'a jingling sound of like endings,' 'a troublesome bondage,' they consider rhyme as essential to poetry.

6.   The only other point which it is necessary to consider in this section is, whether the rhymes of the She were affected by what every Chinese scholar knows as the four tones, and an accurate acquaintance with which is now essential, not only to the making of poetry, but even to speaking so as to be freely and readily understood.   And on this subject there is considerable difference of opinion between those who have most deeply studied it.   One of the cases instanced by Këang Yung in regard to the rhymes, and which I have not adduced in the preceding paragraph, is that characters of the same termination rhyme together though they may be in different tones;[15] and this he endeavours to support by reference to more than 200 stanzas where he contends that the rhymes are altogether independent of the tones.[16]   Këang in

The relation of the ancient poems and the tones.

---

14 句中韻.   15 四聲通韻.   16. *E. g.*   In I. i. I. 3, it is said that 芼 (t. 1) and 樂 (t. 4) rhyme; in IX. 1, 2, 3, 廣 (t. 2), 泳 (t. 3), 永 (t. 2), and 方 (t. 1); in ii. I. 1, 居 (t. 1) and 御 (t. 3); in iv. V. 2, 修 (t. 1), 獻 (t. 3), and 淑 (t. 4); in II. i. II. 5, 駿 (t. 1), 譣 (t. 2.); in III ii. I. 1, 祀 子 止 (all t. 2), and 禝 (t. 4); in st. 3, 字 (t. 3), and 翼 t. 4); in st. 5, 道 草 茂 苞 襃 秀 好 (tt. 1, 2, 3).

this view followed Koo Ning-jin or Koo Yen-woo (A.D.1,603—1682),[17] distinguished by his varied scholarship, and especially by his researches into the ancient rhymes. In opposition to them, Twan Mow-t'ang, or Twan Yuh-tsae (A.D. 1,735—1,815),[18] contends that we ought to acknowledge three tones, the 1st, the 2d, and the 4th, in the She. He says:—'The tones of characters anciently were different from what they are now, just as the ancient rhyming endings were different from the present. Examining the compositions of the Chow and Ts'in dynasties, and the earlier portion of the Han, we find that there were then the 1st, 2d, and 4th tones, but not the 3d. During the dynasties of Wei and Tsin (A.D. 227—419), many words in the 2d and 4th tones assumed the 3d, and many in the 1st tone fell into one or other of the others. In this way there were the four tones complete; but in many cases they were different from what they had anciently been. Characters formerly of the 1st tone were now in one of the others, and many formerly in the 2d and 4th tones were now in the 3d. By diligent research the fact and the process of the change can be ascertained.'[19] Admitting, as I believe we ought to do, what is here claimed, that the tones of many of the characters were different anciently from that they became in the 3d and 4th centuries,·there is not much difficulty in approximating the views of Twan and Koo to each other. The latter says:—'Although the discussion of the four tones arose only when the capital was on the left of the Këang [say in our 5th and 6th centuries], yet the poetical compositions of the ancients had their characters distinguished in pronunciation as slow or rapid, light or heavy, and hence those now in the even tone rhymed together, as did those in the other tones. Yet it was by no means always so. The tones of characters have changed. In fact anciently these tones were simply the variations of pronunciation made by the voice of the singer, now high now low, now repressed now put forth. And thus the four tones could be used to rhyme together.'[20] Three tones existed anciently, according to Twan. 'No,' says Koo, 'there were no tones; but only certain

[17] 顧甯人 or 顧炎武.   [18] 段茂堂, or 段玉裁   [19] See the 六書音均表, 古四聲說; in the 皇清經解, 卷六百五十六, p. 16.
[20] See the 音論, 古人四聲一貫;—In the 皇清經解, 卷四, p. 7.
Koo says that 'the discussion of the four tones arose on the left of the Këang;' i.e., during the time of the various dynasties, which had their capital in the ancient Kin-ling, thence called Nan-king, or the southern capital, during the greater portion of the 5th and 6th centuries. I have translated the rest of the passage according to the sense of it, without attempting to make a literal version.

differences of pronunciation.' Both admit that the tonal system was not completed before our fifth century; and both agree that the tones of characters were liable to change. The difference of opinion between them lies more in words than in things. I concur with Twan in accepting the existence of three tones during the Chow dynasty; and it will be found that the rhymes of the odes, as given at the end of each piece, have more than a sufficient amount of verisimilitude and consistency.

SECTION II.

THE ANCIENT PRONUNCIATION OF THE CHARACTERS, AND THE CLASSIFICATION OF THE RHYMES IN THE SHE.

1. After all that has been said in the preceding section on the rhymes of the She, the student is soon struck by what he cannot at first but regard as the imperfection of many of them. It is evident from the structure of an ode that such and such lines were intended

The actual difficulty with the rhymes in attempting to read the She.

to rhyme; but he can in no way make them do so. Whatever the dialect to which he may have given his special attention, he sees that either the characters were pronounced and toned under the Chow dynasty very differently from the manner in which he has learned to enunciate them, or that the writers of the odes were astonishingly indifferent to the correctness of their rhymes, and content often with a remote approximation to similarity of sound in them. If he have recourse to the aid of the rhyming dictionaries which are current throughout the empire, and which, though representing an older pronunciation than that of the present day, must yet be followed by all poets and poetasters, his difficulty is brought before him with increased definiteness. There is hardly a single ode which will stand the test of an examination by the rhyme-and-tone classes in those dictionaries. We are come to a subject encompassed with perplexity; but much has been done by native scholars to unfold its complications, and to enable us to understand how the Chinese spoke and rhymed in the remote age of the Chow dynasty. I will endeavour to give a brief and clear view of the result of their researches in a few paragraphs, following the method of my own mind in its endeavours to grasp

102]

the subject, and giving in notes the fuller information which will help others to comprehend the processes and acquiesce in the conclusions.

2. In Choo He's edition of the She, we have a multitude of notes to assist us in reading the text, and making out the rhymes. It is always said that such and such a character rhymes with such and

The system of rhyming the She by poetical license. such another; that is, it is to be read different-ly from its ordinary pronunciation that it may give the necessary rhyme; and all these *hëeh yun*, as they are called, are reproduced in the K'ang-he dictionary.[1] This method of rhyming the odes was first reduced to a system by Woo Yih, or Woo Ts'ae-laou,[2] a scholar of the Sung dynasty, a little earlier than Choo He. He published a Work, which I have not seen, under the name of *Yun-poo*, which we may translate 'The Rhyme-mender.' Mr. Wylie observes upon it, that 'it is chiefly valued as being the earliest attempt to investigate the theory of the ancient sounds, but it is said to be a very faulty production.'[3] Whatever conclusions Woo came to as to the ancient sounds, he appears to have de-termined that, in reading the She, the standard pronunciation of his own day was to be adopted, and that, wherever words, evident-ly intended to rhyme, yet did not rhyme according to that stan-dard, then the pronunciation of one or more of them should be changed, and a rhyme effected by *hëeh yun*, or poetical license. Unreasonable as this method was, and impracticable in any alpha-betic language, practicable only in the ideographic Chinese, it found multitudes of admirers and followers. Even Choo He, we have seen, adopted it; and Seu Ch'en of the same dynasty has given it as his opinion, that 'it was not till the Rhyme-mender was published that the pieces in the Book of Poetry could be regarded as poems.'[4]

But the discrepancy between the rhymes of the She and those which had subsequently come to prevail was patent to scholars long before the Sung dynasty. Ch'ing Heuen himself wrote a treatise on the subject;[5] and, all through the time of the Three kingdoms, the Tsin, and other dynasties, on to the T'ang, various writers gave

---

[1] 叶韻. Morrison defines the phrase as—'two syllables that rhyme;' Medhurst as—'rhyme;' and Williams as—'to rhyme; harmonious cadence or tone.' But all these accounts of it fail to indicate its most important and frequent significance, that the rhyme is one of an assumed poetical license, where one of the characters has a pronunciation assigned to it which it does not in other circumstances have.   [2] 吳棫 or 吳才老.   [3] 韻補;—see General Notes ou Chinese Literature, p. 9.   [4] 徐蕆序吳才老韻補曰,自補韻之 書成,然後三百篇始得爲詩.   [5] 毛詩音.

their views upon it. The conclusion in which they rested seems to have been that enunciated by Luh Tih-ming, that 'the ancient rhymes were pliant and flexible, and there was no occasion to make any change in them to suit modern pronunciations.'[6]

The question has received the most thorough sifting during the present dynasty; and Koo Yen-woo, Këang Yung, and Twan Yuh-tsae, all mentioned in the preceding section, endeavouring, one after another, to exhaust the field, have left little to be gleaned, it seems to me, by future labourers. To prepare the reader to appreciate the results at which they have arrived, it will be well to set forth, first, the rhyme-system current at the present day, as given in the Thesaurus of the K'ang-he period, and next, the more extended system given in the *Kwang yun* dictionary, and which represents the rhymes as they were classified in the T'ang and Suy dynasties.

3. In the K'ang-he Thesaurus the rhymes are represented by The rhyme-system current at the present day. 106 characters, no regard being had to the initial consonants of those characters. There are 15 in the upper first tone, as many in the lower first, 29 in the second or ascending tone, 30 in the third or departing tone, and 17 in the 4th, called the entering or retracted tone. Taking the first or even tone as the measure of the endings, this system gives us only 80; and, if we add to them those of the 4th tone, which we must spell differently in English, we obtain 47. But some of those endings, as, for instance the first two, cannot be, and never could have been, represented by any but the same letters in English,—which would reduce their number; while others, as the sixth and seventh, comprehend characters that, as they come upon the ear in conversation and recitation, cannot be represented by the same letters,—which would increase their number.[7] Altogether, Medhurst makes out, upon

6 古人韻緩不煩改字.   7 Those representative words in the Thesaurus are:—

of the upper first tone, 東, 冬, 江, 支, 微, 魚, 虞, 齊, 佳, 灰, 眞, 文, 元, 寒, 刪;

of the lower first tone, 先, 蕭, 肴, 豪, 歌, 麻, 陽, 庚, 青, 蒸, 尤, 侵, 覃, 鹽, 咸;

of the second tone, 董, 腫, 講, 紙, 尾, 語, 麌, 薺, 蟹, 賄, 軫, 吻, 阮, 旱, 潸,

銑, 篠, 巧, 皓, 哿, 馬, 養, 梗, 迥, 有, 寢, 感, 儉, 豏;

of the third tone, 送, 宋, 絳, 寘, 未, 御, 遇, 霽, 泰, 卦, 隊, 震, 問, 願, 翰,

諫, 霰, 嘯, 效, 號, 箇, 禡, 漾, 敬, 徑, 宥, 沁, 勘, 豔, 陷;

of the fourth tone, 屋, 沃, 覺, 質, 物, 月, 曷, 黠, 屑, 藥, 陌, 錫, 職, 緝, 合,

葉, 洽.

this system, 55 finals, or rhyming terminations; and as he makes the initials or consonantal beginnings in the language to amount to 20 and a mute,—say 21, we have 21 × 55 = 1,155, as a near approximation to the number of possible sounds or enunciatrons in Chinese, a little more than one fortieth of the number of characters of which the language is made up. But the actual number is much smaller. Edkins gives the number of syllables, or distinct sounds in the Mandarin dialect, as 522, adding that in the syllabic dictionary of Morrison there are only 411. He says that if we were to accept the final m, and certain soft initials, which were still in existence under the Mongolian dynasty (A.D. 1,280—1,367), there would be at least 700 syllables.[8] Williams states that the possible sounds in the Canton dialect which could be represented by Roman letters would be 1,229, while the actual number of syllables is only 707.[9] It is always to be borne in mind that the rhyming endings, according to the present rules of Chinese poetry, are much fewer than the terminations diversified by the tones.

4. Ascending along the line of centuries from the era of K'ang-he to the time of which the pronunciation is given in the *Kwang-yun* dictionary, a period of nearly a thousand years, we find the rhyming endings represented by nearly twice as many characters as in the Thesaurus, or by 206 in all. There are 28 in the upper first tone and 29 in the lower, 55 in the second tone, 60 in the third, and 34 in the fourth.[10] To the western

The rhyme-system of the T'ang dynasty.

Combining these into groups, according to the tones, we obtain:—

[I.] 東. 董. 送. 屋; 冬. 腫. 宋. 沃; 江. 講. 絳. 覺; 支. 紙. 寘;
微. 尾. 未; 魚. 語. 御; 虞. 麌. 遇; 齊. 薺. 霽; 佳. 蟹. 泰. 卦;
灰. 賄. 隊; 真. 軫. 震. 質; 文. 吻. 問. 物; 元. 阮. 願. 月;
寒. 旱. 翰. 曷; 刪. 潸. 諫. 黠.
[ii.] 先. 銑. 霰. 屑; 蕭. 篠. 嘯; 肴. 巧. 效; 豪. 晧. 號;
歌. 哿. 箇; 麻. 馬. 禡; 陽. 養. 漾. 藥; 庚. 梗......陌;
青......敬. 錫; 蒸. 迥. 徑. 職; 尤. 有. 宥; 侵. 寢. 沁. 緝;
覃. 感. 勘. 合; 鹽. 琰. 豔. 葉; 咸. 豏. 陷. 洽.

This grouping of the characters shows that, though only the division of the first tone into an upper and a lower series is expressly mentioned, yet we must suppose a corresponding distinction carried into the other tones. Thus it is that we have about twice as many representatives of the characters in the 2d and 3d tones as of either of the upper or lower series of those of the 1st tone.

The 4th tone characters are distributed under those of the other tones which end with consonants. This seems natural, and one accustomed to the Canton and other local dialects can hardly suppose that it is not the correct arrangement; yet it was in several instances an innovation, considerably on in the time of our Christian era.

8 Grammar of the Mandarin Dialect, p. 45.   9 Tonic Dictionary, Introduction, p. 23.

10 The Kwang-yun (廣韻) is the oldest of the existing rhyming dictionaries. It appeared early in the Sung dynasty; but was confessedly based on an older work, which is lost, by Luh

student of Chinese the earlier system commends itself as in some
respects preferable to the more condensed one of the present day.
It meets more fully the requirements of the ear in regard to several
endings which we cannot represent by the same letters in any
alphabetic language. On the other hand, however, it multiplies in
several instances endings which we cannot in any way represent but
by the same letters. For instance, the first two endings in the

Fah-yen, a scholar of the Suy dynasty, who had employed the 206 representative characters.
They are:—

of the upper first tone, 東 冬 鍾 江 支 脂 之 微 魚 虞 模 齊 佳 皆
灰 咍 眞 諄 臻 文 欣 元 魂 痕 寒 桓 刪 山;

of the lower first tone, 先 仙 蕭 宵 肴 豪 歌 戈 麻 陽 唐 庚 耕 清
青 燕 登 尤 侯 幽 侵 覃 談 鹽 添 咸 銜 嚴 凡;

of the second tone, 董 腫 講 紙 旨 止 尾 語 麌 姥 薺 蟹 駭 賄
海 軫 準 吻 隱 阮 混 很 旱 緩 潸 產 銑 獮 篠 小 巧 皓 哿
果 馬 養 蕩 梗 耿 靜 迥 拯 等 有 厚 黝 寑 感 敢 琰 忝
儼 豏 檻 范;

of the third tone, 送 宋 用 絳 寘 至 志 未 御 遇 暮 霽 祭 泰 卦
怪 夬 隊 代 廢 震 椁 問 焮 願 恩 恨 翰 換 諫 襇 霰 線 嘯
笑 效 號 箇 過 禡 漾 宕 映 諍 勁 徑 證 嶝 宥 候 幼 沁 勘
闞 豔 㮇 醰 陷 鑑 梵;

of the fourth tone, 屋 沃 燭 覺 質 術 櫛 物 迄 月 沒 曷 末 黠
鎋 屑 薛 藥 鐸 陌 昔 錫 職 德 緝 合 盍 葉 怗 洽 狎
業 乏.

Grouping these characters, according to the tones, we obtain:—

[i.] 東 董 送 屋; 冬 腫 宋 沃; 鍾 … 用 燭; 江 講
絳 覺; 支 紙 寘; 脂 旨 至; 之 止 志; 微 齊
尾 未; 魚 語 御; 虞 麌 遇; 模 姥 暮; 齊
薺 霽 祭; 佳 蟹 卦; 皆 駭 泰 怪 夬; 灰 賄 隊 —
廢; 咍 海 代; 眞 軫 震 質; 諄 準 椁 術; 臻
…, 櫛; 文 吻 問 物; 欣 隱 焮 迄; 元 阮 願
月; 魂 混 恩 沒; 痕 很 恨 曷; 寒 旱 翰; 桓
緩 換 末; 刪 潸 諫 點; 山 產 襇 鎋;

[ii.] 先 銑 霰 屑; 仙 獮 線 薛; 蕭 篠 嘯; 宵 小 笑
肴 巧 效; 豪 養 漾 藥; 歌 哿 箇; 戈 果 過; 庚 梗 映 陌
耕 耿 麥; 清 靜 諍 昔; 青 迥 勁 徑; 庚 梗 映 陌; 燕
證 職; 登 等 嶝 德; 尤 有 宥; 候 厚 候 幽
黝 幼; 侵 寑 沁 緝; 覃 感 勘 合; 談 敢 闞 盍
鹽 琰 豔 葉; 添 忝 㮇 怗; 咸 豏 陷 洽; 銜 檻
鑑 狎; 嚴 儼 醰 業; 凡 范 梵 乏.

Thesaurus, to which I referred in the last paragraph, are expanded
by it into three, and illustrated by characters pronounced *tung, tung,*
and *chung.* The ending is *ung.* Edkins, indeed. is of opinion that
there was a difference anciently in the three sounds. and he represents them by *eng, ang,* and *ong.*[11]   But in the really ancient
times, when the odes of the She were made, there was no such difference, and certainly there is none appreciable now by any ear that
is not of the most exquisite delicacy.   Even Chinese writers of the
highest authority say in reference to them that 'the pronunciation
is the same but the rhyme different.'[12]   I will only further say on
this point, that the manner in which the rhyming dictionaries were
constructed, after the introduction from India of the system of syllabic spelling, by means of the four tones and seven notes of music,
has never yet been fully elucidated by any foreigner.   Nothing satisfactory, so far as I know, has been done to complete what Morrison
said upon the subject in the Introduction to his dictionary.

5.   The reader will, no doubt, now be surprised when he is told
that the result of the investigations of Koo Yen-woo, Këang Yung,
and Twan Yuh-tsae has been to reduce the rhymes of the She to

Rhyme-system propounded } fewer than twenty terminations.   Koo, in-
at the present day.   } deed, allows no more than ten,[13] insisting
on characters of the same ending, whatever be their tones,
rhyming with one another.   Këang, following Koo. in his view
about the tones, yet enlarges his terminations to thirteen.[14]   Twan
Yuh-tsae makes altogether seventeen; but as he contends for the exist-

11 Grammar of the Mandarin Dialect, p. 75.

12 Thus Koo Yen-woo (音論, 古人音緩, 不煩改字) says, 韻書起於
陸法言, 於是有音同韻異, 若東, 冬, 鍾, 魚, 虞, 模, 庚, 耕, 清,
青, 蒸, 登之部, 不可以相雑   13 Koo's system classifies the rhyme-characters
of the *Kwang-yun* thus:—1st, 東, 冬, 鍾, 江; 2d, 支, 脂, 之, 微, 齊, 佳, 皆, 灰, 咍,
質, 術, 櫛, 物, 迄, 月, 沒, 曷, 黠, 鎋, 屑, 薛, 麥, 昔, 錫, 職, 德; 3d,
魚, 虞, 模, 侯, 藥, 鐸, 陌; 4th, 眞, 諄, 臻, 文, 欣, 元, 魂, 痕, 寒, 桓, 刪,
山, 先, 仙; 5th, 蕭, 宵, 肴, 豪, 尤, 幽, 屋, 沃, 燭, 覺; 6th, 歌, 戈, 麻; 7th,
陽, 唐; 8th, 庚, 耕, 清, 青; 9th, 蒸, 登; 10th, 侵, 覃, 談, 鹽, 添, 咸, 銜, 嚴,
凡, 緝, 合, 盍, 葉, 怗, 洽, 狎, 業, 乏.   14 Termination 1, same as Koo's; 2, 支,
脂, 之, 微, 齊, 佳, 皆, 灰, 咍, 咨, 昔, 錫, 職, 德; 3, same as Koo's, omitting 侯;
4, 眞, 諄, 臻, 文, 欣, 魂, 痕, 質, 術, 櫛, 物, 迄, 沒; 5, 元, 寒, 桓, 刪, 山,
先, 仙, 月, 曷, 末, 黠, 鎋, 屑, 薛; 6, 蕭, 宵, 肴, 豪; 7, same as Koo's 6th; 8, same
as Koo's 7th; 9, same as Koo's 8th; 10, same as Koo's 9th; 11, 尤, 侯, 幽, 屋, 沃, 燭, 覺;
12, 侵, 緝; 13, 覃, 談, 鹽, 添, 咸, 銜, 嚴, 凡, 合, 盍, 葉, 怗, 洽, 狎, 業, 乏.

ence of three tones, and that tone rhymes with tone, we may allow $3\times8+2\times9=24+18=42$, as the extreme number of rhyming endings anciently made use of by the Chinese, while the difference between the enunciation of characters in the first and second tones could hardly be appreciable by the ear in singing. Twan's terminations may be approximately represented, in the order in which he gives them, by e (our *e* in *wet*), and eh for his 3d tone; aou (including ëaou); ëw, and its 3d tone ewh (ew in our *new*, and ewt in *newt* are not far from them); ow (as in *now*); u or oo; ăng (the ă approaches to our *a* in *fat*); im and its 3d tone ip (as in our *him* and *hip*); am and its 3d tone ap (as in our *ham* and *hap*); ung (as in our *sung*); ang (as in our *rang*); ing or ĕng; in and its 3d tone it (as in our *sin* and *sit*; un (as in *sun*); an (as in *fan*); ei and its 3d tone eih (nearly as in *scheik*); e or ee (our long *e* as in *me*) and its 3d tone eh; and o (as in *go*).[15]

15 The 1st termination admitted by Twan Yuh-tsae embraces the characters classed in the Kwang-yun under the representatives 之 and 咍 (t. 1), 止 and 海 (t. 2), 志 and 代 (t. 3), and 職 and 德 (t. 4). Under it moreover are comprehended all characters formed from the phonetics in the following list, which, and in the other terminations, includes some derivatives—

絲 台 枲 里 貍 來 思 其 臣 龜 𡥀 𡩡 又 有 尤 右 而 𠚂 迡 坐 事
𧈢 市 某 才 𢦏 在 母 佩 久 臺 式 目 能 矣 疑 亥 郵 牛 茲 㽙 𡧛
寡 不 丕 淄 𢔌 苗 辭 司 丘 采 友 否 音 宰 𡴆 止 齒 巳 己 耳 士 𦰠
𡩡 寺 時 史 吏 𧟌 𠦝 緇 戒 婦 舊 乃 異 北 食 䏌 子 菩 意 再 𦳆 塞
備 直 悳 𡈼 弋 則 賊 革 或 璽 息 亞 力 防 棘 䝵 黑 匿 髟 色 寨
八 失 𡲯 服 麥 克 𦥄 得 伏 牧 墨 茻 荀·

The 2d termination embraces the characters arranged under 蕭, 宵, 肴, 豪 (t. 1), 篠, 小, 巧, 皓 (t. 2), and 嘯, 笑, 效, 号 (t. 3), and those formed from the phonetics—毛 樂 梟 澡 尞 小 丿 少 奐 麃 㬥 𣈙 天 芺 敖 卓 勞 龠 翟 爵 交 虐 高 喬 刀 召 到 兆 苗 番 夒 爻 肴 李 敫 羊 𣍃 巢 吊 羔 𩅧 盜 勺 雀 弱 兒 貌 臬 号 號 了 叜 邑·

The 3d termination embraces the characters arranged under 尤 and 幽 (t. 1), 有 and 黝 (t. 2), 宥 and 幼 (t. 3), and 屋, 沃, 燭, 覺 (t. 4), and those from the phonetics—九 瓜 尻 州 求 流 六 奎 竂 休 舟 憂 汙 游 鬴 攸 條 修 俏 肅 未 叔 戚 奧 秋 李 翏 咎 彡 姦 卯 𠨛 周 矛 柔 敊 包 匋 焦 樵 𧮫 𦥑 報 丂 手 老 牡 畜 𣐒 雔 帚 臿 頁 道 守 ㄐ 自 幵 缶 由 穴 戊 丑 丂 肏 厚 考 族 保 㝛 劉 肘 受 棗 菊 白 學 竹 籀 復 肉 告 育 毒 齒 寶 辱 翏 覉 侯 曲 玉 奥 豸 𣪩 蜀 木 珏 彔 粟 逐 羮 永 卜 支 局 夙 鹿 參 𩏑 秀 目·

The 4th termination embraces the characters arranged under 侯 (t. 1) 厚 (t. 2), and 候 (t. 3), and those formed from the phonetics—婁 句 朱 禺 壴 封 尌 廚 區 蔞 㬰 儿 殳

需須俞叙后取冣聚後臾侮口圍厚付府歪癸、主斗
鞲豆具屚寇畫部盟聮

The 5th termination embraces the characters arranged under 魚, 虞, 模 (t. 1), 語,
麌 (t. 2), 御, 遇, 暮 (t. 3), and 藥, 鐸 (t. 4), and those formed from the phonetics—

姥 祖 者 慮 惡 昇 吾 白
且 虜 奢 廬 魚 異 予 帛
吳 父 盧 鱻 圛 予 魯 尺
亞 甫 穌 乎 乎 午 虍 百
奴 尃 卢 上 午 處 吁 赤
五 浦 古 戶 許 亏 亏 赫
蟲 樂 居 余 尾 武 朔 罭
灷 攀 洛 夕 朔 山 罭 罦
牙 夸 路 素 屋 兎 罭 埊
段 烏 瓜 毋 黍 翠 宋
狎 蔦 賈 巫 罝 罃 霏
家 葛 馬 石 禹 摔 霸
車 岗 鼓 彘 徇 谷 叕
巴 於 鼓 夏 寧 奄 亡
太 与 度 呂 夏 霏
壹 庶 女 寧 卓 霸
雨 卤 下 烏 郙 叕
囫 夏 烏 隻 戟
霏 寜 旅 舊 毛
灷 旅 客 毳
霏 羽 寡 籍

The 6th termination embraces characters arranged under 蒸, 登 (t. 1), 拯, 等 (t. 2), 證,
嶝 (t. 3), and those formed from the phonetics—

曹 夢 蠅 朋 弓 曾 升 雅 丞 朕 與
夌 互 恆 丞 烝 承 徵 薂 厶 玄 众 登 登 樂 仍 再 稱 兂 登

The 7th termination embraces characters arranged under 侵, 鹽, 添 (t. 1), 寢, 琰, 忝 (t. 2),
沁, 豔, 㮇 (t. 3), and 緝, 葉, 帖 (t. 4), and those formed from the phonetics—咸, 鹹, 覃,

林 朓 廉 拾 邑
心 今 替 肰 龜
念 錦 閃 西 華
金 突 丙 入
畬 壬 甜 十
欽 任 卅 卟
歙 品 亶 蠹
凡 至 禀 督
羊 淫 審 爰
南 占 夆 玁
牽 黏 狀 劦
埶 五 歷 協
男 三 戉 麥
琴 參 載 甘
乡 炎 鐵 冊
縛 戍 巳 立
甚 巴 泛 隰
音 州 緳 恳
先 泛 厶 陷
兼 厶
合

The 8th termination embraces characters arranged under 覃, 談, 咸, 銜, 嚴, 凡 (t. 1), 感,
敢, 豏, 檻, 儼, 范 (t. 2), 勘, 闞, 陷, 檻, 釅 (t. 3), and 合, 盍, 洽, 狎, 業,
乏 (t. 4), and those formed from the phonetics—函 臽 臿 監 鹽 炎 刕 熊 灷 毇 嚴
毇 广 詹 斬 亀 甘 奄 雙 欠 尤 妾 甲 枼 涉 灋 業 建 曆 巤 耴 夾
益 昜 函 簶 沓 帀 帀

The 9th termination embraces characters arranged under 東, 冬, 鍾, 江 (t. 1), 董, 腫, 講,
(t. 2), and 送, 宋, 用, 絳 (t. 3), and those formed from the phonetics—中 舟 宮 東 重
童 龍 公 蟲 冬 夆 降 隆 丰 奉 夅 逢 用 甬 庸 从 㕛 囪 恩 同 鳳
邕 雝 宋 戎 封 容 工 巩 空 送 克 共 雙 彖 蒙 凶 匈 兄 夒 宗 崇
蒿 豐 眔 尨 厖 涑 彖 茸 匚

The 10th termination embraces characters arranged under 陽, 唐 (t. 1), 養, 蕩 (t. 2), and 漾,
宕 (t. 3), and those formed from the phonetics—王 行 衡 生 匡 往 狂 网 黃 罔
昜 錫 陽 湯 刲 牆 將 臧 永 方 放 旁 皇 亢 兵 尢 京 羛 巸 舋 兩 凰
庚 康 唐 皀 鄉 卿 上 量 彊 強 兄 桑 爽 小 梁 彭 央 昌 囧 朙 兩 兒
量 奚 誩 競 春 弱 秉 龍 卬 慶 丙 奭 章 商 亡 兂 容 長 皀
The 11th termination embraces characters arranged under 庚, 耕, 清, 青 (t. 1), 梗, 耿,
靜, 迥 (t. 2), and 映, 諍, 勁, 徑 (t. 3) and those formed from the phonetics—熒 丁 成
亭 正 生 盈 鳴 敄 壬 廷 呈 戔 戟 青 鼎 名 平 盈 寧 甯 嬰 粤 敫
宀 冥 霝 爭 頃 开 弁 貞 需 巠 井 耿 門 圝 烝 晶 省

109]

The 12th termination embraces characters arranged under 眞, 臻, 先 (t. 1), 軫, 銑 (t. 2), 震, 霰 (t. 3), and 質, 櫛, 屑 (t. 4), and those formed from the phonetics—秦 卂 人 儿 燊 洤 寅 西 穵 賓 胤 身 旬 夐 信 辛 羍 新 令 天 田 千 年 因 命 民 田 陳 電 仁 眞 顚 侲 匀 訇 門 進 扁 臣 臦 賢 堅 幷 並 緣 民 質 黹 玄 牽 引 矜 禛 八 分 穴 匹 必 宓 瑟 盇 晉 實 吉 壹 頡 質 失 七 憲 冎 卽 節 日 疾 枲 黍 漆 至 室 畢 一 乙 血 徹 逸 印 归 失 刖

The 13th termination embraces characters arranged under 諄, 文, 欣, 魂, 痕 (t. 1), 準 吻, 隱, 混, 很 (t. 2), and 稕, 問, 焮, 恩, 恨 (t. 3), and those formed from the phonetics— 先 辰 晨 盾 困 麇 屯 春 門 殷 分 敦 爨 皀 西 聖 免 昏 孫 奔 賁 君 員 罷 鯤 昆 蕓 璊 川 雲 云 存 巾 侖 蕫 豆 文 彣 吝 閔 豩 蜳 幽 軍 斤 刃 典 盅 溫 緼 亹 熏 焚 彬 豚 盾 多 舜 雧 焝 寸 筋 蜳 耇 慁 隱 乚 困 彖

The 14th termination embraces characters arranged under 元, 寒, 桓, 删, 山, 仙 (t. 1), 阮, 旱, 緩, 潸, 産, 獮 (t. 2), and 願, 翰, 換, 欄, 諫, 線 (t. 3), and characters formed from the phonetics—虔 專 袁 裏 采 弄 卷 凹 舁 厂 尸 彥 雁 鴈 旦 半 平 連 喜 泉 還 歎 難 鴈 緣 官 幵 袞 屡 卵 夋 反 開 曾 宣 桓 見 双 亘 蔑 曼 寬 北 絼 愳 妃 宛 亅 干 岸 旱 攣 妟 宴 圓 安 晏 州 閒 覱 丹 次 羨 白 肰 縣 照 元 完 冠 肙 山 戔 衍 憲 柳 散 潛 柦 樊 延 虘 獻 家 羨 翰 尚 袤 班 建 箕 華 犬 删 片 雋 蚨 允 犮 萭 尊 妟 斷 沿

The 15th termination embraces characters arranged under 脂, 微, 齊, 皆, 灰 (t. 1), 旨 尾, 薺, 駭, 賄 (t. 2), 至, 未, 霽, 祭, 泰, 怪, 夬, 隊, 廢 (t. 3), and 術, 物, 迄 月, 沒, 厶, 曷, 末, 黠, 鎋, 薛 (t. 4), and those formed from the phonetics—妻 飛 皆 自 殺 虫 委 火 季 字 世 辠 畀 朿 刖 歸 豈 詹 回 矢 惠 乂 欬 出 系 勿 骨 突 乞 日 軋 卪 吅 址 厕 嚻 黎 畾 黽 竃 采 貝 貴 聑 乞 夬 賴

The 16th termination embraces characters arranged under 支, 佳 (t. 1), 紙, 蟹 (t. 2), 寘 卦 (t. 3), and 陌, 麥, 昔, 錫 (t. 4), and those formed from the phonetics—支 羈 知 是 紫 羣 智 卑 斯 乀 氏 祇 疧 厂 虒 圭 佳 厄 癸 兒 規 蟜 虒 豪 蠡 瓜 亡 豸 麗 危 爾 只 厲 益 鬲 帝 嗇 適 易 析 皆 束 策 速 賁 刺

110]

Even if we accept these approximations to the ancient rhyming endings of Chinese poetry, we shall still find it extremely difficult to read the odes of the She, as they were no doubt read when they were written; and to enable the student to do so, he would have to unlearn the names of the characters which he has already learned with a great amount of labour, and acquire a set of names which would make him unintelligible to the people and scholars of the present day, thus encountering a toil and expending an amount of time for which there would be no adequate return. All that we can do, is to read the odes as they are now read throughout the nation, making them rhyme imperfectly and often not at all; to be prepared at the same time to maintain that, when they were written, they did come trippingly off the tongue in good rhyme; and then to refer, in proof of our assertion, to the researches of Twan Yuh-tsae.

6. But it is not merely as thus satisfying the cravings of a historical curiosity that those researches are valuable;—they bring

General value of the researches into the ancient rhyme-system. ⎱ before us how it was that rhyme arose in Chinese composition at all, and they carry, in their establishment of that fact, a striking evidence of their own correctness, while showing also how the language has, with the progress of time and the changes growing up in it, become increasingly difficult of acquisition to the people themselves and to foreign students of it.

The written language of China was, I believe, in its first beginnings pictorial, the characters being rude figures of the objects which they were intended to represent. This is a thing sufficiently known; and sufficient illustrations of it are to be found in nearly every book which has been written on the Chinese language.

But there were limits, evidently narrow limits, to this process of representing by pictorial signs the subjects of human thought. The characters speaking to the eye, though their form is now so

囷 罶 朧 簪 昊 鵥 觧 厄 戹 狄 迹 秇 麻 歷 役 圝 畫 扊 㲋 冊 鷇 毄 系 枲 賛

The 17th termination embraces characters arranged under 歌, 戈, 麻 (t. 1), 哿, 果, 馬 (t. 2), and 箇, 過, 禡 (t. 3), and those formed from the phonetics—它 沱 佗 呂 咼 過 哥 爲 皮 己 可 何 离 離 也 地 施 迆 義 儀 羲 加 嘉 多 宜 奇 猗 婺 麻 靡 我 羅 惟 罯 罷 龍 巛 坐 七 化 吹 丆 左 沙 瓦 陸 隋 隋 㐬 坐 禾 和 龢 果 祼 余 崔 貞 瑣 沁 臥 戈 羸 牛 斛

changed that their original nature cannot be discerned, were never more than a few hundred; and most of them are retained in what are generally called radicals, under one or other of which all the other characters of the language are arranged in the K'ang-he dictionary. To meet the requirements of thought and composition, the device was fallen on of forming characters that should be phonetic or representative of sounds,—that should be so, not as embodying in their form the elements of the compound sound as in an alphabetic language, but which should be understood and treasured in the memory as indicative each of its particular sound, whether that was of a single vowel, a dipthong, a triphthong, or a vowel and consonant together. Several of the radicals were set apart for this object; other phonetics had their own individual meaning as ideographs; and some hardly seem to have served any purpose but that of phonetics. By the combination of them with the radicals, the number of ideographs became capable of indefinite multiplication. In fact, the great body of the characters in the language is formed by the union of a radical and a phonetic, the former element giving for the most part some general intimation of the meaning, and the latter of the sound. As Twan Yuh-tsae says, 'In defining dictionaries, the meaning is the principal thing,—the warp, with the sound as the woof; in rhyming dictionaries, the sound is the warp, and the meaning is the woof.'[16] Thus in the *Shwoh-wăn*, as it came from Heu Shin, about A.D. 100, after the lexical definition of the meaning, it is generally added, 'Formed from such a radical, taking its sound from such and such a phonetic.'[17] The spelling by means of an initial and final is an addition by the Sung editor.

It was by means of these phonetic characters that rhyme became possible in Chinese writings. And we may assume it as self-evident, that a phonetic on its first formation had only one sound and one tone; for if it had had many sounds and tones it would have ceased to be a phonetic. Much of this happy simplicity continued well on into the Han dynasty. But later on we find characters into which the same phonetic enters quite variously pronounced, though some one

16 See the 六書音均表, 古諧聲說:- 諧聲之字, 半主義, 半主聲, 凡字書以義爲經, 而聲緯之, 凡韻書以聲爲經, 而義緯之. 17 Callery has called attention to this characteristic of the *Shwoh-wăn* in his *Systema Phoneticum*, p. 16. Twan Yuh-tsae does the same in the paragraph just quoted, adding that there must have been similar dictionaries during the dynasties of Shang and Chow, which are long lost. It may be doubted if such dictionaries ever existed.

or more of them will generally be found to retain the original sound.[18]
How it was that phonetics came in process of time to assume several
different pronunciations or sounds, some of them widely diverse
from the original sound each was intended to suggest, is an
inquiry that has considerable attractions for the minute philologist.
The facts of change may be collected and the dates approximated
to, while the cause was more subtle and is difficult to ascertain; but
it would be foreign to my present purpose to enter on so wide a question. What has been stated affords to my own mind an account
of the peculiarities of the rhymes of the She entirely satisfactory.
We are placed by them near to the fountain-head of the Chinese language. We are shown it in its first appearances; and the one point
of the phonetic having been made to represent only one sound
sufficiently vindicates and establishes the system of the modern researches into the ancient rhymes.

Before leaving the subject of the present section, I will venture to
state my own opinion that the nature of the Chinese language is even
at the best ill-adapted in one important respect for the purpose of
agreeable rhyme. It does not admit the variety that is found in an
alphabetical language, and which is to us one of the charms of poetical
composition. The single rhyming endings in English are 360; and if
we add to them what are called double and triple rhymes, where the
accent falls on the penultimate and antepenultimate syllables, they
cannot come short of 400. In Chinese on the other hand the rhyming
endings are very few, and though there may be a great number
of words to any one ending, yet, through the comparative fewness
of the initial consonants, many rhymes are to a foreign ear
merely assonances, and the effect is that of a prolonged monotony.
This defect, inherent in the nature of the Chinese language, has
been aggravated by the course which poetry has taken for more
than a thousand years. In the She we find characters rhyming with
one another in the different tones, and changes of rhyme in the same
piece, and even in the same stanza; but since the era of the T'ang
dynasty, it has been established that the rhyme in a poem must
always fall on a character in the even tone, and the liberty of the

---

18 Twan instances 某, which originally was sounded *mě*, but is now called *mow*, and classed
under 厚, with 謀, and other derivatives, while 楳 媒, and others, are classed under 灰,
and sounded *mei*; and 每, originally sounded *mě*, some of whose derivatives are sounded *mei*,
one at least (敏) *min*, and several *mow*.

writer is farther cramped by the method of alternating in all the lines, according to certain rules, the even and deflected tones. It is in consequence of this that poetical compositions now are necessarily constrained and brief, and we never meet with the freedom and seldom with the length which we find in the Book of Poetry. Some Christian Chinese of genius, addressing himself to the work of a hymnologist, and breaking down, not rashly but wisely, all restrictions, may yet do more to develope the capabilities of his language for the purpose of poetry than has been hitherto accomplished.

SECTION III.

THE POETICAL VALUE; AND CERTAIN PECULIARITIES OF COMPOSITION IN THE ODES OF THE BOOK OF POETRY.

1. My object in translating the Book of Poetry as a portion of the Chinese classics does not require that I should attempt any estimate of the poetical value of the pieces of which it is composed; Poetical value of the odes. and I touch upon the subject only in a slight and cursory manner. The Roman Catholic missionaries, who were the first to introduce the knowledge of Chinese literature into Europe, expressed themselves with astonishing audacity on the merit of the odes. In the treatise on the antiquity of the Chinese with which the 'Memoires concernant les Chinois' commence, it is said:—'The poetry of the She king is so beautiful and harmonious, the lovely and sublime tone of antiquity rules in it so continually, its pictures of manners are so naive and minute, that all these characteristics give sufficient attestation of its authenticity. The less can this be held in doubt that in the following ages we find nothing, I will not say equal to these ancient odes, but nothing worthy to be compared with them. We are not sufficient connoisseurs to pronounce between the She-king on the one side and Pindar and Homer on the other; but we are not afraid to say that it yields only to the Psalms of David in speaking of the Divinity, of

114]

Providence, of virtue, &c., with a magnificence of expressions and an elevation of ideas which make the passions cold with terror, ravish the spirit, and draw the soul from the sphere of the senses.' Such language is absurdly extravagant, and we are tempted to doubt whether the writer who used it could have had much ao quaintance with the poems which he belauds. And yet it would be wrong to go to the other extreme, and deny to them a very considerable degree of poetical merit. It is true that many of them, as Sir John Davis has said, ' do not rise above the most primitive simplicity,' and that the principal interest which the collection possesses arises from its pictures of manners, yet there are not a few pieces which may be read with pleasure from the pathos of their descriptions, their expressions of natural feeling, and the boldness and frequency of their figures.

The comparison of them to the Psalms of David is peculiarly unfortunate. God often appears in them, indeed, the righteous and sovereign lord of Providence; but the writers never make Him their theme for what He is in himself, and do not rise to the distinct conception of Him as "over all," China and other nations, " blessed for ever," to be approached by the meanest as well as the highest.

2. Sir John Davis contends that ' verse must be the shape into which Chinese, as well as other poetry, must be converted in order

Ought the odes to be translated in verse? } to do it mere justice,'[1] adding that in his own treatise on the Poetry of the Chinese, while giving now *a prose translation*, now *a faithful metrical version*, and anon *an avowed paraphrase*, he has deferred more than his own judgment and inclinations approved to the prejudices of those who are partial to the literal side of the question. It may be granted that verse is the proper form in which to translate verse; but the versifier must have a sufficient understanding of the original before he can do justice to it, and avoid imposing upon his reader. Sir John has rendered in verse two of the odes of the She. Of the former of them, where the meaning of the ode is entirely misapprehended, I have spoken in a note appended to it (p. 21). The second is given with more success; but not in what I can regard as ' a faithful metrical version.' He observes that the style and language of the odes, without the minute commentary which accompanies them, would not always be intelligible at the present day.

1 The Poetry of the Chinese (London, 1870), p. 34.

But the earliest commentary on the odes is modern as compared with their antiquity, and what, it is to be presumed, he calls the minute commentary often differs from it *toto cælo*. Every critic of eminence, indeed, has his own to-say on whole odes and particular stanzas and lines. I have not delivered myself to any commentary. Where the lines are now and then all but unintelligible, we may suspect some error in the text;—no commentary will be found to throw any satisfactory light upon them. But upon the whole, the Book of Poetry is easier to construe than the Book of History;—it is much easier than the poetry of the T'ang and subsequent dynasties.

My object has been to give a version of the text which should represent the meaning of the original, without addition or paraphrase, as nearly as I could attain to it. The collection as a whole is not worth the trouble of versifying. But with my labours before him, any one who is willing to undertake the labour may present the pieces in 'a faithful metrical version.' My own opinion inclines in favour of such a version being as nearly literal as possible. In Bunsen's 'God in History,' Book III., chap. V., poetical versions are given of several passages from the She, which that various writer calls 'The Book of Sacred songs.' Versified, first in German, from the Latin translation of Lacharme, and again from the German version in English, if the odes from which they are taken were not pointed out in the foot-notes, it would be difficult, even for one so familiar with the Chinese text as myself, to tell what the originals of them were. Such productions are valueless, either as indications of the poetical merit of the odes, or of the sentiments expressed in them.

3. Nothing could be more simple than the bulk of the odes in the first Part. A piece frequently conveys only one idea, which is re-

Peculiarities in the structure of the odes. peated in the several stanzas with little change in the language. The writer wishes to prolong his ditty, and he effects his purpose by the substitution of a fresh rhyme, after which the preceding stanza reappears with no other change than is rendered necessary by the new term. An amusing instance is pointed out in the 3d ode of Book XIV., where the poet is reduced, by the necessities of his rhyme, to say that the young of the turtle dove are seven in number.

Some of the pieces in Parts II. and III. are marked by the same characteristics as those of the *Fung*,—the repetition of whole lines and more, merely varied by a change in the rhyme. This peculiarity

116]

belongs especially to what are called the *allusive* pieces. Many odes in these Parts, however, are of a higher order, and furnish the best examples of Chinese poetical ability. The 1st ode of Part III., Book I., is remarkable as constructed in the same way as the 121st and other *step* Psalms, as they have been called, the concluding line of one stanza generally forming the commencing one of the next. In some other odes there is an approximation to the same thing.

Throughout the Book, the occurrence of particles which we cannot translate, and the use of which seems mainly to be to complete the length of the line; the employment of onomatopoetic binomials; the vivid descriptive force of the same character redoubled, or of two characters of cognate meaning together; and the accomplishment of the same purpose by the pronouns 其 and 彼, as pointed out in the notes and in Index III., are peculiarities attention to which will help the student in apprehending the meaning, and appreciating the beauty of the composition.

APPENDIX.

ON THE VARIOUS FORMS IN WHICH POETRY HAS BEEN WRITTEN AMONG THE CHINESE.

1. Lines of four words, with a more or less regular observance of rule, is, we have seen, the normal measure of the ancient odes in the Book of Poetry. I have repeatedly indicated also my opinion that the rules now acknowledged for poetical composition are of a nature to cripple the genius of the writer. A sketch therefore, in as brief compass as possible, of the various measures in which Chinese poets have given expression to their thoughts, and of the laws which the code of poetical criticism now requires them to observe, will form an appropriate appendix to the preceding chapter, and may lead to the fuller treatment of an interesting subject which has not yet received from Sinologues the attention which it deserves. My materials will be drawn mainly from the Works of Chaou Yih (referred to on p. 3 of these proleg.), chapter xxiii., and from a monograph by Wang Tsou.

2. While lines of four characters are the rule in the pieces of the She, I have shown how lines of other lengths, from two characters or syllables up to eight, are interspersed in them. In all these, and still more extensive measures, whole pieces have at different times been attempted.

First, as a specimen of a piece in lines of two characters, there may be given the following on the Posterior Han dynasty (詠蜀漢事) by Yu Pih-săng or Yu Tseih (虞伯生；虞集) of the Ynen dynasty :—

鸞輿 三顧 茅廬 漢祚 難扶 日暮 桑榆 深
渡 南瀘 長驅 西蜀 力柜 東吳 羨平 周瑜
妙術 悲夫 關羽 云殂 天數 盈虛 造物 乘
除 問汝 何如 早賦 歸歟

It may be rendered in English thus :—

The royal carriage	Was Chow Yu,
Thrice visited	With skilful schemes!
The lowly cot.	Alas for
The fate of Han	Kwan yu,
Was irreversible,	Who met his death!
[Like] the evening sun,	The course of Heaven
[Fading from] the mulberries and elms.	Is now favourable, now opposed.
By the deep ford,	The course of events
Southwards he crossed the Leu;	Is now prosperous, now adverse.
By a great effort,	Let me ask you
He took Shuh in the west,	What is best.
And strongly withstood	Early sing—
Woo in the east.	I will retire.
Admirable	

The student who is acquainted with the romance of the Three Kingdoms will have no difficulty in understanding the historical allusions in these lines. The whole may be considered as an advice not to place one's-self, as Mencius says, under a tottering wall,—not to try to maintain a doomed cause.

Second, of a piece in lines of three characters, rhyming, though not all rhyming together as in the above piece, I give the following specimen from the Books of the first Han dynasty (禮樂志 第二), —one of 19 compositions made in the reign of the emperor Woo, and sung by young musicians, male and female, in the night time, at the border sacrifice to Heaven and Earth :—

鍊時日， 侯有望， 炳骨蕭， 延四方， 九重開， 靈
之旂， 垂惠恩， 鴻祜休， 靈之車， 結玄雲， 寫飛
龍， 羽旄紛， 靈之下， 若風馬， 左倉龍， 右白虎，
靈之來， 神哉沛， 先以雨， 般裔裔， 靈之至， 慶至
陰陰， 相膠轕， 震澹心， 已坐， 五音飭， 虞至
且， 承靈億， 牲繭栗， 粢盛香， 尊桂酒， 賓八鄉
靈安留， 吟青黃， 徧觀此， 眺瑤堂， 泉蝶並， 神
奇麗， 顥如茶， 兆逐麛， 被華文， 賜霧轂， 曳阿
錫， 佩珠玉， 俠嘉夜， 苞蘭芳， 澹容與， 獻嘉爝

I venture the following version of it :—

Having chosen this seasonable day,
Here we are expecting.
We burn the fat and the southernwood,
Whose smoke spreads all around.
The nine heavens are opened.
Lo! the flags of the Power,
Sending down his favour,
Blessing, great and admirable.
Lo! the chariot of the Power,
Amidst the dark clouds,
Drawn by flying dragons,
With many feathered streamers.
Lo! the Power descends,
As if riding on the wind;
On the left an azure dragon,
On the right a white tiger.
Lo! the Power is coming,
With mysterious rapidity.
Before him the rain,
Is fast distributed.
Lo! the Power is arrived,
Bright amid the darkness,
Filling us with amazement,
Making our hearts to quake.

Lo! the Power is seated,
And our music strikes up,
To rejoice him till dawn,
To make him well pleased.
With the victim and his budding horns,
With the vessels of fragrant millet,
With the vase of cinnamon spirits,
We welcome all his attendants.
The Power is pleased to remain,
And we sing to the music of all the seasons.
Look here, all,
And observe the gemmeous hall.
The ladies in their beauty,
With wonderful attraction,
Lovely as the flowering rush,
Ravish the beholders; —
In their variegated dresses,
As from out a mist,
Gauzy and light,
With their pendants of pearls and gems;
The Beauty of the night interspersed,
And the *chis* and the *lin*,
With quiet composure,
We offer the cup of welcome.

It will be seen how in this piece words in the other tones, as well as in the first, rhyme with one another just as in the She. But this measure of three words can hardly be said to have been cultivated in later times, though mention is made of a Kin Chih (郭人金埴) of the Ming dynasty, who wrote a thousand pieces in it.

Third, of the measure of four words, so abundant in the She, it is not necessary to give any specimen. It continued a favourite form down to the T'ang dynasty, after which it fell into disuse, though fugitive pieces by famous names may still be culled.

Fourth, the measure of five words for whole pieces took its rise, like that of three, in the Han dynasty under the emperor Woo. The 29th Book of the *Wăn-seuen* (文選; see Wylie's Notes on Chinese Literature, p. 192) commences with a collection of 'Fifteen pieces of ancient Poetry,' attributed to a Mei Shing (枚乘) of Woo's time. The first of them is:—

行行重行行, 與君生別離, 相去萬餘里, 各在天
一涯, 道路阻且長, 會面安可知, 胡馬依北風
越鳥巢南枝, 相去日已遠, 衣帶日已緩, 浮雲蔽
白日, 游子不顧返, 思君令人老, 歲月忽已晚,
棄捐勿復道, 努力加餐飯.

On, on; again, on, on;
Separated am I from you.
Apart more than ten thousand *li*,
We are each at one side of the sky.
The way is rugged and long; —
Shall we ever meet again?
The northern horse loves the winds of the north;
The birds of Yueh nest in the trees of the south.
Many are the days since we parted;
My girdle is becoming daily more loose.
Floating clouds darken the white day;
A wanderer, I do not care to return.
To think of you makes me old;
The years and months hurry to their end.
I will dismiss the subject and say no more,
But do my best at a full board.

119]

It will be seen that here the 2d, 4th, 6th, and 8th lines rhyme, and then the 9th, 10th, 12th, 14th, and 16th;—after the manner of the She. Chaou Yih says that the line of five words is well adapted to the nature of the language, and compares the measure to a flower which will necessarily open at the proper time. We shall find it still in great esteem, but subject to rules of which the early writers in it knew nothing.

Fifth, the measure of six words has never been a favourite, and has been pronounced ill-adapted to the genius of the language. One or more lines of this length occur occasionally in the She, and in what have been called the Elegies of Ts'oo (楚辭), but the first who composed whole pieces in the measure was a Kuh Yung (谷永) of the Ts'in dynasty, whose works are lost. A few fragments of six-words verses are met with in the Books of the Han and succeeding dynasties; but when we come to the dynasty of T'ang, we find that various writers tried to cultivate the measure for short descriptive pieces. The following is by a Wang Wei, or Wang Mo-këeh (王維, 王摩詰), on the morning :—

桃紅復含宿雨, 　柳緑更帶朝烟, 　花落家僮未埽,
鳥啼山客猶眠.

The peach blossom is redder through the rain over-night,
The willow is greener through the mists of the morning.
The fallen flowers are not yet swept away by the servant;
The birds sing, and the guest on the hill is still asleep.

Sixth, the measure of seven words is well adapted to the language, and is that which, subject to certain regulations mentioned below, is preferred above all others at the present day. Instances of its use occur in the She and the Elegies of Ts'oo, and in the pieces in the appendix to chapter I., so that the critics are in error who attribute the origination of the seven-words measure to Pih Lëang (柏梁) of the reign of Woo in the Han dynasty. The following lines were probably made in the Ts'in dynasty, though the speaker in them is supposed to be Hwang Go, the mother of the mythical Shaou Haou (皇娥倚瑟清歌:—

天淸地曠浩茫茫, 　萬象廻薄化無方, 　洽天蕩蕩望
滄滄, 　乘桴輕漾著日旁.

The clear sky and wide earth a boundless prospect give,
Where change and transformation proceed without limit.
Supporting the sky is ocean's vast expanse;—
I will get on a raft, and deftly go to the side of the sun.

Seventh, the measure of eight words is rarely met with. The following quatrain appears as improvised by a Loo K'eun (盧耋) of the T'ang dynasty at a feast :—

祥瑞不在鳳凰麒麟, 　太平須得邊將忠臣, 　但得百
僚師長肝膽, 　不用三軍羅綺金銀.

Good omens are not in the phœnix and the ℎ𝑖𝑛;
But peace comes from your frontier generals and loyal ministers.
Only get your officers and generals to use all their heart,
And you need not spend your silks and treasures on your hosts.

Eighth, longer measures still, of nine, of ten, and of eleven words, are met with very occasionally.

E.g., of nine words :—

120]

昨夜東風吹折中林楠, 渡口小艇滾入沙灘拗 野
樹古梅獨臥寒屋角, 疎影橫斜暗土書窓啟, 半枯
半活幾箇撇倍蕾, 欲開未開數點含香包, 縱使畫
工善畫也縮手 我愛清香故把新詩嘲

Last night the east wind blew and broke the branches in the forest,
And the boats at the ferry were driven inside the shallows.
But this old plum tree, uncared for, slept solitary at the corner of my cold house,
Its sparse shadows, now cross, now slant, beating in the dark at the window of my library;
Half withered, half alive, the few buds upon it,
Inclined to open, yet not opened, so many fragrant knots.
A skilful painter would hold his hand from it,
But I, liking the clear fragrance, take my laugh in these new lines.

A couplet of Le T'ae-pib, in ten words:—

黃帝鑄鼎於荊山錬丹砂, 丹砂成騎龍飛上太清家.

When Hwang-te cast the tripods on mount King, as he melted the vermilion,
The vermilion became a dragon, and flew up to the abode of great purity.

A couplet of Too Foo, in eleven words:—

王郎酒酣拔劍斫地歌莫哀 我能拔爾抑塞磊落之奇才.

Wang Lang when drunk drew out his sword and hewed the ground, singing, 'Don't be sad,
I can draw forth your talents, now repressed, and show their bright and wondrous power.'

These long measures, I may observe, are not suitable to the genius of the Chinese language. It is true that we have only so many syllables in a line; but then every syllable is a word complete, with its meaning entire. Nor is the length of the measure ordinarily eked out as in English by articles, conjunctions, prepositions or any auxiliary words. A single line of Chinese cannot sustain the weight of more characters than eight. The limit perhaps should be placed at seven.

3. We come now to the more prized forms of versification, the establishment of which is generally dated from the beginning of the T'ang dynasty. But they only received then their complete development, having been growing up from the time that the tonal system and the more exact definition of the rhyming endings had been introduced;—that is, all through the many short-lived dynasties which succeeded to that of Tsin.

The measures according to these forms are of five words (五律詩), and of seven words (七律詩); and the length of the piece ought not to exceed 16 lines. All the even lines rhyme together, and in the seven-words measure the first line also. The characters in all the lines must be in certain tones, follow-ing one another with regularity according to prescribed rules; but the rhyme word must always be in the even tone. The characters in the two middle couplets, moreover, of each eight lines ought to correspond to one another:—noun with noun, verb with verb, and particle (including prepositions, conjunctions, adverbs, and in-terjections) with particle. The system is to be learned from examples better than by description.

First, let us take the measure of five words.

[i.] When the piece begins with a character in the even tone, the toning of the lines is as follows:—

平平平仄仄, 仄仄仄平平, 仄仄平平仄, 平平仄
仄平.

E g., we have the following lines from Le T'ae-pih expressing his longing in the west for the arrival of his friend, a magistrate whose gentle rule he admired, where all the characters are toned acc. to the rule, excepting the first; and indeed a deflected tone at the beginning of the first line, and the even tone at the beginning of the second are both allowable.

漢陽江上柳　望客引東枝,　樹樹花如雪,　紛紛亂若絲　春風傳我意,　草木度前知,　寄謝絃歌宰,西來定未遲.

> The willows on the Këang, north of Han-yang,
> Eastward for him who comes their branches spread.
> On every tree the flowers look like snow;
> The numerous hanging twigs are silken thread.
> The winds of spring my longing wish declare;
> My inmost thoughts the trees seem to have read.
> To him of lute-like rule my thanks I send,
> And wish him on his westward journey sped.

[ii.] Where the piece begins with a character in one of the deflected tones, the toning of the lines is as follows :—

仄仄平平仄,　平平,仄仄平,　平平,平仄仄.　仄仄仄平平.

E.g., T'oo Foo describes the pains of military service in a time of decay :—

國破山河在,　城春草木深,　感時花濺淚,　恨別鳥驚心,　烽火連三月,　家書抵萬金,　白頭搔更短,渾欲不勝簪.

> Shattered the State, the hills and streams remain ;
> The walls by spring are clothed with grass and trees;
> Returning flowers constrain my gushing tears;
> The bird's song frightens me, mourning my separation.
> For three months together the beacons have gleamed ;
> A letter from home would be worth ten thousand coins.
> I scratch my head grown grey, till the hair is short,
> And in vain should I try to use a pin.

Secondly, let us take the measure of seven words.

[i.] Where the piece begins with a character in the even tone, the lines are toned thus :—

平平仄仄仄平平,　仄仄平平,仄仄平,　仄仄平平,平仄仄,　平平仄仄,仄平平,　平平仄仄平平仄,　仄仄平平,仄仄平,　仄仄平平,平仄仄,　平平仄仄仄平平.

E g., Ung Hwan (翁綬), one of the T'ang poets, writes:—

徘徊漢月滿邊州　照盡天涯,到隴頭　影轉銀河,寰海靜　光分玉塞古今愁　笳吹遠戍,孤烽滅　雁下平沙,萬里秋　況是鄉園,搖落夜　何堪少婦,獨登樓.

> At length the moon of China doth fill this border-land;
> Its light embracing all beneath the sky has reached Lung-t'ow.
> The shadows have crossed the milky way, and land and sea are still.
> The light penetrating the encampment, as in old times, causes and thoughts.
> The trumpet sounds to the distant wardens, and the solitary beacon is extinguished;
> The geese descend on the level sands, and all round is autumn;
> I think of the desolation in r y village garden;—
> Alas for my young wife going up solitary to the tower!

[ii.] Where the piece begins with a character in a deflected tone, the lines are toned as follow:—

仄仄平平, 仄仄平, 平平仄仄, 仄平平, 平平仄仄平,
平仄, 仄仄平平平, 仄仄平, 仄仄平平, 平仄平平, 平平仄仄,
仄仄, 平仄平平, 平平仄, 平平仄仄, 平平仄, 仄仄平平.

E.g. Fah-chin, a Buddhist priest of the T'ang dynasty, writes the following lines on a friend going from Tan-yang in the interior to a situation on the coast:—

不到終南, 向幾秋　移居更欲近滄洲　風吹雨色, 連
村暗　潮擁菱花, 出岸浮　漠漠望中, 春自艷　寥寥
泊處, 夜堪愁　如君豈得空高枕　只益天書遣遠求.

> For many years you've not been to Chung-nan;
> Changing your place, you towards Ts'ang-chow go,
> Where wind and rain the villages make dark,
> And waves cast up the *king*-flowers on the shore.
> Along the extensive prospect spring shines bright;
> At night sad thoughts 'midst the small anchorage grow.
> Not there will you be left idly to sleep;
> Much more the heavenly charge will find you out.

4. Strictly normal pieces of the above standard measures consist, it has been stated, of 8 couplets, but we often find them of a greater length, in which case they are called 排律詩 or 'Prolonged poems in regular measure.' The marquis D'Hervey-Saint-Denys says, 'Their length consists of twelve lines, subject to the same rhyme, which occurs consequently six times, and is placed always in the second verse of each distich (*L'art Poetique et La Prosodie chez les Chinois*, p. 86.)' But we find them prolonged indefinitely to various lengths. *E.g.*, Maou K'e-ling, at the beginning of the present dynasty, gives us the following piece in 24 lines of seven words, written at the foot of the Tung-kёun mountain, as he was ascending the Kёang

(泝大江泊桐君山下作):—
大江直上泝新安　爲愛桐君縶艭看　幾樹綠蘿懸
露濕　半林黃葉帶霜寒　三時水嶼迷烟市　萬疊秋
山漱錦湍　棃宿影含書閣曉　祈潮聲傍釣臺寬　帆
檣估客歌黃淡　橘柚人家韻綠團　花種上城懷杜牧
草璟故宅問方干　紫巖洞口雲猶閉　烏桕門前雨未
乾　丘壑儼然羞豹隱　江山如此笑龍蟠　望中未嘗
雙峰澗　去後應過七里灘　繡石障村真足美　仙基
布地有誰觀　滔滔木國憑雙槳　渺渺天涯寄一竿
那信戴顒還到此　雙柑斗酒暫盤桓

The famous Too Foo was fond of heaping up pentameters to the extent of 40, 80, and more lines; and in the following piece, addressed to two of his friends Ch'ing Shin and Le Che-fang, high officers at court, and relating to scenes and experiences by the poet in K'wei-chow dept., Sze-ch'uen (秋日夔府, 詠懷率寄鄭監李賓客) he has achieved no fewer than 200 lines, accumulating 100 rhymes of the ending *een*:—(卷十四).

絕塞烏蠻北　孤城白帝邊, 飄零仍百里, 消渴已三
年, 雄劍鳴開匣, 羣書滿繫船, 亂離心不展, 衰謝

123]

日　蕭然，　筋力妻孥間，　菁華歲月遷，　登臨多物色，
陶冶賴詩篇，　峽束滄江起，　巖排古樹圓，　梯雲靄時懸，
氣　潮海蹴吳天，　煮井爲鹽速，　燒畬度地偏，　有壘亦寒花，
鷺疊嶂長似帶，　錦石小如錢，　春草何曾歇，　寒花
碧羅可憐，　獵人吹成火，　野店引山泉，　喚起橈頭急，　交
行幾屐穿，　西京猶薄產，　四海絕隨肩，　幕府初緣，　楠
郎官籍，　幸備員，　瓜時猶旅寓，　萍泛若賓，　目大
餌盧狼高，　諸侯禮，　佳人上客前，　明　歌曲
烟神滿座涕，　南內淩，　開元甲影，　靈州僻，　同腸杜
屋龍威，　莫帶犬戎羶，　耿賈扶王室，　蕭曹
轉　蜂蠆，　魏力劲鹰鸇，　舊物森猶在，　拱凶
令　須行戰伐，　胡星一彗掃，　黔首遂拘攣，　奴僕何知
惡　與煩繪，　苛法令錫，　業成陳始王，　載呂望
宮　側聽千，　台階翊主光，　熊羆不世賢，　音徹一
里　牢沈宋價，　中鄭李聯，　長吟比覺筌，　我先知
省　俱善蹡，　欵惬當禮，　時律久忘，　音如此
流　味蓬題，　隔馬閣南，　置墜血，　視田令境
焉　每逈，　云玄萊壁，　來連湖日，　鶴唳嘹，　羽袍錦
心起　伏顧昔，　孤飛去，　徒梟，　遠遊臨絕涯
郡篁步　論兵戈，　龕涕，　成枕蕡，　慮華生
悵共著　聽腕峰，　幾座漠漠，　蘗曝斑，　池塘作鏡空
蕭平甘　杖予嶺，　仔藥絆蓮，　雕蟲蒙，　富貴月娟娟
西白一　種味柴襦，　心嘗折，　于敬賦，　烹鯉閒
綱廟何　如澁，　馨香，　色好梨，　兒去看魚笱公
章　　　　　三鱓，　九核，　陳圖沙
　　　　　通竹溜，　涓涓，　病即痊

困學違從紞　明公各勉旃　聲華夾宸極　早晚到
星曜戀諫留匡鼎　諸儒引服虔　不過輸鯁直　終畢
會是正陶甄　宵旴憂虞軫　黎元疾苦駢　招尋興已專　七
日晝青簡爲誰編　行路難何有　招尋興已專　門求七
由來具飛梍　暫擬控鳴弦　身許雙峰寺　門求晉
祖禪落帆追夙昔　衣褐向眞詮　安石名高拂雲涎
照王客赴燕　途中非阮籍　查上似張騫　披拂雲涎
宰在淹留景不延　風期終破浪　水怪莫飛國遠
他日辭神女　傷春怯杜鵑　淡交隨聚散　澤國盼多
廻旋本自依迦葉　何曾藉倡佯　鱸峰生轉晚聞
橘井何高賽　東走窮歸鶴　南征盡貼鳶　晚聞鏑任
妙敎　牽踐塞蘭愆　顧慚丹青列　頭陀琬琰鏑清贏任
衆香深霤霜　毿地蕭芊芊　勇猛爲心極　清贏
體屛　金篦空刮眼　鏡象未離銓

Choo E-tsun of the present dynasty, whose name has occurred more than once in the notes to these prolegomena, has strung together a single rhyme to the extent of 200 times.

4. As the normal stanza of eight lines may thus be indefinitely protracted, it is also frequently reduced to half the length, and is then called 絕句詩, or 斷句詩, which we may denominate semi-stanzas. We find this form of ode earlier than the T'ang dynasty. The following lines belong to the period A.D. 560—566 :—送馬猶臨 水, 離旗稍引風, 好看今夜月, 當照紫微宮. It will be seen that the toning is that of a piece of five words beginning with a deflected tone, excepting in the 好 of the 3d line and 當 of the 4th. The following, descriptive of a wife lamenting the absence of her husband, by Yang Keu-yuen (楊巨源) of the T'ang dynasty, is regularly constructed also in five words, beginning in the even tone :—君行登隴上, 妾夢在閨中, 玉筯千行落, 銀牀一半空. As illustrative of a semi-stanza in lines of seven words, the following quatrain lines by Wang Yae, of the T'ang dynasty, and descriptive of the ways of a lady of the harem seeking to attract the notice of the emperor, may be given :—春來新插翠雲釵. 尙着雲頭踏殿鞋, 欲得君 王回一顧, 爭扶玉輦下金堦.

5. It is evident that the tonal rules for these artistically-constructed pieces must sorely embarrass the writer, and even in Le T'ae-pih and Too Foo themselves viola- tions of them are not unfrequent; and the latter morever has many pieces of the meas- ure of seven words, composed after the old fashion, without regard to the tones at all. A line with a character not in the proper tone is described as 拗句, 'irregular.' Attempts have been made to establish permanent alterations in the arrangement of the tones. A Le Shang-yin (李商隱) and others changed the tones of the third and fifth characters; and E Shan (遺山) of the Yuen dynasty proposed to exchange the tones of the 5th and 6th characters. Pieces are sometimes made according to these models, but they are not prized.

And not in the tones of the lines only has there been relaxation. The correspond- ency between the parts of speech, so to speak, of the characters in the middle distiches has also been occasionally dispensed with. This was never rigorously exacted in the first

125]

and last distiches, but for the intermediate two to be without it is a serious blemish. Yet Le T'ae-pih occasionally neglected it in the 3d and 4th lines, as in his ode written on his 'Thoughts of antiquity when anchored at night at the foot of Něw-choo hill:'—

牛渚西江夜， 青天無片雲， 登舟望秋月， 空憶謝
將軍， 余亦能高詠， 斯人不可聞， 明朝挂帆席，
楓葉落紛紛·

Chaou Yih mentions also the occurrence of two rhymes in the same piece; but the cases which he adduces hardly present different rhyming endings;—we have only the same ending, now in the upper first, and now in the lower first tone, variously arranged.

6. Of pieces in measures of unequal length, I may mention one variety, where lines of three, five, and seven words are used together. Le T'ae-pih set the example of it in the following:—秋風清， 秋月明， 落葉聚遷散， 寒
鴉栖復驚， 相思相見知何日， 此時此夜難爲情·

    Autumn's winds keenly blow;
    Bright the autumn moon's glow;
    The leaves fall, heaps here, scattered there;
    Tree-perched cowers still the cold crow.
    I think of you;—when shall I see your loved form?
    At such a season forth regrets freely flow.

7. To go into further details on the measures of Chinese poetry would lead on to a treatise on the subject. In giving the details which I have done, I have had two purposes in view. The one has been to show the missionary that there is abundant precedent and scope for the formation of a Christian hymnology in Chinese in very varied measures. The other has been to provoke some Sinologue to undertake the extensive treatment of Chinese poetry, which deserves much more attention than it has yet met with from foreigners.

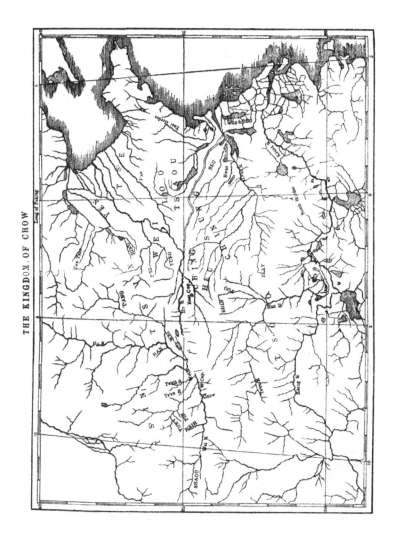

THE KINGDOM OF CHOW

CHAPTER IV.

THE CHINA OF THE BOOK OF POETRY, CONSIDERED IN RELATION
TO THE EXTENT OF ITS TERRITORY, AND ITS POLITICAL
STATE; ITS RELIGION; AND SOCIAL CONDITION.

APPENDIX:—RESEARCHES INTO THE MANNERS OF THE ANCIENT CHI
NESE, ACCORDING TO THE SHE KING. BY M. EDOUARD BIOT.

From the Journal Asiatique for November and December, 1843.

1. A glance at the map prefixed to this chapter will give the
reader an idea of the extent of the kingdom of Chow,—of China as
The territory of the king-
dom of Chow. it was during the period to which the Book of
Poetry belongs. The China of the present day,
what we call China proper, embracing the eighteen provinces, may
be described in general terms as lying between the 20th and 40th
degrees of north latitude, and the 100th and 121st degrees of east
longitude, and containing an area of about 1,300,000 square miles.
The China of the Chow dynasty lay between the 33d and 38th parallels
of latitude, and the 106th and 119th of longitude. The degrees of
longitude included in it were thus about two thirds of the present; and
of the 20 degrees of latitude the territory of Chow embraced no more
than five. It extended nearly to the limit of the present boundaries
on the north and west, because, as I pointed out in the prolegomena
to the Shoo, p. 189, it was from the north, along the course of the
Yellow river, that the first Chinese settlers had come into the country,
and it was again from the west of the Yellow river that the chiefs
of the Chow family and their followers pushed their way to the east,
and took possession of the tracts on both sides of that river, which
had been occupied, nearly to the sea, by the dynasties of Hëa and
Shang. The position of the present departmental city of Pin-chow
in which neighbourhood we find duke Lëw with his people emerging
into notice, in the beginning of the 18th century before our era, is
given as in lat. 35° 04, and long. 105° 46.

The She says nothing of the division of the country under the
Chow dynasty into the nine *Chow* or provinces, of which we read
so much in the third Part of the Shoo, in connexion with the
labours of Yu. Four times in the Books of Chow in the She that

famous personage is mentioned with honour,[1] but the sphere in which his action is referred to does not extend beyond the country in the neighbourhood of the Ho before it turns to flow to the east, where there is reason to believe that he did accomplish a most meritorious work. Twice he is mentioned in the sacrificial odes of Shang, and there the predicates of him are on a larger scale, but without distinct specification; but T'ang, the founder of the dynasty, is represented as receiving from God the 'nine regions,'[2] and appointed to be a model to the 'nine circles'[3] of the land. These nine regions and nine circles were probably the nine *Chow* of the Shoo; and though no similar language is found in the She respecting the first kings of Chow, their dominion, according to the Official book of the dynasty,[4] was divided into nine provinces, seven of which bear the same names as those in the Shoo. We have no Seu-chow, which extended along the sea on the east from Ts'ing-chow to the Këang river, and Chinese scholars tell us, contrary to the evidence of the She and of the Tso-chuen, that it was absorbed in the Ts'ing province of Chow. In the same way they say that Yu's Lëang-chow on the west, extending to his Yung-chow, was absorbed in Chow's Yung. The number of nine provinces was kept up by dividing Yu's K'e-chow in the north into three;—K e to the east, Ping in the west, and Yëw in the north and centre. The disappearance of Seu and Lëang sufficiently shows that the kings of Chow had no real sway over the country embraced in them; and though the names of Yang and King, extending south from the Këang, were retained, it was merely a retention of the names, as indeed the dominion of China south of the Këang in earlier times had never been anything but nominal. The last ode of the She, which is also the last of the Sacrificial odes of the Shang dynasty, makes mention of the subjugation of the tribes of King, or King-ts'oo, by king Woo-ting (B.C. 1,323—1,263); but, as I have shown on that ode, its genuineness is open to suspicion. The 9th ode of Book III., Part III., relates, in a manner full of military ardour, an expedition conducted by king Seuen in person to reduce the States of the south to order; but it was all confined to the region of Seu, and in that to operations against the barbarous hordes north of the Hwae.

1 See II. vi. VI. 1; III. i. X. 5; iii. VII. 1; IV. ii. IV. 1.   2 IV. iii. IV. 1; V. 3.   3
IV. iii. III. l. 7 and IV. 3.   4 Ch. XXXIII. The names of Yu's provinces were—冀. 兗. 青.
徐. 揚. 荊. 豫. 梁. and 雍: those of Chow—并. 幽. 冀. 兗. 青. 揚. 荊. 豫. 雍.

The 8th ode of the same Book gives an account of an expedition, sent by the same king Seuen under an earl of Shaou, to start from the point where the Këang and Han unite, to act against the tribes south of the Hwae, between it and the Këang, and to open up the country and establish States in it after the model of the king's own State. All this was done 'as far as the southern Sea,' which did not extend therefore beyond the mouth of the Këang. Ode 5th, still of the same Book, describes the appointment of an uncle of king Seuen to be marquis of Shin, and the measures taken to establish him there, with his chief town in what is now the department of Nan-yang, Ho-nan, as a bulwark against the encroachments of the wild tribes of the south. Now Seuen was a sovereign of extraordinary vigour and merit, and is celebrated as having restored the kingdom to its widest limits under Woo and Ch'ing; and after his death the process of decay went on more rapidly and disastrously even than it had done during several reigns that preceded his. During the period of the Ch'un Ts'ëw, the princes of Ts'oo, Woo, and Yueh, to whom belonged Yu's provinces of Yang, King, and Lëang, all claimed the title of king, and aimed at the sovereignty of the States of the north,—to wrest the sceptre from the kings of Chow. The China of Chow did not extend beyond the limits which I have assigned it, and which are indicated by the imperfect oval marked red on the map, hardly reaching half way from the Yellow river to what is now called the Yang-tsze Këang. The country held by the kings themselves, often styled the royal State, lay along the Wei and the Ho for about five degrees of longitude, but it was not of so great extent from north to south. It was, moreover, being continually encroached upon by the growing States of Ts'oo on the south, Ts'in on the west, and Tsin on the north, till it was finally extinguished by Ts'in, which subdued also all the feudal States, changed the feudal kingdom into a despotic empire, and extended its boundaries to the south far beyond those of any former period.

2. In the prolegomena to the Shoo, p. 79, I have mentioned the extravagant statements of Chinese writers, that at a great *durbar* held by Yu the feudal princes amounted to 10,000; that, when the Shang dynasty superseded the house of Yu, the princes were reduced to about 3,000; and that, when Shang was superseded in its turn by Chow, they were only 1,773. The absurdity of the lowest of these numbers cannot be exposed better than by the fact that the districts

into which the empire of the present day, in all its eighteen provinces, is divided are not quite 1,300. But in the Book of Poetry, as has been pointed out already, we have odes of only about a dozen States; and all the States or territorial divisions, mentioned in the Ch'un Ts'ew and Tso-chuen, including the outlying regions of Ts'oo, Woo, and Yueh, with appanages in the royal domain, attached territories in the larger States, and the barbarous tribes on the east, west, north, and south. are only 198   In the 'Annalistic Tables of the successive dynasties,' published in 1,803, the occurrences in the kingdom of Chow, from its commencement in B.C. 1,121 down to 403, are arranged under thirteen States, and from 402 down to its extinction in B.C. 225, under seven States.

The principal States which come before us in the She are Ts'in, lying west from the royal domain, a considera-
States mentioned in the She.
ble part of which was granted to it in B.C. 759; Tsin having the Ho on the west, and lying to the north of the royal domain; then to the east, Wei, on the north of the Ho, and Ch'ing on the south of it, with Heu and Ch in extending south from Ch'ing. East from Ch'ing, and south of the Ho, was Sung, a dukedom held by descendants of the royal family of the Shang dynasty. North from Sung was the marquisate of Ts'aou; and north from it again was Loo, held by the descendants of Tan, the famous duke of Chow, to whose political wisdom, as much as to the warlike enterprize of his brother king Woo, was due the establishment of the dynasty. Conterminous with the northern border of Loo, and extending to the waters of what is now called the gulf of Pih-chih-le, was the powerful State of Ts'e. Yen, mentioned in III. iii. VII. 6, lay north and east from Ts'e. The subject of that ode is a marquis of Han, who appears to have played a more noticeable part in the time of king Seuen, than any of his family who went before or came after him did. His principality was on the west of the Ho, covering the present department of T'ung-chow, Shen-se, and perhaps some adjacent territory. The ode commences with a reference to the labours of Yu which made the country capable of cultivation, but much of it must still have been marsh and forest in the time of king Seuen, for mention is made of its large streams and meres, and of the multitudes of its deer, wild-cats, bears, and tigers.

The princes of these States, distinguished among themselves by the titles of Kung, How, Pih, Tsze, and Nan, which may most conveniently be expressed by duke, marquis, earl, count or viscount, and baron, were mostly Kes,[1] offshoots from the royal stem of Chow. So it was with those of Loo, Ts'aou, Wei, Ch'ing, Tsin, Yen, and Han. Sung, it has been stated, was held by descendants of the kings of Shang, who were therefore Tszes.[2] The first marquis of Ts'e, was Shang-foo, a chief counsellor and military leader under kings Wăn and Woo. He was a Këang,[3] and would trace his lineage up to the chief minister of Yaou, as did also the barons of Heu. The marquises of Ch'in were Kweis,[4] claiming to be descended from the ancient Shun. The earls of Ts'in were Yings,[5] and boasted for their ancestor Pih-yih, who appears in the Shoo, II. i. 22, as forester to Shun. The sacrifices to Yu, and his descendants, the sovereigns of the Hëa dynasty, were maintained by the lords of Ke, who were consequently Szes,[6] but that State is not mentioned in the She.

All these princes held their lands by royal grant at the commencement of the dynasty, or subsequently. I have touched slightly on the duties which they owed to the king of Chow as their suzerain in the prolegomena to the Shoo, pp. 197,198; and I do not enter further on them here. A more appropriate place for exhibiting them, and the relations which the States maintained with one another, will be in the prolegomena to my next volume, containing the Ch'un Ts'ëw and the Tso-chuen.

3 The Book of Poetry abundantly confirms the conclusion drawn from the Shoo-king that the ancient Chinese had some considerable knowledge of God. The names given to Him are Te,[1] which we commonly translate *emperor* or *ruler*, and Shang Te,[1] the *Supreme Ruler*. My own opinion, as I have expressed and endeavoured to vindicate it in various publications on the term to be employed in translating in Chinese the Hebrew *Elohim* and Greek *Theos*, is that Te corresponds exactly to them, and should be rendered in English by *God*. He is also called in the She 'the great and sovereign God,'[2] and 'the bright and glorious God;'[3] but, as in the Shoo, the personal appellation is interchanged with T'ëen,[4] *Heaven*; Shang T'ëen,[4] *Supreme Heaven*; Haou T'ëen,[4] *Great Heaven*; Hwang T'ëen,[4] *Great* or *August Heaven*; and Min T'ëen,[4] *Compassionate Heaven*. The two styles are sometimes com-

Religious views.

1 姬   2 子.   3 姜   4 媯   5 嬴   6 姒.
1 帝 and 上帝.   2 IV. ii. IV. 3.   3 IV. i. [ii.] l.   4 天; 上 天; 昊 天; 皇 天; 昊 天:—see 天 in Index III.

bined, as in III. iii. IV., where we have the forms of *Shang Te, Haou T'ëen,* and *Haou T'ëen Shang Te,* which last seems to me to mean—*God dwelling in the great heaven.*

God appears especially as the ruler of men and this lower world.[5] He appointed grain for the nourishment of all.[6] He watches especially over the conduct of kings, whose most honourable designation is that of 'Son of Heaven.'[7] While they reverence Him, and administer their high duties in His fear, and with reference to His will, taking His ways as their pattern, He maintains them, smells the sweet savour of their offerings, and blesses them and their people with abundance and general prosperity.[8] When they become impious and negligent of their duties, He punishes them, takes from them the throne, and appoints others in their place.[9] His appointments come from His fore-knowledge and fore-ordination.[9]

Sometimes He appears to array Himself in terrors, and the course of His providence is altered.[10] The evil in the State is ascribed to Him.[10] Heaven is called unpitying.[10] But this is His strange work; in judgment; and to call men to repentance.[11] He hates no one; and it is not He who really causes the evil time:—that is a consequence of forsaking the old and right ways of government.[12] In giving birth to the multitudes of the people, He gives to them a good nature, but few are able to keep it, and hold out good to the end.[13] In one ode, II. vii. X., a fickle and oppressive king is called *Shang Te* in better irony.

While the ancient Chinese thus believed in God, and thus conceived of Him, they believed in other Spirits under Him, some presiding over hills and rivers, and others dwelling in the heavenly bodies. In fact there was no object to which a tutelary Spirit might not at times be ascribed, and no place where the approaches of spiritual Beings might not be expected, and ought not to be provided for by the careful keeping of the heart and ordering of the conduct.[14] In the legend of How-tseih (III. ii. I.), we have a strange story of his mother's pregnancy being caused by her treading on a toe-print made by God. In III. iii. V. a Spirit is said to have been sent down from the great mountains, and to have given birth to the princes of Foo and Shin. In IV. i. [i.] VIII. king Woo is celebrated as having attracted and given repose to all spiritual Beings,

5 *E.g.*, III. i. VII. 1; iii. I. 1.　　6 IV. i. [i.] X.　　7 *E.g.*, II. i. VIII. 1, 3; IV. i. [i.] VIII.　　8 *E.g.*, II. i. VI. III. i. I.; VII. 7: IV. ii. IV.　　9 III. i. VII. 1, 3.　　10 III. ii. X.; iii. I. 1: II. iv. VII.; and often.　　11 III. ii. X. 8; and often.　　12 II. iv. VIII. 4: III. iii. I. 5; iii. X. 5.　　13 III. iii. I. 1.　　14 III. iii. II. 7.

even to the Spirits of the Ho and the highest mountains. In II. v.
IX., the writer, when deploring the sufferings caused to the States
of the east by misgovernment and oppression, suddenly raises a
complaint of the host of heaven;—the Milky way, the Weaving sisters (three stars in Lyra), the Draught oxen (some stars in Aquila),
Lucifer, Hesperus, the Hyades, the Sieve (part of Sagittarius), and
the Ladle (also in Sagittarius):—all idly occupying their places, and
giving no help to the afflicted country. In no other ode do we
have a similar exhibition of Sabian views. Mention is made in III.
iii. IV. 5 of the demon of drought; and we find sacrifices offered to
the Spirits of the ground and of the four quarters of the sky,[15] to
the Father of husbandry,[16] the Father of war,[17] and the Spirit of
the path.[18]

These last three, however, were probably the Spirits of departed
men. A belief in the continued existence of the dead in a spirit-
state, and in the duty of their descendants to maintain by religious
worship a connexion with them, have been characteristics of the
Chinese people from their first appearance in history. The first
and third Books of the last Part of the She profess to consist of
sacrificial odes used in the temple services of the kings of Chow and
Shang. Some of them are songs of praise and thanksgiving; some
are songs of supplication; and others relate to the circumstances of
the service, describing the occasion of it, or the parties present and
engaging in it. The ancestors worshipped are invited to come and
accept the homage and offerings presented; and in one (IV. i. [i.] VII.)
it is said that 'king Wăn, the Blesser,' has descended, and accepted
the offerings.

The first stanza of III. i. I. describes king Wăn after his death as
being 'on high, bright in heaven, ascending and descending on
the left and the right of God,' and the 9th ode of the same Book
affirms that Wăn, his father, and grand-father, were associated in
heaven. The early Chinese, as I have just said, did not suppose
that man ceased all to be, when his mortal life terminated. We
know, indeed, from the Tso-chuen, that scepticism on this point
had begun to spread among the higher classes before the time of
Confucius; and we know that the sage himself would neither affirm
nor deny it; but that their dead lived on in another State was certainly the belief of the early ages with which we have now to do,

15 II. vi. VII. 2; et al.   16 II. vi. VIII. 2; et al.   17 III. l. VII. 8.   18 III. ii. I.
7. et al.

as it is still the belief of the great majority of the Chinese people. But the She is as silent as the Shoo-king as to any punitive retribution hereafter. There are rewards and dignity for the good after death, but nothing is said of any punishment for the bad. In one ode, indeed (II. v. VIII. 6), a vague feeling betrays itself in the writer, that after every other method to deal with proud slanderers had failed, Heaven might execute justice upon them;—but it may be that he had only their temporal punishment in view. The system of ancestral worship prevented the development of a different view on this subject. The tyrant-oppressor took his place in the temple, there to be feasted, and worshipped, and prayed to, in his proper order, as much as the greatest benefactor of his people. I have pointed out, on III. iii. IV. 5, how king Seuen, in his distress in consequence of the long-continued drought, prays to his parents, though his father king Le had been notoriously wicked and worthless; and how endeavours have been made to explain away the simple text, from a wish, probably, to escape the honour which it would seem to give to one so undeserving of it.

4. The odes do not speak of the worship which was paid to God, unless it be incidentally. There were two grand occasions on which Religious ceremonies. it was rendered by the sovereign,—the summer and winter solstices. The winter sacrifice is often described as offered to Heaven, and the summer one to earth; but we have the testimony of Confucius, in the Doctrine of the Mean, ch. XIX., that the object of them both was to serve *Shang Te*. Of the ceremonies used on those occasions I do not here speak, as there is nothing said about them in the She. Whether besides these two there were other sacrifices to God, at stated periods in the course of the year, is a point on which the opinions of the Chinese scholars themselves are very much divided. I think that there were, and that we have some intimation of two of them. IV. i. [i.] X. is addressed to How-tseih, as having proved himself the correlate to Heaven, in teaching men to cultivate the grain which God appointed for the nourishment of all. This was appropriate to a sacrifice in spring, which was offered to God to seek His blessing on the agricultural labours of the year, How-tseih, as the ancestor of the House of Chow, and the great improver of agriculture, being associated with Him in it. IV. i. [i.] VII., again, was appropriate to a sacrifice to God in autumn, in the Hall of Light, at a great audience to the feudal princes, when king Wăn

was associated with Him, as being the founder of the dynasty of Chow.

Of the ceremonies at the sacrifices in the royal temple of ancestors, in the first months of the four seasons of the year, we have much information in several odes. They were preceded by fasting and various purifications on the part of the king and the parties who were to assist in the performance of them.[1] There was a great concourse of the feudal princes,[2] and much importance was attached to the presence among them of the representatives of the former dynasties;[3] but the duties of the occasion devolved mainly on the princes of the same surname as the royal House. Libations of fragrant spirits were made, to attract the Spirits, and their presence was invoked by a functionary who took his place inside the principal gate.[4] The principal victim, a red bull, was killed by the king himself, using for the purpose a knife to the handle of which were attached small bells.[5] With this he laid bare the hair, to show that the animal was of the required colour, inflicted the wound of death, and cut away the fat, which was burned along with southernwood, to increase the incense and fragrance.[5] Other victims were numerous, and II. vi. V. describes all engaged in the service as greatly exhausted with what they had to do, flaying the carcases, boiling the flesh, roasting it, broiling it, arranging it on trays and stands, and setting it forth.[6] Ladies from the harem are present, presiding and assisting; music peals; the cup goes round [6] The description is as much that of a feast as of a sacrifice; and in fact, those great seasonal occasions were what we might call grand family reunions, where the dead and the living met, eating and drinking together, where the living worshipped the dead, and the dead blessed the living.

This characteristic of these ceremonies appeared most strikingly in the custom which required that the departed ancestors should be represented by living individuals of the same surname, chosen according to certain rules which the odes do not mention. They took for the time the place of the dead, received the honours which were due to'them, and were supposed to be possessed by their Spirits. They ate and drank as those whom they personated would have done; accepted for them the homage rendered by their descendants; communicated their will to the principal in the sacrifice or feast,

1 III. ii. L 7.   2 IV. i. [L] I., IV.; et al.   3 III. i. L 4, 5; IV. i. [ii.] III.   4 II. vi.
V. 2.   5 II. ii. VI. 5.   6 II. vi. V.

and pronounced on him and his line their benediction, being assisted in this point by a mediating priest, as we must call him for want of a better term.   On the next day, after a summary repetition of the ceremonies of the sacrifice, these personators of the dead were specially feasted, and so, as it is expressed in III. ii. IV., 'their happiness and dignity were made complete.'   We have an allusion to this strange custom in Mencius (VI. Pt. i. V.), showing how a junior member of a family, when chosen to represent at the sacrifice one of his ancestors, was for the time exalted above his elders, and received the demonstrations of reverence due to the ancestor.   This custom probably originated under the Chow dynasty,—one of the regulations made by the duke of Chow; and subsequently to it, it fell into disuse.

When the sacrifice to ancestors was finished, the king feasted his uncles and younger brothers or cousins, that is, all the princes and nobles of the same surname with himself, in another apartment. The musicians who had discoursed with instrument and voice during the worship and entertainment of the ancestors, followed the convivial party, 'to give their soothing aid at the second blessing.'[7] The viands, which had been provided, we have seen, in great abundance, and on which little impression could thus far have been made, were brought in from the temple, and set forth anew.   The guests ate to the full and drank to the full; and at the conclusion they all bowed their heads, while one of them declared the satisfaction of the Spirits with the services rendered to them, and assured the king of their favour to him and his posterity, so long as they did not neglect those observances.[7]   During the feast the king showed particular respect to those among his relatives who were aged, filled their cups again and again, and desired that 'their old age might be blessed, and their bright happiness ever increased.'[8]

The above sketch of the seasonal sacrifices to ancestors shows that they were mainly designed to maintain the unity of the family connexion, and intimately related to the duty of filial piety.   Yet by means of them the ancestors of the kings were raised to the position of the Tutelary Spirits of the dynasty; and the ancestors of each family became its Tutelary Spirits.   Several of the pieces in Part IV., it is to be observed, are appropriate to sacrifices offered to some one monarch.   They would be celebrated on particular

7 II. vi V. 6.   8 III. vi. V. 6.

occasions connected with his achievements in the past, or when it was supposed that his help would be specially valuable in contemplated enterprises.

There were also other services performed in the temple of ancestors which were of less frequent occurrence, and all known by the name of *te*.[9]   That term was applied in a restricted sense to the annual sacrifice of the summer season; but there were also 'the fortunate *te*,'[10] when the Spirit-tablet of a deceased monarch was solemnly set up in its proper place in the temple, 25 months after his death; and 'the great *te*,'[11] called also *hëah*,[11] celebrated once in 5 years, when all the ancestors of the royal House were sacrificed to, beginning with the mythical emperor Kuh,[12] to whom their lineage was traced.   There is no description in the She of the ceremonies used on those occasions.

With regard to all the ceremonies of the ancestral temple, Confucius gives the following account of them and the purposes they were intended to serve in the Doctrine of the Mean, ch. XIX. 4:—'By means of them they distinguished the royal kindred according to their order of descent.   By arranging those present according to their rank, they distinguished the more noble and the less.   By the apportioning of duties at them, they made a distinction of talents and worth.   In the ceremony of general pledging, the inferiors presented the cup to their superiors, and thus something was given to the lowest to do   At the [concluding] feast, places were given according to the hair, and thus was marked the distinction of years.'

5.   The habits and manners of the ancient Chinese generally, as they may be learned from the She, will be found set forth in a variety of particulars in the appended essay by M. Edouard Biot, whose
Manners and customs of the Chinese generally. early death was a great calamity to the cause of Chinese study.   It was not possible for him in his circumstances, and depending so much as he did on Lacharme's translation of the odes, to avoid falling into some mistakes.   I have corrected the most serious of these in brief foot-notes, and also several errors—probably misprints—in his references to the odes on which his statements were based.   The pioneers in a field and literature so extensive as the Chinese could not but fall into many devious tracts. It is only by degrees that Sinologues are attaining to the proper accuracy in their representations of the subjects which they take in

9 禘.   10 吉禘.   11 大禘; 祫.   12 帝嚳

137]

hand. On two or three points I subjoin some additional observations.

   i. That filial piety or duty is the first of all virtues is a well-
known principle of Chinese moralists; and at the foundation of a well-
ordered social State they place the right regulation of the relation
between husband and wife. Pages might be filled with admirable
sentiments from them on this subject; but nowhere does a fundamental
vice of the family and social constitution of the nation appear more
The low status of woman,
and polygamy. strikingly than in the She. In the earliest
pieces of it, as well as in the latest, we have
abundant evidence of the low status which was theoretically accord-
ed to woman, and of the practice of polygamy. Biot has referred
to the evidence furnished by the last two stanzas of II. iv. VI. of
the different way in which the birth of sons and that of daughters
was received in a family. The family there, indeed, is the royal
family, but the king to whom the ode is believed to refer was one of
excellent character; and the theory of China is that the lower classes
are always conformed to the example of those above them. The
sentiments expressed in that ode are those of every class of the Chinese, ancient and modern. While the young princes would be
splendidly dressed and put to sleep on couches, the ground to sleep
on and coarse wrappers suffice for the princesses. The former would
have sceptres to play with; the latter only tiles. The former would
be—one of them the future king, the others the princes of the land;
the latter would go beyond their province if they did wrong or if they
did right, all their work being confined to the kitchen and the temple,
and to causing no sorrow to their parents. The line which says that
it was for daughters neither to do wrong nor to do good was translated by Dr. Morrison as if it said that 'woman was incapable of
good or evil;' but he subjoins from a commentary the correct meaning,—that 'a slavish submission is woman's duty and her highest
praise.' She ought not to originate anything, but to be satisfied
with doing in all loyal subjection what is prescribed to her to do.
In II. i. I. a bride is compared to a dove, but the point of comparison
lies in the stupidity of the bird, whose nest consists of a few sticks
brought inartistically together. It is no undesirable thing for a
wife to be stupid, whereas a wise woman is more likely to be
a curse in a family than a blessing. As it is expressed in III. iii.
X. 3,

> 'A wise man builds up the wall [of a city],
> But a wise woman overthrows it.
> Admirable may be the wise woman,
> But she is no better than an owl.
> A woman with a long tongue
> Is [like] a stepping-stone to disorder.
> Disorder does not come down from heaven;—
> It is produced by the woman.
> Those from whom come no lessons, no instruction,
> Are women and eunuchs.'

The marquis D' Hervey-Saint-Denys, in the introduction to his Poetry of the T'ang dynasty, p. 19, gives a different account of the status of the woman anciently in China. He says:—

'The wife of the ancient poems is the companion of a spouse who takes her counsels, and never speaks to her as a master. She chooses freely the man with whose life she will associate her own. Nothing shows us as yet polygamy in the Songs of the *Kwoh Fung*, composed between the 12th and the 8th century before our era.[1] If tradition will have it that Shun gave his two daughters to Yu in choosing him to succeed to the throne;[2] if the Chow Le mentions a grand number of imperial concubines independently of the empress proper:—we may believe that these were only royal exceptions, not in accordance with the popular manners.'

That there was often a true affection between husband and wife in China, in the times of the She-king, as there is at the present day, is a fact to be acknowledged and rejoiced in. Notwithstanding the low estimation in which woman's intellect and character were held, the mind of the wife often was and is stronger than her husband's, and her virtue greater. Many wives in Chinese history have entered into the ambition of their husbands, and spurred them on in the path of noble enterprise; many more have sympathized with them in their trials and poverty, and helped them to keep their little means together and to make them more. I. ii. III.; v. VIII.; vi. II., III., and V.; vii. VIII. and XVI.; viii. I.; x. V. and XI., are among the odes of the She which give pleasant pictures of wifely affection and permanent attachment. I believe also that in those early days there was more freedom of movement allowed to young women than there is now, as there was more possibility of their availing themselves of it so many centuries before the practice of cramping their feet and crippling them had been introduced. But on the other hand there are odes where the wife, displaced from her proper place as the mistress of the family, deplores her hard lot. There is no evidence to show that honourable marriages ever took place without the intervention of the go-between, and merely by the preference and choice of the principal parties concerned; and there can be no doubt that polygamy prevailed from the earliest times, just as it prevails now, limited only by the means of the

1 Between the 12th century and the 6th.   2 The marquis must mean the case of Yaou marrying his two daughters to Shun;—see the first Book of the Shoo.

family.   So far from there being no intimations of it in the odes of
Part I., there are many.   In ode IV. of Book I., the other ladies of
king Wăn's harem sing the praises of T'ae-sze, his queen, the para-
gon and model to all ages of female excellence, because of her freedom from jealousy.   The subject of ode V. is similar.   In ode X.,
Book II., we see the ladies of some prince's harem repairing to his
apartment, happy in their lot, and acquiescing in the difference
between it and that of their mistress.   Every feudal prince received
his bride and eight other ladies at once,—a younger sister of the
bride and a cousin, and three ladies from each of two great Houses
of the same surname.   The thing is seen in detail in the narratives
of the Tso-chuen.   Let the reader refer to the 5th passage which I
have given—on pp. 88. 89—from Han Ying's Illustrations of the She.
The lady Fan Ke there, a favourite heroine of the Chinese, tells the
king of Ts'oo how she had sought to minister to his pleasure, and
had sent round among the neighbouring States to find ladies whom
she might introduce to him, and who from their beauty and docility
would satisfy all his desires.   Nothing could show more the degrad-
ing influence of polygamy than this vaunted freedom from jealousy
on the part of the proper wife, and subordinately in her inferiors.

The consequences of this social State were such as might be expected.   Many of the odes have reference to the deeds of atrocious
licentiousness and horrible bloodshed to which it gave rise.   We wonder
that, with such an element of depravation and disorder working
among the people, the moral condition of the country, bad as it was,
was not worse.   That China now, with this thing in it, can be heartily
received into the comity of western nations is a vain imagination.

ii.   The preserving salt of the kingdom was, I believe, the filial
piety, with the strong family affections of the Chinese race, and
their respect for the aged;—virtues certainly of eminent worth.
All these are illustrated in many odes of the She; and yet there is
a danger of misjudging from them
the actual condition of the country.
In this point the marquis D' Hervey

The filial piety and other virtues of the
Chinese, not conducing to the peace of the
country so much as we might expect.

Saint-Denys has again fallen into error.   Starting from the 14th ode
of Book IX., Part I., he institutes an eloquent contrast between ancient Greece and ancient China (Introduction, p. 15):—

'The Iliad,' says he, 'is the most ancient poem of the west, the only one which can be of use to
us by way of comparison in judging of the two civilizations which developed parallelly under
conditions so different at the two extremities of the inhabited earth.   On one side are a warlike
life ; sieges without end; combatants who challenge one another; the sentiment of military glory

which animates in the same degree the poet and his heroes:—we feel ourselves in the midst of a camp.   On the other side are regrets for the domestic hearth; the home-sickness of a young soldier who ascends a mountain to try and discern at a distance the house of his father; a mother whom Sparta would have rejected from her walls; a brother who counsels the absent one not to make his race illustrious, but above all things to return home:—we feel ourselves in another world, in I know not what atmosphere of quietude and of country life. The reason is simple. Three or four times conquered by the time of Homer, Greece became warlike as her invaders. Uncontested mistress of the most magnificent valleys of the globe, China behoved to remain pacific as her first colonists had been.'

But there are not a few odes which breathe a warlike spirit of great ardour, such as II. iii. III. and IV.: III. i. VII.; iii. VIII. and IX.: IV. ii. III.; iii. IV. and V.   There is certainly in others an expression of dissatisfaction with the toils and dangers of war,—complaints especially of the separation entailed by it on the soldiers from their families. What the speakers in II. iv. I. deplore most of all is that their mothers were left alone at home to do all the cooking for themselves. It may be allowed that the natural tendency of the She as a whole is not to excite a military spirit, but to dispose to habits of peace; yet as a matter of fact there has not been less of war in China than in other lands. During the greater part of the Chow dynasty a condition of intestine strife among the feudal States was chronic. The State of Ts'in fought its way to empire through seas of blood. Probably there is no country in the world which has drunk in so much blood from its battles, sieges, and massacres as this.

iii. The 6th ode of Book XI., Part I. relates to a deplorable event, the burying of three men, brothers, esteemed throughout the State of Ts'in for their admirable character, in the grave of duke Muh, and along with his coffin. Altogether, according to the Tso-chuen, 177 individuals were immolated on that occasion. Following the authority of Sze-ma Ts'ëen, who says that the cruel practice began with duke Ch'ing, Muh's elder brother and predecessor, at whose death 66 persons were buried alive, M. Biot observes that this bloody sacrifice had been recently taken from the Tartars. Yen Ts'an, of the Sung dynasty, of whose commentary on the She I have made much use, says that the State of Ts'in, though at that time in possession of the old territory of the House of Chow, had brought with it the manners of the barbarous tribes among whom its people had long dwelt. But in my mind there is no doubt that the people of Ts'in was made up mainly of those barbarous tribes. This will appear plainly when the Ch'un Ts'ëw and Tso-chuen give

Immolating men at the tombs of the princes, or burying them alive in them.

141]

occasion for us to review the rise and progress of the three great States of Ts'in, Tsin, and Ts'oo. The practice was probably of old existence among the Chinese tribe as well as other neighbouring tribes. A story of Tsze-k'in, one of Confucius' disciples, mentioned in a note on p. 6 of the Analects, would indicate that it had not fallen into entire disuse, even in the time of the sage, in the most polished States of the kingdom. Among the Tartars so called it continues to the present day. Dr. Williams states, on the authority of De Guignes, that the emperor Shun-che, the first of the present Manchëw dynasty, ordered thirty persons to be immolated at the funeral of his consort, but K'ang-he, his son, forbade four persons from sacrificing themselves at the death of his consort.[1]

1 The Middle Kingdom, Vol. I., p. 267.

APPENDIX.

RESEARCHES INTO THE MANNERS OF THE ANCIENT CHINESE, ACCORDING TO THE SHE-KING.

By M. Edouard Biot. Translated from the JOURNAL ASIATIQUE for Novembre and Decembre, 1843.

The She-king is one of the most remarkable Works, as a picture of manners, which eastern Asia has transmitted to us; and at the same time it is the one whose authenticity is perhaps the least contested. We know that this sacred Book of verse is a collection in which Confucius gathered together,[1] without much order, odes or songs, all anterior to the 6th century before our era, and which were sung in China at ceremonies and festivals, and also in the intercourses of private life, as the compositions of the earliest poets of our Europe were sung in ancient Greece. The style of these odes is simple; their subjects are various; and they are in reality the national songs of the first age of China

1 It had not occurred to Biot to question the ordinary accounts of the compilation of the odes by Confucius. While these have been exploded in Ch. I. of these proleg., the antiquity and authenticity of the odes remain, as much entitled to our acknowledgment as before.

The She-king suffered the fate of the other ancient books at the general burning of them, attributed to the first emperor of the Ts'in dynasty, in the third century before our era; but it was natural that the pieces composing it, made in rhyme and having been sung, should have been preserved in the memory of the literati and of the people much more easily than the different parts of the other sacred Works; and hence, on the revival of letters, under the Han dynasty, in the second century before our era, the She-king reappeared almost complete, while the Le Ke and other Works underwent serious alterations. The discovery, a little time before, of Chinese ink and paper, allowed the multiplication of copies; and the text was commented on by several learned scholars. Their commentaries have come down to us; and in the absence of ancient manuscripts the preservation of which is impossible from the bad quality of Chinese paper, these, written at a time not far removed from the first publication of the She-king, afford to us sufficient guarantees that the primitive text has not been altered by the copyist, from antiquity down to our days.

It is evident that this collection of pieces, all perfectly authentic, and of a form generally simple and naive, represents the manners of the ancient Chinese in the purest way, and offers to him who wishes to make a study of those manners a mine more easy to work than the historical books, such as the *Shoo-king*, the *Tso-chuen*, and the *Kwoh-yu*, where the facts relative to the manners and the social constitution of the ancient Chinese are as it were drowned in the midst of long moral discourses. There exist, as we know, two special collections of ancient usages:—the *Le Ke*, or collection of rites properly so called, which has been classed among the sacred Books; and the *Chow Le*, or rites of Chow. A faithful translation of these two Works would throw a great light on the ancient usages of the Chinese; but their extent and the extreme conciseness of the text make such translation very difficult. We can establish in a sure manner the sense of each phrase only by reading and discussing the numerous commentaries found in the imperial editions. M. Stan. Julien has given us hopes of a translation of the *Le Ke*; but the vast labour demands from him a long preparation, and will require perhaps years before it is completely accomplished. While waiting for the publication of this translation so desirable, for that of the *Chow Le* which I have undertaken, and for those of the *Tso-chuen*, and the *Kwoh-yu*, which will perhaps be attempted one day by some patient Sinologues :— while waiting for these things, I have concentrated in this memoir my investigations on the She-king, the reading of which is, to say the least, greatly facilitated by the Latin translation of Lacharme. That translation, made in China by this missionary, has been published by the zeal of M. Mohl; and if we can discover in it some inaccuracies, in consequence of the author's having used in great measure the Manchew version of the original, we owe, as a compensation, to the learned missionary, a series of notes extracted from the commentaries, very useful in throwing light upon the historical allusions, as well as the probable identification of the animals and vegetables mentioned in the text with those with which we are acquainted.

I have explored the She-king as a traveller in the 6th century before our era might have been able to explore China; and to give order to my notes, I have classed the analogous facts which I have succeeded in gathering under different titles which divide my labour into so many small separate chapters. I have indicated the odes from which my quotations are taken, and have thus composed a sort of catalogue of subjects in the *She-king*. This arrangement will allow the reader to glance easily

143]

at the passages which I have brought together, and the results deduced from them; he will be able to verify them, if he desires it, in the text which I have carefully consulted, or at least in the translation of Lacharme. He will be able in the same way to verify, in the text, or in the published translations of them, the occasional quotations which I have made from the *Shoo-king*, the *Yih-king* (that ancient Work on divination, at least as old as the She-king), and finally from the curious work of Mencius. He will thus be placed in the early age of China, and contemplate at his ease the spectacle of the primitive manners of that society, so different from those which were then found in Europe and in western Asia, in that part of the globe designated on our charts by the name of '*The World known to the ancients.*'

PHYSICAL CONSTITUTION OF THE CHINESE.

The epithalamium of the princess of Ts'e (I. v. III.) gives us a portrait. of a Chinese beauty of that period. It is there said :—

> Her fingers were like the blades of the young white grass;
> Her skin was like congealed ointment;
> Her neck was like the tree-grub;
> Her teeth were like melon-seeds;
> Her [fore-] head cicada-like; her eyebrows like [the antennæ of] the silkworm moth.[1]

The form of the head (or forehead), compared to that of a cicada or grasshopper, indicates evidently the rounded temples, which are a characteristic of the portraits that we have of the Chinese of the present day. The slender and long eyebrows were a sign of long life, as we see in II. ii. VII. 4.[2]

In I. iv. III. 2 the beauty of a princess of Wei[3] is mentioned in similar terms. The piece celebrates the whiteness of her temples, and the splendour of her black hair, in masses like clouds. The black colour of the hair is, as we know, habitual among the Chinese of our day. Three odes call the Chinese '*the black-haired nation* (II. i. VI. 5: III. iii. III. 2; IV. 3).' This designation which is found also in the first chapters of the Shoo, in Mencius, in the Tso-chuen, and other ancient Works, is still used in the present day in official publications. The narratives of missionaries inform us that every individual whose hair and eyes are not black is immediately recognized in China as a foreigner.

In I. vii. IX. 1, the complexion of a beautiful lady is compared to the colour of the flower of a tree, analogous to our plum tree.[4] In men they admired a high-coloured complexion as if the face had been rouged (I. xi. V. 1).

We do not find in the She-king any notice about man's height; but I will add here a reference to Mencius, VI. Pt. ii. II. 2, where it is said that king Wǎn was believed to have been 10 cubits high, and T'ang 9 cubits. The speaker in that passage gives his own height as 9 cubits 4 inches. According to the measures of Amyot (Vol. XIII. of the Memoirs by Missionaries), the Chinese cubit, in the time of the Chow dynasty amounted to about 20 *centimetres.* The three preceding numbers therefore correspond to about, in English, 6½ feet, 5 ft. 10 in, and 6 ft. 1 in.

1 M. Biot translates the description in the present tense after Lacharme, after whom also he calls the piece an epithalamium. But the tense does not affect the portrait given us in the description. See the notes on the ode   2 This is a mistake. The slender eyebrows in this ode were a trait of female beauty, different from the bushy eyebrows of men which were a sign of longevity.   3 This princess of Wei was, like the one in I. v. III., a native of Ts'e.   4 Not a plum tree. See the notes on the ode.

Mencius' questioner quotes these heights as remarkable, from which we may presume, with a degree of probability, that man's height has not sensibly varied in China from ancient times.[5]

CLOTHING.

The officers had six sorts of different clothes for the different seasons, or epochs of the year, and the princes had seven (I. x. IX. 1, 2).[1] At the court of king Wăn (in Shen-se) the officers wore habits of wool, embroidered with silk in five different ways (I. ii. VII.).[2] In many courts the garment which was worn uppermost was garnished with cuffs of leopard-skin (I. vii. VI.; x. VII.). In Shen-se, the king[3] of Ts'in wore a garment of fox-fur, with one of broidered silk over it (I. xi. V.). Similar garments of fox-skin were worn at the court of P'ei by the officers (I. iii. XII.). The robes of the feudal princes were generally of embroidered silk (I. xiv. I.: IV. i. [iii.] VII.). Red was adopted by the kings of Chow for the garments of the princes and officers at their court (I. xiv. II. 1: II. iii. V. 4). The officers at the courts of the feudal princes wore a red collar to their principal robe (I. x. III. 1).

One of the feudal princes appears wearing a cap of skin adorned with precious stones (I. v. I. 2). Their officers had in summer a cap woven from the straw of the t'ae plant, and in winter one of black cotton (II. viii. I. 2). Husbandmen wore, in summer, caps of straw (IV. i. [iii.] VL.). These caps were fastened on the head with strings (I. viii. VI. 2), like those of the Chinese at the present day. A princess of the State of Wei had her upper robe of a green colour, and the under one of yellow (I. iii. II.). In a time of mourning the cap and garments were required to be white (I. xiii. II.). Beyond the court, dresses were of various colours with the exception of red. People wore caps of black fur (I. xiv. III. 2).[4] Girdles were of silk (I. xiv. III.), and of various colours, very long, and fastened by a clasp (I. vii. IX.).[5] Men and women who were rich attached to the ends of those girdles precious stones (I. vi. X. 3; v. V. 3).[5] When a rich man wished to do honour to his friends who visited him, he gave them precious stones to adorn their girdles (I. vii. VIII. 3; vi. X. 3).[6]

The princes of the blood wore red shoes (I. xv. VII: III. iii. VII. 2), embroidered with gold (II. iii. V. 4).[7] In general, shoes of cloth made from the dolichos plant (a kind of flax) were worn in summer (I. viii. VI. 2: II. v. IX. 2),[8] and leather shoes in winter. In two odes (I. ix. I. 1 : II. v. IX. 2), men of the eastern districts complain of being reduced by the prevailing misery to have only cloth shoes in winter.[9] Women of the ordinary class wore their garments undyed, and a veil or coiffure of a greyish colour (I. vii. XIX.).

5 Biot might have added that tallness was admired in ladies (I. v. III.)
1 See the notes on I. x. IX. Biot has misunderstood the meaning.   2 I. ii. VII. does not speak of the court of king Wăn, nor of garments of wool worn by the officers at the court in the writer's eye, who has before him their jackets of sheep-skin and lamb-skin.   3 There was no king of Ts'in in the age of the She. The ruler of the State of Ts'in was an earl.   4 This interpretation of the line referred to is very doubtful.   5 The odes here referred to do not speak of the girdle, but of the girdle-pendant; worn by ladies. See on I. vii. VIII.   6 This general conclusion cannot be drawn from these passages.   7 All the feudal princes did the same.   8 The plant, koh, was not a kind of flax; nor could the shoes made of its fibres be said to be made of cloth.   9 In I. ix. I. there is no complaint of the kind intimated.

Princes and dignitaries habitually wore ear-pendants (I. v. I. 2 : II. viii. I. 3).[10] I. iv. III. criticizes the elaborate toilette of a Chinese lady who wore plates of gold in the braids of her hair, and had six precious stones on each of her ear-pendants. Her comb is of ivory, and her robe is embroidered in silk of various colours. The ode says that she wore no false hair, and that she had only her own black hair, thick as clouds.[11] The toilette of Chinese ladies was made before a mirror which must have been of metal (I. iii. I. 2).

The wives of dignitaries twisted their hair on the sides of the head, or they curled it (II. viii. I. 4). As a sign of sadness, they let it hang loose (II. viii. II. 1). Widows cut their hair, preserving a lock on each side of the head (I. iv. I.).[12] The children of the rich wore at their girdle an ivory pin, which was used to open the knot when they undressed, and they wore also a ring of ivory (I. v. VI.).[13] Until their majority the hair was twisted up in two horns on the top of the head (I. viii. VII. 3). We know that this bifurcated coiffure is still that of Chinese maid-servants, often designated, because of this peculiarity, by a character which has the form of our Y. At sixteen, boys assumed the cap called pëen (ib.).

Men and women used pommade for their hair (I. v. VIII. 2), and wore at their side an ivory comb. We know that the practice of having the head shaved was introduced into China by the Manchëw Tartars in the 17th century. A recent traveller, M. Tradescant Lay, has remarked upon the habitually dirty state of the hair of Chinese children ; and he even says that the the hair is of such a nature as easily to become matted, which produces a disagreeable malady. It was probably to avoid this matting that people in easy circumstances carried about them a comb in the times described in the She-king.

BUILDINGS AND DWELLING HOUSES.

The walls of houses were ordinarily made of earth. For the foundations they pounded the soil hard where it was intended to erect the walls (II. iv. V. 3); over this space they placed a frame-work of four planks, two of which corresponded to the two faces of the wall, and were arranged by the help of a plumb-line (III. i. III. 5). The interval between the planks was filled with earth wetted and brought to it in baskets (ib., 6). They rammed in this earth with heavy poles of wood, and thus made a length of wall of a certain height, all the parts of which they brought to the same level, filling up where the earth failed, and paring away where there was too much (ib.; see also the ancient dictionary Urh-ya, Ch. IV.). They then moved the frame-work higher, and proceeded to make the upper part of the wall. It was precisely the same kind of construction which we see in the south of France, and which goes by the name of pisé. Foo Yueh, the minister of the emperor[1] Woo-ting of the Shang dynasty, was at first a pisé-mason (Shoo, IV. viii. Pt. I. 3). The workmen encouraged one another by cries. For the foundation of a town and for the construction of a considerable edifice, the drum gave the signal for the commencement and leaving off of work (III. i. III. 6).[2] The beams were of bamboo, of pine (II. iv.

10, 11. These ear-pendants were the ear-plugs or stoppers, not suspended from the ears, but from a comb in the hair, coming down to cover the ears. See the notes on I. iv. III.   12 See the notes on I. iv. I. The view of it taken by Biot has been maintained.   13 I. v. VI. does not speak of the children (les enfants) of the rich; but of a young dandy. The pin or spike was for loosing knots generally.

1 Woo-ting was not emperor, but king. Emperors should not be spoken of during the Hëa, Shang, and Chow dynasties.   2. The drum in III. i. III. 6 would seem to have sounded to inspirit the workmen.

V), or of cypress (IV. ii. IV. 9). They were cut and planed. The frames of the doors were also made of wood (IV. iii. V. 6). The poor made their cabins of rough planks (II. iv. IV.).[3] In the 14th century before our era, the inhabitants of western China had no houses, but lived in caverns or grottos, a hole at the top of the vault serving as an outlet for the smoke. Such was the first abode of T'an-foo, called also the ancient duke, the grandfather of king Wăn, who inhabited the country of Pin, a district at the present day of the department of Fung-ts'ěang, Shen-se (III. i. III.).[4] 'T'an-foo,' says that ode, 'lived in a cavern like a potter's kiln; there were then no houses.' Another ode, however (III. ii. VI. 3, 4) attributes to duke Lěw, a preceding chief of the same country, buildings considerably extensive, such as large stables and sheep-folds. According to the She-king (III. i. III.), and Mencius (I. Pt. ii. XV. 1, 2) the first establishments of the Chinese in the western regions were destroyed by the Tartars.[5] T'an-foo, the descendant of duke Lěw, was obliged to retire, and to transport his tribe to the south of his earlier settlement. Then he established the new city of which III. i. III. gives the description, and resumed with his people the agricultural labours which had been interrupted by the ravages of the enemy.

The doors of the houses faced the south or the west (II. iv. V. 2), or mid-wise the south-west. They gave them their position by observing the shadow of the sun at noon, or by the culminating of a well-known star (I. iv. VI. 1).[6] In winter the husbandmen ordinarily plastered the doors (I. xv. I. 5) to keep out the cold.

The floor of the house was levelled by beating it, and it was then covered with a coarse kind of dried grass, on which were placed mats of bamboo which served as beds (II. iv. V. 6).[7] People in easy circumstances placed at the south-east corner of their houses a special chamber, called the Hall of ancestors (I. ii. IV. 3). It was adorned with pillars of wood like the entrance-hall. The sovereign, the princes, and the great officers alone had the right of erecting a building dedicated especially to the performance of the ceremonies in honour of their ancestors (III. i. VI. 3 : IV. i. [ii.] VIII.; ii. IV.; iii V.). A path conducted to this building (I. xii. VII. 2), and the approaches to it were required to be carefully cleared of thorns (I. xii. VI.).[8]

The cities were surrounded with a wall of earth, and with a ditch which was dug out first, and furnished the materials for the wall (III. iii. VII. 6; i. X. 3). We read in the Yih king, 'The wall falls back into the moat, if it be badly founded (Diagram 泰, par. 7).'[9]

THE CHASE.

In those times of nascent civilization the chase was an important means of subsistence for the pioneers who were clearing the forests. The habitual arm of the chase was the bow and arrow. The bows were of carved wood (III. ii. II. 3), and adorned with green silk (IV. ii. IV. 5), probably to preserve them from the damp.

---

3 II. iv. V. says nothing of this.   4 The ancient Pin was not in Fung-ts'ěang dept. T'an-foo came from Pin to K'e-chow in Fung-ts'ěang. See the notes on the title of Pt. I, and on III. i. III.   5 Let it not be thought that these Chinese settlers were pushing westwards from the east. They were advancing eastwards from the west, and pushed on by tribes behind them. 6 The mention of the star in I. iv. VI. 1 does not have the meaning here given to it. 7 No. They slept on couches or stands raised from the ground. The mats spread on the ground or floor served as tables, where the meal was set out.   8 Of course a path conducted to the building;—I. xii. VII. 2 describes the tiles with which it was laid. I. xii. VI. speaks of the cemetery, or place of tombs; and not of the temple.   9 The words 'if it be badly founded' are not in the Yih. Biot seems to have misunderstood the text.

They kept them in leather cases (I. vii. IV. 3: II. viii. II. 3). Those of the princes of the blood were painted red, the Chow colour. At certain periods of the year, they observed the ceremony of archery, each archer having four arrows which he discharged at the target (III. ii. II. 3). To aid him in drawing the bow and discharging the arrow, the hunter or archer had a ring of metal on the thumb of his right hand, and threw back his coat upon the other arm (II. iii. V. 5).[1]

Solitary hunters pursued the goose or the wild-duck (I. vii. VIII. 1), the boar (I. ii. XIV.: II. iii. VI. 4), the wolf (I. viii. II. 3), the fox (I. xv. I. 4) in the first month, or at the commencement of our year, the hare (II. v. III. 6; IV. 4).[2] In the chase they used dogs (I. viii. VIII.: II. v. IV. 4).

The great hunts of the chiefs were conducted en battue. They surrounded the woods with large nets, fixed to the ground by stakes, and intended specially to catch the hares, which the beaters forced to throw themselves into them (I. i. VII.).[3] They set fire also to the grass and bushes of a large plain, to collect the game in a place determined on, where they killed it easily with the arrow. We have the description of such a hunt in I. vii. III. and IV. The chief mounted in a carriage and four kills at his ease the game thus collected. The ode eulogizes his courage, and says that he fought against tigers with bare breast.

When they had a considerable number of men, or when the ground was not covered with vegetation high enough to raise a conflagration, they arranged the men in a circle, and made them all march towards a single point, beating back the game (I. xi. II. 2; xv. I. 4: II. iii. V. and VI.). They often formed several circles of beaters, one within another (the Yih, diagram 比, par. 9).[4] These grand hunts took place principally in the second moon, corresponding to our month of February (I. xv. I. 4). They hunted also herds of deer (II. iii. VI. 2), of boars (I. ii. XIV.; xi. II.), of wild oxen (II. iii. VI. 3).[5] The hunters offered to their prince the boars of three years, and kept for themselves the smallest, which were only one year old. To preserve the carcases of the killed deer, they covered them up with straw (I. ii. XII.).[6]

The grand hunts en battue were entirely similar to those which the missionary Gerbillon saw in the 18th century, when accompanying the emperor K'ang-he to Tartary (Duhalde, vol. IV., p. 293, folio edition). At the times described in the She-king, they celebrated them on the two sides of the valley of the Yellow river, about the 35th parallel of latitude, in Ho-nan, in the eastern part of Shen-se, where much of the country was still uncultivated.

FISHING.

Fishing formed also an important means of subsistence. They fished with the line (I. v. V. 1: II. viii. II. 4); but the ordinary method was with nets (I. v. III. 4; viii. IX.). On the banks of large rivers they formed a stockade of wood, in front of which they arranged the nets (I. viii. IX: II. v. III. 8). The English traveller Lay,

1 There is nothing in the ode about the vesture being thrown on the other arm. The poet speaks at once of the ring which was on the thumb of the right hand, and of an armlet of leather which was on the left arm. 2 They hunted also the badger, the deer, the tiger, the panther, the rhinoceros, &c. Some of the odes referred to describe grand hunts, and not those of solitary or isolated individuals. 3 This ode speaks of a solitary hunter or trapper. 4 Biot has misunderstood this passage of the Yih. 5 These wild oxen would seem to be rhinoceroses. 6 This ode has nothing to do with hunting, and the fact of the dead antelope wrapt up with the grass is an inappropriate illustration in this place.

whom I have already quoted, describes, in his visit to Hongkong, the fishing net as it is made in the neighbourhood of Canton. He says that on the borders of the islands in the gulf they form a wooden frame with a wheel and axle to lower and raise the nets which remain under the water. Such appears to have been the kind of apparatus of the She-king. It is said, in II. v. III. 8,

> 'Do not approach my dam,
> Do not loose my nets.'

The nets were made of fine bamboo (I. viii. IX.: II. ii. III.). Like those which were used to take hares, they were fitted with bags (I. xv. VI.), which the fish entered and so was taken. II. ii. III. names several kinds of fish, among which the carp is mentioned (see also I. xii. III.). We find also (IV. i. [ii.] VI.: II. iv. VIII. II) a certain number of fish given as pond-fish.

The habit of fishing had made them construct boats which they directed with oars (II. v. I. 6). The boats were of cypress-wood (I. iii. I. 1; iv. I. 1), and of willow (II. iii. II. 4).[2] III. i. II. 5 mentions a bridge of boats, made by king Woo[3] to pass the river Wei in Shen se.

AGRICULTURE AND PASTURAGE.

According to the *data* furnished by different odes, the system of cultivation with irrigation was established in the vast plain which forms the lower valley of the Yellow river, from the gorge of the Dragon's-gate (in Shan-se) to the gulf of Pih-chih-le, into which this great river then emptied itself (I. iii. XVII.):[1] (II. viii. V.; vi. VIII.: IV. i. [iii.] V. and VI.). Every space of ground assigned to a family of husbandmen was surrounded by a trench for irrigating it, and which formed its boundary (II. vi. VI.); and these trenches communicated with larger canals which were conducted to rejoin the river. The complete system adopted for the purpose of irrigation is expounded in detail in the Chow Le, (Bk. XV. art. 遂人), which confirms the indications in the She-king.

Beyond the great valley, particularly towards the west in Shen-se, and eastwards about the T'ae mountains in Shan-tung, there existed vast forests. The first chiefs of the House of Chow, duke Lëw and T'an-foo, began the clearing of the forests of Shen-se (III. i. III. 8; ii. VI.). We see in IV. ii. IV. that the people of the State of Loo drew materials for building from the neighbourhood of mount T'ae. II. iv. VI. mentions the great herds of cattle and sheep as the chief riches of powerful families;—a natural circumstance among a people still far from numerous, and spread over a vast territory. They fastened the feet of the horses with tethers while they were feeding (II. iv. II.).[2]

We can tell the principal kinds of cereals mentioned in the She-king, and point out the localities where they were cultivated. They were rice, wheat, barley, buck-wheat, two sorts of millet, called *shoo* and *tseih*, which resembled the one the

---

1 I think that M. Biot is wrong in supposing that we have any fishing arrangement indicated in the She-king like that described by Mr. Tradescant Lay, and which is exceedingly common at the present day in China. The odes referred to do nothing more than describe the capture of fish in baskets placed at openings in dams thrown across streams.   2 Boats of pine also are mentioned (I. v. V. 4).   3 Should be king Wăn.

1 This and the other passages adduced are little to the point.   2 The large herds of horses, necessary for the war-chariots, fed at pleasure, without restraint of any kind, in the open territory assigned to them (IV. ii. I.). It was only in the neighbourhood of houses that the horses for use were tethered.

milium globosum, the other the *holcus sorgho*. The labours of cultivation of each month are described for the State of Pin in I. xv. I., and for the territory of the ancient *royaume* of Chang (eastern Ho-nan) in IV. i. [iii.] V. and VI.[3] The rice and the millet were sown in spring, on which occasion there was a ceremony (IV. i. [ii.] I.),[4] the celebrated ceremony of husbandry, the ritual of which is described in the Kwoh-yu (國 語, 上, art 5). II. vi. VI. mentions the furrows traced by the great Yu on the slope of the Nan-shan mountain in the territory of Se-gan dept [5] In autumn took place the ceremony of the ingathering (IV. i. [ii.] IV.). IV. i. [ii.] I. mentions at the beginning of the summer of Chow, *i.e.*, about April, the first harvest of millet and of the winter barley.[4]

The principal instruments of cultivation, the plough with its share, the hoe or spade, the scythe or sickle, are mentioned in different odes (II. vi. VIII.: IV. i. [ii.] I.; [iii.] V. and VI.). Weeding is recommended in a special manner (III. vi. VIII. 2: IV. i. [iii.] V. and VI.). The weeds were gathered in heaps, and burned in honour of the Spirits who presided over the harvest (II. vi. VIII. 2).[6] Their ashes nourished the soil. They prescribed also the destruction of insects or hurtful worms. The assiduous uprooting of weeds has always been recommended by the Chinese government to the cultivators of the ground. It is noted by Confucius and by Mencius as a necessity; and its continuation for twenty centuries is, no doubt, an essential cause of the astonishing fertility of the Chinese soil, from which parasitical herbs have disappeared.

In general they left the land fallow for one year, and then cultivated it for two years. If they still found weeds in it in the second year, they carefully uprooted them (II. iii. IV.). The harvest was a time of great labour and of much rejoicing, just as it is in our country (II. vi. VIII.). This ode says that the reapers left some ears of grain, and even small handfuls of it, for the poor widows who came to glean. The superintendent of agriculture came to the field, and rejoiced with the husbandmen. They then assigned over the share that was due to the State from the returns of the harvest.

We see in the She-king several indications of the agrarian laws established by the dynasty of Chow, and which are explained by Mencius (V. Pt. ii. II.). The division of the land in the tribe of its ancestor duke Lëw is indicated in III. ii. VI. A husbandman in II. vi. VIII. says that the irrigation began with the field of the State (公 田), and thence proceeded to their private fields[7];—in harmony with the ancient system described by Mencius, according to which eight families received a space of ground divided into nine equal portions, the central portion forming the field of the State. IV. i. [ii.] II.[8] shows us Ch'ing, the second of the kings of Chow, naming the officers of agriculture, and ordering them to sow the fields. It mentions the large division of 30 *le*, or more exactly of 33⅓ *le*, which covered a space of about 1,111 square *le*. It places there 10,000 individuals, labouring in pairs, which gives about $\frac{1111}{10000}$ of a *le* to an individual. As the *le* was generally of 300 paces, that would

---

3 No place is specified or indicated in these odes. What is said in them would apply to all the royal domain of Chow. I do not understand what State M. Biot intends by 'the kingdom of Chang.'　　4 There is some confusion in the two references to this ode. See the notes on it.
5 Hardly so much as this. All which the ode says is that the country about Nan-shan was made cultivable by Yu.　　6 No such burning ceremony is here described. The husbandmen only express their wish that the Spirit of husbandry would take the insects and commit them to the flames.　　7 There is no reference to irrigation in this passage; but it implies the existence of the public field or fields, and a loyal wish is expressed that the rain might first descend on them.　　8 See the notes on this ode.

give an individual 9,999 square paces. Taking the ancient acre as 100 square paces, we thus find for an individual about 100 Chinese acres;—the number assigned in several passages of Mencius to every head of a family. The Chow-le, Bk. IX., gives the same number on good lands.

Each house occupied by a family of husbandmen was situated in the midst of the ground assigned to it (II. vi. VI. 4).[9] It had around it its garden supplied with cucumbers, pumpkins, melons, and other kitchen vegetables Each of these houses was surrounded by mulberry trees and jujube trees, and had also its flax-field I. ix. V. speaks of the field of 10 acres, where they cultivated the mulberry-trees;—meaning the plantation near the house [10] The hemp and similar plants, the *ch'oo* (the *boehmeria*), the *keen* (a sort of rush) and the *koh* (the dolichos), were steeped in the moats (I. xii. IV.). The mulberry-leaves served to feed the silk worms (I. xv. I. 2, 3), with which business the women were specially occupied (III. iii. X. 4). In each house, the women span the hemp and the dolichos, and wove cloth and silken stuffs (I. iii. II.).[11] The loom, with the cylinder for the warp, and the shuttle of the woof, are mentioned in II. v. IX. 2.

They cultivated indigo, or some similar plant, from which they extracted a deep blue dye (I. xv. I. 3; II. viii. II. 2). They cultivated also plants which gave a yellow dye and a red (I. xv. I. 3). The dyeing of the stuffs took place in the 8th moon, about the month of September, and also the steeping of the hemp, (I. xv. I. 3).[12] The winter evenings were occupied in spinning, weaving, and making ropes (I. xv. I. 7). They kept themselves warm by burning wood of different kinds (I. xv. I. 6), and among others that of the mulberry tree (II. viii. V. 4)

FOOD AND ITS PREPARATION.

The grains of rice were bruised in a mortar (III. ii. I. 7) to free them from the husk; and when so cleaned, the grain was winnowed, or passed through a sieve (*ib*, and II. v. IX. 7). It was then washed and cooked with the steam of boiling water (III. iii. I. 7). The cakes which were eaten at their ceremonies were thus prepared. Wheat, and the two kinds of millet,—the *shoo* and the *tseih*,—were treated in the same manner; and it is in the same way that bread is made in China in the present day (see the Japanese Encyclopedia, Bk. cv., fol. 18. v., and the memoirs by the missionaries).[1]

The various kinds of flesh were grilled upon live charcoal, or roasted on the spit (III. ii. I. 7; II. 2), or cooked in stew-pans like fish (I. xiii. IV. 3; II. v. IX. 7). They took the meat from the pan (or boiler) by means of spoons made from the wood of the jujube tree (II. v. IX. 1). IV. iii. II.[2] describes the preparation of a

---

9 M. Biot here falls into a mistake: Only huts were in the midst of the territories assigned to the different families,—mere temporary erections occupied by the labourers at the busiest times of the year. They were in a space of 2½ acres, and, no doubt, they cultivated vegetables about them. The proper dwellings were away from the fields, in a space for each family of other 2½ acres, and about the houses they cultivated especially mulberry trees.   10 No conclusion can be drawn from I. ix. V. See the notes upon it. The 10 acres are mentioned in it instead of 20, the space for the homesteads of 8 families,—to show the disorder prevailing in the State of Wei.
11 The statement in this sentence is correct; but I. iii. II.supplies no proof of it.
1 No doubt cakes of rice and wheaten flour were made in China, and may have been used in the ancient religious ceremonies; but the mention of the rice and millet in the She, so far as I recollect, gives the impression of their being boiled in the grain.   2 This is a wrong reference; and I cannot think of any passage which Biot could have had in view.

carp. The stomach and palate of animals were specially esteemed (III. ii. II. 2);[3] —a preference which is still common, as may be seen in the description which Gerbillon gives us of a hunt by K'ang-he (Duhalde, IV., p. 293, fol. ed.). In ordinary houses they reared pigs (III. ii. VI. 4) and dogs to be eaten. The She-king mentions only the watch-dog (I. ii. XII. 3), and the hunting-dog (I. viii. VIII.; II. v. IV. 4): but the habit of eating the dog was very common in China acc. to the Chow Le, *passim*, and the Le Ke, VI. v. 5. In two passages where Mencius describes what is necessary to a family of husbandmen (I. Pt. i III. 4; VII. 24), he notices the raising of dogs and pigs for food. This use of the flesh of the dog is found, we know, among the Indians of north America, and it is still maintained in China. Each house had also its fowl-house, filled with cocks and hens (I. vi. II. 1; *et al.*) The odes of the She and the Book of Mencius do not speak of geese nor of tame ducks. They make frequent mention of these birds in their wild State; and we may thence presume that they were not yet in that age generally domesticated. Nevertheless, an author who lived under the Han dynasty, about 100 years B.C., says that the domestic birds mentioned in the Chow Le, XXXIX. par. 2, were geese and ducks.[4] Beef and mutton were placed only on the table of chiefs and dignitaries who possessed large herds and flocks (II. i V. 2: III. ii. III.). At great feasts, eight different dishes [of grain] were set forth (II. i. V. 2). The turtle was considered a dainty dish (III. iii. VII. 3). The vegetable garden of every husbandman furnished him with cucumbers, pumpkins, and melons (I. xv. I. 6: II. vi. VI. 4). They ate also the jujube-dates, which they struck down in the eighth moon, *i.e.*, about the end of July (I. xv. I. 6). At the same time they cut down the large pumpkins. The cucumbers, melons, and the leaves of the *k'wei* were eaten in the seventh moon (I. xv. I. 6). They ate habitually the tender shoots of the bamboo (III. iii. VII. 3).

In all the descriptions of solemn feasts (I. vii. VIII. 2: II. ii. III.: III. iii. VII., &c.)[5] mention is made of the wine (酒, spirits) as the habitual drink. Men who become unruly in their behaviour are reproached for their love of spirits (III. iii. II. 3.)[6] As at the present day, this wine was a fermented drink extracted from rice (I. xv. I. 6). The preparation of it appears to be indicated in part in III. ii. VII., where it is said:—

'They draw the water from the brook,
And they pass it from vessel to vessel.
Then they can wet with this water the rice cooked by steam.'

And in the second stanza:—

'They draw the water from the brook,
And they pass it from vessel to vessel.
They can wash with it the vases for wine.'

Lacharme has translated the 3d line of the first stanza by:—

3 Here Biot is right in taking 臄 as meaning the *palate*, and not *cheek*, as I have done.

4 Yet in Mencius, III. Pt. ii. X. 5, we have a 鶃, which is the name appropriate to a tame goose, which is cooked and eaten; and in the Tso-chuen, under the 28th year of duke Sëang, mention is made of a 鶩, or tame duck. The common name for the domestic duck—*ah*—does not appear to have been used till the Tsin dynasty. 鶃 and 鶩 are the names employed by Këa Kwei of the Han dyn., to whom M. Biot refers.

5 I. vii. VIII. 2 does not speak of any solemn or extraordinary feast.

6 II. vii. VI. would be a more suitable reference.

'The steam of boiling water is need to make the *vin*;' which would indicate a veritable distillation. The text appears to me less precise;[7] but the making of rice-wine is sufficiently indicated in I. xv. I. 6, where it is said that in the 10th month they reap the rice to make the *vin* for spring. Thus they allowed the fermentation to proceed during the winter, and the *vin* was drunk in the spring of the following year. They separated it from the lees by straining it through herbs, or through a basket with a rough bottom (II. i. V. 3); after which it was fit to be served at feasts (II. i. V. 3 : III. i. V. 4). They mixed Chinese pepper (I. xii. II) with spirits and meats to render them aromatic.

The *vin* was kept in vases or bottles of baked earth (III. ii. VII. 2). The baked earth could not be porcelain, which was not in common use in China till a much later period.[8]

It is to be remarked that milk is not mentioned in the She-king as a drink. The *Yih-king*, diagram 睽, par. 1, mentions the milch cow.[9] We know that the present Chinese in general do not drink milk.

Common people drank from horns, either unpolished or carved (II. vii. I. 4 : I. xv. I. 8). Duke Lëw, the ancestor of the kings of Chow, who lived in the 18th century before our era, after the sovereign T'ae-k'ang, or according to others, after Këeh, the last sovereign of the Hëa dynasty,—duke Lëw drank from a hollow gourd (III. ii. VI. 4). In the times of the Chow dynasty, the princes used cups formed of a precious stone (III. i. V. 2). At solemn feasts, the wine [spirits] was served in large vases called *tow*, *pëen* and *ta-fang*, (III. ii I. 8 : IV. ii. IV. 4),[10] the forms of which can be seen in the work called *Tsi-king-too*, where the famous commentator of the Sung dynasty, Choo He, has represented by figures the vases, the arms, and the dresses, mentioned in the King or Classical books.[11]

METALS IN USE.

The notices furnished by the She-king show us that gold, silver, iron, lead, and copper were then known to the Chinese. IV. iii. III 8 mentions the metal *par excellence* (gold), which was extracted from the mines of the south, and was sent in tribute by the still barbarous tribes of central China.[1] III. i. IV. 5 speaks of ornaments of gold. We read of horses' bits of gold in III. ii. III.,[2] and of lances, the shaft of which was silvered or gilt, in I. xi. III. 3.[3] The breasts of war-horses were covered with [mail of] steel (I. xi. III. 3).[4] Gold and tin, brilliant and purified, are mentioned in I. v. 3. III. ii. VI. 6 speaks of mines of iron worked in Shen-se by duke Lëw in the 18th century before our era. Arms and instruments of iron are mentioned everywhere in the She-king.

7 III. ii. VII. has nothing to do either with the process of fermentation or distillation. See the notes upon it. I believe that 酒 always denotes spirits, the product of distillation. Possibly 醴 may denote the stage of fermentation.   8 At the present day distilled spirits are often kept for a long time in vessels of coarse earthenware.   9 This is a mistake. The text speaks merely of the 牝 牛, or *cow*, with reference to its docility and manageableness.

10 The *tow* and *pëen* were not used to hold wine and spirits, and the *ta-fang* was a stand for meat.   11 I do not know what work M. Biot here calls the *Tsi-king-too*. All the imperial editions of the classics are furnished with plates.

1 The 金 of the south here is plural, meaning gold, silver, and copper.   2 No mention occurs of *freins d'or* in III. ii. III. M. Biot intended, I suppose, ' the ends of the reins with their metal rings,' mentioned in III. iii. VII. 2, *et al.*   3 Only the end of the shaft was gilt.   4 Not the *breast* alone of the war-horse was covered with mail.

ARTICLES MANUFACTURED.

Several odes (I. v. I.: III. i. IV.; iii. II. 5) mention the art of cutting and polishing precious stones. I have referred to the ring of ivory worn by the children of the rich (I. v. VI. 2).[1] IV. ii. III. 8 mentions ivory (elephants' teeth) as being sent, like gold, in tribute by the tribes of central China. The ends of bows were often ornamented with wrought ivory (II. i. VII. 5).

ARMS. WAR.

It has been said that hunting is the image of war. This comparison becomes a reality in the deserts of North America and of Central Asia. When the men of one horde assemble and issue from their place of settlement, their association has two simultaneous objects:—hunting in the vast steppes which have no definite possessors; and war with the other hordes which come to hunt on the same debateable ground. In the times described in the She-king, the greater part of the country surrounding the great cultivated valley of the Yellow river was such a hunting ground, undivided between the Chinese and the indigenous hordes. The Chinese armies, then led against the barbarians, hunted and fought by turns; their warriors used the same arms against the enemies and against the wild animals.[1] Nevertheless several odes give the description of regular expeditions directed by the sovereign, or by a Chinese feudal prince against another prince; several of them depict the posts regularly established upon the frontiers. Some extracts from these odes will give an idea of what was then the art of war in China, and it does not appear that the Chinese have made great progress in that art since this early epoch. Excepting the fire arms which they have now adopted, they have remained stationary in this as in every other thing. The military art of the Chinese, translated by Amyot in the 18th century, and published in the 7th volume of the memoirs by the missionaries, has for its basis an ancient work attributed to Sun-tsze, general of the country of Ts'e, who lived nearly 300 years before the Christian era [2]

The frontier-posts between the States at war with one another, or on the borders of the barbarous regions, were supplied from the peasantry, and were relieved from year to year;—the service at these posts was truly forced, and hence the lamentations of the soldiers who were so stationed (I. vi. IV.: II. i. VII.). The edict which enjoined regular service on the frontiers was inscribed on a bamboo tablet placed at the post (II. i. VIII. 4).[3] In the Chinese armies of this epoch, as in the feudal armies of our middle ages, the infantry was composed of husbandmen taken from their labours, and they complained bitterly of their lot (I. iii. VI.; xv. III. and IV.: II. iv. I.;[4] viii. III.), especially when they formed part of an expedition against the barbarous hordes of the north and the south (II. viii. VIII. and X.). They had the

---

1 It is of an ivory spike at the girdle worn by men that I. v. VI. speaks, and not of a ring for children.

1 No such expeditions, partly for hunting, and partly for war, are described in the She. When the regular huntings were made, opportunity was taken to practise the methods of warfare.

2 Sun-tsze belonged to the State of Woo, (吳), and not to Ts'e; and to the 6th century B.C., and not to the 3d. See Wylie's notes on Chinese Literature, p. 74.   3 II. i. VIII. tells us how the general got his orders on a tablet of bamboo or wood; but nothing about the orders being fixed up at the post.   4 The complaints in II. iv. I. are of a different class.

greatest fear of the Hëen-yun on the north, known afterwards as the Hëung-noo (II. i. VIII.).[5] The principal element of a Chinese army was the chariot drawn by two or by four horses.[6] It carried three mailed warriors, the officer to whom it belonged being in the middle. He had on his right his esquire, who passed to him his arms; and on his left the charioteer (I. vii. V. 3). A troop of soldiers followed the chariot to protect it (II. i. VII. 5 : IV. ii. III. 7). The term chariot was then a collective name like *lance* in our middle ages. The Le Ke reckons for every chariot 3 mailed warriors, 25 footmen in front and at the sides to guide the horses and the chariot, and seventy-two light-armed foot-soldiers following. But this number or company was never complete. IV. ii. IV. 5 counts only 30,000 foot-soldiers for 1000 chariots, making but 30 for a chariot.[7] Another ode (II. iii. IV. 2) speaks of an army of 3000 chariots, which would represent, according to the Le Ke, 300,000 men.[8] Lacharme remarks, and I agree with him, that the numbers in the Le Ke must be very much exaggerated, like all the numbers of armies given by Asiatic authors. The number in the official list was never complete.

The sovereign never marched without a guard of 2,500 men, called *sze*.[9] Every dignitary or great officer had an escort of 500 men called *leu* (II. iii. IV. 3; viii. III. 3)[9] To employ our military terms, *sze* was a regiment, *leu* a battalion. Six *sze*, or 15,000 men, formed an ordinary army (II. vi. IX. 1: III. i. IV. 3).[10] They distinguished the soldiers of the left wing and the right, according to the division long used in the marching and encampments of the Tartar hordes (III. iii. IX. 2). An army was divided into three troops (III. ii. VI. 5).[11] The six *sze* appear also to represent in general six sections of any army (III. iii. IX. 1).[12] In II. iv. III. the commentary explains *sze* by *keun*, which denotes a corps of 12,500 men. The six *sze* are a collective term, like the six *k'ing* mentioned in several chapters of the Shoo-king (III. ii. 1, and V. ii.).[13] The chief of each corps had his place in the middle of it. (I. vii. V.).

The chariot of the sovereign, or of the commander-in-chief, had four or six horses, yoked abreast.[14] When there were four horses, which was the ordinary number, (II. vii. VIII. 2: III. iii. VII. 2), two of them were yoked to the pole, and two to the transverse bar of the chariot (II. vii. VIII.). The horses were covered with mail (I. vii. V.; xi. III.), or protected at the sides by bucklers (I. xi. III. 2).[15] Those

5 The Hëen-yun do not appear an object of fear, so much as a troublesome enemy.   6 I believe the war-chariots had all 4 horses.   7 This description is not quite correct. In an ordinary fighting chariot, the charioteer was in the middle; one warrior, who wielded the spear, was on the right; and the one on the left was an archer. It was only in the chariot of the general that the driver was on the left, while he himself thundered on a drum to urge the troops forward. The spearman on the right was not his esquire to hand him his arms, but a noted warrior of great strength, to protect him, and take part in the battle as he was needed. 8 See the note on IV. ii. IV. 5, where the number of 30,000 is otherwise explained; and the note on II. iii. IV. 1, where the 3,000 chariots may be made out, without any exaggeration. 9 These things do not appear in the odes. In the Tso-chuen, on XI. iv., par. 4, it is said :—

君行師從，卿行旅從，'When the ruler goes, a *sze* (2,500 men) attends him; when a high ministers goes, a *leu* (500 men) attends him;' but the discourse is there of a feudal prince, and the subject is of their going to certain meetings.   10 It should be 5 *sze*, or 12,500 men, which formed a 軍 or army. In both the passages referred to, 六師一六軍, the host which followed the king to the field.   11 See the note on the words referred to. We can draw no conclusion from the passage.   12 See note 10.   13 Only the first reference is applicable. In V. ii., the term does not occur. The six *k'ing* would be the commanders of the six royal armies (六軍 or 六師).   14 The She nowhere mentions 6 horses to a chariot; but the king did have that number.   15 Those bucklers were in the front of the chariot, and not at the sides of the horses.

of the commanders had golden bits (III. ii. III.),[16] with a small bell at each side of the bit (I. xi. II. 3: II. iii. IV. 2: III. iii. VII. 4). The reins were richly adorned (IV. ii. III.),[17] and led through rings of leather on the backs of the horses (I. xi. III. 1: IV. ii. IV. 3). The sides of the chariots were covered with boards as a defence against the arrows of the enemy (I. xi. III.) They were adorned in the inside with mats of bamboo (I. iv. III. 3),[18] or embroidered carpets (I. xi. III. 1).[18] The axle-trees of the chariots of the chiefs were wrapped round with green silk (IV. iii. II.),[20] or with leather (II. iii. IV. 2),[19] probably to strengthen them. The pole was also covered with leather, painted in 5 colours (I. xi. III. 1).[21]

The princes and regular warriors wore helmets. Those of the princes of the blood were adorned with a plume of red silk (IV. ii. IV. 5).[22] The regular warriors had a sword (II. vi. IX. 2: I. vii. V. 3), two lances (or spears) and two bows (I. vii. V. 2: IV. ii. IV. 5).[23] The scabbards of the chiefs' swords were adorned with precious stones (III. ii. VI. 2), or with other ornaments (II. vi. IX. 2). The spears were of three kinds :—the *maou* which was 4 *mètres* long (20 Chow cubits); and the *kih*, 16 cubits (I. xi. VIII. 2). These were set up in the war chariots (*ib.*). The javelin *ko* (*ib.*) was 6 cubits, 6 in. long, and was used by the foot-soldiers.[24] (These lengths are given by the commentary from the Le Ke.) All the lances had red pendants or streamers (I. vii. V 1).

Like the hunting bows, those used in war were of wood adorned with green silk (IV. ii. IV. 5).[25] The bows of the chiefs had ornaments of ivory (II. i. VII. 5). There were also bows of horn, or strong as horn (II. vii. IX. 1: IV. ii III. 7),[26] which discharged several arrows at once.[26] To preserve the bows, they were kept in cases of tiger-skin (I. xi III. 3), or of ordinary leather (I. vii. IV. 3). Every case contained two bows, and they were closely fitted to bamboos, to hinder them from being warped by the damp (I. xi. III. 3: II. viii. II. 3). The bow-cases and the quivers were made of the skin of some marine animal called yu (II. i. VII. 5: iii. IV. 1), which may have been a seal.

The mailed warriors had bucklers (I. i. VII. 1: III. ii VI. 1), and battle-axes with handles of wood (I. xv. IV.: III. ii. VI. 1). The foot-soldiers were usually armed only with javelins and spears (I. xv. IV.). II. iii. V. describes an army in march. The horses in the chariots neigh; the flags and pennons wave in the air; the foot-soldiers and the assistants who guide the horses march in silence.[27] Besides the war-chariots, there followed the army carriages laden with sacks of baggage, and drawn by oxen (II. viii. III. 2. Shoo, V. xxix. 3). These sacks had one or two openings, and contained provisions (III. ii. VI. 1). The chariots were unloaded, and arranged round the place of encampment (Yih-king, ch. VI., diagram *sze*).[28] Then the feeble watched the baggage, while the strong advanced against the enemy.

16 III ii. III. says nothing about horses and their ornaments. The bits were of metal; not necessarily gold; and were fitted with bells. 17 Nor does IV. ii. III. say anything about reins. They are commonly spoken of as soft and glossy; they had rings of metal at their ends. 18 These were screens, not mats, of bamboo, which covered in the carriages of ladies, and some others given to great men by the king. 19 These were mats of tiger-skin. 20 Not with green silk, but only with leather, which was lacquered. The axle-trees, or perhaps only the projecting ends, were bound with this. 21 Only the curved end of the pole. 22 No. The ornament on the helmet consisted of shells strung on red cords. 23 The spear and the bow-case were carried in the chariot. It does not seem to me competent from the odes to say anything about the sword as a regular weapon. 24 It does not appear that the javelin was ever thrown. 25 See notes on I. xi. III. 3. 26 These bows were probably only adorned with horn. The She does not mention the spring-bow, which could discharge more than one arrow at once. 27 This ode is only about a grand hunting-expedition of king Seuen. 28 There is no such statement in the Yih-king.

The expeditions against the indigenous tribes of the centre, the west, and the north, were made in the 6th moon (II. iii. III.), the time of the year corresponding to the end of May and the beginning of June.[29] They marched 30 *le* per day, about 11 kilometres, if we value the *le* at 1,800 cubits of 10 centimetres each (II. iii. III. 2). For a grand army of 300 chariots, 10 chariots formed the advanced guard (*ib.*, 4).

On the banners were figures of birds (*ib.*, 4), and of serpents (II. i. VIII. 2, 3).[30] There were attached to them little bells (II. vii. VIII. 2),[31] and ribbons (III. iii. VII. 2).[32] On the royal standard there was the image of the sacred dragon (IV. i. [ii.] VIII.).[33] The princes of the blood, and secondary chiefs or viceroys had broad pennons or flags (IV. iii. IV. 3). One pennon, formed of an ox-tail upon a pole, was placed behind in the chariot of the chief of a squadron. Figures of these flags are given in the plates published with the imperial editions of the Chow Le and the Le Ke.

The warriors wore coloured cuisses, and buskins on their legs, (II. vii. VIII. 3).[34] Lacharme says that this practice still exists in China with foot-soldiers. In I. xi. VIII. a man of Ts'in engages another to follow him to the war by the promise of clothes, shoes, and weapons, should he need them. This custom of having all their military equipment in common reminds us involuntarily of the miserable equipment of Chinese soldiers at the present day, who, according to many travellers, lend to each other their clothes and weapons for the purpose of passing a review.

The commandant of a *corps d'armée* had the title of K'e-foo (II. iv. I.), or of Shang-foo (III. i. II. 7).[35] Several odes (II. i. VII., *et al*), designate the general by the name of 'the illustrious man;'—meaning the Prince, the Dignitary [36]

The drum gave the signal for departure (I. iii. VI. 1), for attack, and for retreat II. vi. IV. 3).[37] Large drums were covered with the skin of a fish called *t'o* (III. i. VIII. 4), and which appears to have been a crocodile, according to the description in the Japanese Encyclopædia, ch. xiv., fol. 5, and the explanation in the commentary on the Le Ke, VI. iv. 6.[38] Before the battle, the warriors excited one another by mock combats. They leaped, ran, and threatened one another with their weapons (I. iii. VI. 1).[39] Turner, in his Journey to Thibet, gives us a similar description of a sham fight.

In III. i. VII. 7, 8, king Wăn causes the assault of a fortified city, and his soldiers ascend the wall by means of hooked ladders. He takes some prisoners and punishes

29 No. The 6th month in II. iii. III. is mentioned to show the urgency of the occasion, calling for an expedition at an unusual time.   30 The *chaou* was characterized by serpents and tortoises intertwined blazoned upon it.   31 The bells in II. vii. VIII. 2 are probably those at the horses' bits; but there were bells at the top of the flag-staff (IV. i. [ii.] VIII.).   32 I do not know that these ornaments were of ribbons.   33. It is not the royal standard which is here mentioned; but what Biot immediately calls a broad pennon or flag carried by princes of the blood, &c. It was a large flag with dragons figured on it. The royal standard (大 常) had a representation at the top of it of the sun and moon, beneath which and all round were dragons. It is not mentioned in the She.   34. These coloured cuisses, which were a sort of apron or knee-cover, belonged to the dress of ceremony and not of war. The buskins may have been something like the gaiters which I have seen on Chinese soldiers.   35 K'e-foo was a designation of the king's minister of War, and not of the commander of a *corps d'armée*. Shang-foo was the name or designation of a minister of kings Wăn and Woo.   36 'The illustrious man' is merely a title of praise and admiration.   37 A retreat was generally ordered by the gong or some instrument of metal. In II. vi. IV. 3 a light sound of the drum serves the same purpose.   38 The *t'o* was no doubt some kind of saurian; but not the crocodile.   39 I. iii. VI. 1 is not sufficient to bear this remark out. In the Tso-chuen we have numerous instances of individual deeds of daring against the enemy before a battle.

them as rebels, proportioning their chastisement to the gravity of their offence. He causes one ear of his captives to be cut off, and in contenting himself with this punishment he passes for a just and humane man.[40] In the State of Loo (towards the south of Shan-tung), the army, returned from an expedition, is assembled in the parade-ground called Pwan-kung (IV. ii. III.).[41] They present to the prince the ears that have been cut off; they bring the captive chiefs in chains before the judge, by whom they are condemned by regular sentence.[42] Like the tribes of America, the Chinese then made very few prisoners; they put the vanquished chiefs to death, and released the common soldiers after cutting off one of their ears, as a mark of dishonour, or that they might recognize them if they met with them again.

The parade-ground of the capital of Loo was surrounded with a canal, sown with cress and other plants (IV. ii. III. 1, 2).[43] There they practised archery, and the use of other weapons (ib., 7). Near the palace of king Wăn, there was found a similar ground, named Peih yung (the lake of the Round Tablet),[44] and intended for corporal exercises (III. i. VIII.). A similar parade-ground existed under his son, king Woo, at the capital city Haou (III. i. X. 6). The Le Ke, quoted by the commentator on III. i. VIII., and IV. ii. III., affirms that they gave also to the people in this special place lessons in morality (literally, that they taught them the rites). III. i. VI. mentions young men who were educated according to the institutions of king Wăn.

GENERAL ORGANIZATION OF THE GOVERNMENT. DIGNITIES.

The secondary chiefs, feudatories of the sovereign, had the general designation of *how*, assistants (III. iii. II. 5;[1] IV. ii. IV. 2).[2] They were divided into three principal classes,[3] the special titles of which are found in many odes of the She-king, and are well known as they occur in the Shoo-king and the Chow Le. See also these names in the translation of Mencius by M. Stanislas Julien (V. Pt. ii. II.).[4] Among the principal officers attached to the sovereign, the name of *sze*, instructors, is read in the She-king, (II. iv. VII. 2, 3, and III. i. II. 8).[5] Immediately below the *sze* were the ministers designated by the general term of officers of the right and of the left (III. i. IV. 1),[6] according to the place which they occupied in the ceremonies beside the sovereign. The She-king names among them the *sze-t'oo*, charged with the direction of the civil administration and the instruction of the people (III. i. III. 5); the *sze-k'ung*, charged with the public works (ib.); the *how-tseih*, superin-

40 The left ears of the slain. as also often of captives, were cut off.   41 As to what the Pwan-kung really was, and its form, see the notes on IV. ii. III. It is wrong to speak of it as a parade-ground, or place of exercise.   42 This statement appears to have arisen from a misunderstanding of IV.ii.III. 6.   43 No. There was a semicircular pool in front of the Pwan-kung, and in and about the water grew cress and mallows   44 Peih-yung should be called the Hall with the circlet of water.—Neither the Pwan-kung nor the Peih-yung had anything to do with war.

1 諸侯 is the more common term for the feudal princes, or one of their number. 侯 alone however, is so used here. With regard to the meaning of the term, see on Mencius, V. Pt. ii. II. 3. 2 How here has its special meaning of marquis.   3 They are generally reckoned five classes, but M. Biot probably says they were only three, because their territories were assigned them on a three-fold scale;—acc. to the Shoo and Mencius. See my note on the Shoo, V. iii. 10.   4 M. Julien gives the Chinese names, without trying to translate them, or to give their equivalents in Latin. He mentions, but with disapprobation, Noël's rendering of them by duke, prince, count, marquis, and baron. I have called them duke, marquis, viscount, earl, and baron; and any of them, indifferently, prince.   5 The 太師, the grand-master, grand-tutor, or grand-instructor of the Shoo, V. xx. 5.   6 左右, 'those on the right and on the left' was a very general expression, and might be applied to ministers and attendants of almost no rank.

tendent of agriculture (III. ii. I. 1, *et al*.).[7] We find also in the She-king mention of the *ta-foo*, or grand-prefects, placed over the different districts of every principality (III. iii. IV. 8: I. iv. X. 1, 4),[8] and of the *sze*, scholars, or superior secretaries attached to the sovereign (III. i. IV 2). The complete description of the administrative organization of this period cannot be better seen than in the Chow Le. I have said that I have undertaken the translation of this long work; and therefore I will not enter into a larger account of this subject here.

The secondary chiefs, placed at the head of the different principalities, received as the sign of their dignity, two sorts of tablets of precious stone, one of which, called a *kwei*, was oblong, and the other, called a *peih*, was oval (I. v. I. 3: III. iii. V. 5).[9] When they came to court, they held these before the mouth, in speaking to the sovereign (Yih, art. 40; diagram 玤).[10] These visits of the chiefs were made at two seasons of the year,—spring and autumn (II. iii. V. 4.).[11] Various odes of the first and second Parts contain allusions to tours of inspection, which the sovereign himself made at similar periods, through the different principalities.[11] This exchange of visits and of tours is a proof of the small extent of the Chinese empire in the early times described by the She-king. IV. iii. III., which belongs to the times of the Shang dynasty (from the 18th to the 12th century before our era), gives, it is true, to the State of the sovereign the nominal extent of 1,000 *le*. But Part I. v. VII. says that from the chief town of the State of Sung they could see that of the State of Wei; and Mencius (II. Pt. i. I. 10) mentions the small extent of the kingdom of king Wǎn;[11] saying that the crowing of the cocks and the barking of the dogs were heard from the royal residence to the four limits of the kingdom.

RELIGIOUS BELIEFS.

Several odes of the She-king indicate, in an undeniable manner, the belief in one Supreme Being, Shang-te, the Sovereign Lord. III. i. II. 3 says that king Wǎn honoured Shang-te by a reverent worship, and that thence came the prosperity of this prince and of his race. In the same ode (st. 7) the companions of king Woo say to him, before the famous battle of Muh-yay, 'Shang-te is favourable; let not your soul waver between fear and hope.' 'The favour of Shang-te shown to the arms of king Woo is celebrated in the same terms, in IV. ii. IV. 2. III. i. VII. shows Shang-te wearied with the faults of the families of Hëa and Shang, and calling the family of Chow to replace them. It is Shang-te who directs T'an-foo or king T'ae, the ancient chief of this family, in the countries of the west. He seconds his labours

---

[7] *How-tseih* (后稷) was the name of the minister of agriculture in the times of Yaou and Shun. Throughout the She *How-tseih* is simply the name of the ancestor of the house of Chow.   [8] *Ta-foo* is in the She more a name of dignity, than of territorial rule. In II. iv. X. 2 the designation appears as given to the highest ministers of the kingdom.   [9] But of the *kwei* there were three forms, and of the *peih* two; in all five, corresponding to the 5 orders of nobility.   [10] This is probably a wrong reference, as there is nothing under the 40th diagram, relating to the subject in hand. As to how the *kwei* and *peih* were held at court, Confucius has, no doubt, given us an example. See Ana. X. v. 1.   [11] This is a misstatement. See on the Shoo, VI. i. 8, 9: V. xv. 14. And the reasoning from his own mistake to the small extent of the kingdom of Chow falls to the ground. It was not so large as many people vaguely suppose, yet it was not so small as M. Biot would make out. I. v. VII. cannot be strained to the meaning he gives to it, and Mencius. II. Pt. i. I. 10, is speaking not of the kingdom of king Wǎn, but of the State of Ts'e, showing how thickly it was peopled.

[1] I have, after the best Chinese scholars, put this language into the mouth of Shang-foo, a principal adherent of king Woo. This does not affect the sentiment.

to clear the land, and raises him to the dignity of chief. He chooses among his three sons him who shall be the leader. He encourages his grandson, the sage *par excellence*,—king Wǎu.[2]

In the same way, in Part IV. iii., which contains the songs of the Shang dynasty, the 3d ode says that Shang-te chose the illustrious and courageous Ch'ing T'ang, to reign over the four quarters of the land. The 4th ode celebrates the reverence of Ch'ing T'ang for Shang-te, who was touched by it, and called this virtuous prince to the head of the nine regions.

In the odes of the 3d Book of Part III. which deplore the decadence of Chow, and the public misery, the complaints are addressed to *T'ëen* or Heaven, and to *Shang T'ëen*, or High Heaven. The prayers of king Seuen on account of the drought (III. iii. IV.) are addressed to the Supreme Being, designated by the name of *Shang Tëen*, of *Tëen*, and also of *Shang-te*. King Seuen says that Shang-te has withdrawn His regards from the earth, and abandons it.

Many missionaries have thought, and it has again been recently repeated, that the Chinese have never had but a very uncertain belief in a Supreme Being. This opinion is founded on the circumstance that the expression *T'ëen*, Heaven, is found employed by Chinese moralists more often than the expression *Shang-te*, the Supreme Lord. The quotations which I have just made show us the ideas of the ancient Chinese in a more favourable light. Shang-te is represented by the She-king as a Being perfectly just, who hates no one (II. iv. VIII. 4).

The king, the earthly sovereign, had alone the right to sacrifice to Shang-te, the Supreme Lord; and, according to the Kwoh-yu, and the Tso-chuen, the feudal princes lost all respect for their sovereign, when they arrogated to themselves this right. In IV. ii. IV., written during the decadence of Chow, the prince of the eastern State of Loo celebrates the grand solemnities of spring and autumn.[4] He addresses his prayers first to Shang-te, the Supreme Lord who reigns by Himself alone, and then to the famous K'e, also called How-tseih from the name of the office which he occupied under Yaou.[5] The family of Chow pretended to be descended from this illustrious personage, and addressed their prayers to him as their protector next to Shang-te. The duke of Chow in the same ode, Tang the Successful in IV. iii. II., king Wǎn and king Woo, in the odes which celebrate their virtues, are regarded in the same way as heavenly protectors of the Chinese empire.

The Spirits (*génies*, 神) formed a celestial hierarchy around Shang-te like that of the dignitaries around the king.[6] These Spirits inhabited the air, and surveyed the actions of men.[7] Every family had its ancestors for its tutelary Spirits. Thus

2 M. Biot says in a note that towards the latter part of this ode [throughout it in fact], the Supreme Lord is called simply *Te*, the sovereign; *i.e.* instead of 上帝 we have 帝. I have long ago given my reasons for holding that 帝 means God, and 上帝 is merely God emphatic;— corresponding to the *Elohim* and *Ha-Elohim* of the Hebrews.   3 This and the preceding paragraphs would have been eagerly quoted between 20 and 25 years ago by the Protestant missionaries, who were then divided on the question of the name for God in Chinese. The advocates of 上帝 would have been glad to claim the support of Biot's name. Nothing can be more evident in the She and other ancient Books than that Shang-te is the name of the Supreme Being, and a personal name, by which all about God may be taught to the Chinese.   4 They were bound, and all feudal princes were bound, to offer the seasonal sacrifices to their ancestors.   5 It must be remembered that the princes of Loo claimed great privileges, by royal grant to the duke of Chow. in the matter of sacrifices.   6 The She-king does not say so, nor any other of the classics, so far as I recollect.   7 In III. i. I. 1, king Wǎn appears in the presence of God.

160]

How-tseih and the kings Wǎn and Woo were the tutelary Spirits of the family of Chow (II. vi. V.: III. iii. IV.). In III. ii. VIII., made in honour of king Ch'ing, it is said that the Spirits recognize him as sovereign king.[8] In II. i. V. 1, two friends in giving to each other pledges of affection, say:—

> 'The Spirit who hears our words,
> Approves them and confirms the concord of our souls.'[9]

In III. iii. II. 7, we read:—

> 'Do not say, "No one will see it,
> No one will know it."
> We cannot know if the superior Spirits
> Are not looking upon us.'[9]

Besides the tutelary Spirits special to each family, every mountain had its Spirit, and every great river (III. iii. V. 1). Each district even had its protecting Spirit, and the Spirit of the ground was invoked at the solemnities which opened and terminated the agricultural labours of the year. At epochs of great prosperity,[10] the Spirits appeared under the form of a fabulous quadruped, the k's-lin, or of a bird equally fabulous, the fung-hwang. I. i. XI. says that the three sons of king Wǎn represented the feet, the head, and the horn of the k's-lin.[11] III. ii. VIII. celebrates the bird fung-hwang, which appears and walks about during the reign of king Ch'ing. Fung-hwang is the Chinese phœnix.

LOTS. AUGURIES.

At the foundation of a city, and in general for any affair difficult to decide upon, they consulted the lots (I. iv. VI. 2). This was done in two ways:—by a certain plant called she; or by the shell of the tortoise (I. v. IV. 2: II. i. IX. 4; v. I. 3). We do not know well how the divination was performed formerly by the plant she. At the present day, they place on the right and on the left a packet of leaves of this plant; then they recite some mysterious words, and by taking a handful of leaves from each packet, they prognosticate according to their number.[1] The divination by the tortoise was made by placing fire on the tortoise-shell, and auguring by the direction of the cracks made upon it by the heat.[2] In III. i. III. 3 the ancient chief Tan-foo places fire on the tortoise-shell before settling his tribe at the foot of mount K'e. Certain officers had the charge of interpreting the dreams of the king (II. iv. VIII. 5). Soothsayers also interpreted the dreams of men in power (II. iv. VI. 4). The sight of a magpie was a good omen (I. ii. I.)[3] It was on the contrary unlucky to see a black crow or a red fox (I. iii. XVI. 3). They dared not point to the rainbow with the finger (I. iv. VII.).[4]

PRIMITIVE ASTRONOMY.

The first observers of the stars sought to read the future by them; and thus, immediately after the art of augury, I ought to mention the first indications of

---

8 This is a misinterpretation, probably, of st. 3.
10 When a sage monarch was on the throne.
belongs to all the sons of king Wǎn. He had not only three;—I think I have read of their being as many as 80.
1 Perhaps feuilles should here be taken as stalks. Stalks, and not leaves, have always been mentioned to me by Chinese describing the method of divination
ink or some similar substance. See the note on the Shoo. V. iv. parr. 21—23.
nothing in the ode about the sight of the magpie being a good omen.
bow was in the east.

9 See the notes on these two passages.
11 See the ode referred to. Each stanza
2 The shell was smeared with
3 There is
4 Only when the rainbow

astronomy which are found in the She-king. Of the 28 stellary divisions of the Chinese sky, we find 8 mentioned in different odes (I. ii. X.; iv. VI.; x. V.; xv. I.: II. v. VI. and IX);—viz., Ts'an, Maou, Ting or Ying-shih, Ho-sing or San-sing (corresponding to the division Sin), New, T'ëen-peih, Tow, and Ke. We see here also the notion about the constellation Chih-neu (corresponding to Lyra), and the mention of the Celestial river,—the Milky way (II. v. IX.). Finally, in the same ode (st. 6) the planet Venus is indicated by two different names, according as she appears in the east or in the west. The Milky way is again mentioned in several odes (III. i. IV.: iii. IV. 1). II. iv. IX. contains the mention of the celebrated solar eclipse of B.C. 776 [or 775, counting A.D. as 0, as I have done], which is the first certain date of Chinese chronology. The importance attached to the observation of the stars may be deduced from the celebrity of the observatory of king Wăn, called the tower of the heavenly Spirit (III. i. VIII.)[1] The entire population of the tribe had united in its construction.[2] Before king Wăn, his ancestor duke Lëw, referred by tradition to the 17th or 18th century before our era, had already determined the position of his residence by the observation of the solar shadow (III. ii. VI 5).[3]

CEREMONIES AND RELIGIOUS SOLEMNITIES. WORSHIP.

The solemn ceremonies, or sacrifices in honour of Shang-te and of the celestial Spirits, took place at the two solstices and the two equinoxes.[1] The precise determination of these great epochs of the year formed part of the rites, and it is thus that the observation of the length of the shadow of the gnomon at the summer solstice in the capital is mentioned as a sacred rite in the Chow Le, IX. 25.[2] The ceremony of the spring, which commenced at the winter solstice, under the Chow, was called yoh.[3] The ceremony of the summer at the vernal equinox was called sze.[3] The ceremony of autumn at the summer solstice was called ching; and that of winter, at the autumnal equinox, was called shang (II. i. VI. 4; vi. V.).[3] Near the royal palace, (III. i. III. 7) a site named shay was specially consecrated to the Spirit of the ground.[4] About the commencement of the year, a sacrifice was offered in every district to the producing Spirit of the ground, and to the Spirit of the place (II. vi. VII. 2 : III. iii. IV. 6).[5] An analogous sacrifice was presented in autumn after the harvest (IV. i. [ii.] IV.). We see in the Chow Le, XX.—XXVII., that the right to perform sacrifice to the different celestial Spirits was graduated according to the order of dignities and offices. According to this graduation, the lower people of the country districts could sacrifice only to the ground and the secondary Spirits. This regulation must have facilitated the extension of the belief in Spirits so natural to all peoples only a little enlightened.

1 See the notes on III. i. VIII. 1 for the meaning of the phrase 靈 臺   2 This is not said in the ode.   3 Rather had determined the four cardinal points.
1 In this paragraph M. Biot has confounded the sacrifices to Shang-te, and those in the ancestral temple. The She does not speak of the sacrifices to Shang-te, and I need only say that the great sacrifice to Him was at the winter solstice, which was also said to be to the Spirit (or Spirits) of heaven (天 神). At the summer solstice He was also sacrificed to, and the sacrifice was said to be to the Spirit (or Spirits) of earth (地 祇). See on the 'Doctrine of the Mean,' XIX. 6.
2 It does not appear that this had any thing to do with the sacrifice to Shang-te.   3 Yoh, sze, ching, shang were the names of the seasonal sacrifices in the ancestral temple. Yoh was the spring sacrifice, sze that of summer, shang that of autumn, and ching that of winter. They were celebrated not at the equinoxes and solstices; but in the first months of the respective seasons.
4 See on the Shoo, III. i. Pt. i. 35.   5 See the note on II. vi. VII. 2.

At the same great epochs of the year, a ceremony was performed in each family, in honour of its ancestors, which was followed by a grand feast and rejoicings.[6] In this ceremony, the principal ancestor was represented by a child,[7] designated by the name of *she* (尸, literally, the defunct), or of *kung she*, 'the illustrious defunct (II. i. VI.; vi. VI. 3).'[7] This child kept himself motionless while they presented to him viands, fruits, and spirits (II. vi. VI. 3), and they augured the future prosperity of the family from the words which might escape from him (III. ii. III. and IV.). They thought that it was the dead who spoke by his mouth. This child came afterwards to take part in the feast (III. ii. IV.), which endured for at least two days.[8]

They prepared themselves for this ceremony by washing the body, and by abstaining, for several days, from unbecoming words and actions (II. i VI. 4). Prayers were offered at the gate of the Hall of ancestors (II. vi. V. 2),[9] where there was a genealogical table of the family (IV. i. [ii.] VIII.).[10] During these prayers they prepared the solemn repast. Some stript off the skin from the sheep and the oxen, with a knife which was adorned with small bells (II. vi. VI. 5);[11] others roasted and grilled the meats. They extracted the blood and the fat of the slain animals, and seasoned the flesh (II. vi. V. and VI.). The lambs offered by the princes to their ancestors were dyed red,[12] the colour of the Chow dynasty (II. vi. VI. 5). The princes offered also in sacrifice white bulls and red bulls (IV. ii. IV. 4)[13]

They invited to the feast the friends of the family, and gave them presents of pieces of silk in baskets (II. i. I. 1).[14] During the festival they practised shooting with the bow at a target (III. ii. II. 3),[15] and each of those who hit it presented a full cup of wine to those who were unsuccessful (II. vii. VI. 1). At table, they placed the guests on the left and right of the host (II. vii. VI. 1), according to their rank and age (Doctrine of the Mean, XIX). Bells, drums, and other instruments of music sounded in sign of rejoicing (II. vi. V. 6).

These instruments were the same as those which now-a-days are used for the Chinese music. The She-king mentions the *k'in*, a kind of guitar with 5 or 7 strings; the *shih*, another guitar with 25 strings (I. i. I. 3: II. vi. IV. 4); cymbals (I. v. II.);[16] the *sang*, a flute with many tubes, fitted at the opening with a thin metallic plate which vibrated (II. i. I. 1: vi. IV. 4);[17] the *heuen*, a kind of flute with six holes

6 Yes, in each family; but all the illustrations are drawn from what took place in the royal family. The ceremonies took place, it must be borne in mind, not in the house, but in the ancestral temple. 7 No. Possibly, if there were no other member of the family or clan suitable for the position, a child might fill it; but in general the representative of the dead was a grown-up man. M. Biot observes in a note that this custom has always been preserved in China, and that it may be connected with the ideas of the transmigration of souls. He adds that it brings to mind the well known custom in Thibet, where the officers of the court, on the death of every Lama, proceed to choose an infant in the cradle to succeed him, recognizing from divers conventional signs his character as *dalay-lama*. Unfortunately for this ingenious speculation, there are the facts that the personator of the dead was not a child, and that the custom has *not* been preserved in China It did not continue in fact much, if at all, beyond the Chow dynasty.   7 公尸 (kung she) means the representatives of the ancestors,—the former dukes of the House of Chow. See the note on III. ii. III. 3.   8 See the notes, on III. ii. IV.   It must be borne in mind that there was not one personator of the dead only at these ancestral sacrifices.   9 See the note on the passage referred to.   10 Nothing of the kind appears in IV. i. [ii.] VIII.   11 The king, presiding at the sacrifice, used such a knife in killing the bull, or principal victim at the sacrifice.   12 This is a mere imagination of M. Biot.   13 Only to the duke of Chow did the marquises of Loo sacrifice a white bull. See the note on the passage referred to.   14 The feast in II. i. I. was not after a sacrifice;—see the notes upon it.   15 It is very doubtful whether such an exercise was practised in connexion with any sacrificial feast.   16 No instrument of music is mentioned in L v. II. I do not think that cymbals are anywhere mentioned in the She. Possibly M. Biot may have in view the *ching* in II iii. IV. 3, which I have called a *jingle*. It was used in war.   17 The *sang* was a rudimentary organ.

(II. v. V. 7);[18] the *ch'e*, a kind of cornet of baked earth, pierced in the side with six holes *(ib.)*;[19] the *k'ing*, of square shape, and struck with a wand like our triangle, and which was used to accompany the flute (II. vi. IV. 4;[20] IV. iii. I.). Other instruments are called *ch'uh* and *yu* (IV. i. [ii.] V ; they appear to have been flutes with many tubes.[21] There were also several kinds of drums (IV. iii. I.) The Chow Le gives many details about the instruments of music in Book XXII. The large memoir of Amyot on Chinese music, in the 6th volume of the Memoirs by the missionaries, may also be consulted.

The ordinary musicians were blind men (III. i. VIII. 4. IV. i. [ii.] V.). 'The blind man is arrived,' says this last ode; and we call to mind also the passage in the Shoo-king on the famous eclipse of Chung-k'ang :—'The blind man has beaten his drum (Shoo, III. iv. 4).' II. vi. IV. 4 mentions the ritual songs *Ya* and *Nan*, the former meaning, according to the commentary, songs taken from Parts II. and III of the She-king, and the latter songs from the first two Books of Part I., and which belonged to the two ancient States of Chow-nan and Shaou-nan, governed by the early princes of the Chow family.

To the sound of the music they executed various dances. The dance *wan* was grave (I. iii. XIII. 1 : IV. ii IV. 4; iii. I.).[22] In the dance *yoh*[23] they held an instrument in their hands (II. vi. IV. 4). They varied the position of the body by bending and then straightening themselves (II. i. V. 3).[24] They also danced holding a feather in the right hand and a flute in the left (I. vi. III.; iii. XIII, 3). The Chow Le enumerates various kinds of dances in chapter XXII.

The dignitaries received at court said to the sovereign (III. i. VI.) :—'May your happiness be like a large mountain, like an elevated plain, like a perpetual spring; may it increase like the moon going on to be full; like the sun ascending; may your body be preserved like the pine and the cypress whose leaves are always green!'[25] At special entertainments, the guests desired for the master of the house a life of a thousand and ten thousand years (II. vi. IX. 3); that he might have an old age such that his back would be wrinkled like that of a porpoise (III. ii. II. 4); that he might have at the age of 80 the vigour of a man of 50;[26] and finally that he might preserve his health for 11,000 years (IV. ii. IV. 5).[26]

FORMALITIES OF MARRIAGE.

Similar rejoicings took place at marriages. When two families wished to form a matrimonical alliance, the negociation was conducted by a man and a woman, who went to make the proposal to the two Houses (I. viii. VI. 3; xv. V. 1).[1] This

18 The *heuen* was not a flute at all. See the note on II. v. V. 7   19 The *ch'e* was of bamboo; and the *heuen* of baked earth.   20 See Medhurst's dictionary on the *k'ing* (磬).
21 See the notes on IV. i. [ii.] V. The *ch'uh* and *yu* were not flutes, nor indeed instruments of music at all.   22 In these passages M. Biot seems to have taken 萬 舞 as meaning the dance *wan*, whereas *wan* was the name of *military* dances, and *woo* of *civil*.   23 *Yoh* was not the name of a dance, but of the flute which the dancers held in their hands.   24 No doubt they did so; but 蹲 蹲 hardly says so.   25 This was on a particular occasion, at the conclusion, we may suppose, of the feast following the seasonal sacrifices.   26 I do not know any place where this wish is expressed. II. ii. IV. 5, l. 15, desires for the ruler an old age ever vigorous; but without any such specification, as Biot supposes, of the age of 80 and the vigour of 50. I cannot think that 萬 有 千 年 in III. ii. IV. 5. l. 16 is to be thus grotesquely understood of 11,000 years, but, as in my translation, for—thousands and myriads of years.
1 I do not know that there were two go-betweens to a marriage, and certainly the idea of their representing the future partners is imaginary. The go-between might be of either sex.

usage still exists in China, in Tartary, and even in central Russia. The male and female go-betweens were the representatives of the future spouses, as it is expressed in I. xv. V. 1,

> 'In hewing [the wood for] an axe-handle, how do you proceed?
> Without another axe it cannot be done.
> In taking a wife, how do you proceed?
> Without a go-between it cannot be done.'

In the P'e-p'a Ke, a drama of the 9th century, the go-between presents herself with an axe as the emblem of her mission, and cites upon the subject this passage of the She-king. The commentary does not say whether this custom of carrying an axe as an emblem be ancient. The go-between makes even a parade of her learning in explaining to the father of the young lady, whom she is come to ask for, why she carries an axe.

Marriages were arranged at the commencement of the year before the ice was melted by the return of the heat (I. iii. IX. 3); and the ceremony took place at the flowering of the peach tree (I. i. VI.): Mention of these epoques is found in the Hëa Sëaou ching.[2] The songs of rejoicing compare the bride to the flowers of the peach and apricot-trees (I. ii. XIII. 2).

When the bride was of a noble family, she was conducted to her husband (I v. III. 2) in a chariot adorned with feathers of the teih (a kind of pelican according to the description of the commentary).[3] Musicians and a numerous suite accompanied her (I. ii. I. The Yih, art. 54, Diagram 兌).[4] The husband awaited his future wife at the door of the house (I. viii. III.). The arrival of the cortege was the signal for the commencement of the rejoicings (I. i. i., the epithalamium of king Wän).

King Woo and his brother the duke of Chow consecrated by special regulations the sanctity of marriage (I. ii. VI.).[5] This ode speaks of ceremonies of engagement and of the intervention of the magistrate. Every union which had not been so consecrated was declared illegitimate, and the offenders were punished. I. vi. IX. makes allusion to those regulations, and shows us a young lady who refuses to take a husband without fulfilling those formalities.

Generally they preferred marrying in their own district.[6] A princess of the State of Wei (Ho-nan) complains (I. iii. XIV.) of being married outside her own country.[6] I. i. IX. recommends young Chinese not to go to seek for wives on the other side of the Han and the Këang in the country of the barbarians.[7] After having sojourned in the house of her husband, the new wife returned to pass two or three months with her parents.[8] We have an example of this practice in the wife of king Wän (I. i. II. and III.)[9] It exists in China at the present day.

The legitimate wife could not be repudiated but for a very grave cause;—she was then almost dishonoured. Thus in I. iii. X. a rejected wife bitterly bewails her lot, while her husband is espousing another. On no pretext had a wife the right to separate from her husband. A princess of the State of Wei forsaken by her husband, who has taken a mistress, speaks of this mistress as her friend (I. iii. III.).[10] In

2 See the Journal Asiatique, for December, 1840.   3 The teih was a pheasant.   3 The diagram 兌 says nothing on the subject.   5 This ode refers to a time before the duke of Chow had formed the code of Chow laws.   6 It was the contrary with ladies of noble birth. The complaint in I. iii. XIV. is altogether of another matter. 7 The meaning of this ode is quite different.   8 Ode III. says nothing at all on the subject.   9 The return of the wife to visit her parents is a subject on which opinions are much divided.   10 M. Biot has strangely misunderstood this ode.

the China of that time, as in the China of the present day, woman was generally doomed to a state of inferior submission which deprived her of all elevated feeling;—her sole duty was to serve her husband. The practice of having concubines, or wives of a second grade, besides the legitimate wife, was frequent among the chiefs. Concubines are mentioned in the 33d and (?) 37th articles of the Yih-king (the diagrams 漸 and 家人). Every legitimate wife desired to be interred near her husband (I. x. XI. 4, 5.).[11] They esteemed widows who refused to marry again (I. iv. I.). A married woman could not, during the time of the mourning, enter the house of her deceased parents (I. iv. X.)[12];—she was not deemed sufficiently pure to present herself in the place which had for the time become sacred.[12] The ancient Chinese, like those of our days manifested a great indifference for the preservation of female infants. A daughter who was born was regarded as a burden to the family, while they rejoiced in the birth of a son, who would be the future support of his father (III. ii. II.). II. iv. V. establishes perfectly this contrast, representing to us the manner in which they received in the royal family the birth of a boy or of a girl:—

> 'A son is born.
> He is placed upon a bed,
> And clothed with brilliant stuffs.
> They give him a semi-sceptre.
> His cries are frequent.
> They clothe the lower part of his body with red cloth.
> The master, the chief sovereign is born, and to him they give the empire.'

> 'A daughter is born:—
> They place her on the ground;
> They wrap her in common cloths;
> They place a tile near to her.
> There is not in her either good or evil.
> Let her learn how to prepare the wine and cook the food.
> Above all she ought to exert herself not to be a charge to her parents.'[13]

The present Chinese have still this custom of placing a tile upon the clothes of the newly born daughter.[14] They explain it by saying that formerly the women used a tile to press the cloth which they wove, and thus the tile which they place near the infant is an emblem which indicates that the weaving of cloth will be her principal occupation.

DOMESTIC MANNERS AND SLAVERY.

Several odes of the first Part of the She-king express the regrets of wives while their husbands are absent on the service of the prince (I. ii. III. and VIII.; iii. (?).; xi. VII. (?).; xii. X. (?).), and their satisfaction when they return III. viii. IV. (?). Other odes, of a later date, during the decay of the Chow dynasty, deplore on the contrary the relaxation of morality. The men are drunken and debauched, and the women are immodest (I. iii. VII. and IX.; iv. II.—V., VII. and VIII.; xii. IX.).

We do not see in the She-king any notice which points clearly to the existence of slavery properly so called, and this silence agrees with the custom of making few prisoners, which I have noted above. As the two terms *noo* and *pei* (奴, a male slave; 婢, a female slave) are not found in the classes of the population mentioned

11 The conclusion from the ode is too general. See in the Life of Confucius, Vol. I., proleg., p. 15.   12 This again is Biot's own imagination. The case, for illustration of which we may refer to I. iv. X., was, that a lady married into another State could not go back to her native State after her parents were dead.   13 See the translation of these two stanzas at pp. 306, 307.   14 I know of no such practice. M. Biot has misunderstood the lines 載弄之璋. 載弄之瓦.

in the *Chow le* (Ch. II., parr. 44—53), domestics being there designated by the name of *shin ts'ëeh* (臣, a servant, 妾, a wife of the second grade), Chinese authors generally affirm that there were no slaves under the Chow dynasty.[1]   But this assertion is contradicted by a passage of the Shoo-king (V. xxiv. 4), where Pih-k'in, son of the duke of Chow, declares that the valets and women of the second rank who shall have run away must be returned to their masters, and by a passage of the Chow-le itself, (Ch. XIV. par. 22), where the officer in charge of the market is ordered to control the sale of men, cattle, horses, arms, utensils, &c.

PUNISHMENTS.

The punishment of mutilation is mentioned in the She-king.   In II. v. VI. a culprit is condemned to become a eunuch, and laments his lot[1]   He becomes a *sze-jin* (寺 人).[1]   This name, which signifies a man of the palace, and which is also found in I. xii. I. I, has long been the designation for the eunuchs attached to the court.   The commentary on the She-king so explains it, and the complaints of the condemned in II. v. VI. prove that he was about to under go a severe punishment.   Mutilation is mentioned in the Shoo-king, V. xxvii. 3, among the punishments appointed by king Muh.

PROVERBS AND PREJUDICES.

We find some ancient Chinese proverbs quoted in the She-king, all of a very great simplicity, and connected with the habits of a country life.[1]   For example:—'Do not add mud to one in the mud (II. vii. IX. 6);' 'There is no need to teach a monkey to climb trees *(ib.);'* 'The sage himself can speak nonsense (III. iii. II. 1); 'He who takes hold of a piece of hot iron hastens to plunge his hand into water (III. iii. III. 5);' 'He who wishes to remedy a public misfortune is like a man who wishes to march against a violent wind *(ib.* 6); 'Virtue is like a hair; it is as flexible as one (III. iii. VI. 6).'

There are in the She-king other proverbs as simple as these, which I shall not quote; but I will mention two singular sayings which are found in these ancient songs. The one of them occurs in II. v. III. 8:—'The sage does not speak imprudently, for there are ears near the walls of his chamber;'—which corresponds to a common saying in our language.   The other appears to me equally curious.   A man, joyous at seeing once more one of his friends, says (II. iii. II. 3), 'I am as satisfied as if they had given me 100 sets of cowries.'   I would take occasion to notice here both the mention of the ancient practice of using shells for money, and the singularity of this numerical appreciation of joy.   Now-a-days the Chinese still say, in speaking of a fortunate event, ' It is a joy of a thousand or ten thousand;'—meaning so many pieces of money. Chinese romances give us many examples of this mode of speech, which would seem to belong exclusively to the language of financiers.

1 The K'een-lung editors of the *Chow-le* in a note on ch. II. par. 52, refer to this other passage in proof that anciently there were slaves, and also to the Yih, diagram 23, par. 4, proposing a different interpretation of the 妾 in 臣妾.   As the *Chow-le*, XIV. 32. conflicts with the general opinion that anciently there were no slaves, Wang T'aou says that it is not a work sufficiently authenticated to be appealed to for evidence on such a point.

1 See the notes on this ode.

1 It will be well for the reader to refer to the various passages here adduced by M. Biot, and the notes upon them in the body of this volume.

It is common with the Anglo-Americans (?), and characterizes very well the development of the purely material interest among them as among the Chinese.

Such are the principal characteristic traits which may be collected from the She-king to furnish a general sketch of the ancient manners of the Chinese. I consider it useful to add a brief notice of the historical facts which this collection contains. These facts, united with those which are set forth more methodically in the Shoo-king, were the first landmarks of which the famous Sze-ma Ts'ëen availed himself, in the 1st century B.C., to frame in his Historical Records the history of ancient China.

FACTS OF HISTORY.[1]

Several odes mention the name of some of the sovereign chiefs of the early dynasties. The labours of the great Yu are mentioned in II. vi. VI. 1, and III. iii. VII. 1. III. i. X. 5 says that the course of the river Fung in Shen-se was regulated by him. IV. iii. IV. 1 says positively that he delivered the world from the flood. The division of the empire by him into principalities is mentioned in the 6th stanza of the same ode. Këeh, the last sovereign of the dynasty of Hëa, is named in the same stanza. The Book where this ode occurs is composed entirely of odes in honour of the second dynasty, that of Shang;—the most ancient of all the odes. We find there (odes 3 and 4) an account of the miraculous birth of Sëeh, the minister of Shun, to whom the kings of Shang traced their genealogy; the mention of Sëang-t'oo, the grandson of Sëeh (ode 4); the eulogium of Ch'ing-t'ang the first sovereign of Shang (also ode 4); and finally, (in odes 3 and 5), that of Woo-ting, who reigned about 400 years after Ch'ing-t'ang. The 3d ode says, 'The Supreme Lord willed that Ch'ing-t'ang should have under his orders the nine provinces or regions. These are the nine regions of the Shoo-king III. i.; they comprehended all under heaven (下 天), in other words, the world then known to the Chinese. The same ode says, 'What is under the heaven is limited by the four seas.' Among the greater part of the Chinese all geography is still confined to these absurd notions.

The 4th ode of the same Book depicts with extraordinary energy the exaltation of Ch'ing-t'ang, arming himself at the order of Heaven, against the tyrant Këeh:— 'His resolution is taken; he seizes an axe; he rushes forward like a devouring fire; he cries, "Who will dare to resist me?" He defeats the chiefs of Wei and of Koo; he attacks the chief of Keun-woo, and finally Këeh himself, the sovereign-chief of Hëa.' Ch'ing-t'ang cuts down first the three buds which are attached to the new shoot. Këeh is the plant, and the other chiefs who were on his side are represented by the three buds. This comparison is a very singular one.

The expedition of Woo-ting against the strange tribes of Hoo-kwang, those of King-ts'oo, is mentioned in ode 5 of the same Book, and A-hăng, the principal minister of Ch'ing-t'ang in ode 4.

The odes of the first and second Books of Part III. celebrate the origin of the family of Chow, and the great victory of king Woo over the last sovereign chief of the Shang family. II. i. relates the miraculous birth of K'e, the great ancestor of the family and the first minister of agriculture under Shun, from which he derived his name of How-tseih, 'superintendent of millet,' under which he is invoked. Duke

---

[1] I do not offer any criticisms on the statements on this article, but only refer the reader to the odes referred to, and the notes upon them.

Lëw, his descendant, who established himself, on the west of the Yellow river, in Shen-se, is celebrated in ode VI. of the same Book, which is attributed to the duke of Shaou, the second brother of king Woo. According to this ode, duke Lëw founded a city, determined its position or boundaries by the shadow of the sun, built houses for travellers; and knew how to cross rivers with boats or on bridges. Besides this, he extracted iron from mines, and stone from quarries, and regulated the land tax. The text does not indicate the rate of this tax. III. i. does not go higher than T'an-foo, or the ancient duke, the grandfather of king Wăn, and relates that this chief transported his tribe to the foot of mount K'e. I have already cited this ode, which says that T'an-foo and his people lived at first in caves. I have explained, by the devastations of the Tartar hordes, the rapid destruction of the first establishments made by duke Lëw. T'an-foo is also called king T ae, the great king or the great sovereign (III. i. VII.). This ode names his two sons, king Ke or Ke-leih, and T'ae-pih, of whom the younger, king Ke, is chosen to succeed to the command.

Ode VI. contains the eulogium of Chow Këang, wife of T'an-foo, and of T'ae-jin, her daughter-in-law, the mother of king Wăn. This prince and his son king Woo are celebrated in too many odes for me to make extracts from them in detail. The two brothers of king Woo, the dukes of Chow and Shaou, so called from the names of their principalities, Chow and Shaou, are credited with the composition of a great number of the ritual songs of the She-king, and are both celebrated and named in several odes. I will mention, for the duke of Chow, I. xv. IV., and IV. ii. IV., and for the duke of Shaou, I. ii. V., and III. iii. VIII., and XI.

Wei-tsze [the viscount of Wei], the brother of the tyrant Chow, became prince of Sung, on submitting himself to king Woo. His descendants, as well as the princes of Ke, who were descended from the sovereigns of Hëa, always preserved the privilege of taking part, along with the king of the family of Chow, in the ceremony to ancestors (IV. i. [ii.] III.). We find this passage quoted in the Doctrine of the Mean, ch. XXIX. King Ch'ing, the just king, the son of king Woo, is celebrated in III. ii. VII. and VIII. In this same Part of the She-king, iii. I. is directed against king Le, says that the world is filled with robbers, and makes allusion to the disorders which augment through the carelessness of king Le. Ode IV. contains the prayers of his son and successor, king Seuen, requesting from Heaven the end of a great drought. Under the same prince, ode V. celebrates the earl of Shin, king Seuen's uncle, and ode VI., Chung Shan-foo, the grand-master, in the name of the sovereign. Ode VII. describes the visit of the marquis of Han to the royal court, and vaunts the riches of his country of Han. In ode VIII. Hoo, earl of Shaou, a general of king Seuen, marches against the barbarians of the south, on the Këang and the Han, and against the wild E tribes, which occupied the valley of the Hwae. The ode says that after this expedition all was pacified and reduced to order as far as the sea of the south; and here, as in the Historical Records, under the 37th year of the first emperor of Ts'in, this expression, the sea of the south, simply designates the sea which borders Cheh-këang, then the country of Yueh, and extends to the mouth of the Këang.

Ode IX. celebrates another expedition directed by king Seuen in person against the barbarians of the Hwae, in the country of Foo and Seu, the names of which still belong to districts on the left bank of the Hwae. King Seuen subdues everything before him. The style of this ode is very spirited, with a warlike ardour which we see in

169]

three or four odes, all *official*, of the She-king. The expeditions which I have just mentioned took place about the year 826 before our era.

The troubles of the reign of king Yëw are announced in II. iv. IX., with the mention of the solar eclipse of the year B.C. 776, which begins the certain chronology of China. Odes VII., VIII., and IX. of the same Book deplore the wickedness of the beautiful Paou Sze, who proved the destruction of king Yëw, and the general disorder of the kingdom. II. iv. VIII., v. III., and III. iii. VIII. and IX. relate to the same subject. The 10th ode of the 3d Bk. says:—

> 'Never will the misfortunes cease,
> While there shall be at court the wife and the ennuchs.'

These last are designated by the character *sze* (寺), literally officers of the palace ; and the interpretation of the commentators is verified by II. v. VI., where a man is in despair at being condemned to be a *sze* in the palace, as his punishment for a grave fault. After the re-establishment in the capital of king Yëw's son, the feeble king P'ing, we find some *sze* or eunuchs attached to the palace of duke Sëang, prince of Ts'in (I. xi. I.).

In I. xi., which contains the songs of the State of Ts'in, ode VI. deplores the death of three brothers, killed at the tomb of duke Muh, in the year 621 B.C. The Tso Chuen gives 177 individuals as killed or buried alive at the bloody funeral rites of this prince. The ode expresses astonishment at this barbarous sacrifice, a custom which had been recently taken from the Tartars.

I have mentioned the names of several foreign tribes of which we read in the She-king. We see there, on the north and the northwest, the Hëen-yun and the Jung, who occupied the plateau of T'ae-ynen under king Seuen (II. iii. III.); on the south, the Man and the King, settled in the valleys of the Këang and the Han (III. iii. VI. (?); and to the west, the uncivilized tribes of the Hwae and of Seu. These neighbouring savages came to plunder the husbandmen in the lower valley of the Yellow river, and we thus recognize perfectly the limits of the Chinese empire of this period. The first principalities, or feudatory divisions, established by king Woo, were in general of small extent. In I. v. VII. a princess of Wei regrets that she was not able to go to her son, who was become prince of Sung. She says, ' Nevertheless from our district or city of Wei we can see that of Sung by standing on tiptoe. The little river which separates the two countries may be crossed by throwing into it some reeds.'

The wars of one small State with another, which multiplied during the decay of the Chow dynasty, desolated the plains and ruined the small farmers, as we perceive in various odes. In I. iii. XVI. the families of the country of Wei fly to avoid the evils of war. In I. iv. VI. a prince of Wei retreats, in B.C. 660, before the barbarians of the north, and passes to the other side of the Yellow river, to fix himself in the territory of the present department of Kwei-tih. I. vi. VI. and VII. deplore the intestine wars in the time of king P'ing. In ode V. of the same Book a woman is abandoned by her husband, who can no longer support her. The settlers emigrate from the small State of Wei (衛), in the pres. Shan-se, as related in I. ix. VII. Other emigrants bewail their lot in II. iii. VII., and iv. IV. An orphan deplores his isolation in I. x. VI. A poor man laments his condition in II. viii. VI. In ode IX. of the same Book a man cries out, ' If my parents had known that I should be thus miserable, they would not have brought me into the world.' The same weariness life appears in II. iv. VIII. III. ii. X. upbraids the passiveness of certain good men, who kept themselves quiet like the infant *she*, or personator of the dead in the ceremonies; it advises them to listen to the complaints of the poor farmers, who carry on their shoulders the plants they have cut down, *i.e*, who perform painful labours. Ode I. of the next Book regrets the loss of the ancient majesty of the royal court.

Such is a slight sketch of the *data* furnished by the She-king for the history of the wars and revolutions of ancient China. We have seen the notices much more numerous which it supplies us with for the history of the manners of this early age, and which serve to justify or illustrate the fuller exhibitions of the Le Ke, as the others became the base of the memoirs by Sze-ma Ts'öen.

To complete my labour, I had prepared a table of the quadrupeds, birds, fishes, reptiles, and vegetables mentioned in the She-king. As all the odes in this collection relate to the countries comprised between the 33rd and 38th degrees of latitude, it appeared to me desirable to study both the species of the animal kingdom and of the vegetable kingdom, which formerly existed on this zone of eastern Asia, and I should say that this same thought occurred before me to a Chinese author, who has written a special treatise precisely on this subject. M. Julien was good enough to procure for me from his library this Work, adorned with figures, and mentioned in the Chrestomathy of M. Bridgman. I have been able to consult, besides, the identifications given by M. Remusat in his general index to the Japanese encyclopædia, vol. XI. of Notices of Manuscripts. Unfortunately, those helps were still insufficient to afford a sure identification of all the names mentioned in the She-king with the species which we are acquainted with. The animals may generally be recognised, because their names have not varied. The figures of the Japanese Encyclopædia and of the treatise to which I have referred being happily accompanied with descriptions, we learn that different species such as the tiger, the leopard, the rhinoceros, and the jackal, were successively driven from northern and central China by the clearing of the forests. We find unmistakeable mention of the monkey, and the elephant would appear to have existed in eastern China from the 25th to the 28th degree of latitude. But there is still uncertainty about some species of which the description is mingled with fables. As for the vegetables, the figures in the Pun-ts'aou, the Japanese Encyclopædia, and the Chinese treatise, are excessively incorrect, and the descriptions are very vague. The author of the treatise proves even that frequently one and the same name designates different vegetable species in different parts of China, and the commentators themselves often vary in the identification of the name in the She-king with the plants which they know according to their Pun-ts'aou.

With elements so uncertain I believe it more prudent not to publish the table which I had prepared. I refer the reader to the notes appended by Lacharme to his translation of the She-king, and will here terminate my researches on a monument so curious and so authentic of the ancient Chinese civilization.

CHAPTER V.

LIST OF THE PRINCIPAL WORKS WHICH HAVE BEEN CONSULTED IN THE PREPARATION OF THIS VOLUME.

SECTION I.

CHINESE WORKS; WITH BRIEF NOTICES OF THEM.

1. In the 十三經註疏 (see proleg. to vol. I., p. 129):—

[i.] 毛詩註疏, containing Maou's Explanations of the She (see p. 11; but whether this was the work of Maou Chang, as there stated, or of his predecessor Maou Hăng, is not positively determined), and Ch'ing K'ang-shing's 'Supplementary Commentary to the She of Maou (see also p. 11),' with his 'Chronological Introduction to the She (pp. 11, 12).' There are in it also of course K'ung Ying-tah's own paraphrase of Maou and Ch'ing (正義), and supplemental discussions, with citations from Wang Suh's (王肅) Works on the She, from Lëw Choh (劉焯) and Lëw Heuen (劉炫) of the Suy dynasty, and from other early writers. The edition which I have used is beautifully printed, and appeared in 1815 (嘉慶二十年江西南昌府學開雕), under the supervision of Yuen Yuen (see proleg. to vol. I., p. 133). It contains his examination of the text of all K'ung Ying-tah's work (毛詩註疏挍勘記);—a very valuable addition.

[ii.] 爾雅註疏. See proleg. to vol. III. p. 201.

3. 欽定詩經傳說彙纂, 'Compilation and Digest of Comments and Remarks on the She-king. By imperial authority.' In 21 chapters; with an appendix containing the Prefaces, and Choo He's examination and discussion of them,—in whole, and in detail. It was commanded towards the end of the period K'ang-he, and I have generally called it the K'ang-he She; but it did not appear till 1727, the 5th year of the period Yung-ching. The plan of it is similar to the imperial edition of the Shoo-king, which I have described in the proleg. to vol. III., p. 201; and it is entitled to equal praise. The compilers drew in the preparation of it from 260 writers:—1 of the Chow dynasty; 25 of the Han; 3 of the kingdom of Wei; 2 of that of Woo; 4 of the Tsin dynasty; 2 of the Lëang; 1

of the northern Wei; 1 of the Suy; 15 of the T'ang; 1 of the Posterior Tsin; 1 of the southern T'ang; 94 of the Sung; 23 of the Yuen; and 27 of the Ming.

Immediately after the text there follows always the commentary of Choo He in his 'Collected Comments on the She (詩集傳);' and this the editors maintain as the orthodox interpretation of the odes, while yet they advocate, in their own 'decisions,' wherever they can, the view given by Maou in accordance with the Little Preface. Choo's commentary was published in the winter of 1177. My own opinion on Choo's principle of interpretation, and on the Preface, has been given in Chapter II. of these prolegomena, and in many places when treating of particular odes.

4. I have made frequent reference to the imperial editions of the Ch'un T'sëw and the Le Ke;—and also to those of the Chow Le (周禮), and the E Le (儀禮).

8. The 呂氏家塾讀詩記 三十二卷, 'Leu's Readings in the She for his Family School; in 32 chapters.' The author of this work was Leu Tsoo-k'ëen (呂祖謙) or Leu Pih-kung (伯恭), a contemporary of Choo He (born 1137; died 1181). It gives not only the author's view of the text, but those of 44 other scholars, from Maou down to Choo, very distinctly quoted. The peculiarity of it is, that the explanations of Choo He which are adduced are those held by him, at an early period, before he had discarded the authority of the Prefaces. In 1182 Choo wrote a preface to Leu's Work, saying that the views attributed to him in it were those of his youth, 'shallow and poor,' and he regretted that Pih-kung had died before he had an opportunity of discussing them anew with him. To the Work he assigns the characters of comprehensiveness, clearness, and mildness. The edition in my possession is a beautiful one, published in 1811.

9. 詩補傳 三十卷, 'Supplemental Commentary to the She; in 30 chapters.' The writer mentions only his style of Yih-chae (逸齋), but Choo E-tsun and others have identified him with Fan Ch'oo-e (范處義), another great scholar of the 12th century, who took high rank among the graduates of the third degree in the Shaou-hing (紹興) period. He was a vehement advocate of the Prefaces, and of Maou's views; but he was not sufficiently careful in his citation of authorities.

10. 毛詩集解 四十二卷, 'Collected Explanations of Maou's She; in 42 chapters.' By whom this work was first edited I do not know; but it contains the views of three scholars, all of the first half

of the 12th century:—Le Ch'oo (李樗; styled 迂仲 and 若林); Hwang Heun (黃櫄; styled 實夫); and Le Yung (李泳). They were all natives of Fuh-këen province. Ch'oo was a near relative of Lin Che-k'e, of whose commentary on the Shoo I have spoken in the proleg. to vol. III., p. 202;—of vast erudition, yet possessing a mind of his own. Why his interpretations and those of Hwang Heun were edited together, it would be difficult to say, for they do not always agree in opinion. Le Yung's remarks are supplemental to those of the two others.

11. 詩緝三十六卷, 'A Commentary on the She, from all sources; in 36 chapters.' This is the famous commentary on the She, by Yen Ts'an (嚴粲; styled 坦叔, and 華谷), to which I have made very frequent reference. The preface of the author, telling us how he made his commentary in the first place for the benefit of his two sons, is dated in the summer of 1248. In general he agrees with the conclusions of Leu Tsoo-k'ëen; but he was familiar with the labours of all his predecessors, and was not afraid to strike out, when he thought it necessary, independent views of his own. His view of the Prefaces has been mentioned on p. 32. Among all the commentators on the She of the Sung dynasty, I rank Yen Ts'an next to Choo He.

12. 詩傳遺說, 六卷, 'A Supplement to the Commentary on the She; in six chapters.' This is a work by Choo Këen (朱鑑; styled 子明), a grandson of Choo He. It was intended, no doubt, specially to supplement Choo's great Work, and the materials were mainly drawn from his recorded remarks upon the odes, and which were not included in it.

13. 詩說, 一卷, 'Talk about some of the Odes; in one chapter.' This is a small treatise of hardly a dozen paragraphs, on the meaning of passages in a few of the Ya and the Sung, by a Chang Luy (張耒; styled 文潛), a writer of the last quarter of the 11th century.

14. 詩疑二卷, 'Doubts about the She; in two chapters.' By Wang Loo-chae, or Wang Pih, whose 'Doubts about the Shoo' is mentioned in the proleg. to vol. III., p. 203. The author was of the school of Choo He; but he was freer in his way of thinking about the Classical Books even than the great master; contending that many of the present odes were never in the old collection sanctioned by Confucius, and that many more have got transposed from

their proper places. His two chapters are worth reading as specimens of Chinese rationalism.

15, 16. 詩傳一卷; 詩說一卷 'Commentary on the She; in one chapter'; 'Tractate on the She; in one chapter.' Both of these treatises are found in the collection of the 'Books of Han and Wei': —the former ascribed to Confucius's disciple, Tsze-kung; the latter to Shin P'ei, mentioned on p. 8 in connexion with the old Text of Loo. They are acknowledged, now, however, to be forgeries, the work of a Fung Fang (豐坊; styled 存禮), a scholar of the Ming dynasty, in the first half of the 16th century. If the treatise ascribed to Tsze-kung were genuine, we should have to reconsider many of the current opinions about the She; but neither of the forgeries has any intrinsic value.

17. 毛詩六帖講意四卷, 'An Exposition of Maou's She, from six points of view; in four chapters.' This is a more extensive Work than we might suppose from its being merely in four chapters. It is interesting as being the Work of Seu Kwang-k'e (徐光啟; styled 子先), the most famous of the converts of Matteo Ricci; though there is nothing in it, so far as I have observed, to indicate the author's Christianity, if indeed it was written after his conversion. The copy which I have used, belonging to Wang T'aou, is the original one, published, according to a preface by a friend of the author, in 1617. Seu's 'six points of view' are Choo He's interpretations (翼傳); the interpretations of Maou and Ching (存古); new interpretations of others and himself (廣義); illustrations from old poems and essays (肇藻); the names of birds, animals, and plants (博物); and the rhymes (正叶). It is a valuable compilation. It has been republished with considerable alterations by a Fan Fang (范方); of the present dynasty.

19. 詩序廣義二十四卷, 'The She and the Preface to it fully discussed; in 24 chapters.' This may be called the commentary on the She of the present dynasty, by Keang Ping-chang (姜炳璋, styled 石貞 and 白巖), published first in 1762. He would appear to have published an earlier Work, called 詩序補義 of which this is an enlargement. His view of the Preface has been alluded to in p. 32. Though very often opposed to Choo He, he is not slow to acknowledge his great merits, and to adopt in many cases his interpretations in preference to those of the old school. The work is thoroughly honest and able; not without its errors and prejudices, but deserving to rank with those of Maou, Choo He, and Yen Ts'an.

20. 毛詩集釋三十卷, 'Explanations of Maou's She from all sources; in 30 chapters.' This work exists as yet only in manuscript, and was prepared, expressly for my own assistance, by my friend Wang T'aou (王韜; styled 仲弢, and 紫詮). There is no available source of information on the text and its meaning which the writer has not laid under contribution. The Works which he has laid under contribution,—few of them professed commentaries on the She,—amount to 124. Whatever completeness belongs to my own Work is in a great measure owing to this:—the only defect in it is the excessive devotion throughout to the views of Maou. I hope the author will yet be encouraged to publish it for the benefit of his countrymen.

21. 新增詩經補註備旨詳解; 八卷. See the proleg. to vol. I., p. 131. This work is on the same plan as the 'Complete Digest of the Four Books,' there described; by Tsow Shing-mih (鄒聖脈; styled 梧岡), first published in 1763.

22. 增補詩經體註衍義合參; 八卷, 'Supplement to Choo He's commentary on the She, and the Amplification of the meaning; in 8 chapters.' This work, of the same nature as the preceding, but differently arranged;—by a Shin Le-lung (沈李龍), of Hăng-chow. It appeared first in 1689. with a preface by a Koo P'aou-wăn (顧豹文; styled 且菴). There is a very good set of plates at the commencement.

23. 詩經精華, 'The Essence and Flower of the She.' In 8 chapters; by Sëeh Këa-ying (薛嘉穎; styled 悟邨), a scholar of Fuh-këen province;—published in 1825. This is one of the most valuable and useful of all the works on the She which I have consulted. The writer cannot be said to belong to either of the schools, but has honestly and successfully used his own mind, according to the rule of Mencius for the interpretation of the odes, before plunging into the ocean of commentaries.

24. 詩所; 八卷, 'The Correct Meaning and Order of the odes; in 8 chapters.' It is difficult to translate the title (詩所) of this Work, which is taken from Confucius' account of his labours on the She in Ana. IX. xiv. The author, Le Kwang-te (李光地), was one of the great scholars of the K'ang-he period. He began this Work, he tells us in the winter of 1717, and finished it in the spring of 1718. He has many peculiar views about the subjects and arrangements of the odes, but not much that is valuable in the explanation of the text.

176]

25. Maou K'e-ling (毛奇齡;—see proleg. to vol. I. p. 132) has several treatises on the She, most of which were at one time embodied in a large work in 38 chapters, of which he lost the manuscript. They are:—

[i.]   國風省篇一卷·

[ii.] 毛詩寫官記四卷·

[iii.] 詩札二卷·

[iv.] 詩傳詩說駁義五卷· This is occupied with the two forged Works mentioned above (15, 16).

[v.]   白鷺洲 (the name of a college in Këang-se, where the conversations and discussions were held) 主客說詩一卷·

[vi.] 續詩傳鳥名三卷·

32. The 皇清經解 contains a reprint of some of Maou's Treatises, and of many others on the She. I have found assistance in consulting:—

[i.]   毛詩稽古編三十卷· 'Maou's She, according to the views of the old school; in 30 chapters.' I do not know a more exhaustive work than this from the author's point of view. He was a Ch'in K'e-yuen (陳啟源; styled 長發) of Këang-soo. His work was published in 1687, and had occupied him for 14 years, during which he thrice wrote out his manuscripts. He is a thorough advocate of the old school, and is in continual conflict with Choo He, Gow-yang Sëw, Leu Tsoo-k'ëen, Yen Ts'an, and especially Lëw Kin of the Ming dynasty.

[ii.] 毛鄭詩考正四卷· 'An Examination of the She of Maou and Ch'ing; in 4 chapters.' By Tae Chin (戴震; styled 東原, 慎修, and 吉士), a great scholar mainly of the K'ëen-lung period. He carefully examines all the instances where the views of Ch'ing differ from those of Maou, and does not hesitate to decide against the one or the other according to his own views.

[iii.] 詩經補註二卷· 'Supplemental Comments on the She; in 2 chapters.' Also by Tae Chin.

[iv.] 毛詩故訓傳三十卷· This is Maou's commentary on the She, revised and edited by Twan Yuh-tsae (see p. 101); probably the most correct edition of Maou's text which is to be found. It was published first in 1796.

[v.]   詩經小學四卷· 'The rudimentary Learning applied to the She-king; in 4 chapters.' This treatise is also by Twan Yuh-tsae;—an examination of the readings of the She, different from those of Maou, gathered from all sources.

[vi.]　毛詩攷勘記 十卷. See on 1.

[vii.]　毛詩補疏 五卷, 'Supplemental Excursus to Maou's She; in 5 chapters.' By Tsëaou Seun (焦循; styled 里堂 and 理堂), who took his second literary degree in 1801. The name of the Work is taken from K'ung Ying-tah's 註疏, with errors and defects in which, as he fancies, the writer mainly occupies himself.

[viii.]　詩述聞, 三卷, 'Lessons in the She, transmitted; in 3 chapters.' By Wang Yin-che (王引之: styled 伯申), a high officer of the present dynasty, who took the 3d place among the candidates for the Han-lin college in 1799. In this Work he gives the views of the She which he had received from his father, who was also a great scholar;—hence its name.

[ix.]　經傳釋詞, 十卷, 'An Explanation of the Particles employed in the classics and other writings; in 10 chapters.' This work is by the same author; and though not specially on the She, it has been to me of the utmost value. See a full account of it in M. Julien's 'Syntaxe Nouvelle de la Langue Chinoise,' vol. I., pp. 153—231.

[x.]　毛詩紬義 二十四卷, 'The meaning of Maou's She unfolded; in 24 chapters.' By Le Foo-p'ing (李黼平);—on the side of the old school.

[xi.]　詩毛鄭異同辨, 二卷 'On the points of agreement and disagreement between Maou and Ch'ing upon the She; in 2 chapters.' By Tsăng Ch'aou (曾釗; styled 冕士), a native of Nan-hae district, Canton province.

[xiii.]　三家詩異文疏證, 'Exhibition and Discussion of the different readings of the three other Texts and those of Maou. In 2 chapters; by Fung Tăng-foo (馮登府), a scholar and officer of the Taou-kwang period.

44.　重訂三家詩拾遺, 八卷. A work of the same nature as the preceding. By Fan Këa-sëang (范家相) of the period K'ëen-lung; subsequently revised by a Yeh Keun (葉鈞; styled 石亭).

45.　韓詩外傳, 'Han's Illustrations of the She from external Sources.' See on p. 10, and pp. 87—95.

46.　毛詩草木鳥獸蟲魚疏, 二卷, 'On the Plants, Trees, Birds, Animals, Insects, and Fishes, in Maou's She; in two chapters.' By Luh Ke of the kingdom Woo (吳陸機 [more probably 璣]; styled 元恪:—born A.D. 260, died 303). This is the oldest Work on the subject with which it is occupied. The original Work was lost; and that now current was compiled, it is not known when or by whom, mainly from K'ung Ying-tah's constant quotations of it.

47. 毛詩名物解·二十卷, 'Explanation of Names and Things in Maou's She; in 20 chapters.' A Work of the same character as the above, but more extensive; by Ts'ae Pëen (蔡卞; styled 元度), a scholar of the Sung dynasty, in the second half of the 11th century. He commences with the names of heaven; goes on to the cereals; plants and grasses; trees; birds; animals; insects; fishes; horses; and miscellaneous objects, such as garments, the ancestral temple, &c.

48. 埤雅·二十卷, 'Supplement to the Urh-ya, in 30 chapters.' By Luh Tëen (陸佃; styled 農師:—born A.D. 1042, died 1102). Tëen was a disciple of Wang Gan-shih, and a very voluminous writer; but only this *P'e-ya* survives of all his Works. He is less careful in describing the appearance of his subjects than in discussing the meaning of their names. Beginning with fishes, first among which is the dragon, he proceeds to animals; then to birds; then to insects; specially to horses; to trees; to grasses and plants; to the names of heaven, and skyey phænomena. There were originally other chapters; but they are lost.

49. 詩集傳名物鈔·八卷, 'Examination of Names and Things, as given in Choo He's She and Commentary, from all sources; in eight chapters.' By Heu K'ëen (許謙), one of the most famous scholars of the Yuen dynasty, in the first half of the 14th century. He had studied under Wang Pih (see 14), whose 'Doubts' had left their influence on his mind.

50. 毛詩名物略·四卷, 'The Names and Things in Maou's She in brief; in 4 chapters.' Published in 1763, by Choo Hwan (朱桓; styled 拙存). He arranges his subjects under the four heads of Heaven, Earth, Man, and Things (天·地·人·物); that is, celestial Beings and phænomena; the earth, with its mountains, springs, States, &c.; man's works, dignities, garments, &c.; and birds, beasts, plants, trees, insects, and fishes.

51. 毛詩名物圖說·九卷, 'Plates and Descriptions of the objects mentioned in Maou's She; in 9 chapters.' Published in 1769, by Seu Ting (徐鼎; styled 實夫). He tells us that it cost him 20 years' labour. It is a very useful manual on the subject. The author gives a multitude of descriptions from various sources; and generally concludes with his own opinion, occasionally new and reliable. The plates are poor.

179]

52. 毛詩品物圖考, 七卷, 'An inquiry into the various objects mentioned in Maou's She, with plates; in 7 chapters.' This is the work of a Japanese scholar, and physician who calls himself Kang Yuen-fung (岡元鳳) of Lang-hwa (浪華); taking up first the grasses and plants; then trees; birds; animals; insects; and fishes. He seldom gives any other descriptions than those of Maou and Choo. The plates are in general exquisitely done, and would do credit to any wood engraver of Europe. The book, though not containing quite all the objects mentioned in the She, has been of more use to me than all the other books of the same class together. My edition contains a recommendatory preface by a 那波師曾 of 西播, dated in the winter of 1785 (天明四年, 甲辰, 冬十月).

53. 音論; 易音; 詩本音. These three Works are all contained in the 皇清經解, chapters 4 to 19, the productions of Koo Yen-woo, mentioned and made use of in the first and second sections of chapter III. of these prolegomena.

54. 六書音均表. This is the work of Twan Yuh-tsae, mentioned and freely quoted from in the same sections;—on the ancient pronunciation and rhymes of the characters. It also is contained in the same collection, chapters 661—666.

55. 古韻標準, 四卷. 'Adjustment of ancient rhymes; in 4 chapters.' By Këang Yung. See p. 98. I have this Work reprinted in two different Collections. One of them is styled 粵雅堂叢書, which appeared in 1853, published at the expense of a wealthy gentleman of Nan-hae, department Kwang-chow, in Canton province, called Woo Ts'ung-yaou (伍崇曜). It contains upwards of a hundred Works, many of them rare and valuable, mostly of the present dynasty, but others of the T'ang, Sung, Yuen, and Ming dynasties, selected from the publisher's library, called 粵雅堂. One of these, the 疑年錄, and a continuation of it, giving the years of the birth and death of many of the most eminent scholars and others in Chinese history, have been very useful.

The other Collection is styled 守山閣叢書, published in the same way from the stores of his library (守山閣), in 1844, by Ts'ëen He-tsoo (錢熙祚; styled 錫之), a gentleman of Sung-këang dept., Këang-soo. It contains 18 Works on the classics; 28 on the histories; 60 on the philosophers or writers on general subjects; and 4 miscellanies.

The Dictionaries and Books of general reference, mentioned in the list of Works consulted in the preparation of vol. III., have, most of them, been referred to as occasion required; and to them there are to be added the dictionary 玉篇 of the 6th century; the 廣韻 (see on pp. 104—106); the 六書故, written about the close of the Sung dynasty; the 爾雅翼, an appendix [Wings] to the Urh-ya, by Lo yuen (羅願; styled 端良, and 存齋), of the 12th century, —a Work analogous to the 埤雅 above, but superior to it; the 三禮 通釋, an exhaustive Work, in 230 chapters of Description, and 50 chapters of Plates, on the Chow Le, the E Le, and the Le Ke, by Lin Ch'ang-e (林昌彝; styled 薌谿, and 藏谷), a native of Fuh-këen, who was able, after 30 years of labour, to submit his manuscript for imperial inspection in 1852; and the various poets and Collections of poems here and there referred to in these prolegomena.

SECTION II.

TRANSLATIONS AND OTHER FOREIGN WORKS.

Besides most of the Works mentioned in the prolegomena to former volumes, I have used:—

CONFUCII SHE-KING, sive LIBER CARMINUM. Ex Latina P. Lacharme interpretatione edidit Julius Mohl. Stuttgartiæ et Tubingæ: 1830.

SYSTEMA PHONETICUM SCRIPTURÆ SINICÆ. Auctore J. M. Callery, Missionario Apostolico in Sinis. Macao: 1841.

POESEOS SINICÆ COMMENTARII: The POETRY OF THE CHINESE. By Sir John Francis Davis. New and augmented edition. London: 1870.

Notes on Chinese Literature. By A. Wylie Esq. Shanghae: 1867.

POESIES DE L'EPOQUE DES THANG; traduites du Chinois, pour la premiere fois, avec une etude sur l'art Poetique en Chine; par Le Marquis D'Hervey Saint-Denys. Paris: 1862.

CONTRIBUTIONS towards the MATERIA MEDICA AND NATURAL HIS-TORY of China. By Frederick Porter Smith, M.B., Medical missionary in Central China. Shang-hae: 1871.

NOTES AND QUERIES on China and Japan. Edited by N.B. Dennys. Hongkong: 1867 to 1869.

The CHINESE RECORDER and MISSIONARY JOURNAL. Published at Foo-chow. Now in its third year.

GOD IN HISTORY, or The progress of Man's Faith in the Moral Order of the World. By C.J Baron Bunsen. Translated from the German. London: 1870.

FLORA HONGKONGENSIS: a DESCRIPTION of the FLOWERING PLANTS and FERNS of the Island of HONG-KONG. By George Bentham, V.P. L.S. London: 1861.

THE SHE KING.

PART I.
LESSONS FROM THE STATES.

BOOK I. THE ODES OF CHOW AND THE SOUTH.

I. *Kwan ts'eu.*

詩經
國風一
周南一之一

關雎

關關雎鳩。在河
之洲。窈窕淑女
君子好逑。
參差荇菜。左右
流之。窈窕淑女
寤寐求之。求之

1　*Kwan-kwan* go the ospreys,
　　On the islet in the river.
　　The modest, retiring, virtuous, young lady:—
　　For our prince a good mate she.

2　Here long, there short, is the duckweed,
　　To the left, to the right, borne about by the current.
　　The modest, retiring, virtuous, young lady:—
　　Waking and sleeping, he sought her.

TITLE OF THE WHOLE WORK.—詩經. 'The Book of Poems,' or simply 詩. 'The Poems.' By poetry, according to the Great Preface and the views generally of Chinese scholars, is denoted the expression, in rhymed words, of thought impregnated with feeling; which, so far as it goes, is a good account of this species of composition. In the collection before us, there were originally 311 pieces; but of six of them there are only the titles remaining. They are generally short: not one of them, indeed, is a long poem. Father Lacharme calls the Book—'*Liber Carminum*,' and with most English writers the ordinary designation of it has been 'The Book of Odes.' I can think of no better name for the several pieces than *Ode*, understanding by that term a short lyric poem. Confucius himself is said to have 'fitted them to the string.'

TITLE OF THE PART.—國風 一, 'Part I., Lessons from the States. In the Chinese, 一, 'Part I.,' stands last, while our western idiom requires that it should be placed first. The translation of 國風 by 'Lessons from the States' has been vindicated in the notes on the Great Preface. Sir John Davis translates the characters by 'The Manners of the different States' (art. on the Poetry of the Chinese. Transactions of the Royal Asiatic Society; May, 1829). Similarly, the French Sinologues render them by 'Les Mœurs des royaumes.' But in 'Lessons' and 'Manners,' the metaphorical use of 風, 'wind,' is equally unapparent. Choo He says:—'The pieces are called *fung*, because they owe their origin to and are descriptive of the influence produced by superiors, and the exhibition of this is again sufficient to affect men, just as things give forth sound, when moved by the wind, and their sound is again sufficient to move [other] things (謂 之 風者，以其被上之化以有言，而其言又足以感人．如物因風之動以有聲．而其聲又足以動物也). He goes on to say that the princes of States collected such compositions among their people, and presented them to the king, who delivered them to the Board of music for classification, so that he might examine from them the good and bad in the manners of the people, and ascertain the excellences and defects of his own government. 'Lessons from the States' seems, therefore, to come nearer to the force of the original terms than 'Manners of the States.' It will be found, however, that the *lesson* has often to be drawn from the ode by a circuitous process.

The States are those of Chow, Shaou, P'ei, Yung, and the others, which give their names to the several Books.

TITLE OF THE BOOK.—周南 一 之 一, 'Chow Nan, Book I. of Part I.' The first 一 is that of the last title,—國風 一. By Chow is intended the seat of the House of Chow, from the time of the 'old duke, T'an-foo (古公亶父),' in B. C. 1,325, to king Wǎn. The chiefs of Chow pretended to trace their lineage back to K'e, better known as How Tseih, Shun's minister of Agriculture. K'e was invested, it is said, before the death of Yaou, with the small territory of T'ae (邰), referred to the pres. dis. of Woo-kung (武功) in K'een-chow (乾州), Shen-se. Between K'e and duke Lew (公劉), only two names of the Chow ancestry are given with certainty, — Puh-chueh (不窋) and Kuh (鞠, al. 鞠陶). Sz'-ma Ts'een calls the first K'e's son, but can only suppose him to have been one of his descendants. In the disorders of the Middle Kingdom, it is related, he withdrew among the wild tribes of the west and north; and there his descendants remained till the time of duke Lěw, who returned to China in B.C. 1,796, and made a settlement in Pin (豳), the site of which is pointed out, 30 *le* to the west of the present dis. city of San-shwuy (三水) in the small dep. of Pin-chow (邠州). The family dwelt in Pin for several generations, till T'an-foo, subsequently *kinged* by his posterity as king T'ae (太王), moved still farther south in B.C. 1,325, and settled in K'e (岐), 50 *le* to the north east of the dis. city of K'e-shan (岐山), dep. Fung-ts'ëang (鳳翔). The plain southwards received the neme of Chow, and here were the head-quarters of the rising House, till king Wǎn moved south and east again, across the Wei, to Fung (酆), south-west from the pres. provincial city of Se-gan. When king Wǎn took this step, he separated the original Chow—K'e-chow—into Chow and Shaou, which he made the appanages of his son Tan (旦), and of Shih (奭), one of his principal supporters. Tan is known from this appointment as 'the duke of Chow'. The pieces in this Book are supposed to have been collected by him in Chow, and the States lying south from it along the Han and other rivers.— We must supplement in English the bare 'Chow Nan.' of the title, and say—'The Odes of Chow and the South.'

[The above historical sketch throws light on Mencius' statement, in Book IV., Pt II.i., that king Wǎn was 'a man from the wild tribes of the west (西夷之人).' I have translated his words by 'a man near the wild tribes of the west.' But according to the records of the Chow dynasty themselves, we see its real ancestor, duke Lěw, coming out from among those tribes in the beginning of the 17th century before our era, and settling in Pin. Very slowly, his tribe, growing in civilization, and pushed on by fresh immigrations from its own earlier seats, moves on, southwards and eastwards, till it comes into contact and collision with the princes of Shang, whose dominions constituted the Middle Kingdom, or the China of that early time. The accounts of a connection between the princes of Chow and the statesmen of the era of Yaou and Shun must be thrown out of the sphere of reliable history.]

Ode 1.—CELEBRATING THE VIRTUE OF THE BRIDE OF KING WAN, AND WELCOMING HER TO HIS PALACE.

Stanza 1. 關 關 are defined to be 'the harmonious notes of the male and female answering each other.' 關 was anciently interchanged with 管, and some read in the text 管管, with a 口 at the side, which would clearly be onomatopoetic; but we do not find such a character in the Shwǒh-wǎn. It is difficult to say what bird is intended by 雎鳩 Confucius says (Ana. XVII.ix.) that from the

左苻　參三反輾悠悠思寐不
右菜。差。側。轉。哉。哉。服。寐　得。

He sought her and found her not,
And waking and sleeping he thought about her.
Long he thought; oh! long and anxiously;
On his side, on his back, he turned, and back again.

She we become extensively acquainted with the names of birds, beasts, and plants. We do learn *names* enow, but the birds, beasts, and plants, denoted by them, remain in many cases to be yet ascertained. The student, knowing *kew* to mean the wild dove, is apt to suppose that some species of dove is intended; but no Chinese commentator has ever said so. Maou makes it the 王雎, adding 鳥摯 而 有 別, which means, probably, 'a bird of prey, of which the male and female keep much apart.' He followed the Urh-ya, the annotator of which, Kwoh P'oh (郭璞), of the Tsin dynasty, further describes it as 'a kind of eagle (鵰類), now, east of the Kёang, called the *sgoh* (鶚).' This was for many centuries the view of all scholars; and it is sustained by a narrative in the Tso Chuen, under the 17th year of duke Ch'aou, that the Master of the Horse or Minister of War, was anciently styled Ts'eu K'ew (雎鳩氏). The introduction of a bird of prey into a nuptial ode was thought, however, to be incongruous. Even Ch'ing K'ang-shing, would appear to have felt this, and explains Maou's 摯 by 至, as if his words— 'a bird most affectionate, and yet most undemonstrative of desire;'—in which interpretation Choo Ho follows him. But it was desirable to discard the bird of prey altogether; and this was first done by Ch'ing Ts'aou (鄭樵), an early writer of the Sung dyn., who makes the bird to be 'a kind of mallard.' Choo He, no doubt after him, says it is 'a water bird, in appearance like a mallard,' adding that it is only seen in pairs, the individuals of which keep at a distance from each other! Other identifications of the *ts'eu-k'ew* have been attempted. I must believe that the author of the ode had some kind of fish hawk in his mind.

在河之洲 (the Shwoh-wăn has 州, without the 水).—河 is the general denomination of streams and rivers in the north. We need not seek, as many do, to determine any particular stream as that intended. 洲 is an islet, 'habitable ground, surrounded by the water (水中可居之地).

窈窕淑女.—窈 is to be understood of the lady's mind, and 窕 of her deportment.

So, Yang Hёung (楊雄. Died A.D. 18, at the age of 71), and Wang Suh. 淑 (has displaced the more ancient form with 人 at the side) is explained in the Shwoh-wăn by 善, 'good,' 'virtuous.' The young lady, according to the traditional interpretation (on which see below), is T'ae-sz' (太姒), a daughter of the House of Yew-sin (有莘), whom king Wăn married.

君子好逑.—If we accept T'ae-sz' as the young lady of the Ode, then the *keun-tsz'* of course is king Wăn. 逑 and 仇 (in Ode VII.) are interchangeable, = 匹, 'a mate.' K'ang-shing explains the line by 能為君子和好眾妾之怨, 'who could for our prince harmonize the resentments of all the concubines.' He was led astray by the Little Preface. [There is a popular novel called the 好逑傳, the name of which is taken from this line. Sir John Davis has translated it under the misnomer of 'The Fortunate Union.']

St.2. 參差 (read *ch'in ts'ze*) 荇菜—參差 expresses the irregular appearance of the plants, some long and some short. 荇菜 is probably the *lemna minor*. It is also called 'duck-mallows,' that name being given for it in the Pun-ts'aou and the Pe-ya. (埤雅; a work on the plan of the Urh-ya, by Luh Teen (陸佃, of the Sung dyn.).—蕩葵 It is described as growing in the water, long or short according to the depth, with a reddish leaf, which floats on the surface, and is rather more than an inch in diameter. Its flower is yellow. It is very like the *sha*, which Medhurst calls the 'marsh-mallows,' but its leaves are not so round, being a little pointed. We are to suppose that the leaves were cooked and presented as a sacrificial offering. 左右流之,—the analogy of 采之 芼之 in the next stanza, would lead us to expect an active signification in 流, and an action proceeding from the parties who speak in the Ode. This, no doubt, was the reason which made Maou, after the Urh-ya, explain the character

樂 女。窈 右 荇 之。琴 窈 采
之。鐘 窕 芼 菜 參 瑟 淑 之。
　鼓 淑 之。左 差 友 女。窈

3　Here long, there short, is the duckweed;
　　On the left, on the right, we gather it.
　　The modest, retiring, young lady:—
　　With lutes, small and large, let us give her friendly welcome.
　　Here long, there short, is the duckweed;
　　On the left, on the right, we cook and present it.
　　The modest, retiring, virtuous young lady:—
　　With bells and drums let us show our delight in her.

by 求. 'to seek;' but this is forcing a meaning on the term. 流之 simply—'the current bears it about.' The idea of looking for the plant is indicated by the connection. 寤寐 至反側—we have to supply the subject of 求 and the other verbs; which I have done by 'he', referring to king Wăn. The commentators are chary of saying this directly, thinking that such lively emotion about such an object was inconsistent with Wăn's sagely character; but they are obliged to interpret the passage of him. To make, with K'ang-shing and others, the subject to be the lady herself, and the object of her quest to be virtuous young ladies to fill the harem, surely is absurd. 思服.—服=懷, 'to cherish in the breast.' 悠哉=悠, here, acc. to Maou,—思, 'to think.' In other places, in these Odes, it—憂, 'to be anxious,' 'sorrowful'; and also—遠, 'remote,' 'a long distance.' Choo He prefers this last meaning, and defines it by 長, 'long.' The idea is that of prolonged and anxious thought. 輾轉反側—the old interpreters did not distinguish between the meaning of these characters. The Shwoh-wăn, indeed, defines 輾 (it gives only 展) by 轉. Choo He makes 輾=轉之半, 'half a chuen or turning;' 轉=輾之周, 'the completion of the 輾;' while 反 and 側 are the reversing of those processes. This is ingenious and elegant; but the definitions are made for the passage.

St.3. As the subject of 芼 and the other verbs, we are to understand the authors or singers of the Ode,—the ladies of king Wăn's harem.

The Pe-che (備旨), however, would refer all the 之 in the stanza to the young lady, and the verbs to king Wăn, advising him so to welcome and cherish her; and this interpretation is also allowable. Maou, further on, explains 采 by 取, 'to take', and here, 芼 by 擇, 'to pick out', to select' But the selection must precede the taking. It was not till the time of Tung Yëw in the Sung Dyn., that the meaning of 芼, which I have given, and which may be supported from the Le Ke, was applied to this passage. 友之,—'we friend her,' i.e., we give her a friendly welcome. The k'in and shih were two instruments in which the music was drawn from strings of silk. We may call them the small lute and the large lute. The k'in at first had only 5 strings for the 5 full notes of the octave, but two others are said to have been added by kings Wăn and Woo, to give the semi-notes. The invention of a shih with 50 strings is ascribed to Fuh-he, but we are told that Hwang-te found the melancholy sounds of this so overpowering, that he cut the number down to 25.

In Chinese editions of the she, at the end of every ode, there is given a note, stating the number of stanzas in it, and of the lines in each stanza. Here we have 關雎三章一章四句二章章八句, 'The Kwan-tseu consists of 3 stanzas, the first containing 4 lines, and the other two containing 8 lines each.' This matter need not be touched on again.

The rhymes (according to Twan Yuh-tsae, whose authority in this matter, as I have stated in the prolegomena, I follow) are:—in stanza 1, 鳩 洲 逑, category 3, tone 1: in 2, 流 求, ib.; 得 服, 側 cat. 1, t. 3: in 3, 采 友,

ib. t. 2; 芒 樂, . cat. 2. The, after a character denotes that the ancient pronunciation of it, found in the odes, was different from that now belonging to it. A list of such characters, with their ancient names, has been given in the prolegomena, in the appendix to the chapter referred to.

INTERPRETATION OF THE ODE. I have said that the Ode celebrates the virtue of the bride of king Wăn. If I had written *queen* instead of *bride*, I should have been in entire accord, so far, with the schools both of Maou and Choo He. During the dyn. of Han a different view was widely prevalent,—that the Ode was satirical, and should be referred to the time when the Chow dyn. had begun to fall into decay. We find this opinion in Lëw Heang (列女傳, 仁智篇), Yang Heung (法言, 孝至篇), and up and down, in the histories of Sz'-ma Ts'ëen, Pan Koo, and Fan Yeh.—By the E Le, however. IV., ii. 75. we are obliged to refer the *Kwan-ts'eu* to the time of the duke of Chow. That a contrary opinion should have been so prevalent in the Han dyn., only shows how long it was before the interpretation of the odes became so definitely fixed as it now is. Allowing the ode to be as old as the duke of Chow, and to celebrate his father's bride or queen, what is the virtue which it ascribes to her? According to the school of Maou, it is her freedom from jealousy, and her constant anxiety and diligence to fill the harem of the king with virtuous ladies to share his favours with her, and assist her in her various duties; and the ode was made by her. According to the school of Choo He, the virtue is her modest disposition and retiring manners, which so ravished the inmates of the harem, that they sing of her, in the 1st stanza, as she was in her virgin purity, a flower unseen; in the 2d, they set forth the king's trouble and anxiety while he had not met with such a mate; and in the 3d, their joy reaches its height, when she has been got, and is brought home to his palace. In this way, think, Choo, the ode, in reality, exhibits the virtue of king Wăn in making such a choice; and that is with him a very great point.

The imperial editors, adjudicating upon these two interpretations, very strangely, as it seems to me, and will also do, I presume, to most of my western readers, show an evident leaning to that of the old school 'It was the duty,' they say, 'of the queen to provide for the harem 3 wives (三夫人, ranking next to herself), nine ladies of the 3d rank (九嬪), 27 of the 4th (二十七世婦), and 81 of the 5th (八十一御妻).' Only virtuous ladies were fit to be selected for this position. The anxiety of Ts'ae-sz' to get such, her disappointment at not finding them, and her joy when she succeeded in doing so;—all this showed the highest female virtue, and made the ode worthy to stand at the head of all the Lessons from the Manners of the States.

Confucius expressed his admiration of the ode (Ana. III. xx.), but his words afford no help towards the interpretation of it. The traditional

interpretation of the odes, which we may suppose is given by Maou, is not to be overlooked; and, where it is supported by historical confirmations, it will often be found helpful. Still it is from the pieces themselves that we must chiefly endeavour to gather their meaning. This was the plan on which Choo He proceeded; and, as he far exceeded his predecessors in the true critical faculty, so China has not since produced another equal to him.

It is sufficient in this Ode to hear the friends of a bridegroom expressing their joy on occasion of his marriage with the virtuous object of his love, brought home in triumph, after long quest and various disappointments. There is no mention in it of king Wăn and the lady Sz'. I am not disposed to call in question the belief that that lady was the mistress of Wăn's harem; but I venture to introduce here the substance of a note from the 'Annals of the Empire'. Bk. I., p.14. to show how uncertain is the date at least of their marriage.—In the *Le* of the elder Tae, king Woo is said to have been born in Wăn's 14th year, while, in the standard chronology, Wăn's birth is put down in B. C. 1,230, and Woo's in 1,168, when Wăn was 62. But both accounts have their difficulties. First, Wăn had one son—Pih Yih-k'aou—older than Woo, so that he must have married Tae-sz' at the age of 12 or thereabouts, when neither he nor she could have had the emotions described in the *Kwan-ts'eu*. Further, as Wăn lived to be 100 years old, Woo must then have been 85. He died 20 years after, leaving his son, king Ching, only 14 years old. Ching must thus have been born when his father was over 80, and there was a younger son besides. This is incredible. Again, on the other account, it is unlikely that Wăn should only have had Pih Yih-k'aou before Woo, and then subsequently seven other sons, all by the same mother. And this difficulty is increased by what we read in the 5th and 6th Odes, which are understood to celebrate the numerousness of Wăn's children.

These considerations prove that the specification of events, as occurring in certain definite years of that early time, was put down very much at random by the chronologers, and that the traditional interpretation of the Odes must often be fanciful.

CLASS OF THE ODE; AND NAME. It is said to be one of the allusive pieces (興). At the same time a metaphorical element (比) is found in the characters of the objects alluded to:—the discreet reserve between the male and female of the osprey; and the soft and delicate nature of the duckweed. The name is made by combining two characters in the 1st line. So, in many other pieces. Sometimes one character-serves the purpose; at other times, two or more. Occasionally a name is found, which does not occur in the piece at all. The names of the Odes were attached to them before the time of Confucius, of which we have a superfluity of evidence in the Ch'un Ts'ew. From the Shoo, V., vi. 15, some assume that the writers of the pieces gave them their names themselves; and this may have been the case at times.—The subject of the name need rarely be referred to hereafter.

II. *Koh t'an.*

維　施　葛　其　集　黃　維　施　葛　　葛
葉　于　之　鳴　于　鳥　葉　于　之　　覃
莫　中　覃　喈　灌　于　萋　中　覃
莫。谷。兮。喈。木。飛。萋。谷。兮。

1　How the dolichos spread itself out,
　　Extending to the middle of the valley!
　　Its leaves were luxuriant;
　　The yellow birds flew about,
　　And collected on the thickly growing trees,
　　Their pleasant notes resounding far.

2　How the dolichos spread itself out,
　　Extending to the middle of the valley!
　　Its leaves were luxuriant and dense.

Ode 2. CELEBRATING THE INDUSTRY AND DUTIFULNESS OF KING WǍN'S QUEEN. It is supposed to have been made, and, however that was, it is to be read as if it had been made, by the queen herself.

St. 1 葛之覃兮.—葛 is the general name for the dolichos tribe; here the *D. tuberosus*, of whose fibres a kind of cloth is made. 覃 =延, 'to stretch out.' 兮 is of very frequent occurrence in the *she*; a particle of song (歌辭). According to the Shwoh-wǎn and the gloss of Seu in it, it denotes an affection of the mind, over and above what has been expressed in words. 施 (read *e*, =移) 于中谷.—中谷, 'mid-valley,'—谷中, 'the middle of the valley'. Ying-tah says that such inversion of the characters was customary with the ancients, especially in poetry. 維葉萋萋.—維 here, and nearly every where else in the *she*, is simply an initial character which it is not possible to translate. 萋萋 expresses 'the appearance of luxuriant growth.' This repetition of the character is constantly found, giving intensity and vividness to the idea. Often, the characters are different, but of cognate meaning. The compound seems to picture the subject of the sentence to the eye in the colours of its own signification. This is one of the characteristics of the style of the *she*, which the student must carefully attend to. 黃鳥于飛.—'the yellow bird' is, probably, an oriole. It has many names.—博黍. 黃麗.

黃鶯, &c. Twice in this st., 于 occurs as a preposition,—*in, on*; but in this line, we can only take it as a particle which we need not try to translate. So, Wang Yiu-che (王引之); the Urh-ya also, defining it by 曰-聿-欥. Ying-tah erroneously explains it by 往, 'to go.'
L.5. 灌木—'trees growing together,' shrubs.
L.6. 喈喈 is explained as 'their harmonious notes heard far off.' The characters are probably like 關關 in the last ode, onomatopoetic.—I translate the verbs here in the past tense, because the things referred to all belong to the season of the spring, and the speaker is looking back to them.

St.2. L.3. 莫莫 (read *moo* or *mok*) adds the idea of denseness to 萋萋 above. L.4. 蒦-煮, 'to boil.' The boiling was necessary in order to the separation of the fibres, which could afterwards be woven, the finer to form the 絺, and the coarser to form the 綌.

L.5. K'ang-shing takes 服-整 'to make,' 'to work at', giving not a bad meaning.—'T'ae-sz' worked at this cloth-making without weariness.' 斁 is interchanged with 射, both=厭 'to be satiated with,' and then 'to conceive a distaste for,' 'to dislike.'

St.3. Ll.1,2. Choo He takes 言 here as a particle, untranslateable (言, 辭也); Maou and K'ang-shing make it—我 'I,' 'me,' which is a meaning the Urh-ya gives for the term.

歸　害　薄　薄　言　言　服　爲　是
寧　澣　澣　汚　告　告　之　絺　刈
父　害　我　我　言　師　無　爲　是
母。　否。　衣。　私。　歸。　氏。　斁。　綌。　濩。

I cut it and I boiled it,
And made both fine cloth and coarse,
Which I will wear without getting tired of it.

3 I have told the matron,
Who will announce that I am going to see my parents.
I will wash my private clothes clean,
And I will rinse my robes.
Which need to be rinsed, and which do not?
I am going back to visit my parents.

Wang Yin-che coincides with Choo He. Wang T'aou would take it in the 1st line as—我, and as a particle in the 2nd. I regard it as a particle in both. The 師氏 here is difft. from the officer so styled in the Chow Le, Books VIII. and XIII. That was a teacher of morals attached to the emperor and the youths of the State; this was a matron, or duenna, whose business it was to instruct in 'woman's virtue, woman's words, woman's deportment, and woman's work.' Childless widows over 50 were, acc. to Ying-tah, employed for the office. There would be not a few such matrons in the harem, and the one intended in the text would be the mistress of them all. The 1st 告 is to be understood of the lady's announcement to the matron; the 2nd, of the matron's announcement to the king. Maou is led by his interpretation of the whole Ode to understand 歸 as—'to be married,' but we must take it as synonymous with the same term, in the concluding line.

Ll.3,4. 薄, acc. to Choo He,—少, 'slightly.' It is better to take it, as a particle, with Maou, and Wang Yin-che, who calls it 發聲, 'an initial sound.' 汚, 'dirty,' is used for 'to cleanse,' just as we have 亂, 'disorder,' in the sense of 治, 'good order,' 'to govern.' This cleansing was effected by hard rubbing, whereas 澣 denotes a gentler operation, simply rinsing. The 私, as opposed to 衣, is understood of the private or ordinary dress, whereas the other term refers to the robes in which T'ae-sze assisted at sacrificial and other services, or in which she went in to the king. All this and what follows, is to be taken as a soliloquy, and not what T'ae-sz told the matron (乃后妃

自審之詞, 非告師氏也.) L.5. 害 (read hoh)—何, 'what.' 否 simply —不, the negative. L.6. 寧—安, i. e., 問安, 'to inquire after their wellbeing.'

The rhymes are—in Stt.1,2, 谷 谷, cat. 3, t. 3: in 1, 蘽 飛 階, cat. 15, t. 1: in 2, 莫 薄 綌 斁, cat. 5, t. 1: in 3, 歸 私 衣, cat. 15, t.1: 否 母, cat. 1, t. 2.

Interpretation; and Class. The old interpreters held that the ode was of T'ae-sze in her virgin prime, bent on all woman's work; and thus interpreted, it is placed among the allusive pieces. The first two stanzas might be so explained; but the third requires too much straining to admit of a proleptical interpretation as to what the virgin would do in the future, when a married wife.

Choo He makes it a narrative piece (賦), in which the queen tells first of her diligent labours, and then how, when they were concluded, she was going to pay a visit of duty and affection to her parents. If we accept the traditional reference to T'ae-sze, this, no doubt, is the only admissible interpretation. The imperial editors prefer Choo He's view in this instance, and add:—'The Le of Tae only speaks of the personal tendance of the silkworms by the queen and other ladies of the harem; but here we see that there was no department of woman's work, in which they did not exert themselves. Well might they transform all below them. Anciently, the rules to be observed between husband and wife required the greatest circumspection. They did not speak directly to each other, but employed internuncios, thus showing how strictly reserved should be intercourse between men and women, and preventing all disrespectful familiarity. When the wife was

III. *Kewen-urh.*

卷耳

采采卷耳。不盈
頃筐。嗟我懷人。
寘彼周行。

陟彼崔嵬。我馬
虺隤。我姑酌彼
金罍。維以不永
懷。

陟彼高岡。我馬
玄黃。我姑酌彼

1 I was gathering and gathering the mouse-ear,
But could not fill my shallow basket.
With a sigh for the man of my heart,
I placed it there on the highway.

2 I was ascending that rock-covered height,
But my horses were too tired to breast it.
I will now pour a cup from that gilded vase,
Hoping I may not have to think of him long.

3 I was ascending that lofty ridge,
But my horses turned of a dark yellow.

about to lie in, the husband took up his quarters in a side apartment, and sent to inquire about her twice a day. When the wife wished to visit her parents, she intimated her purpose through the matron. Inside the door of the harem, no liberty could be taken any more than with a reverend guest. Thus was the instruction of the people made to commence from the smallest matters, with a wonderful depth of wisdom!'

Ode 3. LAMENTING THE ABSENCE OF A CHERISHED FRIEND Referring this song to T'ae-sz', Choo thinks it was made by herself. However that was, we must read it as if it were from the pencil of its subject.

St.1. L.1. 采, both by Maou and Choo, is taken as in J. 3: the repetition of the verb denoting the repetition of the work; Tae Chin explains 采采 as='numerous, 'were many;' which also is allowable. There are many names for the 卷 (2d tune) 耳. Maou calls it the 苓耳; Choo, the 枲耳, adding that its leaves are like a mouse's ears, and that it grows in bunchy patches. The Pun-ts'aou calls it 苍耳, which, acc. to Medhurst, is the 'lappa minor.' The Urh-ya yih (爾雅翼) says that its seed-

vessels are like a mouse's ears, and prickly, sticking to people's clothes.

L. 2. The 頃筐 was a shallow basket, of bamboo or straw, depressed at the sides, so that it could be easily filled L.3. 我懷人= 我之所懷者, 'the man (or men) of whom I think, whom I cherish in my mind.' Who this was has been variously determined :—see on the Interpretation. L.4. 寘 (now written 置) =舍, 'to set aside.' 周行,—this phrase occurs thrice in the she. Here and in II. v. Ode IX., Choo explains it by 大道, 'the great or high way,' while Maou and his school make it =周之列位. 'the official ranks of Chow.' In II. i. Ode I., they agree in making it=大道 or 至道, meaning 'the way of righteousness.' Tae Chin takes 周=徧 and the whole line='I would place them everywhere in the official ranks.' Choo's explanation is the best here. There was anciently no difference in the sound of 行, however it might be applied. It would rhyme with 筐 in all its significations.

痡　我　瘏　我　砠　陟四葉　傷。　不　維　兒
矣。　僕　矣。　馬　矣。　彼　　　　　永　以　號。

I will now take a cup from that rhinoceros' horn,
Hoping I may not have long to sorrow.

4　I was ascending that flat-topped height,
But my horses became quite disabled,
And my servants were [also] disabled.
Oh! how great is my sorrow!

St 2. L.1. Choo, after Maou, gives 崔嵬 as 'a hill of earth, with rocks on its top,' whereas the Urh-ya gives just the opposite account of the phrase. The Shwoh-wǎn explains 崔 by 'large and lofty,' and 嵬 by 'rocks on a hill'; and I have translated accordingly. L.2. 虺隤 is, with Maou, simply = 病, 'diseased.' Choo takes the phrase as in the translation, after Sun Yen (孫炎) of the Wei dyn. L.3. 姑 = 且, and 姑且 together, indicate a purpose to do something in the meantime, = 'now', 'temporarily'. The 罍 was made of wood, carved so as to represent clouds, and variously gilt and ornamented. L.4. 維 has here a degree of force, = 'only.' Followed by 以, they together express a wish or hope, = 庶幾 永 = 長, 'for long.' L.3. The 兕 is the rhinoceros, 'a wild ox, with one horn, of a greenish colour, and 1000 catties in weight;' and 觥 was a cup made of the horn, very large, sometimes requiring, we are told, 3 men to lift it. L.4. 傷, 'to be wounded,'—here, to be pained by one's own thoughts.

St 3. L.2. 玄黃 is descriptive of the colour of the horses, 'so very ill that they changed colour.'

St.4. L.1. 砠 (Shwoh-wǎn, with 山, instead of 石, at the side) is the opposite of 崔嵬, in st.1, 'a rocky hill, topped with earth.' Here, again, the Urh-ya and the critics are in collision. Ll.2,3. 瘏 and 痡 are both explained in the Urh-ya by 病, 'to be ill', 'sickness.' Horses and servants all fail the speaker. His case is desperate. L.4. 云 must be taken here and in many other places, simply as an initial particle. Wang Yin-che calls it 發語詞. Choo explains 吁—'to sigh sorrowfully.' Maou makes it simply—'to be sorrowful,' as if it were formed from 心 and 于. The Urh-ya quotes the passage—云 何吁矣, which Wang T'aou would still explain in the same way as Maou does his reading.

The rhymes are—in st. 1, 嵬, 行., cat. 10: in 2, 嵬, 隤, 罍, 懷, cat. 15, t. 1: in 3, 岡, 黃, 觥, 傷., cat. 10: in 4, 砠, 瘏, 痡, 吁, cat. 5, t.1.

INTERPRETATION; AND CLASS. The old interpreters thought that this ode celebrated T'ae-sze for being earnestly bent on getting the court of Chow filled with worthy ministers; for sympathizing with faithful officers in their toils on distant expeditions; and for suggesting to king Wǎn to feast them on their return. The 1st st. might be interpreted in this way, taking the 2d and 3d lines as='I sigh for the men I think of, and would place them in the official ranks of Chow' They are quoted in the Tso Chuen. (after IX. xv. 2), with something like this meaning and by Seun K'ing (解蔽篇); though without any reference to T'ae-sze. To make the other stanzas harmonize with this, however, 我 must be taken, now as equal to 我君, 'my prince or husband,' and now as equal to 我使臣, 'my officers abroad on their commissions,' than which no interpretation could be more licentious. It is astonishing that the imperial editors should lean to this view;—on which the piece belongs to the allusive class.

Choo ascribes the ode to T'ae-sze. Her husband, 'the man of her heart,' is absent on some toilsome expedition; and she sets forth her anxiety for his return, by representing herself, first as a gatherer of vegetables, unable to fill her basket through the preoccupation of her mind; and then as trying to drive to a height from which she might see her husband returning, but always baffled. All this is told in her own person, so that the piece is narrative. The whole representation is, however, unnatural; and when the baffled rider proceeds to console herself with a cup of spirits, I must drop the idea of T'ae-sze altogether. and can make nothing more of the piece than that some one is lamenting in it the absence of a cherished friend, —in strange fashion

IV. Këw muh.

云何吁矣。

樛木

南有樛木。葛藟纍之。樂只君子。

福履綏之。南有樛木。葛藟荒之。樂只君子。

福履將之。南有樛木。葛藟縈之。樂只君子。

福履成之。

1   In the south are the trees with curved drooping branches,
With the dolichos creepers clinging to them.
To be rejoiced in is our princely lady·—
May she repose in her happiness and dignity!

2   In the south are the trees with curved drooping branches,
Covered with the dolichos creepers.
To be rejoiced in is our princely lady:—
May she be great in her happiness and dignity!

3   In the south are the trees with curved drooping branches,
Round which the dolichos creepers twine.
To be rejoiced in is our princely lady:—
May she be complete in her happiness and dignity!

Ode 4. CELEBRATING T'AE-SZE'S FREEDOM FROM JEALOUSY, AND OFFERING FERVENT WISHES FOR HER HAPPINESS. So far both the schools of interpreters are agreed on this ode. and we need not be long detained with it. The piece is allusive, supposed to be spoken or sung by the ladies of the harem, in praise of T'ae-sze, who was not jealous of them, and did not try to keep them in the back ground, but cherished them rather, as the great tree does the creepers that twine round it. The stanzas are very little different, the 3rd character in the 2d and 4th lines being varied, merely to give different rhymes.

St.1. L.1. For 'the south' we need not go beyond the south of the territory of Chow. K'ang-shing errs in thinking that the distant provinces of King and Yang, beyond the Keang. are meant. Trees whose branches curved down to the ground were designated 樛木. Such branches were easily laid hold of by creepers.

L.2. The 葛 was, probably, a variety of the 葛; 纍 is explained by 繫, 'to be attached to.' L.3. 只 is another of the untranslateable particles; it occurs both in the middle and at the end of lines. The critics differ on the inter-

pretation of 君子. Maou and his school refer it to king Wăn, and construe the last two lines,—'She is able also to rejoice her princely lord, and make him repose in his happiness and dignity.' Choo refers it to T'ae-sze, and what follows is a good wish or prayer for her. He defends his view of the phrase by the designation of 小君, given to the wife of a prince, (Ana. XVI. xiv.), and of 內子, given to the wife of a great officer. The imperial editors allow his exegesis. It certainly gives a unity to the piece. which it does not have on the other view, and I have followed it. L.4. Choo, after the Urh-ya and Maou, takes 履＝祿, 'e-molument,' 'dignity.' Trying to preserve the proper meaning of 履, 'to tread on', 'foot-steps,' Yen Ts'an (嚴粲; Sung dyn.) and others say, 動罔不吉謂之福履. 'The movements all felicitous are what is meant by 福履.' 綏＝安, 'to give repose to' St.2. 荒＝奄, or 庇覆, 'to cover', 'to overshadow.' The creepers send out their shoots,

V. *Chung-sze.*

福履成之。
螽斯

螽斯羽。薨薨兮。宜爾子孫。繩繩
螽斯羽。詵詵兮。宜爾子孫。振振

1　Ye locusts, winged tribes,
　　How harmoniously you collect together!
　　Right is it that your descendants
　　Should be multitudinous!

2　Ye locusts, winged tribes,
　　How sound your wings in flight!
　　Right is it that your descendants
　　Should be as in unbroken strings!

and cover the branches of the tree. 將 is here best taken as—大, 'to make great.'

St.3. 成=就, 'complete'. The singers wish the happiness of T'ae-sz', 'from first to last, from the smallest things to the greatest', to be complete.

The rhymes are—in st. 1, 累,縈, cat.15, t.1: in 2, 荒,將, cat. 10: in 3, 縈,成, cat. 11.

Ode 5. THE FRUITFULNESS OF THE LOCUST; SUPPOSED TO CELEBRATE T'AE-SZE'S FREEDOM FROM JEALOUSY. The piece is purely metaphorical (比), T'ae-sze not being mentioned in it. The reference to her only exists in the writer's mind. This often distinguishes such pieces from those which are allusive. The locusts cluster together in harmony, it is supposed, without quarrelling, and consequently they increase at a wonderful rate; each female laying, some say 81 eggs, others 99, and others 100.

L.1. in all the stanzas. The 斯 in 螽斯 is by many disregarded, as being merely one of the poetical particles. We shall meet with it as such beyond dispute, and we find 螽 alone, frequently in the Ch'un Ts'ëw. Here, however, it would seem to be a part of the name, the insect intended being the same probably, as the 斯螽, in xv., Ode I.5. Maou gives for it the synonym of 蚣蝑 and Choo calls it 'one of the locusts (蝗 屬).' But 蝗 will include crickets, grasshoppers, and locusts. We cannot as yet do more than approximate to an identification of the insects in the *She*. Williams calls the *chung-sze* one of the *truxalis* locusts; but

in descriptions and plates the length of the antennæ is made very prominent, so that the creature is probably to be found among the *achetidæ*. 羽 is to be taken as in the translation, —羽蟲, and not as meaning 'wings.' So, Ying-tah. The 'Complete Digest' says, 勿作翅說.

L.3. Maou and his school make 爾 to be addressed to T'ae-sze; Choo refers it, better, simply to the locusts. Those who refer it to the lady try to find some moral meaning, in addition to that of multitude, in the concluding lines. The three second lines are all descriptive of the harmonious clustering of the insects. 詵詵 is explained by Choo as the appearance of their 'collecting harmoniously,' and by Maou as meaning 'numerous'. The Shwoh-wǎn gives it as 莘 with 多 at the side. We have the character in the text, the form of the Shwoh-wǎn, 莘 with 羽 at the side, 先 with 馬 at the side, and 生 with another 生 at the side;—all in binomial form with the same meaning. 薨薨 is 'the sound of a crowd of locusts flying.' The bottom of the char. should be 羽, and not 死.

The last lines. 振振, is the 'appearance of their multitude;' Maou makes it—'benevolent and gen erous.' 繩繩,—'the appearance of uninter rupted continuance;' Maou makes it—'cautious,' or 'careful.' 蟄蟄, is the ap-

兮。螽　子　宜　揖　羽。螽^三
　螽　孫。爾　兮。揖　斯

3 Ye locusts, winged tribes,
   How you cluster together!
   Right is it that your descendants
   Should be in swarms!

VI. *T'aou yaou.*

室　宜　于　之　其　灼　夭　桃^一　桃
家。其　歸。子　華。灼　夭。之　　夭

1 The peach tree is young and elegant;
   Brilliant are its flowers.
   This young lady is going to her future home,
   And will order well her chamber and house.

pearance of their being 'clustered together like insects in their burrows.' Maou makes it= 'harmoniously collected.'

The rhymes are—in st.1, 詵 孫 振 cat.13: in 2, 薨 繩 cat.6: in 3, 揖 螽 cat.7.t.3.

The idea of all the critics is that Wăn's queen lived harmoniously with all the other ladies of the harem, so that all had their share in his favours, and there was no more quarrelling among them than among a bunch of locusts. All children born in the palace would be the queen's; and it was right they should increase as they did.— Surely this is sad stuff.

Ode 6. Allusive. PRAISE OF A BRIDE GOING TO BE MARRIED. The critics see a great deal more in the piece than this :—the happy state of Chow, produced by king Wăn (acc. to Choo), or by T'ae-sze (acc. to Maou), in which all the young people were married in the proper season, *i.e.*, in the spring, when the peach tree was in flower, and at the proper age, *i.e.*, young men between 20 and 30, and girls between 15 and 20. It *was* a rule of the Chow dyn. that marriages should take place in the middle of spring (Chow Le. II. vi. 54). This marriage would be about that time, and the peach tree was in flower ; but it was only the latter circumstance which was in the poet's mind.

St.1. L.1. 之 may be taken as the sign of the genitive, the whole line being=' in the young and beautiful time of the peach tree.' Still, 之 is so constantly used throughout the *She* in the middle of lines, where we can only regard it as a particle, eking out the number of feet,

that it is, perhaps, not worth while to resolve such lines as this in the above manner. 夭夭 (Shwoh-wăn, with 木 at the side) denotes 'the appearance of youth and elegance.' L.2. 灼灼 is descriptive rather of the brilliance of the flow- ers than of their luxuriance, as Choo has it. The young peach tree is allusive of the bride in the flush of youth, and its brilliant flowers of her beauty. L.3. 之=是, 'this;' 子='young lady.' Maou and Ch'ing take 于 as=往, 'to go to.' But it is better to regard it as a particle, as in Ode II.1. 歸 here is used of the bride going to her husband's house. As Choo says, women speak of being married as going home (婦人 謂嫁曰歸). Should we take 之子 in the singular or plural? Lacharme translates it by *puella nobiles*, and Heu Hĕen (許謙; Yuen dyn.) says, 'The poet saw the thing going on from the flowering of the peach tree till the fruit was ripe ;—the young ladies were many.' This seems to me very unpoetical. L.4. 室 is the chamber appropriated to husband and wife; 家 is 'all within the door,'—our *house*. 室家 here, 家室 in st.2, and 家人 in st.3, convey the same idea, the terms being varied for the sake of the rhythm. Tso-she says that when a couple marry, the man has a 室, and the woman a 家; so that 室家 are

桃之夭夭。　有蕡其實。　之子于歸。　宜其家室。

桃之夭夭。　其葉蓁蓁。　之子于歸。　宜其家人。

2　The peach tree is young and elegant;
　　Abundant will be its fruit.
　　This young lady is going to her future home,
　　And will order well her house and chamber.

3　The peach tree is young and elegant;
　　Luxuriant are its leaves.
　　This young lady is going to her future home,
　　And will order well her family.

VII.　*T'oo tseu.*

兔罝　肅肅　兔罝　椓之　丁丁。　赳赳　武夫。　公侯　干城。

1　Carefully adjusted are the rabbit nets;
　　Clang clang go the blows on the pegs.
　　That stalwart, martial man
　　Might be shield and wall to his prince.

equivalent to husband and wife. Accordingly, Maou takes the line as meaning, 'Right is it they should be married without going beyond their proper years;' and in this view he is followed by K'ang-shing. But to this there are two objections. 1st the antecedent to 其 is 之子, the girl, and the girl only. 2d, in the 4th line, 宜 must be construed as an active verb. So it is in the 'Great Learning,' Comm. ix.6, where the passage is quoted.

St.2. L.2. Choo says *fun* denotes the abundance of the fruit, intimating that the young lady would have many children. Maou makes the term—' the appearance of the fruit' intimating, that the lady had not beauty only, but also 'woman's virtue.' *Fun* is properly the seeds of hemp, which are exceedingly numerous; and hence it is applied to the fruit of other plants and trees to indicate its abundance. So, Lo Yuen (羅願; Sung dyn.), Wang T'aou, and others.

St.3. L.2. *Ts'in-ts'in* sets forth the luxuriance of the foliage,—至盛貌.

The rhymes are—in st.1, 華, 家, cat. 5, t. 1: in 2, 寶, 室, cat. 12, t. 3; in 3, 蓁, 人, ib., t.1.

Ode 7. Praise of a rabbit-catcher, as fit to be a prince's mate. Whether any particular individual was intended will be considered in the note on the interpretation. The generally accepted view is that the ode sets forth the influence of king Wǎn (acc. to Choo), or of T'ae-sze (acc. to Maou), as so powerful and beneficial, that individuals in the lowest rank were made fit by it to occupy the highest positions.

St.1. L.1. 罝 is defined in the *Urh-ya* as 'a rabbit-net;' to which Le Seun, the glossarist, (李巡; end of the Han dyn.), adds, that the rabbit makes paths underground for itself. 肅肅 descriptive of the careful manner in which the nets were set; Maou, of the reverent demeanour of the trapper. It is difficult to choose between them. On Choo's view the piece is *allusive*; on Maou's, *narrative*.

肅肅　施于　公　赳赳　施于　肅肅
兔罝。　中逵。　侯好　武夫。　中林。　兔罝。
　　　　　公侯　　　　　　　　公侯
　　　　　仇。　　　　　　　　腹心。

（三章）（二章）

2 Carefully adjusted are the rabbit nets,
   And placed where many ways meet.
   That stalwart, martial man
   Would be a good companion for his prince.

3 Carefully adjusted are the rabbit nets,
   And placed in the midst of the forest.
   That stalwart, martial man
   Might be head and heart to his prince.

VIII. *Fow-e.*

采采　有　薄　芣苢。　采采　薄　芣苢。　采　芣苢
采之。　言　　　　　采之。　言

1 We gather and gather the plantains;
   Now we may gather them.
   We gather and gather the plantains;
   Now we have got them.

L.2. 丁 (read *chǎng*) 丁 is intended to represent the sound of the blows (椓) on the pins or pegs (杙) used in setting the nets.

L.3. Both Maou and Choo give 赳赳 as—'martial-like,' while the Shwoh-wǎn defines the phrase by 輕勁有材力, 'light, vigorous, able, and strong.' L.4. 公侯 'duke and marquis;' together,—prince. We are to understand king Wǎn by the designation. At the time to which the ode refers, he was not yet styled king, and, indeed, Choo takes the phrase as one proof that Wǎn never assumed that title. Maou takes 干 = 扞, so that 干城 go together,—'defender,' or 'wall of defence;' probably after Tso-she, in his narrative appended to the 12th year of duke Ching. 'Shield and wall,' however, are suitable enough in the connection.

St.2. L.2. 施 is read *she*, 'to place,' 'to set.' 中逵 and 中林 below,—like 中谷 in Ode II. 逵 = 九達之道, a place

from which 9 ways proceed.' I have asked Wang T'aou and other scholars, whether such a thoroughfare was not an unlikely place to catch rabbits in, and got no satisfactory answer. L.4. 仇 = 逑 in Ode I.

There is a difficulty as to the rhyming of 逵 and 仇. The latter is said to be here read, by poetical license, k'e. A better solution is to adopt the reading of 首 with 九 at the side, instead of 逵, for which there is some evidence.

St.3. L.4. 腹心 — 'confidant and guide;' lit. 'belly and heart.' We do not use 'belly,' as the Chinese do.

The rhymes are—in st.1, 罝, 夫, cat. 5. t. 1; 丁, 城, cat. 11: in 2, 罝, 夫; 逵, 仇, cat. 3 t. 1 (this is a doubtful rhyme): in 3, 夫; 林, 心, cat. 7. t. 1. The alternate lines all rhyme, which is called 隔句韻.

采采芣苢。薄言掇之。采采芣苢。薄言将之。
采采芣苢。薄言祜之。采采芣苢。薄言襭之。

2　We gather and gather the plantains;
　　Now we pluck the ears.
　　We gather and gather the plantains;
　　Now we rub out the seeds.

3　We gather and gather the plantains;
　　Now we place the seeds in our skirts.
　　We gather and gather the plantains;
　　Now we tuck our skirts under our girdles.

IX. *Han kwang.*

漢廣　南有喬木、不可休息。漢有游女、不可求思。漢之廣

1　In the south rise the trees without branches,
　　Affording no shelter.
　　By the Han are girls rambling about,
　　But it is vain to solicit them.

INTERPRETATION. The ordinary view of this ode has been mentioned above. A special interpretation, however, which is worth referring to, has been put upon it. In the 2d of his chapters (尙賢, 上), Mih Teih says that 'king Wăn raised from their rabbit nets Hwang Yaou and T'ae T'een.' We find both those names in the Shoo (V. xvi. 12) as ministers of Wăn. Kin Le-ts'eang (金履祥; Yuen dyn.) and other scholars think, therefore, that this ode had reference to them. This view seems very likely.

Ode 8. Narrative. THE SONG OF THE PLANTAIN-GATHERERS. We are supposed to have here a happy instance of the tranquillity of the times of Wăn, so that the women, the loom and other household labours over, could go out and gather the seeds of the plantain in cheerful concert. Why they gathered those seeds does not appear. From the Preface it appears that they were thought to be favourable to childbearing. They are still thought in China to be helpful in difficult labours. Among ourselves, a mucilage is got from the seeds of some species of the plant, which is used in stiffening muslins.

St. 1. L. 1. 采采,—see on Ode III. The 芣苢 is one of the *plantaginaceæ*; probably our common ribgrass, as in the line of Tennyson, 'The hedgehog underneath the plantain bores.'

L. 2. 薄言,—both of these terms have been noticed, on Ode II., as untranslateable particles. Nothing more can be said of them, when they are found, as here, in combination.

Ll. 2, 4. 采之—'let us go and gather them;' 有之—'we have got them,' here they are. Maou, strangely, takes 有=藏, 'to collect,' 'to deposit.'

St. 2. Ll. 2, 4. 掇=拾, 'to gather,'—meaning the ears. 将=取, 'to take,'—meaning the seeds.

St. 3 祜=執衽, 'to hold up the skirt,'—meaning as in the translation. 襭=扱

方思。　之永矣。不可　馬漢之廣矣。　于歸。言秣其　刈其楚之子　翹翹錯薪言　不可方思　思江之永矣　廣矣。不可泳

> The breadth of the Han
> Cannot be dived across;
> The length of the Këang
> Cannot be navigated with a raft.

2　Many are the bundles of firewood;
　　I would cut down the thorns [to form more].
　　Those girls that are going to their future home,—
　　I would feed their horses.
　　The breadth of the Han
　　Cannot be dived across;
　　The length of the Këang
　　Cannot be navigated with a raft.

衽, 'to tuck the skirt under the girdle;' Medhurst says, 'round the waist.'

The rhymes are—in st. 1, 苜, 采, 苜, 有,—cat. 1, t. 2: in 2, 掇, 捋, cat. 15, t. 3; in 3, 袺, 襭, cat. 12, t. 3.

Ode 9. Allusive, and metaphorical. THE VIRTUOUS MANNERS OF THE YOUNG WOMEN ABOUT THE HAN AND THE KEANG. Through the influence of Wǎn, the dissolute manners of the people, and especially the women, in the regions south from Chow, had undergone a great transformation. The praise of the ladies in the piece, therefore, is to the praise of Wǎn. So say both Choo and Maou, the 'Little Preface' ceasing here to speak of T'ae-sze. The first 4 lines of each stanza are allusive, the poet proceeding always from the first two lines to the things alluded to in them or intended by them. The last 4 lines are metaphorical, no mention being made of the poet's inner meaning in them. To bring that out, we should have to supply,— 'Those ladies are like.' See the remarks of Lëw Kin (劉瑾; Yuen dyn.) appended to Choo's 'Collection of Comments,'—in the Yung-ching She.

St.1. L.1. The south here is difft. from that in Ode II. The connection makes us refer it to the States in Yang-chow and King-chow. 喬

木 means 'lofty trees with few or no branches

low down.' L.2. The 息 unites well enough with 休 of cognate meaning; but it can hardly be other than an error which has crept into the text, instead of 思, the particle with which all the other lines conclude, elsewhere found also at the end of lines. In those lofty trees, giving no shelter, we have an allusion to the young ladies immediately spoken of, virtuous and refusing their favours. L.3. The Han,—see the Shoo, III. i. Pt. ii. 8. L. 6. 泳=潛行. 'to go hidden in the water,' to dive. L.8. Choo defines 方 (or 舫) by 栰, and Maou by 泭; these characters are synonyms, meaning a raft; here—'to be rafted,' to be navigated with a raft. L.7. The Këang,—see the Shoo on III.i. Pt.ii. 9.—Rafts are seen constantly on the Këang. Does not the text indicate that in the time of the poet the people had not learned to venture on the mighty stream?

Stt. 2, 3. The first four lines in these stanzas are of difficult interpretation. 錯 is explained by 雜, 'mixed,' 'made up of different components,' so that 錯薪='bundles of faggots of different kinds of wood, or of wood and grass or brushwood together.' 翹翹 is given by Maou as indicating 'the appearance of the faggots;' but he does not say in what way. Choo

矣。不可　江之永　可泳矣　廣矣漢　駒。言秣　言子于　其蔞歸　薪翹翹　翹翹錯

3 Many are the bundles of firewood;
　I would cut down the southernwood [to form more].
　Those girls that are going to their future home,—
　I would feed their colts.
　The breadth of the Han
　Cannot be dived across;
　The length of the Kĕang
　Cannot be navigated with a raft.

X. *Joo fun.*

怒如　君子。　未見　條枚。　伐其　汝墳。　遵彼　汝墳　方思。

1 Along those raised banks of the Joo,
　I cut down the branches and slender stems.
　While I could not see my lord,
　I felt as it were pangs of great hunger.

says the phrase indicates 'the appearance of rising up flourishingly;' but how can this apply to bundles of faggots? Two other meanings of the phrase are given in the dict., either of which is preferable to this: viz., 'numerous (眾),' which I have adopted; and 'high-like (高貌).' 楚 is a species of thorn-tree (荊屬); and 蔞 is a species of artemisia. It is also called 蔞蒿 and 蔞萿, which last Medhurst calls 'a kind of southernwood.' It is described as growing in low places, and marshy grounds, with leaves like the mugwort, of a light green, fragrant and brittle. When young, the leaves may be eaten, and afterwards, they may be cooked for food. The reference to them in the text, however, is not because of their use for food, but, like the thorns, for fuel. The plant grows, it is said, several feet high; and even, with ourselves, the southernwood acquires a woody stem, after a few years. 秣 (Shweh Wăn, 餗)—'to feed.' 馬 is a full-grown horse, 'six cubits high and upwards;' 駒, is a colt, a young horse, 'between 5 and 6 cubits high;' but stress cannot be laid on the specific differences in the meaning of such terms, which are employed in order to vary the rhymes. But now, what relation was there between the piles of faggots, and cutting down the thorns and the southernwood? and how are the first two lines allusive of what is stated in the next two? Lacharme does not try to indicate this in his notes, and his translation is without Chinese sanction and in itself unjustifiable:—*Ex virgultorum variis fasciculis spinas resecare* '(St. 3, *herbas silvestres avellere) satagunt. Puellæ matrimonio collocantur, et quærunt unde pascant equos suos (St. 3, pullos equinos).*' The nearest approach to a satisfactory answer to those questions that I have met with, is the following:—Cutting down the thorns and the southernwood was a toilsome service performed for the faggots, but such was the respect inspired by the virtuous ladies whom the speaker saw, that he was willing to perform the meanest services for them. This I have endeavoured to indicate in the translation, though the nature of the service done to the faggots is not expressed by any critic as I have done. See the 'Complete Digest' *in loc.*, and the various suggestions in the 'Collection of Opinions (集說),' given in the imperial edition.

The rhymes are—in st. 1, 休, 求, cat. 3, t. 1: in 2, 楚, 馬, cat. 5, t. 2: in 3, 蔞, 駒, cat. 4: in all the stanzas, 廣, 泳, 永, 方, cat. 10.

父　雖　王　魴　不　既　伐　遵　調
母　則　室　魚　我　見　其　彼　飢。
孔　如　如　赬　遐　君　條　汝
邇。燬。燬。尾。棄。子。肄。墳。

2 Along those raised banks of the Joo,
  I cut down the branches and fresh twigs.
  I have seen my lord;
  He has not cast me away.

3 The bream is showing its tail all red;
  The royal House is like a blazing fire.
  Though it be like a blazing fire,
  Your parents are very near.

Ode 10. Mainly narrative. THE AFFECTION OF THE WIVES OF THE JOO, AND THEIR SOLICITUDE ABOUT THEIR HUSBANDS' HONOUR. The royal House, in the last stanza, like a blazing fire, is supposed to be that of Shang, under the tyranny of Chow. The piece, therefore, belongs to the closing time of that dyn., when Wăn was consolidating his power and influence. The effects of his very different rule were felt in the country about the Joo, and animated the wife of a soldier (or officer), rejoicing in the return of her husband from a toilsome service, to express her feelings and sentiments, as in these stanzas.

St. I. L. 1. The Joo is not mentioned in the Shoo. It rises in the hill of T'een-seih (天息), in Joo Chow, Honan, flows east through that province, and falls into the Hwae, in the dep. of Ying-chow (潁州), Ngan-hwui. 墳—大防, 'great dykes,' meaning the banks of the river, raised, or rising high, to keep the water in its channel. Some give the phrase 汝墳 a more definite meaning, and the site of an old city, which was so called, is pointed out, to the north east of the dis. city of Shĕh (葉), dep. Nan-yang. L. 2. 條=枝, 'branches.' 枚='small trees.' The speaker must be supposed to have been cutting these branches and trees for firewood. L. 3. 君子,—the speaker's 'princely man,'—'her husband.' She longed to see him. but she did not do so yet (未). L. 4. 怒 in the Urh-ya is explained both by 思, 'to think,' and by 飢, 'to be hungry.' Maou and Choo unite those definitions, and make it—飢意, 'hungry thoughts.' 調 (chow), with Maou,—朝, 'the morning,' so that the meaning is 'J feel like one hungry for the morning meal.' Much

better it is to adopt, with Choo, the reading of 輖, meaning 重, 'intense,' 'long-continued.'

St. 2. L. 2. 肄—'fresh shoots;' a year had gone by. The branches lopped in the past par. had grown again, or fresh shoots in their place. The husband had long been away; but at length he has returned. So the 既 in L. 3. intimates.

L. 4. 遐=遠='distant,' 'far' 遐棄, together,='to abandon.' 不我遐棄=不遐棄我, 'has not abandoned me'; but whether this expression be='my husband is not dead,' as K'ang-shing and many others take it; or='he comes back, with all the affection of our original covenant,' it would be hard to say. On the latter view the stanza is allusive, and the husband has not yet returned. The fresh shoots awaken the speaker's emotion, and she exclaims, 'Another day, when I shall have seen my husband, perhaps he will not cast me off!' As Yen Ts'an puts it, 他日已見君子,庶幾不遐棄我也.

St. 3. This stanza is metaphorical. L. 1. The fang is the bream called also 鯬 and 魾. 赬—赤, 'red.' The tail of the bream, we are told, is not naturally red like that of the carp; the redness in the text must be produced by its tossing about in shallow water. So was the speaker's husband toiled and worn out in distant service. The other 3 lines are understood to be an exhortation to the husband to do his duty to the royal House of Yin, notwithstanding the oppressiveness of Chow its Head. 燬—火 'a fire,' or to blaze as a fire. K'ang-shing and Ying-tah understand by 'parents' the husbands' parents, so that his wife's idea is that he should do his duty at all risks, and not disgrace his parents whom he should think of as always near him. Choo con-

XI. *Lin che che.*

麟之趾，振振公子，于嗟麟兮。
麟之定，振振公姓，于嗟麟兮。
麟之角，振振公族，于嗟麟兮。

1　The feet of the *lin*:—
　　The noble sons of our prince,
　　Ah! they are the *lin!*
2　The forehead of the *lin*:—
　　The noble grandsons of our prince,
　　Ah! they are the *lin!*
3　The horn of the *lin*:—
　　The noble kindred of our prince,
　　Ah! they are the *lin!*

siders that the phrase is a designation of king Wăn, as the 'parent' of the people; and the wife exhorts her husband ever to think of him, serving the House of Yin loyally, and to copy his example. It may be the best way to accept the view of the old interpreters. 孔=甚, 'very.'

The rhymes are—in St. 1, 枝, 飢, cat. 15, t.1: in 2, 犀, 棄, ib. t.3: in 3, 尾, 燬, 燬, 遁, ib, t.2.

Ode 11. Allusive. CELEBRATING THE GOOD-NESS OF THE OFFSPRING AND RELATIVES OF KING WĂN. The lin (Urh-ya, 麐) is the female of the k'e (麒), a fabulous animal, the symbol of all goodness and benevolence; having the body of a deer, the tail of an ox, the hoofs of a horse, one horn, the scales of a fish, &c. Its *feet* are here mentioned, because it does not tread on any living thing, not even on live grass; its *forehead* (定=題, Maou;—額, Shwoh-wăn), because it does not butt with it; and its *horn*, because the end of it is covered with flesh, to show that the creature, while able for war, wills to have peace. The *lin* was supposed to appear, inaugurating a golden age; but the poet intimates that he considered the character of Wăn's family and kindred as a better auspice of such a time. Choo adopts here the explanation of 振振 given on Ode V.1 by Maou,—仁厚貌 'benevolent and generous-like,' while Maou, I know not for what reason, changes 仁 into 信, and makes the phrase=' sincere and generous-like.' 公子 = the duke's sons' 公

姓=公孫 'the duke's grandsons.' The term 姓, 'surname,' is used for grandsons, because the grandson's descendants became a new clan, with the designation of his grandfather for a clan-name. By 公族 we are to understand all who could trace their lineage to the same high ancestor as the duke.

The rhymes are—in st.1, 趾, 子, cat.1, t.2: in, 2, 定, 姓, cat.11: in 3, 角, 族, cat.3, t.3: the 麟 at the end of each stanza is also considered as making a rhyme.

CONCLUDING NOTE. It is difficult for us to transport ourselves to the time and scenes of the pieces in this book. The Chinese see in them a model prince and his model wife, and the widely extended beneficial effects of their character and government. The institution of the harem is very prominent; and there the wife appears, lovely on her entry into it, reigning in it with entire devotion to her husband's happiness, free from all jealousy of the inferior inmates, in the most friendly spirit promoting their comfort, and setting them an example of frugality and industry. The people rejoice in the domestic happiness of their ruler, and in the number of his children, and would have these multiplied more and more. Among themselves, gravity of manners dignifies individuals of the meanest rank; and the rabbit-trapper is fit to be his prince's friend, guide, and shield. Purity is seen taking the place of licentiousness, both among women and men; and the wife is taught to prefer her husband's honour and loyalty to her own gratification in his society. The 4th Ode gives a pleasant picture of a bride, where yet her future work in her family is not overlooked; and the 8th, with its simple lines, shows to us a cheerful company of rib-grass-gatherers.

BOOK II. THE ODES OF SHAOU AND THE SOUTH.

I. *Ts'ëoh ch'aou.*

召南一之二

鵲巢

維鵲有巢。維鳩居之。之子于歸。百兩御之。

維鵲有巢。維鳩方之。之子于歸。百兩將之。

維鵲有巢。維鳩盈之。之子于歸。百兩成之。

1 The nest is the magpie's;
  The dove dwells in it.
  This young lady is going to her future home;
  A hundred carriages are meeting her.

2 The nest is the magpie's;
  The dove possesses it.
  This young lady is going to her future home;
  A hundred carriages are escorting her.

3 The nest is the magpie's;
  The dove fills it.
  This young lady is going to her future home:
  These hundreds of carriages complete her array.

TITLE OF THE BOOK.—召南一之二, 'Shaou Nan, Book II. of Part I.' On the title of the last Book, it has been stated that king Wăn, on removing to Fung, divided the original Chow of his House into two portions, which he settled on his son Tan, the duke of Chow, and on Shih, one of his principal adherents, the duke of Shaou. The site of the city of Shaou was in dep. of Fung-ts'ëang, and probably in the dis. of K'e-shan. Shih was of the Chow surname of Ke (姬), and is put down by Hwang-poo Meih as a son of Wăn by a concubine; but this is uncertain. After his death, he received the honorary name of K'ang (康公). On the overthrow of the Shang dyn., he was invested by king Woo with the principality of Yen, or North Yen (北燕), having its capital in the pres. dis. of Ta-hing (大興), dep. of Shun-t'ëen, where his descendants are traced, down to the Ts'in dyn. He himself, however, as did Tan, remained at the court of Chow, and we find them, in the Shoo, as the principal ministers of king Ching. They were known as the 'highest dukes (上公),' and the 'two great chiefs (二伯),' Tan having charge of the eastern portions of the kingdom, and Shih of the western.

The pieces in this Book are supposed to have been produced in Shaou and the principalities south of it,—west from those that yielded the odes of the Chow-nan.

Ode 1. Allusive. CELEBRATING THE MARRIAGE OF A BRIDE,—A PRINCESS, TO THE PRINCE OF ANOTHER STATE. The critics will all have it, that the poet's object was to set forth 'the virtue of the lady;' and wherein they find the allusion to that will be seen below. For myself I do not see that the *virtue* of the bride was a point which the writer wished to indicate; his attention was taken by the splendour of the nuptials.

St.1. L.1. 維,—see on i. Ode II.1. The *ts'ëoh* is the magpie. It is common in China, and generally called *he-ts'ëoh* (喜鵲); it makes the same elaborate nest as with ourselves. L.2. 鳩 is the general name for the dove; here, probably, the turtledove, the *she-këw* (鳲鳩). It has many local names. I do not know that it is a fact that the dove is to be found breeding in a magpie's nest, as is here assumed; but Maou K'o-ling vehemently asserts it, and says that any one with eyes may see about the villages a flock of doves contending with as many magpies, and driving the latter from their nests (續詩傳鳥名卷一). The *virtue* of the bride is thought to be emblemed by the quietness and stupidity of the dove, unable to make a nest for itself, or making a very simple, unartistic one. The dove is a favourite emblem with all poets for a lady; but surely never, out of China, because of its 'stupidity.' But says Twan Ch'angwoo (毀昌武), towards the end of the Sung dyn.), 'The duties of a wife are few and confined; there is no harm in her being stupid.'

L.4. 兩——車, 'a carriage,' as being supported on two wheels (兩輪). 御 is commonly read here *ya*, and generally when it has the signification of 'to meet.' But it rhymes here with *kev.* and the variation of its sound, according to its signification, is a device dating only from the Han dyn. The 100 carriages here are those of the bridegroom and his friends, who come to meet the lady, as she approaches the borders of his State.

St.2. L.2. 方之一有之, 'has it.' Yen Ts'an quotes a sentence which ingeniously explains this use of 方 as a verb,—方之以為其所也. L.4. 將—送, to escort.' The carriages here are those of the bride and all her *cortège*.

St.3. L.2. The 'filling' of the nest alludes to the ladies accompanying the bride to the harem. She would be accompanied by two near relatives from her own State, and there would be three ladies from each of two kindred States, so that the prince of a State is described by Kungyang as 'at once marrying 9 ladies (諸侯一娶九女). L.4. The 100 carriages here cover those of each of the previous stanzas. 成之,—as in i. IV. 3,='make her complete.'

The rhymes are—in st.1, 居御, cat. 5. t. 1; in 2, 方將, cat. 10: in 3, 盈成, cat. 11.

NOTE ON THE INTERPRETATION. In his interesting essay on the poetry of the Chinese, (already referred to), Sir John Davis gives the following paraphrase of this ode:—

'The nest yon winged artist builds,
The robber bird shall tear away:
—So yields her hopes the affianced maid,
Some wealthy lord's reluctant prey.

'The anxious bird prepares a nest,
In which the spoiler soon shall dwell:
—Forth goes the weeping bride constrained,
A hundred cars the triumph swell.

'Mourn for the tiny architect;
A stronger bird hath ta'en its nest:
Mourn for the hapless stolen bride,
How vain the pomp to soothe her breast!'

This is paraphrased, he says, 'to convey the full sense of what is only hinted at in the original, and explained in the commentary.' He has made a little poem, more interesting than the original; but altogether away from the obvious meaning of that original, on a view of it not hinted at in any commentary.

II. *Ts'ae fan.*

百兩成之。

采蘩

于以采蘩。于沼
于沚。于以用之。
公侯之事。
于以采蘩。于澗
之中。于以用之。
公侯之宮。
被之僮僮。夙夜
在公。被之祁祁。

1 She gathers the white southernwood,
   By the ponds, on the islets.
   She employs it,
   In the business of our prince.

2 She gathers the white southernwood,
   Along the streams in the valleys.
   She employs it,
   In the temple of our prince.

3 With head-dress reverently rising aloft,
   Early, while yet it is night, she is in the prince's *temple;*
   In her head-dress, slowly retiring,
   She returns *to her own apartments.*

Ode 2. Narrative. THE INDUSTRY AND RE-
VERENCE OF A PRINCE'S WIFE, ASSISTING HIM IN
SACRIFICING. Here we must suppose the ladies
of a harem, in one of the States of the South,
admiring and praising the way in which their
mistress discharged her duties;—all, of course,
add the commentators, through the transforming
influence of the court of Chow. There is a view
that it is not sacrificing that is spoken of, which
I will point out in a concluding note.

St. 1. L. 1. Maou says 于=於, which it is
in the next line; but 于 以 cannot be so construed. K'ang-shing and Ying-tah, seeing this,
made 于=往, which would do in the 1st
line, but not in the 3d. Our best plan is to take
于 and 以 together as a compound particle,
untranslateable; so, Wang T'aou (于 以 猶
薄 言，皆 發 聲 語 助 也). 蘩 is,
no doubt, a kind of *artemisia*, and is defined as
白 蒿, after which Medhurst terms it 'white
southernwood.' Its leaf is coarser than that of
the other *kaou*, with white hairs on it. It does
not grow high, like some other varieties, but

thick. The *fan* was used both in sacrifices, and
in feeding silkworms. L.2. 沼 is a pool or
natural pond, of irregular crooked shape, distinguished from 池, which is round. The
general name for island is 洲; a small *chow* is
called 渚; and a small *choo*, 沚. The *fan* is
not a water plant, so that we must take 于 as
=‘by,’ ‘on.’ L. 4. By 事 we must understand the business of sacrifice, *the* business, by
way of eminence. The sacrifice intended, moreover, must be celebrated in the ancestral temple,
within the precincts of the palace, as the lady
could take no part in sacrifices outside those.

公 侯,—together, as in i. VII. The lady's
husband might be a 公 or a 侯.

St. 2. 澗 is 'a stream in a valley (山夾水).'
Here, however, the idea is more that of a valley
with a stream in it. 宮=廟，'the ancestral
temple;' so, often in the Ch'un Ts'ëw.

III. *Ts'aou-ch'ing.*

憂其陟我見憂阜喓薄
心蕨彼心止。心螽。喓言
惙。南則亦忡未草還
惙。未山。降。既忡。見蟲。歸。
亦見言　觀亦君趯
既君采　止。既子。趯

1   *Yaou-yaou* went the grass-insects,
     And the hoppers sprang about.
     While I do not see my lord,
     My sorrowful heart is agitated.
     Let me have seen him,
     Let me have met him,
     And my heart will then be stilled.

2   I ascended that hill in the south,
     And gathered the turtle-foot ferns.
     While I do not see my lord,
     My sorrowful heart is very sad.
     Let me have seen him,

St. 3. 蔽 is described as 首飾 ‘an ornament for the head,’ and as being made of hair plaited. It was probably the same with what is elsewhere called the 闑, though Ying-tah identifies it with the 夭. 僮僮 (written also without the 人 at the side) is defined by Maou, as—敕敬, ‘standing up high and reverently.’ Then 祁祁 in l.3, is said to be 舒遲貌 ‘the appearance of leisurely ease.’ Both the predicates belong in the construction to the head-dress; in reality to the lady.— 夙夜 is not ‘from morning till night,’ as Lacharme takes it, but early in the morning, while it was yet dark (夙夜，非自夙至夜，乃夜之夙也，昧晦未分爲夜，天光向辰爲夙). The 公 in l.3 = 公所, the prince's place ‘the temple of last st. It must not be taken, says Choo, of ‘the prince's private chamber.’

The rhymes are—in st. 1, 𧎸, 事, cat. 1, t. 2: in 2, 中, 宮, cat. 9; in 3, 僮, 公, ﬦ.; 祁 歸, cat. 15, t. 1.

Note on the interpretation. The interpretation of the ode above given is satisfactory enough. Choo mentions another, however, which would also suit the exigencies of the case pretty well;—that it refers to the duties of the prince's wife in his silk-worm establishment. The *fan* would be useful in this, as a decoction from its leaves, sprinkled on the silkworms' eggs, is said to facilitate their hatching. The imperial editors fully exhibit this view, but do not give it the preference. Le Kwang-te (李光地; of the pres. dyn.) adopts it in his 詩所, and takes no notice of the other.

Ode 3. Narrative. The wife of some great officer bewails his absence on duty, and longs for the joy of his return. All the critics agree that the speaker is the wife of a great officer. According to Choo's view, she speaks as she is moved by the phænomena of the different seasons which she observes, and

見止。
覯止。
則說。

亦旣見止。
亦旣覯止。
我心則說。

陟彼南山。
言采其薇。
未見君子。
我心傷悲。
亦旣見止。
亦旣覯止。
我心則夷。

Let me have met him,
And my heart will then be pleased.

3   I ascended that hill in the south,
And gathered the thorn-ferns.
While I do not see my lord,
My sorrowful heart is wounded with grief.
Let me have seen him,
Let me have met him,
And my heart will then be at peace.

gives expression to the regrets and hopes which she cherished. He compares the piece with the 3d and 10th of last Book. The different view of the older interpreters will be noticed in the concluding note.

St. 1. Ll. 1, 2. 喓 (the Shwoh-wăn does not give the character) 喓 is intended to give the sound made by the one insect; and 趯 趯 represents the jumping of the other. What specific names they should receive is yet to be determined. I have meanwhile, translated 草蟲 literally. It is described as 'a kind of locust, green and with a wonderful note.' The pictures of it are like the *locusta viridissima*. The 阜螽 is, probably, the common grasshopper;—Seu Ting (徐鼎; of the time of K'een-lung) says there can be doubt of it (蚱蜢無疑也). The Urh-ya calls it 蠜 and the former 負蠜 or 'carrier of the *fan*.' These names arose from the belief that when the one gave out its note, the other leaped to it, and was carried on its back. 'They thus,' says K'ang-shing, 'sought each other like husband and wife.' This is the foundation of the old interpretation of the piece.

L. 4, in all the stanzas. 忡 忡 —'to be agitated,' as if it were 衝衝. The Shwoh-wăn explains both 忡 and 惙 by 憂. The predicates in all the three stanzas rise upon each other, as do those in the concluding lines. Ll. 5—7. Of 亦 and 止 we can say nothing but that they are two particles untranslateable; one initial, the other final. So, Wang Yin-che.

The turn in the thought, indeed, makes 亦 一 'but.'

Stt. 2,3. L. 2. 蕨 and 薇 are both ferns. Williams says on the former:—' An edible fern; the stalks are cooked for food, when tender, and a flour is made from the root. The drawing of the plant resembles an *aspidium*.' Choo says, 'The *wei* resembles the *keuoh*, but is rather longer; it has spinous points and a bitter taste. The people among the hills eat it.' The *keueh* is also called 蕨 and 蕨腳, as in the translation.

The rhymes are—in st. 1, 蟲, 螽, 忡, 降, cat. 9: in 2, 蕨, 惙, 說, cat. 15, t.3: in 3, 薇, 悲, 夷, *ib.* t. 1.

NOTE ON THE INTERPRETATION. The old interpreters say, like Choo, that the subject of the ode is 'the wife of a great officer;' but they make the subject of her distress, not the absence of her husband, but the anxiety incident to the uncertainty as to the establishment of her state as his acknowledged wife. According to the customs of those days, ladies underwent a probation of 3 months after their 1st reception by their husbands, at the end of which time they *might* be sent back as 'not approved.' The lady of the ode is supposed to be brooding during this period over her separation from her parents; and then anticipating the declaration of her husband's satisfaction with her, which would be an abundant consolation. I have noticed the *allusion* in the 1st two lines of the 1st st., which may be tortured into a justification of this view; but the other stanzas have nothing analogous. The interpretation may well provoke a laugh. The imperial editors take no notice of it.

IV.　*Ts'ae pin.*

有齊季女。
膈下。誰其尸之。
于以奠之。宗室
維錡及釜。
及筥。于以盛之。維筐
于以湘之。
于彼行潦。
之濱。于以采藻。
于以采蘋。南澗
采蘋

1　She gathers the large duckweed,
　　By the banks of the stream in the southern valley.
　　She gathers the pondweed,
　　In those pools left by the floods.

2　She deposits what she gathers,
　　In her square baskets and round ones;
　　She boils it,
　　In her tripods and pans.

3　She sets forth her preparations,
　　Under the window in the ancestral chamber.
　　Who superintends the business?
　　It is [this] reverent young lady.

Ode 4. Narrative. THE DILIGENCE AND RE-
VERENCE OF THE YOUNG WIFE OF AN OFFICER,
DOING HER PART IN SACRIFICIAL OFFERINGS.
The ancient and modern interpreters are to some
extent agreed in their views of this ode. Wherein
they differ will be noticed under the 3d stanza.

St. 1. 于以.—see on ode 2. The *p'in*
belongs to the same species of aquatic plants as
the 荇菜 of l. 1. The Pun-ts'aou says there
are three varieties of it:—the large, called *p'in*;
the small called 浮萍; and the middle, called
荇菜. Maou makes the *p'in* the large variety,
while Choo and some others make it the 3d.
Yen Ts'an observes that the *p'in* may be eaten;
but not the *fow p'ing*. If the *p'ing* could not be
eaten, it is not likely, he says, it would be gathered, like the plant here, to be used in sacrifice.
The *p'in* is, probably, the *lemna triondos*. The
ts'aou is the tassel-pondweed,—*ruppia rostella-
ta*. Both by Maou and Choo it is called 聚藻,
from the strings of tufts in which it grows. Williams erroneously translates 行潦 by 'a tor-
rent.' 潦 is, primarily, the 'appearance of great

rain; then 行潦, is the rain left after a
heavy fall of it, and by the flooded streams, on
the roads and plains.
St. 2. K'wang and *keu* are distinguished as
in the translation. They were both made of
bamboo. 湘 is defined by 烹 'to boil.' The
vegetables were slightly boiled and then pickled,
in order to their being presented as sacrificial
offerings. The 錡 is distinguished from the
釜, as 'having feet.'

St. 3. 奠=置, 'to place,' 'to set forth.'
室 may be taken as—宮,—廟, so that 宗
室 simply —'the ancestral temple.' More
particularly, however, the phrase may—'the
ancestral chamber,' a room behind the temple,
specially dedicated to the 大宗 or 'ancestor
of the great officer,' whose wife is the subject of
the piece. The princes of States were succeeded, of course, by the eldest son of the wife proper.
Their sons by other wives (庶子) were called
'other sons (別子).' The eldest son by the

V. Kan t'ang.

甘
棠

一章
蔽勿召勿蔽二章勿召蔽三章召勿
芾翦伯翦芾翦伯芾伯翦
甘勿所勿甘勿所甘所勿
棠伐。蔾。說。拜。棠敗。憇。棠。

1 [This] umbrageous sweet pear-tree;—
Clip it not, hew it not down.
Under it the chief of Shaou lodged.

2 [This] umbrageous sweet pear-tree;—
Clip it not, break not a twig of it.
Under it the chief of Shaou rested.

3 [This] umbrageous sweet pear-tree;—
Clip it not, bend not a twig of it.
Under it the chief of Shaou halted.

wife proper of one of them became the 大宗 of the clan descended from him, and the 宗室 was an apartment dedicated to him. The old interpreters, going upon certain statements as to the training of the daughters in the business of sacrifices in this apartment, for 3 months previous to their marriage, contend that the lady spoken of was not yet married, but that the piece speaks of her undergoing this preparatory education. The imperial editors mention their view with respect, but think it better to abide by that of Choo. The door of the 室 was on the east side of it, and the window on the west; and by the 廇下 is to be understood the south corner beyond the window, which was the most honoured spot of the apartment. In l.3, 尸主, 'to superintend.' The 其 is little more than a particle. In cases like the text, Wang Yin-che calls it 擬議之詞, 'a term or particle of deliberative inquiry.' The wife presided over the arrangement of the dishes in sacrifice, and the filling them with the vegetables and sauces. 馨 (read chae) = 敬, 'to respect,' 'reverent.' 茇一少, 'young.' This term gives some confirmation to the old interpretation of the ode.

The rhymes are—in st. 1, 蕷, 濱, cat. 12, t.1; 藾濼, cat.2; in 2, 苫, 釜, cat.5, t.2: in 3, 下 ᵤᵣ 女, ib.

Ode. 5. Narrative. THE LOVE OF THE PEOPLE FOR THE MEMORY OF THE DUKE OF SHAOU MAKES

THEM LOVE THE TREES BENEATH WHICH HE HAD RESTED. 召伯 might be translated 'Shaou, the chief;'—see note on the title of the Book. The nobleman is called pih, not as lord or duke of Shaou, but as invested with jurisdiction over all the States of the west. In the exercise of that, he had won the hearts of the people, and his memory was somehow connected with the tree which the poet had before his mind's eye, who makes the people therefore, as Tso-she says (XI. ix. under p. 1), 'think of the man and love the tree.' Stories are related by Han Ying and Lëw Heang of the way in which the chief executed his functions in the open air; but they owed their origin probably to the ode. We do not need them to enable us to enter into its spirit.

The kan-t'ang is, no doubt, a species of pear-tree. Maou identifies it with the too (杜), after the Urh-ya; others distinguish between them, saying that the fruit of the t'ang was whitish and sweet, while that of the too is red and sour. Maou makes 蔽芾=' small-like;' much better seems to be Choo's view of the phrase, which I have followed. 伐=擊, 'to strike' the tree, 'hew it down;' 敗, acc to Choo,—折, 'to break it;' and 拜=屈, 'to bend it,'—as the body is bent in bowing. The tree becomes dearer, the more the poet keeps it before him. The concluding characters of the stanzas have nearly the same meaning. 茇 is explained by 草舍, 'to halt among the grass;' 說 (read shwuy; al. 稅), simply by 舍, 'to halt,' 'to lodge;' and 憇 (al. 愒), by 息, 'to rest.'

VI. *Hing loo.*

誰謂鼠無牙。何以穿我墉。誰謂
室家不足。c
我獄。雖速我獄。
女無家。何以速
以穿我屋。誰謂
誰謂雀無角。何
夙夜謂行多露。
厭浥行露。豈不
行露

1 Wet lay the dew on the path:—
  Might I not [have walked there] in the early dawn?
  But I said there was [too] much dew on the path.

2 Who can say the sparrow has no horn?
  How else could it bore through my house?
  Who can say that you did not get me betrothed?
  How else could you have urged on this trial?
  But though you have forced me to trial,
  Your ceremonies for betrothal were not sufficient.

3 Who can say that the rat has no molar teeth?
  How else could it bore through my wall?

The rhymes are—in st. 1, 伐 蒺, cat. 15, t. 3; in 2, 敗 蔋, *ib.*; in 3, 拜 說, *ib.*

Ode 6. Narrative; and allusive. A LADY RESISTS AN ATTEMPT TO FORCE HER TO MARRY, AND ARGUES HER CAUSE. The old interpreters thought that we have here a specimen of the cases that came before the duke of Shaou; and Choo does not contradict them. Lëw Heang (列女傳貞順篇) gives this tradition of the origin of the piece:—A lady of Shin was promised in marriage to a man of Fung. The ceremonial offerings from his family, however, were not so complete as the rules required; and when he wished to meet her and convey her home, she and her friends refused to carry out the engagement. The other party brought the case to trial, and the lady made this ode, asserting that, while a single rule of ceremony was not complied with, she would not allow herself to be forced from her parents' house.

St. 1. *Yĕ-yĭ* conveys the idea of 'being wet.' 行=道, 'way,' 'path.' 夙夜,—see on II.3. The difficulty in interpreting and translating this stanza arises from the 豈不 'How not,' which must be supplemented in some way. Maou takes the characters as 有是, 'there was this;' meaning, acc. to K'ang-shing, that she might have been married at this dewy season of the year in the early morning. But on this allusive view, I cannot understand the last line, and hold, therefore, that the lady is here simply giving an illustration of the regard for her safety and character which she was in the habit of manifesting.

Stt. 2, 3 contain the argument. Appearances were against the lady; but to herself she was justified in her course. People would infer from seeing the hole made by a sparrow, that it was provided with a horn, though in reality it had none. Her 2d illustration is defective, if we take 牙 to mean, as is commonly said, only 'the grinders,' in opposition to 齒, the front or incisor teeth, for the rat has both incisors and molars, wanting only the intermediate teeth. But by 牙 is probably to be understood all the other teeth but the incisors. People might infer from seeing what it did, that its mouth was full of teeth, which is not the case. So they might infer, from her being brought by her prosecutors to trial, that their case was complete; but in reality it was not so. The 3d line is very perplexing, 一女 (=汝, 'you') 無家; but

女　亦　我　雖　訟　速　何　家。女
從。不　訟。速　　我　以　　無

Who can say that you did not get me betrothed?
How else could you have urged on this trial?
But though you have forced me to trial,
I will still not follow you.

VII. *Kaou yang.*

自　委　素　羔　委　退　素　羔一章
公　蛇　絲　羊　蛇　食　絲　羊　　　　羔
退　委　五　之　委　自　五　之　　　　羊
食。蛇。緎。革。蛇。公。紽。皮。

1　[Those] lamb-skins and sheep-skins,
　　With their five braidings of white silk!
　　They have retired from the court to take their meal;
　　Easy are they and self-possessed.

2　[Those] lamb-skins and sheep-skins,
　　With their five seams wrought with white silk!
　　Easy are they and self-possessed;
　　They have retired from the court to take their meal.

all the critics agree that we are to understand by 家 all the formalities of engagement and betrothal (以媒聘求爲室家之禮). We must take 室家 in the last line of st.2 in the same way. 速＝召致, 'to summon and bring to.' 獄 and 訟 are both =‘trial.' Maou gives for the former 埆, which should be, as in the Shwoh-wǎn, 确, the place where the defendant was confined while the case was pending.

The rhymes are—in st.1, 露, 夜 ‖ 露, cat.5, t.1: in 2, 角, 屋 獄 獄 足, cat.3, t.8: in 3, 牙 ‖ 家 ‖, cat.5, t.1; 爐 訟 訟 從, cat.9.

Ode. 7. *Narrative.* THE EASY DIGNITY OF THE GREAT OFFICERS OF SOME COURT. The structure of the piece is very simple, the characters and their order in the lines, and the orde-

of the lines themselves, being varied for the sake of the rhythm. By the ‘lamb-skins and sheep-skins' we are to understand the officers wearing such furs. It is better to do so than to take the piece as allusive.

革, in st. 2, is to be taken as = 皮. We cannot give it its proper signification of ‘the hide, with the hair taken off.' Great officers wore such furs;—some say, in court; others, as both Maou and Choo, in their own families. It is not worth while entering here on a discussion of the point. They were often dyed black, and being seamed together with white silk, the hems were conspicuous. 紽, 緎, and 總 all refer to the same thing,—the seams of the furs of which the robes were made. Choo acknowledges that he does not understand 紽 and 總, and Maou explains them both by 數, which is unintelligible.

The meaning of 紽 which I have followed is that given by K'oh King (郝敬; Ming dyn.):—�'s 素絲爲組 拚其縫際,

自 退 委 委 五 素 之 羔
公。食 蛇。蛇 總。絲 縫。羊

3 The seams of [those] lamb-skins and sheep-skins,
  The five joinings wrought with white silk!
  Easy are they and self-possessed;
  They have retired to take their meal from the court.

VIII.   *Yin k'e luy.*

何 南 殷 歸 振 莫 何 南 殷
斯 山 其 哉 振 敢 斯 山 其   殷
違 之 靁。在 歸 君 違 之 靁。   其
斯。側。   哉。子 遑。陽。在   靁

1 Grandly rolls the thunder,
  On the south of the southern hill!
  How was it he went away from this,
  Not daring to take a little rest?
  My noble lord!
  May he return! May he return!

2 Grandly rolls the thunder,
  About the sides of the southern hill!
  How was it he went away from this,

日靁; and for that of 總, I am indebted to Hoo Yih-kwei (胡一桂; Yuen dyn.);—合二爲一謂之總 Maou says 縅 is the same as 縫,—after the Urh-ya.

委蛇 (al. 佗)—自得之貌, 'the app. of self-possession.' Maou says it denotes 'the straight and equal steps with which the officers walked.' 公—公門, 'the duke's gate,' or generally 'the court.'

The rhymes are—in st. 1, 皮 靁. 蛇, cat. 17: in 2, 革 緎 食, cat. 1, t. 3: in 3, 縫 總 公. cat. 9.

Ode. 8. Allude. A LADY'S ADMIRATION OF HER HUSBAND ABSENT ON PUBLIC SERVICE, AND HER LONGING FOR HIS RETURN. The lady, it must be supposed, is the wife of a great officer.

She hears the rolling of the thunder, and is led to think of her absent husband. Yen Ts'an observes that the piece is simply allusive, without any metaphorical element (與之不兼比者); but K'ang-shing and others torture the first two lines into symbols of the officer on his commission. The rhythmical variations in the stanzas are, it will be seen, very small. L. 1. 殷 (sometimes doubled) represents the solemn sound of thunder, heard rolling at some considerable distance off. 其 is the demonstrative,—'the,' or 'that.' 靁 has now given place to the less complicated 雷. L. 2. 'The southern hill' must be one of the hills in the south of the territory of Chow. The southern side of a hill is called 陽. L. 3. The 1st 斯=斯人. So, Maou and Choo; better than Yen Ts'an, who makes it—斯時, 'at this time.' The

歸振莫何南殷三歸振莫
哉振敢斯山其哉振敢
歸君遑違之靁。歸君遑
哉。子。處。斯。下。在哉。子。息。

Not daring to take a little rest?
My noble lord!
May he return! May he return!

3 Grandly rolls the thunder,
At the foot of the southern hill!
How was it he went away from this,
Not remaining a little at rest?
My noble lord!
May he return! May he return!

IX. *P'eaou yew mei.*

庶兮。其標三其庶兮。其標三標
士。求實有有士。求實有有
迨我三梅。吉迨我七梅。梅
兮。 兮。

1 Dropping are the fruits from the plum-tree;
There are [but] seven [tenths] of them left!
For the gentlemen who seek me,
This is the fortunate time!

2 Dropping are the fruits from the plum-tree;
There are [but] three [tenths] of them left!
For the gentlemen who seek me,
Now is the time.

2nd—斯所, 'this place.' 違—去, 'to go away from,' 'to leave.' L. 4. 遑—暇, 'leisure.' The Urh-ya has 偟, but the oldest reading was simply 皇, in the same sense. Wang T'aou, Wang Yin-che, and many others, take 或 here—有, so that the line—不敢有暇. I prefer, however, the construction of Yen Ts'an:—或者閒或之義不敢或違, 則無一時之暇矣. In the other stanzas 違 is used adverbially. L. 5. 振振,—see on i. XI. L. 6. The repetition of 歸哉 is understood to express a wish for the husband's return, but with submission to his absence so long as duty required it.

The rhymes are—in st. 1, 陽, 遑, cat. 10: in 2, 側, 息, cat. 1, t. 3: in 3, 下 or 處, cat. 5, t. 2. In addition to the above, the 1st, 3rd, 5th, and 6th lines of the three stanzas are supposed to rhyme with one another.

$$其今$$

$$標兮$$

$$梅$$

$$之筐$$

$$士我之$$

$$其謂迫庶求塈頃有$$

3 Dropt are the fruits from the plum-tree;
   In my shallow basket I have collected them.
   Would the gentlemen who seek me
   [Only] speak about it!

X. Sëaou sing.

$$小星$$

$$嘒彼$$

$$小星$$

$$三五$$

$$在東。$$

$$蕭蕭$$

$$宵征。$$

$$夙夜$$

$$在公。$$

1 Small are those starlets,
   Three or five of them in the east.
   Swiftly by night we go;
   In the early dawn we are with the prince.
   Our lot is not like hers.

Ode 9. Narrative. ANXIETY OF A YOUNG LADY
TO GET MARRIED. It is difficult for a foreigner
to make anything more out of the piece. The
critics, however, all contend that it is not the
desire merely to be married which is here expressed, but to be married in accordance with
propriety, and before the proper time was gone
by. They mix up two things :—the age when
people should be married, males before 30, and
females before 20 ; and the season of the year,
most proper for marriages,—the season of spring.
We can see an allusion to the latter, in the
stanzas, but none to the former.

L. 1. 摽=落, 'to fall.' It is difficult to
construe the 有, which has no more force
than the 其 in the last ode. See under 有 in
the 3d index to the Shoo, where this peculiarity
of the usage of 有 is pointed out. None of
the critics say a word about it here. The mei is
the general name for the plum tree ; here a species, whose fruit is rather small and sour, and
which ripens earlier than the peach. The falling
of the plums makes the lady think of her own
ripeness, and that it was time she should be
plucked and married.

L. 2. Are we to understand 七 and 三 of 7
plums and 3 plums left on the tree, or as in the
translation ? Maou. Choo, and the commentators
generally understand the single plums ; Ying-tah
adopts the proportional view (十分之中,
倘在樹者七). I agree with him be-
cause of the last stanza, for what need would
there be of a basket to gather 3 plums ?

Ll. 3. 4. The freedom of the lady's expressions in these lines have been a stumbling-block
to many. Ying-tah says, 'We are not to understand that the lady is speaking in her own person (非女自我), but that the poet per-
sonates any marriageable young person.' Hwang
Chin (黃震 ; end of the Sung dyn.) hears in
the words the language of a go-between, expressing the desire of the parents. But the 我
cannot be thus explained away. 迫及,—'till.'
It is here—our 'while.' As Choo expands the
line, 其必有及此吉日而來,
'they must come up to (=while it is now) this
fortunate time.'

In st. 3; 頃筐,—see i.III. 塈 (al. 摡)=
取, 'to take,' 'gather.' 迫其謂之—'if
they would but come to the speaking about it ;'
as Lacharme has it, ' diem dicat ille.' The lady
is prepared to dispense with all previous formalities (但相告語而約可定).

The rhymes are—in st. 1, 七, 吉, cat.12,
t. 3 : in 2, 三, 今, cat. 7, t.1 : in 3, 塈, 謂,
cat.15, t.3.

Ode 10. Allusive. THE THANKFUL SUBMISSION
TO THEIR LOT OF THE INFERIOR MEMBERS OF A
HAREM. We must suppose that we have here
the description by one of the concubines of the
lot of herself and her companions. It is the
early dawn. and she is returning from her visit
to the prince's chamber, which had been allowed

不　裯。抱　蕭　與　星。嘒二章　同。　寔
猶。　寔　衾　宵　昴。　維　彼　　　　命
　　命　與　征。蕭　參　小　　　　不

2　Small are those starlets,
　And there are Orion and the Pleiades.
　Swiftly by night we go.
　Carrying our coverlets and sheets.
　Our lot is not as hers.

XI. *Këang yew sze.*

以。不　以。不　歸　之　氾。江一章　江
我　　我　　　子　　有　　氾
　我　　我　　　　　　　有

1　The Këang has its branches, led from it and returning to it.
　Our lady, when she was married,
　Would not employ us.
　She would not employ us;
　But afterwards she repented.

her by his wife. Only the wife could pass the whole night with her husband. The other members of the harem were admitted only for a short time, and must go and return in the dark. But so had the influence of king Wăn and T'ae-sze wrought, that throughout Shaou and the south the wives of the princes allowed their ladies freely to share the favours of their common lord, only subject to the distinctive conditions belonging to her position and theirs. Hence as *they* were not jealous, *the others* were not envious. Such is the interpretation given to this piece; but there are difficulties, it will be seen, with some of the lines.

L. 1. 嘒=小貌, 'small-like.' L. 2. 三五 are best translated literally, meaning a few. So, Choo. Maou makes them out to be certain stars in Scorpio and Hydra; but it seems decisive against him that those stars are not visible together in the morning, in the same month. There can be no doubt, however, as to the identification of 參 and 昴 in st. 2; but we must not seek, in the 1st line, a special allusion to the mass of the concubines, and in the 2d to those of higher rank among them. Maou explains 蕭蕭 as 'the app. of rapidity,' to which Choo would add that of 'reverence.' 征=往, to go.' 宵=夜, 'at night.' The difficulty to me is with the 4th line. If 宵 denote the

time of the concubines' going, and 夙夜 the time of their return, then they have been the night with the prince. It seems to me that 宵 and 夙夜 must have nearly the same meaning, and that 宵 should be translated—'in the dark.' 在公 is inconsistent with the 4th line's speaking of the return of the ladies. K'ang-shing's view, that 夙夜=或早或夜 'some early, some late,' and that this and the next line set forth the different times at which different ladies were received, ought not to be entertained. It is a strange picture which the 4th line of st.2 gives us, of the concubines carrying their sheets with them to the prince's chamber. L 5. This line expresses the acquiescence of the concubines with their lot. 寔 or 寔 may be taken as=是, 'to be,' 'it is.' The use of 猶 as an adjective is to be noted.

The rhymes are—in st. 1, 星, 征, cat. 11; 東, 公, 同, cat. 9: in 2, 星, 征; 昴, 裯, 猶, cat. 3, t.2.

Ode 11. Allusive. JEALOUSY CURED. THE RESTORATION OF GOOD FEELING IN A HAREM. Acc. to the little Preface, with which Choo in the main agrees, the bride of some prince in the

其嘯也歌。 過。不我過。 之子歸。不我過。 江有沱。三章 其後也處。 與。不我與。 之子歸。不我與。 江有渚。二章 其後也悔。

2 The Këang has its islets.
Our lady, when she was married,
Would not let us be with her.
She would not let us be with her;
But afterwards she repressed [such feelings].

3 The Këang has the T'o.
Our lady, when she was married,
Would not come near us
She would not come near us;
But she blew that feeling away, and sang.

south had refused to allow her cousins, who by rule should have accompanied her, to go with her to the harem; but afterwards, coming under the influence of the govt. of king Wăn and the character of T'ae-sze, she repented of her jealousy, sent for them, and was happy with them. Such is the traditional interpretation of the piece, and the lines suit it tolerably well.

L. 1, in all the stanzas. 汜 is the name for streams derived from larger rivers, flowing through a tract of country, and then conveyed into their mother stream again. From the definition of the term in the Urh-ya, 水決復入爲汜, it would appear that such streams were made in the 1st place artificially. 渚 is 'a small islet.' Rising in the stream, it divides its water s which again unite at the other end of it. 沱 was the name of rivers issuing from the Këang, pursuing a different course from the main stream, but ultimately rejoining it. Two T'os are mentioned in the Shoo (III. i. Pt. i. 64; Pt. ii. 9): These lines conta n the allusive portion of the ode, giving, all of them, the ideas of separation and reunion.

L. 2. The 之子 is, of course, the wife that is spoken of, and in the connection 之子歸 =此子向者于歸之時, 'this lady, formerly, when she went to her home.' Ll. 3, 4 These lines all describe the early conduct of the wife, though it as perhaps too

much to infer, with the critics, from the words, that she left her cousins in their native State. There is nothing in the terms which would not be satisfied with their having in the first place accompanied her to the harem, and then been kept by her in the background. 以 is to be taken in the sense of 用, 'to employ.' 與 is not distinguished by Choo from 以. We may explain it by 'to be with,' 'to associate with.' We hardly know what to make of 過. Choo says, 過謂過我而與俱也, 'to pass close to us, and then to be together with us.' L. 5. describes the wife's subsequent conduct. I cannot follow Choo in his account of 處,—安也; 得其所安也. Maou explains it by 止, 'to stop,' 'to desist;' which K'ang-shing enlarged to 自止, 'she repressed herself.' 嘯 is 'to purse up the mouth and emit a sound,'— 'to blow,' 'to whistle.' Morrison quotes the line under the character, saying, 'K'e seaou yay ko, "whistled and sang," to divert the mind from what vexed it;' but the whistling and singing was an expression rather of relief and satisfaction.

The rhymes are—in st. 1, 汜, 以, 以, 悔, cat. 1, t. 2: in 2, 渚, 與, 與, 處, cat. 5, t 2 in 3, 沱 過 過 歌, cat. 17.

XII. *Yay yew szĕ keun.*

野有死麕

尨感舒有死林吉包野一章
也我而女鹿有士之。有
吠。悅脫如樸誘有死
。兮脫玉。樕之。女麕。
無兮。白野懷白
使無 茅有春。茅
 純
束。

1　In the wild there is a dead antelope,
　　And it is wrapped up with the white grass.
　　There is a young lady with thoughts natural to the spring,
　　And a fine gentleman would lead her astray.

2　In the forest there are the scrabby oaks;
　　In the wild there is a dead deer,
　　And it is bound round with the white grass.
　　There is a young lady like a gem.

3　[She says], Slowly; gently, gently;
　　Do not move my handkerchief;
　　Do not make my dog bark.

Ode. 12. A VIRTUOUS YOUNG LADY RESISTS THE ATTEMPTS OF A SEDUCER. The little Preface says that the piece teaches disgust at the want of proper ceremonies, and belongs to the close of Chow's reign, when the influence of king Wăn was gradually prevailing to overcome the lust and license, through which the Shang dynasty was extinguished. A lady is sought to be won by insufficient ceremonies, yet they were better than none, and showed that the times were mending; and she is willing. He must be clear-sighted who can see traces of all this in the ode. The view which I take of it is substantially the same as Choo's, who inclines to look on it as an allusive piece, but at the same time allows it may be taken as narra ive. It is not worth while to enter on this question.

St. 1. Ll 1,2. 野 denotes 'the open country, beyond the suburbs,' not . yet brought under cultivation. 麕, written also with 君 and with 禾 under the 鹿, is said to be the same as the *chang* (鹿 with 章 under it), which Medhurst calls a kind of musk deer, and Williams, a kind of gazelle. Choo says it is hornless, and Williams thinks therefore it may be the *antilopé gutturosa*, the doe of which has no horns. The figure of the creature, however, in Seu

Ting's plates, has short horns. It has yet to be iden ified. 茅 is a name both of a grass and a rush; here apparently, designa ing the former. We are told that ·it is very common, with a large leaf, soft and white, the lines on it quite straight.' L. 3. We have already seen that the spring was the favourite time for marriages. The ancient legislators of China would have the pairing time of the lower creatures to be also the nuptial season in human societies; 懷春 'cherishing the spring,' therefore = thinking of marriage. L. 4. 吉＝美 'fine' 'elegant;' but we must understand the epithet to be applied ironically. So, Yen Ts'an. I do not see how 誘 can have any other meaning than that given to it in the translation. Maou's explanation of it by 道, so that 誘之＝謂之, in IX. 3, is inadmissible.

St. 2. Ll 1,3. All that we learn from Maou and Choo about the *p'uh-suh* is that it is 'a small tree.' The figure of it in the Japanese plates to the She leaves no doubt that it is a kind of oak. An able botanist in Yokohama to whom it was submitted, pronounced it the *quercus serrata.* · I have ventured, therefore, to translate the name 'by scrubby oaks.' 鹿 is the

XIII.   *Ho pe nung.*

齊 平 華 何二 王 曷 唐 何二   何
侯 王 如 彼穠 姬 不 棣 彼穠   彼穠
之 之 桃 彼穠 之 蕭 之 彼穠   彼穠
子。孫。李。矣。車。雝。華。矣。   矣。

1   How great is that luxuriance,
    Those flowers of the sparrow-plum!
    Are they not expressive of reverence and harmony,—
    The carriages of the king's daughter?

2   How great is that luxuriance,
    The flowers like those of the peach-tree or the plum!
    [See] the grand-daughter of the tranquillizing king,
    And the son of the reverent marquis!

general name for the deer tribe; specially, it is
figured as the spotted axis. 純 (t'un) 束,
'to tie up in a bundle,'—the 包之 of last stanza. L. 4. Choo says that 如玉 intimates
the girl's beauty. I think, with Maou, that the
poet would represent by it her virtue rather.

St.3. We must take these lines as the language of the young lady, warning her admirer
away. Her meaning gleams out indeed but
feebly from them, but I have met with no other
exposition of the stanza, which is not attended
with greater difficulties. The 而, in 舒而
=如, so that the phrase—'slow-like,' 'slowly;'
much the same is the meaning of 脫 (chune) 脫
感—'to move,' 'to touch;' as if the character
were 憾. The napkin or handkerchief (帨
拭物之巾) was worn at the girdle.
'This 2nd line,' says Hoo Yih-kwei. 'warns the
man away from her person, as the next warns
him from her house.' The Shwoh-wän defines
尨, as 'a dog with much hair,'—a tyke; but
we may take it with Choo as simply a
synonym of 犬. The student will do well to
refer to the application which is made of this
line in the 1st narrative subjoined by Tso-she to
par. 8 of XI. i., in the Ch'un Ts'ëw.

The rhymes are—in st. 1, 蕐 春. cat. 13;
包, 誘, cat. 3, t. 2: in 2, 穠, 鹿, 束, 玉
孫, t. 8: in 3, 脫, 帨, 狀, cat. 15, t. 3.

Ode 13. Allusive. THE MARRIAGE OF ONE
OF THE ROYAL PRINCESSES TO THE SON OF ONE
OF THE FEUDAL NOBLES. The critics, of course,
all see a great deal more in the piece than this,
and think that it celebrates the wifely dignity
and submissiveness of the lady. Whether any-
tning can be determined as to who she was will
be considered on the 2d stanza.

Stt.1,2. Ll.1,2. 穠 (or in Maou, with 衣 at
the side) denotes 'the appearance of abundance.'
There are great differences of opinion about the
tree called t'ang-te. Maou, after the Urh-ya, calls it
the e (移), and is followed by Choo, who adds that
it is like the white willow (白楊). Descriptions
are given of the constant motion and quivering
of its leaves, which would make us identify it
with the aspen, a species of the poplar. But the
flowers of the tree are what the writer has in
view, and this forbids our taking it for a willow
or a poplar. Wang T'aou argues moreover that
the 移 in the Urh Ya and Maou is a mistake
for 棣. Evidently, from the 2d line of st. 2,
the tree in the ode is akin to the peach and the
plum. And so say many commentators. Luh
Ke (陸璣; during the time of the 'Three
Kingdoms') makes it out to be the same as the
yuh li (薁李), called also the 'sparrow's plum,'
and other names. The flowers of this are both
white and red, and the fruit is distinguished in
the same way. I suspect the tree here is the
white cherry.

Ll.3,4. 蕭 is explained by 敬, 'to be re
verent' and 雝 by 利. 'to be harmonious,
And say the critics, 'reverence and harmony

之　平　之　齊　伊　維　維　其^{三章}
孫。王。子。侯　緡。絲　何。釣

3　What are used in angling?
　　Silk threads formed into lines.
　　The son of the reverent marquis,
　　And the grand-daughter of the tranquillizing king!

XIV　*Tsow-yu.*

虞。于　壹　彼^{二章}虞。于　壹　彼^{一章}
　嗟　發　苗　　嗟　發　苗　　騶虞
　乎　五　者　　乎　五　者
　騶　豵。蓬，　騶　豝。葭。

1　Strong and abundant grow the rushes;
　　He discharges [but] one arrow at five wild boars.
　　Ah! he is the Tsow-yu!

2　Strong and abundant grows the artemisia;
　　He discharges [but] one arrow at five wild boars.
　　Ah! he is the Tsow-yu!

are the chief constituents of wifely virtue.' What there was about the carriages to indicate these virtues in the bride, we are not told. She is called a royal *Ke,* 姬 being the surname of the House of Chow. Evidently she was a king's daughter. Most naturally we should translate the 2d and 3d line of st. 2,

'The grand-daughter of king P'ing.
And the son of the marquis of Ts'e;'

but, so taken, the piece must be dated about 400 years after the duke of Shaou, and is certainly out of place in this Book of the She. Choo, indeed, is not sure but they may be correct who find here king P'ing and duke Seang of Ts'e; but the imperial editors sufficiently refute that view. We must take 平 and 齊 as two epithets, the former designating. probably, king Wǎn, and the latter some one of the feudal princes.

St. 3　L. 2. 伊 has no more force here than the 維. Yin-che says it is synonymous with 維, but the examples he adduces have the sense of 'but,' 'only.' The case in the text is sufficient to show that the two particles are synonymous only when they have that sense.

緡—綸, 'a cord' 'a string. The allusion in the silk twisted into fishing lines would seem to be simply to the marriage—the union—of the princess and the young noble. I cannot follow Maou and his school, when they make it out to be to the lady's ' holding fast of wifely ways to complete the virtues of reverence and harmony.'

The rhymes are—in st. 1, 綸, 絲, cat. 9; 華, 車, cat. 5, t. 1: in 2, 何, 李 子, cat. 1, t. 2: in 3, 緡, 孫, cat. 13.

Ode 14. Narrative. CELEBRATING SOME PRINCE IN THE SOUTH FOR HIS BENEVOLENCE. There is a general agreement as to the object of this short piece, though there are great differences, as we shall see, in the explanation of it in detail. Its analogy to the concluding ode in the 1st Book is sufficiently evident, and must be allowed to have the turning weight in settling the interpretation.

Ll. 1. 苗 expresses the fresh, vigorous appearance of plants, as they first rise above the ground. 葭 is another name for 蘆, which Williams calls—' high rushes along river courses.' When full-grown and flowered, they are called 葦.

We must suppose that the prince, who is the subject of the ode, is hunting in spring, by some lake or stream where such rushes were common. Maou and Choo say nothing more about 蘩 than that it is the name of a grass. According to the Shwoh-wǎn, it should be a kind of artemisia. One account of it says that its flowers grow like the catkins of the willow, and fly about in the wind, like hair.

Ll. 2. Maou gives 豝 as 'the female of the swine;' and in the connection we must understand the wild animal. Choo makes it just the opposite,—the male, Maou took his account from the Urh-ya; but in both cases I imagine there is an error of the text,—牝 for 牡. To shoot female animals would be inconsistent with the benevolence which the piece is understood to celebrate. The Kwang-ya, without reference to the sex, says, 'the *pa* is a pig two years old,' and all authorities agree in taking *ts'ung*, as one, 'one year old.' But we cannot suppose that the poet laid any stress on these special distinctions of the terms. He varied them to suit his rhymes merely. —發—'by one discharge,' *i.e.*, of his arrows, acc. to Choo. The prickers, it is understood, had driven together a herd of the animals; but the noble would not kill them all. He contented himself with discharging the four arrows, which constituted what we may call a round. But could he kill 5 boars with 4 arrows? Choo supposes that one of the arrows transfixed two of them. This does not seem very likely; and I am inclined to adopt the view of K'ang-shing, as expounded by Ying-tah, that out of 5 boars driven together the prince would shoot only one (君止一發,必翼五 豝者,中則殺一而已.)

Ll. 3. The great battle of the ode, however, is over 騶虞. Maou and Choo. after him, take these terms as the name of a wild beast, 'a righteous beast; a white tiger, with black spots, which does not tread on live grass, and does not eat any living thing, making its appearance when a State is ruled by a prince of perfect benevolence and sincerity. Being a tiger, it might be expected to kill animals, like other tigers, but it only eats the flesh of such as have died a natural death.' This view of the terms was not challenged till Gow-yang Sëw of the Sung dyn., who contended that we are to understand by them the huntsmen of the prince's park. Since his time this interpretation has been variously enlarged and insisted on. One of the ablest asserters of it is Yen Ts'an, who appeals to the fact that the Urh-ya says nothing of the fabulous animal, as a proof that it was not heard of before Maou. The imperial editors. however, refute this statement, and I agree with

them that the old view is not to be disturbed. The analogy of the *Lin che che* is decisive in its favour. 于嗟乎 here—于嗟... 分 of that ode.

The rhymes are—in st. 1, 葭 . 豝 . 虞 and 虞 of st. 2, cat. 5, t. 1: in 2, 蓬, 縱, cat. 9.

CONCLUDING NOTE. Confucius once (Ana. XVII. x.) told his son to study the Chow-nan and Shaou-nan, adding that 'the man who has not done so is like one who stands with his face right against a wall.' Like many more of the sayings of the sage, it seems to tell us a great deal, while yet we can lay hold of nothing positive in it.

Choo He says, 'The first four odes in this 2d Book speak of the wives of princes and great officers, and show how at that time princes and great officers had come under the transforming influence of king Wǎn. so that they cultivated their persons and regulated rightly their families. The other pieces show how the chief prince among the States spread abroad the influence of king Wǎn, and how other princes cultivated it in their families and through their States. Though nothing is said in them about king Wǎn, yet the wide effects of his brilliant virtue and renovation of the people appear in them. They were so wrought upon, they knew not how. There is only the 13th piece which we are unable to understand, and with the perplexities of which we need not trouble ourselves.' One of the Ch'ings says, 'The right regulation of the family is the first step towards the good govt. of all the empire. The two *Nan* contain the principles of that regulation, setting forth the virtues of the queen, of princesses, and the wives of great officers, substantially the same when they are extended to the families of inferior officers and of the common people. Hence these odes were used at courts and village gatherings. They sang them in the courts and in the lanes, thus giving their tone to the manners of all under heaven.'

These glowing pictures do not approve themselves so much to a western reader. He cannot appreciate the institution of the harem. Western wives cannot submit to the position of T'ae-sze herself. Western young ladies like to be married 'decently and in order,' according to rule, with all the ceremonies; but they want other qualities in their suitors more important than an observance of formalities. Where purity and frugality in young lady and wife are celebrated in these pieces, we can appreciate them. The readiness on the part of the wife to submit to separation from her husband, when public duty calls him away from her, is also very admirable. But upon the whole the family-regulation which appears here is not of a high order, and the place assigned to the wife is one of degradation.

BOOK III. THE ODES OF PEI.

I. *Pih chau.*

邶一之三

柏舟

往　不　以　我　無　如　其　汎一
愬　可　茹　心　酒　有　流　彼章
　　以　亦　匪　以　隱　耿　柏
逢　據　有　鑒　敖　憂　耿　舟
彼　　二　　　　　　
之　薄　章　　　　　　亦
怒　言　兄　不　以　微　不　汎
　　　弟　可　遊　我　寐　汎

1　It floats about, that boat of cypress wood;
　　Yea, it floats about on the current.
　　Disturbed am I, and sleepless,
　　As if suffering from a painful wound.
　　It is not because I have no wine,
　　And that I might not wander and saunter about.

2　My mind is not a mirror;—
　　It cannot [equally] receive [all impressions].
　　I, indeed, have brothers,
　　But I cannot depend on them.
　　If I go and complain to them,
　　I meet with their anger.

TITLE OF THE BOOK.—邶, 一之三 'P'ei,
Book III. of Part I.' Of P'ei which gives its
name to this Book, and of Yung which gives its
name to the next, we scarcely know anything.
Long before the time of Confucius, perhaps before the date of any of the pieces in them, they had
become incorporated with the State of Wei, and
it is universally acknowledged that the odes of
Books III., IV., and V. are odes of Wei. Why
they should be divided into three portions, and
two of them assigned to P'ei and Yung is a
mystery, which Choo declares it is impossible
to understand. It would be a waste of time to
enter on a consideration of the various attempts

which have been made to elucidate it. In the
long narrative which is given by Tso-she under
p.8 of the 29th year of duke Seang, they sing
to Ke-chah. their visitor from Woo at the court
of Loo, the odes of P'ei, Yung, and Wei, and
that nobleman exclaims, 'I hear and I know:—
it was the virtue of K'ang-shuh and of duke
Woo, which made these odes what they are,—
the odes of Wei.' This was in B. C. 543, when
Confucius was 8 years old. Then there existed
the division of these odes into 8 Books with the
names of different States, all, however, acknowledged to be odes of Wei.
　　When king Woo overthrew the dynasty of
Shang, the domain of its kings was divided by

憂四章 可 棣 也。 不 心 轉 石。 我三章
心 選 棣。 威 可 也。 不 心
悄 也。 不 儀 卷 席。 我 可 匪
　 也。 不 威 卷 席。 我 可 匪

3 My mind is not a stone;—
It cannot be rolled about.
My mind is not a mat;—
It cannot be rolled up.
My deportment has been dignified and good,
With nothing wrong which can be pointed out.

him into three portions. That north of their
capital was P'ei; that south of it was Yung;
and that east of it was Wei. These were constituted into three principalities; but who among
his adherents were invested with P'ei and Yung
has not been clearly ascertained. Most probably they were assigned to Woo-kăng, the son of
the last king of Shang, and the 3 brothers of
king Woo, who were appointed to oversee him.
What was done with them, after the rebellion
of Woo-kăng and his overseers, is not known;
but in process of time the marquises of Wei
managed to add them to their own territory.

The first marquis of Wei was K'ang-shuh, a
brother of king Woo, of whose investiture we
have an account in the Shoo, V. ix., though whether he received it from Woo, or in the next
reign from the duke of Chow, is a moot point.
The first capital of Wei was on the north of the
Ho, to the east of Ch'aou-ko, the old capital of
Shang. There it continued till B. C. 659. when
the State was nearly extinguished by some
northern hordes, and duke Tae (戴公) removed across the river to Ts'aou (漕邑); but
in a couple of years, his successor, duke Wăn (文
公), removed again to Ts'oo-k'ew (楚邱),
—in the pres. dis. of Shing-woo (城武) dep.
Ts'aou-chow, Shan-tung. The State of Wei embraced the territory occupied by Hwae k'ing.
Wei-hwuy, Chang-teh,—all in Ho-nan, and
portions of the depp. of K'ae-fung in the same
province, of Ta-ming in Chih-le, and of Tung-
chang in Shan-tung.

Ode 1. Mostly narrative. Aɴ ᴏꜰꜰɪᴄᴇʀ ᴏꜰ
ᴡᴏʀᴛʜ ʙᴇᴡᴀɪʟꜱ ᴛʜᴇ ɴᴇɢʟᴇᴄᴛ ᴀɴᴅ ᴄᴏɴᴛᴇᴍᴘᴛ
ᴡɪᴛʜ ᴡʜɪᴄʜ ʜᴇ ᴡᴀꜱ ᴛʀᴇᴀᴛᴇᴅ. Such is the
view taken of the piece by Maou, who refers it
to the time of duke K'ing (頃 公: B.c. 866—
854); of the difft. view of Choo I will speak
in a concluding note.

St. 1. Ll. 1, 2. 汎 denotes 'the app. of floating about.' 柏 is the cypress, whose wood
is said to be good for building boats. The two
lines are, by the school of Maou, understood to
be allusive, representing the 'state of the officer
unemployed, like a boat floating uselessly about
with the current.' Yen Ts'an thinks the allusion
is to the sad condition of the State left to go to
ruin, as a boat must do with no competent person
in it to guide it. Choo takes the lines as metaphorical. Ll. 3, 4. Maou takes 耿耿 as =
微微, meaning 'restless,' 'disturbed.' 隱
—痛, 'a pain.' Ll. 5, 6. 微一非 'not,'
'it is not that.' The two lines are construed
together,—as Choo explains them, 非爲無
酒可以遨遊而解之也.' 'It is
not because I have no spirits, or that I could
not dissipate my grief by wandering about.' To
the same effect Yen Ts'an:—'This sorrow is not
such as can be relieved by drinking or by rambling.' Lacharme quite mistakes the meaning:
—ego deambulo, ego iter facio, non quia vino careo.
St. 2. Ll. 2. The difficulty in these lines is
with 茹, which both Maou and Choo explain
here by 度, 'to estimate,' 'to measure,' as if
the meaning were, 'A glass can only shew the
outward forms of things; but there is more than
what appears externally in my case, and the
causes of my treatment are too deep to be examined by a glass.' I must adopt another meaning
of 茹, which is also found in the dict.,—that
of 受 or 容, 'to receive,' 'to admit.' A
glass reflects all forms submitted to it, with indifference; but the speaker acknowledged only
the virtuous. Bad men he rejected, and would
have nothing to do with them.

Ll. 3—6. Here, and in st. 1, we can allow
some connective force to 亦.' By 'brothers'

悄。慍于群小。覯閔既多。受侮不少。靜言思之。寤辟有摽。日居月諸。胡迭而微。心之憂矣。如匪澣衣。靜言思之。不能奮飛。

4　My anxious heart is full of trouble;
　　I am hated by the herd of mean creatures;
　　I meet with many distresses;
　　I receive insults not a few.
　　Silently I think of my case,
　　And, starting as from sleep, I beat my breast.

5　There are the sun and the moon,—
　　How is it that the former has become small, and not the latter?
　　The sorrow cleaves to my heart,
　　Like an unwashed dress.
　　Silently I think of my case,
　　But I cannot spread my wings and fly away.

we must understand 'officers of the same surname with the speaker (同姓臣).' Choo's view of the ode enables him to take 兄弟 in its natural meaning. 據＝依, 'to rely, or be relied, on.' 薄言,—as in i. VIII.

St. 3. In the first 4 lines, the speaker says his mind was firmer than a stone, and more even and level than a mat. 威儀 denotes his whole manner of conducting himself. 棣棣 (read tae)＝'the app. of complete correctness and long practice.' 選＝'to select.' The meaning is that nothing in the speaker's deportment could be picked out, and made the subject of remark.

St. 4. 悄悄 denotes 'the app. of sorrow.' The 于 after 慍 gives to that term the force of the passive voice. 羣小, 'the herd of small people,' denotes all the unworthy officers who enjoyed the ruler's favour. 閔＝病 'distress;' here probably meaning blame or slander. In l. 5, 言 is the particle, so frequent in the She. L. 4, 辟 is explained by 拊心, 'to lay the hand on the heart,' or ' to beat

the breast, and 摽, as 'the app of doing so.' In this acceptation the 有 may have its meaning of 'having'; but it rather has a descriptive power, making the word that follows very vivid, as if it were repeated.

St 5. Ll. 1, 2. 居 and 諸 are used as particles which we cannot translate, unless we take them as＝平, and render,—'O sun,' 'O moon.' So, Choo on ode 4, where he says 日居月諸, 呼而訴之也. 迭＝更, 'to change,' 'in altered fashion.' The meaning seems to be:—The sun is always bright and full, while the moon goes through regular changes, now full, and now absent from the heavens. In Wei the ruler was at this time obscured by the unworthy officers who abused his confidence and directed the govt. The sun had become small, and the moon had taken its place.

The rhymes are—in st. 1, 舟, 流, 憂, 游, cat. 3, t. 1; in 2, 茹, 據, 愬, 怒, cat. 5, t. 2; in 3, 石, 席, ib., t. 3; 轉, 卷, 選, cat. 14; in 4, 悄, 小, 少, 摽, cat. 2. in 5, 微, 衣, 飛, cat. 15 t. 1.

II. Luh e.

綠　曷　心　綠　綠　曷　心　綠　綠
兮　維　之　衣　兮　維　之　衣　兮　　綠
綠　其　憂　黃　衣　其　憂　黃　衣　　衣
兮。亡。矣。裳。兮。已。矣。裏。兮。

1　Green is the upper robe,
　　Green with a yellow lining!
　　The sorrow of my heart,—
　　How can it cease?

2　Green is the upper robe;
　　Green the upper, and yellow the lower garment!
　　The sorrow of my heart,—
　　How can it be forgotten?

NOTE ON THE INTERPRETATION. Choo He, in his Work on the *She*, contends that we have in this ode the complaint of Chwang Këang, the wife of one of the marquises of Wei, because of the neglect which she experienced from her husband;—as will be explained on the next ode. He was preceded in the view that the subject of the ode was a lady by Han Ying and Lëw Heang: but they referred it to Seuen Këang, the circumstances of whose history, as related by Tso-she under the 11th year of Chwang, p.5, and the 2d year of Min, p.7, would not harmonize with the spirit of this piece. Choo, therefore, discarded her, adopted Chwang Këang, and argues at great length, in his notes on the 'Little Preface,' against Maou's view. His work on the *She* was published A. D. 1,177; but in his work on the 'Four Books,' completed about 12 years afterwards, he seems to have returned to the view of the older school. See his remarks on the first two lines of st. 4, in Mencius, VII. Pt. ii. XIX. Mencius at any rate, by applying those lines to Confucius, sanctions the view of the ode which regards it as the complaint of a worthy officer, neglected by his ruler, and treated with contempt by a host of mean creatures.

Ode 2. Metaphorical. THE COMPLAINT, SAD BUT RESIGNED, OF A NEGLECTED WIFE. We said that the last piece was explained by Choo of Chwang Këang, one of the marchionesses of Wei. This ode and several others are, by the unanimous consent of the critics, assigned to her. though it is only in ode 3 that we have internal evidence of the authorship, or subject at least, that is of weight.

The marquis Yang (揚), or duke Chwang (莊), succeeded to the State of Wei in B.C. 756. In that year, he married a Këang, a daughter of the House of Ts'e,—the Chwang Këang of history. She was a lady of admirable character.

and beautiful; but as she had no child, he took another wife, a Kwei (厲媯) of the State of Ch'in. She had a son, who died early; but a cousin who had accompanied her to the harem, called Tae Kwei (戴媯), gave birth to Hwan (完), whom the marquis recognized as destined in due time to succeed him. At his request, and with her own good will, Chwang Këang brought this child up as her own. Unfortunately, however, another lady of the harem, of quite inferior rank, bore the marquis a son, called Chow-yu (州吁), who became a favourite with him. and grew up a bold, dashing, unprincipled young man. The marquis died in 734, and was succeeded by his son Hwan, between whom and Chow-yu differences soon arose. The latter fled from the State; but he returned, and in 718 murdered the marquis, and attempted, without success, to establish himself in his place.—The above details we have from Sze-ma Ts'ëen, and from Tso-she under the 3d and 4th years of duke Yin. The odes lead us further into the harem of Wei, and show us the dissatisfactions and unhappiness which prevailed there.

Stt.1,2. Ll.1.2. 'Yellow' is one of the 5 'correct' colours of the Chinese (see on Ana. X. vi.), and 'green' is one of the 'intermediate,' or colours that are less esteemed. Here we have the yellow used merely as a lining to the green, or employed for the lower and less honourable part of the dress;—an inversion of all propriety, and setting forth how the concubine, the mother of Chow-yu, had got into the place of the rightful wife, and thrust the latter down. The old interpreters take the lines as allusive. while with Choo they are metaphorical; but they understand them in the same way. Choo's view seems the preferable.—'Like a green robe with

女 所 思 治
今。我 俾
古 人。思
無 訧 人。
絺 兮 綌
兮。凄 兮。
以 風。凄
思 古 其
實 獲 我
心。 我 絺

3 [Dyed] green has been the silk;—
It was you who did it.
[But] I think of the ancients,
That I may be kept from doing wrong.

4 Linen, fine or coarse,
Is cold when worn in the wind.
I think of the ancients,
And find what is in my heart.

III. *Yen-yen.*

于 遠 于 之 其 差 于 燕 燕
野。送 歸。子 羽。池 飛。燕 燕

1 The swallows go flying about,
With their wings unevenly displayed.
The lady was returning [to her native state],
And I escorted her far into the country.

yellow lining, &c, *so is the state of things with us.'* Ll.3.4 describe Chwang Kĕang's feelings. 已 —止, 'to stop;' 亡 is equivalent to 忘, 'to forget,' 'to be forgotten.'

St.3. The green garment was originally so much silk on which the colour had been superinduced by dyeing;—intimating how the marquis had put the concubine in the place of the wife. 女—汝, 'you,' referring to the marquis or husband. So, Choo;—better than K'ang-shing, who takes 女=女人. 治 has the meaning of 'to do,' 'to bring about.' The 'ancients' are wives of some former time, who had been placed in similarly painful circumstances, and set a good example of conduct in them. K'ang-shing makes them out to be simply the ancient authors of the rules of propriety, with whom Chwang Kĕang was in accord, while the marquis had turned those rules upside down. 訧—尤, 'extraordinary,' 'to go beyond what is right.'

St.4. 絺 and 綌,—see on i.II.2. 'Linen' in the translation is not quite accurate, as this cloth was made of dolichos fibre. 凄 is the rec. text; but we should read 凄, meaning 'cold'; 凄 denotes 'the app. of clouds rising.' See K'ang-shing, as quoted by Yen Ts'an *in loc.* It is not easy to construe the 2nd line. Wang T'aou would take both 其 and 以 as particles; but we might give it literally:—'cold is it because of the wind.' The speaker represents herself as wearing a cold dress in cold weather, when she should be warmly clad. All things are against her. 實(=是)獲我心, 'and get my mind'; meaning apparently that, by her study of the examples of antiquity, Chwang Kĕang found herself strengthened to endure, as she was doing, her own painful experience.

The rhymes are—in st.1, 裳, 已, cat.1, t 2; in 2, 裳, 亡, cat.10: in 3, 絲 治 訧 ＊, cat.1, t.1; in 4, 風 ＊, 心, cat.7, t.1.

Ode 3. Narrative and allusive. CHWANG KĔANG RELATES HER GRIEF AT THE DEPARTURE OF TAE KWEI, AND CELEBRATES THAT LADY'S VIRTUE. It has been related on the last ode, how Tae Kwei bore Hwan to duke Chwang of Wei; and how ho was brought up by Chwang Kĕang and final

瞻望弗及。泣涕
如雨。
燕燕于飛。頡之
頏之。之子于歸。
遠于將之。瞻望
弗及。佇立以泣。
燕燕于飛。下上
其音。之子于歸。
遠送于南。瞻望
弗及。實勞我心。

I looked till I could no longer see her,
And my tears fell down like rain.

2 The swallows go flying about,
Now up, now down.
The lady was returning [to her native state],
And far did I accompany her.
I looked till I could no longer see her,
And long I stood and wept.

3 The swallows go flying about;
From below, from above, comes their twittering.
The lady was returning [to her native state],
And far did I escort her to the south.
I looked till I could no longer see her,
And great was the grief of my heart.

ly succeeded to his father. In B. C. 718, he— duke Hwan, 桓公 — was murdered by his half brother Chow-yu, and his mother then re- turned—was obliged, probably, to return—to her native State of Ch'in. Chwang Këang con- tinued in Wei, the marchioness-dowager; and she is understood to bewail, in this piece, her sorrow at the departure of her cherished and virtuous companion.

Stt. 1, 2, 3. Ll. 1, 2. 燕 is still the common name in China for the swallow. Maou and Choo take the reduplication of the character here as still singular;—after the Urh-ya. It seems more natural, however, to take it as plural. So, Yen Ts'an, and others. The figure of the creature in illustrations of the She is that of the *Hirundo daurica.* Synonyms of 燕 are 鳦 and 玄鳥. 差 (read as in i. l.) 泚— 'the app. of being uneven.' To the spectator, the wings of the swallow, in its rapid and irregular flight, often present this appearance. 頡頏 (al, with 羽 on the right) denote the app. of the birds in flying, their darting upwards being specially signified by the former character, and their sudden turns downwards by the latter. So

says Maou, 飛而上曰頡, 飛而下曰頏. Wang T'aou, however, calls attention to an argument of Twan Yuh-tsae, that 上 and 下 should here change places. '頡,' he says, 'takes its meaning from 頁,—頭, "the head," and 頏 its meaning from 亢—頸, "the neck." When a bird is flying downwards, we see its head; when it is rising in the air, we see its neck. And moreover, that it is the down- ward flight which is first described appears from the 下上 of the next stanza.' It is not worth while to try and settle the point, The migratory habits of the swallow, probably, lie at the basis of the allusion. Chwang Këang and Tae Kwei had been happy together as two swallows, and now one of them was off to the south, and the other was left alone.

Ll. 3, 4. 歸 is here 'the great return (大 歸)'; not the visit of a wife to see her parents, but her return for good to her native State. 之 于,—于 is here 'a lady,' one who was a widow

仲氏任
只。其心
塞淵。終
溫且惠。
淑慎其
身。先君
之思。以
勗寡人。

四章

4 Lovingly confiding was the lady Chung;
Truly deep was her feeling.
Both gentle was she and docile,
Virtuously careful of her person.
In thinking of our deceased lord,
She stimulated worthless me.

IV. *Jeh yueh.*

日居月
諸照臨
下土。乃
如之人
兮。逝不
古處。胡
能有定。
寧不我
顧。

一章

日月

1 O sun, O moon,
Which enlighten this lower earth!
Here is this man,
Who treats me not according to the ancient rule.
How can he get his mind settled?
Would he then not regard me?

In 于歸, 于將, 于 is the particle. 將
=送, 'to escort.' Ch'in lay south from Wei,
and therefore we have 于南.

Ll. 5, 6. We must take 涕 and 泗 together
as='to weep'; though 泗 is defined as 'the
emission of tears without any sound.' 行=
久, 'a long time.'

St. 4. By 仲氏, 'the lady Chung,' we are to
understand Tae Kwei. She was called 仲, as
the 2d of sisters or of cousins, to distinguish
her in the family and the harem; and the designation becomes here equivalent to a surname.
只 occurred before, an untranslateable particle,
in i. IV., in the middle of a line; here it is at
the end. We find it with 尺 and 車 at the
side, used in the same way, and also interchanged with 旨. 任 has the meaning in the translation One definition of it is—信于友道,

'sincere in the ways of friendship.' 塞=實,
'really.' Throughout the She, 終, followed by
且, is merely=既, and may be translated
by 'both.' We must not give it the sense of
'ever.' By 先君 is intended duke Chwang.
Considering all the evils which he had brought
on the two ladies, it is matter of astonishment
that they should be able to think of him with
any feeling but that of detestation. But, according to Chinese ideas, though the husband have
failed in every duty the wife must still cherish
his memory with affection.

The rhymes are—in st. 1, 羽, 野 *, 雨,
cat. 5, t. 2: in 2, 頎, 將, cat. 10; 及 泣, cat.
7, t. 3: in 3, 音, 南 *, 心, *ib.*, t. 1: in 4, 淵,
身, 人, cat. 12, t. 1. 飛 歸 make a rhyme
also in *st.* 1—3, cat. 15, t. 1.

Ode 4. Narrative. CHWANG KËANG COM-
PLAINS OF AND APPEALS AGAINST THE BAD
TREATMENT SHE RECEIVED FROM HER HUSBAND.
Both the old interpreters and Choo give this

日 土 之 相 定 日 自 之 無 定。
居 是 人 好。宅 居 東 人 良。俾
月 冒。兮 胡 不 月 方。兮。胡 也
諸 乃 逝 能 我 諸。乃 德 能 可
下 如 不 有 報。出 如 音 有 忘。

2 O sun, O moon,
　Which overshadow this lower earth!
　Here is this man,
　Who will not be friendly with me.
　How can he get his mind settled?
　Would he then not respond to me?

3 O sun, O moon,
　Which come forth from the east!
　Here is this man,
　With virtuous words, but really not good.
　How can he get his mind settled?
　Would he then allow me to be forgotten?

interpretation of the piece; but the former refer it to the time when she was suffering from
the usurpation and oppressive ways of Chow-yu,
long after the death of duke Chwang. To this
view Choo very properly objects; the individual
of whom the piece complains is evidently still
alive, and a faint hope is intimated that he
would change his course. It is strange that
critics like Yen Ts‘an should still hold to the
opinion of Maou. Choo is also correct in saying that the whole is narrative. There is no
allusion, as the old school thinks, in the sun
and moon to the marquis and his wife. The
suffering lady simply appeals to those heavenly
bodies, as if they were taking cognizance of the
way in which she was treated. As well might
it be said that there is a similar allusion in her
appeal to her parents in the last stanza.

Ll. 1, 2, in all the stt. 居 and 諸,—see
on I. 5. I have not translated 臨, but it has
its meaning of ‘a superior‘s regarding those below him.’ 冒＝覆, ‘to cover,’ ‘to overshadow.’ In stt. 3, 4, the writer is thinking of the
sun as it rises daily in the east, and of the moon
as it does so when it is full. Obs. how in st. 4 the
自 follows the noun which it governs.

Ll. 3,4. 乃如 must be taken as a compound
conjunction, nearly equivalent to our ‘but.’
乃 alone has often this meaning, indicating ‘a

turn in the narration or discourse (乃, 轉
語 詞 也)‘; and Wang Yin-che takes 乃
如, here and elsewhere, in the same way (乃
如 亦 轉 語 詞 也). So, he adds, 乃若
in Mencius, IV. Pt. ii. XXVIII. 7, et al., though
the characters are also found at the beginning of
paragraphs. 之人,—之=此 or 是, ‘this.’
逝 by Choo and Wang Yin-che, is taken as
simply an initial particle. This is better than
to try, with Maou and Wang T‘aou, to explain
it by 逮 or 及. Instead of 逝 we also find
噬 and 遾, used in the same way. Choo acknowledges that he does not understand 古
遾, but he gives the explanation of some other
critic—以古道相處, as in the trans-
lation:—which is the best that can be made of
it. Chwang Këang was not treated as the ancient rules laid down that a wife should be. In
德音, the 音=言語, ‘words.’ So, Choo
and Yen Ts‘an. Wang T‘aou prefers to take the
phrase in the sense. which it sometimes has, of
令名, ‘a good name, or reputation.’ In 畜
我不卒, 畜=養, ‘to nourish;’ and 卒
一終, ‘end,’ or ‘conclusion.’ The ‘Complete

我　有　卒。畜　兮　自　諸。日　〔四章〕
不　定。胡　我　母　出。東　居
述。報　能　不　今。父　方　月

4　O sun, O moon,
From the east which come forth!
O father, O mother,
There is no sequel to your nourishing of me.
How can he get his mind settled?
Would he then respond to me, contrary to all reason?

V. *Chung fung.*

是　中　笑　謔　則　顧　且　終　〔一章〕終
悼。心　敖。浪　笑。我　暴。風　風

1　The wind blows and is fierce.
He looks at me and smiles,
With scornful words and dissolute,—the smile of pride.
To the centre of my heart I am grieved.

Digest' expands the line very well:—今我中道見棄,何父母養我不終也.

Ll. 5,6. Both 胡 and 寧 have the sense of 何, 'how.' So, Choo. Maou explains 胡 in the same way by 何; but he says nothing of 寧. Wang Yin-che takes 寧 here in the sense of 乃 or 曾, denoting 'a turn in the discourse'; but the meaning comes to the same thing, the 5th and 6th lines being construed closely together. The mind of the marquis was all perverted; could it but get settled as it ought to be, he would treat the speaker differently. To quote again from the 'Complete Digest:'—心志同惑,亦胡能有定哉,使其有定,則古道之善,宜知之也,何爲獨不我顧也. 報一荅, 'to respond to.' The speaker did her duty as a wife. She longed for the marquis to respond to her with the duty of a husband. The last line in st. 3 is difficult to construe It is still interrogative like those of the preceding stanzas:—' would it be given to me to be forgotten?' As Choo expands it:—何獨使我爲可忘者耶. So also the last line in st. 4 may be regarded as interrogative, though we are able to translate it as it stands. 述=循, 'to be in accordance with,' i. e., with the principles of reason. So, both Maou and Choo. According to Choo's interpretation of this ode and the next, which I believe to be correct, they ought to take precedence of the last.

The rhymes are—in st. 1, 土,處,顧, cat. 5, t. 2: in 2, 冒,好,報, cat. 3, t. 2: in 3, 方,良,忘, cat. 10: in 4, 出,卒,述, cat. 15, t. 3.

Ode 5. Metaphorical. CHWANG KEANG BEMOANS THE SUPERCILIOUS TREATMENT WHICH SHE RECEIVED FROM HER HUSBAND. The old interpreters think the lady is bemoaning the cruel treatment which she received from Chow-yu. The imperial editors approve of Choo's view, but have in their edition preserved also the earlier. If Choo's interpretation be correct, the ode should, like the last, be placed before the 3d; 'he did not venture,' say the editors, to alter the existing order of the pieces;'—because to do so would have brought him into collision with the authority of Confucius.

終風且霾。惠然
肯來。莫往莫來。
悠悠我思。

終風且曀。不日
有曀。寤言不寐。
願言則嚏。

曀曀其陰。虺虺
其雷。寤言不寐。
願言則懷。

2   The wind blows, with clouds of dust.
    Kindly he seems to be willing to come to me;
    [But] he neither goes nor comes.
    Long, long, do I think of him.

3   The wind blew, and the sky was cloudy;
    Before a day elapses, it is cloudy again.
    I awake, and cannot sleep;
    I think of him, and gasp.

4   All cloudy is the darkness,
    And the thunder keeps muttering.
    I awake and cannot sleep;
    I think of him, and my breast is full of pain.

Maou treats the piece as allusive; it seems better to understand with Choo that the stanzas all begin with a metaphorical description of the harassing conduct of duke Chwang.

Stt. 1. 2. Ll. 1. Maou and Choo both explain 終風 by 終日風, 'wind through all the day.' Wang Yin-che, as has already been observed, takes 終 here, and generally in the She, as =既; which is ingenious, and probably correct. 暴=疾, 'rapid,' 'fierce.' The Urh-ya says, 風而雨土爲霾, 'wind after which the dust descends like rain is 霾.'

Stt. 3, 4. Ll. 1, 2. 曀 denotes 'dark and windy';—the wind blowing, and clouds at the same time obscuring the sun. In 不日有曀, the 有=又, 'further,' 'again.' I translate the 1st line of st. 3 in the past tense. We are then led to think of the sky clearing for a time; but before a day elapses (不日), it is again overcast. The reduplication of 曀 in st. 4 denotes 'the app. of the darkness or cloudiness,' and 虺虺 signifies, acc. to Choo, the

muttering of thunder before it bursts into a crash, while Maou makes it the crash itself.

Stt. 1, 2. Ll. 2—4. The 2d line describes some titful gleams of kindness shown by duke Chwang; and the 3d line, how-they were only deceitful and mocking. 謔=戲言, 'sportive, or scornful words.' 浪=放濤, 'dissolute,' 'unlicensed,' The Urh-ya explains 謔浪笑敖 all together by 戲謔. 莫往莫來 express the uncertainty and changeableness of duke Chwang's moods. He would neither go nor come; was neither one thing nor another. Maou's explanation of the line is very far-fetched.— 'Chuw-yu did not come as a son to serve Chwang Kĕang, and she could not go and show to him the affection of a mother.' 悼=傷, 'to be wounded,' i. e., with grief. 悠悠—see on i. I.

Stt. 2, 3, 4, Ll. 3, 4. 言 must be treated simply as a particle. Here it is in the middle of the line as in ode I., stt. 4, 5. Taking 言 as a particle, we cannot explain 願 by 'to wish.' Maou says nothing about it, but Choo defines it

VI. *Keih koo.*

擊鼓

憂心有忡。
不我以歸。
平陳與宋。
從孫子仲。 二章
我獨南行。
土國城漕。
踊躍用兵。
擊鼓其鏜。 一章

1   Hear the roll of our drums!
    See how we leap about, using our weapons!
    Those do the fieldwork in the State, or fortify Ts'aou,
    While we alone march to the south.

2   We followed Sun Tsze-chung,
    Peace having been made with Ch'in and Sung;
    [But] he did not lead us back,
    And our sorrowful hearts are very sad.

by 思, 'to think.' There is a difficulty with *te*, which means 'to sneeze;' and Morrison, under the character, translates the line,—'I think with anxiety, till indisposition makes me sneeze.' We must cast about surely for some other meaning. Now Maou has 疐 without the 口 by the side, and it would appear that this was the reading till the time of Wan-ts'ung (文宗) of the T'ang dynasty (A.D. 827-840), when 疐 got into the stone tablets of the classics which were then cut. Maou further explains 疐 by 跲, or, acc. to Luh Teh-ming, by 欶 meaning 'to open the mouth wide,' 'to gape.' I venture, therefore, to give the meaning in the translation.

Maou explains 懷 by 傷, 'to be pained'; and Choo, by 思, 'to think.' The speaker cherished her husband despairingly in her thoughts.

The rhymes are—in stt. 1, 暴笑敖悼, cat. 2: in 2, 歸 ,, 來, 來, 思, cat. 1, t. 1: in 3, 疐 ,, 疐 ,, 疐 ,, cat. 12, t. 3: in 4, 靁, 懷, cat. 15, t. 1.

Ode 6. Narrative. SOLDIERS OF WEI REPINING BITTERLY OVER THEIR SEPARATION FROM THEIR FAMILIES, AND ANTICIPATING THAT IT WOULD BE FINAL. We read in the Ch'un Ts'ew (I. iv. 4,5) that, in B. C. 718, Wei twice joined in an expedition against Ch'ing. Chow-yu had just murdered duke Hwan, and the people were restless under his rule. He thought it would divert their minds, and be acceptable to other States. if he attacked Ch'ing; and having made an agreement with Sung, Ch'in and Ts'ae, a combined force marched against that State. Its operations lasted only 5 days; but very soon, in autumn, the troops, having been joined by a body of men from Loo, returned to the south, and carried off all the grain of Ch'ing from the fields.—It is supposed that it is to these operations that the ode refers, and I would assign it to the period of the second expedition. The soldiers had hoped to return to their families at the conclusion of the former service; and finding that another was to be performed, they gave vent to their aggrieved feelings in these stanzas. We must bear in mind, however, that this interpretation of the piece is only traditional.

St. 1. 鏜 denotes the sound of the drums. The line is twice quoted in the Shwoh-wan, and once we have this character with 鼓 instead of 金,—probably the more correct form. The demonstrative force of the 其 justifies the translation 'Hear!' 兵 denotes sharp, pointed weapons. The drum gave the signal for action or advance. The troops are here represented as bestirring themselves on hearing it. 土—土 功, 'field labour.' 國—國 中 'in the State.' 漕 was the name of a city of Wei, that to which duke Tae removed the capital for a short time in B. C. 659, as mentioned in the note on the title of the Book. It was in the pres. dis. of Hwah (滑), dep. Wei-hwuy. The 獨 in the last line leads us to refer this 3d line away from the troops which were in march southwards to Ch'ing, to the rest of the people

不我信兮。　活兮。于嗟洵兮。不我　于嗟闊兮。與子偕老。不我　成說。執子之手。　死生契闊。與子　于林之下。　其馬。于以求之。　爰居爰處。爰喪

五章　四章　三章

3　Here we stay; here we stop;
　　Here we lose our horses;
　　And we seek for them,
　　Among the trees of the forest.

4　For life or for death, however separated,
　　To our wives we pledged our word.
　　We held their hands;—
　　We were to grow old together with them.

5　Alas for our separation!
　　We have no prospect of life.
　　Alas for our stipulation!
　　We cannot make it good.

As the 'Complete Digest' expands it,—顧彼
衞國之民，或役土功於國，
或築城於漕．They were toiled too,
but not to the peril of their lives, as the troops
were.

St. 2. Sun Tsze-chung was the name of the
commander. Maou, in his introductory note on
the ode, says he was the Kung-sun Wăn-chung.
There was a noble family in Wei having the
surname of Sun, of which we read much in the
Ch'un Ts'ëw. L. 2. See the note above, on the
interpretation of the piece. L. 3, 以 is here
explained by 與, 'with.' See the same note.
L. 4. Maou explains 有忡 by 忡忡然,
'very sad-like.' It is another of the many instances where 有 makes the word that follows
it vividly descriptive.

St. 3. 爰 is defined by Choo by 於, which
he immediately expands to 於是, 'here.' We
must take it as a particle,—于, which takes
the place of it in the 3d line. So, Wang Yin-
che. 于以—see on ii. II. 1, 2. This stanza
sets forth, acc. to Choo, the disorder in the ranks

of the troops, who had no heart to fight. Wang
Suh (王肅；of the kingdom of Wei) considered that in this and the two next stanzas we
had the words of the farewell taken by the
soldiers of their families:—'We shall not return
from this expedition. We know not where we
shall finally rest ourselves, nor where we shall
lose our horses. You will have to look for us
and them in the forests.'

St. 4. The soldiers think here of their engagements with their wives at the time of their
marriage, and go on, in the next stanza, to mourn
because they cannot now be carried out. 契
(read k'ĕoh) 闊 express the idea of separation.
Maou explains the phrase by 勤苦, 'toil and
suffering.' The dict., on 契, gives both this
meaning of the phrase and that which I have
adopted. 與子，—子 must refer to their
wives. The last two lines seem to necessitate
this. K'ang-shing, very unnaturally, refers it to
the 'comrades' of the speakers, (從軍之
士，與其伍約云云). Perhaps this
was the idea of Maou, who explains 說 by 數,
as if the 與子成說—'with you we will

VII. K'ae fung.

凱風

凱風自南。吹
彼棘心。棘心
夭夭。母氏
劬

勞。

凱風自南。吹
彼棘薪。母氏
聖善。我無令
人。

爰有寒泉。在

1 The genial wind from the south
Blows on the heart of that jujube tree,
Till that heart looks tender and beautiful.
What toil and pain did our mother endure!

2 The genial wind from the south
Blows on the branches of that jujube tree,
Our mother is wise and good;
But among us there is none good.

complete the number in our ranks.' 成說一 ' we pledged our word.'

St. 5. 不我活,—'there is now no living for us.' 洢.—'to be true.' It is often used adverbially, and here it has a substantive meaning, referring to the engagements in the previous stanza. 信一伸, 'to stretch out,' 'to make good;'—an established usage of the term. 于 嗟,—as in i. XI.

The rhymes are—in st. 1, 鎧, 兵., 行., cat. 10: in 2, 仲, 宋, 忡, cat. 9: in 3, 處, 馬., 下., cat. 5, t. 2: in 4, 闊, 說, cat. 15, t. 3; 手, 老., cat. 3, t. 2: in 5, 闊, 活, cat. 15, t. 3; 洢, 信, cat. 12, t. 1.

Ode 7. Metaphorical and allusive. SEVEN SONS OF SOME FAMILY IN WEI BLAME THEMSELVES FOR THE RESTLESS UNHAPPINESS OF THEIR MOTHER. The 'Little Preface' says that the mother could not rest;—we must suppose in her state of widowhood, and wanting to marry a second time; and that her sons, by laying the blame of her restlessness upon themselves, recalled her to a sense of duty. There is nothing in the ode, as Choo says, to intimate that the mother was thus wrought upon: and he might have added that there is nothing in it to suggest that it was her wish to marry again which troubled the sons. However, he accepted the traditional interpretation so far. Mencius, VI.

Pt. ii. III., alludes to the ode, but he merely says that the fault of the parent referred to in it was small, and it was proper therefore that the dissatisfaction with her expressed by the sons should be slight.

St. 1, 凱風, 'the triumphant or pleasant wind,' is a name given to the south wind from its genial influence on all vegetation. By the kih we are, probably, to understand the zizyphus jujuba, a small thorny tree, bearing a fruit the size of a cherry, which is mealy and eatable, and goes among foreigners by the name of the Chinese date. The name of this is generally written 棗; but Heu Shin says that 棘 is applied to a smaller variety of the tree or shrub whose fruit is more acid. By the 'heart' of the tree are intended the inner and hidden shoots, which it is more difficult for the genial influence to reach. 夭夭,—see i. VI. 母氏.—氏 is used much as in III. 4. We cannot translate it, and say 'our mother, of such and such a surname.' 劬勞一病苦, 'to have distress and toil.' In this 4th line, the sons, acc. to Choo, refer to their mother's toil in their nurture and upbringing.—He makes this stanza to be metaphorical, agreeing with the old interpreters in regard to the allusive character of the others. See in justification of this, the remarks of Lёw Kin on the next stanza.

St. 2. Maou explains 薪 of the shoots of the tree, now grown into branches (其成就者). They might be used for firewood. 聖

心。莫 子 其 鳥。睍￼勞 人。有 浚
慰 七 音。載 睆 苦。母 子 之
母 人。有 好 黃 氏 七 下。

3 There is the cool spring
Below [the city of] Tseun.
We are seven sons,
And our mother is full of pain and suffering.

4 The beautiful yellow birds
Give forth their pleasant notes.
We are seven sons,
And cannot compose our mother's heart.

VIII. *Heung che.*

伊 自 懷 我 其 泄 于 雄￼ 雄
阻。詒 矣。之 羽。泄 飛。雉 雉

1 The male pheasant flies away,
Lazily moving his wings.
The man of my heart!—
He has brought on us this separation.

一叡, 'wise.' 善 and 令 are synonyms. Lew Kiu (劉瑾; Yuen dyn.) says:—'The former stanza speaks of the genial wind, and the heart of the jujube tree, but afterwards does not mention what was in the poet's mind corresponding to these things, so that the verse is metaphorical. This stanza speaks of the wind and jujube tree, and then mentions the mother and the sons which correspond to these, so that it is allusive. There is a similarity between the two, but they are not of the same character.'

St. 3. 爰.—see on st. 3 of last ode. Tseun was a city of Wei.—in the pres. Puh Chow, dep. Ts'aou-chow, Shan-tung. Near it was a famous spring, to the virtue of which the sons refer as a contrast to their own uncleanness. The spring refreshed the people of Tseun, while they could not keep their mother from trouble and pain.

St. 4. 睍睆 is explained by Maou as meaning 好貌, 'good-like.' Choo understands the phrase of the notes of the orioles, 'clear and twirling.' It may be doubted if either of them have brought out the meaning correctly. One would expect some description of the eyes in the characters. 載 must be taken simply as a particle. Wang Yin-che explains it by 則, but there is not that force of meaning in it. The birds were useful in their way, contributing to the pleasure of men; but the sons failed to comfort their mother's heart. The old interpreters have a great deal more to say on the allusion; but it would be a waste of time and space to dwell on their views.

The rhymes are—in st. 1, 南, 心, cat. 7, t. 1; 天, 勞, cat. 2: in 2, 薪, 人, cat. 12: in 3, 下, 苦, cat. 5, t. 2: in 4, 音, 心, cat. 7, t. 1.

Ode 8. Allusive and narrative. A WIFE DEPLORES THE ABSENCE OF HER HUSBAND, AND CELEBRATES HIS VIRTUE. The 'Little Preface' says that this ode was composed by the people of Wei against duke Seuen,—the marquis (晉), called to the rule of the State on the death of Chow-yu (B.C. 718—699). His dissoluteness and constant wars distressed and widowed the people, till they expressed their resentment in this ode.

何　德　百　曷　我　瞻　實　其　雄
用　行　爾　云　思　彼　勞　音　雉
不　　　君　能　　　日　我　　　于
臧　不　子　來　道　月　心　展　飛
　　忮　　　　　之　　　　　矣　　
　　不　不　　　云　悠　　　君　下
　　求　知　　　遠　悠　　　子　土

2 The pheasant has flown away,
　But from below, from above, comes his voice.
　Ah! the princely man!—
　He afflicts my heart.

3 Look at that sun and moon!
　Long, long do I think.
　The way is distant;
　How can he come to me?

4 All ye princely men,
　Know ye not his virtuous conduct?
　He hates none; he covets nothing;—
　What does he which is not good?

Choo well observes that there is nothing in the piece about the dissoluteness of duke Seuen, or to indicate that it was made in his time; that we ought not to hear in it the voice of the people, but of a wife deploring the absence of her husband. The imperial editors in this case fully agree with him.

Stt. 1, 2, Ll. 1, 2. 于 is the particle. 泄泄 describes the slow flight of the pheasant moving, not under alarm, from one place to another. So, l. 2 in st. 2, is understood to shew the feeling of security enjoyed by the bird. Yen Ts'an observes that here, in v. VI, and some other odes, where the subject is an officer engaged on military duty, the male pheasant is introduced, because of the well-known fighting character of that bird. It may be so; but here it is the contrast between the ease and security of the pheasant and the toils and danger of her husband, which is in the speaker's mind. 我之懷=我懷人 in I. i. III. 1 伊 is the particle. K'ang-shing says it should be 繄, and explains it by 'this;'—which is unnecessary. 阻 means 'to hinder,' 'to obstruct;' hence 'an impediment,' that by which communication is prevented. Here Choo explains it by 隔, 'to be separated.' This is

better than Maou's 難, 'difficulty,' 'hardship.' 詒=遺, simply =='to occasion.' There is some difficulty with the 自. Yen Ts'an's reference of it to the speaker—the wife—is inadmissible. 'She attributes,' says Foo K'wang, 'their separation to her husband, not wishing to blame others for it.' 君子 denotes the husband,—as in i. X., et al. 展=誠, 'sincere,' 'sincerely.' Choo observes that the 展 and 實 give strong emphasis to these lines of st. 2.

Stt. 3, 4. These are simply narrative. The sun and moon are spoken of as the measurers of time. Many revolutions had they performed since the husband went away. The 云 in ll. 3 and 4 is merely a particle. It is found both at the beginning and in the middle of lines. Wang Yin-che says on this passage, 云 語助詞也，詩雄雉曰道之云遠曷云能來言道之遠何能來也. Lacharme, endeavouring to translate the 云, has,—'Viam longam esse aiunt; quid igitur memorant eum advenisse posset!' The

IX.　*P'aou-yew-koo-yeh.*

匏有苦葉

一章
匏有苦葉。
濟有深涉。
深則厲。
淺則揭。

二章
有瀰濟盈。
有鷺雊鳴。
濟盈不濡軌。
雊鳴求其牡。

1　The gourd has [still] its bitter leaves,
And the crossing at the ford is deep.
If deep, I will go through with my clothes on ;
If shallow, I will do so, holding them up.

2　The ford is full to overflowing;
There is the note of the female pheasant.
The full ford will not wet the axle of my carriage ;
It is the pheasant calling for her mate.

君子 in st. 4 must be taken as addressed to the brother officers of the husband, who is described, though he is not named explicitly, in the 3d and 4th lines. The 2d line is taken interrogatively. The last 2 lines are quoted by Confucius (Ana. IX. xxvi), as illustrated in the character of Tsze-loo. Le Hung-tsoo (李閎祖; Sung dyn.) distinguishes the force of 枝 and 求 ingeniously :—'枝 indicates hatred of men because of what they have; 求, shame, because of what we ourselves have not.' 用一行 or 爲, 'to do.'

The rhymes are—in st. 1, 羽, 阻, cat. 5, t. 2: in 2, 音, 心, cat. 7, t. 1: in 3, 思, 來, cat. 1, t. 1: in 4, 行, 臧, cat. 10.

Ode 9. Allusive and narrative. AGAINST THE LICENTIOUS MANNERS OF WEI. According to the 'Little Preface,' the piece was directed against duke Seuen, who was distinguished for his licentiousness, and his wife also. Choo demurs to its having this particular reference, which, however, the imperial editors are inclined to admit. Duke Seuen was certainly a monster of wickedness. According to Tso-she (on p. 5 of the 16th year of duke Hwan), his first wife was a lady of his father's harem, called E Këang (夷姜), by an incestuous connection with whom he had a son called Keih-tsze (急子), who became his heir-apparent. By and by he contracted a marriage for this son with a daughter of Ts'e, known as Seuen Këang (宣姜);

but on her arrival in Wei, moved by her youth and beauty, he took her himself, and by her he had two sons,—Show (壽) and Soh (朔). E Këang hanged herself in vexation, and the duke was prevailed on, in course of time, by the intrigues of Seuen Këang and Soh, to consent to the death of Keih-tsze, Show peristing in a noble, but fruitless, attempt to preserve his life. In the next year, the duke died, and was succeeded by Soh, when the court of Ts'e insisted on Ch'aou-peh (昭伯), another son of Seuen, marrying Seuen Këang. From this connection sprang two sons, who both became marquises of Wei, and two daughters, who married the rulers of other States;—see Tso-she on p.7 of the 2d year of duke Min.

When such was the history of the court of Wei, we can well conceive that licentiousness prevailed widely through the State. The particular reference of the ode to duke Seuen must remain, however, an unsettled question. The explanation of the different stanzas is, indeed, difficult and vexatious on any hypothesis about the ode that can be formed.

St.1. The *p'aou* is no doubt, the bottle gourd, called also 葫, or 壺蘆. When the fruit has become thoroughly hard and ripe, the shell, emptied of its contents, can be used as a bladder. We often see one or more tied to boat-children on the Chinese rivers, to keep them afloat, should they fall into the water, till they can be picked up. The gourd in the text had still its leaves on it; the fruit was not yet hard enough to serve the purpose of a bladder in crossing a stream. 濟=渡處, 'a ford or ferry.' So, both Maou and Choo. Le Kwang-te takes the character as the name of the river Tse. 涉 means 'to wade,' to cross the ford on foot.

卬　人　人　招四　迨　士　旭　雝三
須　涉　涉　招章　冰　如　日　雝章
我　卬　卬　舟　　未　歸　始　鳴
友。否。否。子。泮。妻。旦。鴈。

3 The wild goose, with its harmonious notes,
  At sunrise, with the earliest dawn,
  By the gentleman, who wishes to bring home his bride,
  [Is presented] before the ice is melted.

4 The boatman keeps beckoning;
  And others cross with him, but I do not.
  Others cross with him, but I do not;—
  I am waiting for my friend.

In st.4, however, we must take it differently. 鴈 means to go through the water, without taking one's clothes off; while 揭 (*k'e*) denotes to go through, holding the clothes up. The Urh-ya says that when the water only comes up to the knees, we may *k'e* it; when it rises above the knees, we can wade it (涉); but when it rises above the waist, we must *le* it. The 3d and 4th lines are quoted in the Ana. XIV. xiii. to illustrate, apparently, the propriety of acting according to circumstances; and so Maou and Choo try to explain them here. Yen Ts'an, however, seems to me to take them more naturally. The first two lines are intended to show the error of licentious connections. The ford should not be attempted, when there are not the proper appliances for crossing it. The last two lines show the recklessness of the parties against whom the piece is directed. They are determined to cross in one way or another.

St. 2. 瀰 denotes 'the full or swollen appearance of the water.' 有 is used as in 有 狔, in VI. 2. It gives a vivid or descriptive force to the character that follows it,—as in the reduplication of adjectives which is so common. 有鷕 in the same way denotes the note of the female pheasant. 軌 is here the axle of the carriage; not as Choo says, the rut or trace of the wheel. The character should be 軏. Both Maou and Choo take 牡 as—'a male quadruped,' saying that the male and female of birds are expressed by 雄 and 雌, while for quadrupeds we have 牡 and 牝; but this distinction is not always observed. We have in the She itself 雄狐 for 'a male fox,' and in the Shoo, 牝鷄 for 'a female fowl.'

To suppose that the female pheasant is here calling to her a male quadruped *is too extravagant*.—The explanation of the stanza is substantially the same as that of the preceding.

St. 3. This stanza is of a different character, and indicates the deliberate formal way in which marriages ought to be contracted,—in contrast with the haste and indecencies of the parties in the poet's mind. When the bridegroom wanted to have the day fixed for him to meet his bride and conduct her to his house, he sent a live wild goose, at early dawn, to her family. Why that bird was employed, and why that early hour was selected for the ceremony, are points on which we need not here enter. This was done, it is said, 'before the ice was melted' implying that the concluding ceremony would take place later. The meaning is that no forms should be omitted, and no haste shown in such an important thing as marriage.

According to this view, the stanza is parenthetical and explanatory. 雝雝 denotes 'the harmony of the goose's notes,' which may be doubted. 鴈, from the pictures of it, should be the Bean goose, *Anser segetum*. 旭 is 'the appearance of sunrise.' 如—'if,' almost—our 'when.' 歸妻—'to bring his wife home.' (使之來歸於已). 迨—as in ii. IX.

St. 4. 招 is 'to beckon,' 'to call with the hand.' The repetition of it vividly represents the calling. 舟子,—'boat-son,'—the master of the ferry boat. 涉 is here to cross the ferry in the boat, and not to wade through it on foot. Yen Ts'an keeps here, indeed, the latter meaning of the term, which is the only one given in the dict.; but to do so, he is obliged to construe the first line,—'I keep beckoning to the boatman,' in which it is impossible to agree with him. 卬

X. *Kuh fung.*

谷風

習習谷風。以陰
以雨。黽勉同心。
不宜有怒。采葑
采菲。無以下體。
德音莫違。及爾
同死。
行道遲遲。中心
有違。不遠伊邇。
薄送我畿。誰謂

1 Gently blows the east wind,
 With cloudy skies and with rain.
 [Husband and wife] should strive to be of the same mind,
 And not let angry feelings arise.
 When we gather the mustard plant and earth melons,
 We do not reject them because of their roots.
 While I do nothing contrary to my good name,
 I should live with you till our death.

2 I go along the road slowly, slowly,
 In my inmost heart reluctant.
 Not far, only a little way,
 Did he accompany me to the threshold.

一我. 'L' The meaning of the stanza is, that people should wait for a proper match, and not hurry on to form licentious connections.

The rhymes are—in st. 1, 葉。涉, cat. 8, t. 3; 雷。揭, cat. 15, t. 3: in 2, 盈。鳴, cat. 11; 軌 (prop. 軌, cat. 7), 牡。cat. 3, t. 2: in 3, 雁旦。泙, cat. 14: in 4, 于。否。, 否。, cat. 1, t. 2.

Ode 10. Metaphorical, allusive, and narrative. THE PLAINT OF A WIFE REJECTED AND SUPPLANT-ED BY ANOTHER. Thus much we learn from the ode itself. There can be no doubt that the manners of the court of Wei injuriously affected the households of the State; but this does not appear in the piece, though Maou seems to say that it does.

St 1. Maou and Choo take 習習 as describing the 'gentle breath' of the wind. 谷風 is taken by them, after the Urh-ya, as meaning 'the east wind.' This brings clouds and rain, and all genial influences. Ying-tah explains 谷 as if it were 穀, 'living.' We may tal e these

two lines either as metaphorical or allusive, referring to what the harmony and happiness of the family should be. Yen Ts'an explains them very differently, as referring to the angry demonstrations of the husband, like gusts of wind coming constantly (習習＝連續不斷), from great valleys, and bringing with them gloom and rain. Who shall decide on the comparative merits of the two views thus conflicting? 黽勉＝勉勉, 'to exert one's self.' Maou gives 黽 with 人 at the side, which is also found in the same sense. 葑 and 菲 are, probably, two species of Brassica; Williams calls 葑, 'vegetables resembling mustard.' Maou says it is the *seu* (須) and Choo the *man-tsing* (蔓菁); others make it the *woo-tsing* (蕪菁); and others again the *kae* (芥), or mustard plant. These are but different names for varieties of the same plant. In the Japanese plates, the figure of the *fung* is that of a sorrel or dock,—*rumex persicariodes*; and the author says he does

我　躬　母　以　新　湜　涇　如　薈　荼
後　不　發　毋　昏　其　以　兄　宴　苦
　　閱　我　逝　不　沚　渭　如　爾　其
　　遑　笱　我　我　宴　濁　弟　新　甘
　　恤　我　梁　屑　爾　涇　　　昏　如

Who says that the sowthistle is bitter?
It is as sweet as the shepherd's purse.
You feast with your new wife,
[Loving] as brothers.

3　The muddiness of the King appears from the Wei,
But its bottom may be seen about the islets.
You feast with your new wife,
And think me not worth being with.
Do not approach my dam,
Do not move my basket.
My person is rejected;—
What avails it to care for what may come after?

not know the *fei*. After the Urh-ya, Maou calls *fei* the *wuh* (芴) 'a sort of turnip, the flower of which is purple.' The root is red. It is, no doubt, what Kwoh Poh calls it 'the earth melon (土瓜);' and so I have translated it. The leaves, stalk, and root of the *fung* and *fei* are all edible; and if sometimes the root or lower part—下體—be bad, yet the whole plant is not on that account thrown away. From this the wife argues that though her beauty might in some degree have decayed, she should not on that account be cast off. 德音 is explained by Choo by 美譽, 'admirable praise,'=good character or name. K'ang-shing and Yen Ts'an, however, take the phrase here as in IV. 3;—'Husband and wife should speak kindly to each other.' Choo's view suits the connection best.

St. 2. The first 4 lines describe the cold manner in which the wife was sent away, and her reluctance to go. The 2d line says that while her feet went slowly on the way, her heart was all the while rebelling, and wished to turn back. 伊 —惟, almost—'only.' Both Maou and Choo explain 畿 by 門內, 'the inside of the door.' The word is used in the sense of 限, a limit or boundary, which, from the 3d line, we infer would here be the threshold.

The last 4 lines describe the bitterness of the wife's feelings at seeing herself supplanted. Medhurst is probably correct in calling the *t'oo* the sowthistle. I was inclined, from the descriptions of it, to call it a sort of lettuce. 'Its leaf exudes a white juice, which is bitter. Its flowers are like those of an aster. It is edible but bitter.' The pictures of the *tse* are those of the shepherd's purse. They say that the seeds of it are sweet. 昏 is used for a marriage, because it was in 'the dark,' at night, that the wife was brought home. Here it—妻, 'wife.'

St. 3. The King and the Wei;—see the Shoo, on III. Pt.i.73, Pt.ii.12. 湜湜—'clear-looking.' The Shwoh-wăn defines the term as 'clear water, where the bottom can be seen.' 'The waters of the King,' says Choo, 'are muddy, and those of the Wei are clear, and the muddiness of the King appears more clearly after its junction with the Wei; yet where its channel is interrupted by islets, and the stream flows more gently, it is not so muddy but that the bottom may be seen. So, with the rejected and the new wife. The former was thrown into the shade by the latter. Yet if the husband would only think, he might know that she still had her good qualities.' Yen Ts'an here again construes differently. With him the new wife is the King, well known for its muddiness, representing her, the clear Wei, to be muddy;—a misrepresentation which inspection or reflection would readily refute. In l. 4 不屑,—'you

就其深矣。方
之舟之。就其
淺矣。泳之游
之。何有何亡。

黽勉求之。凡
民有喪。匍匐
救之。

不我能慉。反
以我為讎。既
阻我德。賈用

四章　五章

4   Where the water was deep,
I crossed it by a raft or a boat.
Where it was shallow,
I dived or swam across it.
Whether we had plenty or not,
I exerted myself to be getting.
When among others there was a death,
I crawled on my knees to help them.

5   You cannot cherish me,
And you even count me as an enemy.
You disdain my virtues,—
A pedlar's wares which do not sell.

do not think it right to demean youself to.'
See, by help of the index, the use of 不屑 in
Mencius. Both by Maou and Choo, 屑 is correctly explained by 潔, 'pure;' but Choo is
wrong when he construes 不我屑,—不
以我為潔, 'you do not consider me to
be pure;' such is not the usage of 不屑.
We must, then, look out for a substantive
meaning to the concluding 以. K'ang-shing
explains it by 用, 'to employ,' which is allowable. It is better, however, to take it, with
Choo, as = 與, 'with,' 'to associate with.'
Though he errs with the 不屑, his expansion
of the whole line is not far wrong:—不以
我為潔而與之. Chaou K'e on
Mencius, II. Pt.i.IX, quotes the line as 不我
屑已; but we cannot argue from that.
潔 is a stone dam in the stream, with open
spaces, through which the fish might pass, or
where they might be taken by means of baskets
(笱). 逝—之, 'to go to,' 'to approach.'
The wife is suddenly excited to address her
enemy, and order her away from her place and

her property; but she as suddenly checks herself. Her person rejected, she could hereafter
have no interest in anything that had belonged
to her. 閱 is explained by 容, 'to bear, be
borne, with;' 遑, 'leisure,' is, as often, taken
interrogatively:—'what leisure have I to—,' or
'of what use will it. be to.—' 我後—我
已去之後, 'what will happen after I am
gone.'
St.4. The wife here sets forth how diligent
and thoughtful she had been in her domestic
affairs, ever consulting for the prosperity of
her husband.
方 and 泳,—see on i. IX. 1. 之 after these
characters, and also 舟 and 游,—as in 顛之,
顛之, in III. 2. 何有 何亡—不
論貧富, 'without regard to our being rich
or poor.' 'If they had plenty,' says K'ang-shing,
'she sought that they might have more; if they
wanted, she sought that they might have enough.'
And not in her own family only was she thus
sedulous. She was ever ready to help in the
need of her neighbours, thus consulting for her
husband's popularity and comfort.
St. 5. The wife dwells on her husband's hostile
feeling to her in his prosperity, in contrast with
what had been her interest in his early struggles.
We may accept Ying-tah and Choo's explanation of 慉 by 養, 'to nourish.' 阻—'to hinder

來 不 有 以 御 我 毒。生 鞠 不
塈。念 潰。我 冬。有 既 及 售。
　 昔 既 御 宴 旨 育。爾 昔
　 者。詒 窮。爾 蓄。比 顛 育
　 伊 我 有 新 亦 予 覆。恐
　 余 肄。洸 昏。以 于 既 育

Formerly, I was afraid our means might be exhausted,
And I might come with you to destitution.
Now, when your means are abundant,
You compare me to poison.

6   My fine collection of vegetables
Is but a provision against the winter.
Feasting with your new wife,
You think of me as a provision [only] against your poverty.
Cavalierly and angrily you treat me;
You give me only pain.
You do not think of the former days,
And are only angry with me.

or impede.' Choo explains it here by 却, 'to reject.' The idea is that of an impediment or obstruction between the wife's virtues and the husband's mind, so that he would give no recognition of them. 賈 is read koo, 'a shopman' 'a trader.' 用 may be taken as 一以 or 因, and the whole line is—'The trader therefore does not sell his wares.'

In the last 4 lines, there is a difficulty with the two 育 in l. 5 and 既生既育 in l. 7. Yen Ts'an thinks the former 育 refers to the business of child-bearing, after the marriage of the parties, when the wife was always fearing that the number of mouths would be more than they could feed, and the 7th line says that that business was all over;—the children were grown up and there was prosperity. Few will be inclined to accept this exegesis, and I can make nothing out of Maou, who explains 育 by 長. We must be content to accept the construction of of Choo. The 1st 育 is the struggle for a livelihood, and the 2nd is the means of that livelihood. Then 既生既育 expresses the idea that that livelihood has been abundantly secured. 鞠一窮, 'to be exhausted.' 顛

覆 means 'to be overthrown;' here—to come to destitution. Yen Ts'an and Ying-tah are both obliged to force upon the terms the meaning of 'did my utmost.'

St. 6. The wife repeats the plaint of last stanza, and concludes by deploring her husband's angry mood. 蓄 is understood to be 'the collection,' of vegetables which the wife has made against (御一禦 or 當) the winter. In the spring, when new vegetables were produced, she would not need it. So she herself had been cherished by her husband only when he had need of her in his poverty. The text has thus to be supplemented considerably in order to get a meaning out of it. 有洸一 'fierce-like.' 有潰一'angry-like.' 肄一 勞, 'pain,' 'toil.' Both Maou and Choo take 塈 in the sense of 息 'to rest,' so that the 7th and 8th lines—'you do not think of the former days, when I came to rest.' Much better is the exegesis of Wang Yin-che, which I have followed. He explains 伊 by 惟, 來 by 是, and 塈 by 愾,—'to be angry.' This usage of 來 is not infrequent.

XI. *Shih Wei.*

式微

式微式微。胡不歸。微君之故。胡爲乎中露。

式微式微。胡不歸。微君之躬。胡爲乎泥中。

1 Reduced! Reduced!
Why not return?
If it were not for your sake, O prince,
How should we be thus exposed to the dew?

2 Reduced! reduced!
Why not return?
If it were not for your person, O prince,
How should we be here in the mire?

XII. *Maou-k'ew.*

旄丘

旄丘之葛兮。何誕之節兮。叔兮伯兮。何多日也。

1 The dolichos on that high and sloping mound;—
How wide apart are [now] its joints!
O ye uncles,
Why have ye delayed these many days?

The rhymes are—in st. 1, 風, 心, cat. 7, t. 1; 雨, 怨, cat. 5, t. 2; 菲, 體, 死, cat. 15, t. 2: in 2, 遲, 違, 畿, ib., t. 1; 薺, 弟, ib., t. 2: in 3, 沚, 以, cat. 1, t. 2; 筍, 後, cat. 4, t. 2; in 4, 舟, 游, 求, 救, cat. 3, t. 1: in 5, 愊, 讐, 售, cat. 3, t. 2; 鞠, 覆, 育, 毒, ib., t. 3: in 6, 冬, 窮, cat. 9; 潰, 肆, 壺, cat. 15, t. 3.

Ode 1₁. Narrative. THE OFFICERS OF SOME STATE WHO WERE REFUGEES AND IN DISTRESS IN WEI, EXHORT THEIR RULER TO RETURN HOME WITH THEM. The 'Little Preface' says that the prince addressed was the marquis of Le (黎侯), a State adjoining Wei, who had taken refuge from the Teih, in the time of duke Seuen. His officers feel themselves in very reduced circumstances, and advise their ruler to return with them.

In l. 1, 式, is an initial particle. 微微, 'to be decayed.' The repetition shows the extent of the decay. Comp. 悠哉悠哉, in i. I. 2. The parties had come refugees to Wei, and there perhaps they were slighted, and little cared for. The 微 in l. 3,—無, 'but for.' It is difft. from 微=非, in l. 1. In l. 4, 中露 =露中, like 泥中 in the 2d st. Maou says Chung-loo and Ne-chung were two towns of Wei that had been assigned to the refugees. Even the imperial editors allow that it is better to take the characters as I have done.

The rhymes are—in st. 1, 微, 歸, cat. 15, t. 1; 故, 露, cat. 5, t. 1: in 2, 微, 歸; 躬, 中, cat. 9.

何其處也。必有
與也。何其久也。
必有以也。
狐裘蒙戎。匪車
不東。叔兮伯兮。
靡所與同。
瑣兮尾兮。流離
之子。叔兮伯兮
褎如充耳。

2 Why do they rest without stirring?
It must be they expect allies.
Why do they prolong the time?
There must be a reason for their conduct.

3 Our fox-furs are frayed and worn.
Came our carriages not eastwards?
O ye uncles,
You do not sympathize with us.

4 Fragments, and a remnant,
Children of dispersion [are we]!
O ye uncles,
Notwithstanding your full robes, your ears are stopped.

Ode 12. Abusive and narrative. COMPLAINT OF THE MINISTERS OF LE AGAINST THOSE OF WEI FOR NOT ASSISTING THEM. The piece, acc. to the 'Little Preface' is directed against the marquis of Wei, though only his officers are spoken of. In this interpretation of it both the old school and the new agree. We shall find, however, that Maou and Choo differ considerably in their explanations of many of the lines.

St.1. In the Urh-ya 旄丘 is defined as 'a mound, the front of which is high;' and the current definition now is—'a mound high in front, and low behind.' It is said that the very mound thus described is to be recognized in K'ae-chow (開州), dep. Ta-ming, Chih-le. The speakers in the ode refer to the length of the joints of the koh, to show how long they had been waiting in vain in Wei. We need not, like Maou, seek in the intertwining of the creepers the close alliance which should subsist between the different States. 誕=闊, 'wide apart.' 節 is 'the joints' of the creeping plant. By 叔伯 'uncles,' we are to understand the ministers of Wei, thus honourably designated by those of Le. The complaint against them is in reality intended for their ruler. 何多日也=何其久而不見救乎, 'How is it that we are left unhelped so long?'

St.2. The officers of Wei are spoken of, if not directly addressed; and the speakers seem to be trying to account for their dilatoriness, in itself so strange and unworthy. 處=安處, 'to dwell quietly,' i.e., to make no movement in favour of Le. 與=與國, 'cooperating States,' i.e., allies who would act with them. 以,='a reason,' something by which their conduct was regulated. Maou says that 與 denotes 'benevolence and righteousness' and 以, 'serviceable kindness (功德);'—which is surely wide of the mark. Attempting to show the application of these interpretations, K'ang-shing takes the stanza as addressed to the marquis of Le:—'Why do you stay here? You must be [vainly] thinking that Wei has benevolence and righteousness;' &c.

St.3. The speakers advance here to a charge against the officers of Wei of a want of sympathy with their distress. They had long been waiting;—so long that their fox-furs were worn out. 蒙戎 denotes 'the appearance of disorder,' i.e. says Choo, 'of being worn out.' Le was on the west of Wei, and they had come east in their carriages, imploring help. 靡所與同= 'have nothing (no feeling) in common with us.' The old interpreters consider all the stanza as

XIII. *Kёen he.*

左 執 有 公 碩 在 日 方 簡
手 轡 力 庭 人 前 之 將 兮
執 如 如 萬 俁 上 方 萬 簡
籥。組。虎。舞。俁。處。中。舞。兮。

簡
兮

1 Easy and indifferent! easy and indifferent!
   I am ready to perform in all dances,
   Then when the sun is in the meridian,
   There in that conspicuous place.

2 With my large figure,
   I dance in the ducal courtyard.
   I am strong [also] as a tiger;
   The reins are in my grasp like ribbons.

spoken of the officers of Wei, whose disordered dresses were an emblem of their disordered minds, and who had carriages in which they might have come eastwards to the help of Le; but they were not so inclined. That Le was on the west of Wei is a sufficient refutation of this view.

St. 4. The 1st two lines describe the piteous condition of the officers of Le. 瑣細, 'anything small,' a fragment. 尾, 'the tail,'=末, 'the end,' or last, of anything. 流離之子=children carried by a current and dispersed. Again Maou takes these lines of the officers of Wei. 瑣尾 is with him 'the app. of being good-looking when young.' Then 流離 is the name of a bird, a kind of owl (梟), which is beautiful when young, and ugly when grown. So had Wei falsified its promises. Wang T'aou spends pages in vindicating this absurd explanation. 裒 is defined by Choo 多笑貌 'the app. of many smiles.' K'ang-shing seems to justify this definition, taking 如充耳='like a deaf man.' 'Such a person,' he says, 'not hearing what you say, generally answers with a smile.' This account of the term, however, cannot be supported, and the dict. does not recognize it. We must take 裒 (jew) and 如 together (see Wang Yin-che on 如), as meaning 'the app. of being in full dress.' 充—'to fill up,' meaning to stop.

The rhymes are—in st. 1, 葛 (prop. cat. 15), 節, 日, cat. 12, t. 3; in 2, 處, 與, cat. 5,

t. 2; 久, 以, &c. cat. 1, t. 2: in 3, 我, 東, 同, cat. 9: in 4. 子, 耳, cat. 1, t. 2.

Ode 13. Narrative and allusive. HALF IN SCORN, HALF IN SORROW, AN OFFICER OF WEI TELLS OF THE MEAN SERVICE IN WHICH HE WAS EMPLOYED. The 'Little Preface' says the piece censures Wei for not giving offices equal to their merit to its men of worth, but employing them as dancers. This is a correct view of the scope of the piece; but in bringing out the meaning of the different stanzas of it Maou and Choo are wide apart. The imperial editors do not touch upon their differences, and only call attention to Maou's peculiar interpretations in a portion of the 2d stanza, intimating in this way their opinion that they may without loss be consigned to oblivion. I shall copy their example, and make little reference to the old school in the notes. I believe with Le Kwang-te that in this instance, 'only Choo has caught the spirit of the ode.'

St. 1. 簡簡=簡易, giving the idea or taking things easily. 萬 is 'a general name for dancing,' or posture-making, for such the dancing of the Chinese was and is. There were the civil and the military dances, 萬 being applied more expecially to the latter, when it and 舞 are contrasted. 方 in L 2 can hardly be translated. K'ang-shing says that 方將=方且, which Williams translates—'about to do,' 'just then.' The phrase is in accordance with the idea of the speaker's indifference, which the 1st line gives. In L 3, 方 has the sense of 今, 'now.' Shin Le-lung (沈李龍, pres. dyn.) observes that

右手秉翟。
赫如渥赭。
公言錫爵。
山有榛。
之苨。云誰
美人。彼美
人兮。西方
之人兮。

3 In my left hand I grasp a flute;
   In my right I hold a pheasant's feather.
   I am red as if I were rouged;
   The duke gives me a cup [of spirits].

4 The hazel grows on the hills,
   And the liquorice in the marshes.
   Of whom are my thoughts?
   Of the fine men of the west.
   O those fine men!
   Those men of the west!

the 3d and 4th lines are to be taken together, as indicating that the speaker would dance in a conspicuous place, and not as describing the former the time and the latter the place of his performance. 前上處 is, lit. 'the' high place in front.'

St. 2. 碩—大, 'large.' There is no idea of 'virtue' in it, as Maou says. 俁俁—'stout-like.' 公庭,—the open court of the duke or marquis. Here, and often elsewhere, we might render 公 by palace;—as in Ana. X. 4. The speaker, in this stanza, is merely describing his various qualities which might have attracted the attention of the marquis of Wei, and made him aware of his abilities. The old school got great mysteries out of the last two lines, that the neglected officers of Wei had great military vigour and great civil capacity. This civil capacity is indicated, they thought, in the warp and woof of the ribbons to which the reins are compared!

St. 3. 簥, acc. to Williams, is 'a reed or pipe with 3 or more holes, resembling a flageolet.' It is more like a flute. 翟—雉羽, 'a pheasant's feather.' The flute and the feather were carried in the hand in the civil dances (文舞). 赭 is the name of red ochre. Here, however, Choo defines it as simply 赤色 'a red colour.' The speaker's countenance was red and flushed as if rouged with some red pig-

ment;—with the spirits given him by the marquis, says Le Kwang-te. Rather, we may say, with his exercise in dancing, which the marquis rewarded with a cup. 渥—'to moisten,' 'to be moistened.'

St.4. The 榛 is described as a small tree, like the chestnut. Lacharme, however, translates the term by corylus arbor. It may, however, be a small variety of the castaneoea. The 苨, acc. to the Pun-ts'aou, which is followed by Choo, is the 甘草 'sweet grass,' or liquorice. Maou calls it 大苦, 'the great bitter,' which Seu Ting thinks may, notwithstanding the dissonance, be another name for the same plant. The hazel and the liquorice were to be found in the places proper to them; but it was not so with the speaker.

The last 4 lines show us the true character of all that precedes. The dancer might speak jestingly of his position, but he felt the degradation of it. He passes in thought from Wei to the early seat of the House of Chow, and from the incapable ruler who neglected him to the chiefs of that western region, who sought out merit, appreciated and rewarded it.

The rhymes are—in st. 1, 舞,處, cat. 5, t.2: in 2, 俁舞,虎,組, ib.: in 3, 簥, 翟, 爵, cat. 2: in 4 榛苨, 人人人 cat. 12, t.1.

XIV. *Ts'euen shwuy.*

泉水

毖彼泉水。亦流
于淇。有懷于衞。
靡日不思。孌彼
諸姬。聊與之謀。
出宿于泲。飲餞
于禰。女子有行。
遠兄弟父母。問
我諸姑。遂及伯
姊。

1　How the water bubbles up from that spring,
　　And flows away to the K'e!
　　My heart is in Wei;
　　There is not a day I do not think of it.
　　Admirable are those, my cousins;
　　I will take counsel with them.

2　When I came forth, I lodged in Tse,
　　And we drank the cup of convoy at Ne.
　　When a young lady goes [to be married],
　　She leaves her parents and brothers;
　　[But] I would ask for my aunts,
　　And then for my elder sister.

Ode 14. Allusive and narrative. A DAUGHTER OF THE HOUSE OF WEI, MARRIED IN ANOTHER STATE, EXPRESSES HER LONGING TO REVISIT WEI. The 'little Preface' does not say who this princess was, nor into what State she married; but it assumes that her parents were dead. It would have been allowable for her, according to the custom at least which prevailed in the Ch'un Ts'ew period, to visit them at stated times, so long as they were alive.

St. 1. 毖 (al. 必 with 水, 示, and 目 at the side) denotes 'the app. of water issuing from a spring.' 泉水 is taken by K'ang-shing and Choo as the name of a stream,—the 'Hundred springs (百泉)' of the pres. day. But it is better to take the characters as in the translation. Those waters, wheresoever they rose, flowed into the K'e, and so traversed Wei. The speaker, debarred from Wei, could have wished that her lot had been theirs. I can make out no reasonable allusion to her condition in the fact of one river of Wei running into another. The K'e was a famous river of Wei, rising at the hill of Ta-haou (大號), and flowing eastwards from the pres. dis. of Lin (林), dep. Chang-tih.

The Shwoh-wǎn says it fell into the Ho, but it now pursues a difft. course to the sea. 有懷 —'I have my cherishings,' i.e., my affections. 孌 = 'good-like' and may be used with reference to the body or mind. 諸姬—'all the Ke.' The lady herself was a Ke, for that was the surname of the House of Wei. By 'all the Ke' she means her cousins, and the other ladies from States of the same surname, who had accompanied her to the harem. 聊 is explained by Maou by 願, 'to wish.' Its meaning is not so substantive. K'ang-shing calls it 且略之辭 'a particle lightly indicating a purpose.' The lady will consult with her cousins on the subject of her wish to revisit Wei.

St. 2. K'ang-shing says that Tse and Ne were places in the State where the lady was married. Rather we may think, with Choo, that they were in Wei, not far from its capital city, and that the speaker is referring to her departure from her native State. People going on a journey offered a sacrifice to the spirit of the way, and when that was concluded, the friends who had escort-

以　悠　之　我　不　邁　載　餞　出
寫　駕　永　思　瑕　遄　舝　于　宿
我　言　歎　肥　有　臻　還　言　于
憂　出　思　泉　害　于　車　載　干
　　遊　須　茲　　衞　言　脂　飲

3　I will go forth and lodge in Kan,
　And we will drink the cup of convoy at Yen.
　I will grease the axle and fix the pin,
　And the returning chariot will proceed.
　Quickly shall we arrive in Wei;—
　But would not this be wrong?

4　I think of the Fei-ts'euen,
　I am ever sighing about it.
　I think of Seu and Ts'aou,
　Long, long, my heart dwells with them.
　Let me drive forth and travel there,
　To dissipate my sorrow.

ed them so far, drank with them, and feasted them close by. This was called 飲餞行—出嫁, 'to go or come forth to be married.' There is a difficulty with the 4th line, and to see its connection with the whole piece, we must supplement it by the assumption which I have noticed above, that the speaker's parents were dead. Thus Choo explains, and adds:—'When I came here to be married, I left my parents and brothers; how much more can this be said, now that my parents are dead? Can I in this case return to Wei again?' He then takes the last two lines as equivalent to the last two of the prec. stanza. The aunts and the elder sister here are the same, he says, as the cousins there. It is impossible to agree with him in this. From Tso-she's narrative on p. 6 of the 2d year of duke Wăn, we see that he understood 姑 and 姊 as really meaning 'aunts and sisters.' We cannot suppose that any of these had accompanied the lady to the harem. As the imperial editors say, Choo can adduce no usage of terms in support of his view. We must then take 問 not in the sense of 'asking and consulting with,' but of 問安, 'asking about their welfare.' The lady allows that she cannot see her parents and brothers; but there are aunts remaining and her sister. May she not go to Wei and see them?

St. 5. The lady supposes now that she can accomplish her purpose, and is on the way to Wei,

her departure to it escorted as that from it had been. Kan and Yen are two places outside the capital of the State where she was married. 舝 is the iron ends of the axle, that enter the nave of the wheels. If we suppose that only one act is described in the 3d line, the lady says that she will grease the ends of the axle. If there are two acts in it, as the repetition of the particle 載 suggests, the meaning must be that which I have given. 還車.—K'ang-shing and Choo supposes that the carriage is called 'returning,' because the lady purposed to go back to Wei in the same carriage that she had come from it in. This does not seem to be necessary. 邁=行, 'to go,' 'to proceed.' 遄=疾, 'rapidly.' 臻=至, 'to come to.' The last line has greatly vexed the critics. Maou took 瑕 in the sense of 遠 'to be far from,' as if the meaning were—'For me thus to go back to Wei will not be anything so injurious as going far from what is right.' Ying-tah also adduces Wang Sub in support of this view; but it is too strained. Choo takes 瑕 as—何, 'how,' and makes the moral value of the whole ode then turn on the line, The lady has in fancy arrived in Wei, but she suddenly arrests her thoughts and says to herself,—'But would not this be injurious to—contrary to—right and reason?' And so she will not think seriously any more of going back to

XV. *Pih mun.*

我入自外。室　事一埤益我　王事適我。政　何哉。　實爲之。謂之　艱。已焉哉天　且貧。莫知我　心殷殷。終窶　出自比門。憂　比門

1　I go out at the north gate,
　　With my heart full of sorrow.
　　Straitened am I and poor,
　　And no one takes knowledge of my distress.
　　So it is!
　　Heaven has done it;—
　　What then shall I say?

2　The king's business comes on me,
　　And the affairs of our government in increasing measure.
　　When I come home from abroad,

Wei. K'ang-shing took 瑕 in its ordinary sense of 'a flaw,' 'a fault'; and though his explanation of the line (taking 害—何) is otherwise inadmissible, he probably suggested to Yen Ts'an a view of it, according to which we should translate,

'It would not be wrong with any harm in it.'

The difficulty, however, with this is that we cannot so translate the same words elsewhere, as in XIX. 2, where we are forced to take 不瑕 as—何不, a question, expressing a doubt in the mind. So Wang Yin-che, on the term 還.

St. 4. In this the lady repeats her longing desire to revisit Wei; and we cannot say from it positively whether her desire was gratified or not. The *Fei-ts'uen* was a river of Wei, which she had crossed, probably, on her departure from it. Many identify it with what is now called 'the Water of a hundred streams.' The account of it given by Maou, from the Urh-ya, is all but unintelligible; and does not affect our understanding of the ode 茲—此;—'this is what I am ever sighing for.' Sou and

Ts'aou were two cities of Wei which the lady had passed on her leaving. Ts'aou—see on VI. 1. 駕,—'to yoke,' 'to put the horses to the carriage.' 寫,—lit., 'to overturn,' as a vessel, and so empty it of its contents,—'to remove,' 'to dissipate.'

The rhymes are—in st. 1, 淇. 思 姬 謀,* cat. 1, t. 1: in 2, 沛. 禰 弟 姊, cat. 15, t. 2: in 3, 干 言, cat. 14; 牽 邁 儇 害, cat. 15, t. 3: in 4, 泉 歎 cat. 14; 漕* 悠 游 憂 cat. 3, t. 1.

Ode 15. Metaphorical and narrative. AN OFFICER OF WEI SETS FORTH HIS HARD LOT, AND HIS SILENCE UNDER IT IN SUBMISSION TO HEAVEN. The object of the piece, acc. to Maou, is to expose the government of Wei, which neglected men of such worth.

St. 1. The south is the region of brightness, and the north of darkness; and so the officer here represents himself as passing from light to darkness. So, Maou and Choo. If we suppose, with Yen Ts'an and others, that the speaker had quitted the capital by the north gate on

哉。實摧自一王謂焉人
　爲我室外事之哉交
　之。已外。敦何。偏
　謂焉室我。哉。天讁
　之哉人政　實我。
　何天交事　爲已
　　實偏我　之。

The members of my family all emulously reproach me.
So it is!
Heaven has done it;—
What then shall I say?

3　The king's business is thrown on me,
　And the affairs of our government are left to me more and more.
　When I come home from abroad,
　The members of my family all emulously thrust at me.
　So it is!
　Heaven has done it;—
　What then shall I say?

some public service, then the ode is all narrative. 殷殷=憂, 'sorrowful'; it denotes 'the app. of grief.' 終,—see on V. 1. This line should be decisive as to the meaning of 終 in the *She* when followed by 且. 窶 and 貧 are of cognate signification. The critics try to distinguish between them here, and say that the former denotes 'the want of money to make presents,' and the latter, 'the want of it to supply one's own wants.' In l.4 the ruler of Wei may be understood; but the terms are quite general. 已焉哉=既然哉, 'it is so!' or 'since it is so.' The 'Complete Digest' says, 'Take care and not make Heaven here equivalent to Fate;' but it does not say what the word really indicates. The idea is our 'Providence.' 謂 in l.7=如, as often.

St. 2. 王事=王所命之事, 'affairs ordered by the king.'—committed by him to Wei for execution. 政事 refers to the affairs of the government of Wei. We must suppose, however, that they are not great affairs which are intended, but vexatious and trivial

matters. The speaker would not have been in such poverty if he had been high in office. 適 =至, 'to go or come to.' —— both by Choo and Wang Yin-che, is explained by 皆, 'all.' Wang T'aou prefers the meaning of 乃, 'are,' which —— also has. 埤=厚 or 增, as in the translation. 室人=家人, 'the members of the family.' 謫,—as in Mencius I. Pt. i. I. 4. 讁=責, 'to reproach.'

St. 3. Choo follows K'ang-shing in reading 敦 *tuy*, and explaining it by 投擲—as in the translation. Maou's 敦 (*tun*),—=厚, is not so appropriate. 遺, 'to be left to,'—加, 'to be laid upon.' 摧, both by Maou and Choo is explained by 沮, 'to repress.' The word means 'to press upon,' 'to throw down,' 'to push.'

The rhymes are—in st. 1, 門, 殷, 貧, 艱, cat. 13; in 2, 適, 益, 讁, cat. 15, t. 3; in 3, 敦 (prop. cat. 13), 遺, 摧, cat. 15, t. 1: in all the stt., 哉, 之, 哉, cat. 1, t. 1.

XVI. *Pih fung.*

比風

其風
雩。其
比其涼。雨雪

其其
邪。雩。惠而好我。
既亟只且。攜手同行。其虛

其霏。比風其喈。
惠而好我。雨雪
攜手同歸。

其邪。其虛
既亟只且。

莫赤匪狐。
莫黑
其邪。既亟只且。

1 Cold blows the north wind;
   Thick falls the snow.
   Ye who love and regard me,
   Let us join hands and go together.
   Is it a time for delay?
   The urgency is extreme!

2 The north wind whistles;
   The snow falls and drifts about.
   Ye who love and regard me,
   Let us join hands, and go away for ever.
   Is it a time for delay?
   The urgency is extreme!

Ode. 16. Metaphorical. Some one of Wei presses his friends to leave the country with him at once, in consequence of the prevailing oppression and misery. St. 1. 雩 is the 'app. of much snow.' The first two lines in all the stanzas are a metaphorical description of the miserable condition of the State. Choo explains 惠 by 愛, 'to love.' K'ang-shing makes it—'ye who are of a loving nature.' Yen Ts'an well explains the line by 以恩惠相與者, 'ye who have kindly intercourse with me.' We might translate the whole by 'O friends.' 攜 is 'to lead by the hand'; 攜手 here, 'to take one another by the hand.' The 5th line is the difficulty of the ode. The 其 is both graphic and interrogative, which decides against the explanation of K'ang-shing:—'The forbearing and good all think things have come to a climax, and that they should leave. We also ought to go.' The Urh-ya quotes the line as

其虛其徐, and so 邪 is here read. How it comes to have that pronunciation and meaning—'slow,' 'leisurely'—is a point on which pages are written. But 邪 being taken in this sense, we are led to give a cognate one to 虛, and Choo, after one of the Ch'ings, explains it by 寬貌 'forbearing-like.' I have no doubt the translation gives the idea of the line correctly. Lacharme has '*nullus mora datur locus.*' 既—已, in last ode. 亟—急, expressing 'extreme urgency.' 只且 (*tsu*) go together, particles untranslateable.

St. 2. 喈,—see i. II. 1. It here represents the rapid whistling of the wind, which is the reason, probably, that it is made to rhyme with 霏 and 歸. 霏 denotes 'the app. of the falling snow, scattered about.' Choo takes 歸 here in the sense of 大歸, 'going away for good.'

匪 惠 好 攜 同 其 其 旣 只
鳥。而 我。手 車。虛 邪。亟。且。

3 Nothing red is seen but foxes,
   Nothing black but crows.
   Ye who love and regard me,
   Let us join hands, and go together in our carriages.
   Is it a time for delay?
   The urgency is extreme!

XVII. *Tsing neu.*

靜 靜 俟 於 隅 而 見。首 踟
女 女。姝。我 城 愛 不 搔 蹰。

1 How lovely is the retiring girl!
   She was to await me at a corner of the wall.
   Loving and not seeing her,
   I scratch my head, and am in perplexity.

St. 3. Foxes and crows were both creatures of evil omen. Every thing about Wei was of evil auspice. 莫赤匪狐,—無有赤而非狐, 'there is nothing red which is not a fox.'

The rhymes are:—in st. 1, 涼,雾,行。, cat. 10: in 2,嗜,霏,歸, cat. 15, t. 1: in 3, 狐, 烏,車。, cat. 5, t. 1: in all the stanzas, 邪, 且。, *ib.*

Ode 17. Narrative. A GENTLEMAN DEPLORES HIS DISAPPOINTMENT IN NOT MEETING A LADY ACCORDING TO ENGAGEMENT, AND CELEBRATES HER GIFTS AND BEAUTY. This is the first of many odes, more or less of a similar character. In the interpretation of which the new and old schools greatly differ. Acc. to Maou, it describes the virtues of a correct and modest lady, who would make a good mate for a prince; acc. to Choo, it refers to a licentious connection between two young persons. The account of it in the 'little Preface' may be made to agree with either interpretation. All that is there said is that 'the piece is directed against the age. The marquis of Wei had no principle, and the marchioness no virtue.' On Choo's view we have only to say, 'Like rulers, like people.' On Maou's that we have a description of what the marchioness should have been.

The imperial editors give both views in their notes, inclining themselves to maintain that of Maou. It will be seen from the notes below that

I do not agree with them. It is allowed on all hands that Choo's interpretations are the most natural deductions from the words of the odes; but it is alleged that he is superficial, and that the deeper we dig, the more do we find to support the older views. Here and elsewhere I have tried to follow Maou and his advocates in all their researches; but it is often impossible to assent to their conclusions without the entire surrender of one's own judgment.

St. 1. 靜 means 'still,' 'quiet,' 'retiring.' The idea which it conveys is of one who is modest and correct; and this is held to be inconsistent with Choo's view. Still, the speaker would not be likely to give a bad character to the lady, who was bestowing her favours on him. Ts'aou Suy-chang (曹粹中; Sung dyn.) distinguishes between 靜女 and 游女, or 'the rambling girls' of LIX. The latter were girls of the common people, whose circumstances did not allow them to keep themselves immured in the harem, whereas the former were daughters of officers' families, who could and did keep themselves so retired. On this view 靜 in the text need not say anything of the character of the lady. 姝 =美色, 'beautiful.' 城隅,—'a corner of the city wall.' 踟蹰 denotes the 'app of a man stopping as he walks,' and hence is used to signify 'irresolute,' 'perplexed.'—Morrison quotes the stanza under 姝, and remarks on

貽。美　匪　洵　自三章　說　貽　靜二章
美　女　美　牧　懌　我　女
人　之　且　歸　女　彤　其
之　爲　異。荑。美。管　變。
　　　　　　　　有
　　　　　　　　煒。

2　How handsome is the retiring girl!
　　She presented to me a red tube.
　　Bright is the red tube;—
　　I delight in the beauty of the girl.

3　From the pasture lands she gave me a shoot of the white grass,
　　Truly elegant and rare.
　　It is not you, O grass, that are elegant;—
　　You are the gift of an elegant girl.

the last line:—'It is curious to mark the similarity which exists among men of every clime and every age. Man, when vexed and embarrassed, scratches his head with his hand, in China as in Europe, both in ancient and modern times.'

Let us see what Maou makes of the stanza. '靜' denotes correct and quiet. When a lady's virtue is correct and quiet, and she acts according to law and rule, she is one to be pleased with. 姝 means beautiful; 俟 means to wait. We have "a corner of the city wall" to express what was high and could not be passed over.' This is all we have from Maou. Expanding and explaining his view, Ying-tah says, 'The meaning is, There is a correct and modest girl, who is beautiful, and could be submissive and obedient to her husband, waiting till she is assured of its propriety before doing anything, guarding herself as by a city wall, which is high and cannot be passed over. Such is her virtue, and therefore I love her, and wish she were the ruler's mate. Since I love her in my heart, and cannot see her, I scratch my head, and look perplexed.' I am persuaded the student who cares to read this with attention will pronounce it to be mere drivelling. The meaning which it is thus attempted to force on the 2d line is simply ridiculous.

St. 2. 孌.—as in XIV. 1. 貽—'to present to.' 彤管 is 'a red reed or tube;' but what article is denoted by it, we of course, cannot tell. The bamboo tubes, with which pencils are now made, are called 筆管. There might

be many things of small tubes, painted or varnished red, among a young lady's possessions, one of which she might present to a friend or admirer. Maou makes the 'red reed' to have been an instrument used by a literate class of ladies in the harem, who acted as secretaries to the mistress, and recorded the rules and duties for all the inmates; and then he says that the presenting the red reed is equivalent to acquainting the speaker with the exact obedience she paid to the ancient regulations of the harem! The mere statement of this view is its refutation. Choo says that 煒 means 'red-like;' but it is the brilliance of the colour, and not the colour itself, which is intended. 說, (=悅) and 懌 are cognate in meaning, 'to be pleased with,' 'to delight in.' 女美=女之美, 'the beauty of the girl.'

St. 3. 牧=牧地, 'pasture grounds.' 歸 =貽, 'to give,' or 'to send to;'—as in Ana. XIII. i. l. 荑 means 'a plant just sprouting.' It is accepted, here, that the plant was the 茅, or 'white grass' of ii. XII. 洵—here, as often, an adverb, meaning 'truly.' 女=汝, 'you,' addressed to the grass. 匪,—非, 'it is not,' not simply=不, 'not,' as frequently.

The rhymes are—in st. 1, 姝,*偶*,,* 鼳*,,* cat. 4, t. 1; in 2, 孌, 管, cat. 14; 煒, 美, cat. 15, t. 2: in 3, 異, 貽, cat. 1, t. 1.

XVIII. *Sin-t'ae.*

新臺

得此戚施。 離之燕婉之求。 魚網之設鴻則 三章 蓬篠不珍。 逸逸燕婉之求。 二章 新臺有洒。河水 三章 蓬篠不鮮。 瀰瀰燕婉之求。 一章 新臺有泚。河水

1 Fresh and bright is the New Tower,
  On the waters of the Ho, wide and deep.
  A pleasant, genial mate she sought,
  [And has got this] vicious bloated mass!

2 Lofty is the New Tower,
  On the waters of the Ho, flowing still.
  A pleasant, genial mate she sought,
  [And has got this] vicious bloated mass!

3 It was a fish net that was set,
  And a goose has fallen into it.
  A pleasant, genial mate she sought,
  And she has got this hunchback.

Ode 18. Narrative and allusive. SATIRIZING THE MARRIAGE OF DUKE SEUEN AND SEUEN KEANG. In the introduction to the notes on ode 9, it has been stated how duke Seuen took to himself the lady who had been contracted to marry his son Keih. It is only necessary to add here, that to accomplish his purpose, he caused a tower to be built on the Ho, where he received the lady on her way from Ts'e and forced her. The general opinion of scholars is that the tower was in the pres. dis. of Kwan-shing (觀城), dep. Ts'aou-chow, Shan-tung.

St. 1. 泚=鮮明, 'fresh and bright.' The Shwoh-wän quotes the line with 玼, which is, probably, the more correct reading. 瀰瀰 denotes 'the full appearance of the stream.' 燕婉 is explained by 安順, 'quiet and docile,' and is understood as descriptive of Keih-tsze, whom Seuen Kăng should have married. Two meanings are given in the dict. to 籧篠. The first is, 'a coarse bamboo mat;' the 2d, 'an ugly disease, which is said to prevent its subjects from stooping down.' Choo observes that if you roll up a bamboo mat, so as to form a sort of grain-barrel, it presents the appearance of a man bloated and swollen, so that he cannot stoop down, and hence the characters were used as a designation of that disease. However we may account for the applications of the terms, they were so employed.—so long ago. The disease must have been dropsy. We are not to suppose that duke Seuen did suffer from this; he is here spoken of as doing so, to indicate his loathsomeness. Choo explains 鮮 by 少, 'few;' but I do not see how the word can here be construed with that meaning. I take it with K'ang-shing, as—善, 'good.'

St. 2. 洒=高峻, 'lofty.' 逸逸 denotes 'the app. of a stream flowing quietly.' Yen Ts'an accepts the account of it as the 'app. of a muddy stream.' Such should be its signification if the character be read *mei*; but the pronunciation here is *zăen*; 珍 means 'to cut off,' 'to exterminate,'—a meaning which is inapplicable here. I must again agree with K'ang-shing, who thinks 珍 was an old form of 腆 =善, 'good.'

XIX. *Urh-tsze.*

不　願　汎　二　中　願　汎　二
瑕　言　汎　子　心　言　汎　子
有　思　其　乘　養　思　其　乘
害　子　逝　舟　養　子　景　舟

1 The two youths got into their boats,
　Whose shadows floated about [on the water].
　I think longingly of them,
　And my heart is tossed about in uncertainty.

2 The two youths got into their boats,
　Which floated away [on the stream].
　I think longingly of them;—
　Did they not come to harm?

St. 3. The *kung* is described as a large species of the *yen* (鴈); see on IX.3. 離—遇, 'to meet with;' here—'to come or fall into.' 戚 施 is the name for another 'ugly infliction' of an opposite nature to that denoted by *k'eu-ch'oo.* That prevents a man from bending down; this prevents him from standing up straight. It is what is now called 駝背, or hunch-back. The 得此 shows how we should supplement the last line of the other stanzas.

The rhymes are—in st.1, 汎。瀰。鮮 (prop. cat.14), cat.15, t.2: in 2, 酒。涘。 矣。, cat. 15: in 3, 離。施。, cat.17.

Ode 19. Narrative. SURMISES AS TO THE DEATH OF TWO SONS OF DUKE SEUEN. See again the introductory note to ode 9. Seuen Këang and Soh, one of her sons, had long plotted to get rid of Keih-tsze, the duke's son by E Këang, to clear the way for Soh's succession to the State; and at last the duke was prevailed on to send him on a mission to Ts'e, having arranged beforehand that he should be waylaid by ruffians and murdered, soon after he landed on the northern bank of the Ho. Show, Seuen Këang's other son, became aware of this design, and as there was a close, brotherly, intimacy between him and Keih-tsze, he told him of it, and exhorted him to make his escape to another State. Keih-tsze being resolved to meet his fate

rather than run away, the other made him drunk, took his boat, personated him, and was murdered by the ruffians:—thus endeavouring by the sacrifice of himself to save his brother. When Keih-tsze recovered from the effects of his intoxication, and found that Show was gone, he divined his object, and followed after him in another boat. It was too late. He approached the spot, crying out in language which must always recal to a western reader the words of Nisus,

'*Me, me! adsum qui feci; in me convertite ferrum.*'

But Show was already murdered, and the ruffians, 'that they might make no mistake,' put Keih-tsze to death also.

The duke gave out that his sons had been killed by bandits, but the people had their suspicions, and they are supposed to have expressed them enigmatically in the two verses of this ode.

St. 1. The 二子 are Show and Keih-tsze.

汎 see on I.1. The repetition of the term sets the vessels vividly before us, floating on the water. The idea of 'floating about,' without direction, which 汎 is said to express, does not apply, however to the 2d l. of the next stanza. 景 is the old form *t* 影, 'a shadow.' The 彡 was first added by Koh Hung (葛洪) of the Tsin dynasty. 願言,—as in V. 3, 4; but the 則 there makes us look more for a substantive meaning in 願. In this and many other places 願言 appears to me to have no more meaning than 薄言. 每.—'every time,' 'whenever.' 養養 is explained as 'the app. of sorrow and perplexity.' Choo says the characters are equivalent to 濛濛. Others would read 恙恙, and 洋洋.

St. 2. 逝—往, 'to go,' 'to proceed to.' 不瑕有害,—see on XIV. 3. The 害 indeed in that case is said of wrong,—what is injurious to the right; in this 'of harm,'—what is injurious to the person. No better meaning, however, can be drawn out of the line.

The rhymes are—in st. 1, 景, 養, cat. 10: in 2, 逝, 害, cat. 15, t. 3.

CONCLUDING NOTE ON THE BOOK. The odes of Wei have the 1st place in those which are styled 'Lessons of Manners, Degenerate (變風).' Certainly they are of a different character from those of the two former Books, which contain the 'Lessons of Manners, Correct.' The influence of king Wăn and his queen, and of the dukes of Chow and Shaou, had left no very beneficial effects in Wei. And yet, the horrible licentiousness and atrocious crimes which disgraced the State of Wei were mainly the fruit of the polygamy which the founders of the Chow dynasty approved and exemplified.

Lëw Kin observes that as the odes of Wei occupy the first place in the 'Lessons, Degenerate,' so that division of them which is assigned to P'ei takes precedence of the others, because no disorders of the social state, and no neglect of the principles of good government, greater than what appear in them, could be found.

I. *Peh chow.*

只。只。他。之實髧在汎^章 鄘
不母死維彼彼彼 一
諒也矢我中柏 柏 之
人天靡儀。髦。河。舟。舟。 四

1 It floats about, that boat of cypress wood,
   There in the middle of the Ho.
   With his two tufts of hair falling over his forehead,
   He was my mate;
   And I swear that till death J will have no other.
   O mother, O Heaven,
   Why will you not understand me?

TITLE OF THE BOOK.—鄘一之四.
'Yung; Book IV. of Part I.' There is little to
be said here beyond what has been stated on the
title of the last Book. The statistical account of
the pres. dynasty says that the capital of Yung was
in the north-east of the pres. dia. of Keih (汲),
dep. Wei-hwuy. Some writers refer it to the
south-west of the dis. of Sin-heang (新鄉),
which would bring us to about the same spot.

Ode 1. Allusive. PROTEST OF A WIDOW
AGAINST BEING URGED TO MARRY AGAIN. Acc.
to the 'Little Preface,' this ode was made by
Kung Këang, the widow of Kung-peh, son of the
marquis He (僖侯; B.C. 854—813). Kung-
peh dying an early death, her parents (who must
have been the marquis of Ts'e and his wife or
one of his wives) wanted to force her to a second
marriage;—against which she here protests.
Choo says this account rests on the sole authority of the Preface, but he is content to follow

it. It is not, however, without its difficulties.
Acc. to Sze-ma Ts'een, Kung-peh was attacked
at their father's grave by his younger brother Ho
(和), and killed himself. Ho then took his
place, and had a very long rule in Wei of. 55
years (he is known as duke Woo;—武公)
dying at the age of 95;—see the 'Narratives of
the States,' VI. Pt.i.6. Duke Woo then must
have been 40, when he came to the marquisate,
and Kung-peh must have been older. If the
reference in the ode be to him, the Preface is incorrect, when it says that 'he died an early
death.'

In both att., ll.1,2. See on III. l. and xix. 'The
middle of the Ho,' and 'the side of the Ho,' are
simply rhythmical variations. The allusion is
probably to the speaker's widowhood, which left
her like 'a boat floating about on the water.'
K'ang-shing interprets it rather differently:—
'A boat on the river is like a wife in her husband's family;—each is in the proper place.'

汎^{二章}彼柏
舟。在彼
河側。彼髧
兩髦。
實維我
特之死
矢靡他。
母也天
只。不諒
人只。

2 It floats about, that boat of cypress wood,
There by the side of the Ho.
With his two tufts of hair falling over his forehead,
He was my only one;
And I swear that till death I will not do the evil thing.
O mother, O Heaven,
Why will you not understand me?

II. *Ts'eang yew ts'ze.*

牆^{一章}有茨，
不可埽也。
中冓之言。
不可道也。
所可道也。
言之醜也。

1 The tribulus grows on the wall,
And cannot be brushed away.
The story of the inner chamber
Cannot be told.
What would have to be told
Would be the vilest of recitals.

Ll. 3. 4. 髦 denotes 'the app. of the hair hanging down or forward;' 髧 describes the mode in which the hair was kept, while a boy or young man's parents were alive, parted into two tufts from the *pia mater*, and brought down as low as the eyebrows on either side of the forehead. Both Maou and Choo take 儀 as=匹, 'mate;' thus making both the lines refer to the deceased husband. Similarly they explain 特 also by 匹. Han Ying read 值.—'the price or equivalent of.' The term indicates that which stands out alone, and, as Hwang Tso (黃佐; Ming dyn.) says, is appropriately used by a wife of her husband. Yen Ts'an understands these two lines of the lady herself, wearing her hair this way. u token of her widowhood. 儀 would suit this view, if it were otherwise tenable; but 特 must be strained to comport with it.

Ll. 4, 5. 之=至, 'to,' 'till;' 矢=誓, 'to swear.' 也 and 只 must both be taken as particles of exclamation. Maou says that by 'Heaven' the father is intended, while Choo says that the mother is here called Heaven by the distressed lady, and supposes that her father may have been dead. Why may we not suppose that she really appeals to Heaven? 諒 is hardly sufficiently exhausted by the 信, 'to believe,' of Maou and Choo. Its meaning is 'to believe and sympathize with,'—our 'to understand.' 慝=邪, 'that which is evil or depraved.' In thus characterizing a second marriage, the lady expresses her abhorrence of such a thing in the strongest way; and Confucius, it is said, preserved such an instance of virtue, as an example to all future ages. One of the Ch'ings gives his opinion on the point thus:—'It may be asked whether a widow left solitary and poor, with none to depend on, may not marry again, to which I reply that such is

牆有茨。不可
襄也。中冓之
言。不可詳也。
所可詳也。言
之長也。
牆有茨。不可
束也。中冓之
言。不可讀也。
所可讀也。言
之辱也。

2   The tribulus grows on the wall,
    And cannot be removed.
    The story of the inner chamber
    Cannot be particularly related.
    What might be particularly related
    Would be a long story.

3   The tribulus grows on the wall,
    And cannot be bound together, [and taken away].
    The story of the inner chamber
    Cannot be recited.
    What might be recited
    Would be the most disgraceful of things.

the suggestion of subsequent times through fear
of want and starvation. But to die of want is
a very small matter, while the loss of chastity
is a very great matter!' But why should Chinese moralists mete out different measures for
the widow and the widower?

The rhymes are:—in st. 1 舟, 瞢 (prop. cat.
2), cat. 3, t. 1; 河, 儀, 他, cat. 17; 天
人, cat. 12, t. 1: in 2, 舟, 瞢; 側, 特,
慝, cat. 1, t. 3; 天, 人.

Ode 2. Allusive. THE THINGS DONE IN THE
HAREM OF THE PALACE OF WEI WERE TOO SHAME-
FUL TO BE TOLD. This piece is supposed, on
the authority of the 'Little Preface,' to have
reference to the connection between Ch'aou-peh,
or duke Seuen's son Hwan (頑), and Seuen
Këang, which has been mentioned on the 9th
ode of last Book.

In all the stt., ll. 1, 2. The ts'ze is said in
the Urh-ya, to be the tsib-le (蒺藜), which
Williams simply calls a 'very spinous plant.'
Medhurst says it is the 'tribulus terrestris,'
which is probably a correct identification. It is
described as a creeper, growing along the ground,
with a small leaf, and triangular seeds or seed-
vessels, armed with prickles. There are two
varieties of it: one bearing a small yellow flower;
the other having a purple flower. From the
picture of the plant in the Japanese plates, the
botanist whom I have already referred to, judged

that it was the trapa bicornis; but that is an
aquatic plant, and would not be spoken of as
'growing on a wall.' 掃 is interchanged with
埽 'to brush or sweep away.' 襄=除,
'to remove.' 束=束而去之.—as
in the translation. A plant like the tribulus
on the wall was unsightly and injurious to it;
but the attempt to remove it would be still more
injurious, and it is therefore let alone. So with
the deeds done in the harem, vile and disgusting,
so that it was better not to speak of them
openly.—The allusive portion of the stanzas is
thus explained.

Ll. 3, 4. All that Maou says of 中冓 is
內冓, leaving 冓 unexplained. K'ang-shing
tries to explain the phrase by taking the term
as 構=成, 'to complete,' 'to do.' The
Shwoh-wăn seems to make it the name of the
couples of a roof, or of all its wooden structure
(中冓交積材). Whatever difficulty
there may be with the term, the phrase is
acknowledged to mean the inside of the palace,
in opposition to the wall, and not only so, but
the most secret and retired part of the interior,
—the harem. 言 is not to be taken of the
words spoken in the harem, but of the deeds
done there, put into words and told. Yen Ts'an
says well:—中冓之言, 但謂閨門

III. *Keun-tsz' kēae laou.*

君子偕老

一章 君子偕老。副笄六珈。委委佗佗。如山如河。象服是宜。子之不淑。云如之何。

二章 玼兮玼兮。其之翟也。

1 The husband's to their old age;
In her headdress, and the cross-pins, with their six jewels;
Easy and elegant in her movements;
[Stately] as a mountain, [majestic] as a river,
Well beseeming her pictured robes:—
[But] with your want of virtue, O lady,
What have you to do with these things?

2 How rich and splendid
Is her pheasant-figured robe!

之事,不必以爲煩與夫人淫昏之言. 道—言, 'to speak about.' 詳,—'to speak about particularly.' 讀, 'to read,' here—'to recite.' Maou explains the term by 抽, which K'ang-shing explains again by 出, 'to give forth,' 'to publish.'

Ll. 5, 6. 所可道,—可 has to be taken in the conditional mood, past complete tense,—'what would have to be told.' 言之長,—'would be the longest of stories.' 'The speaker,' says Choo, 'does not wish to enter on the story, and so he excuses himself by saying that if he once began, it would be difficult for him to end.'

The rhymes are—in st. 1, 埽., 道., 道., 醜, cat. 3, t. 2: in 2, 襄, 詳, 詳, 長, cat. 10: in 3, 束, 讀, 讀, 辱, cat. 3, t. 3.

Ode 3. Narrative. CONTRAST BETWEEN THE BEAUTY AND SPLENDOUR OF SEUEN KEANG, AND HER VICIOUSNESS. This piece like the last is supposed to be directed against Seuen Kēang, the true spirit and meaning of it coming out in the last two lines of the 1st stanza.

St. 1. 君子 is here, as often, the designation of 'the husband.' 偕老, see iii. VI. 4. We must understand an 與 before 君子. The subject of the line is the lady of whom the ode speaks, though she does not directly appear in it till the 6th line. 'Woman is born,' says Choo He,' for the service of the man with her person, so that the wife draws out her life with her husband, and should die with him. Hence when her husband dies, she calls herself "The person not yet dead." She henceforth is simply waiting for death, and ought not to have any desire of becoming the wife of another.' 副 (*fow*) was the head-dress worn by the queen or the princess of a State, when taking part in sacrifices. It was made of hair. 笄 was 'a hair-pin;' here a special article of the kind, used in connection with the *fow*, and adorned with six gems (珈—玉之加, gems attached). To the end or head of the pin was attached the string of the ear-plug, and hence I imagine we must take 笄 in the plural, a pin crossing from each side of the head. 委委 is referred by Maou to the elegance of the lady's movements, and 佗佗 to her virtuous appearance. The Urh-ya makes the whole line to mean 'elegant,' or 'beautiful' (美). Comp. 委蛇 in ii. VII. 象服,—see on the Shoo, II. iv. 4; and the 2d line of next stanza. 子 is to be taken as addressed to Seuen Kēang. Notwithstanding the splendour of her array and the elegance of her carriage, she was 不淑 'not good.' Yen Ts'an directs attention to v. III, and to viii. XI, as two odes constructed on the same model as this, in which the spirit and design of the piece comes out in a single line, 'one or two words coolly interjected.'

St. 2. 玼 denotes what has a rich lustre. 翟 is what is called 'the Tartar pheasant.' Here the term denotes the robe of the princess used in sacrificing, which had such a pheasant

鬒髮如雲。不
屑髢也。玉之
瑱也。象之揥
也。揚且之晳
也。胡然而天
也。胡然而帝
也。
瑳兮瑳兮。其
之展也。蒙彼
縐絺是紲袢

Her black hair in masses like clouds,
No false locks does she descend to.
There are her ear-plugs of jade,
Her comb-pin of ivory,
And her high forehead, so white.
She appears like a visitant from heaven!
She appears like a goddess!

3   How rich and splendid
Is her robe of state!
It is worn over the finest muslin of dolichos,
The more cumbrous and warm garment being removed.

brilliantly represented upon it. 鬒—黑,
'black.' 不屑—see on iii. X. 8. 髢 is defined in the Shwoh-wăn by 益髮, 'an increase
of the hair.' It is our 'false hair.' 瑱—塞
耳, 'ear-stoppers.' We shall speak of them
hereafter. The 揥 is described by Williams
as 'a hair-pin, which was used to secure the hair
in a knot.' But it was not used to secure the
hair at all, but 'to scratch the head (搔首)'.
It was, in fact, a rudimentary comb, consisting
of a single tooth, and is said therefore to correspond to 'the present comb (若今之篦
兒).' Being elegantly made of ivory (象—
象骨), it was worn on the hair, as an ornament. 揚 is given in the dict. as meaning
'the space above and below the eyebrows,' but
Maou, who is followed by Choo, simply calls it
眉上廣, 'being broad or high above the
eyebrows.' 且 is taken by Choo as the particle. Yen Ts'an says it is the conjunction
'and;' but I cannot follow him in his explanation
of 揥 on that view. Wang Yin-che and Wang
Tsun also say 之, in this and the other
lines of the stanza, is merely 'a helping particle;'
and it is better to rest in that view, than to try

to keep its common meaning;—'The whiteness
of her high forehead!' In the last two lines,
而—如, 'as.' This may be said to be universally acknowledged, and there is also a
general agreement as to the meaning, though it
is variously expressed without an attempt to
define the force of the other terms. Choo says
一見者驚猶鬼神也. 'Beholders
are struck with awe, as if she were a spiritual
being.' Hoo Hëen (許謙: Yuen dyn.) says,
'With such splendour of beauty and dress, how
is it that she is here? She has come down from
heaven! She is a spiritual being!' Lacharme
takes 帝 in the sense of emperor:—Tu prim
aspectu coeles (pulchritudine) et stupendum (ma-
jestatis), adaques! But 帝 was not in use at
this time in the sense of emperor. The rulers
of China were only kings. I take 胡然,
'how so,' as an expression of surprise and admiration. 天—天人, 'a heavenly person.'
帝—' a goddess.' Elsewhere we have 帝女
in this sense.

St. 3. 瑳 has the same meaning as 璀, in
the last st. 展 (in the 3d tone) was the name
of 'a robe worn at ceremonial interviews with
the ruler, and in receiving guests.' K'ung-ching
points out that the character should be 襢;
which we have in the Le Ke. 蒙, 'covering.'

也。之兮。之展顏且揚。之也。
媛邦人如也。之揚清子

Clear are her eyes; fine is her forehead;
Full are her temples.
Ah! such a woman as this!
The beauty of the country!

IV. *Sang-chung.*

上要乎矣。美誰鄉矣。爰　桑
宮。我桑期孟之矣。沬采　中
送乎中。我姜思。云之唐

1   I am going to gather the dodder,
    In the fields of Mei.
    But of whom are my thoughts?
    Of that beauty, the eldest of the Këang.
    She made an appointment with me in Sang-chung;
    She will meet me in Shang-kung;
    She will accompany me to K'e-shang.

=='worn over.' 絺 is the name for crape, a
crinkled fabric; but I do not understand how
that could be made from the fibres of the dolichos. I therefore adopt the explanation of Ying-
tah, that the term denotes here 'the finest quality
of fine dolichos cloth.' 是絺紳也 is
almost unintelligible. Choo takes 絺紳 in
the sense of 'to bind tightly,' as if the robe were
worn tightly over the muslin; but in doing this
he, as if unconsciously, changes 紳 into 絆.
絆 has the sense of 'hot with garments,' 'abundance of clothing' (see Morrison, *in ver.*). Maou
keeps the meaning of 紳, but does not explain
絺, for which Ying-tah gives 去, 'to remove,'
thereby changing it into 潔. This view seems
the better of the two, as the fine dolichos was
worn in summer. Both Maou and Choo think
they have sufficiently explained 清 by 觀清
明, 'seeing clearly.' 'We do so,' says Ying-tah,
'with the eyes. Hence 清 is used as a name for
them.' 顏, denotes 'fulness about the temples.' 展如=='really,' and Yen-Ts'an carries

on the line to the next as its subject,— 'Really
this woman is the beauty of the country.' It
seems better, however, to make the meaning of
the line complete in itself,—as in the translation. A beautiful woman is called 媛.

The rhymes are—in st.1, 珈 佗 河 宜 何,
何, cat.17; in 2 翟 (prop. cat.2). 髢 (should
have 易 below). 揥 哲 帝 ** cat. 16,
t.3: in 3, 展 紳 顏 媛, cat.14.

Ode 4. Narrative. A GENTLEMAN SINGS OF
HIS INTIMACY AND INTRIGUES WITH VARIOUS
NOBLE LADIES. The piece, acc. to the 'Little
Preface,' was directed against the lewd customs
of Wei. This Choo He denies. It will be well
to remit the question of the interpretation to a
concluding note.

In all the stt., ll. 1, 2. 爰.—see on iii. VI. 3.
The t'ang is a parasite growing on plants and
trees, and yielding a seed, 'like the grub of the
silk worm,' which is used in medicine. Maou
improperly calls it the *mung* (蒙) vegetable,
and Medhurst says, perhaps after him, that it
is 'a culinary vegetable;' but the plant is not
eaten as food. It has many names in the Pun-
ts'aou, and I was disposed to call it by one of them,

美孟庸矣。期我
東矣。云誰之思。
爰采葑矣。沬之
之上矣。三章
上宮送我乎淇
乎中要我乎
美孟弋矣。期我
比矣。云誰之思。
爰采麥矣。二章 沬之
我乎淇之上矣。

2   I am going to gather the wheat,
     In the north of Mei.
     But of whom are my thoughts?
     Of that beauty, the eldest of the Yih.
     She made an appointment with me in Sang-chung;
     She will meet me in Shang-kung;
     She will accompany me to K'e-shang.

3   I am going to gather the mustard plant,
     In the east of Mei
     But of whom are my thoughts?
     Of that beauty, the eldest of the Yung.

一金線草, 'the gold thread.' The Japanese plates, however, leave no doubt as to the plant's being the dodder (*cuscuta*). 麥 is the general name for grain with an awn. 葑 see iii. X. 1. 沬,—see on the Shoo, V. X. 1, the 妹 there and the 沬 in the text being different forms of the same name. The tract of Mei had belonged in the first place, after the extinction of the Shang dyn., to Yung, but it fell afterwards under the power of Wei, and both Maou and Choo say upon the text that 'Mei was a city or tract of Wei.' 鄉 is here=所. It is better translated by 'parts' or 'fields,' than by 'villages.'

Ll. 3,4. The nature of the ode now begins to come out. The gentleman proposed to gather the wheat and other things, and would seem to be doing so, but it was not for them that he cared; his thoughts were differently occupied. Këang, Yih and Yung are all surnames of ladies,—ladies from other States who were married in distinguished families of Wei, and they are called 孟, as being 'the eldest' of their respective surnames.—'the beautiful' eldest Këang,' &c. The Këang must have been a daughter of the ruling House of Tse; Yung is supposed by some to have been the surname of the original holders of Yung (鄘), some branch-

es of whom would be remaining in the State; Yih takes the place of 姒, in Kung-yang and Kuh-lëang's text of the Ch'un Ts'ëw, so that the Yih here may, possibly, have been a lady of Ke (杞), the seat of the descendants of the House of Hea.

Ll. 5-7, Sang-chung, Shang-kung, and K'e-shang were all the names of small places in the district of Mei, the last name being prolonged by the insertion of 之 between 淇 and 上, unless we translate—'above the K'e.' 期 means 'a set time;' here, used as a verb—'to set a time.' 要 has the force of 迎, 'to meet.' These lines are best connected together by 或, 'or.' So, Yen Ts'an.

The rhymes are—in st. 1, 唐,鄉,姜, cat. 10; 中, 宫, cat. 9: in 2, 麥, 北, 弋, cat. 1, t.3; 中 宫 : in 3, 葑, 東, 庸,中, 宫, cat. 9: and the final 上 in all the stanzas.

NOTE ON THE INTERPRETATION. It has been stated above, that Maou considers the piece as satirical, directed against the lewd practices of the wealthy and official classes of Wei. But there is not a word in it to indicate directly a satirical purpose. The actor in it, or the author personating him, describes his various intrigues,

俏 零。靈 允 吉。卜 觀 與 堂 望
人。命 雨 臧。終 云 于 京。景 楚
星 彼 旣   然 其 桑。降 山 與

He surveyed Ts'oo and T'ang,
With the high hills and lofty elevations about:
He descended and examined the mulberry trees;
He then divined, and got a fortunate response;
And thus the issue has been truly good.

3 When the good rains had fallen,
   He would order his groom,

from Ts'aou, to rebuild from it, as a centre, the ruins of the broken State. He was assisted in doing so by the other States, under the presidency of duke Hwan of Ts'e; but the ode takes no notice of this. K'ang-shing understands by 宮, 'the ancestral temple,' and by 室 in l. 4, 'the residences.' Maou and Choo, however, do not distinguish between the two terms, and Choo says that 室 takes the place of 宮, merely for the sake of the rhythm with 日. 揆一度, 'to measure,' or 一考, 'to examine.' The meaning is that he determined the aspects, east and west, of the site which he had chosen, by means of the sun. How he did so, we need not inquire here. The trees mentioned in ll. 5, 6, would be planted about the moat and wall of the city principally. The selection of the different trees is understood to shew the duke's foresight of his future wants. 榛 and 栗—see on iii. XIV. 4., The t'ung is said by Choo to be the woo-t'ung (梧桐), the *Eleococcus oleifera*, or the *Dryandra cordifolia* of Thunberg. This identification is generally regarded as incorrect, the *woo-t'ung* being of no use for the making of lutes. The tree here mentioned was probably what is called the 'white t'ung (白桐).' The Urh-ya makes the *e* and *tsze* to be the same tree, but the mention of both in the text seems to show that they were different, —varieties probably of the same tree which is elsewhere called the *ts'ew* (梂);—with Medhurst, 'a kind of fir;' with Williams, 'like a yew or cypress.' They are both wrong, however. In the Japanese plates, in those of Seu, and in the 'Cyclopædia of Agriculture,' the tree is figured with large leaves. As it appears in the Japanese plates, the *t'ung* is the *bignonia*. The last line is too condensed to admit of a close translation. Choo says 爰一於, but that will give no meaning. We must take it, with K'ang-shing as —日, and call it a mere particle. K'ang-shing expands the whole line, 其長

大可伐以爲琴瑟—as in the translation. This extends only to the trees in the last line. The best lutes are said to be those of which the upper part is made of *t'ung* wood, and the bottom of that of the *tsze*.

St. 2. 盧—故城, 'old walls,' 'the ruins of Ts'aou,' acc. to Maou. We read in iii. VI. 1, of the walling of this place, in B. C. 718. A hundred and fifty years had elapsed since that time, and now Ts'aou had become a ruin. For 盧, in the sense of the text, the same character with 土 at the side is now used. The Ts'oo is Ts'oo-k'ew, as in the last st. T'ang was the name of a town not far from Ts'oo-k'ew, which, we here see, could not be far from the old site of Ts'aou. Choo makes 景 a verb, meaning to determine the position of the hills by means of their shadows. It is simpler to take it with Maou as an adj., meaning 'great,' 'high.' Others take it as the name of a hill. 京 means 'a high mound,' whether natural or artificial. Here we must understand it of the natural elevations or heights in the neighbourhood. This survey would assist duke Wān in fixing on the site of his new capital. He then descended and examined the mulberry trees, to see whether the ground was well adapted for their growth; and assured of this, he further consulted the tortoise shell (卜), to get the sanction of Spiritual Beings (稽之于神), to this site. 卜云 其吉, 'he consulted the tortoise-shell; and it was fortunate.' 終一旣. 終然—'having done thus.' 允—'truly.'

The 3d st. celebrates Wān's subsequent diligence in the duties of his position, after the new settlement was made. 靈一善, 'good referring to the rains of spring. 零一落, 'to fall.' 俏人 is explained by 主駕者, 'the

千。牝　淵。心　人。直　田。于　駕。言
三　驂　塞　秉　也　匪　桑　說　夙

By starlight, in the morning, to yoke his carriage,
And would then stop among the mulberry trees and fields.
But not only thus did he show what he was;—
Maintaining in his heart a profound devotion to his duties,
His tall horses and mares amounted to three thousand.

VII. *Te tung.*

弟。母　遠　有　女　敢　莫　在　蝀ㅡ章　蝀
兄　父　行。子　指。之　東。棟　棟

1　There is a rainbow in the east,
　And no one dares to point to it.
　When a girl goes away [from her home],
　She separates from her parents and brothers.

superintendent of the carriage;' but this meaning of the phrase is only known from the next line. 星—見星, 'when he saw the stars.' 夙 = 'the early dawn.' 說—as in ii. V. 3. All this was to stimulate and encourage the silk cultivators and husbandmen in their labours. The 5th line has vexed the critics. Maou explains 直 by 徒, which he takes as an adj.— 庸. 'ordinary,' and he refers the 人 to duke Wăn:—'no ordinary ruler was this.' Choo also refers the 人 to Wăn; and taking 匪直 in the meaning of 'not only,' as Mencius in II. Pt. ii. VII. 2, he seems vaguely to bring out the meaning which I have given in the translation, and which Hwang Ch'un (黃樣; Sung dyn.) more clearly expresses:—不直其爲人也如此. 秉—操, 'to grasp, or hold fast.' 塞—誠 or 實, 'sincere.' 淵—深, 'deep.' The line might be rendered, 'In his steadfast heart he was sincere and profound.' The consequence of this was a great accession of general prosperity, one instance of which is given in the last line. Horses seven feet high and upwards are called *lae.* Maou says 驂馬與牝馬, showing that he considered the 牝 to be distinct from the *lae.* At the end of the 2d year of duke Min in the Ch'un Ts'ew, Tso-she praises very highly the merits of duke Wăn, and says that while his war chariots in the 1st year of his rule were only 30, they amounted in his last year to 300.

The rhymes are—in st.1, 中 宮, cat.9; 日, 室, 栗, 漆, 瑟, cat.12, t.3: in 2, 虛, 楚, cat.5, t. 2; 堂, 京, 桑, 藏, cat.10: in 3, 霥•, 人, 田, 淵, 千, cat.12, t.1.

Ode 7. Metaphorical and narrative. AGAINST LEWD CONNECTIONS. Maou thinks the piece celebrates the stopping of such connections by duke Wăn's good example and government. But there is nothing in it to indicate that it belonged to the time of Wăn, or had anything to do with him. It condemns an evil that is existing before the eyes of the writer, instead of expressing any joy that such an evil was a thing of the past.

Stt. 1, 2, ll. 1. 2. The Urh-ya has 蝃蝀 instead of the name in the text. The characters denote a rainbow. Why the radical element in the name should be 虫, 'an insect,' I have been unable to discover. A rainbow is regarded as the result of an improper connection between the *yin* and the *yang* the light and the dark, the masculine and feminine principles of nature; and so it is an emblem of improper connections between men and women. Lacharme says that the superstition still prevails among the Chinese of holding it unlucky to point to a rainbow in the east:—an ulcer will forthwith be produced in the offending hand. The meaning then of these lines in the 1st st. is, that as the rainbow in the east was not fit to be pointed to. so the woman who formed an improper connection was not fit to be spoken about. In the 2d st. 隮—升, 'to ascend,' but the subject is still a rainbow,

矣。 之 乎 送 上 我 中。 乎
上 淇 我 宮。 乎 要 桑

She made an appointment with me in Sang-chung;
She will meet me in Shang-kung;
She will accompany me to K'e-shang.

V. *Shun che pun-pun.*

我 人 鶉 鵲 我 人 鵲 鶉 鶉
以 之 之 之 以 之 之 之 之
為 無 奔 彊 為 無 彊 奔 奔
君。 良。 奔。 彊。 兄。 良。 彊。 奔。 奔

1   Boldly faithful in their pairings are quails;
    Vigorously so are magpies.
    This man is all vicious,
    And I consider him my brother!

2   Vigorously faithful in their pairings are magpies,
    Boldly so are quails.
    This woman is all vicious,
    And I regard her as marchioness!

and so far Choo is correct, when he says 'it was
made by the adulterer himself.' Yen Ts'an vainly
endeavours to get over the 我, 'I,' by distin-
guishing between the writer and the individual
concerned, so that the 'I' is really equivalent to
汝, 'you,' as if the meaning were,—'You say
that you are going to gather the wheat; but you
have quite another intention. I know what intrigues you have in hand.' Such an exegesis is
grammatically inadmissible, and takes all the
spirit out of the piece.

The questions then arise— How did Confucius
give such a vile piece a place in the She? and
how is its existence reconcileable with his statement that all the odes might be summed up in
one sentence,—'Have not a single depraved
thought?' It is replied that the sage introduced
this ode, showing, without blaming, the evil of
the time, just as he related the truth of things
in the Ch'un Ts'ew, not afraid to leave his readers to form their own opinion about them.

After all, looking at the structure of this ode,
I think we may believe that it was made with a
satirical design. If the speaker in it had confined
himself to one 'beauty,' or one locality, it would
not have been possible to regard it as other than
a base love song. Seeing that a new lady comes

up in every stanza, it is possible to conceive of
the piece as having been thus constructed to
deride the licentiousness which prevailed. This
view occurred to me long ago, and I am glad to
see something like an approximation to it in the
remarks of Tang Yuen-seih (鄧元錫; Ming
dyn.), appended by the imperial editors to their
collection of notes on the piece.

Ode. 5. Allusive. AGAINST SEUEN KEANG AND
HWAN AS WORSE THAN BEASTS. So the 'little
Preface' interprets the piece, and Choo accepts
the interpretation.

Ll. 1, 2. In explaining these, Maou simply
says that 'quails are *pun-pun*-like, and magpies
are *k'eang-k'eang*-like,' without indicating the
significance of the terms. Choo, after K'ang-
shing, says that 奔奔 and 彊彊 denote 'the
app. of the birds dwelling together, and flying together in pairs.' This idea of faithfulness between
pairs of the quail and the magpie is imported
into the words however, from the known or supposed habits of the birds. 奔奔 denotes the
boisterous vehement manner in which the quail
rushes to fight;—to maintain, it is believed, its
exclusive title to its mate; and 彊彊 denotes

VI. *Ting che fang chung.*

以望楚矣。　升彼虛矣、　爰伐琴瑟。　椅桐梓漆、　樹之榛栗、　揆之以日。　作于楚室。　作于楚宮。　定之方中。

1 When *Ting* culminated [at night-fall],
　He began to build the palace at Ts'oo.
　Determining its aspects by means of the sun,
　He built the mansion at Ts'oo.
　He planted about it hazel and chesnut trees,
　The *e*, the *t'ung*, the *tsze*, and the varnish-tree,
　Which, when cut down, might afford materials for lutes.

2 He ascended those old walls,
　And thence surveyed [the site of] Ts'oo.

the strong vigour with which the magpie does the same. We may construe 之 as meaning 'of,' but here, as so often in other odes, it has perhaps only the force of a particle, giving a descriptive vividness to the line.

Ll. 3, 4. The 人 in the first stanza is referred to the prince Hwan, and that in the second to Seuen Kĕang. The one duke Seuen's son, and the other his wife, they were cohabiting together. The 我 is referred to duke Hwuy, or Soh, Seuen Kĕang's son. He was himself vile enough to consent to any wickedness about his palace; and we must suppose that the piece sends a shaft against him as well as his mother and brother. 君 is in the sense of 小君;—see Ana. XV. xiv.

Morrison translates the 1st stanza under the character 奔:—

'The quails fly together,
The magpies sort in pairs.
When man is dissolute,
Shall I yet call him brother?'

The rhymes are—in st. 1, 彊, 艮, 兄; cat. 10: in 2 彊, 艮; 奔, 君, cat. 13.

Ode 6. Narrative. The praise of duke Wan:—his diligence, foresight, sympathy with the people, and prosperity. The last ode, we have seen, makes reference to the marquis Soh, or duke Hwuy. He died in B.C. 668, and was succeeded by his son Ch'ih (赤), known as duke E (懿公), who perished in fighting with the Teih in B.C. 659. Wei was

then reduced to extremity, and had nearly disappeared from among the States of China. The people destroyed all the family of Hwuy, and, what we cannot but be surprised at, called to their head Shin (申), a son of Seuen Kĕang and Ch'aou-pih Hwan, He was duke Tae (戴公), and crossed the Ho with the shattered remnant of the people, with whom he camped in the neighbourhood of Ts'aou. Dying that same year, his brother Wei (燬), known as duke Wan, was called to his place, and became a sort of second founder of the State. It is of him that this ode speaks.

St. 1. *Ting* is the name of a small space in the heavens, embracing α Markab (室宿) and another star of Pegasus. It culminated at this time of the Chow dyn. at night-fall, in the 10th Hea or the 12th Chow month, and was regarded as the signal that now the labours of husbandry were terminated for the year, and that building operations should be taken in hand. The urgency was great for the building of Ts'oo-k'ew, his new capital, but duke Wan would not take it in hand, till the proper time for such a labour was arrived. 方='then.' 中, 'to be on the middle;' *i. e.*, here, 'on the meridian.' We have to understand 昏 'at dusk or night-fall.' As K'ang-shing has it, 於此時定星昏而正中. Maou takes 方 and 中 differently.

楚宮=楚邱之宮, 'the palace of Ts'oo-k'ew;'—see note on the title of Book 3d. It was to Ts'oo-k'ew that duke Wan removed

也。　也。三　也。　也。　乃三章　母。　遠　女　崇　朝二草
不　　大　　懷　　如　　　　二章　　兄　子　隮　隮
知　　無　　昏　　之　　　　　　　弟　朝　其　于
命　　信　　姻　　人　　　　　　　父　有　雨。 西。
　　　　　　　　　　　　　　　　　　 行。

2   In the morning [a rainbow] rises in the west,
And [only] during the morning is there rain.
When a girl goes away [from her home],
She separates from her brothers and parents.

3   This person
Has her heart only on being married.
Greatly is she untrue to herself,
And does not recognize [the law of] her lot.

VIII.   *Seang shoo.*

何　不　無　人　無　人　有　相一草　相
爲。死。儀。而　儀。而　皮。鼠　　鼠

1   Look at a rat,—it has its skin;
But a man shall be without dignity of demeanour.
If a man have no dignity of demeanour,
What should he do but die?

'suddenly appearing as if it had risen from beneath.' 崇朝＝終朝, 'all the morning,' *i. e.*, the space between dawn—and breakfast. The phrase seems here to be equivalent to 'for a short time,' or 'only for a short time,' like 終食之閒, in Ana. IV. vii. 3. Choo He and others bring out the meaning by saying, 'In the course of (in all) the morning, the rain will cease.' So fleeting were the pleasures of unlawful love. The old interpreters take a different view of these two lines, but I need not dwell on it. Even the imperial editors do not call attention to it.

Ll. 3, 4. Comp. iii. XIV. 2, ll. 3 4. Ying-tah brings out the meaning clearly enough:—'It is in the order of things for a young lady to go and be another's; she will as a matter of course leave her parents and brothers. But she ought to marry acc. to propriety. Why should she fear she will not get married, and be guilty of that licentious course?'

St. 3. Dropping all metaphor, the poet here proceeds to direct reproof. 乃如,—see on

iii. IV. 之人＝是人,—as frequently. We must refer it to the lady in the connection which is the subject of the ode. 懷昏姻 'cherishes marriage,' *i. e.* thinks of being married, and of that only. 大無信, 'is greatly without faith;' and for a girl to have faith, we are told, is 'not to lose herself (女子以不自失爲信)' I take 命 in the sense of 'lot,'—as in ii. X. Choo makes it—正理 and 天理之正, 'the correctness of heavenly principle.' Maou and K'ang-shing take it as 'the orders of the parents.' The different views come to the same thing. Young people, and especially young ladies, have nothing to do with the business of being married. Their parents will see to it. They have merely to wait for their orders. If they do not do so but rush to marriage on the impulse of their own desires and preferences, they transgress the rules of Heaven, and violate the law of their lot.

胡　人　人　相　不　人　人　相
不　而　而　鼠　死　而　而　鼠
遄　無　無　有　何　無　無　有
死。禮。禮。體。俟。止。止。齒。

2　Look at a rat,—it has its teeth;
　　But a man shall be without any right deportment.
　　If a man have not right deportment,
　　What should he wait for but death?

3　Look at a rat,—it has its limbs;
　　But a man shall be without any rules of propriety.
　　If a man observe no rules of propriety,
　　Why does he not quickly die?

IX.　Kan maou.

彼　四　良　純　素　之　在　干　旄　干
姝　之。馬　之。絲　郊。浚　旄。　　旄

1　Conspicuously rise the staffs with their ox-tails,
　　In the distant suburbs of Tseun,
　　Ornamented with the white silk bands;
　　There are four carriages with their good horses,
　　That admirable gentleman,—
　　What will he give them [for this]?

The rhymes are—in st. 1, 弟 楷, cat. 15,
t. 2: in 2, 雨, 母, (prop. cat. 1), cat. 5, t. 2: in
3, 人, 姻, 信, 命, ㄨ cat. 12, t. 1.

VIII. Allusive. A MAN WITHOUT PROPRIETY IS
NOT EQUAL TO A RAT. This piece is also referred to the time of duke Wän, through whose
influence his people condemned not only licentiousness, as in the last ode, but also the want of
propriety in the general carriage and demeanour.

In all the stanzas, l. 1. 相＝視, 'to see,'
'look at.' The Shwoh-wän explains it by 省
視,＝'to mark.' A rat is a small and despica-
ble creature, but it has its skin, its teeth, and its
separate limbs (體＝支體),—all that it
ought to have. So it is better than a man, who
does not know to behave himself as a man ought
to do.

L. 2. This line is generally explained as if it
contained a question, 'Ought a man to be, or

can he be a man who is, without propriety?' The
rendering I have given brings the meaning out
better. The next line proceeds on the supposi-
tion of such a case, and then it is added that
such a man is not fit to live. 儀＝威儀,
'dignity of demeanour,' conduct which is becoming. 無止＝無所止息, 'nowhere to
rest;' i. e. all the movements are disordered and
disjointed. See what Confucius is made to say
on propriety in the Le Ke, XXVIII. 8. 禮 is
the general term for propriety, expressing, as in
the passage just referred to, 事之治, 'the
good order or government of all one does.'
L. 4. The meaning is, as expressed by K'ang-
shing,—不如其死, 'he had better die.'
遄＝速, 'quickly.'

The rhymes are—in st. 1, 皮ᵃ, 儀ᵃ, 儀ᵃ,
爲ᵃ, cat. 17: in 2, 齒, 止, 止, 俟, cat. 1,
t. 2: in 3, 體, 禮, 禮, 死, cat. 15, t. 2.

者子。何以畀之。

孑孑干旟。在浚

（二章）

之都。素絲組之。彼姝

良馬五之。彼姝

者子。何以予之。

孑孑干旌。在浚

（三章）

之城。素絲祝之。彼姝

良馬六之。彼姝

者子。何以告之。

2 Conspicuously rise the staffs with their falcon-banners,
　In the nearer suburbs of Tseun,
　Ornamented with the white silk ribbons ;
　There are five carriages with their good horses.
　That admirable gentleman,—
　What will he give them [for this]?

3 Conspicuously rise the staffs with their feathered streamers,
　At the walls of Tseun,
　Bound with the white silk cords.
　There are six carriages with their good horses.
　That admirable gentleman,—
　What will he tell them [for this]?

Ode 9. Narrative. THE ZEAL OF THE OFFICERS OF WEI TO WELCOME MEN OF WORTH. This piece, like the two preceding, is held to show the good influence of duke Wǎn. 'His officers,' says the Little Preface, 'loved to learn good principles and ways, and men of worth rejoiced to instruct them.' Choo accepts this account of the ode, but he differs much from Maou in the explanation of many parts of it. There is, indeed, great difficulty with some of the lines.

Maou treats the whole as if proceeding from some man of talents and virtue, expressing his admiration of an officer of Wei, and wondering what lessons of government he would be glad to instruct him about. But this view only distresses the student by the astonishing confusion and absurdities in which it lands him. Even the imperial editors take no notice of Maou's views here, fond as they are of upholding them in general; and I shall not further advert to them.

Acc. to Choo He, the first 4 lines describe an officer or officers of Wei, meeting the man of worth, a recluse, or a visitor from another State, in the neighbourhood of Tseun. This man of worth is then introduced in the 子 of the 4th line. In this way some consistent explanation can be given of the piece, though the language, we shall find, is still attended with difficulties.

In all the stt.,ll.1,2. 孑孑 denotes 'the appearance of the flag or banner rising up on its staff.' 干旄 denotes the staff and pennon of a great officer, which was displayed from his chariot. The top of the staff was adorned with feathers. It was carved into the figure of some animal, or had such a figure set upon it; and the pennon hung down, consisting of ox-tails, dressed and strung together. The yu was a flag with falcons represented on it. It might be borne by great officers of the highest rank, and ministers of the States. The tsing was like the maou, but instead of the ox-tails, the pennon was composed of feathers of different colours, skilfully disposed in spreading plumes. I have translated 干旄 and the other phrases in the plural, in consequence of the view which I take of the 4th line. Tseun,—see on iii.VII.8. The flags appear first in the suburbs, the open country, some distance beyond the city, and finally by the walls. This suggests to us the idea of a distinguished visitor from another State travelling to the capital of Wei; and as he passes through the district of Tseun, the officers of Wei pour out from it to greet him. None of the explanations given of 都 in the dict. meet the exigency of its occurrence here, nor does Maou or Choo say anything about it to the point. Ho K'ëae (何楷; Ming dyn.) observes that, on comparing the 3 stanzas, we perceive that the too was inside the suburbs and outside the walls.' I would venture, therefore, to identify it with the foo (邨) of the Ch'un Ts'ew, and translate it accordingly.

X. *Tsae ch'e.*

心　跋　漕。言　馬　衞　驅。載一
則　涉。大　至　悠　侯。馳　載章
憂。我　夫　於　悠　驅　歸　載載馳馳

I I would have galloped my horses and whipt them,
Returning to condole with the marquis of Wei.
I would have urged them all the long way,
Till I arrived at Ts'aou.
A great officer has gone, over the hills and through the rivers;
But my heart is full of sorrow.

L. 3. This line is descriptive of certain cords or bands, woven of white silk thread, and used about the staff, or in some other conspicuous way. The dict. defines 紕 by 飾 'to ornament;' but Choo calls it simply 織組 'woven bands or ribbons.' Then 組 in the 2d st. is properly a noun, denoting the woven fabric. And in the same way we must take 祝一鳳, as simply meaning 'bands.' The 之 gives the whole line a verbal force (if we are to seek any meaning in that term at all), and refers it to the 1st line, without indicating the use of the ribbons or bands.

L. 4 is perhaps still more troublesome and difficult. That in st. 1 is easy enough, as 4 horses were yoked in a chariot; but 5 horses, as in st. 2, and 6 as in the 3d, were not used. The numbers therefore cannot be applied to the horses; and to say that they are varied merely for the sake of the rhyme, as Choo He does in one place, is to set very little store by the sound sense of the writer. It remains, then, to take the horses, by synecdoche, for the horses and chariots together. The number of carriages meeting the visitor gets more numerous, the nearer he comes. As above, the 之 gives a verbal force to 四, 五, and 六. This is the view of Yen Ts'an.

Ll. 5, 6. The distinguished visitor at last appears in these lines, and the writer asks himself what he can give to the officers, or what he can teach them, for the enthusiastic welcome with which they have received him. 姝一美 'admirable.'

Yen Ts'an instances the cases of Ke-chah, a prince of Woo, who is mentioned in the Tso Chuen, as visiting many States, and imparting of his wisdom to their ministers; and of Tsze-ch'an of Ching, who is ever ready with his lessons at the court of Tsin. The arrival of some such visitor in Wei, he thinks, may be here celebrated.

The rhymes are—in st. 1, 旄, 郊, cat. 2; 紕, 四, 畀, cat. 15, t. 3: in 2, 旗, 都, cat. 5, t. 1; 組, 五, 予, ib. t. 2: in 3, 旌, 城, cat. 11; 祝, 六, 告, or. cat. 3, t. 3.

Ode 10. Narrative. THE BARONESS MUH OF HEU COMPLAINS OF NOT BEING ALLOWED TO GO TO WEI, TO CONDOLE WITH THE MARQUIS ON THE DESOLATION OF HIS STATE, AND APPEAL TO SOME GREAT POWERS ON ITS BEHALF. The wife of the baron of Heu was one of the daughters of Seuen Keäng and Ch'aou-pih Hwan (see on iii.IX.), and a sister consequently of the dukes Tae and Wan of Wei. Sorry for the ruin which the Teih had brought on Wei, she had wished, while the remnant of the people was collected about Ts'aou, to go and condole with her brother (probably duke Wän), and consult with him as to what had best be done in his desperate case. It was contrary, however, to the rules of propriety for a lady in her position (see on iii.XIV.) to return to her native State, and she was not allowed to do so. In this piece we have, it is supposed, her complaint, and the vindication of her purpose.

St. 1. 載 can here, standing at the beginning of the ode, be taken simply as an initial particle. Its position renders the explanation of it by 則, which we find in K'ang-shing and Choo, inapplicable. 馳一走馬, 'to race the horses;' and 驅一策馬, 'to whip them,' 'to urge them.' Choo would construe this line in the indicative mood, as if the lady had actually driven a long way on the road to Wei, until she was stopped by a great officer sent to recal her. It is better to construe it in the conditional mood,—with Ying-tah and Yen Ts'an. The baroness relates what she wished to do, and not what she did. 唁 is 'to condole with the living,' on occasion of their misfortunes; condoling on occasion of a death is expressed by 弔 言

旣
不
我
嘉
不
能

旋
反。
視
爾
不
臧。

我
思
不
遠
旣
不

我
嘉
不
能
旋
濟。

視
爾
不
臧。
我
思

不
閟。

陟
彼
阿
丘。
言
采

其
蝱。
女
子
善
懷

亦
各
有
行。
許
人

尤
之。
衆
穉
且
狂。

2 You disapproved of my [proposal],
   And I cannot return [to Wei];
   But I regard you as in the wrong,
   And cannot forget my purpose.
   You disapproved of my purpose,
   And I cannot return across the streams;
   But I regard you as in the wrong,
   And cannot shut out my thoughts.

3 I will ascend that mound with the steep side,
   And gather the mother-of-pearl lilies.
   I might, as a woman, have many thoughts,
   But every one of them was practicable.
   The people of Heu blame me,
   But they are all childish and hasty [in their conclusions].

in l. 4, is the particle. 跋涉 denotes a toilsome journey, now over hills and across grassy plains (草行曰跋), now through rivers (水行曰涉). Who the great officer of this line was is much disputed. Ying-tah thinks he was the messenger from Wei who had brought the news of its desolation. Choo thinks he was an officer of Heu, who had pursued her to stop the return which the baroness was attempting. Yen Ts'an thinks he was the messenger who had been despatched to express the condolences of Heu in the circumstances of Wei. This last seems the preferable view. Such an officer had been sent, but the lady thinks it would have been better for her to go, and is sad.

St. 2. 嘉=善, used as a verb, 'to approve of.' Choo takes the 3rd line as meaning—'Though I see that you do not approve of my movement (雖視爾不以我爲善).' I prefer the construction in the translation, which is, again, that of Ying-tah and Yen Ts'an. 爾 is to be referred to 許人, 'the people, and more especially the ministers, of Heu.' 遠 may be taken as equivalent to 忘, 'to forget.'

濟 refers to some stream or streams in the route between Heu and Wei. 閟=閉, 'to shut up;' also, 'to repress.'

St. 3. The Urh-ya defines 阿丘 as 'a mound high on one side.' The difference between this and 旄丘, in iii.XII., does not immediately appear. It must depend on the spectator's point of view 言 is the particle. 蝱, or 蝱, is a lily, called the 'mother of pearl,' from the appearance of its shining bulbous roots, or as others say, from that of its flower. It is the fritillaria Thunbergiæ; and I should have called it the fritillary, if I had met anywhere with the term. Many medical qualities are ascribed to the root: among them that of dissipating melancholy;—for which the baroness proposes to use it. If we attempt, with the old interpreters, to treat these two lines allusively, we experience great difficulties. In l. 3, 善 is considered as equivalent to 多, 'many.' A woman is 'good at fancying things with an anxious mind.' The people of Heu, it would appear, had charged this on the baroness; and she vindicates herself. 行 is explained by 道

四章

之。不如我所 百爾所思。 無我有尤。 大夫君子。 誰因誰極。 控于大邦。 芃芃其麥。 我行其野。

4 I would have gone through the country,
　Amidst the wheat so luxuriant.
　I would have carried the case before the great State.
　On whom should I have relied? Who would come [to the help
　　of Wei]?
　Ye great officers and gentlemen,
　Do not condemn me.
　The hundred plans you think of
　Are not equal to the course I was going to take.

'Every one of her ideas,' she says, 'had a principle of reason in it.' This does not seem to be necessary. 尤 has the sense of 訧, with which it is interchangeable,—'a fault,' and here, 'to count as a fault.'—as in Ana. V. xxi.

St. 4. The lady here speaks more fully of what her purpose had been, and again asserts its superiority to the course taken by the State. We must take the first four lines in the conditional mood as in st. 1. 芃芃 expresses the luxuriant appearance of the wheat in the fields. 野 is evidently 'the country' simply; not a wild, uncultivated tract. Maou explains 控 by 引, 'to lead,' which we find also in the Shwoh-wăn; but that meaning of the term is not applicable here. Han Ying made it 赴, 'to go to,' and we find 告 'to inform,' as one of the definitions of it in the dict. The meaning evidently is that in the translation. I translate 大邦 by 'the great State,' because the baroness could only have meant Ts'e, which at this time had the presidency of all the States of the kingdom. At a later time we find the same designation often applied in the Tso Chuen to Tsin, after it had taken the place of Ts'e. It may be worth while to give here an account of the lady, as related by Lëw Heang (列女傳). He says: 'The wife of Muh of Heu was a daughter of duke E of Wei. [This is an error. Tso-she is a better authority in such a matter, and acc. to him was a daughter of Ch'aou-pih Hwan and Seuen Këang,—as I have said. See Këang Ping-chang on this ode]. She was sought in marriage both by Heu and Ts'e; and when her father was about to assent to the proposals of Heu, the young lady sent a message to him by her instructress in the harem, to the effect that Heu was a small and distant State, while Ts'e was large and near to Wei; and that, as there was trouble from the Jung on the borders of Wei, when he wanted to apply to "the great State (赴告大邦)," it would be better for her to be married there. Duke E, however, did not act according to her suggestion.' 因—as in Ana. I xiii. 極—至, 'to come to.' 誰極 has been explained as meaning, 'Who would have been willing to come?' (So, Yen Ts'an); or, 'To whom should I have gone?' (So, Hwang Yih-ching, 黃一正; Ming dyn). 無—毋, 'do not;' imperative. Choo thinks the 大夫 is the same as that in st. 1, and that 君子 refers to 'all the people of the State of Heu.' I think he is wrong, and that the lady is here addressing generally the ministers and officers of the court of Heu. 百—the hundred things or plans. 之—往 or 適, so that the line might be translated—'Are not equal to my going,'—what my going would have accomplished.

In Maou, the ode is divided into 5 stanzas: the 1st of 6 lines; the 2d and 3d of 4 each; the 4th of 6; and 5th of 8. In the Tso-chuen, however, under the 13th year of duke Wăn, an officer is made to sing the 4th stanza of this ode, which it appears must then have contained the lines 控于大邦誰因誰極. This suggested to Soo Ch'eh (蘇轍) to combine Maou's

2d and 3d stanzas in one; and Choo He adopted his arrangement.

The rhymes are—in st. 1, 驅 ., 侯, cat. 4, t. 1; 悠 滫 ., 憂, cat. 3, t. 1: in 2; 反 遠 . cat. 14; 濟 閟 (prop. cat.12), cat. 15, t. 2: in 3, 巔 ., 行 ., 狂, cat.10 : in 4, 麥 ., 極, cat. 1, t. 3; 尤 ., 思 之, ib., t.1.

CONCLUDING NOTE. The best of the odes of Yung is the 6th, celebrating the praise of duke Wăn. A retributive providence is to be recognised in the overthrow of Wei by the Teih; the iniquity of the ruling House had become full. That its restoration should come from a son of Seuen Këang is surprising. That two of her sons by Ch'aou-pih Hwan should have been accepted by the people of Wei as their marquises, and that their two daughters should have become the wives of the princes of other States, would seem to indicate a very low state of public feeling.

And yet those children proved themselves not unworthy. The praise of duke Wăn is recorded; and we cannot but sympathise with the baroness of Heu in the last ode, in her sisterly affection, and her regard for her native State. Though she did feel the rules of female propriety more strict than she was willing to submit to, we cannot wonder at it. The lady of the 1st ode is a true Chinese heroine, rejoicing in her chains, and preferring to remain single in her widowhood, even against the wishes of her parents. Similar conduct continues to this day in the greatest estimation. We can understand a widow remaining single from devoted attachment to the memory of her husband. That a widow should be expected to do so from a feeling that she cannot serve two masters —from a feeling of duty, into which the element of affection does not enter, seems to arise from the lower position assigned to woman, as compared with man, in the social scale.

I. K'e yuh.

衞一之五

瞻彼淇奧。

綠竹猗猗。

有匪君子。

如切如磋。

如琢如磨。

瑟兮僩兮。

赫兮咺兮。

有匪君子。

終不可諼兮。

1 Look at those recesses in the banks of the K'e,
   With their green bamboos, so fresh and luxuriant!
   There is our elegant and accomplished prince,—
   As from the knife and the file,
   As from the chisel and the polisher!
   How grave is he and dignified!
   How commanding and distinguished!
   Our elegant and accomplished prince,—
   Never can he be forgotten!

TITLE OF THE BOOK.—衞，一之五，'Wei; Book V. of Part I.' To what has been said on Wei on the title of the 3d Book, it may be added here, that the State had a longer history, under the descendants of K'ang-shuh, its first marquis, than any of the other States of the Chow dynasty. It outlasted that dynasty itself,—through a period of 905 years, when the last prince of Wei was reduced to the ranks of the people under the 2d of the emperors of Ts'in.

Ode 1. Allusive. THE PRAISE OF DUKE WOO,—HIS ASSIDUOUS CULTIVATION OF HIMSELF; HIS DIGNITY; HIS ACCOMPLISHMENTS. The critics all agree to accept duke Woo as the subject of this ode. He has been referred to already, in the note on the subject of the 1st ode in the last Book. What is said of him there is not to his credit; but his rule of Wei subsequently was of unusual length (B. C. 811—757) and unusual success. 'He cultivated the principles of govt.,' says See-ma Ts'een, 'of which K'ang-shuh had

given the example. The people increased in number, and others flocked to the State. In his 42d year (B. C. 770), when the "dog Jung" killed king Yew (幽王), he led a body of soldiers to the assistance of Chow, and did great service against the Jung, so that king P'ing appointed him a duke of the court.' The 'Little Preface' says this ode was made when duke Woo entered the court of Chow, and was a minister there; but whether he had acted in this capacity before the time of king P'ing or not, we cannot determine.

Ll. 1, 2, in all the stanzas. 淇,—see on iii.

XIV. 奧 means a recess, or little bay, made in the bank by the stream. Maou explains it by 隈; but the Urh-ya distinguishes between the two terms, saying that the former denotes 'a recess in the banks,' and the latter 'an advance of them into the channel of the stream.'

瞻二章彼淇奧。綠竹
青青。有匪君子。
充耳琇瑩。會弁
如星瑟兮。僩兮。有匪
赫兮咺兮。有匪
君子。終不可諼
瞻三章彼淇奧。綠竹
如簀。有匪君子。
如金如錫。如圭

2　Look at those recesses in the banks of the K'e,
　　With their green bamboos, so strong and luxuriant!
　　There is our elegant and accomplished prince,—
　　With his ear-stoppers of beautiful pebbles,
　　And his cap, glittering as with stars between the seams!
　　How grave is he and dignified!
　　How commanding and distinguished!
　　Our elegant and accomplished prince,—
　　Never can he be forgotten!

3　Look at those recesses in the banks of the K'e,
　　With their green bamboos, so dense together!
　　There is our elegant and accomplished prince,—
　　[Pure] as gold or as tin,

綠 =' green,' though Maou makes it the name
of a plant called 'king grass (王芻). 猗
猗 denotes 'the fresh and luxuriant' appearance of the bamboos; 青青, their 'strong
and luxuriant appearance;' and 如簀, 'their
denseness.' Choo, indeed, takes this last phrase
as—狀牀, 'bed boarding,' but all poetic feeling
revolts from such a view. Maou explains
簀 by 積, 'collected together,'—thick as the
stalks of grain in a field. The K'e was famous
in old times for the luxuriance and quality of
its bamboos. The sight of them, so rich and
beautiful, suggested to the poet the idea of
king Woo, with his admirable and attractive
qualities.

Ll. 3,—5, in all the stt. 匪—斐, which we
find for it in the 'Great Learning,' Comm. III.. 4,
where all this st. is quoted,—meaning 'elegant
and accomplished.' The 君子 is duke Woo.
Ll. 4, 5, in st. 1, tell how he had cultivated
himself, as men work on bone or horn with
the knife and file (切磋), and on stones
and jade, with the chisel and hammer, and

sand (琢磨). In st. 2, they set Woo before us as he appeared in court in full dress.
充耳, lit. 'filling the ears,'—the 瑱 of
iv. III. 2. Wang T'sou asserts that notwithstanding the name of this article, it was worn
more for ornament than use,—that in fact it
was not employed to stuff the ears. The ear-
plugs of the king were made of jade; those of
the princes of stones, precious but not so valuable
as jade. All that the dictionaries tell us about
琇 and 瑩 is that they are 'stones like jade.'
The 弁 was a cap of leather, made, according
to the Chinese shape, of several separate pieces
sown together; and 會 (kwae) was the name
of those pieces, or the space between the seams;
such is the account of it by K'ang-shing (弁
中之縫). Maou, however, makes it a
separate thing from the cap, a pin used in fas-
tening up the hair. The cap, between the seams,
was stuck over with gems, 'like stars,' or the
cap and this pin, if so we are to take 會, were
so. In st. 3. these lines bring the duke before
us, pure like gold and tin that have come from

虐　不　謔　善　較　猗　綽　寛　如
兮。為　兮。戲　兮。重　兮。兮　璧。

[Soft and rich] as a sceptre of jade!
How magnanimous is he and gentle!
There he is in his chariot with its two high sides!
Skilful is he at quips and jokes,
But how does he keep from rudeness in them!

II. *K'aou pwan.*

之　阿。考　諼。永　寐　之　澗。考
蕑　碩　槃　矢　寤　寛。碩　槃
獨　人　在　弗　言。獨　人　在

考
槃

1 He has reared his hut by the stream in the valley,
—That large man, so much at his ease.
Alone he sleeps, and wakes, and talks.
He swears he will never forget [his true joy].

2 He has reared his hut in the bend of the mound,
—That large man, with such an air of indifference.

the furnace, soft and rich like the jade formed into the sceptre-tokens of rank (see on the Shoo II. i. 7).

Ll. 6-9 in all the stt. The writer seems here hardly to be able to find words to express his admiration of the appearance and character of duke Woo. 瑟 sets forth, his 'gravity;' 僩 his 'awful dignity;' 赫, his 'glowing ardour;' 咺, the 'proclamation,' as it were, of all those qualities. 諼=忘, 'to forget' or 'be forgotten.' Again, 寛 sets forth his 'magnanimity,' and 綽 his 'slow and leisurely manner.' 猗 is an exclamation. 重較 (now read *ch'ung keoh*) has reference to the form of the carriage used by high ministers of the royal court. As this is represented in the 三禮通釋, the sides of the box were in this form ⌐, the raised portion bring called 較; as in iv. X. 3. 戲謔,—see, on iii. V. 1. The meaning of 虐 here does not amount to more than 'rude,' 'rudeness.'

The rhymes are—in st. 1, 猗., 磋, 磨, cat. 17; 僩, 咺, 諼, cat. 14: in 2, 青, 瑩, 星, cat. 11; 僩, 咺, 諼 in 8. 簀, 錫, 璧, cat. 16, t. 3; 綽., 較., 謔., 虐., cat. 2.

Ode 2. Narrative. A HAPPY RECLUSE. This is all which we can gather from the ode itself. Maou says that it was directed against duke Chwang, who did not walk in the footsteps of his father Woo, and by his neglect of his duties led men of worth to withdraw from public life into retirement. But this is mere speculation, and gives no assistance in the interpretation of the piece.

L. 1, in all the stt. There is much difficulty with the first two characters. 考=成, 'to complete.' This meaning is sufficiently supported, and we find it used of the completion of buildings; e. g., in the Ch'un Ts'ew, I. v. 4. 槃 is more perplexing. The meaning of it which I have given may be said to have been made for the ode; Hwang Yih-ching says, 槃 者 架 木 爲 屋. Choo endeavours to get this sense out of another which the term has,—that of stopping in a given space and not advancing, which brings

告。永 寐 之 陸。考╤過。永 寐
矢 寤 軸。碩 槃 矢 寤
弗 宿。獨 人 在 弗 歌。

Alone, he sleeps and wakes, and sings.
He swears he will never pass from this spot.

3   He has reared his hut on the level height,
—That large man, so self collected.
Alone, he sleeps and wakes, and sleeps again.
He swears he will never tell [of his delight].

III. *Shih jin.*

之 儕 之 齊 褧 衣 其 碩╤ 碩
妻。侯 子。侯 衣。錦 頎。人 人

1   Large was she and tall,
In her embroidered robe, with a [plain] single garment over it:—
The daughter of the marquis of Ts‘e,
The wife of the marquis of Wei,

us to something like the idea of a hermitage. Maou makes it—樂, as if it were 盤; but 成樂, 'he has completed his joy,' is an awkward phrase, and seems unnatural in this place. Choo mentions a view which takes 考=扣, and 樂=器, 'an article of furniture;' which brings the recluse before us enjoying himself in beating his table, or something else, as music to his singing! 澗—as in ii. II. The Shwoh-wăn defines 阿 by 曲阜, 'a curved mound.' 陸 denotes 'what is high and level,' a table-ground.

L. 2. 碩人,—as in iii. XIII. 2. 寬 much as in the last st. of the prec. ode. 之 here, and in a multitude of similar constructions, is most simply treated as a particle. There is, however, an echo of its meaning of 'of,' which adds to the descriptive force of the lines. Choo acknowledges that he does not know the meaning of 薖. Chaou explains it by 寬大貌—as in the translation. 軸 means 'the roller of a map,' or, of anything else; here, the self-collectedness of the recluse, rolled up on himself.

L. 3. We can conceive the recluse singing, as in st. 2; his 'talking' all 'alone,' as in st. 1, is more perplexing. The meaning of 'to sleep again' in 宿 was devised by Choo for the passage, which it suits well. None of the meanings of the term in the dict. is applicable here,—not even 安, 'to rest in.'

L. 4. 矢,—as in iv. I. 諼—'to forget,' as in the last ode; but we want an object for the verb, and also for 過 and 告, which we must supply, as we think most suitable. K'ang-shing is blamed for finding in all the lines the resentment of the recluse against his ruler, whose wickedness he would never forget, whose court he would never again pass, to whom he would never more offer good counsel. A man of this character, it is said, could never have found a place in the She.

The rhymes are—in st. 1, 澗,寬,言,諼, cat. 14: in 2, 阿,過,歌,薖, cat. 17: in 3, 陸,軸,宿,告, cat. 3, t. 3.

Ode 3. Narrative. CHWANG KEANG AS SHE APPEARED ON HER ARRIVAL IN WEI. HER GREAT CONNECTIONS; HER BEAUTY; HER EQUIPAGE; THE RICHES OF TS'E. From the ode itself it is plain that the subject of it is Chwang Kĕang, the principal points in whose unhappy history have been noticed on the 2d and some other odes of Book 3d. A difficulty arises as to the tense in which the greater part of the piece should be

東宮之妹。邢侯之姨。譚公維私。手如柔荑。膚如凝脂。領如蝤蠐。齒如瓠犀。螓首蛾眉。巧笑倩兮。美目盼兮。碩人敖敖。說

The sister of the heir-son of Ts'e,
The sister-in-law of the marquis of Hing,
The viscount of T'an also her brother-in-law.

2 Her fingers were like the blades of the young white-grass;
  Her skin was like congealed ointment;
  Her neck was like the tree-grub;
  Her teeth were like melon seeds;
  Her forehead cicada-like; her eyebrows like [the antennæ of]
      the silkworm moth;
  What dimples, as she artfully smiled!
  How lovely her eyes, with the black and white so well defined!

translated;—in the present? or in the past? The 'Little Preface' says it was made 'in commiseration of the lady,' and this view is supported by an expression of Tso-she, in a narrative at the conclusion of the 3d year of duke Yin. There is little or nothing, indeed, in the ode to indicate this intention, though Yen Ts'an, as we shall see, finds a hint of it in the last two lines of the 3d stanza; but I have deferred to the general opinion of the Chinese critics, and have employed the past tense. Lacharme uses the present, and calls the piece an 'Epithalamium.'

St. 1. 碩人—as in iii. XIII. 2. 頎 denotes 'the app. of being tall.' The 錦 was 'an embroidered robe,' worn by the princess in travelling from Ts'e to Wei. Over it she wore a plain single garment (褧=襌), made probably of linen. Tsze-sze quotes this line, in somewhat diff. words,- in 'The Doctrine of the Mean,' XXXIII. 1, and draws a moral from it, about the avoiding of all display. The remaining 4 lines exalt Chwang Këang on the ground of her birth and her connections. 東宮, 'eastern palace,' is a designation of the eldest son, or heir-apparent of a State, from the part of the palace buildings which he occupied. Chwang Këang, it thus appears, was the daughter of the marquis of Ts'e by his wife proper, and not by any lady of inferior rank. Hing was a marquisate, held by descendants of the duke of Chow, of which we read in the Ch'un Ts'ew, till it was absorbed by Wei in B.C. 634. T'an was a small State, whose lords were viscounts (子), adjacent to Ts'e. Why the viscount of T'an should here be called duke (公), we cannot well tell, as it is not likely that he was dead at this time. 公 must be taken generally as=the ruler of a State. A husband calls his wife's sisters 姨, and a lady calls her sisters' husbands 私.

St. 2 is occupied with the personal beauty of Chwang Këang. 手 is here not the 'hand,' but 'the fingers,'—soft, delicate, and white. 荑 —as in iii. XVII. 3. L. 2 describes the whiteness of her skin, and l. 3 that of her neck. 蝤蠐 is the name for the larva of a beetle which bores into wood, and deposits its eggs in trees. The larvæ are remarkable for their whiteness and length, and hence poets turn them to account as here! 瓠犀 is 'the section of a melon,' (Williams strangely calls it 'the carpel'), showing the seeds regular and white; such were the lady's teeth. 螓 is the name of one of the cicadæ, rather small, but remarkable for the broad and square formation of its head; such was Chwang Këang's forehead, like Seuen Kë-ang's in iv. III. 楊且之皙, 楊且之顏. 蛾 is here the moth of the silkworm, whose small curved antennæ are a favourite figure for the eyebrows of ladies. 倩 denotes 'the app. of the dimple in smiling.' This exact significance of the term has been missed in all

施　比　河　使　夫　蒲　幩　牡　于
罛　流　水　君　夙　以　鑣　有　農
濊　活　洋　勞。　退。　朝。　鑣。　驕。　郊。
濊。　活。　洋。　　　　無　大　翟　朱　四

3　Large was she and tall,
　　When she halted in the cultivated suburbs.
　　Strong looked her four horses,
　　With the red ornaments so rich about their bits.
　　Thus in her carriage, with its screens of pheasant feathers,
　　　she proceeded to our court.
　　Early retire, ye great officers,
　　And do not make the marquis fatigued!

4　The waters of the Ho, wide and deep,
　　Flow northwards in majestic course.
　　The nets are dropt into them with a plashing sound,

our Chinese-and-English dictionaries. 盼 denotes the black and white of the eyes clearly defined.

St. 3 describes the appearance and equipage of Chwang Këang as she drew near to the capital of Wei. 敖敖 has the same meaning as 其頎 in st. I. 說,—as in ii. V. 3. 農郊 are the suburbs, not far distant from the capital, which husbandmen had brought under cultivation. 四牡 are the four horses or stallions of the carriage; 有驕 expresses their 'appearance as strong.' Maou explains 幩 simply by 飾, 'to ornament,' or 'an ornament;' Choo, more fully, by 鑣飾, 'the ornament of a bridle,' meaning more particularly the iron parts outside the bit in the mouth. In princely equipages these were twisted round with red cloth, both for ornament and a protection from the foam. Yen Ts'an takes 幩鑣 as denoting 'all the bits;' Maou and Choo, better, as a descriptive adj., expressing the rich appearance of the ornamented instruments. 蒲=蔽, 'a screen.' The front and rear of ladies' carriages were furnished with screens, made, in the case of princesses, with pheasants' feathers. The ruler of a State gave audience, with the dawn, to his ministers, and then withdrew to 'the small chamber,' and changed his robes. The last two lines are understood as the expression of the people's feelings, when they saw the beauty and splendour of Chwang Këang.—Such a wife was to be cherished by the marquis. Let not the ministers fatigue him with business, so

as to unfit him for showing due attention to her. The poet, it is supposed, repeats the words here, to insinuate his regret for the neglect with which the lady had come to be treated.

St. 4 is understood to indicate the rich resources and strength of Ts'e in the Ho, which then flowed northwards along the west of the State. 洋洋 describe the vastness of the stream, and 活活 'the appearance of its current.' 罛=魚罟, 'a fish net.' 濊濊 express the sound of the nets entering the water. 鱣 is, no doubt the sturgeon. It is described as having a short snout, with the mouth under the chin, covered with bony plates, instead of scales. The flesh is yellow, in consequence of which one name of it is the 'yellow fish.' It is found sometimes of an immense size, and weighs 1,000 pounds. Of the 鮪 I was not so sure. It is described as like a sturgeon, but much smaller, the snout longer and more pointed, with the flesh white. Williams erroneously calls it 'a kind of eel or water snake, found in the Yangtsze Këang.' The fish is common enough at Han-k'ow, Kew-këang, and other places on that river. We should no doubt find it also in the Ho. It is described in Blakiston's 'Five months on the Yang-tsze,' p.77. Figures of it are given on p.88 to help naturalists to identify the species. He says 'it had somewhat the appearance of a dogfish or shark;' but I believe the Chinese are correct in saying that it

鱮鮪。　發發。　葭菼。　揭揭。　庶姜。　孽孽。　庶士。　有朅。

Among shoals of sturgeon, large and small,
While the rushes and sedges are rank about.
Splendidly adorned were her sister ladies;
Martial looked the attendant officers.

IV. *Măng.*

氓之蚩蚩。　抱布貿絲。　匪來貿絲。　來即我謀。　送子涉淇。　至于頓丘。　匪我愆期。　子無良媒。　將子無怒。

氓

1 A simple-looking lad you were,
Carrying cloth to exchange it for silk.
[But] you came not so to purchase silk;—
You came to make proposals to me.
I convoyed you through the K'e,
As far as Tun-k'ew.
'It is not I,' [I said],' who would protract the time;
But you have had no good go-between.
I pray you be not angry,
And let autumn be the time.'

is a kind of sturgeon. The line might be translated, 'Amid shoals of sturgeon, the large and the snouted.' 發發 may describe the abundance of the fishes, or their struggles in the nets. 葭,—as in ii. XIV. 1. 菼 is a kindred plant; other names for it are 薍 and 荻. 揭揭 express the rank high growth of the rushes. The marchioness of Wei was a Kĕang (姜); by 庶姜 must be intended her cousins, attending her from Ts'e to her harem,—'the virgins, her companions;' 孽孽 expresses the richness of their array. 庶士 are the officers escorting Chwang Kĕang and her companions from Ts'e; 有朅 expresses their martial appearance.

The rhymes are—in st. 1, 頎 (prop. cat. 15), 衣,妻,姨,私, cat 1 t. 1: in 2, 薲,脂,

蠐,犀,眉, ib; 倩,盼,。, cat. 13: in 3, 敖,郊,驕,鑣,朝,勞, cat. 2; in 4, 沽, 渶,發,揭,孽,朅, cat. 15, t. 3:

Ode 4. Narrative, with metaphorical and allusive portions interspersed. A WOMAN, WHO HAD BEEN SEDUCED INTO AN IMPROPER CONNECTION, NOW CAST OFF, RELATES AND BEMOANS HER SAD CASE. Maou refers the piece to the time of duke Seuen, of whose dissolute character notice has already been taken. He thinks, accordingly, that the piece was directed against the times, and holds up to approval the woman who relates her case in it, as a reformed character. The ode, however, gives no note of the time when it was composed, nor does anything more appear in it beyond what I have expressed in the above summary.

St. 1. Ll. 1—4 describe the way in which the seduction was accomplished. The 子 in l. 5 shows that we should translate them in the 2d

來　咎　卜　載　漣　復　望　乘　秋
以　言　爾　笑　。　關　復　彼　以
我　以　筮　載　既　泣　關　垝　爲
賄　爾　體　言　見　涕　不　垣　期
遷　車　無　。　復　漣　見　以　。
。　　　　　爾　關

2　I ascended that ruinous wall,
　　To look towards Fuh-kwan;
　　And when I saw [you] not [coming from] it;
　　My tears flowed in streams.
　　When I did see [you coming from] Fuh-kwan,
　　I laughed and I spoke.
　　You had consulted, [you said], the tortoise-shell and the reeds,
　　And there was nothing unfavourable in their response.
　　'Then come,' [I said],' with your carriage,
　　And I will remove with my goods.'

person. The whole piece, indeed, is addressed to the man, who had first led astray, and then cast off. 氓=民, 'one of the people.' The woman intimates by the term 'that at first she, did not know the man nor anything about him.' 蚩 蚩 describes his 'ignorant look;' Maou says his 'honest looks.' 'Simple-looking' gives the meaning. 布 = 'cloth,' without saying of what material. The critics define it here by 幣 'pieces of woven silk,' 絲 is the raw silk. 貿, =='to barter,' 'to exchange.' 即=就, 'to come to.'—'You came to me to consult,' i. e. to propose that I should at once elope with you. The other lines show how far the woman was wrought upon, and how, though yielding to some extent, she tried to bring about a regular marriage. Tun-k'ew was a place in Wei, but it cannot be identified. The last 4 lines are the substance of the woman's parting words. 愆=過, 'to go beyond;' here, ='to protract.' 將=請, 'to beg,' 'to ask.' The man must have made his first approach in the beginning of summer, when the silk from the cocoons was ready for sale.

St. 2 describes the elopement, how anxious the woman was, when the time came, to see her lover, and how she sought, notwithstanding, to get some justification of her deed. 垝=毀, 'broken down,' 'dilapidated.' 垣=牆, 'a

wall.' Choo says that Fuh-kwan was 'the place where the man lived;' Maou, 'a place near which he lived.' The characters would appear to be the name of a barrier-gate, through which the visitor must come. Through modesty, she mentions the place, and not the person. The Urh-ya defines 漣漣, as 'the appearance of weeping;' but we must not lose the significance of 連 連, denoting continuity. Choo supposes the last 4 lines to have been spoken by the woman, questioning the visitor. K'ang-shing, better, it appears to me, refers the first two to the man, and the others to the woman. 卜 is used of divination by the tortoise-shell, and 筮 of divination by the reeds or milfoil. 體.—see on the Shoo, V.vi.9,10. It properly belongs to the form on the burnt shell, but is here applied also to the diagrams indicated by the reeds. 賄=財, 'wealth, substance.' It does not appear in what the woman's wealth consisted. There was probably little of it, notwithstanding her use of the term. 'The man,' says Ying-tah, 'had never divined about the matter, and he only said so to complete the process of seduction. The critics dwell on the inconsistency of the parties' having recourse to divination in their case. 'Divination is good only if used in reference to what is right and moral.'

車帷裳。女也不爽。
食貧。淇水湯湯。漸
隕。自我徂爾。三歲
桑之落矣。其黃而
兮。不可說也。
猶可說也。女之耽
與士耽。士之耽
桑葚于嗟女兮。無食
若于嗟鳩兮。無食
桑之未落。其葉沃
四章
三章

3　Before the mulberry tree has shed its leaves,
　　How rich and glossy are they!
　　Ah! thou dove,
　　Eat not its fruit [to excess].
　　Ah! thou young lady,
　　Seek no licentious pleasure with a gentleman.
　　When a gentleman indulges in such pleasure,
　　Something may still be said for him;
　　When a lady does so,
　　Nothing can be said for her.

4　When the mulberry tree sheds its leaves,
　　They fall yellow on the ground.
　　Since I went with you,
　　Three years have I eaten of your poverty;
　　And [now] the full waters of the K'e
　　Wet the curtains of my carriage.
　　There has been no difference in me,

In st. 3, the woman is conscious of the folly she had committed. 沃若, = 沃然, 'glossy-like.' The dove here is not the turtle-dove of ii. 1. but another species, called the *kwuh kiw* (鶻鳩), 'rather smaller than a pigeon, marked with greenish black spots, having a short tail, and noisy, from which it is named the chattering dove (鳴鳩). It appears in the spring, and goes away in the winter.' 葚 denotes the berries of the mulberry tree. This dove is very fond of them, and they are supposed to intoxicate it. Here the allusive and metaphorical element comes in. The dove, drunk with the berries, represents the young lady who has been indiscreet. 耽 = 樂, 'to take pleasure,' or, as Yen Ts'an has it, 溺好,

'to be sunk—over head and ears—in love.' 說 is explained by. 解, 'to explain,' found where we might render it by—'to give satisfaction for.' A man's sphere, it is said, is wide, and by good services and deeds he may expiate his indiscretion; but in a woman's limited sphere, if she lose her virtue, she loses all. The speaker in the ode finds this out—too late.

In st. 4 the woman appears cast off, and returning to her original home. In l. 2, 而 = 且, 'and.'—'The leaves become yellow and fall.' So was it now with her a faded beauty. In l. 3, 爾 is best taken as a particle, = 矣. 徂 = 往, 'to go away.' 湯 (shang) 湯 is descriptive of the full waters of the stream. 漸 = 漬 'to wet.' A woman's carriage was curtained

士貳其行。士也罔
極。<small>五章</small>二三其德。
三歲爲婦。靡室勞
矣。夙興夜寐。靡有
朝矣。言既遂矣。至
于暴矣。兄弟不知。
咥其笑矣。靜言思
之。<small>六章</small>躬自悼矣。
及爾偕老。老使我
怨。淇則有岸。隰則
有泮。

But you have been double in your ways.
It is you, Sir, who transgress the right,
Thus changeable in your conduct.

5　For three years I was your wife,
And thought nothing of my toil in your house.
I rose early and went to sleep late,
Not intermitting my labours for a morning.
Thus [on my part] our contract was fulfilled,
But you have behaved thus cruelly.
My brothers will not know [all this],
And will only laugh at me.
Silently I think of it,
And bemoan myself.

6　I was to grow old with you;—
Old, you give me cause for sad repining.
The K'e has its banks,
And the marsh has its shores.

at the sides. The curtains were to the carriage what the lower garment (裳) was to the body, and hence they were called 帷裳女, of course, is the woman herself, and 士 the gentleman. We might translate in the 3d person:—'It was not the woman, who,' &c. 爽—差, 'different.' Maou explains 極 by 中正.—'the path of the correct mean;' Choo, by 至, meaning the 'perfect' rule of conduct. 二三 have a verbal force, 'now two, now three,' i. e. varying.

St. 5. 靡室勞—不以室家之務爲勞,—as in the translation. L. 4, lit.,—

'did not have a morning.' 夙 and 夜, separated, as in l. 3, are difft. from the phrase 夙夜 in ii. II. 3, et al. In l. 5, K'ang-shing makes 言—我, 'I' and 遂—久, 'long.'—'I have thus been long with you.' But we cannot so explain the terms. 言—相約之言 'the words of their covenant,' and 遂—成, 'to complete,' 'to be complete.' Driven away, as she was, her brothers ignorant of all the circumstances, would not acknowledge her. It is to be supposed her parents were dead. 咥 (he) is intended to express a sneering laugh. In l. 9, 言 is the particle.

St. 6. 老 in l. 2 is a stumbling block to the critics, as the woman had been the man's no-

焉　思。反　思　且　晏　言　角　有
哉。亦　是　其　且。信　笑　之　泮。
　　已　不　反。不　誓　晏　宴。總

In the pleasant time of my girlhood, with my hair simply
　　　gathered in a knot,
Harmoniously we talked and laughed.
Clearly were we sworn to good faith,
And I did not think the engagement would be broken.
That it would be broken I did not think,
And now it must be all over!

V.　*Chuh kan.*

致　遠　爾　豈　于　以　竹　籊　竹
之。莫　思。不　淇。釣　竿。籊　竿

1　With your long and tapering bamboo rods,
　　You angle in the K'e.
　　Do I not think of you?
　　But I am far away, and cannot get to you.

minal wife for only 3 years. I conceive, however, we are not to press a term in such a piece.
泮＝涯, 'a bank or shore.' The K'e had its
banks, and the marsh its shores; people knew
where to find them. But it was not so with the
man who acknowledged no rules nor bounds in
his conduct. 總角 describes the hair gathered, without any pins, into two horn-like
knots. Lads wore their hair so, till they were
capped, and girls, till they were married.
晏晏＝和柔, 'harmonious and soft.' 且
旦＝明, 'clearly.'—'Our faithful oaths (pledges) were distinct.' 不思其反, 'I did not
think of the going contrary,' i. e., of the possibility of the engagement's being broken.' Choo
expands the last line, 則亦如之何哉,
亦已而已矣. 'What then can be done?
It is all over; yes, all over.'

　The rhymes are—in st. 1, 蚩絲絲謀 *,
淇丘 *, 媒 *, 期, cat. 1, t. 1: in 2, 垣,關,
關,漣,關,言,言,遷, cat. 14: in 3, 落,
若 *, cat. 5, t. 3; 葚,耽 (prop. cat. 8), cat. 7,
t. 1; 說,說, cat. 15, t. 3: in 4, 隕,貧 *, cat.

13; 湯,裳,爽,行, cat. 10; 極,德, cat. 1,
t. 3: in 5, 勞,朝,暴 *, 笑,悼, cat. 2;? 寐,
遂, cat. 15, t. 3: in 6, 怨,岸,泮,宴 *, 晏
旦,反, cat. 14,; 思,哉, cat. 1, t. 1.

Ode 5. Narrative. A DAUGHTER OF THE
HOUSE OF WEI, MARRIED IN ANOTHER STATE,
EXPRESSES HER LONGING TO REVISIT WEI. The
argument of this ode is thus the same with that
of iii. XIV. This, however, is shorter and simpler. The 'Little Preface' says, indeed, that
the lady here was unhappy in her marriage, and
that she was able by a sense of propriety to
repress her longing. But neither of these things
appears in the piece. She thinks of the scenes
of her youth, and longs that she were back
among them. That cannot be, she is now so
far removed from them; and with an expression
of regret she submits to her lot. This is the
substance of the poem.

St. 1. 籊籊＝'long and tapering.' I translate the first 2 lines in the 2d person, because of
the 爾 in the 3d line. When young, the

以寫我憂。　松舟。駕言出遊。　^{四章}淇水滺滺。檜楫　佩玉之儺。　在左。巧笑之瑳。　^{三章}淇水在右。泉源　遠兄弟父母。　在右。女子有行。　^{二章}泉源在左。淇水

2 The Ts'euen-yuen is on the left,
   And the waters of the K'e are on the right.
   But when a young lady goes away, [and is married],
   She leaves her brothers and parents.

3 The waters of the K'e are on the right,
   And the Ts'euen-yuen is on the left.
   How shine the white teeth through the artful smiles!
   How the girdle gems move to the measured steps!

4 The waters of the K'e flow smoothly;
   There are the oars of cedar and the boats of pine.
   Might I but go there in my carriage and ramble,
   To dissipate my sorrow!

speaker had been pleased to look at the fishers, and she would be glad to be able to do so again. 遠莫致之 'from the distance, there is no bringing it about,' i. e., there is no getting a sight of the Wei anglers. As Gow-yang Sëw expands it, 遠適異國不得見焉.

Stt. 2, 3. The Ts'euen-yuen is 'The Hundred Springs,' referred to on iii. XIV. 1. It flowed 1st on the northwest of the capital of Wei, and then, after a southeast course, joined the K'e, which came from the southwest. The north was held to be 'on the left,' and the south 'on the right.' Hence the rivers are spoken of thus relatively. The lady remembers the pleasures she had experienced between those streams, and mourns that she no longer resided in Wei. If we seek for any allusive element in the two rivers, as the old interpreters do, we only fall into absurdities. 女子, 云云,—see on ii. XIV. 2. The last two lines of st. 3 indicate more particularly what the lady's pleasures had been,—rambling with her companions, in happy converse and elegant dress. 瑳 is here explain-

ed by Maou, as 'the appearance of an artful smile;' but the word properly denotes the brilliant, white appearance of a gem.' Here it signifies the ivory of the teeth displayed in smiling. 佩玉—'the gems attached to a girdle.' An ornament of various gems, variously strung together, was worn anciently by ladies at the girdle. We shall have occasion to speak of it again. The gems struck against each other, and made a noise in walking. 儺 means 'to walk with measured steps (行有節).'

St. 4. 滺滺 denotes the 'app. of the flowing current.' 檜, called also 栝, is probably a cedar, 'having the leaf of the cypress, and the trunk of a pine.' 松 is the pine. 駕言, 云云,—as in iii XIV. 4.

The rhymes are—in st. 1, 淇, 思, 之, cat. 1, t. 1: in 2, 右。, 母。, ib., t. 2: in 3, 左, 瑳, 儺 (prop. cat. 14), cat. 17: in 4, 滺, 舟, 游, 憂, cat. 3, t. 1.

VI. *Hwan-lan.*

芄蘭

能不我甲。容兮。
遂兮。垂帶悸兮。
佩韘。佩韘雖則佩韘。
芄蘭之葉。童子
二章

能不我知。容兮。
遂兮。垂帶悸兮。
佩觿。佩觿雖則佩觿。
芄蘭之支。童子
一章

1　There are the branches of the sparrow-gourd;—
There is that lad, with the spike at his girdle.
Though he carries a spike at his girdle,
He does not know us.
How easy and conceited is his manner,
With the ends of his girdle hanging down as they do!

2　There are the leaves of the sparrow-gourd;—
There is that lad with the archer's thimble at his girdle.
Though he carries an archer's thimble at his girdle,
He is not superior to us.
How easy and conceited is his manner,
With the ends of his girdle hanging down as they do!

Ode 6. Allusive. PICTURE OF A CONCEITED YOUNG MAN OF RANK. Acc. to the 'Little Preface,' the subject of this piece is duke Hwuy of Wei,—Soh, the son of Seuen and Seuen Kĕang, who succeeded to the State after the murder of his brothers, Keih-tsze and Show;—see on iii.XIX. He was then 'young,' acc. to the Tso-chuen;—Too-yu says 15 or 16. Choo says he cannot tell who is the subject, and does not think it worth his while to attempt an application of it to any one in particular. Nothing more than what I have stated can be deduced from the language of the two stanzas.

L.1 in both stanzas. The *hwan lan* is a creeping plant, the stalk of which, when broken, exudes a white juice. Its leaves may be eaten, both raw and cooked. It has the names also of 雀, 蘿藦, and 雀瓢; by the last of which I have translated it. From the Japanese plates, we might conclude that it was a *tylophora*. Some explain 支 by 荚, 'pods,' those of the plant, several inches long, hanging

down from among the leaves, 'like an awl.' The *weakness* of the plant, unable to rise from the ground without support, is supposed to be the reason why it is introduced here, with an allusion to the weak character of the youth who is spoken of.

L.2. 童子 may be used of any one under 19. The *hwuy* was an ivory spike, worn at the girdle for the purpose of loosening knots. It belonged to the equipment of grown up men, and was supposed to indicate their competency for the management of business, however intricate. The youth in the ode had assumed it from vanity. The *sheh* was an instrument, also of ivory, worn by archers on the thumb of the right hand, to assist them in drawing the string of their bow. A ring of jade is now used for this purpose. K'ang-shing makes the *sheh* to have been a sort of glove, made of leather, and worn with the same object on 3 fingers of the right hand.

L.4. I agree with Wang Yin-che in taking 能 here as = 而, 'and yet,' responding to 雖 in

VII. *Ho kwang.*

二章　曾不崇朝。
　　　誰謂宋遠。
　　　曾不容刀。
　　　誰謂河廣。
二章　跂予望之。
　　　誰謂宋遠。
　　　一葦杭之。
一章　誰謂河廣。

河廣

1　Who says that the Ho is wide?
　　With [a bundle of] reeds I can cross it.
　　Who says that Sung is distant?
　　On tiptoe I can see it.

2　Who says that the Ho is wide?
　　It will not admit a little boat.
　　Who says that Sung is distant?
　　It would not take a whole morning to reach it.

1.3. The line is condemnatory of the youth, pretending to be a man, but without a man's knowledge or ability; but I cannot get Maou's idea of it in st.1.—'He does not say (=think) that he has no knowledge, but is proud and insolent to others(不自謂無知,以驕慢人),' nor follow him in taking 甲 in st.2 as = 狎. The lines are at least translateable, as they are, and 甲 = 長, ' to be superior to,' 'to rule over.'

Ll.5,6. 容 is 'the manner,' or 'air,' of the youth; and 遂, the appearance of it, as in the translation. 悸 expresses the appearance of his girdle hanging down,—' in a jaunty manner.'

The rhymes are—in st.1, 支, 䑡 or 艫, 知, cat.16, t.1; 遂, 悸 (and in st.2), cat.15, t.3: in 2, 葉 or 葦, 䑞, 甲, cat.8, t.3.

Ode 7. Narrative. OTHER THINGS, MORE DIFFICULT TO OVERCOME THAN DISTANCE, MAY KEEP ONE FROM A PLACE. Both Maou and Choo refer this short piece to a daughter of Seuen Kёang, who was married to duke Hwan of Sung;—see on iii.IX. After giving birth to a son, who became duke Sёang, she was divorced, and returned to Wei. When that son succeeded to Sung, she wished to return to that State; but the rules of propriety forbade her, as having been divorced, to do so; and she is supposed to have made

these verses to reconcile herself to her circumstances. They are supposed, therefore to be much to her honour, as showing how she could subordinate her maternal longings to her sense of what was proper! Yen Ts'an started a difficulty about the time when the lines were written, making them earlier than the accession of duke Sёang, and this would affect the general interpretation. It is hardly worth while, however, to discuss this point.

Ll. 1, 2, in both stt. 葦,—' a reed or rush.' 杭=渡, 'to cross over.' I agree with Ying-tah in taking 一 葦 as meaning, not 'a single reed,' but 'a bundle of reeds.' 曾=則 We can hardly translate it. If we try to do so, *but* would come nearest to its meaning:—'It is not wide, but,' &c. 刀 means a small boat. A more modern form of the character has 舟 at the side. It is not true that the Ho is so narrow, or that we could cross it with the help of a bundle of reeds; but the speaker thus intimates that if nothing but the stream of the Ho stood in her way, she could easily get across it. So, in the other lines.

Ll.3,4. 跂 (k'e, 2d tone)=舉踵, 'to raise the heel,' i.e. to stand on tiptoe. 崇朝, —see on iv. VII. 2.

The rhymes are—in st.1, 杭, 望, cat.10; in 2, 刀, 朝, cat.2.

VIII. *Pih he.*

伯兮

甘　出　其　誰　飛　自　為　桀　伯
心　日　雨　適　蓬　伯　王　兮　兮
首　願　其　為　豈　之　前　伯　朅
疾　言　雨　容　無　東　驅　也　兮
　　思　杲　　　膏　首　　　執　邦
　　伯　杲　　　沐　如　　　殳　之

1 My noble husband is how martial-like!
  The hero of the country!
  My husband, grasping his halberd,
  Is in the leading chariot of the king's [host].

2 Since my husband went to the east,
  My head has been like the flying [pappus of the] artemisia.
  It is not that I could not anoint and wash it;
  But for whom should I adorn myself?

3 O for rain! O for rain!
  But brightly the sun comes forth.
  Longingly I think of my husband,
  Till my heart is weary, and my head aches.

Ode 8. Narrative and metaphorical. A WIFE MOURNS OVER THE PROTRACTED ABSENCE OF HER HUSBAND ON THE KING'S SERVICE. Maou thinks that this piece was directed against the warlike character of the times, when officers were long kept on service away from their families. K'ang-shing, more particularly, and I believe correctly, referred it to the year B. C. 706, when, as we learn from the Ch'un Ts'ew (II. v. 6), Wei and some other States did service with the king against the State of Ch'ing. That was in the time of duke Seuen of Wei.

St. 1. Choo takes 伯 as a designation of her husband by the lady. This is much better than to take it, with Maou, as a designation of him by his office, which he supposes to have been the presidency or charge of a district (州伯) 朅—武貌, 'martial-like.' 桀—'one of a myriad,'—a hero. The *shoo* was a clab or halberd, 10 or more cubits long, made of wood, thick and heavy towards the point, but without a sharp edge. It was used to strike down, not to pierce. The lady sees her husband in his chariot, and in the front of the king's host,—the post of daring and danger.

St. 2. Ch'ing lay to the south-west of Wei The troops of Wei and the other States must first have marched west to the capital, to join the royal army, and then gone east to attack Ch'ing. 蓬,—see on ii. XIV. 2. It is here called 'the flying *fung*,' with reference to its bristly or feathery *pappus*, through which its seeds are dispersed by the wind. Such had the lady's hair become. 膏沐 are both nouns;— 'Have I no ointment and wash?' The wash for the head was congee water. Both Maou and Choo explain 適 (*tch*) by 主, 'to pay chief attention to,' 'to set the mind on,'—as in Ana. IV. x. 為 is in the 3d tone,—'for.' 容 妝飾容貌 'to adorn the person.' The 'Complete Digest' expands the line,—今君子在外我固無所主矣…… 則誰所主而為之容耶

St. 3. 其雨,—其 has here the optative or imperative force, which is so common in the Shoo. Wang Yin-che explains it, in this signifi-

心使思願之言諼焉[四章]得
痗。我伯。言背。樹草。

4 How shall I get the plant of forgetfulness?
I would plant it on the north of my house.
Longingly I think of my husband,
And my heart is made to ache.

IX. Yëw hoo.

有狐綏綏，[一章]
在彼淇梁。
心之憂矣，
之子無裳。

有狐綏綏，[二章]
在彼淇厲。
心之憂矣，……[三章]

1 There is a fox, solitary and suspicious,
At that dam over the K‘e.
My heart is sad ;—
That man has no lower garment.

2 There is a fox, solitary and suspicious,
At that deep ford of the K‘e.

cance, by 尚, and 庶幾. 杲杲=日色明, 'the sun looking bright.' These two lines are metaphorical.—As, when one longs for rain, and day after day is disappointed by a brilliant sun, so was it with the lady longing for the return of her husband, while yet that return was continually delayed. 甘心 generally means—'with a pleased or contented mind;' but that signification cannot well be applied here. Maou explains 甘 by 厭, 'to be satiated, or surfeited,' and Wang T‘aou observes that 'satisfaction of mind is expressed by 甘心, and so is also is a fulness of anxious thoughts (快意謂之甘心憂念之思滿足於心亦謂之甘心).' 願言, —see on iii. XIX. 1.

St. 4. 諼,—as in I. 1, 'to forget.' There is a plant which is fancied to have the quality of making people forget their sorrows, for which purpose the flowers and leaves are cooked together. It is cal ed 萱草 and 諼草 and also 鹿葱, 'stag's onions.' In the Japanese plates it is the *hemerocalta Japonica*, or Day lily. 背, 'the back,' is considered to be 'the north of the body.' Here the term denotes 'the part of a house behind the apartments and chambers, which was called 北堂, 'the north hall.' Outside and below this was a small piece of ground, where a few flowers and shrubs could be planted; and here the lady says she would plant 'the grass of forgetfulness.' 痗=病, 'to be sick,' 'to ache.'

The rhymes are—in st. 1, 揭, 桀, cat. 15, t. 3; 又, 里, cat. 4, t. 1: in 2, 東, 蓬, 容, cat. 9: in 3, 日, 疾, cat. 12, t. 3: in 4, 背, 痗, cat. 1, t. 2.

Ode 9. Metaphorical. A WOMAN EXPRESSES HER DESIRE FOR A HUSBAND. She does so certainly in a singular way, and there is considerable difficulty in explaining satisfactorily these few lines. The 'Little Preface' says the piece is directed against the times.—Through the misery and desolation of Wei, many, both men and women, were left unmarried, or had lost their partners; and in such circumstances, ace. to ancient practice, the marriage rules might have been relaxed, and made more simple and easy, to encourage unions and the increase of the people. Because the government took no action in this direction, this piece was written to censure it.

心之憂矣、之子無帶。
有狐綏綏、在彼淇側。
心之憂矣、之子無服。

My heart is sad;—
That man has no girdle.

3 There is a fox, solitary and suspicious,
By the side there of the K'e.
My heart is sad;—
That man has no clothes.

X.　*Muh kwa.*

木瓜

投我以木瓜、報之以瓊琚。
匪報也、永以為好也。

1 There was presented to me a papaya,
And I returned for it a beautiful *keu*-gem;
Not as a return for it,
But that our friendship might be lasting.

But, as Choo observes, there is nothing in the language of the ode to suggest to us that such was its design. The language, indeed, must be strained to reconcile it with this interpretation.

Ll.1,2, in all the stt. 綏 is read *shwuy*, and the dict. Yuh-p'een (玉篇; A.D. 523) quotes l.2 of viii.VI., with 夊夊, instead of 綏綏. The K'ang-he dict. refers to the line under this sound of the character, and would fain deduce the meaning of the phrase from that of 鬕鬕 'having long hair,' or 'fox-like.' It concludes however, with giving the explanation of it by Maou,—匹行貌 'the app. of walking in pairs.' The lst line then, is with Maou= 'There is a pair of foxes;' and the piece becomes allusive. It is all as it should be with the foxes. Those unmarried multitudes are worse off. Choo on the other hand makes 綏綏 to mean 'the app. of walking solitary, seeking a mate (獨行求匹之貌);' so that the piece becomes metaphorical.—'As is the fox, so is the individual, who is in the speaker's eye.' The 'seeking a mate' is imported into the phrase. Yen Ts'an seems to give the best account of it.—'The fox is by nature suspicious. 綏綏 describes one walking soli-tary, slowly and suspiciously.' 梁—as in iii.X.3. 厲,—see on iii.IX.1, where the character is used as a verb, meaning 'to go through deep water with the clothes on.' Here it is a noun, meaning a deep ford, which must be crossed in such a way. Two other significations of the term are given in the dict., to which some critics hold here. One is 'stepping stones;' the other, 'a high and dangerous bank.'

Ll.3,4. 心之憂矣 must be understood of the speaker, or of the writer. 之子—是人, as in i.VI., *et al.* It is most natural-ly taken as masculine. Maou's interpretation of the ode requires the phrase to be taken in the plural:—'those parties,' the men and women, who were left, through the unhappiness of the times, without partners. 無裳，無帶, and 無服 describe the desolate appearance of the wifeless man, and intimate that the speaker would be glad to supply his wants,—make him lower garments, a girdle, and clothes in general; *i. e.*, would be glad to become his wife. It is a strange way of intimating her wish. 裳 it is supposed, is used in the 1st. st., because a man walks along the top of a dam with his lower garment on; and 帶 in the 2d,

好也永以爲　也。　瓊玖。　李報之以　投我以木　三章

好也。永以爲　也。　瓊瑤。匪報　桃。報之以　投我以木　二章

2 There was presented to me a peach,
  And I returned for it a beautiful *yaou*-gem;
  Not as a return for it,
  But that our friendship might be lasting.

3 There was presented to me a plum,
  And I returned for it a beautiful *këw*-stone;
  Not as a return for it,
  But that our friendship might be lasting.

because he would have taken off his girdle in crossing the ford.

The rhymes are—in st. 1, 梁 裳, cat. 10: in 2, 厲 帶, cat. 15, t. 3: in 3, 偪 服。, cat. 1, t. 3.

Ode 10. Metaphorical. SMALL GIFTS OF KIND-NESS SHOULD BE RESPONDED TO WITH GREATER; BUT FRIENDSHIP IS MORE THAN ANY GIFT. When Wei was nearly extinguished by the Teih, duke Hwan of Ts'e, as the leading prince among the States, came grandly and munificently to its help; and Maou finds in this ode the grateful sentiments of the people of Wei towards him. We can hardly conceive that this is the correct historical interpretation of the piece. If it be so, Hwan's all but royal munificence and favour is strangely represented by the insignificant present of fruit. Choo compares the piece with ii. XVII., and thinks it may refer to an interchange of courtesies between a lover and his mistress. We need not seek any particular interpretation of it. What is metaphorically set forth may have a general application.

Ll. 1, 2 in all the stt. 投 means, properly, 'to throw at or to;' but here=='to present.' 木瓜 is the well-known *carica papaya;* called a 瓜, we presume, from its gourd-like fruit. We must understand the terms here of the fruit, and not of the tree. But what are we to make of the 木桃 and 木李 in the other stanzas? Neither Maou nor Choo says anything in explanation of the 木, nor does the Urh-ya mention such trees. The probability is, therefore, that we are to understand by the phrases simply the peach proper and the plum proper. The *Pun-ts'aou,* indeed, gives the name of 木桃 to the *cha-tsze* (樝子) 'a kind of bad

pear,' and of 木李 to the *ming cha* (榠樝) which is described as an inferior variety of the *muh kwa.* But these identifications have been made for the sake of the texts before us. Maou quotes a saying of Confucius, that in this od he saw 'the ceremony of sending presents in bundles made of rushes (苞苴之禮行),' which might lead us to translate 'a bundle of the papaya,' &c.; but where Maou found the saying, we do not know. It appears, indeed, in the fabrication by Wang Suh, attributed to K'ung Ts'ung (孔叢子); but it was stolen, probably, by Suh from Maou. The Shwoh-wǎn defines 瓊 as 'a gem of a carnation colour;' but in this ode the term is used as an adj.,== 'beautiful (玉之美名).' 瑤 is the name of a gem. Two square *këw* formed part of the furniture of the girdle appendages;—see on V. 3. The *yaou* was another prized gem, or stone, acc. to the Shwoh-wǎn; and the *këw* was a stone, ranking in value immediately after the gems.

Ll. 3, 4. As expanded by Yen Ts'an, these two lines are—此非足爲報欲以結好於永久。 'This is not sufficient to be a return. but I wish by means of it to tie the bonds of friendship for ever.'

The rhymes are—in st. 1, 瓜。, 瑤。, cat. 5, t. 1; (and in 2, 3), 報。好。, cat. 3, t. 2: in 2, 桃。瑤。cat. 2: in 3, 李玖。, cat. 1, t. 2.

CONCLUDING NOTE. We have thus arrived at the end of the odes of Wei. Those in this 3d Book of them do not differ much in character from those in the others, though there is less in them of the licentiousness which often disgraced the court, and of the oppression of the government. The 3d and 4th pieces are the most

interesting and ambitious. Chang Tsae, a friend
of Choo He's, says, 'The State of Wei lay along
the banks of the Ho. The soil was not deep,
and the disposition of the people was volatile;
the country was level and low, and so the people
were soft and weak; it was fertile, and did not
require much agricultural toil, so that the people were indolent. Such was the character
of the inhabitants, and their songs and music
were licentious and bad. To listen to them
would induce idleness, insolence, and depravity.
So is it also with the odes of Ch'ing.'

More favourably, Choo Kung-ts'een says,
Wei had many superior men. In the odes there
appear duke Woo (v.L.) a ruler whose equal is
hardly to be found in other States; and duke
Wän (iv. VI.), the restorer of the State. Besides
these, we have the filial sons of iii. VII., the

faithful minister of iii. XV., the wise man of
iii. XVI., the worthy great officers of iv. IX., the
worthy musician of iii. XIII., and the recluse of
v. II. All these stand eminently out in a time
of degeneracy. Next to them are to be ranked
the two princes of iii. XIX., striving to die for
each other. Then there are the six worthy
princesses:—Chwang Këang, Kung Këang, the
wives of Muh of Heu and Hwan of Sung, and
the two heroines of iii. XIV., and v. V. There
are, moreover, in addition to these, Tae Kwei of
iii. III., virtuously careful of her person; the
lady of v. VIII., so devoted to her husband; she
of iii. VIII., so well acquainted with what constituted virtuous conduct; and she of iii. X., cast
off, and yet maintaining her good name. Wei had
thus not only many superior men, but many
wives of ability and virtue.'

I. *Shoo li*

王一之六

黍離

彼黍離離。彼
稷之苗。行邁
靡靡。中心搖
搖。知我者。謂
我心憂。不知
我者。謂我何
求。悠悠蒼
天。此何人哉。

1 There was the millet with its drooping heads;
There was the sacrificial millet coming into blade.
Slowly I moved about,
In my heart all-agitated.
Those who knew me
Said I was sad at heart.
Those who did not know me
Said I was seeking for something.
O distant and azure Heaven!
By what man was this [brought about]?

TITLE OF THE BOOK.—王一之六 'Wang; Book VI. of Part I.' By *Wang* (King or King's) we are to understand the territory which constituted the royal domain or State, attached to Loh, or the eastern capital of Chow. At the beginning of that dynasty, king Wăn occupied the city of Fung, from which his son moved the seat of govt. to Haou (see the Shoo on V. iii. 6). In the time of king Ching, a city was built by the duke of Chow, near the pres. Loh-yang, and called 'the eastern capital.' Meetings of the princes of the States assembled there, but the court continued to be held at Haou, till the accession of king P'ing, who removed to the east in B.C. 769. From this time the kings of Chow sank nearly to the level of the princes of the States; and the poems collected in their domain were classed among the 'Lessons of Manners,' though still distinguished by the epithet of 'Royal,' prefixed to them.

Ode 1. Narrative. AN OFFICER DESCRIBES HIS MELANCHOLY AND REFLECTIONS ON SEEING THE DESOLATION OF THE OLD CAPITAL OF CHOW. There is nothing in the piece about the old capital of Chow, but the schools both of Maou and Choo are agreed in this interpretation of it. In Han Ying and Lëw Hëang we find it differently attributed, and with more than one meaning; but we need not enter on their views, which are valuable only as showing that the historical interpretation of the odes was made, in the end of the Chow and the beginning of the Han dyn., by different critics, according to their own ability and presumptions. The place of the piece, at the commencement of this Book, should be decisive in favour of the common view.

Ll. 1—4, in all the stt. describe what the writer saw, and how he felt. Maou makes 彼, —'there,' the site of the ancestral temple and the buildings of the old palace, from which they had disappeared. We must construe it,

悠蒼天。此何人哉。　知我者。謂我何求。悠　知我者。謂我心憂。不　行邁靡靡。中心如噎。　彼黍離離。彼稷之實。〔三章〕　悠蒼天。此何人哉。　知我者。謂我心憂。不　知我者。謂我何求。悠　行邁靡靡。中心如醉。　彼黍離離。彼稷之穗。〔二章〕

2 There was the millet with its drooping heads;
There was the sacrificial millet in the ear.
Slowly I moved about,
My heart intoxicated, as it were, [with grief].
Those who knew me
Said I was sad at heart.
Those who did not know me
Said I was seeking for something.
O thou distant and azure Heaven!
By what man was this [brought about]?

3 There was the millet with its drooping heads;
There was the sacrificial millet in grain.
Slowly I moved about,
As if there were a stoppage at my heart.
Those who knew me
Said I was sad at heart.
Those who did not know me
Said I was seeking for something.
O thou distant and azure Heaven!
By what man was this [brought about]?

however, with 黍 and 稷,—'that millet,' &c.,
meaning, no doubt that which the writer had
seen where the seat of the kings formerly was.
Shü and *tseih* are both varieties of the millet,
黍 acc. to Williams, being *milium nigricans*,
and 稷 simply *milium*. The *Pan-ts'aou* makes
the essential difference between them to be that
'the grains of the *shü* are glutinous, and those
of the *tseih* not.' A spirit is distilled from the
former; the latter are more used for food. The

稷 is also called 明粢, and 穄, and was
used much as a sacrificial offering. Until the
plants are authoritatively identified, I call 黍
'millet' simply, and 稷, 'sacrificial millet.'
離離 is descriptive of 'the drooping appearance (垂貌)' of the heads of the *shü*, which is
very characteristic in the best pictures of the
plant. 苗 is the plant shooting up in the blade;

II. *Keun-tsze yu yih.*

君子于役

君子于役　　不

知其期。曷至

哉。雞棲于塒。

日之夕矣。牛

羊下來。君子

于役。如之何

勿思。

君子于役。

日不月。曷其

1　My husband is away on service,
　　And I know not when he will return.
　　Where is he now?
　　The fowls roost in their holes in the walls;
　　And in the evening of the day,
　　The goats and cows come down [from the hill];
　　But my husband is away on service.
　　How can I but keep thinking of him?

2　My husband is away on service,
　　Not for days [merely] or for months.
　　When will he come back to me?

穗, the inflorescence, or the plant in the ear;
and 實, the plant when the grain is fully formed. The *shŭ* ripens much earlier than the *tseih*,
and there is supposed to be a reference to this
in st. 1; but the other stt. seem to make this
point doubtful. 邁,—as in iii. XIV. 3. 靡
靡=遲遲. 'slowly.' 搖搖—'tossed
about,' 'agitated.' 醉,—'intoxicated;' 'intoxicated with sorrow,' Maou says. 'The officer,'
says Le Kung-k'ae, 'lost in his sorrow all consciousness, as if he had been intoxicated with
spirits.' 噎,—'an interruption of breathing,'
as in sobbing from grief. Morrison says, 'The
line here denotes deep sorrow, or, as we express
it. A load or weight upon the mind.'—Choo He
finds an allusive element between the 1st and
2d lines and the 3d and 4th. This does not
seem to be necessary.
Ll. 5—8 describe the different judgments suggested by the movements and appearance of the
writer to those who saw him, according as they
sympathized with his feelings or not.
Ll. 9, 10 contain the writer's appeal to Heaven
on the desolation before him. 悠悠=遠貌
'the app. of distance.' 蒼 is the azure of the
lofty, distant sky. 蒼天 is used by metony-

my for providence, the Power supposed to dwell
above the sky.
　The rhymes are—in st. 1. (and in 2, 3), 離,
靡, cat. 17; 苗, 搖, cat. 2; (and in 2, 3),
憂, 求, cat. 3, t. 1; (and in 2, 3),
天, 人,
cat. 12, t. 1: in 2, 穗, 醉, cat. 3, t. 1: in 3, 實,
噎, cat. 12, t. 3.

Ode 2. Narrative. THE FEELINGS OF A WIFE
ON THE PROLONGED ABSENCE OF HER HUSBAND
ON SERVICE, AND HER LONGING FOR HIS RETURN.
This is the interpretation of the piece given by
Choo, and even the imperial editors approve of
it, as more natural than that of Maou, who
attributes the ode to the great officers who
remained at court, and, indignant at the protracted service on which their companion was
employed, thus expressed their disapprobation of
king P'ing.
Ll. 1—3 in both stt. 君子,—as in LX., ii.
III, et al. 于役 might be construed, taking
于 in the meaning of 往, 'to go away,' which
K'ang-shing always gives it; but it is better to
consider 于 as the mere particle, as in 于
飛 in I. II., et al. 其期=其反還之

渴。苟 子 下 矣。日 棲 有
無 于 括。牛 之 于 佸。
飢 役。君 羊 夕 桀。雞

The fowls roost on their perches;
And in the evening of the day,
The goats and cows come down and home;
But my husband is away on service.
Oh if he be but kept from hunger and thirst!

III. *Keun-tsze yang-yang.*

其 招 左 君 其 招 左 君
樂 我 執 子 樂 我 執 子
只 由 翿。陶 只 由 簧。陽
且。敖。右 陶。且。房。右 陽。
　　　　右　　　　　右　　陽
　　　　陶。　　　　　陽。

1 My husband looks full of satisfaction.
In his left hand he holds his reed-organ,
And with his right he calls me to the room.
Oh the joy!

2 My husband looks delighted.
In his left hand he holds his screen of feathers,
And with his right hand he calls me to the stage.
Oh the joy!

期, 'the time of his return.' 不日不
月,—as in the translation. Choo says, 'The
length of his service is not to be calculated by
days and months (不可計以日月).
曷至哉 is taken by Choo of the place where
the officer was at the time. As the 'Complete
Digest' expands it, 且今何所至哉,
其所至之地, 吾亦不得而
知之也. K'ang-shing connects the line
closely with the preceding:—'I do not know the
set time of his return,—the time when he
ought to come.' That is the meaning of the
3d line in st. 2, where 佸=會, 'to assemble,'
'to meet.' In st. 1, 曷—'where;' in 2,—'when.'

Ll. 4,6. The creatures around her had their
nightly resting places, while her husband had

none. 塒 is the name for holes made in the
walls for fowls,—'chiselled out,' as Maou says,
from the walls of earth and lime, of which the
houses were built. 桀—杙, 'a post;' but
we must think rather of 'a perch.' K'ang-shing,
unnaturally, explains 下來 by 從下牧
地而來, 'come from their low pasture-
grounds.' 括—至, 'to come,' 'to arrive.'

Ll. 7,8. 苟, 'if,' must be taken as expressing
a wish or prayer. As Le Kung-k'ae puts it,
既不得歸, 則庶幾其在道
路之間, 且無飢渴之患亦
可矣, 'Since he cannot come immediately,
if peradventure in his travelling he escape the
suffering of hunger and thirst, so far well.'

IV. *Yang che shwuy.*

揚　薪。不　揚　與　申。懷　月　歸
之　彼　流　之　我　懷　予　哉。
水。其　水。子。成　哉。曷　還
　　　束　流　之　我　懷　　
　　　　　　　　　　　　　　

1　The fretted waters
　　Do not carry on their current a bundle of firewood!
　　Those, the members of our families,
　　Are not with us here guarding Shin.
　　How we think of them! How we think of them!
　　What month shall we return home?

The rhymes are—in st. 1, 期 哉 辮 來,
思, cat. 1, t. 1: in 2, 月, 佸, 桀, 括, 渴,
cat.15, t.3.

Ode 3. Narrative. THE HUSBAND'S SATIS-
FACTION, AND THE WIFE'S JOY, ON HIS RETURN.
This again is the view of Choo He, who regards
this ode as a sequel of the preceding one; and
I do not think anything better can be made of
it. Still it does not carry with itself the witness
of its own correctness, so much as the interpretation of ode 2. Choo refers, as if with some
doubt of his own view, to that of the old school,
that the piece is expressive of commiseration
for the disordered and fallen condition of Chow,
and that it shows us, more especially, the officers
encouraging one another to take office, for the
sake of preserving their lives. To my mind the
piece, as a whole and in its details, is accompanied with greater difficulties on this interpretation than on the other.

Both stanzas. 陽 陽 = 得 志 之 貌,
'the appearance of satisfaction, having got one's
will.' So, Choo. Maou's explanation is nearly
the same,—'not exercising the mind on anything.'
陶 陶 indicates 'the app. of harmony and
joy.' 簀 is used for 笙, an instrument in
which the ancient Chinese had the rudiments of
the organ. It consisted of 13 or of 19 tubes, set
up in the shell of a gourd, each with an orifice
near the bottom, to which a moveable tongue of
metal called 簧 was fitted. The whole was
blown by the mouth. 翻 was a sort of flag or
screen carried by dancers, with which they could
screen themselves at parts of their performance.
The 3d lines are the most difficult, and none of
the critics throw much light upon them. Acc.
to Maou, by 房 we are to understand 'the
music in the apartment,' and 由 = 用, 'to use.'
The king, it is said, had the pieces of the *Chow
Nan* sung to him with music in an inner apartment of the palace, and the officer of the ode is
made to appear beckoning to his friends to

follow him, and take part in the performance,
all unworthy, as it was, of his and their position
and abilities. In the 2d stanza, he beckons to
them, in the same way, to follow him to the
place where the dancers or pantomimes performed
their part;—敖 = 舞 位, 'the places for the
dancers.' All this is very harsh and forced;
and could hardly be followed by the expression
of delight in the last line. Choo contents himself with simply explaining the terms, and that
obscurely. He defines 由 by 從, which we
must take as meaning 'to follow to,' in order
to construe it similarly in both stanzas. The
general meaning is plain enough. The husband,
returned from his long service, forgets all his
toils, and is ready to express his pleasure by
music and dancing; and his wife shares in his
joy. 只 且 —as in iii. XVI.

The rhymes are—in st. 1, 陽, 簀, 房, st.
10: in 2, 陶, 翿, 敖 (prop. cat. 2), cat. 3,
t. 2: in the two stanzas, 樂, 樂, cat. 2.

Ode. 4. Allusive. THE TROOPS OF CHOW,
KEPT ON DUTY IN SHIN, MURMUR AT THEIR SEPA-
RATION FROM THEIR FAMILIES. The mother of
king P'ing was a Këang, a daughter of the
House of Shin. That State had suffered repeatedly from the attacks of Ts'oo, and the king,
after removing to the eastern capital, sent his
own people to occupy and defend it, and kept
them long absent from their homes on the service. The piece contains their murmurings at
their separation from their families. This is
the interpretation given by Maou, and adopted
by Choo,—with differences in the details. Gow-
yang Sëw had proposed, before Choo's time, a
somewhat different view, which has had many
followers. L.3 is to be taken, they think, not of
the families of the troops employed in Shin, nor
of other troops of Chow which were left at home,
but of the troops of other States, which should
have been called forth by the king for the duty.
This modification of the interpretation shows us
better the nature of the allusion in the 1st two
lines, but does not agree so well with the last

歸哉。懷哉。與我戍許。蒲。彼其之子。不揚三之水。不流束　歸哉。懷哉。與我戍甫。楚。彼其之子。不揚二之水。不流束

2　The fretted waters
　　Do not carry on their current a bundle of thorns!
　　Those, the members of our families,
　　Are not with us here guarding P'oo.
　　How we think of them! How we think of them!
　　What month shall we return?

3　The fretted waters
　　Do not carry on their current a bundle of osiers!
　　Those, the members of our families,
　　Are not with us here guarding Heu.
　　How we think of them! How we think of them!
　　What month shall we return?

two. I feel unable myself to express any decisive opinion in the case.

Ll. 1, 2. in all the stt. 揚 is explained by Maou by 激揚, 'to impede and excite,'—as rocks do the waters of a stream; but he does not explain the nature of the allusion which underlies the statement that a stream thus fretted is yet not able to carry away so slight a thing as a bundle of firewood. Acc. to K'ang-shing, it is that, though the king's commands were so urgent and exacting, no kindness flowed from him to the people. This is unsatisfactory; and Ying-tah and Wang Taou insist that the lines should be taken interrogatively, or that ll. 2 and 4 should be understood as strong assertions, and not negations. Carrying out this view, Wang would farther refer the 之子 in l. 3 to king P'ing, and take 與 in l. 4 as = 用, ' to employ.' This would meet the difficulty about the allusion; but the murmuring of the troops becomes thus very violent. It is inconsistent with the spirit of the odes to express disapprobation of the king so directly; and the last two lines seem to require us to interpret l. 3 of the families of the soldiers.

Choo adopts a different exegesis of l. 1. Referring to a phrase, 悠揚, meaning the ' long and rippling' course of a stream, he explains 揚之水 as ' the appearance of water flowing gently;'—so gently and feebly in this case, that the current would not bear away a small bundle of anything. How the lines thus understood bear allusively on the rest of the stanza, he does not at all make clear, saying that it is to be found in the two 不,—in lines 2 and 4. Gow-yang and those who follow him, taking yang in the same way, make out the allusion to be to the feebleness of king P'ing, who could not command the services of the States to guard Shin, but was obliged to lay the duty on his own people.—This meaning of 揚 is not given in K'ang-he's dict., and I feel constrained to keep to Maou's account of the term with all its difficulties. 薪 and 楚.—see on i. IX. 2. Maou takes 蒲 in the sense of ' rushes;' but it also means 'osiers,' from which arrow-shafts could be made, which seems more suitable here.

Ll. 3, 4. The 其 is read ke, and is treated as a mere particle. Wang Yin-che gives 記, 忌, 已 and 迅, as synonyms of it, which are found used (and are interchanged) in the same way. 之子 = 是子, ' those parties,'—' the fami-

V. *Chung kuh.*

嘆其脩矣。　中谷有蓷　難矣。遇人之艱　嘅其嘆矣。　嘅其嘆矣。　有女仳離　嘆其乾矣。　中谷有蓷

1　In the valleys grows the mother-wort,
　　But scorched is it in the drier places.
　　There is a woman forced to leave her husband;
　　Sadly she sighs!
　　Sadly she sighs!
　　She suffers from his hard lot.

2　In the valleys grows the mother-wort,
　　But scorched is it where it had become long.

lies of the absent soldiers, 'their parents, wives, and children,' acc. to K'ang-shing. It has been mentioned that king P'ing's mother belonged to Shin,—a marquisate held by Këangs, the capital of which was near the site of the pres. dep. city of Nan-yang, Ho-nan. P'oo is identified by Ying-tah and Choo with Leu (see note on the name of the 22d Bk. of the Shoo, Pt. V.) It was also a marquisate held by Këangs, and adjoined Shin. Heu was another Këang State, in the pres. Heu Chow, Ho-nan. Shin and P'oo were contiguous, but Heu was at some considerable distance from them. Heu K'ëen (許謙; Yuen dyn.) thinks that the troops of Chow were not really guarding the territories of P'oo and Heu; but that the poet, to vary his rhymes, introduces the names of those other States, as belonging to Këangs. We may rather suppose, however, that through the consanguinity of their chiefs, the three States were confederate, all threatened by Ts'oo, and all hence requiring aid. 戍申甫兵以守, 'to station troops throughout a country to maintain it.'

Ll. 5, 6. The object of 懷 is to be sought in the parties intended by 之子, and this term, as well as the line that follows, are in favour of the interpretation of the piece adopted by Maou and Choo. The soldiers did not wish their families to be with them, keeping guard in Shin,—such a thing would have been contrary to all rules of propriety; but they grudged their prolonged absence from them, and wished that they might soon return to Chow.

The rhymes are—in st. 1, (and in 2, 3), 水, 子 (prop. cat. 1), cat. 15, t. 2; 薪, 申, cat 12, t. 1; (and in 2, 3), 懷, 歸, cat. 15, t. 1: in 2, 楚, 甫, cat. 5, t. 2: in 3, 蒲, 許, *ib.*, t. 1.

Ode 5. Allusive. THE SAD CASE OF A WOMAN FORCED TO SEPARATE FROM HER HUSBAND THROUGH PRESSURE OF FAMINE. Maou says the piece is expressive of pity for the suffering condition of Chow. Many later critics seek to find in it a condemnation of the govt. of king P'ing, and of the morals of the people; but this has to be argued out of the language, and is not implied in it. Choo attributes the composition to the suffering wife herself; but I agree with Heu K'ëen in attributing it to another, who has her case—one of many—vividly before him (詳味其辭人在言外蓋當時君子之言，非婦人所自作也).

Ll. 1, 2 in all the stt. The 蓷 has many names, of which the most common are 茺蔚, and 益母草. Medhurst calls it the 'bugloss;' but I should have preferred to call it by its popular name of 'mother's help,' if it did not clearly appear in the Japanese plates as the *leonurus sibiricus*, or mother-wort. It is described as having a square stem, and white flowers which grow between the sections of the stem. The seeds, stalk, flowers, and leaves are all believed to have medical virtues, and to be specific in

何嗟及矣。
矣。嘅其泣矣。
此離。嘅其泣
其溼矣。有女
中谷有蓷。
不淑矣。
歗矣。遇人之
其歗矣。條其
有女仳離。條

There is a woman forced to leave her husband,
Long-drawn are her groanings!
Long-drawn are her groanings!
She suffers from his misfortune.

3　In the valleys grows the mother-wort,
But scorched is it even in the moist places.
There is a woman forced to leave her husband;
Ever flow her tears!
Ever flow her tears!
But of what avail is her lament?

VI.　*T'oo yuen.*

生之
爲我。
尚無
之初。
我生
于羅。
雉離
爰爰。
兔爰
有兔
爰爰。

1　The hare is slow and cautious;
The pheasant plumps into the net.
In the early part of my life,
Time still passed without commotion.
In the subsequent part of it,

many troubles of women, before and after child-
birth; hence, its common name. The plant
grows best in moist situations, and Maou erred
greatly in supposing that a high situation and
dry soil suited it best, so that the decay of it,
spoken of here, was owing to its situation in
a valley. That decay is evidently ascribed
to the prevailing drought, killing it first in the
drier grounds; next, where it had attained a
good height and was vigorous; and finally, even
in damp places, best adapted for it. Such a
plant drooping and dying in the valleys, we may
conceive how all other vegetation was scorched
up, and famine, with its miseries, desolated
the country. 暵=燥, 'to dry up,' 'to be
dried up or scorched.' 其乾=生於乾
者,—as in the translation. 脩=長, 'long.'

Ll. 3—6. 仳—別, 'to be separated.' 仳
離 does not mean that the woman had been
cast off by her husband, but that they had been
obliged to separate from each other, and try if
they could manage to subsist apart. 嘅 is
designed to give 'the sound of her sighing.' 歗
is synonymous with 嘯 in ii.XI. 3; not, however,
meaning, here, 'to whistle,' but an audible
sound emitted from the mouth, and long-pro-
tracted. This idea of 'long-drawn' is conveyed
by 條—長. 嘅 denotes 'the appearance
of weeping.' In l. 4 we must understand 人 of
the husband of the woman. K'ang-shing explains
it by 君子, which we have often met with in

百　庸。罝。有　百　造。罼。有　無　後。
凶　我　我　兔　憂　我　我　兔　吪。逢
尚　生　生　爰　我　生　生　爰　　此
寐　之　之　爰。生　之　之　爰。　百
無　後。初。雉　之　後。初。雉　　罹。
聰。逢　尚　離　初。逢　尚　離　　尚
　　此　無　于　尚　此　無　于　　寐
　　　　覺。　　寐　　　　　　　　無
　　　　　　　無

We are meeting with all these evils.
I wish I might sleep and never move more.

2　The hare is slow and cautious;
　　The pheasant plumps into the snare.
　　In the early part of my life,
　　Time still passed without anything stirring.
　　In the subsequent part of it,
　　We are meeting with all these sorrows.
　　I wish I might sleep, and never wake more.

3　The hare is slow and cautious;
　　The pheasant plumps into the trap.
　　In the early part of my life,
　　Time still passed without any call for our services.
　　In the subsequent part of it
　　We are meeting with all these miseries.
　　I would that I might sleep, and hear of nothing more.

the sense of husband. It might also be taken generally:—'she has met with—fallen on—a time when people are in distress.' 不淑 is the 'evil' lot, not evil conduct.

The rhymes are—in st. 1, 乾, 嘆, 嘆, 難, cat. 14: 僾, 歇., 獻., 淑, cat. 3, t. 1: 濕, 泣, 泣, 及, cat. 7, t. 3.

Ode 6. Metaphorical. AN OFFICER OF CHOW DECLARES HIS WEARINESS OF LIFE BECAUSE OF THE GROWING MISERIES OF THE STATE. The 'Little Preface' refers this piece to the time of king Hwan, the grandson of king P'ing (B.C.718—696), who became involved in hostilities with the State of Ch'ing in B. C. 706, and received a severe defeat from his feudatory; but there is nothing in it to indicate such a reference. The growing misery of the country, and the writer's weariness of his life, are all that is before us.

Ll.1,2. in all the stt. 爰爰 conveys the meaning of being 'slow and cautious.' The rabbit or hare is said to be of a secret and crafty nature, while the pheasant is bold and determined. The former, consequently, is snared with difficulty, while the latter is easily taken. 羅= 網, the general name for a net. 罦 and 罿 are terms for nets with some peculiarity in their construction, but they are used, not because of that, but to vary the rhythm. Indeed, the Urh-ya gives 罬, 罿, 罦, and 罦, all as names of the same thing, which is also called 覆車, 'an inverted carriage.' It seems to have been a net extended between, or a noose suspended from, two poles, which were made to close by a spring when the rabbit or bird entered. 離,—as in iii. XVIII. 3. In the crafty hare, acc. to Choo, we have the mean men, who stirred up disorder,

VII. *Koh-luy.*

葛
藟

人　謂　之　縣一章　人　謂　之　縣二章
母　他　涘　縣　父　他　涘　縣
。　人　。　葛　。　人　。　葛
亦　母　終　藟　亦　父　終　藟
莫　。　遠　。　莫　。　遠　。
我　謂　兄　縣　我　謂　兄　在
有　他　弟　縣　顧　他　弟　河
。　人　。　葛　。　人　。
　　　　　　藟　　　　　　之
　　　　　　。　　　　　　滸
　　　　　　在　　　　　　。
　　　　　　河　　　　　　終
　　　　　　　　　　　　　遠
　　　　　　　　　　　　　兄
　　　　　　　　　　　　　弟
　　　　　　　　　　　　　。
　　　　　　　　　　　　　謂
　　　　　　　　　　　　　他

1   Thickly they spread about, the dolichos creepers,
    On the borders of the Ho.
    For ever separated from my brothers,
    I call a stranger father.
    I call a stranger father,
    But he will not look at me.

2   Thickly they spread about, the dolichos creepers,
    On the banks of the Ho.
    For ever separated from my brothers,
    I call a stranger mother.
    I call a stranger mother,
    But she will not recognize me.

and then contrived to escape from its consequences; in the bold and impetuous pheasant, the superior men, who would do their duty in the disorder,—and suffered. Maou and others make these two lines allusive.

Ll. 3—6. 尚=猶, 'still.' The speaker, it would appear, had seen the time when the royal House was strong, and able to control the various States. 無爲=無事, 'there was nothing doing,' 'there was no trouble;' 無造, the same; 無庸=無用, 'no service.' 罹 is synonymous with 憂, 'sorrows,'—things falling out untowardly.

L. 7. 尚 here is different from that in l.3, and has the same force as 其, used optatively,—庶 幾, or 寧 可. 吪=動,—'to move;' 覺=寤, to 'awake;' 聵=聞, 'to hear.' The line, in its various forms, expresses the idea that the speaker had no enjoyment of his life, and would prefer to die.

The rhymes are—in st. 1, 羅, 爲, 罹, 吪, cat. 17; 罩, 造, 憂, 覺, cat. 3, t. 2: in 3, 罿, 庸, 凶, 聵, cat. 9.

Ode 7. Allusive. A WANDERER FROM CHOW, SEPARATED FROM HIS KIN, MOURNS OVER HIS LOT. The 'Little Preface' says the piece was directed against king P'ing, who had thrown aside all care for the nine classes of his kindred (see on the Shoo, I.2). Nothing more, however, than what I have stated can be concluded from the piece itself.

Ll.1,2. 葛藟,—as in i.IV. 縣縣 is descriptive of the dolichos, spreading and intertwining its branches, all connected together. There is little difference between 滸涘, and 漘. It is said, 'The space above, on the banks,' is called 滸; and 'where the banks are level, but underneath the earth caves in, and the banks hang over like lips,' is called 漘. The thick, continuous growth of the creepers, on the soil proper to them, is presented by the speaker in contrast to his own position, torn from his family and proper soil.

縣縣葛藟，在河之滸。終遠兄弟，謂他人昆。謂他人昆，亦莫我聞。

3 Thickly they spread about, the dolichos creepers,
   On the lips of the Ho.
   For ever separated from my brothers,
   I call a stranger elder-brother;
   I call a stranger elder-brother,
   But he will not listen to me.

VIII. Ts'ae koh.

采葛

彼采葛兮，一日不見，如三月兮。彼采蕭兮，一日不見，如三秋兮。彼采艾兮，一日不見，如三歲兮。

1 There he is gathering the dolichos!
   A day without seeing him
   Is like three months!

2 There he is gathering the oxtail-southernwood!
   A day without seeing him
   Is like three seasons!

3 There he is gathering the mugwort!
   A day without seeing him
   Is like three years!

Ll. 3—6. Following out the view of the Pre-face, K'ang-shing takes 遠 actively, with 王 or 'the king,' as its subject; but the view in the translation is more simple and natural, and agrees better with the usage of 遠,—as in iii.XIV., iv.VII., et al. 他人, 'another man,' = 'a stranger.' 昆 = 兄, 'an elder brother.' 莫我有,—'does not have me.' K'ang-shing and Choo explain 有 by 識有, 'to remem-ber that there is such a person.'

The rhymes are—in st. 1, 藟, 弟 (and in 2, 3), cat. 15, t. 2; 滸父父顧, cat. 5, t. 2: in 2, 滸母母有, cat. 1, t. 2: in 3, 滸昆昆聞, cat. 13.

Ode 8. Narrative. A LADY LONGS FOR THE SOCIETY OF THE OBJECT OF HER AFFECTION. So Choo interprets this little piece; and his view of it is more natural than that of the old interpreters, who held that it indicates the fear of slanderers, entertained by the officers of Chow. So bad, they say, was the gov't of king Hwan, that if any of the ministers, great or small, was sent away on duty for however short a time, a crowd of slanderous parasites was sure to sup-plant him, or injure him in some way. The 1st line, on this view, is allusive of the services on which a minister might be commissioned; and it is the king that is spoken of in the other lines. This interpretation is, surely, imported very violently into the simple verses. Choo's is more natural. A short absence from the loved object seems to be long, and longer the more it is dwelt upon. The lady fancies her lover engaged as the first lines describe, and would fain go and join him in his occupations.

IX. *Ta keu.*

大車

大車檻檻。毳衣如菼。豈不爾思。畏子不敢。

大車啍啍。毳衣如璊。豈不爾思。畏子不奔。

穀則異室。死則同穴。謂予不信。有如皦日。

1 His great carriage rumbles along,
  And his robes of rank glitter like the young sedge.
  Do I not think of you?
  But I am afraid of this officer, and dare not.

2 His great carriage moves heavily and slowly,
  And his robes of rank glitter like a carnation-gem.
  Do I not think of you?
  But I am afraid of this officer, and do not rush to you.

3 While living, we may have to occupy different apartments;
  But when dead, we shall share the same grave.
  If you say that I am not sincere,
  By the bright sun I swear that I am.

彼 is best taken as demonstrative of the individual thought of,—with K'ang-shing; though we may also understand it, with Yen Ts'an, as ='there.' 蕭—荻, which Medhurst calls 'southernwood.' It is understood to be here what is called the 牛尾蒿,—as in the translation; 'with whitish leaves, the stalk brittle, bushy and fragrant.' 艾 is the mugwort, the down of which yields the moxa, which is burnt upon the skin to produce counter-irritation. 三秋, 'three autumns'—三時, 'three seasons.' Ying-tah points out that 三春 and 三夏 are employed in the same way.

The rhymes are—in st. 1, 葛, 月, cat. 15, t. 3: in 2, 蕭, 秋, cat. 3, t. 1: in 3, 艾, 歲, cat. 15, t. 2.

Ode 9. Narrative. THE INFLUENCE OF A SEVERE AND VIRTUOUS MAGISTRATE IN REPRESSING LICENTIOUSNESS. According to the old school, this piece should be translated in the past tense, as setting forth the manners of a former time, when licentiousness was repressed by virtuous magistrates, and did not dare to show itself; and this, it is supposed, is done, as a lamentation over the different state of things under the eastern Chow. Nothing is gained by thus dragging antiquity into the ode, and the explanation of it is only thereby made difficult and unnatural. The whole is simple, if we take it, with Choo, as spoken by some lady of the eastern Chow, that would fain have gone with her lover, but was restrained by her fear of some great officer, who, amid the degeneracy of the times, retained his purity and integrity. Both interpretations, however, admit the licentiousness of the age; and the character of this piece supplies an argument for the correctness of the view which we took of the preceding.

Ll. 1, 2 in stt. 1, 2. 檻檻 (hěen) denotes the noise made by the carriage of the officer, the 于 of the 4th line. It is called 'a great carriage,' because great officers of the court, when travelling in the discharge of their duties, were privileged to ride in a carriage of the same materials and structure as that of a prince of a State. They wore also the robes of a viscount or baron, which are here called 毳衣. These

X. *K'ew chung yĕw me.*

丘　彼　彼　丘　施。將　彼　彼　將
中　留　留　中　　　其　留　留　其
有　子　子　有　丘　來　子　子　來
麻　嗟。嗟。麻。中　施。國。國。食。
　　　　　　　　有
　　　　　　　　麥。

I   On the mound where is the hemp,
    Some one is detaining Tsze-tsëay.
    Some one is there detaining Tsze-tsëay;—
    Would that he would come jauntily [to me]!

2   On the mound where is the wheat,
    Some one is detaining Tsze-kwoh.
    Some one is there detaining Tsze-kwoh;—
    Would that he would come and eat with me!

had five of the emblematic figures mentioned in the Shoo, II. iv. 4 upon them:—the temple-cup, the aquatic grass, and the grains of rice, painted on the upper robe; and the hatchet, and the symbol of distinction, embroidered on the lower. 黺 means the down of birds, or the fine under-growth of hair on animals, and those robes were so denominated, probably, from the materials of which they were made, but we lack information on this point;—see the Chow Le, XXI. 8 and 17. The painting and embroidery were in all the five colours; hence the green is described as being equal to that of a young sedge (see v. III. 4), and the red to that of a *moon*, a gem of a carnation colour. 摩摩 is descriptive of the 'slow and heavy motion' of the carriage.

Ll. 3, 4. 爾 思, 'think of you,'—'wish to be with you,' or, 'to follow you.'

St. 3. The lovers might be kept apart all their lives, but they would be united in death, and lie in the same grave. So the lady gives expression to her attachment. 穀生, 'to be living.' 穴, 'a cave;' here,—'the grave.' 有 如 in l. 4 is the common form of an oath among the Chinese. 'The Complete Digest' thus expands it,—此子由衷之言也. 若以子言爲不信，則有如皦日在上以鑒我矣，予言豈不信者哉. 'These are words from my heart. If you think that my words are not sincere, there is a *Power* above like the bright sun observing me. How should my words not be sincere?' Acc. to the old interpreters, this stanza is addressed to the magistrates of Chow. 'In the old days,' it is said, 'husbands and wives kept to their separate

apartments, and only in death were they long together.' It was difficult for an officer in the degenerate times of Chow to believe that there had ever been such purity of manners: but verily there had been!

The rhymes are—in st. 1, 檻 萋 敢, cat. 8, t. 1: in 2, 庤 瑞 奔, cat. 13: in 3, 室, 穴, 日, cat. 12, t. 3.

Ode 10. Narrative. A WOMAN LONGS FOR THE PRESENCE OF HER LOVERS, WHO, SHE THINKS, ARE DETAINED FROM HER BY ANOTHER WOMAN. This interpretation of the ode lies upon the surface of it, and is that given by Choo He. We might have expected a different view from the old interpreters, and we have one. They refer the piece to the time of king Chwang (B. C. 695—679), who drove away from their employments officers of worth through his want of intelligence. The people, they say, mourned the loss of such men, and expressed their desire for their return in these verses. The imperial editors indicate their approval of this view, and say that many scholars have doubted the correctness of Choo's interpretation, on the ground that Confucius would not have admitted so licentious a piece into his collection of ancient poems. If the books to which Maou had access had been preserved, they think, there would have been sufficient evidence of the correctness of his view. But the difficulty here, and in other odes, lies in reconciling the words before us with the interpretation put upon them. The writers, to convey the ideas in their minds, must have used language the most remote from that calculated to do so. As to the unlikelihood of Confucius giving a place to a licentious piece like this in the *She*, if he admitted so the ode that precedes, even taking Maou's interpretation of it, I do not see that he need have been squeamish about this.

丘中有李。彼留之子。彼留之子。貽我佩玖。

3 On the mound where are the plum trees,
  Some one is detaining those youths.
  Some one is there detaining those youths;—
  They will give me *këw*-stones for my girdle.

Ll. 1,2 in all the stt. No special meaning is to be sought in the mention of the mound, and the things growing on it. The lady misses her friend, and she supposes he may be detained on such a place in a way she does not approve of. 彼 — 'there.' 留 — 有留者, 'there is some one detaining.' 子嗟 is the designation of the friend who does not make his appearance. 子國 is the designation of another similar friend. With this we may compare the variation of the surnames in the different stanzas of iv.IV.

Acc. to Maou, 留 is the clan-name of the officers introduced, and Tsze-kwoh is the father of Tsze-tsëay. A mound is a stony, barren spot, where we do not look for hemp or wheat or plum-trees. Yet these Lëws, banished from the court, had laboured on such a spot, and made it fruitful, in consequence of which the people longed the more to see them back in office!

In st.3, 之于, — 是于, 'those gentlemen,' — referring to Tsze-tsëay and Tsze-kwoh.

L.4. 將, — as in v.IV.1. 施施, — as in Mencius, IV. Pt.ii.XXXIII.1. The line in st.3 is also to be taken as a wish; Choo says, 冀其有以贈已, 'she hopes that they will have gifts for her.' 玖, — as in v.X.3:

Maou says nothing on the 將, but seems to take it as the sign of the future. 施施, he says, means 'the difficulty of advancing,' of which it is difficult to see the significancy in the case. On 將其來食 he says, 'when Tsze-kwoh comes again, we shall get food!' His misapprehension of the nature of the ode makes it impossible for him to explain its parts satisfactorily.

The rhymes are — in st. 1, 麻, 嗟, 嗟, 施,., 17: in 2, 麥,, 國國, 食,, cat. 1, t. 3: in 3, 李, 子, 子, 玖,, ib., t. 2.

CONCLUDING NOTE. The odes of the Royal domain afford sufficient evidence of the decay of the House of Chow. They commence with a lamentation over the desolation of the ancient capitals of Wăn and Woo, and, within the territory attached to the eastern capital, we find the people mourning over the toils of war and the miseries of famine. The bonds of society appear relaxed, and licentiousness characterizes the intercourse of the sexes. There are some odes, however which relieve the picture. The 2d and 3d show us the affection between husband and wife, and the pleasantness of their domestic society, while the 9th tells us that amid abounding licentiousness there were officers who helped to keep it in check.

I. *Tsze e.*

鄭一之七

緇衣

緇衣之宜兮。
敝予又改為兮。
適子之館兮。
還予授子之粲兮。

緇衣之好兮。
敝予又改造兮。
適子之館兮。
還予授子之粲兮。

1　How well do the black robes befit you!
　　When worn out, we will make others for you.
　　We will go to your court,
　　And when we return [from it], we will send you a feast!

2　How good on you are the black robes!
　　When worn out, we will make others for you.

TITLE OF THE BOOK. 鄭一之七 'Ch'ing; Bk. VII. of Pt. I.' The State of Ch'ing was not one of the oldest fiefs of the Chow dyn. King Seuen (B. C. 826—781) conferred on his brother Yëw (友), in B. C. 805, the appanage of Ch'ing, a city and district adjoining,—in the pres. Hwa Chow (華州), dep. T'ung-chow (同州), Shen-se. This Yew, who is called duke Hwan in the list of the lords of Ch'ing (桓公), acted as minister of Instruction at the royal court, and was killed, in B. C. 773, not long before the Jung hordes took the capital, and put to death king Yëw (幽王). His son Keuh-t'uh (掘突) was of great service to king P'ing when he moved the capital to the east, succeeded to his father's office, and becoming possessed of the lands of Kih and K'wei (虢檜之地), 'south of the Ho, north of the Ying, east of the Loh, and west of the Tse,' he removed there, and called his State 'New Ch'ing,' which is still the name of one of the districts in the dep. of K'ae-fung, Ho-nan. He is duke Woo (武公) of Ch'ing. For further information about Ch'ing see on the title of Bk. XIII.

Ode 1. Narrative. THE PEOPLE OF CHOW EXPRESS THEIR ADMIRATION OF AND REGARD FOR DUKE WOO OF CH'ING. We have the authority of Confucius for understanding this piece as expressive of the regard that is due to virtue and ability;—see the Le Ke, Bk. XXXIII. 2. The critics agree that it is to be interpreted of the admiration and affection which the people of Chow had for duke Woo, son of the founder of the House of Ch'ing. He had so won upon them in the discharge of his duties as a minister, that they ever welcomed his presence, and would gladly have retained him at the court. The structure of the piece is exceedingly simple. The stanzas are varied merely by the change of two characters in each, without giving any new meaning,—to produce a variety of rhymes. The 'Little Preface' is wrong in attributing the ode to the people of Ch'ing.

Ll. 1, 2, in all the stt. 緇 denotes the deepest black,—that which has been subjected to the dye seven times. Ministers of the court wore robes of this colour,—not in the king's court, when having audience of him; but in their own courts or offices, to which they proceeded after the morning audience, and discharged their several duties. 宜=稱, 'to be fit,' 'to correspond to.' As Yen Ts'an expands the line, 'That duke Woo should be a minister of the king and wear

還子授
子。
子之粲
兮。

緇三章
衣
之
蓆
兮。

子
之
粲
兮。

還子授
子。

改
作
兮。
適

兮。
敝子又

子
之
館
兮。

還子授
子

之粲
兮。

We will go to your court,
And when we return [from it], we will send you a feast!

3   How easy sit the black robes on you!
    When worn out, we will make others for you.
    We will go to your court.
    And when we return [from it], we will send you a feast!

II.   *Tsëang Chung-tsze.*

也。
父
母

仲
可
懷

我
父
母。

愛
之
豈
敢

杞。
折
我

我
里。
無

兮。
將二
無仲
子踰

將
仲
子

1   I pray you, Mr. Chung,
    Do not come leaping into my hamlet;
    Do not break my willow trees.
    Do I care for them?
    But I fear my parents.
    You, O Chung, are to be loved,

these black robes is most proper; his virtue corresponds to his robes (甚宜. 德稱其服). We may construe 之 as the sign of the genitive;—'O the befittingness of the black robes!' But it is better to take it as a particle,—'How befitting are they!' 好 and 蓆 in the other stanzas must convey a similar meaning to 宜. There is no difficulty with the former, but Maou and Choo both explain the latter by 大, 'great,' which Ying-tah expands by 服緇衣. 大得其宜. 'In him to wear the black robes is *greatly* befitting.' I prefer the meaning of 安舒, 'easy and natural,' given by one of the Ch'ings. In the 2d line the people express their affection for duke Woo by saying they would make new robes for him, when those were worn out. 改=更. 'a

change,'—others. 爲. 造, and 作 all mean 'to make.'

Ll. 3, 4, 適=之, 'to go to.' 館=舍, 'a lodging house;' but the idea is more that of a hotel in the sense which that term has in France. It was the residence assigned to the minister during his residence at the capital, where he lived with his retinue and had his own office or court. The 子 leads us to translate the whole piece in the 2d person, as if it were addressed to duke Woo,—the welcome of the people of Chow to him. The people would go to his court, to see that he was lodged there comfortably on his arrival from Ch'ing. We learn from narratives of Tso-she on the Ch'un Ts'ëw, that the govt. of the capital was sometimes remiss in keeping these public buildings in proper repair. The people go on to say, that when they were satisfied the building was all in good order, they would send him viandas. To the present day, the good will of the people of China, of all

可畏也。　諸兄之言。亦　兄。仲可懷也。諸　愛之。畏我諸　我樹桑。豈敢　踰我牆。無折　將仲子今。無　也。　之言。亦可畏

But the words of my parents
Are also to be feared.

2   I pray you, Mr. Chung,
     Do not come leaping over my wall;
     Do not break my mulberry trees.
     Do I care for them?
     But I fear the words of my brothers.
     You, O Chung, are to be loved,
     But the words of my brothers
     Are also to be feared.

ranks, expresses itself in this form. Fowls, ducks, geese, flesh, cakes, and fruits, figure largely in complimentary offerings.

The rhymes are—in st. 1, 宜., 爲., cat. 17; 館, 粲 (and in 2, 3), cat. 14: in 2, 好., 造., cat. 3, t. 2: in 3, 蕭., 作., cat. 5, t. 3.

Ode 2. Narrative. A LADY BEGS HER LOVER TO LET HER ALONE, AND NOT EXCITE THE SUSPICIONS AND REMARKS OF HER PARENTS AND OTHERS. Such is the interpretation of this piece, given by Choo, after Ch'ing Ts'eaou (鄭樵), an earlier critic of the Sung dynasty; and no one, who draws his conclusion simply from the stanzas themselves, can put any other upon it. The 'Little Preface,' however, gives an historical interpretation of it, which is altogether different, and for which something like an argument has been constructed. To understand it, some details must be given.—Duke Woo of Ch'ing, the subject of the last ode, was succeeded, in B.C. 742, by his son Woo-shang, known as duke Chwang, to whom his mother had a great dislike, while a brother, named Twan (段), was her favourite. At the mother's solicitation, Twan was invested with a large city; and he proceeded, in concert with her, to form a scheme for wresting the earldom from duke Chwang The issue was the ruin of Twan; but his brother was dilatory, as it appeared to his ministers, in taking measures against him, and Maou understands the piece as the duke's reply to Chung of Chae (祭仲), one of his ministers, whose advice that he should take swift and summary

measures with Twan he declined to follow. At the same time, he had no more liking for Twan than his minister had. Acc., then, to this view, the Chung of the ode is Chung of Chae, the minister; the 2d and 3d lines are metaphorical ways of telling him not to incite the duke to injure his brother; the 4th line tells the duke's own disregard for and dislike of his brother; and the 6th line, 'You, O Chung, are to be cherished,' is taken of 'the words of the minister,' which the duke would keep in mind. The lesson of the whole, acc. to the 'Little Preface,' is that duke Chwang, not venturing to follow the advice given him, which would have needed but little exertion of power, had afterwards to deal with Twan by calling into requisition all the resources of the State. It must be said, without hesitation, that if this be the correct interpretation of it, then the piece is a riddle, which only appears the more absurd, when the answer to it is told.

The imperial editors are willing to admit that Choo's interpretation is the more natural, but they find strong confirmation of the older view, in a passage of Tso-she's commentary on the Ch'un Ts'ew IX.xxvi. 5.—In B.C. 548, the marquis of Wei was kept a prisoner in Tsin, and the lords of Ts'e and Ch'ing went to the court of that State to intercede for him; and in their negotiations for that purpose, the minister, who was in attendance on the earl of Ch'ing, sang this piece, as suggesting a reason why the prisoner should be let go. But the only sentiment in the ode applicable to that occasion, as Too Yu points out, is that the general feeling and remarks of men are not to be disregarded. So far, the use of it was appropriate in the circumstances, whichever interpretation we adopt. Even Yen Ts'an, who follows Maou's view, thinks

畏　多　懷　多　之。檀。無　無　將
也。言。也。言。畏　豈　折　踰　仲
亦　人　仲　人　人　敢　我　我　子
可　之　之　可　之　愛　樹　園。兮。

3　I pray you, Mr. Chung,
　Do not come leaping into my garden;
　Do not break my sandal trees.
　Do I care for them?
　But I dread the talk of people.
　You, O Chung, are to be loved,
　But the talk of people
　Is also to be feared.

III. *Shuh-yu-t'ëen.*

仁。　洵　如　居　人。　巷　叔　叔
美　叔　人。　人。　豈　無　于　于
且　也。　不　無　居　田。　田

1　Shuh has gone hunting;
　And in the streets there are no inhabitants.
　Are there indeed no inhabitants?
　[But] they are not like Shuh,
　Who is truly admirable and kind.

that the lesson of the piece mentioned in the 'Little Preface' is wide of the mark. I do not see why the use of the piece, as preserved by Tso-she, nearly 200 years after it was written, should make us reject the only view on which it can be naturally and simply explained.

Ll 1—3 in all the stt. 將,—as in vi.X., et al. 仲子,—仲 is the designation of the person addressed,—indicating his place among his brothers. The 子 is equivalent to our 'Mr.' 里 may be translated 'hamlet.' Anciently. '5 families constituted a *neighbourhood* (鄰), and 5 neighbourhoods constituted a *le*, or hamlet.' The 杞 was a species of willow, 'growing by the water-side, the leaves whitish, with the lines in them slightly red.' The wood of it was valuable for bowls and other articles of use. 'These willows,' says Choo, 'would be those planted about the ditch that surrounded the

hamlet.' 樹 = 'planted.' Ying-tah says 無 揬折我所樹之杞木. 'Do not injure or break the willows which I planted.' I have translated 檀 by 'sandal trees' not meaning the sandal-wood tree of commerce, which is called *t'an-heang* (檀香). The Pan-ts'aou says on the *t'an*, that it is found on the hills about the Këang, the H'wae, and the Ho, and is of the class of the *t'an-heang*, but without its fragrance.

L.4 'How dare I love them?' but 愛 is to be taken in the sense of 'to grudge,' which it often has. Of course, on the old and orthodox view, the 之 must be referred to duke Chwang's brother, and there is no antecedent to it in the ode.

Ll.5—9. There is a difficulty with 父 on the old view, because duke Chwang's father was dead, and with 兄, because his cousins—his

叔一
于
狩。

無
飲
酒。
巷

無
飲
酒。
豈

如
叔
也。
不

美
且
好。
洵

叔三
適
野。
巷

無
服
馬。
豈

無
服
馬。
不

如
叔
也。
洵

美
且
武。

2. Shuh has gone to the grand chase;
And in the streets there are none feasting.
Are there indeed none feasting?
[But] they are not like Shuh,
Who is truly admirable and good.

3   Shuh has gone into the country;
And in the streets there are none driving about.
Are there indeed none driving about?
[But] they are not like Shuh,
Who is truly admirable and martial.

ministers who were his kin—were all urging him to take summary measures with Twan. 人之 多言,—'men's many words,'—'people's talk.'

The rhymes are—in st.1, 子, 里, 杞, 母, cat.1, t.2; 懷, 畏 (and in 2,3), cat.15 t.1: in 2, 牆, 桑, 兄, cat.10: in 3, 園, 檀, 言, cat.14.

Ode 3. Narrative. THE ADMIRATION WITH WHICH SHUH-TWAN WAS REGARDED. The Shuh of this ode is the Twan, the brother of duke Chwang, of whom I have spoken on the interpretation of the last piece. His character was the reverse of being worthy of admiration; and we must suppose that this ode and the next express merely the sentiments of his parasites and special followers. His brother conferred upon him the city of King, where he lived in great state, collecting weapons, and training the people to the use of them, with the ulterior design of wresting the State from his brother. The Preface says that the piece was directed against duke Chwang, but there is not a word in it, which should make us think so. Choo has animadverted on this, but he agrees with the Preface in referring the ode to the people of Ch'ing generally, as being smitten with the dash and bravado of Twan, and inclining to support him. On this point, the view of Yen Ts'an is more likely,—that the piece does not express the sentiments of the people generally, but of the people of King, and only of those among them who were Twan's partizans and flatterers. The mass fell off from him, when the duke took active measures against him.

L.1, in all the stt. 叔 is tne designation of Twan as being younger than duke Chwang. The eldest of 4 brothers is called pih (伯): the 2d, chung (仲); the 3d, shuh (叔); the 4th, ke (季). Frequently, however, we find the younger brothers called shuh indiscriminately. 于 is the particle. 田,—'to hunt.' Maou explains it here by 取禽, 'to take birds;' but it is best regarded as a general name for hunting. 狩 was the term appropriate to the winter hunt; but the idea of winter need not be expressed in a translation. Too Yu finds in the character the idea which I have indicated. 野 is the country beyond the suburbs, where the hunting was carried on.

Ll. 2—5. 巷 is defined as 里塗, 'the way or road of the le.' The le, we saw on the last ode, was a hamlet of 25 families, which would have, probably, their houses on either side of a street running through them, and we must understand here, I think, that the speakers have in view the quarter of King, or perhaps a hamlet outside it, where Twan had his residence. He had gone into the country hunting; and the street seemed quite empty. The life and glory of it had departed. Those who remained were not worthy of being taken notice of. 無飲 酒,—'no drinking of spirits,'— no feasting. 無服馬—'no subjugating of horses,'—無 乘馬, 'no riding with horses.' We must not understand the phrase of riding on horseback, —a thing which was all but unknown in those early times, but of driving in chariots. 仁 can here only have the modified signification of 'kind.' Choo explains it by 愛人, 'loving people.'

IV. *Shuh yu t'een.*

大叔于田

叔于田。乘乘

馬。執轡如組。

兩驂如舞。叔

在藪。火烈具

舉。襢裼暴虎。

獻于公所。將

叔無狃。戒其

傷女。

1   Shuh has gone hunting,
     Mounted in his chariot and four.
     The reins are in his grasp like ribbons,
     While the two outside horses move [with regular steps], as
        dancers do.
     Shuh is at the marshy ground;—
     The fire flames out all at once,
     And with bared arms he seizes a tiger,
     And presents it before the duke.
     O Shuh, try not [such sport] again;
     Beware of getting hurt.

The rhymes are—in st. 1, 田, 人, 人, 仁,
cat. 12, t. 1: in 2, 狩, 酒, 酒, 好。, cat. 3,
t. 2: in 3, 野。, 馬。, 馬。, 武, cat. 5, t. 2.

Ode 4. Narrative. CELEBRATING THE CHA-
RIOTEERING AND ARCHERY OF SHUH-TWAN.
Twan, the brother of duke Chwang, is the subject of this piece as of the last; and the two
are much of the same character. The 'Little
Preface' says this also was directed against duke
Chwang,—with as little foundation. To the
title of it the Preface prefixes the character
大, or 'great,' to distinguish it from ode 3;
and in many editions this is admitted, by mistake, into the 1st line of st. 1.

Ll. 1–4, in all the stt. 叔于田,—see on
last ode. The hunting there, however, was presided over by Twan himself, followed by his
own people from his city of King. Here, it appears from l. 8, st. 1, the hunting is presided over
by the duke, and Twan is in his train. 乘乘
馬,—the 1st 乘 is a verb,—'to mount,' 'to
ride in,' 'to drive;' the 2nd (3d tone), is a noun,
—'a team of 4 horses.' 執轡如組,—
see on iii. XIII. 2. The 4 horses were driven all
abreast; the two inside ones, which were called
服, being kept a little ahead of the others,

which were called *ts'an* (驂). In st. 1 the two
outsides are driven so skilfully, that they move
like dancers,—*i. e.*, with regular and harmonious
step. In st. 2. they move 'in goose column,' *i. e.*
keeping behind the leaders, acc. to the order
observed in a flock of wild geese in the sky; and
in st. 3, they are behind them, as the same may
be said to be behind the head. The 'yellow'
colour of the horses in st. 2 is a light bay, said
to be the best colour for horses. 上襄 may
be translated—'of a superior yoke;' for 襄—
駕, 'to put to a carriage.' K'ang-shing says,
'The phrase means the very best horses.' In
st. 3 鴇 is a kind of wild goose, of a grey colour; and the term is used here to describe the
colour of the horses, 'black and white mixed together,'=grey. The characters are varied; now
=='yellow,' now=='grey,' for the rhythm,—which
is so common a characteristic of these odes.

Ll. 5, 6. 藪 is defined by 澤, 'a marsh;' but
that does not give us a correct idea of what
the term conveys. Williams calls it 'a marshy
preserve in which game is kept and fish reared.'
In hunting during the winter, fire was set to
the grass, which drove the birds and beasts
from their coverts, and gave the hunters an opportunity of discharging their arrows at them.
烈 is best taken with Choo as 熾盛貌

叔二章
于
田。
乘
乘
黃。
兩

服
上
襄。
兩
驂
鴈
行。

叔
在
藪。
火
烈
具
揚。

叔
善
射
忌。
又
良
御

忌。
抑
磬
控
忌。
抑
縱

送三章
忌。

叔
于
田。
乘
乘
鴇。
兩

服
齊
首。
兩
驂
如
手。

叔
在
藪。
火
烈
具
阜。

2 Shuh has gone hunting,
Mounted in his chariot with four bay horses.
The two insides are the finest possible animals,
And the two outsides follow them regularly as in a flying
    flock of wild geese.
Shuh is at the marshy ground;—
The fire blazes up all at once.
A skilful archer is Shuh!
A good charioteer also!
Now he gives his horses the reins; now he brings them up;
Now he discharges his arrow; now he follows it.

3 Shuh has gone hunting,
Mounted in his chariot with four grey horses.
His two insides have their heads in a line,
And the two outsides come after like arms.
Shuh is at the marsh;—
The fire spreads grandly all together.

'the appearance of the spreading flames.' Maou explains it by 列, 'rows,' and K'ang-shing says that 'men were arranged in order carrying fire;' but why should we depart from the proper meaning of the term, which is quite applicable in the case? 具=俱, 'all at once,' 'all together.' 阜=盛, 'abundantly,' 'grandly.'

Ll. 7—10. In st. 1, 襢裼 means to strip off the clothes, so as to leave the upper part of the body bare. 暴=空手搏獸, 'with unarmed hands to attack and seize a wild beast.' Comp. Mencius, VII. Pt.ii. XXIII. 2. Ll. 9,10 are to be taken as spoken by the people. affectionately cautioning Twan against such perilous displays of his courage and strength.

狃=習, 'to practise,' or, as the Urh-ya defines it, 復, 'to repeat.'

In stt 2, 3, 抑 and 忌 are to be taken as two particles, which cannot be translated:—the former initial; the other final. In st. 2, these lines describe Twan's action, when the chase was at its height; in st. 3, when it was drawing to a close. 磬=騁馬, 'to gallop his horses,' making them in their action resemble a k'ing. 控=止馬, 'to stop, or check, his horses.' 縱 is 'the discharge of the arrow;' the meaning of 送 in this connection is not so clear. Maou understands it in the sense of 'following the arrow to make sure of the game;' but it is evidently, like 縱, descriptive simply of Twan's

弓 柳 搠 柳 罕 叔 慢 叔
忌。 閟 忌。 釋 忌。 發 忌。 馬

His horses move slowly;
He shoots but seldom;
Now he lays aside his quiver;
Now he returns his bow to the case.

V. Ts'ing jin.

河 二 駟 清 翔 河 二 駟 清
上 矛 介 人 。 上 矛 介 人   清
乎 重 麃 在 乎 重 旁 在   人
逍 喬。 麃。 消。 翱 英。 旁。 彭。

1 The men of Ts'ing are in P'ang;
   The chariot with its team in mail ever moves about;
   The two spears in it, with their ornaments, rising, one above
      the other.
   So do they roam about the Ho.

2 The men of Ts'ing are in Seaou;
   The chariot with its team in mail looks martial,
   And the two spears in it, with their hooks, rise one above the
      other.
   So do they saunter about by the Ho.

shooting, and indicates something done with the
left hand, which held the bow, that was called
'escorting the arrow.' 釋 拥—the critics all
take ping as 'the cover of the quiver.' We must
suppose that this was tied up somehow during
the chase, that the arrows might be readily taken
out; when they were no more wanted, the fas-
tening was 'loosed,' and the quiver closed. We
find in the Tso Chuen 冰 instead of the character in the text. 閟=韔, 'a bow-case.' It
is here used as a verb;—' He cases his bow.'

   The rhymes are—in st. 1, 馬、 組、 舞、
舉 虎、 所、 女、 cat. 5, t. 2: in 2, 黃 襄、
行、 楊、 cat. 10; 射 御、 cat 5, t. 2; 控
送、 cat. 9; in 3, 搋 首、 手、 阜、 cat. 3, t. 2;
慢 罕、 cat. 14; 拥 弓、 cat. 6.

   Ode 5. Narrative. THE USELESS MANŒUV-
RING OF AN ARMY OF CH'ING ON THE FRONTIERS.

The Tso-chuen, on the 2d year of duke Min, pp.
7, 8, that 'the Teih entered Wei,' and 'Ch'ing
threw away its army,' says that 'the earl of
Ch'ing hated Kaou K'ih, and sent him with an
army to the Ho,' (to resist the Teih), ' where he
was stationed for a long time, without being
recalled. The troops dispersed and returned to
their homes. Kaou K'ih himself fled to Ch'in;
and the people of Ch'ing, with reference to the
affair, made the Ts'ing-jin.' This account of the
piece is adopted substantially in the 'Little
Preface,' which adds, what does not appear
from the piece itself, that it was directed against
duke Wan, who took this method of getting rid
of Kaou K'ih, a minister who was distasteful to
him.—Duke Wan ruled in Ch'ing, B.C. 662—
627). The attack of Wei by the Teih was
often referred to in Bkk. IV.—VI. It took
place in B.C. 659.

   L. 1, in all the stt. Ts'ing was a city of Ch'ing,
—that belonging. it is supposed, to Kaou K'ih,
the people of which he had been ordered to lead
to defend the frontiers of the State against the
Teih. P'ang, Seaou, and Chow, were all cities
near the Ho, which flowed through both the

遙 清 在 駟 陶 左 右 中 作
人 軸 介 陶 旋 抽 軍 好

3　The men of Ts'ing are in Chow;
　　The mailed team of the chariot prance proudly.
　　[The driver] on the left wheels it about, and [the spearman]
　　　　on the right brandishes his weapon,
　　While the general in the middle looks pleased.

VI. *Kaou k'ew.*

羔 羔 如 洵 且 彼 之 舍 不
裘 裘 濡 直 侯 其 子 命 渝

1　His lamb's fur is glossy,
　　Truly smooth and beautiful.
　　That officer
　　Rests in his lot and will not change.

States of Ch'ing and Wei. Maou seems to say that P'ang was in Wei, as if the troops of Ch'ing had passed into that State, to intercept any movement of the Teih to the south.

Ll. 2, 3. 駟 as the composition of the character intimates, denotes 'four horses,'—the number driven in one chariot. 介一甲, 'mail,' and here—被甲, 'clothed with mail,'—referring to a defensive armour against the spears and arrows of the enemy, with which war-horses were covered. We are to understand by this mailed team that of the chariot of Kaou K'ih, who commanded the troops of Ch'ing. I may say that we must do so in the 3d st., and the conclusion there must be extended to the other stanzas. Of course, where the chariot of the leader was, there also would the rest of his force be. 旁旁 is explained as 'the appearance of racing about without ceasing;' 麃麃 as 'martial-looking;' and 陶陶 as 'the appearance of being pleased and satisfied.' The 'two spears' were set up in the chariot. Maou says nothing about them, but Choo follows K'ang-shing in saying they were the *ts'ew* (酋) spear, and the *e* (夷),—the former 20 cubits long, and the latter 24. Hwang Yih-ching says that the *maou* was pointed, and had also a hook, near the point, so that it could be used both for thrusting and piercing, and for laying hold. From this hook there was hung an ornament of feathers dyed red, which was called 英. Owing to the diff. length of the spears, these ornaments fluttered 'one above the other (重 疊

而見).' In the 2d st., only the 'hooks of the spears (喬)' are seen, the ornaments having disappeared in consequence of the length of time that the troops were kept on service. Maou took the 3d line in st. 3 as describing the movements of the whole army; but K'ang-shing, more correctly, understood the 左 of the driver of the chariot, who sat on the left of the general, and the 右 of the spearman, who sat on his right. In this way the chariot of Kaou K'ih is represented as moving about with a vain display. 旋一還車 'turns the chariot;' 抽一拔刃, 'draws and brandishes his weapon.'

L. 4. 翱翔 and 逍遙 are of cognate signification, the former representing the wheeling about of a bird in the air, and the latter the aimless sauntering of a man. In st. 3, 中軍 points out K'aou K'ih, occupying the central place in his chariot, and supposed to be the centre of his army. He made it his business simply 'to act the pleased.'—Nothing could be expected from an army thus commanded.

The rhymes are—in st. 1, 彭., 旁, 英., 翔, cat. 10: in 2, 消. 麃 喬遙 cat. 2: in 8, 軸 陶., 抽 好., cat. 3, t. 2.

Ode 6. Narrative. CELEBRATING SOME OFFICER OF CH'ING. No conjecture even can be hazarded as to the officer whom the writer of this piece had in mind, but that can be no reason for adopting any other interpetation of it than

羔裘豹飾。
孔武有力。
彼其之子。
邦之司直。

羔裘晏兮。
三英粲兮。
彼其之子。
邦之彦兮。

2 His lamb's fur, with its cuffs of leopard-skin.
   Looks grandly martial and strong.
   That officer
   In the country will ever hold to the right.

3 How splendid is his lamb's fur !
   How bright are its three ornaments!
   That officer
   Is the ornament of the country.

VII. *Tsun-ta loo.*

大遵
  路

遵大
路兮。
摻執
子之
袪兮。
無我
惡兮。
不寔
故也。

1 Along the highway,
   I hold you by the cuff.
   Do not hate me;—
   Old intercourse should not be suddenly broken off.

what I have given. The 'Little Preface' makes the same mistake here as in its account of the 9th ode of last Book, and refers the subject to some officer of a former time, who is here praised, to brand more deeply the court of Ch'ing, which had come to be without such men. —There are two other odes having the same title as this, x. VII., and xiii. I. They are distinguished by prefixing to the title the name of the Book to which they belong. This is *Ch'ing Kaou-k'ew.*

Ll.1,2, in all the stt. 裘 signifies 'fur garments, furs after they are made up.' Here it is used for the upper garment or jacket, worn at audiences, both by the princes of States and their officers, and made of lamb's fur. The jackets of the officers, however, were distinguished by cuffs—in st.2, called 'ornaments'—of leopard-skin. 如濡 'glossy,'—as if wet and shining with ointment. 晏 in st.3 is defined by Maou and Choo as meaning 'fresh and rich-looking.' The 2d line is best treated as descriptive of the lamb's fur. Maou explains it of the character of the officer; but st.3 would seem to be decisive in favour of Choo's view, which I have followed. Moreover, the officer comes in directly in L3. 直=順, 'straight,' 'all in order.' 侯=美 'admirable.' This explanation of 侯 appears in Han Ying. 三英 is descriptive of ornaments sewn upon the jacket, but we have not the means of describing them. Comp. 素絲五紽, &c., in ii.VII. This meaning of 英 would come under the definition of that term by 美 in the dict.

Ll.3,4. 彼其之子,—see on vi.IV. 舍命—命 here='the lot,' and all the duties belonging to it; 舍, in the 3d tone, =處, 'to occupy,' 'to rest in.' 渝=變, 'to change.' *i. e.,* in this case, to deviate from his principles. 邦之司直—'the country's master of the right,'—one who makes the right his constant aim, as if for 司 we had 主. 彦,—as in the Shoo, IV.v. Pt.i.5, *et al.*

好不讒無手子摻路遵
也。訾兮。我兮。之執兮。大

2   Along the high way,
     I hold you by the hand.
     Do not think me vilè;—
     Old friendship should not hastily be broken off.

VIII.   *Neu yueh ke ming.*

有明視子昧士雞女
爛。星夜興旦。曰鳴曰

雞女
鳴曰

1   Says the wife, 'It is cock-crow;'
     Says the husband, 'It is grey dawn.'
     'Rise, Sir, and look at the night,—
     If the morning star be not shining.

The rhymee are—in st. 1, 濡、侯、渝、 cat. 4, t. 1: in 2, 飾、力、直, cat. 1, t. 3: in 3, 晏、粲、彥, cat. 16.

Ode 7. Narrative. OLD FRIENDSHIP SHOULD NOT BE HASTILY BROKEN OFF. 1 will not venture any interpretation of this brief and trivial ode. Choo hears in it the words of a woman entreating her lover not to cast her off. Maou understands it of the people of Ch'ing wishing to retain the good men who were dissatisfied with duke Chwang, and leaving the public service. So far as the language of the ode is concerned, we must pronounce in favour of Choo; but the 'highway' is a strange place for a woman to be detaining her lover in, and pleading with him. He, however, fortifies his view by the opinion of Sung-yuh (宋玉), a poet of the end of the Chow dyn.;—see the 登徒子好色賦, in the 19th Book of Seaou T'ung's 'Literary Selections.' The imperial editors evidently incline to the old view. Choo He, they say, at one time held it himself; and few of the scholars of the Sung, Yuen, and Ming dynasties adopted his interpretation.

Ll. 1,2 in both stt. 遵,—as in i.X. 大路, 'the grand road,' = the high or public way. 摻=擥, 'to hold,' 'to grasp.'

Ll. 3,4. 無=毋, 'do not.' 讒 is another form of 醜, 'ugly,' and this would seem to be decisive in favour of Choo's interpretation:—'Do not look on me as ugly.' Still, I have not pressed this. The Shwoh-wăn quotes the line with another variation of the character, and explains the term by 棄, 'to reject.' The 4th line is not a little difficult. 不 is for the most part our negative 'not,' and is not to be taken imperatively. So Maou appears to take it here,—as indicative. 疌=速, 'hurriedly,' or 'to do anything hurriedly.' K'ang-shing explains the lines in the 1st st. thus:—'Do not hate me for trying thus to detain you; it is because duke Chwang is not swift to pursue the way of our former ruler that I do so.' Similarly he deals with them in the next stanza, taking 好 in the 2nd tone,—'good ways.' Even the scholars who reject Choo's view shrink from thus explaining 疌. They take 不 imperatively; which is allowable:—see Wang Yin-che on the term. Then 故=舊, 'old intercourse,' and 好='friendship,' in 3d tone:—'Do not deal thus hastily with old intercourse.'

The rhymes are—in st. 1, 路, 祛, 故, cat 5, st.1: in 2, 手, 魗, 好, cat.3, t.2.

Ode 8. Narrative. A PLEASANT PICTURE OF DOMESTIC LIFE. A WIFE SENDS HER HUSBAND FROM HER SIDE TO HIS HUNTING, EXPRESSES HER AFFECTION, AND ENCOURAGES HIM TO CULTIVATE VIRTUOUS FRIENDSHIPS The 'Little Preface' falls into the same absurdity here, as in the interpretation of ode 6, and says we have in the piece a description of the better morals of a past age, by way of contrast to the lascivious indulgences which characterized the domestic life of Ch'ing when it was written. The first ode of next book is something akin to this; but the parties there are a marquis and ma chioness of Ts'e, while here we have simply an officer (not

知　雜　知　莫　老　飲　子　弋　鳧　將
子　佩　子　不　琴　酒　宜　言　與　翱
之　以　之　靜　瑟　與　之　加　鴈　將
順　贈　來　好　在　子　宜　之　　　翔
之　之　之　　　御　偕　言　　　　　弋

Bestir yourself, and move about,
To shoot the wild ducks and geese.

2　‘When your arrows and line have found them,
I will dress them fitly for you.
When they are dressed, we will drink [together over them],
And I will hope to grow old with you.
Your lute in your hands
Will emit its quiet pleasant tones.

3　‘When I know those whose acquaintance you wish,
I will give them of the ornaments of my girdle.
When I know those with whom you are cordial,

of high rank) of Ch‘ing and his wife; and to suppose, with Maou, that the wife rouses her husband that he may go to court destroys the life and spirit of the ode.

St. 1. The 曰 in ll. 1, 2, is evidently the verb, and not the particle. It = ‘says.’ 昧旦, ‘dark and bright,’ denotes the early dawn, when the first beams of light are making the darkness visible. The dawn is subsequent to the time of cock-crowing. The husband does not here, as in viii.I., show any unwillingness to get up. We must take l. 3 and all the rest of the piece, as spoken by the wife who occupies the prominent place. 明星有爛—‘the bright star is shining.’ By ‘the bright star’ we are to understand the morning star. Maou does not say so expressly, but his words, that ‘the small stars had now disappeared,’ are not inconsistent with the view. 翱翔—as in v. I. 2. The terms are appropriate to describe the motions of a hunter, moving from place to place in quest of his game. 將 has a little of the imperative force, and of its meaning of the future. The ‘Complete Digest’ gives for the 5th line,— 於斯時當翱翔而往, ‘At this time you ought to be moving about and going.’ 弋—as in Ana. VII.xxvi.

St. 2. The 言 in ll. 1, 3, is the particle; the 子 in ll. 2, 4, must refer to the husband, the

子 of st. 1; the 之, to the wild ducks and geese. K‘ang-shing takes it of the husband’s guests, and makes the whole st. to be spoken by him, having no perception of the unity of the piece The wife supposes that the husband’s shooting is sure to be successful. The string attached to his arrows is securely fixed on his game (加諸鳧鴈之上), which is brought home: and then her task with it commences. 宜之,—‘will deal fitly with it;’ i. e., will cook it, and serve it up with its proper accompaniments. The 3d and 4th lines express the happiness of the couple, and the affection especially of the wife; the 5th and 6th indicate more particularly the enjoyment of the husband. 琴瑟 is not to be taken as plural, or denoting both instruments so called; but either the one of them or the other. The phrase 在御 is difficult to construe, though the meaning is obvious enough. We may refer 御 to the definition of it in the dict. by 進, ‘put forward, = ‘to use.’ The superior man, acc. to the rules of antiquity, was never, without some urgent reasons, to be without his lute by his side, so that it might always be at hand for his use. The quiet harmony of the lute was a common image for conjugal affection.

St. 3. While the wife was so fond of her husband, she did not wish to monopolize him; and she here indicates her sympathy with him in cultivating

之。以 雜 好 子 之。以 雜
報 佩 之。之 知 問 佩

I will send to them of the ornaments of my girdle.
When I know those whom you love,
I will repay their friendship from the ornaments of my girdle.'

IX. *Yew neu t'ung keu.*

瓊 佩 將 將 舜 顏 同 有ᵇ   同 有
琚。玉 翔。翱 華。如 車。女   車 女

1   There is the lady in the carriage [with him]
    With a countenance like the flower of the ephemeral hedge-tree.
    As they move about,
    The beautiful *keu*-gems of her girdle-pendant appear.

the friendship—we must suppose of men of worth like himself, his friends. She would despoil herself of her feminine ornaments to testify her regard for them. The 之 at the end of the lines, is to be taken of the friends, whose acquaintance the husband enjoyed or wished to cultivate. 來 is to be taken with a *hiphil* force,—'to make to come,' 'to draw to one's-self.' 順, 'to accord with,'—here, 'to find one's-self in cordial sympathy with.' 問, 'to ask,' was used also of the offerings which were sent, by way of compliment, along with the inquiries or messages which were sent to individuals. 雜佩 means the various appendages which were worn at the girdle. Maou 'and Choo understand the phrase here of the gems and pearls, worn by ladies of rank and wealth, and called 佩玉, see on v. V. 2, VI. 1, 2, *et al.* These are all represented in the annexed figure, in which the strings connecting the different gems are all strung with pearls.

Others, arguing from the supposed position of the husband in this piece, hold that we are not to think of anything so valuable as these ap-

pendages; and I incline to their view.—See the translation of the ode, and the remarks on it in the introduction to Le Marquis D'Hervey-Saint-Denys' 'Poésies de l'epoque des Thang;' where the author has been misled by the version of P. Lacharme.

The rhymes are—in st. 1, 且, 爛, 扅, cat. 14: in 2, 加, 宜, cat. 17; 酒, 老, 好, cat. 3, t. 2: in 3, 來 (prop. cat. 1), 贈, cat. 6; 順, 問, cat. 13; 好, 報, cat. 3, t. 2.

Ode 9. Narrative. THE PRAISE OF SOME LADY. I cannot make any more out of the piece than this. The old school, of course, find a historical basis for it. Hwuh, the eldest son of duke Chwang, twice refused an alliance which was proffered to him by the marquis of Ts'e, and wedded finally a lady from a smaller and less powerful State. His counsellors all wished him to accept the overtures of Ts'e, which would have supported him on his succession to the marquisate. As it turned out, he became marquis of Ch'ing in B. C. 700; was driven out by a brother the year after; was restored in 696; and murdered in 694. He is known as duke Ch'aou (昭). The Preface says that in this piece the people of Ch'ing satirize Hwuh for his folly in not marrying a daughter of Ts'e. But there is no indication of satire in the ode; and neither by ingenuity nor violence can an explanation of the lines be given, which will reasonably harmonize with this interpretation. I will not waste time or space by discussing the different exegeses, on this view, of Ying-tah and Yen Ts'an. Dissatisfied with the old interpretation, Choo had recourse to his usual solvent, and makes the ode to be spoken by a lover about his mistress. But the language is that of respect more than of love.

彼美孟姜。 洵美且都。 有女同行。二章 顏如舜英。 將翶將翔。 佩玉將將。 彼美孟姜。 德音不忘。

That beautiful eldest Këang
Is truly admirable and elegant.

2   There is the young lady walking [with him],
    With a countenance like the ephemeral blossoms of the hedge-
    As they move about,   [tree.
    The gems of her girdle-pendant tinkle.
    Of that beautiful eldest Këang
    The virtuous fame is not to be forgotten.

X.   *Shan yew foo-soo.*

山有 扶蘇 山有 扶 隰有 荷華。 不見 子都。 乃見 狂且。

1   On the mountains is the mulberry tree ;
    In the marshes is the lotus flower.
    I do not see Tsze-too,
    But I see this mad fellow.

We must take the piece as it is, and be content to acknowledge our ignorance of the special object of the author in it.

Ll. 1, 2, in both stt. 同行 must be taken as in the translation, because of the 4th line. The lady is seen first sitting in a carriage, and then walking along the road. The *shun*, generally and more correctly written with 艹 at the top, is, no doubt, one of the *malvaceæ*, noted for the beauty of its fugitive flowers. It has many names;—木槿、槻桹、and 王蒸. It is also called 日及, 'the ephemeral,' with reference to the fall of its five-petalled flowers in the evening of the day when they open, and 藩籬草, 'fence' or 'hedge-plant,' from its being much used for hedges, especially in Hoo-nan and Hoo-pih. I have combined those two names in the translation. 英=華, 'flower,' or 'blossoms.'

Ll. 3, 4. L. 3, as in st. 1 of last ode. The 將 approaches our 'whenever.' 佩玉,—as in v.

V. 3. 瓊琚,—see on v. X. 1. 將將 is intended to denote the tinkling of the gems.

Ll. 5, 6   The surname *Këang* indicates that the lady was of Ts'e; and 孟, that she was the eldest daughter of the family. I must understand, contrary to the opinion of Yen Ts'an, that this Këang is the same with the lady in the previous lines. 都 means 'of an elegant carriage (閒雅).' 德音,—as in iii X. 1.

The rhymes are—in st. 1. 車、, 華、, 琚, 都, cat. 5, t. 1; 翔 姜, cat. 10: in 2, 行、, 英、, 翔 將、姜 忘, *ib.*

Ode 10. Allusive. A LADY MOCKING HER LOVER. This is Choo's interpretation of the piece, but it is much demurred to. The Preface says the piece is directed against the marquis Hwuh.—duke Ch'aou, who gave his confidence to men unworthy of it. The same difficulty attaches to this as to so many other of the old interpretations, that make the odes into riddles, which we are obliged, when the answer

狹 乃 子 不 游 隰 橋 山 ^二^章
童。見。充。見 龍。有 松。有

2　On the mountains is the lofty pine;
　　In the marshes is the spreading water-polygonum.
　　I do not see Tsze-ch'ung,
　　But I see this artful boy.

XI. T'oh he.

倡 叔 風 蘀 倡 叔 風 蘀 ^一^章
子 兮 其 兮 子 兮 其 兮 蘀
要 伯 漂 蘀 和 伯 吹 蘀 兮
女。兮。女。兮。女。兮。女。兮。

1　Ye withered leaves! Ye withered leaves!
　　How the wind is blowing you away!
　　O ye uncles,
　　Give us the first note, and we will join in with you.

2　Ye withered leaves! Ye withered leaves!
　　How the wind is carrying you away!
　　O ye uncles,
　　Give us the first note, and we will complete [the song].

has been told us, to pronounce to be very badly constructed ones.

Ll.1,2, in both stt. 扶蘇 is evidently the name of a tree; but of what tree is not well ascertained. Choo, following Maou, says it is 扶胥, 'a small tree;' but the best editions of Maou throw the 'small' out of his text,—and with reason. Kwei Wǎn-ts'an (桂文燦; pres. dyn) has a long criticism which it is not worth while to repeat here, arguing that the mulberry tree is meant. 荷 is the nelumbium, or lotus. 華 indicates that it is spoken of as in flower. 喬,—as in i.IX.1. 龍 is one of the *polygonaceæ*,—the *polygonum aquaticum*, called 'wandering,' from the way in which its branches and leaves spread themselves out. It has many names, particularly 紅花 and 水紅, from the reddish colour of the leaves.—The mountains and the marshes were all furnished with what was most natural and proper to them. It was not so with the speaker and her friends.

Ll.3,4. Tsze-too is understood, in both interpretations, to be a designation expressive of the beauty of the individual to whom it is applied, derived from the Tsze-too referred to in Mencius, VI. Pt.i. VII. 7, so that we might translate—'I do not see a Tsze-too.' Consistently enough with the character of the original, Choo understands that it was merely the beauty of the outward form from which the speaker had in view. Most inconsistently with that character, the other interpretation renders it necessary to suppose the idea is of moral beauty or goodness. But if Tsze-too is thus to be taken as a metaphorical designation, so must Tsze-ch'ung in st.2 be taken; and existing records do not supply us with any individual so styled before the date of the ode. Why should we think that the two are more than the current designations of two gentlemen, known to the lady and her lover, whom she calls, mockingly, 'foolish,' and 'an artful boy?' Maou takes the artful boy intended to be duke Ch'aou; but even those who adopt his general view of the piece see the inapplicability of such a reference.

The rhymes are—in st.1, 蘇, 華., 都且., cat.5, t.1: in 2, 松, 龍, 充, 童, cat.9.

XII. *Këaou t'ung.*

狄童

彼狄童兮。
與我言兮。
子之故。
使我
維不

彼狄童兮。
不能餐兮。
與我食兮。
子之故。
使我
維

不能息兮。
子之故。
與我食兮。
彼狄童兮。
不能餐兮。

1 That artful boy!
   He will not speak with me!
   But for the sake of you, Sir,
   Shall I make myself unable to eat?
2 That artful boy!
   He will not eat with me!
   But for the sake of you, Sir,
   Shall I make myself unable to rest?

Ode 11. Metaphorical. AN APPEAL FROM THE INFERIOR OFFICERS OF CH'ING TO THEIR SUPERIORS ON THE SAD CONDITION OF THE STATE. This interpretation is a modification of that given in the 'Little Preface,'—elaborated mainly by Yen Ts'an. Maou treats the ode as allusive, the first two lines introducing the exposition of the abnormal relations between the marquis Hwuh and his ministers, as indicated in the last two. This view cannot be sustained, and Yen himself is wrong in continuing to say that the piece is allusive. Choo hears in it the words of a bad woman soliciting the advances of her lovers, and offering to respond to them. This does not appear, however, on the surface of the words. We have already in iii. XII. met with 叔 分 伯 分 in the sense which the characters have on Yen's view, while on Choo's we should have to translate the 3d line—'O Sir! O Sir!' It is not *necessary here* to follow Choo in the peculiar interpretation which he adopts of many of these odes of Ch'ing; where there is not more difficulty in following a more honourable one, it should be done.

Ll. 1, 2, in both stt. 蘀 is used of a tree whose leaves are withered and ready to fall. Elsewhere, it is explained by 落, 'to fall.' 漂 is cognate with 摽, in ii. IX. Maou says it is synonymous with 吹 in st. 1, and Choo takes it as equivalent to 飄, 'blown about.' These two lines are metaphorical of the state of things in Ch'ing, all in disorder and verging to decay.

Ll. 3, 4. 叔 分 伯 分.—as in iii. XII. The high officers of Ch'ing, we are to suppose, are thus addressed by those below them, who go on to exhort them to take the initiative in encountering the prevailing misgovernment, and promise to second their efforts. 倡 is 'to lead in singing,' and to take the lead generally. 要 =成, 'to complete,' 'to carry out.' 和 in 3d tone,—'to join in with,' 'to second.'

The rhymes are—in st. 1, 蘀 伯。(and in 2), cat. 5, t. 3; 吹., 和. cat. 17: in 2, 漂 要, cat. 2.

Ode 12. Narrative. A WOMAN SCORNING HER SCORNER. Here again I follow the interpretation of Choo. As between it and the interpretation of Maou, we cannot hesitate; but Yen Ts'an has here again modified the old view so as to give a not unreasonable exegesis of the ode. The Preface says it was directed against Hwuh, who would not consult with men of worth about the affairs of the State, but allowed the young and arrogant minions about him to take their own way. Those men of worth consequently gave expression to their sorrow and apprehension in these lines. Adopting this explanation, Maou makes both 'the artful boy,' and the 'you, Sir,' to refer to Hwuh, as if any officer of worth would have permitted himself to apply such a term as 校 童 to his ruler! The K'ang-he editors allow that this is inadmissible. To obviate this difficulty, Yen Ts'an pro-

XIII. K‘ëen chang.

褰裳

子惠思我、褰裳
涉溱。子不我思、
豈無他人。狂童
之狂也且。

子惠思我。褰裳
涉洧。子不我思。
豈無他士。狂童
之狂也且。

1   If you, Sir, think kindly of me,
     I will hold up my lower garments, and cross the Tsin.
     If you do not think of me,
     Is there no other person[to do so]?
     You, foolish, foolish fellow!

2   If you, Sir, think kindly of me,
     I will hold up my lower garments, and cross the Wei.
     If you do not think of me,
     Is there no other gentleman [to do so]?
     You, foolish, foolish fellow!

posed to take 狡童 in the plural,—of 'the crafty youths,' the unworthy ministers who ruled in Hwuh's court, and the 子 in l. 3 of Hwuh himself, still dear to those who cared for the welfare of the State, so that in their anxiety for him they were hardly able to take their food or to rest. The editors think this gives a sufficient explanation of the piece. To my mind, the referring 狡童 in l. 1, and 子 in l. 3 to different subjects is unnatural and forced,—to get over a difficulty. At the same time Choo's exegesis of ll. 3, 4, which I have indicated by translating them interrogatively, goes on a foregone conclusion as to the meaning of the whole.

The rhymes—are in st. 1, 言, 餐, cat. 14:
食, 息, cat. 1, t. 3.

Ode 13. Narrative. A LADY'S DEFIANT DECLARATION OF HER ATTACHMENT TO HER LOVER. Here, as in most of the odes hereabouts, Choo and the critics of the old school widely differ. The Preface understands the piece as the expression of the wish of the people of Ch'ing that some great State would interfere, to settle the struggle between the marquis Hwuh and his brother Tuh. Hwuh succeeded to his father in B. C. 700; and that same year he was driven from the State by his brother Tuh. In 696, Tuh had to flee, and Hwuh recovered the earldom, but before the end of the year Tuh was again master of a strong city in Ch'ing, which he held till Hwuh was murdered in 694. The old school holds that Tuh is 'the madman of all mad youths' in the 5th lines; but how an interpretation of the other four lines, acc. to the view of the Preface, was ever thought of as the primary idea intended in them, I cannot well conceive. The K'ang-he editors appeal to the use which is made of the ode in a narrative introduced into the Tso Chuen under X.xvi. 2, as a proof that, in the time of Confucius, it was not considered a love song. A minister of Ch'ing there repeats it to an envoy of Tsin, to sound him whether that State would stand by Ch'ing. Why might he not turn the piece in which a lady is sounding her lover to that application? It seems to me very natural that he should do so. 子 is the party whom the speaker addresses;—acc. to the old school, the chief minister of some other State; but this is quite inconsistent with the 人 and 士 in the 4th lines. Tsin and Wei were two rivers in Ch'ing. See them mentioned in Mencius, IV. Pt. ii. II. 1, in connection with fords over their separate streams, or a ford over their united waters after their junction. 且 at the end is the particle.

The rhymes are—in st. 1, 溱, 人, cat. 12, t. 1: in 2, 洧, 士, cat. 1, t. 2: in both st., 狂, 狂, cat. 10.

XIV. *Fung.*

丰

子之丰兮。俟我乎巷
兮。悔子不送兮。
子之昌兮。俟我乎堂
兮。悔子不將兮。
衣錦褧衣。裳錦褧裳。
叔兮伯兮。駕予與行。
裳錦褧裳。衣錦褧衣。
叔兮伯兮。駕予與歸。

1 Full and good looking was the gentleman,
Who waited for me in the lane!
I repent that I did not go with him.

2 A splendid gentleman was he,
Who waited for me in the hall!
I regret that I did not accompany him.

3 Over my embroidered upper robe, I have put on a [plain]
　　single garment;
Over my embroidered lower robe, I have done the same.
O Sir, O Sir,
Have your carriage ready for me to go with you.

4 Over my embroidered lower robe, I have put on a [plain]
　　single garment;
Over my embroidered upper robe, I have done the same.
O Sir, O Sir,
Have your carriage ready to take me home with you.

Ode 14. Narrative. A WOMAN REGRETS LOST OPPORTUNITIES, AND WOULD WELCOME A FRESH SUITOR. In the interpretation of this piece the old and new schools approach each other. The former finds in it a lady regretting that she had not fulfilled a contract of marriage; the latter, a lady regretting that she had not met the advances of one who sought her love. But there is nothing in the stanzas to indicate that there had been a previous contract of marriage between the lady and the gentleman who waited for her. Had there been so, the matter would have been out of her hands, and she could not have refused to go with him when he came in person for her. Choo's interpretation is the preferable. The imperial editors speak of the piece as, on either view, an illustration of the light and loose manners of Ch'ing. With this ode before us, we need not to be stumbled at the view which Choo gives of several others in the Book.

XV *Tung mun che shen.*

東門之墠
茹藘在阪。
東門之墠
其室則邇
其人甚遠。
有踐家室。
豈不爾思。
子不我即。

1 Near the level ground at the east gate,
   Is the madder plant on the bank.
   The house is near there,
   But the man is very far away.

2 By the chestnut trees at the east gate,
   Is a row of houses.
   Do I not think of you?
   But you do not come to me.

Stt. 1, 2. 丰 describes the plumpness and good looks of the gentleman; 昌, the richness and splendour of his appearance. 之 is the particle, giving a vividness to the description. 巷 is the lane, or street, outside the house where the lady lived; 堂, the hall, or raised floor, to which visitors ascended as the reception-room. 送 and 將 are synonyms,—as in ii.I.

Stt. 3, 4. 衣錦褧衣, see on v. III. 1. The 裳, or lower garment is here introduced also, to vary the rhythm in the two stt. Comparing this ode and v.III., we understand that it was the fashion of ladies, when travelling, to dress in the style described. 叔兮伯兮 is here evidently equivalent to our 'O Sir, O Sir,' or 'any Sir.' The same mode of mentioning gentlemen, or speaking to them, is still common. Maou thinks the gentleman, who had previously come to meet her, in a lawful way, is intended; but the indefiniteness of the 3d line is against this, and moreover, it requires us to construe 駕 in the imperative mood. Maou's construction makes the piece more licentious than Choo's. Le Hoo (李樗; Sung dyn.) says: 'The woman, having refused to go with her bridegroom, and yielded herself to another man, now wishes him to come for her again. This is a specimen of the manners of Ch'ing.'

The rhymes are—in st. 1, 丰, 巷, 送, cat. 9: in 2 昌, 堂, 將, cat. 10: t: in 3, 裳, 行., ib.: in 4, 衣, 歸, cat. 15, t. 1.

Ode 15. Narrative. A WOMAN THINKS OF HER LOVER'S RESIDENCE, AND COMPLAINS THAT HE DOES NOT COME TO HER. In the interpretation of this, even more than of the last piece, there is an agreement.

Ll. 1, 2, in both stt. The east gate is that of the capital of Ch'ing,—the principal gate of the city. From the Tso Chuen, on the 4th year of duke Yin, we know that there was an open space about it, sufficient to receive a numerous enemy, which may explain the reference to 'the level ground.' 墠 is explained as 'the levelling of the ground, and removing the grass.' Sometimes it is used of 'the level ground at the foot of an altar;' but we must think here of a larger space. Near this was a bank (陂者曰阪), where the madder plant was cultivated. The 茹藘 has other names,—茅蒐, 蒨草, 茜, &c. On the space also was a road, along which chestnut trees were planted, and by one or more of them was a row of houses. 踐—行列貌, 'the appearance of things in a row.' In this row lived the object of the lady's affection.

Ll. 3, 4. The house was near, but the man was distant;—not really so, but as she did not see him, it was the same to her, as if he were far away. 即,—as in v. IV. 1.

The rhymes are—in st. 1, 墠, 阪, 遠, cat. 14: in 2, 栗, 室, 即., cat. 12, t. 3.

XVI. *Fung yu.*

風雨

風雨凄凄。雞鳴喈喈。既見君子。云胡不夷。

風雨瀟瀟。雞鳴膠膠。既見君子。云胡不瘳。

風雨如晦。雞鳴不已。既見君子。云胡不喜。

1 Cold are the wind and the rain,
   And shrilly crows the cock.
   But I have seen my husband,
   And should I but feel at rest?

2 The wind whistles and the rain patters,
   While loudly crows the cock.
   But I have seen my husband,
   And could my ailment but be cured?

3 Through the wind and rain all looks dark,
   And the cock crows without ceasing.
   But I have seen my husband,
   And how should I not rejoice?

Ode 16. Narrative. A WIFE IS CONSOLED, UNDER CIRCUMSTANCES OF GLOOM, BY THE ARRIVAL OF HER HUSBAND. I venture, in the interpretation of this ode, to depart both from the old school and from Choo. On the view of the former, the speaker is longing for 'superior men (君子)' to arise and settle the disturbed state of Ch'ing, men who should do their duty as the cocks in the darkest and stormiest night;—so that the piece is allusive. Choo thinks the speaker tells in it of the times of her meeting with her lover, and of the happiness their interviews gave her. It has been urged that on this view the appellation of 君子 is inappropriate, such a name being inapplicable to one indulging in an illicit connexion. I have been led to the view which I have proposed, mainly by a comparison of the piece with ii. III. 君子 is there used of a husband, and the structure and sentiment of the two are very much akin.

Ll. 1, 2, in all the stt. 凄凄,—see on iii. II. 4. The reduplication of the term describes, as it were, the feeling of the cold. 瀟 (should, probably, be without the 艸 at the top) 瀟 gives the sound of the wind and rain; and 膠 (elsewhere, and better, with 口 at the side) 膠, that of the cock's crowing.

Ll. 3, 4. 君子 is used for 'husband,' as in ii. III, et al. 云 is the particle. Maou explains 夷 by 悅, 'to be pleased;' but its common meaning of 平, 'to be pacified,' 'made quiet,' answers sufficiently well. 瘳.—'to be cured.' Her anxieties had been as troublesome to her as if she had been labouring under disease.

The rhymes are—in st. 1, 凄, 喈, 夷, cat. 15, t. 1: in 2, 瀟, 膠, 瘳, cat 3, t. 1: in 3, 晦, 已, 子, 喜, cat. t. 2.

XXVII. *Tsz' K'en.*

子衿

青青子衿。悠悠
我心。縱我不往。
子寧不嗣音。
青青子佩。悠悠
我思。縱我不來。
子寧不來。
挑兮達兮。在城
闕兮。一日不見。
如三月兮。

1 O you, with the blue collar,
　 Prolonged is the anxiety of my heart.
　 Although I do not go [to you],
　 Why do you not continue your messages [to me]?

2 O you with the blue [strings to your] girdle-gems,
　 Long, long do I think of you.
　 Although I do not go [to you],
　 Why do you not come [to me]?

3 How volatile are you and dissipated,
　 By the look-out tower on the wall!
　 One day without the sight of you
　 Is like three months.

Ode 17. Narrative. A LADY MOURNS THE INDIFFERENCE AND ABSENCE OF HER LOVER. I cannot adopt any other interpretation of this piece than the above, which is given by Choo. The old interpreters find in it a condemnation of the neglect and disorder into which the schools of Ch'ing had fallen. The attendance at them was become irregular. Some young men pursued their studies, and others played truant; and one of the former class is supposed to be here upbraiding a friend in the second. The imperial editors approve of this view, and say that Choo himself once held it; but the language of the ode is absurd upon it.

Ll. 1, 2, in all the stt. 衿, i. q. 襟, is the collar of the jacket or upper garment. 青 denotes a light green, or blue inclining to green, like the azure of the sky. The repetition of the term does not here, as often, give intensity to the meaning;—see Ying-tah *in loc.* Up to the time of the present dyn., students wore a blue collar, and the phrase 青衿 is a designation for a graduate of the 1st degree. The gentleman spoken of in the piece was probably a student. By 佩 is understood 佩玉, 'the gems worn at the girdle;' and 青青 is taken as descriptive of the colour of the strings on which they were worn (士佩繻珉而青組綬也，故云青青，謂組綬也). 悠悠—as in i. I. 2, 挑 expresses the idea of 'lightness in leaping about;' 達 that of 'dissipation (放恣).' Maou explains them both together as denoting 'the app. of coming and going.' 闕 was a tower or look-out on the top of the city-wall,—a place where idle people were likely to collect.

Ll. 2, 3. 寧—何, 'why.' 嗣音—繼續其聲問. 'to continue communication and inquiries.' Maou explains 嗣 by 習, 'to practise,' and understands 音 of the lessons of music which the truant had learned at school! Even Yen Ts'an, however, who adheres to the old interpretation, understands this phrase as Choo does:—汝寧不繼聲以間我乎.

XVIII.   *Yang che shwuy.*

揚之水

之言。人實不信。
予二人。無信人
薪。終鮮兄弟。維
揚之水。不流束
之言。人實迋女。
予與女。無信人
楚。終鮮兄弟。維
揚之水。不流束

1   The fretted waters
Do not carry on their current a bundle of thorns.
Few are our brethren;
There are only I and you.
Do not believe what people say;
They are deceiving you.

2   The fretted waters
Do not carry on their current a bundle of firewood.
Few are our brethren;
There are only we two.
Do not believe what people say;
They are not to be trusted.

The rhymes are—in st. 1, 衿, 心 音, cat. 7, t. 1: in 2, 佩, 思 來, cat. 1, t. 1: in 3, 達, 闊, 月, cat. 15, t. 3.

Ode 18. Allusive. ONE PARTY ASSERTS GOOD FAITH TO ANOTHER, AND PROTESTS AGAINST PEOPLE WHO WOULD MAKE THEM DOUBT EACH OTHER. Who the parties are we really cannot tell. Choo thinks, in his commentary on the *She* (he has elsewhere expressed a different view), that they are two lovers, warning each other against some who were attempting to sow doubt and jealousy between them. Maou and his school say the piece was directed against the weakness of the marquis Hwuh, and the faithlessness of his officers and counsellors. Both interpretations have difficulties, and it is better not to insist on either, but to leave the question as to the aim of the writer undetermined.

Ll. 1, 2, in both stt. See on vi. IV.

Ll. 3, 4. 終 一 既, as when it is followed by 且. We can hardly translate it. 鮮, in the 2d tone,—'few.' 兄弟 would be very perplexing on Choo's view. He takes the phrase as meaning *relatives*, and refers to a passage in the Le Ke, VII. Pt. i. 17, where 兄弟 is used for husband and wife, or the affinities formed by a marriage. 人 一 他人, 'other men,' 'people.' 迋 一 誑, 'to deceive.'

The rhymes are—in st 1 (and in 2), 水, 弟, cat. 15, t. 2: 楚, 女, 女, cat. 5, t. 2: in 2, 薪, 人, 信, cat. 12, t. 1.

XIX. *Ch'uh k'e tung mun.*

出其東門

一章 出其東門。有女如雲。雖則如雲。匪我思存。縞衣綦巾。聊樂我員。

二章 出其闉闍。有女如荼。雖則如荼。匪我思且。縞衣茹藘。聊可與娛。

1 I went out at the east gate,
Where the girls were in clouds.
Although they are like clouds,
It is not on them that my thoughts rest.
She in the thin white silk, and the grey coiffure,—
She is my joy!

2 I went out by the tower on the covering wall,
Where the girls were like flowering rushes.
Although they are like flowering rushes,
It is not of them that I think.
She in the thin white silk, and the madder-[dyed coiffure],—
It is she that makes me happy!

Ode 19. Narrative. A MAN'S PRAISE OF HIS OWN POOR WIFE, CONTRASTED WITH FLAUNTING BEAUTIES. The 'Little Preface' says this piece was directed against the prevailing disorders, in consequence of which families were divided and scattered, and the people kept anxiously thinking how they could preserve their wives. The K'ang-he editors rightly condemn this interpretation, and approve of that of Choo, saying that the language of the ode is the reverse of what we should expect, if it had reference to contentions and abounding misery.

Ll. 1, 2, in both stt. 闉 was an outer wall built in a curve from the principal one, in front of the gates, to which it served as a curtain or defence; 闍 was a tower on this wall over against the gate. We are to understand that these terms belong to the east gate of st. 1. Choo takes the 'like clouds' as descriptive of the 'beauty,' as well as of the 'number,' of the ladies about the gate. 荼 is 'a kind of flowering rush (野菅白華),' and not the sow-thistle of iii. X. 2. Choo seems to go too far in setting down all these ladies as of loose character (淫奔之女); it is enough to say their manners were free.

Ll. 3—6. 匪我思存,—非我思之所存, 'She of whom I think is not among them,' or 'they are not those on whom my thoughts rest.' I prefer the former construction. In st. 2, 且 is the particle. The 5th line is descriptive of the speaker's wife in poor, unassuming dress. 縞 is a fabric of thin silk, in its natural colour, undyed. 衣 is the upper garment. 巾 is a napkin or kerchief, frequently denoting a handkerchief or towel; here it seems to be used of a head-dress, the kerchief being employed for that purpose. The dict. gives this meaning of the character;—but without reference to this passage. 綦 denotes the colour of the kerchief, 'light blue, with a whitish tint, like the colour of mugwort.' 茹藘,—as in XV. 1. We must bring on the 巾 of st. 1,—here dyed with madder. 聊,—as in iii. XIV. 1. 員—云, and so read, is the particle. 娛—樂, 'to rejoice,' 'have pleasure.'

XX. *Yay yew man ts'aou.*

野有蔓草

相　婉　瀼　野　相　清　溥　野
遇　如　瀼　有　遇　揚　兮　有
。　清　。　蔓　。　婉　。　蔓
與　揚　有　草　適　兮　有　草
子　。　美　。　我　。　美　。
偕　邂　一　零　願　邂　一　零
臧　逅　人　露　兮　逅　人　露
。　　　。　　　。

1 On the moor is the creeping grass,
 And how heavily is it loaded with dew!
 There was a beautiful man,
 Lovely, with clear eyes and fine forehead!
 We met together accidentally,
 And so my desire was satisfied.

2 On the moor is the creeping grass,
 Heavily covered with dew.
 There was a beautiful man,
 Lovely, with clear eyes and fine forehead!
 We met together accidentally,
 And he and I were happy together.

The rhymes are—門, 雲雲存, 巾
員 &c., cat. 13: in 2, 闌茶茶且·, 慮
娛, cat. 5, t. 1.

Ode. 20. Narrative and allusive. A LADY
REJOICES IN AN UNLAWFUL CONNECTION WHICH
SHE HAD FORMED. This is the view, substantially, which Choo takes of this piece; and the
K'ang-he editors allow that the language in itself bears it out. Twice, however, the ode is
introduced by Tso K'ew-ming.—under the 4th
year of duke Chwang, and the 27th year of duke
Sëang; where the application of such a piece
seems out of place. Han Ying also puts it into
the mouth of Confucius (外傳, II. 14), to illustrate the accidental meeting of himself and
another worthy. Even Maou's account of it is
as hard to reconcile with those citations of it,
as Choo's, for he thinks that it expresses the
wish of the bachelors and spinsters of Ch'ing to
get married in any way, the disorders of the
state having made them pass the flower of their
age unmarried. Yen Ts'an says that Maou
mistook the meaning of the 1st sentence in the
'Little Preface' about it, and then of the ode
itself; and then proceeds to explain it himself in

harmony with the passages in the Tso Chuen;
but it is not worth while trying to unravel all
the perplexities of the interpretation.

Ll.1,2, in both stt. 零,—as in iv. VI. 3. 零
露—'the fallen dew.' 溥 denotes ' the app.
of much dew;' and so, 瀼瀼

Ll.3,4. 清揚—see on iv. III. 3. 婉—
'beautiful;' 婉如, 'beautiful-like.' The analogy of iv. III. would make us understand
清揚 of a lady, and translate the 3d line—
'There was a beautiful lady.' So, Yen Ts'an.
But the 子 in the last line of st.2 will not allow us to do so.

Ll.5,6. 邂逅—'accidentally,' or, as Choo
and Maou say, 'a meeting not previously arranged for.' 適—'to accord with,' 'be according to.' 臧—善, 'good,' or 'to esteem
good.'

The rhymes are—in st.1, 溥, 婉, 願, cat.
14: in 2, 瀼, 揚, 臧, cat.10.

XXI. *Tsin Wei.*

之以勺藥。　女。伊其相謔。贈　訏且樂。維士與　觀乎。洧之外。洵　士曰既且。且往　蕑兮。女曰觀乎。　兮。士與女。方秉　溱與洧。方渙渙　溱洧

1　The Tsin and the Wei
　　Now present their broad sheets of water.
　　Ladies and gentlemen
　　Are carrying flowers of valerian.
　　A lady says, 'Have you been to see?'
　　A gentleman replies, 'I have been.'
　　'But let us go again to see.
　　Beyond the Wei,
　　The ground is large and fit for pleasure.'
　　So the gentlemen and ladies.
　　Make sport together,
　　Presenting one another with small peonies.

Ode 21. Narrative. A FESTIVITY OF CH'ING, AND ADVANTAGE TAKEN OF IT FOR LICENTIOUS ASSIGNATIONS. The old and new schools are, happily, agreed in their interpretation of this piece. Choo says there is an allusive element in it, but I am unable to perceive it. The introduction of it would only lead to perplexity.

Ll. 1—4, in both stt. The Tsin and the Wei, —see on XIII. 1, 2. 方 —'now;' an indication of time. 渙渙 (Han Ying gives 洹 洹; and the Shwoh-wan, 汍汍, where 汍 should, perhaps, be 汎) denotes 'the appearance of swollen waters.' The ode is understood to have reference to the 3d month of the year, when the streams were all swollen by the melting of the ice and snow. 瀏 is defined as 'the appearance of depth.' 蕑, both by Maou and Choo, is defined by 蘭, but we are not much helped thereby to an identification of the plant; for that term enters into the names of a multitude of flowers. Williams says that it is a general name for gynandrous flowers, and others with a single flower on a peduncle. The particular plant here intended is also called 'the fragrant grass (香草),' but that name is also variously given. The stalk and leaf are like those of the 'marsh lan (澤蘭);' the joints are wide apart, and the stalk between them is red. The plant grows in marshy places, and near rivers, and rises to a height of 4 and 5 feet. The Pun-ts'aou kang-muh gives 8 different names for it, one of them being 孩兒菊, or 'child's chrysanthemum' which I should have adopted, but that in the Japanese plates the plant plainly appears to be valerian, *valeriana villosa.* It was a custom in Ch'ing for men and women, on the 1st *sze* (巳) day of the 3d month, to gather it, for the purpose of driving away pestilential influences, and of using it in baths; and the custom had become one of festivity and dissipation. 殷 —衆 'a multitude.' 盈 says that the banks of the streams were 'full,'— covered with the festive companies.

Ll. 5, 6. The 乎 is not so much interrogative, as an exclamation. Both Choo and Yen Ts'an explain 觀乎 by 盍往觀乎, 'why not go and see?' The 且 in l. 6 is the particle.

溱　清　殷　曰　既　乎　訏　與　藥。
與　矣。　其　觀　且。　洧　且　女。　謔。
洧。　士　盈　乎　且　之　樂。　伊　贈
瀏　與　矣。　士　往　外。　維　其　之
其　女。　士　曰　觀　洵　士　將　以
　　　　與　　　　　　　　　　　勺
　　　女。　　　　　　　　　　　　

2 The Tsin and the Wei
Show their deep, clear streams.
Gentlemen and ladies
Appear in crowds.
A lady says, 'Have you been to see?'
A gentleman replies, 'I have been.'
'But let us go again to see.
Beyond the Wei,
The ground is large and fit for pleasure.'
So the gentlemen and ladies
Make sport together,
Presenting one another with small peonies.

Ll. 7—9. 且 (*ts'ëng*) in l.7 = 姑, having the force of 'but let us.' We are to understand that these lines were spoken by the lady, as if they were preceded by another 女日. 訏一大, 'large.' 洵訏,—'truly large.' 且 樂一且—'and.'

Ll. 10—12. 維 is here = 於是, 'on this.' I think we should take 士 and 女 in the plural, so that the conversation in 5—9, between one lady and one gentleman, is but a specimen of what was generally going on. 伊 is here simply an initial particle. 將 in st. 2 is probably a mistake for 相. 勺 (generally 芍) 藥 is the small peony. *pæonia albiflora*. 贈之, 'gifting it,'—'presenting it to one another.'

The rhymes are—in st. 1, 渙, 蕑, 觀, 觀, cat 14; 樂, 謔, 藥, (and in 2), cat. 2: in 2, 清, 盈, cat. 11; 觀, 觀.

CONCLUDING NOTE ON THE BOOK. Choo He says, 'The music of Ch'ing and Wei was noted for its licentious character; and when we examine the odes of the two States, a fourth only of the 39 pieces of Wei are of a lewd nature, while more than five sevenths of the 20 pieces of Ch'ing are so. Moreover, in the odes of Wei. the language is that of the men expressing their feelings of delight in the women, and there is in many of them an element of satire and condemnation; whereas in those of Ch'ing we have mostly the women leading the men astray, and giving expression to their feelings, without any appearance of shame or regret. In this way the lewdness of the music of Ch'ing was greater than that of Wei, and hence, the Master, in speaking of how a State should be administered (Ana. XV.x.), warned against the music of Ch'ing only, without speaking of Wei, mentioning simply that in which what he condemned was most apparent.'

The language of Confucius, to which Choo He thus refers, is confirmatory of the view which he took of most of the odes of Ch'ing, in opposition to the interpretation of them in the 'Little Preface,' and by Maou and his school. Yen Ts'an endeavours to meet this by saying that though the odes of Ch'ing of a lewd character, which we have in the She, are more than those of Wei, Confucius is speaking of the multitude of others which he excluded from his collection;—which is very unlikely.

The 8th ode and the 19th, however, stand out conspicuously among the others.

BOOK VIII. THE ODES OF TS'E.

I. *Ke ming.*

齊一之八

雞鳴

雞既鳴矣。朝
既盈矣。匪雞
則鳴。蒼蠅之
聲。

東方明矣。朝
既昌矣，匪東
方則明。月出
之光。

1 'The cock has crowed;
 The court is full.'
 But it was not the cock that was crowing;—
 It was the sound of the blue flies.

2 'The east is bright;
 The court is crowded.'
 But it was not the east that was bright;—
 It was the light of the moon coming forth.

TITLE OF THE BOOK.—齊一之八. 'The *odes of* Ts'e; Bk. VIII. of Pt. I.' Ts'e was one of the great fiefs of the kingdom of Chow. King Woo, on his overthrow of the Shang dynasty, appointed Shang-foo (尚父), one of his principal ministers, known also as 'Grand-father Hope (太公望),' marquis of Ts'e, his capital being at Ying-k'ёw (營邱),—in the pres. dis. of Lin-tsze, dep. Ts'ing-chow, Shan-tung. The State greatly increased in population and territory, having the Ho on the west, the sea on the east, and Loo on the south. Shang-foo claimed to be descended from Yaou's chief minister; hence the family surname was Kёang (姜). Sometimes we find the surname of Leu (呂), from a State so called in the Shang dynasty, of which his ancestors had been chiefs. The Kёangs ruled in Ts'e for about six centuries and a half. Their last representative died in B. C. 378.

Ode 1. Narrative. A MODEL MARCHIONESS STIMULATING HER HUSBAND TO RISE EARLY, AND ATTEND TO HIS DUTIES. So far Choo and the early critics agree in their view of this piece. The Preface, however, refers it further to the time of duke Gae (B. C. 934—894), who, it says, was 'licentious and indolent,' so that this ode was made to admonish him by a description of the better manners of an earlier time. Yen Ts'an agrees in this reference, for which there is no historical ground, but interprets differently the verses, as will be pointed out below.

Stt.1,2, ll.1,2. These lines are to be taken as the language of the good wife, thinking it was time for her husband to be stirring, and give audience in his court. Yen Ts'an puts them into the mouth of the grand-master, whose duty it was to announce cock-crow to his ruler, and call him to the court. 昌 is explained by 盛, 'all-complete.' It is a stronger term than 盈 of st.1.

子　庶　矣。且　夢。子　甘　薨　蟲
憎。子　無　歸　會　同　與　薨。飛

3 'The insects are flying in buzzing crowds;
　It would be sweet to lie by you and dream,
　But the assembled officers will be going home.—
　Let them not hate both me and you.'

II.　*Seuen.*

之　遭　子　我　兮。驅　之　遭　子
道　我　之　儇　揖　從　閒　我　之　　還
兮。乎　茂　兮。我　兩　兮。乎　還
並　猶　兮。　謂　肩　並　猶　兮。
　　猶　　　　　　　　猶

1　How agile you are!
　You met me in the neighbourhood of Naou,
　And we pursued together two boars of three years.
　You bowed to me, and said that I was active.

2　How admirable your skill!
　You met me in the way to Naou,

LL. 3,4. In the translation these lines are
from the writer of the piece. The lady was
wrong, and mistook the noise of flies for the
crow of the cock, &c.; but that only showed her
anxiety that the marquis should not lie in bed
too long. Yen-she takes the lines as the reply
of the marquis to the call to get up, indicative of his habits of luxurious self-indul-
gence and indolence. The 匪 .... 則 seems to
suit better the former view, 則 = 'and so,' or
'so that.'

St. 3 is to be taken as. all, the language of the
wife, coaxing the marquis to get up. Yen-she
understands the lines as addressed by him to
her. He is obliged unwillingly to rise, and thus
excuses himself, so betraying his uxoriousness.
This is unnatural, and should put his view of
the latter part of the other stanzas out of court.
薨薨—see on i.V. 3. 甘 is used as a verb,
—樂, 'to rejoice,' 'to like.' 夢 'to dream;'
here. evidently,—' to lie in bed.' L. 3 speaks of
the ministers or officers assembled in the court.
If the marquis did not soon appear, they would
return to their own houses or offices. 無—
毋, 'do not.' 庶 is here adverbial,—'thus

peradventure.' Most commentators give to the
line this meaning—'Do not let them, on my account, make you also the object of their dislike.'

The rhymes are—in st. 1, 鳴, 瑂, 鳴, 聲,
cat. 11: in 2, 明,, 昌, 明,, 光, cat. 10: in
3, 薨, 夢,, 憎, cat. 6.

Ode 2. Narrative. FRIVOLOUS AND VAIN-
GLORIOUS COMPLIMENTS INTERCHANGED BY THE
HUNTERS OF TS'E. The piece is of little value.
It is referred, in the Preface, to duke Gae. like
the last, and is said to be directed against his
inordinate love of hunting, which infected the
manners of the officers and people. Chang
Hwang (章潢; Ming dyn.) says, 'In the 1st
line of each stanza, the speaker praises another;
in the last, that other praises him; in the 3d, he
takes credit to himself and the other for ability.
The poet simply relates his words, without any
addition of his own;—a specimen of admirable
satire, through which the boastful manners of
the people of Ts'e are clearly exhibited.'

LL 1 and 4 in all the stt. 還 (*seuen*) is defined as 'the app. of being nimble,' and the
meaning of 儇 is akin to it. There is the same

我　兮。　驅　之　遭　子　我　兮。　驅
臧　揖　從　陽　我　之　好　揖　從
兮。　我　兩　兮。　乎　昌　兮。　我　兩
　　謂　狼　並　猗　　　　謂　牡

And we drove together after two males.
You bowed to me, and said that I was skilful.

3　How complete your art!
You met me on the south of Naou,
And we pursued together two wolves.
You bowed to me, and said that I was dexterous.

III.　*Choo.*

而。　瓊　尚　素　充　著　俟　　著
　　華　之　乎　耳　乎　我
　　乎　以　而。以　而。於

1　He was waiting for me between the door and screen.
The strings of his ear-stoppers were of white silk,
And there were appended to them beautiful *hwa*-stones.

relation between 茂 and 好, and 昌 and 臧.
The terms must all be taken of the skill and
dexterity of the parties in driving their chariots
and hunting.

Ll. 3, 4. Naou was a hill in Ts'e, not far
from the capital. 閒 must be translated—
'neighbourhood,' some point *between* Naou'And
the city. 陽,—as in ii. VIII. 1. 驅 expresses
their urging on of their horses; and 從＝逐,
'followed,' 'pursued.' 肩 is explained by 獸
三歲, 'a beast of three years;' in this sense
the term is interchanged with 豜, from which
I render it by 'boars.' 牡,—'males,' without
saying of what animal.

The rhymes are—in st. 1, 還, 閒, 肩, 儇,
cat. 14: in 2, 茂., 道., 牡., 好., cat. 3, t.
2: in 3, 昌, 陽, 狼, 臧, cat. 10.

Ode 3. Narrative. A BRIDE DESCRIBES HER
FIRST MEETING WITH THE BRIDEGROOM. The
critics, old and new, suppose that the piece was
directed against the disuse of the practice which
required the bridegroom, in person, to meet his
bride at her parents' house, and conduct her to
her future home. This does not appear, however, in the piece itself; and indeed. there is
nothing in it about a bride and bridegroom,
though it is not unnatural to suppose that the
speaker in it is a bride. Some suppose that we
have three brides and as many bridegrooms, the
latter all of different rank; but I prefer to think
that the places where they meet, and the colour
of the stones of the ear-stoppers, are varied
simply to prolong the piece, and give new
rhymes. We have found this a characteristic
of many previous odes.

L. 1, in all the stt. 著 (al. 箸) is defined
as 'the space between the door and the screen
(門屏之閒),' called also 宁. Passing
round the screen, one would advance on to the
庭, 'the open court' of the mansion, in front
of the 堂, the raised 'hall,' or reception-room,
from which the chambers led off. The 而 is
used simply as a final particle (句絕之辭;
Wang Yin-che); and 乎 is a particle of admiration.

俟[二章]我於庭　乎而。充耳　以青乎而。　尚之以瓊　瑩乎而。　俟[二章]我於堂　乎而。充耳　以黃乎而。　尚之以瓊　英乎而。

2 He was waiting for me in the open court.
  The strings of his ear-stoppers were of green silk,
  And there were appended to them beautiful *yung*-stones.

3 He was waiting for me in the hall.
  The strings of his ear-stoppers were of yellow silk,
  And there were appended to them beautiful *ying*-gems.

IV. *Tung fang che jih.*

東[二章]方之日　東[二章]方之日　兮。彼姝者　子。在我室　兮。在我室　兮。履我卽　兮。　東[二章]方之月

1 The sun is in the east,
  And that lovely girl
  Is in my chamber.
  She is in my chamber;
  She treads in my footsteps, and comes to me.

L. 2. 充耳,—see on v. I. 2. We must understand the line of the strings or ribbons by which the ear-stoppers were suspended, which were called *tan* (紞);—in st. 1, of white silk, in 2, of green; in 3, of yellow.

L. 3 is most naturally taken of the stones which formed the ear-stoppers, the *teen* of iv. III. 2. 尚=加, 'to add, or append to.' 瓊,—as in v. X, an adjective. It is commonly construed with the terms following, as a compound name of the precious stones used for the ear-stoppers. Maou erroneously takes those stones as belonging to the girdle-pendant.

The rhymes are—in st. 1, 著, 素, 華., cat. 5, t. 1: in 2, 庭, 青, 瑩, cat. 11: in 3, 堂, 黃, 英., cat. 10.

Ode 4. Narrative. THE LICENTIOUS INTERCOURSE OF THE PEOPLE OF TS'E. I do not see how this short piece is to be understood in any other way. Choo, indeed, agrees with the old interpreters, in taking the 1st line as allusive; but the question then occurs,—allusive of what? which has been very variously answered. At the same time there are difficulties about the view which I have followed. That the lady should seek her lover in the morning, and leave him at night, is not in accordance with the usual ways of such parties. Kĕang Ping-chang (姜炳璋; pres. dyn.) observes that the incongruousness of this should satisfy us that, under the figuration of these lovers, is intended a representation of Ts'e, with bright or with gloomy relations between its ruler and officers. But when we depart from the more natural interpretation of the lines, we launch out on a sea of various fancies and uncertainties.

彼姝者子。在我闥兮。在我闥兮。履我發兮。

2　The moon is in the east,
　　And that lovely girl
　　Is inside my door.
　　She is inside my door;
　　She treads in my footsteps, and hastens away.

V.　*Tung fung ming.*

東方未明。顛倒衣裳。顛之倒之。自公召之。
東方未晞。顛倒裳衣。倒之顛之。自公令之。

1　Before the east was bright,
　　I was putting on my clothes upside down;
　　I was putting them on upside down,
　　And there was one from the court calling me.

2　Before there was a streak of dawn in the east,
　　I was putting on my clothes upside down;
　　I was putting them on upside down,
　　And there was one from the court with orders for me.

L. 1, in both stt. This has no difficulty in st. 1, as the sun always rises in the east; but why the action of the piece is fixed to the time when the moon rises there, is a question. Does it not indicate that the lines are narrative, and not allusive?

L. 2. This must be understood here of a lady; but in iv. IX., we were obliged to interpret the same terms of 'an admirable officer.'

L. 3. 室,—'a chamber,' a room for refreshment and repose. 闥 is explained by Luh Tih-ming in the same way as 著 in the last ode,—'the space between the door and the screen.' We must understand the door as that leading from the hall to the chambers.

Ll. 4, 5. These lines are enigmatical in their brevity. 履—躡, 'to tread on.' 我—我之跡, 'my footsteps.' 卽—相就, 'to come to.' 發—行去, 'to go away.'

The rhymes are—in st. 1, 日,室,室,卽。cat. 12, t. 3: in 2, 月,闥,闥,發。cat. 15, t. 3.

Ode 5. Narrative and metaphorical. THE IRREGULARITY AND DISORDER OF THE COURT OF TS'E. Maou thinks that in the 3d stanza especially there is reference to the officer of the clepsydra, who did not keep the marquis of Ts'e sufficiently informed of the time; but this is by no means apparent. The piece is evidently directed against the irregularity of the marquis's relations with his officers.

Stt. 1,2. The officer, who, we must suppose, is the writer, was not inattentive to his duties; but was hurriedly making preparations to attend the morning audience, when a summons came to him,—All out of time. Ying-tah defines 晞 by 日之光氣, 'the rays of the sun,' the first streaks of dawn. 衣裳, varied for the sake of the rhyme to 裳衣, 'the upper garment and the lower,'='clothes.' The anxiety of the speaker to be in time for the audience is graphically set forth by the 顛倒, 'to turn upside down.' 公—公所, 'duke's place,' the court;—see ii.II.3, et al. 召之, 'sum-

則　不　辰　不　瞿　狂　樊　折
莫。夙　夜。能　瞿。夫　圃。柳

3　You fence your garden with branches of willow,
　　And the reckless fellows stand in awe.
　　He, [however], cannot fix the time of night;
　　If he be not too early, he is sure to be late.

VI.　Nan shan.

又　歸　歸。齊　道　綏　崔。南　南
懷　止。既　子　有　綏。雄　山　山
止。曷　曰　由　蕩。魯　狐　崔

1　High and large is the south hill,
　　And a male fox is on it, solitary and suspicious.
　　The way to Loo is easy and plain,
　　And the daughter of Ts'e went by it to her husband's.
　　Since she went to her husband's,
　　Why do you further think of her?

moning him to the audience;' 令 之,—'with
some orders to be executed.' I translate the
之 in the 1st person; but the whole ode might
be given in the 3d.

St. 3. This st. is metaphorical. A feeble
fence served to mark the distinction between
forbidden and other ground, and the most reckless paid regard to it; in the court of Ts'e, however, the evident distinction of morning and
night was disregarded, and times and seasons
confounded. 柳 is the drooping willow, the
wood of which has little strength. 樊=蕃,
'a fence' or 'to fence:'—'Break a willow tree
and fence your garden.' 瞿瞿 is 'the appearance of looking at with awe.' 辰=時, 'time,'
used here as a verb, 'to time,' 'to fix the time of.'
莫,—read as, and=暮 'late.'

The rhymes are—in st. 1, 明。, 裳, cat. 10;
倒, 召, cat. 2: in 2, 瞮, 衣, cat. 1, t. 1; 顡
令。, cat. 12, t. 1: in 3, 圃, 瞿, 夜, 莫,
cat. 5, t. 1.

Ode 6. Allusive. ON THE DISGRACEFUL CON-
NECTION BETWEEN WAN KEANG, THE MAR-
CHIONESS OF LOO, AND HER BROTHER:—AGAINST
SEANG OF TS'E AND HWAN OF LOO. There is

a substantial agreement among the critics as to
the intention of this piece, though they differ
in the interpretation of several of the lines. In
B.C. 708, Kwei, the marquis of Loo, known as
duke Hwan, (軌桓公), married a daughter
of the House of Ts'e, known as Wan Keang
(文姜). There was an improper affection
between her and her brother; and on his succession to Ts'e, the couple visited him. The
consequences were—incest between the brother
and sister, the murder of the husband, and a
disgraceful connection, long continued, between
the guilty pair. The marquis of Ts'e is known
in history as duke Seang (襄公). If we
translate the verbs in the last lines in the present tense, the time of the piece must be referred
to the visit to Ts'e,—before the death of the
marquis of Loo. The first two stt. are commonly taken as directed against duke Seang,
and the last two as against duke Hwan. It is
not worth the space to point out other constructions of the words, which slightly modify this
view.

St. 1. 'The south hill' is the New hill (牛山)
of Mencius, VI. Pt. i. VIII. 崔崔 describe
its appearance as high and large. The allusion
in it is understood to be to the greatness of the
State of Ts'e. L. 2,—see on v. IX. 1. 雄, properly the male of birds, is here used of a quad-

鞠止。 既曰告止。曷又 之何。必告父母。 從其畝。取妻如 蓺麻如之何。衡 庸止。曷又從止。 齊子庸止。既曰 雙止。魯道有蕩。 葛屨五兩。冠緌

2　The five kinds of dolichos shoes are [made] in pairs,
　　And the string-ends of a cap are made to match;
　　The way to Loo is easy and plain,
　　And the daughter of Ts'e travelled it.
　　Since she travelled it,
　　Why do you still follow her?

3　How do we proceed in planting hemp?
　　The acres must be dressed lengthwise and crosswise.
　　How do we proceed in taking a wife?
　　Announcement must first be made to our parents.
　　Since such announcement was made,
　　Why do you still indulge her desires?

ruped,—the fox. Duke Sëang is understood to be thus contemptuously alluded to. L.3. 蕩 is explained by 平易 'level and easy.' L.4. The daughter of Ts'e is Wăn Këang, who had gone to Loo by this way (由一從) to her husband's (歸,—as in i.VI.) The 止 in lines 5, 6, and below, is the final particle. So, the 曰 is only a particle. The subject of 懷 is most naturally understood to be duke Sëang.

St.2. 兩 (3d tone), is explained of two, or a pair of shoes. 五兩, 'five pairs,' must be taken as in the translation, the 'five' referring, probably, to the five different colours of which shoes were made of the dolichos fibre. What the writer would say, is simply that shoes were made in pairs,—alluding to the union of man and wife. L.2. 緌 denotes the ends of the strings, by which the cap was tied under the chin, which were then left hanging down of equal lengths (雙). The line thus conveys the same idea, and contains the same allusion, as the former one. L.4. 庸一用, 'to use,'—

here applied to travelling the road to Loo. L.6. 從, like 懷 above, is to be understood of duke Sëang, following his sister, unable to leave her to her husband.

St.3. L.1. 蓺一樹, 'to plant, or sow.' L.2. For hemp the ground had to be carefully prepared, and was ploughed both cross-wise (衡 一橫), or from east to west, and length-wise, or from north to south. L.3. 取一娶, 'to marry.' L.4. 告, is now in the 4th tone. The 'parents' are those of the bridegroom. As the parents of the marquis of Loo were dead, he had announced his intention to marry a princess of Ts'e to their spirits in the ancestral temple his intention to marry a princess of Ts'e. He thus obtained their sanction to the union. The marriage was concluded with every formality. It was for him to maintain it as strictly; but instead of this, he weakly allowed his wife to visit her brother. The 鞠 of l.6 is understood of duke Hwan, 'allowing his wife to carry out her licentious desires (使之得窮其 欲).'

極 止。既 媒 之 取 斧 之 析 四
止。曷 曰 不 何。妻 不 何。薪 章
又 得 得。匪 如 克。匪 如

4 How do we proceed in splitting firewood?
    Without an axe it cannot be done.
    How do we proceed in taking a wife?
    Without a go-between it cannot be done.
    Since this was done,
    Why do you still allow her to go to this extreme?

VII. *Foo t'ëen.*

勞 無 維 無 勞 無 維 無
心 思 莠 田 心 思 莠 田   甫
怛 遠 桀 甫 忉 遠 驕 甫   田
怛。人。桀。田。忉。人。驕。田。

1 Do not try to cultivate fields too large;—
    The weeds will only grow luxuriantly.
    Do not think of winning people far away;—
    Your toiling heart will be grieved,

2 Do not try to cultivate fields too large;—
    The weeds will only grow proudly,
    Do not think of winning people far away;—
    Your toiling heart will be distressed.

St. 4. Here another formality in contracting a marriage is mentioned, and illustrated by an indispensable condition in the splitting of firewood. This also had been complied with by the marquis of Loo; and as he had begun his marriage, so he should have continued it. 極 r—as 殛 in the former stanza.

The rhymes are—in st. 1, 崔, 綏, 歸, 歸, 懷, cat. 15, t. 1: in 2, 兩, 雙, 蕩, cat. 10; 庸, 庸, 從, cat. 9: in 3, 何, 何, (and in 4), cat. 17; 麻 ., 母 ., cat. 1, t. 2; 告 ., 鞠, cat. 3, t. 3: in 4, 克, 得, 得, 極, cat. 1, t. 3.

Ode 7. Metaphorical. THE FOLLY OF PURSUING OBJECTS BEYOND ONE'S STRENGTH. So, Choo. The Preface refers the piece to duke Seang, possessed by a vaulting ambition which over-leapt itself. It may be applied to the insane course which he pursued to acquire the foremost place among the States, but there is nothing in the language to indicate that it was in the first place directed against him.

Ll. 1, 2, in stt. 1, 2. 無—毋, though we might also translate it as a simple negative—'There is no such thing,' &c. 田 (read *teen*, in 3d tone) is a verb,—'to cultivate,' i. q. 畋 in 畋爾田, Shoo, V.xviii. 21. Ying-tah, indeed, quotes that passage here as 田爾田. 甫—大, 'large.' Maou explains it by 'large beyond measure,' so that the labour put forth on it is inadequate to secure any return. 莠—see Men. VII. Pt.ii. XXXVII. 12. 驕驕

弁 突 見 未 卯 總 孌 婉
兮。而 兮。幾 兮。角 兮。兮

3   How young and tender
    Is the child with his two tufts of hair!
    When you see him after not a long time,
    Lo! he is wearing the cap!

VIII. *Loo ling.*

且 其 盧 且 其 盧 且 其 盧
偲。人 重 孌 人 重 仁。人 令 盧
美 鋂   美 環。   美 令。   令

1   *Lin-lin* go the hounds;—
    Their master is admirable and kind.

2   There go the hounds with there double rings;—
    Their master is admirable and good.

3   There go the hounds with there triple rings;—
    Their master is admirable and able.

expresses the 'app. of luxuriant growth.' So, 樷樷 Leu Tsoo-k'een says that both combinations give us to see the darnel growing luxuriantly, to the injury of the good grain.

Ll. 3, 4. 遠人, 'distant men,' are people removed from us so far as to be beyond our influence. 切切 and 怛怛 (*tah*) express 'the app. of being grieved and distressed.'

St. 3, 婉 and 孌—'young and tender-like.' 總—聚, 'to gather.' 角,—'a horn.' Yen-Ts'an says, 'The hair of a child was gathered into two tufts, so as to have the form of the character 卯. 突—忽, conveying the ideas of suddenness and growth. 而—然. 弁 is here simply—冠, 'a cap,' worn by the youth grown up. In this st. we have an instance of natural and legitimate development, surely taking place;—in contrast with the fruitless strain and effort indicated in the other stanzas.

The rhymes are—in st. 1, 田, 人 (and in 2), cat. 12, t. 1; 驕, 忉, cat. 2: in 2, 樷 怛 (prop. cat. 14), cat. 15, t. 3: in 3, 孌, 卯, 見., 弁, cat. 14.

Ode 8. Narrative. THE ADMIRATION IN TS'E OF HOUNDS AND HUNTERS. This piece is akin to ode 2. We are only to find in it the foolish estimation in which hunting was held in Ts'e. The Preface makes it out, indeed, to have been directed against duke Sëang's wild addiction to hunting, and to set forth the sympathy which the people had with their good rulers of a more ancient time in their hunting expeditions (See Men I. Pt. ii. II. 6), as a lesson to him. This, however, is much too far-fetched.

L. 1, in all the stt. 盧 (more fully with 犬 at the side) is the name for a hunting dog (田犬). 令令 is intended to give the sound of the rings which the hounds carried at their necks. The Shwoh-wǎn gives 獜, 獜 with 犬 at the side,—meaning 'strong.' 重環, 'a double ring,' denotes a large ring carrying a smaller one attached; and 重鋂, a larger ring with two smaller ones attached. L. 2. The 人 is best taken of the owner of the hounds, and not of the hunters generally. 美且仁,— see on vii. III. 1. Here, as there, the application of 仁 is an exaggeration. We may accept Maou's explanation of 鬈 by 好貌, 'good-like,' and of 偲 by 才, 'able,' 'talented.' Choo explains these terms by 'whiskered,' 'bearded.'

IX. *Pe kow.*

敝笱

敝笱在梁。
其魚鲂鰥。
齊子歸止。
其從如雲。

敝笱在梁。
其魚鲂鱮。
齊子歸止。
其從如雨。

敝笱在梁。
其魚唯唯。
齊子歸止。
其從如水。

1 Worn out is the basket at the dam,
  And the fishes are the bream and the *kwan.*
  The daughter of Ts‘e has returned,
  With a cloud of attendants.

2 Worn out is the basket at the dam,
  And the fishes are the bream and the tench.
  The daughter of Ts‘e has returned,
  With a shower of attendants.

3 Worn out is the basket at the dam,
  And the fishes go in and out freely.
  The daughter of Ts‘e has returned,
  With a stream of attendants.

The rhymes are—in st. 1, 令 ., 仁, cat. 12, t. 1: in 2, 瀴, 罄, cat. 14: in 3, 鑄, 偶, cat. 1, t. 1.

Ode 9. Metaphorical. THE BOLD LICENTIOUS FREEDOM OF WAN KEANG IN RETURNING TO TS‘E. The Preface says, further, that the piece was directed against duke Hwan of Loo, unable in his weakness to impose any restraint on his wife;—see on ode 6. Choo, on the contrary, makes it to be directed against their son, duke Chwang;—and with reason. All critics understand the 歸, in the 3d lines, of Wăn Kĕang's repeated returns to Ts‘e after her husband's death, to carry on her intrigue with her brother, duke Sëang. If any marquis of Loo, therefore, was in the writer's mind, it must have been the son, unable to control the conduct of his mother.

敝,—see on vii. I. 笱 and 梁—see on iii. X. 3. 鲂,—see on i. X. 3. 鰥 is the tench.

described as 'like the bream, but with a large head, and weak scales.' The 鰥 has not been identified. The Shwoh wăn simply calls it 'a fish.' Maou calls it 'a large fish;' and a story is given by K‘ung Ts‘ung (孔叢子.抗志篇) of a kwan being taken in Wei, large enough to fill a cart. K‘ang-shing says the word means 'spawn.' Neither of these accounts is admissible in the connection. 唯唯 in st. 3 denotes the freedom with which the fishes went in and out of the broken basket (唯唯者,惟所出入,而無忌之貌) The concluding lines set forth the multitude of the marchioness's followers,—'like clouds,' 'like rain,' 'like water.'

The rhymes are—in st. 1, 鰥, 雲, cat. 13; in 2. 鱮雨, cat. 5, t. 2: in 3, 惟, 水, cat. 15, t. 2.

X. Tsae k'eu.

載驅

載驅薄薄。簟茀
朱鞹。魯道有蕩。
四驪濟濟。垂轡
齊子發夕。
灑灑濟濟。魯道有蕩。
齊子豈弟。
汶水湯湯。行人
彭彭。魯道有蕩。
齊子翱翔。

1　She urges on her chariot rapidly,
　　With its screen of bamboos woven in squares, and its vermilion-
　　　　coloured leather.
　　The way from Loo is easy and plain,
　　And the daughter of Ts'e started on it in the evening.

2　Her four black horses are beautiful,
　　And soft look the reins as they hang.
　　The way from Loo is easy and plain,
　　And the daughter of Ts'e is delighted and complacent.

3　The waters of the Wăn flow broadly on;
　　The travellers are numerous.
　　The way from Loo is easy and plain,
　　And the daughter of Ts'e moves on with unconcern.

Ode 10. Narrative. THE OPEN SHAMELESS-
NESS OF WAN KEANG IN HER MEETINGS WITH
HER BROTHER. There is an agreement among
the critics that this is the subject of the piece.
Maou differs, however, from Choo in referring
the first two lines of the stanzas to duke Sëang,
driving to the place of assignation; but even
Yen Ts'an agrees in this point with Choo. The
ode has thus a better unity, and Sëang had no
need to cross the Wăn.

St. 1, 載 is the initial particle,—as often.
薄薄 expresses the sound of the carriage
driven rapidly, and so seeming to touch the
ground *slightly*. 茀,—as in iii. X. 3. Here the
screen is made of 簟, 'slender bamboos,' which
were made or woven in squares. 鞹 is the
name for hides dressed and curried,=leather.
This was employed in the construction of the
carriage, but for what part of it, it is difficult
to say. In this case it was painted vermilion. As that colour was used in one of the carriages of the princes of States, Maou contends
that the 1st and 2d lines should be referred to
duke Sëang; but there is no evidence that their
wives might not ride in chariots of the same
colour. 發,—nearly as in IV. 2. I follow
Maou in taking 夕 as the time when Wăn
Këang commenced her journey (自夕發至
旦). Choo makes it the place where she had
passed the night,—as Lacharme translates, '*ex
diversorio capescit iter*.'

St. 2. 驪 tells the black colour of the horses;
Maou only says their rich and well-groomed
appearance. 濟濟＝美貌, 'the app. of
beauty.' 灑灑, acc. to Choo,＝柔貌, 'soft-
like;' this gives a better meaning than Maou's
衆, 'numerous;'—Maou reads simply 爾爾.
豈弟＝樂易, 'pleased and easy,' setting
forth the complacency with which Wăn Këang
went on her way of vice.

遊 齊 有 魯 儦 行 滔 汶 ^四_章
敖。子 蕩。道 儦。人 滔。水

4 The waters of the Wăn sweep on;
　The travellers are in crowds.
　The way from Loo is easy and plain,
　And the daughter of Ts'e proceeds at her ease.

XI. E tseay.

則 蹌 兮。美 若 長 兮。猗 ^一_章
臧 兮。巧 目 揚 兮。頎 嗟
兮。射 趨 揚 兮。抑 而 昌

猗
嗟

1 Alas for him, so handsome and accomplished!
　How grandly tall!
　With what elegance in his high forehead!
　With what motion of his beautiful eyes!
　With what skill in the swift movements of his feet!
　With what mastery of archery!

Stt. 3, 4. 汶，—see on Ana. VI. vii. The Wăn divided Ts'e and Loo, and it was necessary that Wăn Kĕang should cross it. 湯湯 denotes the 'full appearance of the waters;' and 滔滔, 'the app. of their flow.' 彭彭 and 儦儦 both denote the multitude of the travellers on the way, whom the lady might have been afraid to face. But instead of this, she went on with unconcern, as described in the synonymous phrases with which the stt. conclude.

The rhymes are—in st. 1, 薄，鄰，, cat. 5, t. 3: in 2, 濟，濔，弟, cat. 15, t. 2: 湯，彭，, 蕩，翔, cat. 10.

Ode 11. Narrative. LAMENT OVER DUKE CHWANG, NOTWITHSTANDING HIS BEAUTY OF PERSON, ELEGANCE OF MANNERS, AND SKILL IN ARCHERY. The Preface and subsequent critics are, probably, correct in their account of this piece as referring to duke Chwang of Loo, notwithstanding his various accomplishments, yet allowing his mother to carry on her disgraceful connection with her brother, and himself joining the marquis of Ts'e in hunting, oblivious of his mother's shame and his father's murder. Some say the piece should have a place in 'Lessons from Loo;' but to this it is replied that here is the wisdom of Confucius, who would

not directly publish the shame of his native State, and yet took care, by giving this and the other pieces about Wăn Kĕang a place in the odes of Ts'e, that that shame should not be concealed. All these odes, however, were, no doubt, written in Ts'e. The point of this one is found in the exclamation with which all the stanzas commence.

St. 1. 猗嗟 'oh alas!'—an exclamation of lamentation. The prefixing of this to the praises which follow shows the writer's opinion of the deficiencies of Chwang's character, notwithstanding his various accomplishments. 昌, —as in II. 3. It covers all the lines that follow. L. 2. 頎而 describes 'the app. of Chwang's tallness.' 而一然. The combination is adverbial.

L. 3 若, like 而，一然, and 抑若, describes the beauty or elegance of the high forehead. Maou defines 抑 by 美色, 'admirable beauty,' where 色 is probably a misprint for 兒 or 貌; and accepting this account of 抑, we must take 揚 as in iv. III. 2, et al. To account for this meaning of 抑, Wang Taou says that the character may originally have been 懿, homophonous with it, and having the signification of

猗嗟名兮。美
目清兮。儀既
成兮。終日射
侯。不出正兮。
展我甥兮。

猗嗟孌兮。清
揚婉兮。舞則
選兮。射則貫
兮。四矢反兮。
以禦亂兮。

2 Alas for him, so famous!
His beautiful eyes how clear!
His manners how complete!
Shooting all day at the target,
And never lodging outside the bird-square!
Indeed our [ruler's] nephew!

3 Alas for him, so beautiful!
His bright eyes and high forehead how lovely!
His dancing so choice!
Sure to send his arrows right through!
The four all going to the same place!
One able to withstand rebellion!

美 L. 4. Choo defines 揚 here as 目之
動, 'the movement of the eyes;' and this we
may accept, as the term would hardly be repeated
with the same meaning as in the preceding line.
   L. 5. 蹌 describes 'the app. of his artful and
quick walk (巧趨);'—Choo says, 'as if he
were on wings,' i.e., equable and graceful. L. 6.
'When he shoots, then he is skilful.'
   St. 2. L. 1. 名, 'famous,' or rather 'worthy
of fame,' is evidently like 昌, in st. 1, covering
the rest of the stanza. This is decisive against
Maou's definition of it as 目上為名,
'above the eyes is called 名.' L. 2. 成
with Yen Ts an, as—備, 'complete.' Ll. 3.
Ying-tah observes that, at trials of archery, the
parties engaged thrice discharged their arrows,
each time four, and then stopped. The 'whole
day' mentioned here is an exaggeration; what
we are to think of is Chwang's skill, and the
length of time for which he could exhibit it.
正 (1st tone) denotes the square in the centre
of the target, in the centre of which again was
the figure of a bird called ching. L. 6. 展—
誠, 'truly.' The 我 proves that the writer
was a native of Ts'e; and by his words he
refutes a calumny which was current, that
Chwang was the son of duke Sëang.

St. 3. L. 2.—see on vii. XX. 1. L. 3. 選,
'choice,'—異於眾, 'different from—better
than—all others.' L. 5. 反—復, 'again;' i.e.
arrow after arrow went to the same place.
(皆得其故處). L. 6. We have an in-
stance of duke Chwang's prowess with his arrows in the Tso-chuen, under the 10th year of
his rule.
   The rhymes are—in st. 1, 昌, 長, 揚, 揚,
蹌, 臧, cat. 10: in 2, 名, 清, 成, 正, 甥,
cat. 11: in 3, 孌, 婉, 選, 貫, 反, 亂, cat. 14.
   CONCLUDING NOTE ON THE BOOK. The odes
of which duke Sëang is. more or less directly,
the subject, are the only pieces in this Book,
the time of which can be determined. It is
strange that from none of the others do we get
any definite ideas of the history of the State
before him, and still more strange that there is
no celebration of the famous duke Hwan. subsequent to him.—the hero of Ts'e. His exploits,
it has been said, would be sung of in a boasting
style, and the sage therefore purposely excluded
them from his collection; but much more might
we have expected him to exclude the odes about
duke Sëang. Only the 1st ode presents us with a
pleasing picture. The 2d and 8th show us the
vaingloriousness of the officers of the State,
and their excessive estimation of skill in hunting. The 6th seems to give an indication of
lewd manners; and the 5th, of how ill the court
was regulated.

I. *Koh keu.*

魏一之九

葛屨

絿絿葛屨　可以履霜。

摻摻女手　可以縫裳。

要之襋之　好人服之。

好人提提

1 Shoes thinly woven of the dolichos fibre
 May be used to walk on the hoarfrost.
 The delicate fingers of a bride
 May be used in making clothes.
 [His bride] puts the waistband to his lower garment and the
   collar to his upper,
 And he, a wealthy man, wears them.

THE TITLE OF THE BOOK.—魏一之九，
'*The odes of* Wei; Book IX. of Part I.' In B.C.
660, duke Hëen of Tsin extinguished the State of
Wei, and incorporated it with his own dominions.
At the division of the kingdom, after the subjugation of the Shang dynasty, Wei had been
assigned to some chief of the Ke stock; but no
details of its history have been preserved. In
consequence of this, many critics are of opinion
that the odes of Wei are really odes of Tsin,
and that they are here prefixed to those of
T'ang, just as those of P'ei and Yung are prefixed to the odes of Wei, all really belonging to
that Wei (衞). We shall find expressions in
some of the odes which bear this view out; but,
as Choo observes, the question cannot be positively settled. The territory of Wei was small,
and the manners of the people were thrifty and
industrious. It was within the present Këae-
chow (解州) of Shan-se, but did not extend
over all the territory now forming that department.

Ode 1. Narrative. THE EXTREME PARSI-
MONIOUSNESS EVEN OF WEALTHY MEN IN WEI.
The piece explains itself in a way which no
other ode has yet done, the last two lines stating
plainly the reason of its condemnation of its
subject This has been accounted for on the

ground that in the Chinese code of morals,
sanctioned afterwards by Confucius, an excessive
economy even was commended; and the writer
therefore felt it necessary to point out that he
branded it as interfering with generosity of soul.

St. 1. Ll. 1, 2, 絿絿 are explained by
Maou as = 繚繚, which was in use in his
time;—the combination denotes the thin texture
of the woven fibres (稀疎之貌; Ying-tah).
Dolichos shoes were for summer wear; yet
necessity might require and justify the use of
them in winter. These two lines are taken as
allusive, introducing the next two; but I prefer
to regard them as narrative, giving an instance
of allowable economy. Ll. 3, 4. 摻摻 = 纖
纖, 'small,' 'delicate.' 女 is 'a bride,'—a wife
during the three months that elapsed between
her presentation in the ancestral temple of her
husband's family, which ceremony was the full
and solemn recognition of her in the new relation. Until it took place, it was not the rule
for her to engage in all the domestic work of
the family; but still circumstances might justify her in doing so. 裳 = 衣裳, 'clothes,'
generally. Ll. 5, 6. 要, (or with 衣 at the

為是褊維象佩左宛
刺。以心。是掃。其辟。然

> 2　Wealthy, he moves about quite at ease,
> And politely he stands aside to the left.
> From his girdle hangs his ivory comb-pin.
> It is the narrowness of his disposition,
> Which makes him a subject for satire.

II.　*Hwun tseu-joo.*

彼言彼乎無美彼言彼
其采汾公度無其采汾
之其一路。度。其其沮
子。桑。方。殊度。之莫洳
　　　　異美子。　　
　　　　美　　　　汾
　　　　　　　　　沮
　　　　　　　　　洳

> 1　There in the oozy grounds of the Hwun
> They gather the sorrel.
> That officer
> Is elegant beyond measure.
> He is elegant beyond measure
> But, perhaps, he is not what the superintendent of the ruler's
> 　　carriages ought to be.
>
> 2　There along the side of the Hwun,
> They gather the mulberry leaves.
> That officer

side) 之襫 之 have a verbal force. 好人
一大人 or 貴人, 'a great or noble man,'
i. e., one occupying a high position in society.
Whatever poverty might justify, it was not for
one like him to be wearing dolichos shoes in
winter, or to put his bride to such tasks.

St. 2, 提提 is descriptive of 'the gentle-
manly ease' of the husband. The right was
the place of honour anciently in China; the
husband therefore is represented as moving to
the left, to give the precedence to others. 掃,
—see iv.III.2.　The man's manners and dress in
public were such as became his position. The
facts in st.1, however, showed a stinginess of
disposition in his family which made him a
proper subject for reprehension.

The rhymes are—in st. 1, 霜, 裳, cat. 10;
襫, 服。, cat. 1, t. 3: in 2, 提。, 辟, 掃。
刺。, cat. 16, t. 3.

Ode 2. Allusive. AGAINST THE PARSIMONI-
OUSNESS OF THE OFFICERS OF WEI. The argument of this piece is akin to that of the last;
only the 'good' or wealthy man there appears
here as a high officer of the State. It belongs to
the allusive class, and we are not to suppose
that the officer or officers spoken of actually did
the things mentioned in the second lines, but
only that they did things which parties per-
forming such tasks might have done. If we
make 彼其之子 the subject of 采, as
K'ang-shing does, then the ode will be narrative.
Ll. 1, 2, in all the stt. The Hwun rises in the
pres. dis. of Tsing-loh (靜樂), E Chow (忻

乎公族。 如玉。殊異美 美如玉。 彼其之子。 言采其薁。 彼汾一曲。 乎公行。 如英。殊異美 美如英。

Is elegant as a flower.
He is elegant as a flower;
But, perhaps, he is not what the marshaller of the carriages
  ought to be.

3 There along the bend of the Hwun,
  They gather the ox-lips.
  That officer
  Is elegant as a gem.
  He is elegant as a gem;
  But, perhaps, he is not what the superintendent of the ruler's
    relations should be.

III. *Yuen yew t'aou.*

士也驕。 者。謂我 不知我 歌且謠。 憂矣。 殺心之 其實之 園有桃。 園有桃

1 Of the peach trees in the garden
  The fruit may be used as food.
  My heart is grieved,
  And I play and sing.
  Those who do not know me
  Say I am a scholar venting his pride.

州), and flows into the Ho, in the dis. of Yungho (榮 河), dep. P'oo-chow (蒲 州). The capital of Wei was near its junction with the Ho. 沮洳 — 'low and oozy.' 一方一邊, 'one side;' but the 一 is not to be pressed, as appears from the 一 曲, designating the bend of the Hwun where it joins the Ho. The 莫 (moo) is, perhaps, the *rumex acetosa*. Medhurst, after Luh Ke, says—'A kind of sorrel, the stalk of which is as large as a goose-quill, of a red colour, and giving out at every joint a leaf like the willow; it is provided with hairy prickles, sour, and when young, can be boiled into soup.' The Urh-ya calls the 薁 the 牛脣, which I have adopted in the translation. Medhurst says,—'water plantago;' and Williams,—'a marshy, grassy, and (?) climbing plant, with leaves like purslane, called also cow's lips.'

Ll.3,4. 彼其之子,—as in vi.VI. 其 is the particle; 彼 and 之, a double demonstrative. 無度 is laudatory. Maou takes

彼人是哉。子曰
何其。心之憂矣。
其誰知之。其誰
知之。蓋亦勿思。
園有棘。其實之
食。心之憂矣。聊
以行國。不知我
者。謂我士也罔
極。彼人是哉。子

'Those men are right;
What do you mean by your words?'
My heart is grieved;
Who knows [the cause of] it?
Who knows [the cause of] it?
[They know it not], because they will not think.

2   Of the jujube trees in the garden
The fruit may be used as food.
My heart is grieved,
And I think I must travel about through the State.
Those who do not know me
Say I am an officer going to the verge of license.
'Those men are right;

英 in the sense of 'a man of ten thousand;' but the 如, and 如玉 of st.3, require the meaning I have given.

L.6. 公路=掌公之路車者,— as in the translation. 公行 is another name for the same officer, as regulating the order of the carriages (以其主兵車之行列. 公族=掌公之宗族者 'the superintendent of the branches of the ducal family.' There were, as we learn from the Tso-chuen, such officers in the state of Tsin; and hence it is contended that this piece is really an ode of Tsin. But there may have been officers so called in Wei, at an earlier time. The appointment of them in Tsin took place 54 years after its extinction of the ancient Wei. The 公族 were more honourable than the 公行. It seems very unnatural to refer the 3d and 6th lines to different subjects,—as Ho K'ëae (何楷) does.

The rhymes are—in st. 1, 沮,莫,度,度,路. cat. 5, t. 1: in 2, 方,桑,英,英.,

行., cat. 10: in 3, 曲,賣,玉,玉,族 cat. 3, t. 3.

Ode 3. Allusive. AN OFFICER TELLS HIS GRIEF BECAUSE OF THE MISGOVERNMENT OF THE STATE, AND HOW HE WAS MISUNDERSTOOD. The idea of the misgovernment of the State is not evident, but it is found in the allusion in the first two lines. 'The peach,' says Ch'ing E, 'is but a poor fruit; but while there are peach-trees in the garden, their fruit can be used as food. This suggests the idea of the people of the State as few, and yet, if they were only rightly used and dealt with, good government would ensue.' This may seem far-fetched, yet it is the most likely interpretation of the words. The ode may be compared with the first of the 6th Book; but there the speaker is mourning over ruin accomplished, and makes his moan to Heaven, while here the speaker is grieved by the prospect of ruin approaching, and indicates the authors of it.

Ll.1—4, in both stt. 殽, 'viands,' is here = 食 in st. 2, 'to eat,' or 'to use as food.' The 之 in l. 2 is a difficulty; we must call it a mere particle, and translate as I have done. The 'Complete Digest' gives—其實可爲殽

思。亦之。誰之。誰矣。之其。曰
勿蓋知其知其憂心何

What do you mean by your words?'
My heart is grieved.
Who knows [the cause of] it?
Who knows [the cause of] it?
[They do not know it], because they will not think.

IV. *Chih hoo.*

來陟已。夙子曰父兮。陟
無哉。上夜行嗟兮。瞻彼
止。猶愼無役。予父望陟岵

陟
岵

1　I ascend that tree-clad hill,
　　And look towards [the residence of] my father.
　　My father is saying, 'Alas! my son, abroad on the public service,
　　Morning and night never rests.
　　May he be careful,
　　That he may come [back], and not remain there!'

In l.3 also, 之 may be taken as a particle. 歌 is distinguished from 謠, as 'singing with the accompaniment of an instrument, while the latter term denotes singing simply.' Standing alone, 歌 does not necessarily imply playing, as well as singing. 聊,—as in vii. XIX. 1, 2; *et al.* 行國 indicates that the speaker thought of travelling about to dissipate his grief (出遊於國中以忘憂). L1.5—8. The speaker's dissatisfaction is perceived. but not understood. People say he is conceited and 罔極, 'without a well-balanced judgment,' taking 極=中, according to Maou; or 'without any bounds to his condemnation of the government' (so, Choo). Ll.7,8 give their words directly. 彼人,—'those men.'—meaning the conductors of the govt. 是,—'to be right.' 其 is a final particle, used in interrogations, to be distinguished from that in Ll.3 last ode.

L.12. 蓋 takes up the question in the preceding lines, as if it were said directly,—They do not know me, for'———. 勿 is used as an indicative negative,—非 or 不. 亦 is a mere particle. Wang Yin-che makes a rule that 亦 preceded by 蓋 has never any substantive force.

The rhymes are—in st. 1, 桃, 殽, 謠, 驕, cat. 2; 哉, 其, 之, 之, 思, (and in 2), cat. 1, t. 1: in 2, 棘, 食, 國, 極, *ib.*, t. 3.

Ode 4. Narrative. A YOUNG SOLDIER ON SERVICE SOLACES HIMSELF WITH THE THOUGHT OF HOME. The marquis D'Hervey-Saint-Denys, having translated into French Lacharme's very inaccurate Latin translation of this ode, proceeds to found on it some ingenious reflections on the unwarlike character of the Chinese. He finds in it 'regrets for the loss of the domestic hearth; the longing of a young soldier who ascends a mountain to try to discover in the distance the house of his father; a mother whom Sparta would have driven from its walls; a brother who counsels the absent one, not to make his race illustrious. but before every thing to come back.' 'We feel ourselves.' he adds, 'in I know not what atmosphere of quietude and rural life.' The sentiment of the piece, however, should not make such an impression upon us. According

來無死。偕。上慎旃哉。猶弟行役夙夜必兄兮兄日嗟予陟彼岡兮、瞻望〔三章〕來無棄。寐。上慎旃哉。猶季行役夙夜無母兮母日嗟予陟彼屺兮、瞻望〔二章〕

2 I ascend that bare hill,
And look towards [the residence of] my mother.
My mother is saying, 'Alas! my child, abroad on the public
    service,
Morning and night has no sleep.
May he be careful,
That he may come [back], and not leave his body there!'

3 I ascend that ridge,
And look towards [the residence of] my elder brother.
My brother is saying, 'Alas! my younger brother, abroad on
    the public service,
Morning and night must consort with his comrades.
May he be careful,
That he may come back, and not die!'

to the Preface, the service in which the young soldier was engaged was service exacted from Wei by a more powerful State, in which there was no room for patriotism, no opportunity for getting glory. The sentiment is one of lamentation over the poor and weak Wei whose men were torn from it to fight the battles of its oppressors.

L.1, in all the stt. 岵 and 屺 are defined in the Urh-ya, as I have translated them. Maou strangely reversed the definitions, and Choo followed him. I cannot but agree with Ying-tah in thinking that in Maou's account of the characters we have errors of transcription.

L.2. 瞻 is properly ' to look up to,' and 望, ' to look out to,' or ' to look towards.'

L.3. 行役, 'has gone away on service,' or ' is doing public service.' 季=少子, 'younger son,'=child. This term is appropriately put into the mother's mouth. 無已=不得 止息 'gets no rest.' The mother says, naturally again, 無寐, 'gets no sleep.' 必偕—

必與同役者偕,—as in the translation. This language is natural from the elder bother.

L1.4,5. 上=尚, with the optative force of that term. 旃=之. It gives force to the verb. 猶—' still,' ' and so, notwithstanding.' It carries on the wish, and converts it into a hope. The 'Complete Digest' says, 猶來不敢必之詞. 無止,—as in the translation, or according to a meaning of 止, to which Choo refers, ' not be taken prisoner.' 棄=棄其尸, ' cast away his corpse.' Yen Ts'an observes that we are not to suppose that the soldier ascended three different heights;—the writer merely, as is usual in these odes, varied his terms for rhyme's sake.

The rhymes are—in st.1, 岵, 父, cat.5, t.3; 子, 已, 止, cat.1, t.2: in 2, 屺, 母, ib.; 季, 寐, 棄, cat.15, t.3: in 3, 岡, 兄, cat. 10: 弟, 偕, 死, cat.15, t.2.

V. *Shih mow che këen.*

子　泄　兮。　十　子　閑　兮。　十　十
逝　兮。　桑　畝　還　兮。　桑　畝　畝
兮。　行　者　之　兮。　行　者　之　之
　　與　泄　外　　　與　閑　間　間

1　Among their ten acres
　　The mulberry-planters stand idly about.
　　'Come,' [says one to another], 'I will return with you.'

2　Beyond those ten acres,
　　The mulberry-planters move idly about.
　　'Come,' [says one to another], 'I will go away with you.'

VI. *Fah t'an.*

猗。　且　水　兮。　之　之　兮。　伐　坎　伐
不　漣　清　河　干　河　寘　檀　坎　檀

1　*K'an-k'an* go his blows on the sandal trees,
　　And he places what he hews on the river's bank,
　　Whose waters flow clear and rippling.

Ode 5. Narrative. THE STRAITS OF THE PEASANTRY OF WEI. The interpretation of this short piece is not a little difficult. Acc. to the Preface, it was directed against the times when the State of Wei was so much reduced by the loss of territory, that there was not room for the people to live in it. Acc. to Choo, on the other hand, a worthy officer, disgusted with the irregularities of the court, proposes to his companion to withdraw from the public service to a quiet life among the mulberry trees in the country. The old view seems to me the preferable.

L. 1, in both stt. Why *ten* acres are here specified, or what ten acres are meant, cannot be determined. According to the ancient regulations, often spoken of by Mencius, each farmer, the head of a family, received 100 acres. Here, it is said, so much was Wei reduced, that such a man could only receive a tenth part of his proper allotment. But those hundred acres were for the cultivation of grain; the mention of the mulberry trees in the 2d line shows that the farm is not intended here. Rather must we think of the 'homesteads with their five acres' (Men. I. Pt. i. VIII. 24), about which mulberry trees were planted. Those 5 acres were divided into two portions, half in the fields, and half in

the villages. The eight families which constituted a *tsing* (井) had thus 20 acres of mulberry ground in each place, which here appear, it is supposed, reduced to 10. This is more likely. 畝 was anciently written 畮. Six cubits (尺) formed a pace (步), and 100 paces was the length of an acre.

L. 2. 桑者,—'mulberriers.' We are to understand, probably, the gatherers of the mulberry leaves. 閑閑 or 閒閒,—as in the translation. Choo makes it—'placidly or contentedly going about.' 泄泄 may be regarded as synonymous with 閑閑. Maou makes it mean—'the app. of a multitude,' the people being too numerous for the space.

L. 3 is to be taken as the language of the mulberry planters to one another. They have no work to do, and think they may as well go home empty-handed, or go and amuse themselves in the neighbouring lot. 行, acc. to Choo,—將, the sign of the future. 逝=往.

稼不穡。胡取禾三百
廛兮。不狩不獵。胡瞻
爾庭有縣貆兮。彼君
子兮。不素餐兮。
二章
坎坎伐輻兮。寘之河
之側兮。河水清且直
猗。不稼不穡。胡取禾
三百億兮。不狩不獵。
胡瞻爾庭有縣特兮。
彼君子兮。不素食兮。

You sow not nor reap;—
How do you get the produce of those three hundred farms?
You do not follow the chase;—
How do we see the badgers hanging up in your court-yards?
O that superior man!
He would not eat the bread of idleness!

2 K'an-k'an go his blows on the wood for his spokes,
And he places it by the side of the river,
Whose waters flow clear and even.
You sow not nor reap;—
How do you get your three millions of sheaves?
You do not follow the chase;—
How do we see those three-year-olds hanging in your court-yards.
O that superior man!
He would not eat the bread of idleness!

'to go to another place.' The use of 還 and 逝 respectively respondst o the 間 and 外 of ll. 1, the ground of the speakers, and the ground beyond it.

The rhymes are—in st. 1, 間, 閑, 還, cat. 14: in 2, 外, 泄, 逝, cat. 15, t. 3.

Ode 6. Allusive. AGAINST THE IDLE AND GREEDY MINISTERS OF THE STATE. CONTRAST BETWEEN THEM AND A STALWART WOODMAN. Choo does not, in his work on the She, admit the allusive element, and puts the lines from the 4th downwards into the mouth of the woodcutter, solacing himself under his toil, and with the results to which it might lead. The interpretation which I have given, more in accordance with the Preface, seems preferable; Choo himself held it, when commenting on Mencius, VII. Pt. i. XXXII.

Ll. 1—3, in all the stt. 坎坎 is intended to convey the sound of the woodman's blows;—like 丁丁 in i. VII. 檀,—see on vii. II. 3. The wood was prized for making carriages, and was specially good for the spokes and other parts of the wheels. 干—厓, 'a river's bank.' 淯,—as in vi. VII. 3. 漣 is the 'rippling' appearance of the water; 直, its being 'even and unagitated;' 淪, the 'rippling circles' caused by a slight wind. Choo thinks the third line always describes the condition of the river,

坎坎伐輪兮。寘之河之漘兮。河水清且淪猗。不稼不稽。胡取禾三百囷兮。不狩不獵。胡瞻爾庭有縣鶉兮。彼君子兮。不素飧兮。

3 *K'an-k'an* go his blows on the wood for his wheels,
And he places it by the lip of the river,
Whose waters flow clear in rippling circles.
You sow not nor reap;—
How do you get the paddy for your three hundred round binns?
You do not follow the chase;—
How do we see the quails hanging in your court-yards?
O that superior man!
He would not eat the bread of idleness!

VII. *Shih shoo.*

碩鼠碩鼠。無食我黍。三歲貫女。莫我肯顧。逝將

1 Large rats! Large rats!
Do not eat our millet.
Three years have we had to do with you,
And you have not been willing to show any regard for us.

unfit to carry away the wood which the worker's toil produced. 猗 is used as 兮.

Ll. 4—7. 稼 is properly 'the spike' of grain, and 穡, the grain fit to be reaped. 稼穡 intimates the business of husbandry; but from the constant use and order of the terms, they have come to get the respective meanings in the translation. So in l. 6. 狩 and 獵 together denote hunting. 廛 denotes the ground assigned for the dwelling of a farmer, and the land, or 100 acres, attached to it, so that we can render it here by 'farms.' 取禾三百廛＝取三百廛所出之禾. The 3 millions of st. 2. are understood to refer to the sheaves or bundles in which the cut paddy was gathered (禾秉之數); and the binns (囷 denotes their round form) of st 4, the repositories in which the grain was stored. 貆 is a species of 貉;—see on Ana. IX. xxviii. Here, as there, it might mean badgers' skins, but for the 特 and 鶉 below. Maou gives the former of those terms as meaning any animal of the chase, three years old. These four lines set forth the great revenues of the officers intended in the ode, acquired and enjoyed without any proper services performed for them.

Ll. 8, 9, return to the woodman, as truly a superior man, earning his support. 素＝空 'emptily,' or 'idly.' 飧＝食, 'to eat.'

The rhymes are—in st. 1, 檀, 干, 漣, 廛, 貆, 飧, cat. 14: in 2, 輻, 側, 直, 億, 特, 食, cat. 1, t. 3: in 3, 輪, 漘, 淪, 囷, 鶉, 殑, cat. 13.

去女。適彼樂土。樂土

樂土。爰得我所。

碩鼠碩鼠無食我麥。

三歲貫女。莫我肯德。

逝將去女。適彼樂國。

樂國樂國。爰得我直。

碩鼠碩鼠無食我苗。

三歲貫女。莫我肯勞。

逝將去女。適彼樂郊。

樂郊樂郊。誰之永號。

> We will leave you,
> And go to that happy land.
> Happy land! Happy land!
> There shall we find our place.

2　Large rats! Large rats!
　Do not eat our wheat.
　Three years have we had to do with you,
　And you have not been willing to show any kindness to us.
　We will leave you,
　And go to that happy State.
　Happy State! Happy State!
　There shall we find ourselves right.

3　Large rats! Large rats!
　Do not eat our springing grain!
　Three years have we had to do with you,
　And you have not been willing to think of our toil.
　We will leave you,
　And go to those happy borders,
　Happy borders! Happy borders!
　Who will there make us always to groan?

Ode 7. Metaphorical. AGAINST THE OPPRESSION AND EXTORTION OF THE GOVERNMENT OF WEI. The piece is purely metaphorical, the writer, as representative of the people, clearly having the oppressive officers of the govt. before him, under the figure of *large rats*. The Preface is wrong in supposing it to be intended directly against the ruler of Wei. It would serve as an admonition to him, but it would be too licentious if it designated him as the *large rat*.

Ll. 1, 2, in all the stt. 無＝毋, imperative. The term 'millet' is varied by the others, merely for the sake of the rhythm.

Ll. 3, 4. There must have been a reason for specifying 'three years;' so long, probably, had the ministers complained of been in office. Choo defines 貫 by 習, 'to practise,' 'to be accustomed to;' and Maou by 事, 'to serve.' The translation gives the exact idea. 顧＝念, 'to think of,' 'to regard;' 德,—used as a verb, 'to show kindness to;' 勞我＝以我爲 勤勞, 'to consider our toil.'

Ll. 5, 6. 逝,—a particle, as in iii. IV. 去, —'to go away from,' 'to leave.' 'That happy land' was, probably, some neighbouring State, where there was kindly government.

Ll. 7, 8. 爰—'there,' as iii. VI. 3, *et al.* 我 所,—'our place,' *i. e.*, our right place. 我 直, 'our right,' *i. e.*, be dealt with right- eously. 誰之永號,—號—呼, 'to cry out;'—'whose will be our constant crying out?' As Choo expands it—當復爲誰而永 號乎.

The rhymes are—in st. 1, 鼠, 黍, 女, 顧, 女, 土, 土, 所, cat. 5, t. 2: in 2, 鼠, 女, 女, (and in 3), 麥, 麥, 德, 國, 國, 直, cat. 1, t. 3: in 3, 苗, 勞, 郊, 郊, 號, cat. 2.

CONCLUDING NOTE ON THE BOOK. Yen Ts'an calls attention to the fact that there are no licentious songs among the odes of Wei. The characteristics of excessive parsimony in the higher classes, and oppressive extortion practised by them on the people, leave no room for sur- prise at the early extinction of the State as an independent fief. The best pieces are IV. and VI.

I. *Sih-tsuh.*

良士瞿瞿。
好樂無荒。
職思其居。
無已大康。
日月其除。
今我不樂。
歲聿其莫。
蟋蟀在堂。

蟋蟀

唐一之十

1 The cricket is in the hall,
And the year is drawing to a close.
If we do not enjoy ourselves now,
The days and months will be leaving us.
But let us not go to great excess;
Let us first think of the duties of our position;
Let us not be wild in our love of enjoyment.
The good man is anxiously thoughtful.

TITLE OF THE BOOK.—唐一之十, '*The odes of* T'ang; Book X. of Part I.' The odes of T'ang were the odes of Tsin,—the greatest, perhaps, of the fiefs of Chow, until the rise and growth of Ts'in. King Ching, in B. C. 1106, invested his younger brother, called Shuh-yu (叔虞), with the territory where Yaou was supposed to have ruled anciently as the marquis of T'ang;—in the pres. dep. of T'ae-yuen, Shan-se, the fief retaining that ancient name. In the south of the territory was the river Tsin (晉水), and Shih-foo (燮父), the son of Shuh-yu, gave its name to the marquisate. Choo He says that 'the soil was thin and the people poor; that they were diligent, thrifty and plain in their ways, thinking deeply and forecasting;—characteristics which showed the influence among them of the character and administration of Yaou.' It is difficult to say why the name of the State, which had gone into disuse, was given to the collection of its poems. We should set it down, probably, to a fondness for ancient legends and traditions. The State of Tsin developed greatly, having the Ho as its boundary on the west, and extending nearly to it on the south and east.

Ode 1. Narrative. THE CHEERFULNESS AND DISCRETION OF THE PEOPLE OF TSIN, AND THEIR TEMPERED ENJOYMENT AT FITTING SEASONS. The Preface refers the piece to the time of the marquis He (僖侯; B.C. 839-822), who was too parsimonious, and did not temper his economy by the rules of propriety. This ode therefore, it says, was made, through compassion for him, and to suggest to him to allow himself proper indulgences. But there is nothing in the language to make us think of the ruler of the State; we have only to see in it a pleasant picture of the manners of the people.

Ll. 1—4, in all the stt. The 蟋蟀, no doubt, is the cricket. It has many names. In xv. I. 5, it is said in the 9th month to be at the door, and in the 10th under the bed. By the door we must understand that of the bedchamber, so that the 在戶 there and 在堂 here are equivalent, and we conclude that the time intended is the 9th month, when the year had entered on its last quarter. 聿 is used as a particle, synonymous with 于, 曰, 奧, and 越. Choo defines it by 遂. 莫=暮, 'late.'

二章
蟋蟀在堂。歲聿其逝。今我不樂。日月其邁。無已大康。職思其外。好樂無荒。良士蹶蹶。

三章
蟋蟀在堂。役車其休。今我不樂。日月其慆。無已大康。職思其憂。好樂無荒。良士休休。

2   The cricket is in the hall,
    And the year is passing away.
    If we do not enjoy ourselves now,
    The days and months will have gone.
    But let us not go to great excess;
    Let us first send our thoughts beyond the present;
    Let us not be wild in our love of enjoyment.
    The good man is ever diligent.

3   The cricket is in the hall,
    And our carts stand unemployed.
    If we do not enjoy ourselves now,
    The days and months will have gone by,
    But let us not go to an excess;
    Let us first think of the griefs that may arise;
    Let us not be wild in our love of enjoyment.
    The good man is quiet and serene.

其 in the 4th line is by Wang Yin-che brought under the category of 將,—'will.' In the 2d line we may take it as descriptive, or emphatic, equivalent to our use of the subject proper and of the 3d personal pronoun in the same sentence. 除 —去, 'to go,' 'pass away;' so also, both 逝 and 邁. 慆—過, 'to pass by,' 役車, 'service carriages,'—our 'carts,' or perhaps, only 'barrows.'

Ll. 5—8. The first four lines are to be taken as the language of a party of the people, as there rises among them the idea of their having a jovial time. At this point we may suppose that one among them, of a more serious and thoughtful character, interjects the remarks that follow, in order to temper their mirth. 已 is defined by Maou as meaning 甚, 'greatly.' 康—樂, 'pleasure.' 大康—過於

樂. 職—主, 'to make the first business.' 其居, 'where we dwell,' 'where we occupy;'—as in the transl. 其外, 'what is beyond,' i. e., what yet may remain for us to do. 荒,—'to go wildly to excess;'—comp. Men. I.Pt.i.IV. 良士,—士 is here not more than our 'man.' 蹶蹶 denotes 'the app. of looking round and out;' 蹶蹶, that of 'sedulous movement;' and 休休, that of 'calm composure.'

The rhymes are—in st.1, 堂, 康, 荒 (and in 2, 3), cat.10; 莫, 除, 居, 瞿, cat. 3, t.1: in 2, 逝, 邁, 外, 蹶, cat.15, t. 3: in 3, 休, 慆, 憂, 休, cat.3, t.1.

II. *Shan yëw ch'oo.*

山有樞

山有樞。隰有榆。子
有衣裳。弗曳弗婁。
子有車馬。弗馳弗
驅。宛其死矣。他人
是愉。

山有栲。隰有杻。
子有廷內。弗洒弗埽。
子有鐘鼓。弗鼓弗
考。宛其死矣。他人

1　On the mountains are the thorny elms,
In the low, wet grounds are the white elms.
You have suits of robes,
But you will not wear them;
You have carriages and horses,
But you will not drive them.
You will drop off in death,
And another person will enjoy them.

2　On the mountains is the *k'aou,*
In the low wet grounds is the *nëw.*
You have courtyards and inner rooms,
But you will not have them sprinkled or swept;
You have drums and bells,
But you will not have them beat or struck,
You will drop off in death,
And another person will possess them.

Ode 2. Allusive. THE FOLLY OF NOT EN-
JOYING THE GOOD THINGS WHICH WE HAVE, AND
LETTING DEATH PUT THEM INTO THE HANDS OF
OTHERS. The Preface says that this piece was
directed against the marquis Ch'aou (B. C. 744-
738), who could not govern the State well, nor
use the resources which he had, so as to secure
himself against the enemies who were plotting
his ruin. I must believe, with Choo, that such
an interpretation is ‘very wrong.’ He considers it himself to be a response to the previous
ode, bringing in the idea of death, to remove all
hesitation in accepting the counsel to enjoyment
there given. The two pieces would seem to
have some connection.

Ll.1,2, in all the stt. 荎 is another name
for the 樞 which is described as ‘the thorny

elm (刺榆).’ I have seen the tree, with its
trunk all covered with spinous protuberances,
making it very difficult to climb, 榆 is the
general name for elms. The one intended in
the text is understood to be ‘the white elm
(白枌).’ The 栲 is said to be like the varnish tree; the 杻 affords good material for bows.
It goes also by the name of ‘the myriad years
(萬歲),’ or ‘the everlasting.’ 山 and 隰
—see iii.XIII. 4. These two lines are allusive,
but they suggest no idea apropriate to the
subject which they introduce. As Choo says,
刪無意義只是與起下面
子有車馬子有衣裳耳.

三章

人　其　以　以　日　酒　有　山　是
入　死　永　喜　鼓　食　栗　有　保。
室。矣。日。樂。瑟。何　子　漆。
　　他　宛　且　且　不　有　隰
　　　　　　　　　　　　　　　有

3　On the mountains are the varnish trees,
　　In the low wet grounds are the chestnuts.
　　You have spirits and viands ;—
　　Why not daily play your lute,
　　Both to give a zest to your joy,
　　And to prolong the day ?
　　You will drop off in death,
　　And another person will enter your chamber.

III.　*Yang che shuy.*

二章

沃。子　襮。衣　鑿。石　水。揚
既　于　從　朱　鑿　白　之　揚
　　　　　　　　　　　　　　之水

1　Amidst the fretted waters,
　　The white rocks stand up grandly.
　　Bringing a robe of white silk, with a vermilion collar,
　　We will follow you to Yuh.

Ll. 3–6. 子—'you,' any one to whom we
may suppose the speaker to be addressing himself. 曳 and 婁 are synonyms, signifying ' to
drag or trail along.' The two terms together
give us the idea of the man's moving along in
full dress. 馳驅—see iv. X. 1. 廷=庭;
內 is probably the hall and apartments, inside
from the courtyard. 考=擊, to 'strike.'
This term is more appropriate to the bells,
though in the 3d st. 鼓 is used for to play on
the lute. In l.4 of st. 3, 日, on Choo's view of
the piece, is taken to mean 'the days of the year
that remain ;' but that is not necessary. Moreover, to explain 以永日 he says that
' when men have many anxieties, the days seem
short,' whereas the contrary is the case.
Ll. 7, 8. 宛, with Choo, is 坐見貌 'the
app. of sitting and seeing,' i.e., anything happen-
ing without warning or excitement. 愉—

樂, 'to enjoy ;' 保=居有, 'to dwell in the
possession of.'
　　The rhymes are—in st. 1, 樞,榆,婁,
驅,愉, cat. 4, t. 1 : in 2, 栲,杻,栳,
考,保, cat. 3, t. 2 : in 3, 漆,栗,瑟,日,
室, cat. 12, t. 8.

Ode 3. Allusive. REBELLION PLOTTED A-
GAINST TSIN BY THE CHIEF OF K'EUH-YUH AND
HIS PARTIZANS. At the beginning of his rule,
the marquis Ch'aou invested his uncle, called
Ching-sze (成師) and Hwan-shuh (桓叔)
with the great city of K'euh-yuh, thus weaken-
ing greatly his own power ; and from this proceeding there resulted long disorder in the State
of Tsin. A party was soon formed to displace
the marquis, and raise Hwan-shuh to his place.
The piece is supposed in the Preface, and by
Choo, to describe the movement for this object,
the people declaring in it their devotion to the
chief of K'euh-yuh, who is intended by the 君

敢　粼　揚　子　皓　揚　樂　見
以　我　之三　于　素　之二　　　君
告　聞　水章　鵠　衣　水章　　　子
人　有　白　既　朱　白　　　云
。　命　石　見　繡　石　　　何
　　不　粼　君　從　皓　　　不

When we have seen the princely lord,
Shall we not rejoice?

2   Amidst the fretted waters,
The white rocks stand glistening.
Bringing a robe of white silk, with a vermilion collar, and
    embroidered,
We will follow you to Kaou.
When we have seen the princely lord,
What sorrow will remain to us?

3   Amidst the fretted waters,
The white rocks clearly show.
We have heard your orders,
And will not dare to inform any one of them.

子 of the first two stanzas. But, as a matter of fact, the conspiracy against Ch'aou was the affair of a faction, and not shared in by the mass of the people. I prefer, therefore, to adopt the view of Yen Ts'an, that the piece describes the plottings of conspirators in the capital of Tsin. The 'we,' the speakers, are only the adherents of the conspiracy, and the 子 in l.4 is an emissary of Hwan-shuh, who is the 君子 of l. 5. The object of the piece, therefore, was to warn the marquis Ch'aou of the machinations against him. The K'ang-he editors rather incline in favour of this interpretation.

Ll. 1, 2, in all the stt. 揚之水,—see on vi. IV., and vii. XVIII. 鑿鑿,—'the rugged, lofty app. of the rocks;' 皓皓,—'their shining appearance;' 粼粼 is obscure. The Shwoh-wǎn explains it as 'the water about the banks and rocks;' Maou, as—'clear;' Choo, as 'the stones visible amid the clear water' What meaning we are to get from these allusive lines, it is as difficult to determine as in the previous odes which began with 揚之水.

Ll.3–6 in stt.1,2. The robe described in l.3 was one worn by the princes of States in sacrificing. It was an inner robe, made of white silk, with a collar which is here called poh. On this were embroidered the axes of authority, and it was fitted also with a hem or edging of vermilion-coloured silk. Hwan-shuh had no right to such a robe; and the people of the capital, in saying to his emissary (子) that they would go with one to Yuh, promise, in effect, to make him the marquis of Tsin. 鵠 was the name of a town or city in the territory of K'ëuh-yuh. 云 in l.6 is the particle. In stanza 3, 'we have heard your orders,' means the orders from Hwan-shuh communicated to his partizans in Tsin.—Lacharme has erred egregiously in translating the 3d and 4th lines of stt.1,2, and the 3d line of st.3.—' Homines simplici cultu induti, in vestibus quibus collare rubrum assuitur, &c., se deduct viro cuidam in regione Kou dicto.'...'Ego quæ audivi Imperatoris mandata,' &c.

The rhymes are—in st. 1, 鑿,襮,沃,樂, cat. 2: in 2, 皓,繡,鵠,憂, cat. 3, t. 2: in 3, 粼,命,人, cat.12, t. 1.

IV. *Tsëaou lëaou.*

椒聊

椒聊之實，蕃衍
盈升。彼其之子，
碩大無朋。椒聊
且。遠條且。

椒聊之實，蕃衍
盈匊。彼其之子，
碩大且篤。
且。遠條且。

1　The clusters of the pepper plant,
Large and luxuriant, would fill a pint.
That hero there
Is large and peerless.
O the pepper plant!
How its shoots extend!

2　The clusters of the pepper plant,
Large and luxuriant, would fill both your hands.
That hero there
Is large and generous.
O the pepper plant!
How its shoots extend;

V. *Chow-mow.*

綢繆

綢繆束薪。三星
在天。今夕。何夕。
見此。良人。子
兮。

1　Round and round the firewood is bound;
And the Three Stars appear in the sky.
This evening is what evening,
That I see this good man?

Ode 4. Allusive and metaphorical. SUPPOSED TO CELEBRATE THE POWER AND PROSPERITY OF HWAN-SHUH, AND TO PREDICT THE GROWTH OF HIS FAMILY. The Preface gives this interpretation of the piece, and Choo allows that he does not know to what to refer it.

Ll. 1, 2, in both the stt. 椒 is the pepper plant; 聊 is to be taken as a mere particle. 蕃=茂, 'luxuriant;' 衍=廣, 'wide,' 'large.' 升 is a pint measure, and 匊 is the two hands full. Both words express the great productiveness of the plant; and as Yen-she observes, it is folly to go about trying to determine the size of the old pint. Evidently there is a metaphorical element in the allusion in these lines, and the two last.

Ll. 3, 4. 彼其之子 has often been met with. 碩 and 大 intensify each other. 朋=比, our 'peer.' 篤=厚, 'generous.'

Ll. 5, 6. 且,=as in iv. III. 2, et al. It here gives the sentiment a tinge of regret.

此粲者何。
粲者。子兮子兮。如
戶。今夕何夕。見此
綢繆束楚。三星在
此邂逅何。
邂逅。子兮子兮。如
隅。今夕何夕。見此
綢繆束芻。三星在
子兮。如此良人何。

O me! O me!
That I should get a good man like this!

2 Round and round the grass is bound;
And the Three Stars are seen from the corner.
This evening is what evening,
That we have this unexpected meeting?
Happy pair! Happy pair!
That we should have this unexpected meeting!

3 Round and round the thorns are bound;
And the Three Stars are seen from the door.
This evening is what evening,
That I see this beauty?
O me! O me!
That I should see a beauty like this!

The rhymes are—in st.1, 升朋, cat. 6; 聊，
條。(and in 2), cat. 3, t. 1 : in 2, 芻, 篤, ib., t. 3.

Ode 5. Allusive. HUSBAND AND WIFE EX-
PRESS THEIR DELIGHT AT THEIR UNEXPECTED
UNION. The Preface says that the piece was
directed against the disorder of Tsin, through
which the people were unable to contract marriages at the proper season assigned for them.
Hence Maou would make it out that we have
here the joy of husband and wife, as married at
the fitting time, in contrast with the existing
disappointment and misery. Choo, on the contrary, says we have here simply the joy of a
newly married pair. So far I must agree with
Choo; the joy indicated is not that of a past
age, but of the time then being. The pair,
however, would seem to rejoice in the realiza-
tion of a happiness from which they had seemed
hitherto debarred.

L. 1 in all the stt. 綢繆 denotes 'the app.
of the bundles bound or tied together.' 芻

means 'grass,' generally fodder; but here we
must think of it as gathered for the purpose of
fuel. The point of the allusion in this line is
hard to tell. The idea of union, in the bringing
things together, may, possibly, be it.

L. 2. By the 'Three Stars,' we are to understand a constellation so denominated. Maou
understood by it the constellation of Ts'an (參
宿) in Orion; and K'ang-shing, whom Choo
follows, that of Sin (心宿) in Scorpio.
The Ts'an would be visible at dusk in the horizon in the 10th month, a proper time according
to Maou for contracting marriage;—hence his
view of the ode. The Sin would be visible in
the 5th month, when, acc. to Ch'ing, the proper
season was past. The mention of the constellation as opposite the corner (i. e., the south-east
corner of the house), and the door, ought not to
be pressed to a special significance. It is only
the usual variation for the sake of rhythm.

Ll.3—6. In st.1 the lady is supposed to be
soliloquizing, and calls her husband 良人.

VI. *Tĕ too.*

他人。不如我同姓。

菁。獨行睘睘。豈無

有杕之杜。其葉菁

佽焉

焉。人無兄弟。胡不

嗟行之人。胡不比

他人。不如我同父。

湑。獨行踽踽。豈無

有杕之杜。其葉湑

杕杜

1　There is a solitary russet pear tree,
　　[But] its leaves are luxuriant.
　　Alone I walk unbefriended;—
　　Is it because there are no other people?
　　But none are like the sons of one's father.
　　O ye travellers,
　　Why do ye not sympathize with me?
　　Without brothers as I am,
　　Why do ye not help me?

2　There is a solitary russet pear tree,
　　[But] its leaves are abundant.
　　Alone I walk uncared for;—
　　Is it that there are not other people?
　　But none are like those of one's own surname.

'the good man.' Mencius, IV.Pt.ii.XXXIII.. is decisive in favour of this view; and the opinion of Maou, that it is a designation of the wife, must be rejected. In st.2, both husband and wife are supposed to be the speakers, congratulating each other. 邂逅 gives the idea of 'a meeting,' and one which is unexpected, 'not previously arranged.' Maou erroneously understands it of 'mutual delight.' In st.3, the husband solilo-quizes. 粲—美 'beautiful.' Maou, from an expression in the 國語, that 'three ladies make a ts'an,'—a bevy of beauties, understands the term of the wife and two concubines of a great officer! The 如...何 in all the stanzas expresses the delight of the parties.

The rhymes in st. l are—薪 天, 人, 人, cat. 12, t. 1 ; in 2, 芻, 隅, 逅 逅, cat. 4, t. 1 : in 3, 楚, 戶, 者, 者, cat. 5, t 2.

Ode 6. Allusive. LAMENT OF AN INDIVIDUAL DEPRIVED OF HIS BROTHERS AND RELATIVES, OR FORSAKEN BY THEM. A historical interpretation of the piece is given, as we should have expected, in the Preface, which refers it to the marquis Ch'aou, opposed by his uncle of K'ŭh-yuh, and plotted against by other members of his House. This, however, is only conjecture. The words may have a manifold application.

Ll. 1, 2. in both stt. 杜.—see on li. V. 杕 =特 'the app. of standing alone.' 有 is, I think, the descriptive, to be construed with 杕. 湑湑 and 菁菁 are synonymous, and describe the abundant frondage of the tree. The allusion is understood to be by way of contrast. —The tree, though solitary, was covered by its leaves; the speaker was solitary and desolate of friends.

侁焉。 胡不 兄弟。 人無 比焉。 胡不 之人 嗟行

O ye travellers,
Why do ye not sympathize with me?
Without brothers as I am,
Why do ye not help me?

VII. *Kaou k'ew.*

羔裘

羔裘豹袪（一章） 自我人居居 豈無他人 維子之故。

羔裘豹褎（二章） 自我人究究 豈無他人 維子之好。

1 Lamb's fur and leopard's cuffs,
 You use us with unkindness.
 Might we not find another chief?
 But [we stay] because of your forefathers.

2 Lamb's fur and leopard's cuffs,
 You use us with cruel unkindness.
 Might we not find another chief?
 But [we stay] from our regard to you.

Ll. 3—5. 踽踽,—see Men. VII. Pt. ii. XXXVII. 9. Ll. 4, 5 express the speaker's pain in being forsaken by his brothers and relatives. 同父='brothers by the same father,' 同姓 =blood relations, 'descended from the same ancestor.'

Ll. 6—8. 嗟行之人=嗟歎行路之人, 'O ye wayfaring men!' 比 and 侁 are both explained by 'to help;' but the former is referred to the sympathy of the mind, the latter to its demonstration in the act.

The rhymes are—in st. 1, 杜, 湑, 踽, 父, cat. 5, t. 2: in 2, 菁, 睘 (prop. cat. 14), 姓, cat. 11: in both stt., 比, 侁, cat. 15, t. 3.

Ode 7. Narrative. THE PEOPLE OF SOME GREAT OFFICER COMPLAIN OF HIS HARD TREATMENT OF THEM, WHILE THEY DECLARE THEIR LOYALTY. Choo does not attempt to interpret these verses, but dissents from the view of the Preface which I have followed.

L. 1, in both stt.—See on vii. VI. The great officer, to whose territory the speakers belonged, is here indicated by his dress. 袪 and 褎 are synonyms, signifying the cuff of the jacket. L. 2. Maou explains 自 by 用, 'to use.' He also says that 居居 and 究究 are synonyms, denoting 'the app. of evil intentions, and of want of sympathy.'

Ll. 3, 4 tell how the speakers might seek the lands of some other great officer, who would treat them better, but that they felt an attachment to the family of their chief, and even to himself. 故=于故舊之人.—as in the translation.

The rhymes are in st. 1—袪, 居, 故, cat. 5, t. 1: in 2, 褎, 究, 好, cat. 3, t. 2.

VIII. *Paou yu.*

鴇羽

一章
肅肅鴇羽。集于苞栩。
王事靡盬。不能蓺稷
父母何怙。悠悠蒼
天。曷其有所。

二章
肅肅鴇翼。集于苞棘。
王事靡盬。不能蓺黍
父母何食。悠悠蒼
天。曷其有極。

1　*Suh-suh* go the feathers of the wild geese,
As they settle on the bushy oaks.
The king's affairs must not be slackly discharged,
And [so] we cannot plant our sacrificial millet and millet;—
What will our parents have to rely on?
O thou distant and azure Heaven!
When shall we be in our places again?

2　*Suh-suh* go the wings of the wild geese,
As they settle on the bushy jujube trees.
The king's affairs must not be slackly discharged,
And [so] we cannot plant our millet and sacrificial millet;—
How shall our parents be supplied with food?
O thou distant and azure Heaven!
When shall [our service] have an end?

Ode 8. Allusive or metaphorical. THE MEN OF TSIN, CALLED OUT TO WARFARE BY THE KING'S ORDER, MOURN OVER THE CONSEQUENT SUFFERING OF THEIR PARENTS, AND LONG FOR THEIR RETURN TO THEIR ORDINARY AGRICULTURAL PURSUITS. The piece is referred, we may presume correctly, to some time after duke Ch'aou, when, for more than 50 years, a struggle went on between the ambitious chiefs of K'euh-yuh, and the marquises proper of Tsin. The people were in the main loyal to Tsin, and one king and another sent expeditions to support them. There were of course great trouble and confusion in the State, and the work of agriculture was much interfered with. Këang Ping-chang compares the ode with the 4th of last Book. The strength of the home feeling in the ancient Chinese appears in both pieces. 'Here,' says Këang, ' the interest turns more on the destitution of the parents, because the filial son of Wei could rely on his elder brother at home, to provide for the wants of the family.'

Ll. 1, 2, in all the stt. The *paou* is described as similar to a wild-goose, but larger, without any hind toe. The last particular may be doubted. I think the bird intended may be the Grey Lag. 行, in st. 4, is descriptive of the rows or orderly manner which distinguishes the flight of wild geese. *Suh-suh* is intended to give the sound of the birds in flying. 集。—as i. II.

1. 苞=叢生, 'growing thickly together,' 'bushy.' 栩 is a species of oak; 棘.—as in iii. VII. The *paou* is said not to be fond of lighting on trees, the attempt to perch occasioning it trouble and pain. That is not the proper

有天。悠母稻不事苞行。肅_{三章}
常。曷悠何粱。能靡桑。集蕭
其蒼嘗。父蓺鹽。王于鴇

3　*Suh-suh* go the rows of the wild geese,
　　As they rest on the bushy mulberry trees.
　　The king's business must not be slackly discharged,
　　And [so] we cannot plant our rice and maize;—
　　How shall our parents get food?
　　O thou distant and azure Heaven!
　　When shall we get [back] to our ordinary lot?

IX. *Woo e.*

且子六豈且子七豈
煥之兮。日吉之兮。日　無
兮。衣。不無兮。衣。不無　衣
　　安如衣。　安如衣。
　　安如　　安如

1　How can it be said that he is without robes?
　　He has those of the seven orders;
　　But it is better that he get those robes from you.
　　That will secure tranquillity and good fortune.

2　How can it be said that he is without robes?
　　He has those of the six orders;
　　But it is better that he get those robes from you.
　　That will secure tranquillity and permanence.

position for it; and Choo thinks that the soldiers introduce it in this position as metaphorical of the hardship of their lot.
Ll. 3—5. The 'king's business' was the operations of his commissioners aginst K'euh-yuh, in which the men of Tsin were, of course, required to take part. 鹽 is defined as 'not strong or durable;' and also by 略, 'perfunctory,' 'slackly performed.' 靡＝無, and must here be construed as in the translation. 黍 and 稷,—see on vi.I. 稻 is paddy; and 粱＝粟類, 'a kind of maize.' 嘗＝食, 'to eat.'

Ll.6,7. L.6,—see on vi.I. 曷, 'when,'—as in vi.II. 2. 其 must be translated 'in the 1st person; or we might keep its demonstrative force,—'when shall there be this, the getting the [proper] place [for us]?' &c.
The rhymes are—in st.1, 羽, 栩, 鹽, 黍, 枯, 所, cat. 5, t. 2: in 2, 翼, 棘, 稷, 食, 極, cat. 1, t. 3: in 3, 行,, 桑, 粱, 嘗, 常, cat.10.
Ode 9. Narrative. A REQUEST TO THE KING'S ENVOY FOR THE ACKNOWLEDGMENT OF DUKE WOO AS MARQUIS OF TSIN. In B. C. 678, the struggle between the branches of the House of

X. *Yëw te che too.*

有杜之杜

好之。曷飲食之。
噬肯來遊。中心
道周。彼君子兮。
有杕之杜。生于

好之。曷飲食之。
噬肯適我。中心
道左。彼君子兮。
有杕之杜。生于

1 There is a solitary russet pear tree,
　Growing on the left of the way.
　That princely man there!
　He might be willing to come to me.
　In the centre of my heart I love him,
　[But] how shall I supply him with drink and food?

2 There is a solitary russet pear tree,
　Growing where the way makes a compass.
　That princely man there!
　He might be willing to come and ramble [with me].
　In the centre of my heart I love him;
　[But] how shall I supply him with drink and food?

Tsin was brought to a termination, and Ching, earl of K'euh-yuh, called after his death duke Ching (成公), made himself master of the whole State, 67 years after the investiture of his grandfather, Hwan-shuh. It was an act of spoliation, but the usurper bribed the reigning king, He (僖王), and got himself acknowledged as marquis of Tsin. In this piece we must suppose that an application is made in his behalf, by one of his officers, to an envoy from the court, for the royal confirmation. The daring of the application is equalled by the arrogance of its terms. Choo supposes the application was made directly by Woo himself, so that by the 于 of L2 the emperor is meant. This is not likely. The remark of the Preface, that the piece is expressive of admiration for duke Woo, is not worth discussion.

Ll.1,2, in both stt. The different ranks in ancient China were marked by the number of carriages, robes, &c., conferred by the king. The prince of a great State had *seven* of the symbols of rank or, as we may call them here, orders, on his robes: on the upper robe three; on the lower robe four. Those robes had previously belonged to the marquisate of Tsin, which Woo had now seized; and he might have pro-

ceeded to assume them at once, but he preferred to get the sanction of the king to his doing so, because that would tranquillize the minds of men, and strengthen his own position. The prince of a State, when serving at court as a minister of the crown, was held to be of lower rank by one degree; hence the seven orders of st.1 appear in st.2 as only 6. 日,—as in the translation; it is not a particle merely. 于—'you;'—spoken to the king's envoy.

L.3. 燠=煖, 'warm;' but Choo makes it 久, 'long-lasting;'—in consequence, that is, of the thickness of the robes, and their good quality. Others give the character the meaning of 安, 'tranquil,' 'secure.'

Both Maou and Choo note that each stanza consists of three lines; but the rhythm shows that each should be arranged in 4 lines, 七兮 and 六兮 forming lines themselves.

The rhymes then are—in st.1 衣, 衣 (and in 2), cat.1, t.1; 七, 吉, cat.12, t.3: in 2, 六, 燠, cat.3, t.3.

XI. *Koh sang.*

葛生

誰爛角誰于葛誰于葛
與兮枕與域生與野生
獨予粲獨。蒙獨。蒙
旦美兮息予棘處予楚
。亡錦。美。。美。
此衾于蘞蘞
。蒙蔓蔓
爛予蔓
兮美
亡
此
。

1　The dolichos grows, covering the thorn trees;
　　The convolvulus spreads all over the waste.
　　The man of my admiration is no more here;—
　　With whom can I dwell?—I abide alone.

2　The dolichos grows, covering the jujube trees;
　　The convolvulus spreads all over the tombs.
　　The man of my admiration is no more here;
　　With whom can I dwell?—I rest alone.

3　How beautiful was the pillow of horn!
　　How splendid was the embroidered coverlet!
　　The man of my admiration is no more here;—
　　With whom can I dwell?—Alone [I wait for] the morning.

Ode 10. Metaphorical. SOME ONE REGRETS THE POVERTY OF HIS CIRCUMSTANCES, WHICH PREVENTED HIM FROM GATHERING AROUND HIM COMPANIONS WHOM HE ADMIRED. The Preface finds in this piece a censure of duke Woo, who did not seek to gather worthy officers around him. Choo repudiates, correctly, such an interpretation, and the K'ang-he editors make no attempt to support it.

Ll. 1, 2, in both stt. L. 1,—see on the 6th ode. The 'left' of the road means the east, 周 is explained by 曲, 'a bend.' 'The way went round the spot (周繞之),' says Ying-tah. Such a solitary tree would afford little or no shelter, and so the speaker sees in it a resemblance to his own condition.

Ll. 3—6. 噬 is an initial particle. We have previously had 逝, with the same pronunciation, used in the same way; and Han Ying here read 逝. 飲 and 食 are now both in the 3d tone, with the meaning which I have given.

The rhymes are—in st. 1, 左, 我, cat. 17: in 2, 周, 遊, cat. 3, t. 1. The last two lines

Ode 11. Allusive and narrative. A WIFE MOURNS THE DEATH OF HER HUSBAND, REFUSING TO BE COMFORTED, AND WILL CHERISH HIS MEMORY TILL HER OWN DEATH. The Preface says that the piece was directed against duke Heen (獻公; B. C. 675—650), who occasioned the death of many by his frequent wars. This charge could, indeed, be made against him; but there is nothing in the piece to make us refer it to his time.

Ll. 1, 2, in stt. 1, 2. With the names 葛, 楚, and 棘 we are by this time familiar 蘞 is a convolvulus; probably the *ipomœa pentadactylis*,—a creeper found abundantly in Hongkong, and called by the common people, from the way in which its leaves grow, 五爪龍, 'the five-clawed dragon.' 域 is in the sense of 塋域, 'a place of graves.' These two lines are taken by Maou and Choo as allusive; the speaker being led by the sight of the weak plants supported by the trees, ground, and tombs, to think of her own

do not rhyme, unless we make those in the one stanza rhyme with those in the other.

其 後。 百 夏 冬 _{五章} 其 後。 百 冬 夏 _{四章}
室。 歸 歲 之 之   居。 歸 歲 之 之
于 之 日。 夜。   于 之 夜。 日。

4 Through the [long] days of summer,
   Through the [long] nights of winter [shall I be alone],
   Till the lapse of a hundred years,
   When I shall go home to his abode.

5 Through the [long] nights of winter,
   Through the [long] days of summer [shall I be alone],
   Till the lapse of a hundred years,
   When I shall go home to his chamber.

XII. *Ts'ae ling.*

人 亦 舍 信。 苟 之 之 苓。 采 采
之 無 旃。 舍 亦 爲 巓。 首 苓 苓
爲 然。 苟 旃 無 言。 人 陽 采

1 Would you gather the liquorice, would you gather the liquorice,
   On the top of Show-yang?
   When men tell their stories,
   Do not readily believe them;
   Put them aside, put them aside.
   Do not readily assent to them;

desolate, unsupported condition. But we may also take them as narrative, and descriptive of the battle ground, where her husband had met his death.

Ll. 3, 4, 予美一我 所美之人,—as in the translation, a designation of the husband. Yen Ts'an makes 亡此一死於 此, 'died here;' but I prefer the version I have adopted. 誰與獨處一誰與乎獨 處而已,—as is the translation. Some critics call attention to the rhyme between 與 and 處 in the line; but it is not carried out in st. 2.

St. 3. The pillow of horn and embroidered coverlet had been ornaments of the bridal chamber; and as the widow thinks of them, her grief becomes more intense. 獨旦一獨處至 旦, 'I dwell alone till the morning.' Some would construe ll. 1, 2 in the pres. tense, and

infer that the speaker had not been long married. Maou takes the pathos out of the stanza by explaining it of some ancient sacrificial usages. Stt. 4, 5. The lady shows the grand virtue of a Chinese widow, in that she will never marry again. And her grief would not be assuaged. The days would all seem long summer days, and the nights all long winter nights; so that a hundred long years would seem to drag their course. The 'dwelling' and the 'chamber' are to be understood of the grave.

The rhymes are—in st. 1, 楚, 野, 處, cat. 5, t. 2: in 2, 棘, 域, 息, cat. 1, t. 3: in 3, 粲, 爛, 旦, cat. 14: in 4, 夜, 居, cat. 5, t. 1: in 5, 日, 室, cat 12, t. 3.

Ode 12. Metaphorical. AGAINST GIVING EAR TO SLANDERERS. This piece, like the last, is supposed to have duke Hëen for its object; but such a reference is open to the same remark as there.

言，胡得焉。

采苦采苦，首陽之下。
人之爲言。苟亦無與。

人之爲言。胡得焉。

采葑采葑，首陽之東。
人之爲言。苟亦無從。

舍旃舍旃。苟亦無然。

人之爲言。胡得焉。

And, when men tell their stories,
How will they find course?

2 Would you gather the sowthistle, would you gather the sow-
thistle,
At the foot of Show-yang?
When men tell their stories,
Do not readily approve them;—
Put them aside, put them aside.
Do not readily assent to them;
And, when men tell their stories,
How will they find course?

3 Would you gather the mustard plant, would you gather the
mustard plant,
On the east of Show-yang?
When men tell their stories,
Do hot readily listen to them;—
Put them aside, put them aside.
Do not readily assent to them;
And, when men tell their stories,
How will they find course?

<hr>

Ll. 1, 2, in all the stt. These lines are metaphorical of baseless rumours, carrying their
refutation on the face of them. The plants
mentioned were not to be found about Show-
yang. That any one might know, and a person,
asked to look for them on it, would never think
of doing so. In the same way baseless slanders
might, by a little exercise of sense and discrimination, be disregarded. The lines are in the
imperative mood, but I have translated them
interrogatively, the better to indicate their relation to those that follow. 荼,—see on iii. XIII.

4; 苦,—i. q. the 荼 of iii. X. 2; 葑,—see on
iii. X. 1. Show-yang,—see on Ans. XVI. xii.

Ll. 3–5. 之 may be construed as the sign
of the genitive. 爲言,—'make words,'—
tell their stories. Some take 爲=僞 'hy-
pocritical,' 'false;' but it is not necessary to do
so. Maou takes 苟 in the sense of 誠 'really'
or 'if really.' It is better to take it in the sense
of 且, as I have done, and treat 亦 as a

particle; unless, indeed, we take the two terms
as a compound particle, as Wang Yin-che says
that 蓋亦 always is, and not attempt to
translate them at all. 與=許, 'to grant,'
'to approve of;' 從, 'to follow,' is here, both
by Maou and Choo, explained by 聽 'to
hearken to.' 庶,—as in ix. IV.

Ll. 6—8. 然 — 'to account correct.' Choo
makes 人 the nominative to 得,—'How will
those men attain to spread their slanders.?' I
think we should take the whole of the 7th line
as the subject. The meaning comes to the same.

The rhymes are—in st. 1, 苓, 巔, 信, cat.
12, t. 1: in 2, 苦, 下., 與, cat. 5, t. 2: in 3,
蒲, 栗, 從, cat. 9: and in all the stanzas, 庶,
言, 然, 焉, cat. 14.

CONCLUDING NOTE ON THE BOOK. As the
omission in Book VIII. of all odes about duke
Hwan was matter of surprise, so in this Book
we must think it strange that there is silence
about duke Wăn, the hero of Tsin. In the odes,
as we have them, there is a good deal that is
pleasing, and has more than a local interest.
The 1st, as a picture of cheerful, genial ways;
the 8th, as an exhibition of filial regard and anxiety; and the 11th, as a plaintive expression of
the feelings of a lonely widow, bear to be read
and read again. The 2d, in the view which it
gives us of death, and the 5th, in the joy which
it describes of a union unexpectedly attained,
have a human attraction. And in none of the
others is there any of the lewdness which de-
files so many of the odes of Wei and Ch'ing.

I. *Keu lin.*

秦一之十一

車鄰

有車鄰鄰。有
馬白顛。未見
君子寺人之
令。

阪有漆。隰有
栗。既見君子。
並坐鼓瑟。今
者不樂。逝者

1 He has many carriages, giving forth their *lin-lin*;
  He has horses with their white foreheads.
  Before we can see our prince,
  We must get the services of the eunuch.

2 On the hill-sides are varnish trees;
  In the low wet grounds are chestnuts.
  When we have seen our prince,
  We sit together with him, and they play on their lutes.
  If now we do not take our joy,
  The time will pass till we are octogenarians.

TITLE OF THE BOOK.—秦一之十一, *The odes of Ts'in; Book XI. of Part I.* The State of Ts'in took its name from its earliest principal city,—in the pres. dis. of Ts'ing-shwuy (清水), Ts'in-chow (秦州), Kan-suh. Its chiefs claimed to be descended from Yih, or Pih-yih (伯益), Shun's forester, and the assistant of the great Yu in his labours on the deluge, from whom he got the clan-name of Ying (嬴). Among his descendants, we are told, there was a Chung-keueh (仲潏), who resided among the wild tribes of the west for the protection of the western borders of the kingdom of Shang. The sixth in descent from him, called Ta-loh (大駱), had a son, Fei-tsze (非子), who had charge of the herds of horses belonging to king Hëaou (B.C. 908—894), and in consequence of his good services was invested with the small territory of Ts'in, as an attached State. His great-grandson, called Ts'in-chung, or Chung of Ts'in (秦仲), was made a great officer of the court by king Seuen, in B.C. 826; and his grandson, again, known as duke Sëang (襄公), in consequence of his loyal services, in 769, when the capital of Chow was moved to the east, was raised to the dignity of an earl, and took his place among the great feudal princes of the kingdom, receiving a large portion of territory, which included the ancient capital of the House of Chow.—In course of time, Ts'in, as is well known, superseded the dynasty of Chow, having gradually moved its capital more and more to the east, after the example, in earlier times, of Chow itself. The people of Ts'in were, no doubt, composed of the wild tribes of the west, though the ruling chiefs among them may have come originally from the more civilized China on the east. The descent from Pih-yih belongs to legend, not to history.

亡。逝 者 鼓 子。既 隰 阪^三其
者 不 簧。並 見 有 有 墊。
其 樂。今 坐 君 楊。桑。

3 On the hill-sides are mulberry trees;
In the low wet grounds are willows.
When we have seen our prince,
We sit together with him, and they play on their organs.
If now we do not take our joy,
The time will pass till we are no more.

II. *Sze t'ëeh.*

于 從 媚 公 在 六 孔 駟^二 駟
狩。公 子。之 手。轡 阜。驖 驖

1 His four iron-black horses are in very fine condition;
The six reins are in the hand [of the charioteer].
The ruler's favourites
Follow him to the chase.

Ode 1. Narrative and allusive. CELEBRATING THE GROWING OPULENCE AND STYLE OF SOME LORD OF TS‘IN, AND THE PLEASURES AND FREEDOM OF HIS COURT. The Preface says that the lord of Ts‘in here intended was Ts‘in-chung, mentioned in the note above. Choo, however, remarks that there is nothing in the piece to make us refer it to Ts‘in-chung. This is true; but we must believe it was made at an early period, when the State was emerging from its obscurity and weakness.

St. 1. 鄰 鄰 is defined as 'the noise of many chariots.' The character here was probably formed originally by 車, with the phonetic on the right. 顚, here, = 顙, 'forehead.' The horses would have a white spot in their foreheads. By 君子 we are to understand 'the ruler of Ts‘in.' 寺人 = 閹官 'a eunuch-officer.' There were eunuchs about the court of Chow, though not in any great number. From the Tso-chuen we know that in the Ch‘un-ts‘ëw period, they were in the great feudal courts. The mention of one here, whose services were necessary to announce the wish of a high officer (such we must suppose the speaker to have been) to have an interview with the ruler, is intended to show that the court of Ts‘in was now assuming all the insignia of the other States of the kingdom.

Stt. 2, 3, ll. 1, 2. Perhaps the allusion here is to indicate that as the hill-sides and low grounds had their appropriate trees, so music was appropriate to the court. 阪,—see vii. XV. 1. Here 'banks,' however had better give place to 'hill-sides.' The Shwoh-wǎn defines the term by 山脅.

Ll. 3, 4. Hwang Tso observes on 並坐, that it is to be understood of the ruler and his guests, sitting together in the same apartment, but not of their doing so, 'shoulder to shoulder,' without distinction of rank. We are not to suppose that the ruler and his guests played themselves on the instruments mentioned; the music was from the proper officers, an accompaniment of the feasting which was going on. 簧,—see on vi. III. 1.

Ll. 5, 6. 今者 makes the meaning of 逝者 plain enough. In x. l. 2, 逝 is used of the passing away of the year. We might translate 逝者 by 'hereafter;'—comp. 往者 in Men. VII. Pt. ii. XXX. 2. I take 其 as in x. l., —將. Eighty years old is called 耋.

The rhymes are—in st. 1, 鄰 顚 令 &c. cat. 12, t. 1: in 2, 漆 栗 室 耋 ib., t. 3: in 3, 桑 楊 簧 亡 cat. 10.

載　輶　四　遊三　舍　公　辰　奉二
獫　車　馬　于章　拔　曰　牡　時章
歇　鸞　既　北　　則　左　孔　辰
驕。鑣。閑。園。　獲。之。碩。牡。

2　The male animals of the season are made to present themselves,
　　The males in season, of very large size.
　　The ruler says, 'To the left of them;'
　　Then he lets go his arrows and hits.

3　He rambles in the northern park;
　　His four horses display their training.
　　Light carriages, with bells at the horses' bits,
　　Convey the long and short-mouthed dogs.

Ode 2. Narrative. CELEBRATING THE GROWING OPULENCE OF THE LORDS OF TS'IN, AS SEEN IN THEIR HUNTING. The Preface refers this piece to duke Sĕang, also mentioned in the introductory note, on his being raised to the dignity of earl by king P'ing, and assuming the style becoming his rank; but such a reference is entirely outside the piece itself.

St. 1. 鐵 is descriptive of the colour of the horses. Lŭh Tëen says that the term has reference not only to their iron colour, but also to their iron strength (堅壯如鐵). Maou explains 阜 by 'large (大);' Choo adds 肥, 'fat.' L. 2. We must understand that the reins were in the hand of the charioteer; but I do not see, with Maou, that the line is intended to indicate his skill, but simply his holding the reins in his hand. With a team of 4 horses, there were of course 8 reins, but the two inner reins of the outsiders were somehow attached to the carriage; so that the driver held only 6 in his hand. L. 3. 公,—as in iii.XIII. 3, et al. We need not translate it by 'duke.' 媚 is in the sense of 愛, 'to love.' Yen Ts'an and Choo both understand the line as in the translation; Maou's view of it is much too far-fetched,—'the duke's officers, who love him above them, and the people below them.' L. 4. 狩, 'the winter hunt,' is here probably=·the chase,' generally.

St. 2 describes the action of the chase. As a nominative to 奉 we must understand 虞人, 'the forester,' and his attendants, who have surrounded the animals in season, so as to afford plenty of sport. 時＝是 'these;' 辰＝時, 'season;' 牡＝獸之牡者, 'the males of the animals.' The 'these' represents the scene graphically, as if passing before the speaker's eye. L. 3. 左之, 'left it,'—to

the left with the carriage. L. 4. 拔＝矢 末, 'the end of an arrow,' not 'the barb,' as Williams says; so that 舍拔＝放矢, 'he discharges his arrows.'

St. 3 supposes the hunting finished. The action is now transferred to some park, north of the capital of Ts'in. 園 is here evidently synonymous with 囿, 'a park,' though it is now confined mainly to the signification of 'garden.' Ying-tah says that the difference between them was in their being enclosed, the 囿 by a wall, and the 園 by a hedge or fence. L. 2. 閑＝習 or 調習, 'to put through their practice.' The horses now went gently along, not driven about as in the chase, and displayed the skill with which they had been trained. 輶＝輕, 'light.' These were used to prevent the animals of the chase from escaping out of the circle in which they were enclosed, and for the purpose here mentioned. On each side of the bits (鑣) of the horses in them were suspended bells, called here 鸞, being supposed to emit a sound like that of the fabulous bird so called. L. 4. Both Maou and Choo say that 獫 was the name for 'long-muzzled dogs,' and 歇驕, that for 'dogs with short muzzles.' These last characters, if we are to accept this explanation of them, should be formed with 犬, instead of 欠 and 馬, as indeed they are in the Shwoh-wăn.

The rhymes are:—in st. 1, 阜手狩, cat. 3, t. 2: in 2, 碩獲, cat. 5, t. 3: in 3, 園閑, cat. 14; 鑣驕, cat. 2, t. 1.

III. *Sëaou jung.*

小戎

小戎俴收。
五楘梁輈。
游環脅驅。
陰靷鋈續。
文茵暢轂。
駕我騏馵。
言念君子。
温其如玉。
在其板屋。

1 [There is] his short war carriage;—
With the ridge-like end of its pole, elegantly bound in five places;
With its slip rings and side straps;
And the traces attached by gilt rings to the masked transverse;
With its beautiful mat of tiger's skin, and its long naves;
With its piebalds, and horses with white left feet.
When I think of my husband [thus],
Looking bland and soft as a piece of jade;
Living there in his plank house;
It sends confusion into all the corners of my heart.

Ode 3. Narrative. THE LADY OF AN OFFICER ABSENT ON AN EXPEDITION AGAINST THE TRIBES OF THE WEST GIVES A GLOWING DESCRIPTION OF HIS CHARIOT, AND PRAISES HIMSELF, EXPRESSING, BUT WITHOUT MURMURING, HER OWN REGRET AT HIS ABSENCE. The Preface says the piece is in praise of duke Sëang; which is altogether foreign to its spirit, though it may, or may not, have belonged to his time. He received a charge from king P‘ing to subdue the tribes referred to in it, and the struggle between them and Ts‘in long continued. Both the Preface and Choo suppose two speakers in each stanza, referring the 1st six lines to the followers of the officer, and the last four to his wife. This destroys the unity of the verses. They are, evidently, all the language of the wife. and we thus have in her a fine specimen of a Ts‘in matron, public-spirited and tender-hearted;— see Këang Ping-chang, *in loc.*

St.1. L.1. 戎 here denotes the ordinary war-chariot, called 'small (小),' to distinguish it from a larger one, which we shall by and by meet with. 收 is used in the sense of 軫, 'the boards forming the back and front of the carriage.' They are called 'shallow (俴＝淺),' or short as we must translate, because the war chariot was much shorter than the carriage or waggon used for ordinary purposes. The width of both was the same,—6 ft. 6 in ; but the latter was 8 ft. long, and the former only 4 ft. 4 in. L.2. 輈 was the end of the pole, where the yoke for the two inside horses was attached. It rose in a curve, like the ridge of a house (梁),

and was bound in 5 places with leather, which gave it an elegant appearance. 楘 ＝'ornamental bands of leather.' L. 3. 'The slip (游 ＝moving) rings' were attached somehow to the backs of the inside horses, and the off reins of the outsides were drawn through them, so that the driver could keep those horses in control, if they tried to start off from the others. 'The side straps,' it is said, were fixed to the ends of the yoke and the front of the carriage, running along the 'sides' of the insiders, and so preventing the other horses from pressing in upon them. The force of the 驅 I cannot discover.—The student must bear in mind, that in those times the team of a chariot consisted of 4 horses, which were driven abreast or nearly so, and not yoked two behind, and two in front. L.4. 靷 means a trace (所以引). What is here spoken of are the traces attached in front to the necks or breasts of the outsiders, and behind to the front of the chariot. The places where they were so attached to the carriage were somehow masked or concealed (陰); the attachment (續) was made by means of gilt rings. L.5. 文茵 is the mat of tiger's skin' which was spread in the carriage. 暢 ＝長, 'long,' For the sake of greater strength the naves of the wheels in a warchariot were made of extraordinary size. L.6. 'Yoked in it are our piebalds,' &c. The terms descriptive of the horses are defined as in the translation.

鋈錞。蒙伐有苑。　俴駟孔群。厹矛（三章）　胡然我念之。　在邑。方何為期。　言念君子。溫其　之合。鋈以觼軜。　騧驪是驂。龍盾　在手。騏駵是中。　四牡孔阜。六轡（二章）　亂我心曲。

2　His four horses are in very fine condition,
And the six reins are in the hand [of the charioteer].
Piebald, and bay with black mane, are the insides;
Yellow with black mouth, and black, are the outsides;
Side by side are placed the dragon-figured shields;
Gilt are the buckles for the inner reins.
I think of my husband [thus],
Looking so mild in the cities there.
What time can be fixed for his return?
Oh! how I think of him!

3　His mail-covered team moves in great harmony;
There are the trident spears with their gilt ends;
And the beautiful feather-figured shield;

Ll. 7—10. 言 is the particle. 君子,— 'husband,' as in i. X., *et al.* The 其 in l. 8, and in the next st., increases the descriptive force of 溫. The tribes of the west lived in plank houses or log huts. The lady sees her husband in one, which he had taken, we may suppose, from the enemy. 心 曲,—' bends of the heart.'

St. 2. 四牡,—the horses were entire. 孔 阜,—as in II. 1. L. 3. 駵 is 'a red horse, with a black mane.' 中 denotes the 'middle' horses, the insiders, called 服馬. L. 4. The outsiders were called *ts'an*. Maou defines 騧 as in the transl. L. 4. The shields are called 'dragon,' from having the figure of a dragon drawn upon them. They were set up in the front of the carriage, and helped to protect those in it from the missiles and arrows of the enemy.

L. 6. By 軜 is meant the two inner reins of the outsiders, which were attached by buckles (觼=環之有舌者) to the front of the carriage, leaving only 'six reins' for the driver to manage.—以 must be disregarded, as a mere particle, and the line='the reins with their gilt buckles.'

Ll. 7, 10. 邑 may be taken of the cities or towns on the western border of Ts'in, or those of the western tribes. 方—將, 'there will be.' 胡然,—as in iv. III. 2.

St. 3. L. 1. 俴 has here the sense of 'mailed,' the mail for the horses being made of 'thin' plates of metal, scale-like. 羣=和, 'harmonious,' referring to the unison of their movements. L. 2. The *k'ew maou* is defined as 'a three cornered spear (三隅矛)'; but it is figured as a trident. The end of its shaft (錞) was gilt. L. 3. 伐 is here used in the sense of 'shield,' specifically one of middle size. The Shwoh-wǎn gives the character as 旱 with 戈 on the right. 蒙 denotes the feathers, which were fixed (Maou), or painted (Ch'ing), on the shield. 有苑 describes the effect as elegant (文貌). L. 4. 韔 was the 'bow-case (弓

音。秩厭載子。言閉二膺。虎
秩良興。載念繩弓。交鞃
德人。厭寢君縢。竹鞃鋈

With the tiger-skin bow-case, and the carved metal ornaments
    on its front.
The two bows are placed in the case,
Bound with string to their bamboo frames.
I think of my husband,
When I lie down and rise up.
Tranquil and serene is the good man,
With his virtuous fame spread far and near.

IV.   Kĕen kĕa.

遡 一 在 伊 所 爲 白 蒼 蒹 一章 兼
洄 方。水 人。謂 霜。露 蒼。葭 葭

1   The reeds and rushes are deeply green,
   And the white dew is tnrned into hoarfrost.
   The man of whom I think
   Is somewhere about the water.
   I go up the stream in quest of him,

室),' 鋈膺,—lit., 'engraven breasts.' Maou
and Choo take the phrase of the carved metal
ornaments on the horses' breast-bands; but I
agree with Yen Ts'an that it is very unlikely the
speaker should start off from the bow-case to
the breast-bands of the horses, and then in the
next line return to the bow-case again. We must
take the phrase as descriptive of the ornaments
on the front of the case.

L.5. 交鞃二弓=交二弓於
鞃中. 'there were placed together two bows
in the case.' L.6. The 閉 (composed elsewhere of 韋 and 必) was an instrument of
bamboo, strapped to the bow when unstrung, to
keep it from warping. It appears here, as so
strapped to it with string (縢), and placed
along with it in the case.

L1.6—7. 載,—as in iii.XIV. 8. 厭厭
describes 'the tranquil serenity of the husband's
virtue.' 秩秩 — 'orderly.' Choo Kung-
ts'een says, 'The manifestation of his virtuous
fame proceeded from the inside to the outside,

from near to far. This is what is meant by its
being *an orderly fame.*'

The rhymes are—in st. 1, 收, 轕, cat. 3, t. 1;
驅, 續, 轂, 舜, 玉, 曲, *ib.,* t. 3 (驅
prop. belongs to cat. 4): in 2, 阜, 手, *ib.* t. 2;
中, 驂 (this is very doubtful); 合, 軜 (prop.
cat. 15), 邑, cat. 7, t. 3: in 3, 羣, 錞, 苑
(prop. cat. 14), cat. 13, t. 1; 膺, 弓,, 縢, 興
and 音 (prop. cat. 7), cat. 6, t. 1.

Ode 4. Narrative. SOME ONE TELLS HOW HE
SOUGHT ANOTHER WHOM IT SEEMED EASY TO
FIND, AND YET COULD NOT FIND HIM. This
piece reads very much like a riddle, and so it
has proved to the critics. The Preface says it
was directed against duke Sĕang, who went on
his course to strengthen his State by warlike
enterprises, without using the proprieties of
Chow, and so would be unable to consolidate it.
In developing this interpretation, on which the
first two lines are allusive, Ch'ing K'ang-shing
makes 'the man' in the 3d line to be a man or
men versed in the proprieties; Gow-yang and

従之。道阻且長。遡
游従之。宛在水中。
央。蒹葭凄凄。白露未
晞。所謂伊人。在水
之湄。遡洄従之。道
阻且躋。遡游従之。
宛在水中坻。
蒹葭采采。白露未
已。所謂伊人。在水

But the way is difficult and long.
I go down the stream in quest of him,
And lo! he is right in the midst of the water.

2　The reeds and rushes are luxuriant,
And the white dew is not yet dry.
The man of whom I think
Is on the margin of the water.
I go up the stream in quest of him,
But the way is difficult and steep.
I go down the stream in quest of him,
And lo! he is on the islet in the midst of the water.

3　The reeds and rushes are abundant,
And the white dew has not yet ceased.
The man of whom I think
Is on the bank of the river.

others think duke Seäng himself is meant; and Lën Tsoo k'een takes 'the man' as 'the proprieties of Chow.' All this is what Choo well calls 'chiselling.' and gives no solution of the riddle. He himself takes the whole as narrative, and does not attempt any solution;—nor do I venture to propose one.

LL. 1, 2, in all the stt. The këen is described as like the hwan (萑), which Medhurst calls a tough sedge or rush, but smaller, though it rises to the height of several feet. For the këa, see on ii. XIV. 蒼蒼 describes their appearance of a deep green. Maou and Choo say that 凄凄 is synonymous with this;—comp. 萋萋 in i. II. 1. 采采 must have a similar meaning; Choo tries to keep to the meaning in it of 采, 'to gather.' The 2d line indicates the time as towards the close of autumn, when frost was beginning to make itself felt;

and the time of the day as in the morning, when the dew still lay in hoarfrost, or a semblance of it. 乾.—'to be dry.'

Ll. 3. 伊人—彼人, 'that man.' Maou makes 伊—維, as in ii. XIII. 3, but the term has here a demonstrative force. Wang Yin-che explains it by 是. 一方, 'one quarter,'—somewhere. 湄 is the margin, 'the place where the water and grass meet.' 涘.—as in vi. VII.

2. To go up against the stream is called 遡 (or with 水 at the side) 洄; to go down with the stream is called 遡游;'—so, the Urh-ya. 従之—'follow him,' i.e., go in quest of him. 阻—險, 'dangerous,' 'precipitous and difficult.' 躋—升, 'ascending,' 'steep.'

沚。水宛從遡且道從遡之
中在之游右。阻之洄洟。

I go up the stream in quest of him,
But the way is difficult and turns to the right.
I go down the stream in quest of him,
And lo! he is on the island in the midst of the water.

V. *Chung-nan.*

有　終　其　顏　錦　君　有　終　終
紀　南　君　如　衣　子　條　南　南
有　何　也　渥　狐　至　有　何
堂。有。哉。丹。裘。止。梅。有。

1　What are there on Chung-nan?
　　There are white firs and plum trees.
　　Our prince has arrived at it,
　　Wearing an embroidered robe over his fox-fur,
　　And with his countenance rouged as with vermilion.
　　May he prove a ruler indeed!

2　What are there on Chung-nan?
　　There are nooks and open glades.

右,—'to the right.' The meaning is, as Choo says, that 'he did not meet with the man, and turned away to the right of him.' 坻 and 沚 both mean 'islet;' but 坻 is the smaller of the two. 宛—as in x. II.

The rhymes are—in st. 1, 蒼, 霜, 方, 長, 央, cat. 10; it is not worth while to put down ll. 5 and 7 as rhyming: in 2, 淒, 晞, 湄, 躋, 坻, cat. 15, t. 1: in 3, 采, 已, 涘, 右, 沚, cat. 1, t. 1.

Ode 5. Allusive. CELEBRATING THE GROWING DIGNITY OF SOME RULER OF TS'IN, AND ADMONISHING, WHILE PRAISING, HIM. The piece is akin to the first and second. The Preface refers it to duke Sëang, who was the first of the chiefs of Ts'in to be recognized as a prince of the kingdom, and we need not question the reference.

Ll. 1, 2, in both stt. Chung-nan was the most famous mountain in the old demesne of Chow, lying south of the old capital of Haou,—in the pres. dep. of Se-gan, in Shen-se. It came to belong to Ts'in, when king P'ing had granted to duke Sëang the old possessions of Chow The t'éou is another name for 'the mountain ts'ëu (山楸),' 'a kind of fir,' distinguished by the whiteness of its bark, and leaves, and affording good materials for making chariots, coffins, &c. Choo defines 紀 by 山之廉角, 'corners of a hill,' and 堂 by 山之寬平處, 'open, level, places.' It is hard to tell in what the allusion in these two lines lies.

Ll.3-5. I construe 止 as the particle, and suppose that the lines are descriptive of the prince of Ts'in's arrival in the neighbourhood of the mountain, from a visit to the court of Chow, or in some progress through his territories. On l.4, st.1, Ying-tah says that the prince of a State wore a white fox-fur at the royal court, and on his return to his own dominions when he announced in his ancestral temple what gifts he had received from the son of Heaven; after which he no more wore it. The same would probably be true of the dress mentioned in the corresponding line of st.2. On the

不 壽 將 佩 繡 黻 至 君
忘。考 將。玉 裳。衣 止。子

Our prince has arrived at it,
With the symbol of distinction embroidered on his lower garment,
And the gems at his girdle emitting their tinkling.
May long life and an endless name be his?

VI. *Hwang nëaou.*

黃
鳥

者 其 其 夫 此 車 從 止 交 一
天。慄。穴。之 奄 奄 穆 于 交 黃
殲 彼 惴 特 息。息。公 棘。黃 鳥
我 蒼 惴 臨 百 維 子 誰 鳥。

1 They flit about, the yellow birds,
And rest upon the jujube trees.
Who followed duke Muh [to the grave]?
Tsze-keu Yen-seih.
And this Yen-seih.
Was a man above a hundred.
When he came to the grave,
He looked terrified and trembled.
Thou azure Heaven there!

symbol of distinction, see the Shoo on II.iv. 4. Ying-tah, after Ch'ing, observes that as the symbol was represented on the lower garment, we are not to find two article of array in this line. The 黻衣 and the 繡裳 are merely variations of expression for the same thing. We have indeed, two articles in st.1, and we know that the embroidered robe was worn over the fur. 渥丹,—comp. on iii.XIII. 3. 將將 gives the sound of the gems.

L.6. expresses a wish, in which a warning or admonition is also supposed to be conveyed. The 其, as optative, may be pleaded in favour of the admonition in st.1, and Këang finds the same in 2, by taking 不忘 as—自始至終, 時以王命爲念. 'from first to last, ever mindful of the king's orders.' I prefer to take the 忘 passively. Elsewhere in

Ptt. II. and III., we find 壽考 combined, in the sense of 'to live long.'

The rhymes are—in st.1, 梅裳, 哉, cat. 1.t.1: in 2, 堂, 裳, 將, 忘, cat.10: 有, 止 may also be taken as rhymes in both stt., cat. I, t. 2.

Ode 6. Allusive. LAMENT FOR THREE WORTHIES OF TS'IN WHO WERE BURIED IN THE SAME GRAVE WITH DUKE MUH. There is no difficulty or difference about the historical interpretation of this piece; and it brings us down to the year B.C. 620. Then died duke Muh, after playing an important part in the northwest of China for 39 years. The Tso-chuen, under the 6th year of duke Wăn, makes mention of his requiring the three officers here celebrated to be buried with him, and the composition of the piece in consequence. The 'Historical Records' say that the barbarous practice began with duke Ching.

良人。如可贖兮。人百

其身。

交交黃鳥。止于桑。

從穆公。子車仲行。

此仲行。百夫之防。臨

其穴。惴惴其慄。彼蒼

者天。殲我良人。如可

贖兮。人百其身。

交交黃鳥。止于楚。誰

從穆公。子車鍼虎。維誰

Thou art destroying our good men.
Could he have been redeemed,
We should have given a hundred lives for him.

2　They flit about, the yellow birds,
And rest upon the mulberry trees.
Who followed duke Muh [to the grave]?
Tsze-keu Chung-hang.
And this Chung-hang
Was a match for a hundred.
When he came to the grave,
He looked terrified and trembled,
Thou azure Heaven there!
Thou art destroying our good men.
Could he have been redeemed,
We should have given a hundred lives for him.

3　They flit about, the yellow birds,
And rest upon the thorn trees.
Who followed duke Muh [to the grave]?

Muh's predecessor, with whom 66 persons were buried alive, and that 170 in all were buried with duke Muh. The death of the last distinguished man of the House of Ts'in, the emperor I., was subsequently celebrated by the entombment with him of all the inmates of his harem. Yen Ts'an says that though that House had come to the possession of the demesne of Chow, it brought with it the manners of the barbarous tribes among which it had so long dwelt.—Have we not in this practice a sufficient proof that the chiefs of Ts'in were themselves sprung from those tribes?

In all the stt. Ll. 1, 2. I take 交交 in the sense adopted by Choo, 'the app. of flying about, coming and going.' Maou makes it='small-like.' The allusion is variously explained, some say there is in it the idea of the people's loving the three victims as they liked the birds; others, that the birds among the trees were in their proper place,—very different from the worthies in the grave of duke Muh. 從=從死, 'to follow in death.' 殉 is the more common term in this sense. L. 4. 子車 was the clan-name of the victims, brothers, whose names follow in

百 贖 人。殲 蒼 其 穴。禦 百 此
其 兮。如 我 者 慄。惴 臨 夫 鍼
身。人 可 良 天。彼 惴 其 之 虎。

Tsze-keu K‘ëen-hoo.
And this Tsze-keu K‘ëen-hoo
Could withstand a hundred men.
When he came to the grave,
He looked terrified and trembled.
Thou azure Heaven there!
Thou art destroying our good men.
Could he have been redeemed,
We should have given a hundred lives for him.

VII. *Shin fung.*

如 欽 憂 君 未 比 鬱 晨 鴥 晨
何 欽。心 子。見 彼 林。彼 風。彼 風

1 Swift flies the falcon
   To the thick-wooded forest in the north.
   While I do not see my husband,
   My heart cannot forget its grief.
   How is it, how is it,
   That he forgets me so very much?

the several stanzas. L. 6. 特 gives the idea
of 'standing out eminent;' 防, that of 'a dyke
or bulwark;' 禦, that of 'a combatant.' Ll. 7,
8. 穴 is explained by 壙, 'the pit of a tomb.'
惴惴 —'terrified-like.' I follow Choo in understanding these lines of the victims themselves. Ch'ing is followed by Yen Ts'an in
taking them of the spectators. The other view
is more natural. L. 9. This line is equivalent
to 悠悠蒼天 in x, VIII. *et al.* The appeal is, literally, to 'that which is azure, the
sky,' but we must understand really to the
Power dwelling in the heavens. 殲＝盡, 'to
make an end of.' L. 12. Choo makes this—'men
would all have wished to make their lives a
hundred to give in exchange for him.' But the
construction is, perhaps,—'*The price would have
been* of men a hundred.'

The rhymes are—in st. 4, 棘. 息. 息. 特,
cat. 1, t. 3: in 2, 桑. 行。 行。防, cat. 10:

in 3, 楚. 虎. 虎。禦, cat. 5, t. 2. Also 穴
慄, and 天. 人. 身, in all the stt.

Ode 7. Allusive. A WIFE TELLS HER GRIEF
BECAUSE OF THE ABSENCE OF HER HUSBAND, AND
HIS FORGETFULNESS OF HER. Such is the account of the piece given by Choo, drawn from
the language of the different verses. The Preface says it was directed against duke K‘ang (B.
C. 619—608), the son and successor of Muh,
who alighted the men of worth whom his father
had collected around him, leaving the State
without those who were its ornament and
strength. But there is really nothing in the
piece to suggest this interpretation;—it is, indeed,
far-fetched.

Ll. 1,2, in all the stt. 鴥 expresses 'the app.
of the rapid flight of a bird.' 晨風 is a
name for the 鸇, which Williams calls 'a falcon, goshawk, or kite.' It is described as 'ful-
vous, with a short swallow-like neck, and a
hooked beak, flying against the wind with great

如何。忘我實多。

山有苞櫟。隰有　（二章）

六駮。未見君子。

憂心靡樂。如何。忘我實多。

山有苞棣。隰有　（三章）

樹檖。未見君子。

憂心如醉。如何忘我實多。

2 On the mountain are the bushy oaks;
In the low wet grounds are six elms.
While I do not see my husband,
My sad heart has no joy.
How is it, how is it,
That he forgets me so very much?

3 On the mountain are the bushy sparrow-plums;
In the low wet grounds are the high, wild pear trees.
While I do not see my husband,
My heart is as if intoxicated with grief.
How is it, how is it,
That he forgets me so very much?

VIII. *Woo e.*

無衣

豈曰　（一章）

無衣

與子同袍。

王于興師。

修我戈矛。

1 How shall it be said that you have no clothes?
I will share my long robes with you.
The king is raising his forces;
I will prepare my lance and spear,
And will be your comrade.

rapidity.' 樾 describes 'the thick and extensive growth of the forest.' In st.2 there is
great difficulty with 六駮, and there is, probably, a corruption of the text. Acc. to Maou,
駮 is the name of an animal, 'like a white
horse, with a black tail, and strong teeth like
a saw, which eats tigers and leopards!' But an
animal of any kind is entirely out of place here.
We must take the term as the name of a tree,
and Luh Ke says the *pok* is a kind of elm.
Why *six* trees are mentioned we cannot tell,
unless it were that a meadow with that number
of elms in it was in the writer's view or in his
mind's eye, when he wrote the verse. In the
Japanese plates the tree would seem to be the *celtis
muku*. The 檖 is the 唐棣 of ii.XIII. The 苤
yields a fruit like a pear, but smaller and sour. It
is called 'the hill, or wild pear tree,' 'the deer pear
tree,' 'rat pear tree,' &c. 樹苞 must have a meaning, to correspond to the 苞 of the prec. line,
and 六 in st 2. I translate it by 'high.' The
allusion in all the stt. seems to be simply in the
contrast between the falcon and the trees, all in

與子同仇。

豈曰無衣。同澤。王于興師。修我矛戟。與子偕作。

豈曰無衣。同裳。王于興師。修我甲兵。與子偕行。

2 How shall it be said that you have no clothes?
   I will share my under clothes with you.
   The king is raising his forces;
   I will prepare my spear and lance,
   And will take the field with you.

3 How shall it be said that you have no clothes?
   I will share my lower garments with you.
   The king is raising his forces;
   I will prepare my buffcoat and sharp weapons,
   And will march along with you.

the places and circumstances proper to them, and the different condition of the speaker.

Ll. 3–6. 君子,—in the sense of 'husband,' as often. 欽欽 represents the speaker to us as 'unable to forget' her grief. 未見, 'not yet seen,' suggests the thought that the husband had been long absent. 靡樂,—'with no joy.' All was grief.

The rhymes are—in st. 1, 風 (all through the She, 風 rhymes thus), 林, 欽, cat. 7, t. 1: in 2, 檖, 駭, 樂, cat. 2; in 3, 棣, 檖, 醉, cat. 15, t.3: also in all the stt., 何, 多, cat. 17.

Ode 8. Narrative. THE PEOPLE OF TS'IN DECLARE THEIR READINESS, AND STIMULATE ONE ANOTHER, TO FIGHT IN THE KING'S CAUSE. I can get no other meaning but the above out of this perplexing piece. The Preface says it is condemnatory of the frequent hostilities in which the people were involved by a ruler who had no fellow feeling with them; but I can see no trace in it of such a sentiment. Some refer it to duke K'ang; others to Sëang; others to Chwang. With some it expresses condemnation; with others praise. Evidently it was made at a time when the people were being called out in the king's service; and the loyalty which they had felt, when they were subjects of Chow, still asserted its presence, and made them forward to take the field.

Ll.1,2 in all the stt. Here we have one of the people stimulating another who had been excusing himself, perhaps, from taking the field on the ground that he had but a scanty wardrobe. The friend will share his own with him. 袍 is the term for a long robe or gown. The critics all speak of it here as quilted. Choo, after Ch'ing, defines 澤 as in the translation. The Shwoh-wăn gives the character with 衣 at the side,—no doubt correctly.

Ll.3–5. 于 must be taken as the particle. I translate both 戈 and 戟 by lance. The former is said to have been of all spear-like weapons the most convenient for use. It was 6 ft. 6 in. long, and you could pound, cut, smite, and hook with it. The kih here is said to have been that used in the chariot, 16 feet long, used both for thrusting and hooking. 甲 is the corselet, made in those days of leather. 兵 means sharp weapons generally. I take 仇, with Maou, in the sense of 匹, 'mate,' 'comrade,'—like 逑 in i.I. 作, 'to rise to action,'—to take the field.

The rhymes are—in all the stt. 衣, 師, cat. 15, t. 1: in 1, 袍, 矛, 仇, cat. 3, t. 1: in 2, 澤, 戟, 作, cat. 5, t. 3; in 3, 裳, 兵, 行, cat. 10.

IX.　*Wei yang.*

渭陽

我送舅氏　日至渭陽　何以贈之　路車乘黃　我送舅氏　悠悠我思　何以贈之　瓊瑰玉佩。

1　I escorted my mother's nephew,
　　To the north of the Wei
　　What did I present to him?
　　Four bay horses for his carriage of state.

2　I escorted my mother's nephew;
　　Long, long did I think of him.
　　What did I present to him?
　　A precious jasper, and gems for his girdle-pendant.

X.　*K'euen yu.*

權輿

於我乎夏屋　渠渠　今也每　食無餘　于嗟　乎不承　權輿。於我乎每　食四簋　今也每　食不飽　于嗟　乎不承　權輿。

1　He assigned us a house large and spacious;
　　But now at every meal there is nothing left.
　　Alas that he could not continue as he began!

2　He assigned us at every meal four dishes of grain;
　　But now at every meal we do not get our fill.
　　Alas that he could not continue as he began!

Ode 9. Narrative. THE FEELINGS WITH WHICH DUKE K'ANG ESCORTED HIS COUSIN, DUKE WAN, TO TSIN, AND HIS PARTING GIFTS. Duke Hëen of Tsin had a daughter who became the wife of Muh of Ts'in, and was the mother of his son who became duke K'ang. The eldest son and heir of Hëen was driven to suicide by the machinations of an unworthy favourite of his father, and his two sons fled to other States. One of them, Ch'ung-urh, afterwards the famous duke Wăn of Tsin, took refuge finally in Ts'in, and by the help of duke Muh was restored to his native State, and became master of it, after he had been a fugitive for 19 years. K'ang was then the heir-apparent of Ts'in, and escorted his cousin into the State of Tsin when he undertook his expedition to recover it. These verses are supposed to have been written by him at a subsequent time, when he recalled with interest the event.

Ll. 1, 2, in both stt. 舅 denotes a mother's brothers, and 舅氏 will therefore be one bearing their surname, and little removed from them; here it=‘cousin.’ Lacharme translates it *avunculus*, which is here incorrect. 渭,—see iii.X. 3. The north of a river is called 陽. The capital of Ts‘in at this time was Yung (雍), in pres. dis. of Hing-p‘ing, dep. Se-gan. The one prince accompanied the other to the territory of the pres. dis. of Heen-yang (咸陽). 悠悠我思,—see iii. V. 2, Maou says that he thought of his mother, now long dead. But whether she were dead or not at this time does not appear;—the line simply expresses the anxious regard which he felt for his cousin, embarked on a hazardous enterprize.

Ll. 3, 4. We are not to understand that the carriage was given by the prince of Ts‘in. Such a carriage the princes of States received from the king. If Ch‘ung-urh succeeded, he would have such a carriage as the marquis of Tsin; and now his cousin, anticipating his success, gave him the horses for it. 瑳 as in v.X. *et al.* Williams says the 瓌瑰 was ‘a kind of jasper.’ We cannot tell whether this jasper was to be worn at the girdle-pendant, or whether it was given in addition to the usual stones worn there.

The rhymes are—perhaps, in both stanzas 氏, 之 (not given by Twan): in 1, 陽, 黃, cat. 10: in 2, 思, 佩, cat. 1, t 1.

Ode 10. Narrative. SOME PARTIES COMPLAIN OF THE DIMINISHED RESPECT AND ATTENTION PAID TO THEM. The Preface says the complainers were men of worth, old servants of duke Muh, in his attentions to whom K‘ang, his successor, gradually fell off. It may have been so, but we cannot positively affirm it. In the common editions, the stanzas are printed in 5 lines, 於我乎 and 于嗟乎 being each regarded as one. Koo-she observes that these expressions can hardly be treated as separate lines.

In both stt., l. 1. 於我乎 is an exclamation, —‘for us,’ ‘in the treatment of us.’ 夏 =大, ‘large.’ 渠渠 expresses ‘the appearance of being deep and wide.’ The 簋 were vessels of earthenware or wood, round outside, and square inside, in which grain was set forth at sacrifices and feasts. A prince, in entertaining a great officer, had two of these dishes on the mat, or, as we should say, on the table, and the dishes of meat and other viands corresponded. Here there are 4 such dishes, intimating the abundance of the entertainment which was provided.

L. 2. The student will observe the appropriateness of 無 in st. 1, and of 不 in 2.

L.3. 承—繼, ‘to continue.’ 權輿—始, ‘a beginning.’ How the two characters have this signification is attempted to be made out in this way. 權 is the weight or stone attached to a steel yard, and with a stick and stone the first rude attempts at weighing were made; 輿 is the bottom of a carriage, and the first attempts at conveying things were made on a board. However this be, the two characters are now recognized as meaning ‘the beginnings of things.’

CONCLUDING NOTE ON THE BOOK. From the first three odes, the fifth, and the seventh, we get the idea of Ts‘in as a youthful State, exulting in its growing strength, and giving promise of a vigorous manhood. The people rejoice in their rulers; wives are proud of the martial display of their husbands, while yet they manifest woman's tenderness and affection. The sixth ode shows what barbarous customs still disfigured the social condition; but there is in the whole an auspice of what the House of Ts‘in became,—the destroyer of the effeminate dynasty of Chow, and the establisher of one of its own, based too much on force to be lasting. Many of the critics think that Confucius gave a place in his collection of odes to those of Ts‘in, as being prescient of its future history!

The rhymes are—in st. 1, 渠, 餘, 輿, cat. 5, t. 1: in 2, 簋, 龜, cat. 3, t. 2. The 輿 in st. 2 rhymes with 1.

I. *Yuen-kew.*

羽。無丘坎望有子一章宛陳一之十二
夏。之其兮。情之丘
值下擊望兮。湯兮。
其。無鼓。兮。而兮。宛
鷺冬宛無洵宛

1 How gay and dissipated you are,
   There on the top of Yuen-k'ëw!
   You are full of kindly affection indeed,
   But you have nothing to make you looked up to!

2 How your blows on the drum resound,
   At the foot of Yuen-k'ëw!
   Be it winter, be it summer,
   You are holding your egret's feather!

TITLE OF THE BOOK.—陳, 一之十二.
'The odes of Ch'in; Book XII. of Part I.' Ch'in
was one of the smaller feudal States of Chow,
and its name remains in the dep. of Ch'in-chow
(陳州), Ho-nan. It was a marquisate, and its
lords traced their lineage up to the verge of his-
toric times, and boasted of being descended from
the famous emperor Shun, so that they had the
surname of Kwei (媯). At the rise of the
Chow dynasty, one of Shun's descendants, called
Ngoh foo (閼父), was potter-in-chief to king
Woo, who was so pleased with him that he gave
his own eldest daughter (大姬) to be wife to
his son Mwan (滿), whom he invested with the
principality of Ch'in. He is known·as duke
Hoo (胡公), and established his capital near
the mound called Yuen-k'ew, in the present

district of Hwae-ning (淮寧), dep. Ch'in-
chow. His marchioness is said to have been
fond of witches and wizards, of singing and
dancing, and so to have affected badly the manners and customs of the people of the State;—a
character of her, a daughter of king Woo, which
perplexes many of the critics.
   Ode 1. Narrative. THE DISSIPATION AND
PLEASURE-SEEKING OF THE OFFICERS OF CH'IN.
The Preface says the piece was directed against
duke Yew (幽公, B. C. 850–834), and Maou
interprets the 子 in st. 1 of him. Choo, however, says that there is no evidence of Yew's
dissipation but in the bad title given to him
after his death, and that 'he does not dare to
believe' that the ode speaks of him. To make
the 子 refer to him supposes a degree of
familiarity with his ruler on the part of the
writer, which is hardly admissible. Yet we

坎 其 三章 擊 缶 宛 丘 之 道 無 冬 無 夏 值 其 鷺 翿

3 How you beat your earthen vessel,
  On the way to Yuen-k'ëw!
  Be it winter, be it summer,
  You are holding your egret-fan!

II. *Tung mûn che fun.*

東 門 之 枌 東 一章 門 之 粉 宛 丘 之 栩 子 仲 之 子 婆 娑 其 下 穀 二章 旦 于 差 南 方 之 原 不 績 其 麻 市 也 婆 娑

1 [There are] the white elms at the east gate.
  And the oaks on Yuen-k'ew;
  The daughter of Tsze-chung
  Dances about under them.

2 A good morning having been chosen
  For the plain in the South,
  She leaves twisting her hemp,
  And dances to it through the market-place.

may infer from st. 1, l. 4 that the subject of the piece was an officer, a man of note in the State, and a representative, I assume, of his class.

St. 1. I have mentioned that Maou refers the 于 to duke Yëw. Ch'ing, however, supposes it is addressed to some 'great officer;'—which is more likely. 湯 is taken as = 蕩, 'dissipated,' 'unsettled.' Maou, after the Urh-ya, understands 宛丘 as 'a mound, high on the 4 sides, and depressed in the centre;' while Kwoh Puh gives just the opposite account of the name, as 'a mound rising high in the centre.' Evidently, however, we need not try to translate the words. Whatever was its shape, Yuen-k'ew was the name of a mound, inside, some say, the chief city of Ch'in, certainly in its immediate neighbourhood, and a favourite resort of pleasure-seekers. 有情 is here about = our word 'jolly.'

Stt. 2,3. 坎, followed by the descriptive 其, is intended to give the sound of the blows on the instruments. 缶 is a vessel of earthen-ware. We find it used of a vessel for holding wine, and a vessel for drawing water. It is used also, as here, for a primitive instrument of music. 無冬無夏一無聞(or 論), 冬夏.—with the meaning I have given. 值 —植 or 持, 'to hold in the hand.' We generally translate 鷺 by 'beron;' but according to Kwoh, who says that both from the crest and from the back arose a plume of long feathers, we must understand the bird here to be the Great White Egret (*Ardea Egretta*). Those feathers, either single or formed into fans, were carried by dancers, and waved in harmony with the movements of the body.

The rhymes are—in st. 1, 湯, 上, 望, cat. 10: in 2, 鼓, 下, 夏, 羽, cat. 5, t. 2: in 3, 缶, 道, 翿, cat. 3. t. 2.

Ode 2. Narrative. WANTON ASSOCIATIONS OF THE YOUNG PEOPLE OF CH'IN. The Preface says the piece was intended to express detestation of the lewd disorder of the State. Këang

握 貼 如 視 闟 越 于 穀^三
椒。我 荍。爾 邁。以 逝。旦

3　The morning being good for the excursion,
　　They all proceed together.
　　'I look on you as the flower of the thorny mallows;
　　You give me a stalk of the pepper plant.'

III. Hăng mûn.

樂 可 洋 泌 樓 可 之 衡^一 衡
飢。以 洋。之 遲 以 下。門 門

1　Beneath my door made of cross pieces of wood,
　　I can rest at my leisure;
　　By the wimpling stream from my fountain,
　　I can joy amid my hunger.

Ping-chang explains it of some celebration by witches and wizards, of which I can discover no trace in the language.

St. 1. Going out at the east gate, it would appear, parties proceeded, to the mound of Yuen-k'ëw, as the great resort of pleasure-seekers. 栩,—i. q. 榆, x. II. 1; 椒,—see x. VIII. 1. The Tsze-chung was one of the clans of Ch'in, and we must understand that a daughter of it is here introduced. This is much more likely than the view of Ch'ing, who takes 之子 as —'that man (男子).' Indeed, we must take 子 as feminine, if the same person be the subject of the 3d line in st. 2. 婆娑 is explained as—'舞貌, 'the app. of dancing.' The action in this stanza is subsequent to that in the two others.

Stt. 2, 3. 穀=善, 'good;' here = bright. 差 is explained by 擇, 'to choose.' The dict. refers to this passage, under the pronunciation of 差 as ch'ae, which it cannot have here. 于 is the expletive particle. L. 2, st. 2. Maou takes 原 as a surname or clan-name, and understands by the line—'a lady of the Yuen clan living in the south.' Gow-yang was the first to discard this unnatural construction. 'The plain in the south' was, probably, at the foot of Yuen-k'ëw, and to reach it, the parties went through the city, and out at the east gate. In st. 3, 越以 must be taken as a compound particle; like 于 以 in ii. II., et al. 逝=往, 'to go,' — to

make the excursion. 闟=衆, 'all,' or, as Ch'ing says, 總, 'all together.' 邁=行, to go.' lLL3, 4 in st. 3 give the words of some gentleman of the party addressed to a lady. There is a difficulty about them, because l. 3 is directly addressed to the lady, whereas l. 4 is narrative, unless 貽 be taken in the imperative which no critic has ventured to do. I have called 荍, 'the thorny mallows,' after Medhurst. This is, indeed, a literal translation of another name for the same plant,—荊葵. The figure of it is evidently that of one of the malvaceæ.

The rhymes are—in st. 1, 栩 下 ., cat. 5, t. 2: in 2, 差 麻 娑, cat. 16; Twan also makes 原 rhyme here, by poetic license, but unnecessarily: in 8, 逝 邁, cat. 15, t. 3; 荍 椒., cat. 3, t. 1.

Ode 3. Narrative. Tʜᴇ ᴄᴏɴᴛᴇɴᴛᴍᴇɴᴛ ᴀɴᴅ ʜᴀᴘᴘɪɴᴇss ᴏғ ᴀ ᴘᴏᴏʀ ʀᴇᴄʟᴜsᴇ. These simple verses, sufficiently explain themselves. The Preface, however, finds in them advice, thus metaphorically suggested to duke He (傳公; B. C. 830—795), whom some one wished to tell that, though Ch'in was a small State, he might find it every way sufficient for him. We need not take that view, and go beyond what is written.

St. 1. 衡門 is an apology for a door.—one or more pieces of wood placed across the opening in a hut or hermitage. The meaning of 下 is not to be pressed. 樓遲,—lit., 'roost

豈其食魚。　　必河之鲂。　　豈其取妻。　　必齊之姜。　　豈其食魚。　　必河之鯉。　　豈其取妻。　　必宋之子。

2 Why, in eating fish,
 Must we have bream from the Ho?
 Why, in taking a wife,
 Must we have a Këang of Ts'e?

3 Why, in eating fish,
 Must we have carp from the Ho?
 Why, in taking a wife,
 Must we have a Tsze of Sung?

IV. *Tung mûn che ch'e.*

東門之池　　東門之池。　　可以漚麻。　　彼美淑姬。　　可與晤歌。　　東門之池。　　可以漚紵。　　彼美淑姬。　　可與晤語。

1 The moat at the east gate
 Is fit to steep hemp in.
 That beautiful, virtuous, lady
 Can respond to you in songs.

2 The moat at the east gate
 Is fit to steep the bœhmeria in.
 That beautiful, virtuous, lady
 Can respond to you in discourse.

and be at leisure.' 泌一毖 in iii. XIV. 1, 'the app. of water bubbling up from a spring.' The term here, however, refers us more to the spring itself. 洋洋 gives the idea of a gentle flow of the water, which then spreads itself out (安流廣長貌). The last line is expanded by Choo—亦可以玩樂而忘飢也. 'I can still enjoy myself, and forget my hunger.' Stt. 2, 3. The marquises of Ts'e had the surname of Këang, and the dukes of Sung that of Tsze. Not bream or carp only could be eaten; one might be satisfied with fish of smaller note.

And so, one could be happy with a wife, though she were not a noble Këang or Tsze.

The rhymes are—in st. 1, 遲, 飢, cat. 15, t. 1: in 2, 鲂, 姜, cat. 10: in 3, 鯉, 子, cat. 1, t. 2.

Ode 4. Allusive. THE PRAISE OF SOME VIRTUOUS AND INTELLIGENT LADY. Choo thinks that in this piece we have a reference to a meeting between a gentleman and lady somewhere near the moat at the eastern gate; but the K'ang-he editors remark correctly that there is nothing in the language indicating any undue familiarity. The Preface says it was directed

東門之池。可以漚菅。彼美淑姬。可與晤言。

東門（三章）之池。可以漚菅。彼美淑姬。可與晤言。

3 The moat at the east gate
   Is fit to steep the rope-rush in.
   That beautiful, virtuous lady
   Can respond to you in conversation.

V.   *Tung mûn che yang.*

東門之楊。其葉牂牂。昏以為期。明星煌煌。東門之楊。其葉肺肺。昏以為期。明星哲哲。

1 On the willows at the east gate,
   The leaves are very luxuriant.
   The evening was the time agreed on,
   And the morning star is shining bright.

2 On the willows at the east gate,
   The leaves are dense.
   The evening was the time agreed on,
   And the morning star is shining bright.

against the times, and the writer is thinking of the weak character of the ruler, and wishing that he had a worthy partner, like the lady who is described, to lead him aright. This view has been variously expanded; but I content myself with the argument of the piece which I have given.

Ll. 1, 2, in all the stt. From its association with the east gate, the 池 here is understood of the 城池, or moat surrounding the wall. 漚—漬, 'to soak,' 'to steep.' The stalks of the hemp had, of course, to be steeped, preparatory to getting the threads or filaments from them. 紵 is described as 'a species of hemp,' a perennial, and not raised every year from seed. In the Japanese plates, it is, evidently, the bœhmeria, or nettle from which the grass-cloth is made. The 菅 resembles the 茅. Strings, and cordage generally, could be made from the fibres of the long leaf. It produces a white flower.

Ll.3,4. 姬—Ke was the surname of the House of Chow.—of all who could trace their lineage, indeed, up to Hwang-te, just as Kēang was the surname of the House of Ts'e, and of all descended from the still more ancient Shin-nung. These were the most famous surnames in China; and hence to say that she was 'a Ke,' or 'a Kēang,' was the highest compliment that could be paid to a lady. So Ying-tah explains the 姬 here. Choo explains 晤 by 解 'to explain,'—intelligently. I prefer the explanation of Ch'ing,—對,—'responsively.'

The rhymes are—in st. l, 池 漚 歌, cat. 17: in 2, 紵 語, cat. 5, t.2: in 3, 菅 言, cat. 14.

Ode 5. Allusive. THE FAILURE OF AN ASSIGNATION. The old and new schools differ here as they do in the interpretation of vii.XIV. Here, as there, I prefer the view of Choo. Why should we suppose that there had been any contract of marriage between the parties? or embarrass ourselves with speculations as to the time of the year for the regular celebration of marriages?

VI. *Moo mûn.*

墓門

墓門有棘。斧以
斯之。夫也不良。
國人知之。知而
不已。誰昔然矣。

墓門有梅。有鴞
萃止。夫也不良。
國人訊之。訊予
不顧。顛倒思予。

1 At the gate to the tombs there are jujube trees;—
They should be cut away with an axe.
That man is not good,
And the people of the State know it.
They know it, but he does not give over;—
Long time has it been thus with him.

2 At the gate to the tombs there are plum trees,
And there are owls collecting on them.
That man is not good,
And I sing [this song] to admonish him.
I admonish him, but he will not regard me;—
When he is overthrown, he will think of me.

Both stanzas. 拜拜 and 肺肺 are
synonymous expressions, denoting the dense
and luxuriant appearance of the foliage. 明
星,—as in vii.VIII.1. 煌煌 and 晢晢
are also synonymous.

The rhymes are—in st. 1, 楊, 拜, 煌, cat.
10: in 2, 肺, 晢, cat. 15, t. 3.

Ode 6. Allusive. ON SOME EVIL PERSON WHO
WAS GOING ON OBSTINATELY TO HIS RUIN. The
Preface gives an historical interpretation of this
piece which Choo at one time accepted. It was
directed, we are told, against T'o of Ch'in.
This T'o was a brother of duke Hwan (B.C.
743—706), upon whose death, he killed his eldest son, and got possession of the State,—to
come to an untimely end himself the year after.
Yet the critics do not refer the third line directly
to him, but to his tutor and guardian, who was
unfaithful to his duty, and ruined the prince,
who was naturally well inclined. The two first
or allusive lines in the stanzas are explained so
as to support this view, but it is too complicated. Choo did right in changing his opinion.

Ll.1,2, in both stt. Maou understands by 墓
門 'the gate at the path leading to the tombs;'
and this interpretation need not be questioned,
though Wang Taou tries to make out that one
of the gates of the capital of Ch'in was thus
named,—'Tomb-gate.' 斯=析, 'to split
wood,' 'to lop.' 鴞, also called 鵬, appears
to be the barn owl,—'a bird of evil voice.'
萃=集, 'to collect.' 止 is the particle.
The thorns about the gate of the tombs, and the
owls collected on the plum trees, were both
things of evil omen; and thence are here employed to introduce the subject of the ode.

Ll 3—6. 夫 is here the demonstrative,—'this,'
—the individual in the speaker's mind. The
'Complete Digest' says that 不已=不改,
'does not alter.' That is the meaning, but we
cannot define 已 by 改. 誰 must be taken
here as merely an introductory particle. The
Urh-ya says that 誰昔 is no more than 昔.
The wickedness of the person referred to was in-
grained, had matured for long, and was now not

VII. *Fang yĕw ts'ĕoh ch'aou.*

心　誰　邛　中　心　誰　邛　防
焉　侜　有　唐　焉　侜　有　有
惕　予　旨　有　忉　予　旨　鵲
惕。美。鷊。甓。忉。美。苕。巢。巢

1 On the embankment are magpies' nests;
   On the height grows the beautiful pea.
   Who has been imposing on the object of my admiration?
   —My heart is full of sorrow.

2 The middle path of the temple is covered with its tiles;
   On the height is the beautiful medallion plant.
   Who has been imposing on the object of my admiration?
   —My heart is full of trouble.

sensible to shame. Ch'ing refers 歌 to the present ode (作此詩);—most naturally I think. 訊＝告, 'to inform,'—to admonish. 顛倒＝至 於顛倒之時, 'when he is overthrown.'

The rhymes are—in st. 1, 斯, 知, cat. 16, t. 1; 已, 矣, cat. 1, t. 2: in 2, 萃, 訊 (this rhyme, however, is attained by reading 誶 for 訊; the text is, no doubt, corrupted), cat. 15, t. 3; 顇, 子, cat. 5, t. 2.

Ode 7. Allusive. A LADY LAMENTS THE ALIENATION OF HER LOVER BY MEANS OF EVIL TONGUES. The Preface says we have here 'sorrow on account of slanderous villains,' and goes on to refer the piece to the time of duke Seuen (宣公; B C. 691—647), who believed slanderers, filling the good men about his court with grief and apprehension. Much more likely is the view of Choo, that the piece speaks of the separation between lovers effected by evil tongues. He does not give his opinion as to the speaker, whether we are to suppose the words to be those of the gentleman or of the lady. In this I have ventured to supplement his interpretation.

Ll. 1, 2 in both stt. 防 and 邛 are taken by some as the names of places in Ch'in. There might be places so styled, the speaker having in view what were known as 'the embankment' and 'the height;' but the spirit of the ode does not require as to enter on this question. 邛 (the radical is 邑, not 阝, as in Williams)＝邱 'a mound.' Maou here simply explains 苕 by 草, 'a grass or plant.'—It is different from the same character in II. viii. IX., and is figured as a pea. 旨＝美 'beautiful.' 唐 was the designation of the path in a temple from the gate up to the hall or raised platform; and 甓, of the tiles with which it was paved;—tiles of a peculiar and elegant make. I do not know where Williams got his account of the term as—'a sort of tiles which is to be partly covered with other tiles, and in which lines are made.' Maou explains 鷊 as 'the ribbon plant.' The character is properly the name of the medallion pheasant (*tragopan satyrus*), and the plant may have got its name from its resemblance to the neck of that bird. It should be written in the text with 卄 at the top.—I cannot tell wherein lies the point of the allusion in these lines to those that follow.

Ll. 3, 4. 侜,—'to cover,'—to impose upon. 子美,—see on x. XI.; here ＝ 'my lover.' 忉 忉 and 惕惕 are synonymous, denoting 'the app. of sorrow or trouble.'

The rhymes are—in st. 1, 巢, 苕, 忉, cat. 2; in 2, 甓, 鷊, 惕, cat. 16, t. 3.

VIII. *Yueh ch'uh.*

月出

勞心慘兮。
燎兮。舒夭紹兮。
月三章出照兮。
勞心慅兮。
懰兮。舒懮受兮。
月二章出皓兮。
勞心悄兮。
僚兮。舒窈糾兮。
月一章出皎兮。
佼人
佼人
佼人

1 The moon comes forth in her brightness;
  How lovely is that beautiful lady!
  O to have my deep longings for her releved!
  How anxious is my toiled heart!

2 The moon comes forth in her splendour;
  How attractive is that beautiful lady!
  O to have my anxieties about her relieved!
  How agitated is my toiled heart!

3 The moon comes forth and shines;
  How brilliant is that beautiful lady!
  O to have the chains of my mind relaxed!
  How miserable is my toiled heart!

Ode 8. Allusive. A GENTLEMAN TELLS ALL THE EXCITEMENT OF HIS DESIRE FOR THE POSSESSION OF A BEAUTIFUL LADY. There is no difference of opinion as to the character of the piece, only the Preface moralizes overs it, according to its wont, and says that it was directed against the love of pleasure.

L. 1, in all the stt. 皎 and 皓 both describe the bright, 'white,' light of the moon; and 照, its 'enlightening.' The speaker is supposed to be led on from his view of the moon to speak of the object of his affections.

L. 2. 佼=美, 'beautiful;'—comp. 姣 in Men. VI. Pt. i. VII. 7. 僚 and 懰 are both explained by 好貌, 'good, elegant-like.' 燎 =明, 'bright,' 'brilliant.' In this line we have the description of the lady.

L. 3 is more difficult than the others. Maou interprets it as a continuation of the description of the lady, explaining 舒 by 遲, 'leisurely,' and understanding it of her movements. 窈糾, he says, denotes 'the elegance of those movements.' He does not touch the other lines, but Yen Ts'an and other critics of the Maou school interpret them in the same way. Choo on the other hand interprets the line of the gentleman,—as in the translation. 舒 has the meaning of 解, 'to relieve,' 'to untie;' and the other two characters describe his feelings towards the lady, pent up, and chain-bound. 窈 is descriptive of their depth, and 糾 of their intensity, as if they were knotted together in his breast; 懮受, of the grief with which they possessed him; and 夭紹, of the sorrowful desire in which they held him fast.

L. 4. describes the gentleman's feelings unable to compass the object of his desire, rising from the condition of sorrowful anxiety to that of misery.

The rhymes are—in st. I, 皎, 僚, 糾 (prop. cat. 3), 悄, cat. 2: in 2, 皓, 懰, 受, 慅, cat. 3, t. 2: in 3, 照, 燎, 紹, 慘 (this character ought to be 懆. In the Han. dyn. 參 and 桌 were constantly confounded), cat. 2.

IX.   *Choo-lin.*

朝　乘　說　駕　從　匪　林。胡　　株
食　我　于　我　夏　適　從　爲　　林
于　乘　株　乘　南。株　夏　乎　
株。駒。野。馬。　　林。南。株

1　What does he in Choo-lin?
　　He is going after Hëa Nan.
　　He is not going to Choo-lin;
　　He is going after Hëa Nan.

2　'Yoke for me my team of horses;
　　I will rest in the country about Choo.
　　I will drive my team of colts,
　　And breakfast at Choo.'

X.   *Tsih p'o.*

泗　無　何。傷　美　與　陂。彼　　澤
滂　爲。　寤　如　荷。有　澤　　陂
沱。涕　寐。之　一　　蒲　之
　　　　人。有

1　By the shores of that marsh,
　　There are rushes and lotus plants.
　　There is the beautiful lady;—
　　I am tortured for her, but what avails it?
　　Waking or sleeping, I do nothing;
　　From my eyes and nose the water streams.

Ode 9. Narrative. THE INTRIGUE OF DUKE
LING WITH THE LADY OF CHOO-LIN. Choo observes that this is the only one of the odes of
Ch'in, of which the historical interpretation is
certain. The intrigue of duke Ling (B.C. 612
—598) with the lady Hëa makes the filthiest
narrative, perhaps, of all detailed in the Tso-
chuen. She was one of the vilest of women;
and the duke was killed by her son Hëa Nan,
who was himself put to a horrible and unde-
served death, the year after, by one of the
viscounts of Ts'oo.

St. 1. We have here the people of Ch'in intimating, with bated breath, the intrigue carried
on by their ruler. Choo-lin was the city of
the Hëa family,—in the pres. dis. of Se-hwa (西
華), dep. Ch'in-chow　乎 may be taken as—
於, 'in,' 'at.' The question is put as to what
the duke meant by being constantly at Choo-
lin, and the answer is given that he was cultivating the acquaintance of Hëa Nan, the writer
not daring to say openly, that the object of attraction was Nan's mother. The son's name
was Ching-shoo (徵 舒), and his designation,
Tsze-nan.

St. 2. I think we should take these lines as
spoken by the duke. The critics all refer them
to the people, and interpret them as narrative;
but the 我 becomes in that case very awkward. 說—舍, to rest;' here meaning to
pass the night, in opp. to 朝食, in l. 4. Maou
interprets 駒, of the 'horses of a great officer,' probably finding in l. 3 a reference to two
officers of Ch'in, each of whom had an intrigue

輾轉伏枕。｜儼。窹寐寐無爲。｜一人。碩大且｜蒲菡萏。有美｜彼澤之陂。有（三章）｜中心悁悁。｜卷。窹寐無爲。｜一人。碩大且｜蒲與蘭。有美｜彼澤之陂。有（二章）

2 By the shores of that marsh
There are rushes and the valerian.
There is the beautiful lady,
Tall and large, and elegant.
Waking or sleeping, I do nothing;
My inmost heart is full of grief.

3 By the shores of that marsh,
There are rushes and lotus flowers.
There is that beatiful lady,
Tall and large, and majestic.
Waking or sleeping, I do nothing;
On my side, on my back, with my face on the pillow I lie.

at the same time with the lady; but it is simpler to suppose that the character is synonymous with 馬. The stanza indicates the frequency with which the duke sought the company of his mistress.

The rhymes are—in st. 1, 林, 南 ., cat. 7, t. 1: in 2, 馬 ., 野 ., cat. 5, t. 2; 駒 ., 株 ., cat. 4, t. 1.

Ode 10. Allusive. A GENTLEMAN'S ADMIRATION OF AND LONGING FOR A CERTAIN LADY. Choo observes that the piece is of the same nature and to the same effect as the 9th. It is of no use seeking for a historical interpretation of it, as the Preface does, in the lewd ways of duke Ling and his ministers.

Ll. 1, 2, in all the stt. 陂 is here explained by 障, 'a dyke,' 'an embankment;' but it is better to take it as the natural shores, 蒲,—not as in vi. IV. 8. but—'rushes.' Mats were made of them. 荷 is the nelumbium or lotus plant. Its flower, unopened, is callen as in the 3d st. 蘭,—as in vii. XXI. From the pool and its beautiful flowers, the writer is led to think of the object of his affection.

Ll. 3–6. Choo expands ll. 3, 4 of st 1 thus: 有美一人而不可見,則雖憂傷而如之何哉, 'there is that

beautiful lady, but I cannot see her, so that, though I am wounded in consequence with grief, it is of no avail.' L. 4 in stt. 2, 3 describes the person of the lady. 卷=好貌 'beautiful-like.' Choo explains it of the fine appearance of the hair; and the critics refer us to 鬈 in viii. VIII. but that term is there used of a gentleman. 窹寐,—as in i. I. 2; so also 輾轉. 涕 is used of tears; 泗, of water from the nose. 滂沱 indicates the abundance of the tears. 悁悁, like 悒悒,—'the app. of grief or disquiet.' 伏枕,—'I lie prostrate on the pillow.'

The rhymes are—in st. 1, 陂 荷 何 爲 ., 沱, cat. 17: in 2, 蘭, 卷, 悁, cat. 14: in 3, 菡, 儼, 枕, cat. 8; 陂 in stt. 2, 3, is supposed to rhyme with the same character in st. 1.

CONCLUDING NOTE ON THE BOOK. The odes of Ch'in are of the same character as those of Wei and Ch'ing, and the manners of the State must have been frivolous and lewd. Only in the 8d, 4th, and 6th pieces have we an approach to correct sentiment and feeling. The 9th is the latest of all the odes in the Classic, as if the sage had intended to represent duke Ling as the ne plus ultra of degeneracy and infamy.

I. *Kaou k'ĕw.*

羔裘逍遙。狐
裘以朝。豈不
爾思勞心忉
忉。

羔裘翱翔。狐
裘在堂。豈不
爾思我心憂
傷。

檜一之十三
羔裘

1 In your lamb's fur you saunter about;
In your fox's fur you hold your court.
How should I not think anxiously about you?
My toiled heart is full of grief.

2 In your lamb's fur you wander aimlessly about;
In your fox's fur you appear in your hall.
How should I not think anxiously about you?
My heart is wounded with sorrow.

TITLE OF THE BOOK.—檜，一之十三, 'The odes of Kwei; Book XIII. of Part I.' Kwei was originally a small State, in the pres. Ch'ing Chow (鄭州), dep. K'ae-fung, Ho-nan, or acc. to others, in the dis. of Meih (密), same dep. Its lords were Yuns (妘云), and claimed to be descended from Chuh-yung (祝融), a minister of the ancient emperor Chuen-hёuh. Before the period of the Ch'un-ts'ёw, it had been extinguished by one of the earls of Ch'ing, the one, probably, who is known as duke Woo (武公; B.C. 770—743), and had become a portion of that State. Some of the critics contend that the odes of Kwei are really odes of Ch'ing, just as those of P'ei and Yung belonged to Wei. It may have been so; but their place, away from Bk. VII., instead of immediately preceeding it as Bkk. III. and IV. do Bk. V., may be accepted as an argument to the contrary.

Ode 1. Narrative. SOME OFFICER OF KWEI LAMENTS OVER THE FRIVOLOUS CHARACTER OF HIS RULER, FOND OF DISPLAYING HIS ROBES, INSTEAD OF ATTENDING TO THE DUTIES OF GOVERNMENT. The Preface says further that the officer, rightly offended by the ruler's ways, left his service; but this does not appear in the piece.

Ll. 1, 2, in all the stt. A jacket of lamb's fur was proper to the prince of a State in giving audience to his ministers; but should have been changed when that ceremony was over. One of fox's fur was proper to him, when he appeared at the court of the king; but it was irregular for him to wear it in his own court. 逍遙 —as in vii. V. 2. 翱翔—as in viii. X. 3, et al. 堂 is here the hall or State-chamber, to which the ruler retired, after giving audience to his officers, and where he transacted business with them. 有曜—有光, 'to have effulgence,' i. e., 'to glisten.'

羔裘二章
如膏。
日出
豈不曜。
爾思、
中心
是悼。

3　Your lamb's fur, as if covered with ointment,
　　Glistens when the sun comes forth.
　　How should I not think anxiously about you?
　　To the core of my heart I am grieved.

II.　*Soo kwan.*

素冠

庶見素冠
兮。
棘人欒
欒
兮。勞心
慱慱
兮。

庶見
素衣
兮。我心傷
悲兮。聊
與
子同
歸兮。

1　If I could but see the white cap,
　　And the earnest mourner worn to leanness!—
　　My toiled heart is worn with grief!

2　If I could but see the white [lower] dress!—
　　My heart is wounded with sadness!
　　I should be inclined to go and live with the wearer!

Ll. 3, 4. 思 has here the meaning, as frequently, of 'to think of with interest and longing.' 怐怐,—as in xii. VII. 1. 悼, 'to be pained in mind,' 'afflicted.'

The rhymes are in st. 1, 膏, 朝, 怐, cat. 2: in 2, 翔, 堂, 傷, cat. 10: in 3, 膏, 曜, 悼, cat. 2.

Ode 2. Narrative. SOME ONE DEPLORES THE DECAY OF FILIAL FEELING, AS SEEN IN THE NEGLECT OF THE MOURNING HABIT. Both Maou and Choo quote, in illustration of the sentiment of the piece, various conversations of Confucius on the three years' mourning for parents;—see Ana. XVII. xxi.

St. 1. 庶,—as in viii. I. 3. It is here defined from the Urh-ya by 幸 'fortunately,' 'luckily; but it has also an optative or conditional force. By the 'white cap' we are to understand the cap worn by mourners for their parents at the end of two years from the death (大祥之後), and which was properly

called 縞冠 Maou supposes it was another, called 練冠 which was assumed in the 13th month;—but this is not so likely. 棘 —急; 'earnest,' 'forward.' 棘人 is a man earnest to observe all the prescribed forms of mourning. 欒欒—瘠貌 'thin and worn-like,' i.e., by grief and abstinence. 慱慱 —憂勞之貌 'the app. of sorrow and toil.'

St. 2. 素衣 was the proper accompaniment of the 素冠 The skirt or lower robe was then also of plain white silk. Ying-tah observes that 衣, as the general name for any article of dress, is here used for 裳, for the sake of the rhyme. 傷悲—as in ii. III. 3. 聊—as in iii. XIV. 1, et al. 子 must here be translated in the 3d person, meaning 'such a mourner.' The 同歸 expresses the speaker's love and admiration of him.

三章 庶見素韠兮。我心蘊結兮。聊與子如一兮。

3 If I could but see the white knee-covers!—
Sorrow is knotted in my heart!
I should almost feel as of one soul with the wearer!

III. *Sih yĕw ch'ang-ts'oo.*

隰有萇楚

一章 隰有萇楚。猗儺其枝。夭之沃沃。樂子之無知。

二章 隰有萇楚。猗儺其華。夭之沃沃。樂子之無家。

三章 隰有萇楚。猗儺其實。夭之沃沃。樂子之無室。

1 In the low wet grounds is the carambola tree;
Soft and pliant are its branches,
With the glossiness of tender beauty.
I should rejoice to be like you, [O tree], without consciousness.

2 In the low, damp grounds is the carambola tree;
Soft and delicate are its flowers,
With the glossiness of its tender beauty.
I should rejoice to be like you, [O tree], without a family.

3 In the low, damp grounds is the carambola tree;
Soft and delicate is its fruit,
With the glossiness of its tender beauty.
I should rejoice to be like you, [O tree], without a household.

St. 3. The 'white 韠,' was a sort of leather apron covering the knee,—also the accompaniment of the white cap and skirt. 我心蘊結,—lit., 'my heart is a collection of knots.' 如一, 'as one,'—其志同, 'of the same mind.'

The rhymes are—in st. 1, 冠, 欒, 慱, cat. 14: in 2, 衣, 悲, 歸, cat. 15, t. 1: in 3, 韠, 結, 一, cat. 12, t. 3.

Ode 3. Narrative. SOME ONE, GROANING UNDER THE OPPRESSION OF THE GOVERNMENT, WISHES HE WERE AN UNCONSCIOUS TREE. The Preface says the piece was composed to indicate the writer's disgust at the licentiousness of his ruler. On this view, the 子 in the 4th line must be referred to the ruler, and the piece becomes allusive. In carrying out this interpretation, however, Maou and his followers are put to such straits, that the K'ang-he editors content themselves with giving Choo's view, and do not refer to the older one at all.

IV. *Fei fung.*

匪風

一章
匪風發兮。
匪車偈兮。
顧瞻周道。
中心怛兮。

二章
匪風飄兮。
匪車嘌兮。
顧瞻周道。
中心弔兮。

三章
誰能亨魚。
漑之釜鬵。
誰將西歸。
懷之好音。

1   Not for the violence of the wind;
    Not for the rushing motion of a chariot;—
    But when I look to the road to Chow,
    Am I pained to the core of my heart.

2   Not for the whirlwind;
    Not for the irregular motion of a chariot;—
    But when I look to the road to Chow,
    Am I sad to the core of my heart.

3   Who can cook fish?
    I will wash his boilers for him.
    Who will loyally go to the west?
    I will cheer him with good words.

All the stt. The *ch'ang-ts'oo* is also called 羊桃, 'the goat's peach.' I agree with Williams in identifying it with the *averrhoa carambola*, though Medhurst calls it 'a sort of cherry.' 猗儺 is explained as meaning 'soft and pliant-looking,' 'soft and delicate.' Luh Ke says that 'the leaves of the plant are long and narrow, its flowers of a purplish red, and its branches so weak, that, when they are more than a foot long, they go creeping along on the grass.' 夭,—as 夭夭 in i.VI. 沃沃,— 'glossy-like.' The point of the ode is in the 4th line. So grew the plant in beauty and exuberance;—It was better under such a government to be a plant than a man. 無家 and 無室 are synonymous,—'without a family' to care for.

The rhymes are—in st. 1, 枝, 知, cat. 16 t. 1: in 2, 華,, 家., cat. 5, t. 1: in 3, 實, 室, cat. 12, t. 3.

Ode 4. Narrative and allusive. SOME ONE TELLS HIS SORROW FOR THE DECAY OF THE POWER OF CHOW. The difference between Choo's view of this piece and that of the Preface will appear in the interpretation of the phrase 周道.

Stt. 1, 2. 風發, 'a wind rushing forth,'— a violent wind; 風飄,—'a wind whirling about.' 偈 denotes 'the app. of a chariot driven along furiously;' 嘌, 'the app. of one driven irregularly.' 周道,—'the way to Chow,' acc. to Choo; acc. to Maou, 'the way of Chow.' On this latter view, the sorrow which the ode expresses is because of the misgovernment of Kwei, contrary to the good rules of the Chow dynasty. 顧瞻, however, agree better with Choo's view, and the 3d line of st. 3 is decisive in its favour. Maou defines both 怛 and 弔 by 傷, 'to be pained,' 'wounded.'

St. 3. It is certainly a homely subject which the writer employs to introduce the expression

of his sympathy with the friends of Chow. 烹,
'to boil or stew;'—to cook. The 釜, was a
deep pan or boiler without feet;—see ii. IV. 2;
the 鬵 was a utensil of the same kind, larger
at the mouth than at the bottom. 溉之,
'clease him,' i.e., cleanse for him. The capital of
the western Chow lay west from Kwei; hence
the expression 西歸. 懷—安 'to cheer
or comfort.' 音—語, 'words.' The writer
means, probably, this ode which he had made.

The rhymes are—in st. 1, 發, 偈, 怛 (prop.
cat. 14), cat. 15, t. 3: in 2, 飄, 嘌, 用, cat. 2:
in 3, 鬵. 音, cat. 7, t. 1.

CONCLUDING NOTE ON THE BOOK. In these
few odes of Kwei we have the picture of a small
State, misgoverned and hastening to ruin.
Dissoluteness, decay of filial affection, and oppression are sapping its foundations; yet there
are men in it, who are painfully conscious of
these evils, and see that the decay of Kwei is but
a part of the general decay that is at work in
the whole kingdom. Of the four odes the third
has the greatest merit.

Kĕang Ping-chang says, 'Kwei became a part
of Ch'ing, at the time of king P'ing's removal
to the east. When duke Woo extinguished the
independent existence of the State, these four
odes were carried with king P'ing to the east,
and afterwards the Grand Recorder found them
in the archives of the kingdom. Thus it was that
Confucius was able, in his labours on the poems,
to give them a place in the Classic. Ah! Kih
(檜) and Kwei were both extinguished by
Ch'ing; but while no odes of Kih remain, we
have these four odes of Kwei.—Such was the
good fortune of this State!'

I. *Fow-yĕw.*

曹一之十四

蜉蝣

蜉蝣之羽。
裳楚楚。心之
憂矣。於我歸
處。

蜉蝣之翼。采
采衣服。心之
憂矣。於我歸
息。

1 The wings of the ephemera
  Are robes, bright and splendid.
  My heart is grieved;—
  Would they but come and abide with me!

2 The wings of the ephemera
  Are robes, variously adorned.
  My heart is grieved;—
  Would they but come and rest with me!

TITLE OF THE BOOK.—曹, 一之十四. ‘*The odes of* Ts‘aou;’ Book XIV. of Pt. I.’ Ts‘aou was a small State, corresponding to the pres. dep. of Ts‘aou-chow, Shan-tung, having as its capital T‘aou-k‘ew,—in the pres. dis. of Ting-t‘aou (定陶). Its lords were earls, the first of them, Chin-toh (振鐸), having been a younger brother of king Woo. It continued for 646 years, when it was extinguished by the larger Sung.

Ode 1. Metaphorical. AGAINST SOME PARTIES IN THE STATE, OCCUPIED WITH FRIVOLOUS PLEASURES, AND OBLIVIOUS OF IMPORTANT MATTERS. The Preface says the piece was directed against duke Ch‘aou (昭公; B. C. 660—652), who indulged in a vainglorious extravagance, and gave his confidence to mean and unworthy creatures. Maou tries to interpret it on this view, and makes it allusive, the second line being descriptive of the *dandyism* of Ch‘aou and his officers. There is nothing in the words, however, nor in any existing records, to lead us to refer it to duke Ch‘aou; and Choo, therefore, gives the argument of it which I have proposed. On this view the piece is metaphorical, and the first two lines belong to the beetle, which is the emblem of the parties intended.

Ll. 1, 2. in all the stt. Williams says that the *fow-yĕw* is ‘a dung-fly,’ and Medhurst calls it ‘a sort of *aleochora*, or tumble dung.’ The name originally was 浮游, ‘floating wanderer,’ and the 水 gave place to 虫, only to make it clear that the character was the name of an insect. No doubt one of the coleoptera is intended,—‘narrow and long, the wing-cases yellow and black, produced from dung and the ground, coming out in the morning, and dying in the evening.’ Though its wing-cases are so splendid, it is only an ephemera. 羽 and 翼 are

歸 於 憂 心 如 麻 掘 蜉
說。我 矣。之 雪。衣 閱。蝣

3 The ephemera bursts from its hole,
   With a robe of hemp like snow.
   My heart is grieved;—
   Would they but come and lodge with me!

II. How-jin.

赤 三 之 彼 與 何 人 彼 候
芾。百 子。其 殳 戈 兮。候 人

1 Those officers of escort
   Have their carriers of lances and halberds.
   But these creatures,
   With their three hundred red covers for the knees!—

synonymous, being varied for the sake of the rhyme. Choo says he does not understand 掘 閱. 閱 may be taken as=穴, 'a hole,' and 掘, as—堀, which, indeed, the Shwoh-wǎn gives, of the same meaning. The phrase will then indicate the insect making its first appearance out of the ground. 楚楚='fresh and bright-looking.' 采采,—'variegated.' Both these phrases are descriptive of the wing-cases of the creature. L. 2 in st. 3 is descriptive of the wings, under the cases, like snow-white linen.

Ll. 3, 4. The 4th line is all but unintelligible. It must be taken as optative. If the speaker could only get the parties he is complaining of to go with him, and take his counsels, he would guide them to a better way. But the 於我 is a great difficulty. 於我乎 in xi. X. does not help us here. The critics have various ways of developing the meaning, but none satisfactory. Kǎng Ping-chang says 君於我 謀歸處之道, 'if the ruler would consult with me (chez moi) about the way of coming to a permanent security,'—. Le Kwang-te (李光地) says,—我心於何歸乎 於我之所歸宿者爾, 'About what is my heart grieved? About where I shall turn to for rest.' It is of no use quoting more attempts to throw light on the darkness.

The rhymes are—in st. 1, 羽, 楚, 處, cat. 5, t. 2: in 2, 襄, 服。, 息, cat. 1, t. 3: in 3, 閱, 雪, 說, cat. 15, t. 3.

Ode 2. Allusive and metaphorical. LAMENT OVER THE FAVOUR SHOWN TO WORTHLESS OFFICERS AT THE COURT OF TS'AOU, AND THE DISCOUNTENANCE OF GOOD MEN. The Preface refers this piece to the time of duke Kung (共公; B. C. 651—617), and he was chargeable, no doubt, with the error which is here condemned, for we are told in the Tso-chuen, that when duke Wǎn of Tsin entered Ts'aou in B. C. 631, his condemnation of its ruler was based on the ground of his having about him 300 worthless and useless officers. It has been argued, however, that when duke Wǎn specified the number of 'three hundred,' he was speaking from this ode, previously in existence. But we may contend, on the other hand, that it had only become current in the previous years of Kung.

St. 1. 候人 was an officer for the reception and convoy of guests or visitors. There were six of them of the 1st degree (上士), and twelve of a lower (下士), attached to the court of Chow,—with their attendants. The number at the court of Ts'aou would be smaller. 何 (2d tone)—揭, 'to carry.' 殳=殳, as in v. VIII. 1. The second line is to be understood of the attendants of the officers. These all had their use, and from them the writer goes on to point out the useless favourites. L. 3,—as in vi. IV, but is here to be understood as the expression of contempt. 芾—韠, in xiii. II. 3.

維鵜在梁。不濡
其翼。彼其之子。
不稱其服。

其咮。彼其之子。
不遂其媾。

薈兮蔚兮。南山
朝隮。婉兮孌兮。
季女斯飢。

2 The pelican is on the dam,
  And will not wet his wings!
  These creatures
  Are not equal to their dress!

3 The pelican is on the dam,
  And will not wet his beak!
  These creatures
  Do not respond to the favour they enjoy.

4 Extensive and luxuriant is the vegetation,
  And up the south hill in the morning rise the vapours.
  Tender is she and lovely,
  But the young lady is suffering from hunger.

III. *She-kĕw.*

鳲鳩
在桑。鳲鳩
七兮。其子
淑人
君子
其儀
一兮。其儀
儀兮。

1 The turtle dove is in the mulberry tree,
  And her young ones are seven.
  The virtuous man, the princely one,
  Is uniformly correct in his deportment.

Ying-tah observes that when the two terms are to be distinguished, the former is the name of the article in sacrificial dress, and the latter, as worn on other occasions. Great officers and those of higher rank were entitled to this appendage to their dress. The '300' is not to be pressed. It indicates the multitude of the 'creatures' spoken of.

Stt. 2, 3. The 鵜 is the pelican, called also 鴮鸅, and by other names. It is here represented as sitting on a dam, contriving somehow to get its food, without effort or labour of its own;—resembling the useless officers who had

their salaries and positions, without doing anything for them. 稱 (3d tone),—'to weigh;' hence meaning 'to balance,' 'to be equal to.' 媾 is here defined by 厚 and 寵, 'the favour' which the 'creatures' enjoyed. 遂,—'to be according to,' synonymous with 稱.

St. 4 is metaphorical:—the first two lines, of the number and forwardness of the 'creatures;' the last two, of the men of worth, kept in obscurity and poverty, or of the poor, weak people, suffering from the misgovernment of the State. These interpretations are forced out of

一兮。心如結兮。

鳲鳩〔二章〕在桑。其子

在梅。淑人君子。

其帶伊絲。其弁

伊絲。其弁伊騏

鳲鳩〔三章〕在桑。其子

在棘。淑人君子

其儀不忒。其儀

不忒。正是四國。

鳲鳩〔四章〕在桑。

其子

He is uniformly correct in his deportment,
His heart is as if it were tied to what is correct.

2　The turtle dove is in the mulberry tree,
And her young ones are in the plum tree.
The virtuous man, the princely one,
Has his girdle of silk.
His girdle is of silk,
And his cap is of spotted deer-skin.

3　The turtle dove is in the mulberry tree,
And her young ones are in the jujube tree.
The virtuous man, the princely one,
Has nothing wrong in his deportment.
He has nothing wrong in his deportment,
And thus he rectifies the four quarters of the State.

the words; but we must be content with them. 菁莪 are taken to denote 'the app. of vegetation, luxuriant and abundant.' 隮=升, 'to ascend,' is taken of vapours or clouds. 婉孌—as in viii. VII. 8. 季女—see ii. IV. 3; but it is not necessary to understand here that the lady is married. 斯—'this,' giving emphasis to the antecedents.

The rhymes are—in st. 1, 蔚 莪, cat. 15, t. 3: in 2, 翼 服, cat. 1, t. 3: in 3, 隮 饑, cat. 4, t. 2: in 4, 隮 饑, cat. 15, t. 1.

Ode 3. Allusive. Tʜᴇ ᴘʀᴀɪꜱᴇ ᴏꜰ ꜱᴏᴍᴇ ᴏɴᴇ, ꜱᴏᴍᴇ ʟᴏʀᴅ, ᴘʀᴏʙᴀʙʟʏ, ᴏꜰ Tꜱ'ᴀᴏᴜ, ᴜɴɪꜰᴏʀᴍʟʏ ᴏꜰ ᴠɪʀᴛᴜᴏᴜꜱ ᴄᴏɴᴅᴜᴄᴛ ᴀɴᴅ ᴏꜰ ᴇxᴛᴇɴꜱɪᴠᴇ ɪɴꜰʟᴜᴇɴᴄᴇ. Acc. to the Preface, the praise in this piece is of some early ruler of Ts'aou, who is celebrated by way of contrast with the very different characters of the writer's time. But we can gather nothing of this from the language of the piece;—nor from history.

Ll. 1, 2, in all the stt. The she-kew is, no doubt, the turtle dove, the same as the kew in ii. I. There is a difficulty, indeed, in the statement that the young ones of the bird amount to 'seven,' as the turtle dove, like all other birds of the same species, has only two young at a time. It is highly characteristic of the critics, that the only one I have met with who touches on this point is Maou K'e-ling. He observes that we have the 七 simply because it rhymes with 一, and are not to understand the text as if it gave definitely the number of the turtle's young! As if this misstatement in the text were not enough, almost all the critics, follow the old Maou in saying that the dove has a uniform method in feeding her young, giving them their food in the evening in the reverse order of that in which she had supplied them in the morning! And this equality and justice form the ground of the allusion in the piece, they say, the dove being thus the counterpart of the uniformly virtuous man. Something of the same kind is brought out from the 2d and other stanzas, the mother dove always appearing in a mulberry tree, while her young continually change their place. All this seems to be mere fancy.

萬　胡　國　正　國　正　君　淑　在
年。不　人。是　人。是　子。人　榛。

4　The turtle dove is in the mulberry tree,
　　And her young ones are in the hazel tree.
　　The virtuous man, the princely one,
　　Rectifies the people of the State.
　　He rectifies the people of his State:—
　　May he continue for ten thousand years!

IV. *Hëa ts'euen.*

念　愾　浸　冽　念　愾　浸　冽
彼　我　彼　彼　彼　我　彼　彼　下
京　寤　苞　下　周　寤　苞　下　泉
周。嘆。蕭。泉。京。嘆。稂。泉。

1　Cold come the waters down from that spring,
　　And overflow the bushy wolf's-tail grass
　　Ah me! I awake and sigh,
　　Thinking of that capital of Chow.

2　Cold come the waters down from that spring,
　　And overflow the bushy southernwood.
　　Ah me! I awake and sigh,
　　Thinking of that capital of Chow.

Ll. 3—6. 君子 would here seem to be not only one in authority (在位), but one in the highest authority, whose influence extends to the whole State (正是四國). The meaning of 儀, 'deportment,' is well illustrated by referring to Ana. VIII. iv. 3. 一 gives the ideas of uniformity, and equality or correctness. 如結—'as if tied;' i.e., the mind is tied to what is correct, as things are tied together so that they cannot separate. It is a great descent from this, when we come in st. 2 to read of the girdle and cap. 伊,—as in ii. XIII. 3. 騋弁, i.q. 綦弁, in the Shoo, V. xxii. 21. 忒, 差忒, 'error.' 四國=曹四境, 'all within the four borders of Ts'aou. 胡不萬年 is a wish for the long life of one so worthy (顧其壽考之詞).

The rhymes are—in st. 1, 杞, 一, 一 結, cat. 12, t. 3: in 2, 梅, 絲 絲 騏, cat. 1, t. 1: in 3, 棘, 忒, 忒, 國, cat. 1, t. 3: in 4, 榛, 人, 人, 年, cat. 12, t. 1.

Ode 4. Metaphorical-allusive. THE MISERY AND MISGOVERNMENT OF TS'AOU MAKES THE WRITER THINK OF CHOW, AND OF ITS FORMER VIGOUR AND PROSPERITY.

Ll. 1, 2 in stt. 1—3. 冽 (formed from 冫) is descriptive of the coolness of the waters. 下泉—'descending spring,' i.e., a spring whose waters flow away downwards. Both Maou and Choo seem to take 苞 as—'bushy grass,' diff. from the other productions mentioned; but it is better to follow the analogy of x. VIII., and other places, where we have met with the term as an adjective 稂 is explained by some as 'blasted ears of grain;' but it is better

冽　浸　愾　念　芃^{四章}　陰　四　郇
彼^{三章}　彼　我　彼　芃　雨　國　伯
下　苞　寤　京　黍　膏　有　勞
泉。　蓍。　嘆。　師。　苗。　之。　王。　之。

3 Cold come the waters down from that spring,
  And overflow the bushy divining plants.
  Ah me! I awake and sigh,
  Thinking of that capital-city.

4 Beautifully grew the fields of young millet,
  Enriched by fertilizing rains.
  The States had their sovereign,
  And there was the chief of Seun to reward their princes.

taken as a kind of weed or darnel. I have translated it by one of the names which it receives. 蕭,—see on vi. VIII. 2. 蓍 is a plant said by the Chinese to be of the same order as 蕭,—one of the *artemisia*. Its stalks were used for the purpose of divination. In the Japanese plates it is the *achillea*. The cold water overflowing these plants only injured them;—an image of the influence of the government of Ts‘aou on the people.

Ll. 3, 4. 愾 is onomatopoetic of a sigh. 周 京 appears in st. 2 as 京周 for the rhyme; the same may be said of 京師 in st. 3, though those characters are often associated in the sense of 'a capital-city.'

St. 4. The writer here speaks of the former and prosperous period of the House of Chow, and we must translate in the past tense. 芃 芃—'beautiful-like.' 苗 is not to be taken of other grain, besides the millet 黍苗=黍 之苗). The millet is metaphorical of the States of the kingdom. 陰雨,—compare 以 陰以雨, iii. X. 1. The phrase denotes abundant and fertilizing rains, rains impregnated with

the masculine, generating influences of nature. 膏, 'to anoint.'='to moisten and enrich. 四 國=四方之國, 'the States in the four quarters of the kingdom.'

Seun was a small State,—in the pres. district of Lin-tsin (臨晉), dep. P‘oo-chow (蒲州), Shan-se. It was first conferred on a son of king Wǎn, one of whose descendants was the chief mentioned in the text,—so called, as presiding with viceregal authority over a district embracing many States. We do not know when he lived.

The rhymes are—in st. 1, 泉, 歎, cat. 14, 稂 京。, cat. 10: in 2, 泉, 歎; 蕭。, 周, cat. 3, t.1: in 3, 泉, 歎; 蓍, 師, cat. 15, t.1: in 4, 苗, 膏, 勞, cat. 2.

Concluding Note upon the Book. To none of the odes of Ts‘aou does there belong any great merit. The second, taken in connection with the statement in the Tso-chuen referred to in the notes on it, shows one of the principal reasons of the decay and ruin of the State,—the multiplication of useless and unprincipled officers. The last ode is strikingly analogous to the last in the preceding Book. In both, the writers turn from the misery before their eyes, and can only think hopelessly of an earlier time of vigour and prosperity.

I. *Ts'ih yueh.*

幽　七　七　衣　七　褐　日　趾　南
一　月　月　一　月　何　于　同　畝
之　　　流　之　　　以　耜　我　田
十　　　火　日　　　卒　四　婦　畯
五　　　九　觱　　　歲　之　子　至
　　　　月　發　　　三　日　饁　喜
　　　　授　無　　　之　舉　彼
　　　　　　衣　　　　　　　
之　　　　　無　　　　　　　
日　　　　　二　　　　　　　
栗　　　　　　　　　　　　　
烈　　　　　　　　　　　　　

1　In the seventh month, the Fire Star passes the meridian;
　In the 9th month, clothes are given out.
　In the days of [our] first month, the wind blows cold;
　In the days of [our] second, the air is cold;—
　Without the clothes and garments of hair,
　How could we get to the end of the year?
　In the days of [our] third month, they take their ploughs in
　　hand;
　In the days of [our] fourth, they take their way to the fields.
　Along with my wife and children,
　I carry food to them in those south-lying acres.
　The surveyor of the fields comes, and is glad.

THE TITLE OF THE BOOK.—幽，一之十
五，'The odes of Pin; Book XV. of Part I.' Of
Pin I have spoken sufficiently in the note on the
title of Book I. There the chiefs of the House
of Chow dwelt for nearly five centuries, from
B. C. 1796—1825. The first piece in this Book
is accepted as a description by the famous duke
of Chow of the ways of the first settlers in Pin,
under Kung-lëw, and hence the name of Pin is
given to all the odes in the Book. No other of
them, however, is descriptive of so high an antiquity. They were made by the duke of Chow
about matters in his own day, or they were
made by others about him, and, it would be
difficult to say for what reason, were arranged
together under this common name of Pin.
The character 幽 is now 邠, the form having
been changed in the period K'ae-yuen (開元;
A. C. 713-741) of the T'ang dynasty. From a
narrative in the Tso-chuen, under B. C. 543, it

appears that at that time the odes of Pin followed those of Ts'e. That its place now is at the end of the 'Lessons from the States' is attributed to the arrangement of Confucius, 'showing,' says Yen Ts'an, 'the deep plan of the sage.' What that deep plan was I have not been able to ascertain.

Ode 1. Narrative. LIFE IN PIN IN THE OLDEN TIME ; THE PROVIDENT ARRANGEMENTS THERE TO SECURE THE CONSTANT SUPPLY OF FOOD AND RAIMENT,—WHATEVER WAS NECESSARY FOR THE SUPPORT AND COMFORT OF THE PEOPLE. I do not wish to deny here this universally accepted account of the ode; but it is not without its difficulties. Pin is not once mentioned in it, nor Kung-lëw. The note of time with which the first three stanzas commence is not a little perplexing :—'In the seventh month, the Fire star, or the Heart of Scorpio (see on the Shoo, I. 5), passes on,' i.e., passes to the westward of the meridian at night-fall. Mr. Chalmers has observed that this could not have been the case if the year of Chow commenced, as it is said to have done, with our December ; but the critics meet this difficulty by saying that in this ode, and indeed throughout the She, the specification of the months is according to the calendar of the Hëa dyn., and not that of Chow. They add, moreover, that it was proper in this piece, occupied with the affairs of Pin during the Hëa dynasty, to speak of its months. This is granted ; but it only leads us to a greater difficulty. Scorpio did pass to the westward in August, or the 7th month of the Hëa dynasty, in the time of the duke of Chow,—say about B. C. 1114 ; but it did not do so in the time of Kung-lëw, or B. C. 1,796. Lew Kin (劉瑾) observes on this :—'In the Canon of Yaou it is said, "The day is at its longest, and the star is Ho. You may thus exactly determine midsummer." In the time of Yaou, the sun was, at midsummer, in Cancer-Leo, and the Ho star culminated at dusk. More than 1,240 years after came the regency of the duke of Chow during the minority of king Ching ; and the stars of the Zodiac must have gone back during that time, through the retrocession of the equinoxes, 16 or 17 degrees. It would not be till the sixth month, and after, therefore, that the sun would be in the same place, and the Ho star pass away to the westward at nightfall. But in this poem which relates the customs of Pin in the times of Hëa and Shang, it is said that the star passed in the 7th month, the duke of Chow mentioning the phænomenon, as he himself saw it.' We are thus brought to one of two conclusions :—that the piece does not describe life in Pin about 700 years before the duke of Chow's time ; or that he supposed the place of the sun in the heavens in the time of Kung-lëw to have been the same as it was in his own days. I think we must adopt the latter conclusion, nor need we be stumbled by the lack of astronomical science in the great statesman. I adhere to the ordinary view of the ode, mainly because of the 2d line in the stanzas already referred to, that clothes were given out in the 9th month. In anticipation of the approaching winter. This must evidently be the 9th month of Hëa, and not of Chow. Were the author telling of what was done in his time, soon after the commencement of the Chow dyn., we cannot conceive of

his thus expressing himself. Why then should we not translate the piece in the past tense, as being a record of the past ? I was for some time inclined to do so. The 9th and 10th lines of st. 1 determined me otherwise. The speaker there must be an old farmer or yeoman of Pin, and the whole ode must be conceived of as coming from him.

St. 1. 流 'flows down,' is explained by 下, 'descends,' i.e., goes on towards the horizon. The giver out of the clothes was the head of each family, distributing their common store according to the necessities of the household (授者家長，以與家人也). The expressions, 一之日，二之日, &c., 'the days of the first, of the second, &c., are taken on all hands as meaning the days of the 1st month, of the second month, &c., according to the calendar of Chow. I accept the conclusion, without attempting to explain the nomenclature, and have indicated it by the addition of 'our' in the translation. The use of the two styles in the same piece, and even in the same stanza, is certainly perplexing. 觱發 are explained together, as 風寒 'winds cold,' and 栗烈 as 氣寒, 'the air cold.' 觱 was the name of a horn blown by the Këangs to frighten the horses of the Chinese, and is here used as giving the sound of the wind as it began to blow in December. 烈 should, probably, be 洌, as in the last of the pree. Book. 褐—毛布, 'cloth of hair,' of which the clothes of the inferior members of the household were made. But a supply of clothes was necessary for all, in order to get through the rigour of the second month of Chow, and so conclude the year of Hëa. L. 7 brings us to the 3rd month of Chow, and the 1st of Hëa, when the approach of spring required preparations to be made for the agricultural labours of the year. 耜, the part of the plough which enters the ground, is here used for the plough, and agricultural implements in general ; I take 于 as a particle, as in i. II., et al. Choo explains it here by 往 'to go to ;' but even then we should have to supply another verb to indicate that 'they went to prepare their ploughs.' 舉趾, 'lifted up their toes,'—the meaning is as in the translation. In l. 9, the narrator appears in his own person, an aged yeoman, who has remained in the house, with his wife (or 婦 may mean the married women on the farm generally) and young children, while the able-bodied members of the household have all gone to work in the fields. 饁—餉田, 'to carry food to those in the fields.' 畯田 was an officer who superintended the farms over a district of considerable extent. It is a pleasant picture of agricultural life which these last five lines give us.

崔　七　公　女　遲　爰　懿　有　授　七
葦　月　子　心　遲　求　筐　鳴　衣　月
蠶　流　同　傷　采　柔　遵　倉　春　流
月　火　歸　悲　蘩　桑　彼　庚　日　火
條　　　　　殆　祁　春　微　女　載　九
桑　八　七　及　祁　日　行　執　陽　月
　　月　月
　　　　流
　　　　火
　　　　八
　　　　月

2　In the seventh month, the Fire Star passes the meridian;
　　In the ninth month, clothes are given out.
　　With the spring days the warmth begins,
　　And the oriole utters its song.
　　The young women take their deep baskets,
　　And go along the small paths,
　　Looking for the tender [leaves of the] mulberry trees.
　　As the spring days lengthen out,
　　They gather in crowds the white southernwood.
　　That young lady's heart is wounded with sadness,
　　For she will [soon] be going with one of our princes as his wife.

3　In the seventh month the Fire Star passes the meridian;
　　In the eighth month are the sedges and reeds.
　　In the silkworm month they strip the mulberry branches of
　　　　their leaves,

St. 2. *Care of the silkworm.* L. 3. 載＝始,
'to begin.' 陽＝温和, 'genial.' L. 4. The
ts'ang-kāng is, probably, the same as the 'yellow
bird' of i. II.;—a kind of oriole. It begins its
song contemporaneously with the hatching of
the eggs of the silkworm. L. 5. I translate
女 by 'young women,' in consequence of its
recurrence in l. 10. L. 6. 'The small paths' are
those about the homesteads, around which the
mulberry trees were planted;—see Men. I. Pt.
i. VII. 24. L. 7. 爰—as in iii. VI. 3, *et al.* L. 8.
Maou explains 遲遲 by 舒緩, 'slow and
easy.' The meaning is what I have given. L. 9.
蘩,—as in ii. II. Choo says that the leaves of
this were used to feed the young worms which
were later in being hatched. More correctly,
Seu Kwang-k'e (徐光啟) says that the
eggs are washed with a decoction from the
leaves to assist their hatching. 祁祁＝衆
多, 'all;' meaning that all the ladies, of noble
families as well as of others, engaged in this

work. The last two lines are variously explained.
I have adopted the view of Choo which is certainly the most poetical, and I believe is correct
also. He says, ' At that time the princes of the
State still married ladies of it; and those of noble families, who might be engaged to be married
to them, took their share of the labour of feeding the silkworms. Hence at this time, those
of them who were so engaged, thinking of the
time when they would be going home with their
husbands and leave their parents, felt sad!'
Maou explains l. 10 of sorrow from the fatigue
of the labour, and l. 11 of returning home along
with the princes who came to see the labour, as
the surveyor of the fields had done in st. 1. Others
take 公子 of the daughters of the ruling
House. 殆＝將然之詞, 'a word indicating what will be.'
St. 3. *Further labour with the silkworms, and
the weaving of silk.* L. 2. Choo observes that
崔葦＝蒹葭 in xi. IV. These things
are mentioned here, it is said, simply as a note
of time. The leaves were made into baskets for
collecting the mulberry leaves, and also into the
frames on which the silkworms were placed.

取彼斧斯。以伐遠
揚狗彼女桑。七月
鳴鵙。八月載績。載
玄載黃。我朱孔陽。
爲公子裳。
四月秀葽。五月鳴
蜩。八月其穫。十月
隕蘀。一之日于貉。
取彼狐貍。爲公子
裘。二之日其同。載

And take their axes and hatchets,
To lop off those that are distant and high;
Only stripping the young trees of their leaves.
In the seventh month, the shrike is heard;
In the eighth month, they begin their spinning;—
They make dark fabrics and yellow.
Our red manufacture is very brilliant,
It is for the lower robes of our young princes.

4 In the fourth month, the Small grass is in seed.
In the fifth, the cicada gives out its note.
In the eighth, they reap.
In the tenth, the leaves fall.
In the days of [our] first month, they go after badgers,
And take foxes and wild cats,
To make furs for our young princes.
In the days of [our] second month, they have a general hunt,

L. 3. No month is specified, as the eggs might be hatched, now in one month, now in another, according to the heat of the season. 條桑—'branch the mulberry trees,' i. e., bring down the branches to the ground, and then strip them of their leaves.

L. 4. The *foo* and the *ts'ang* were both axes, differing in the shape of the hole which received the handle;—in the former it was oval, in the latter, square. L. 6. 猗 should be 掎, which the Shwoh-wǎn defines as 'to draw on one side.' It means here, says Choo, 'to take the branches and preserve the branches.' 女桑—小桑, 'small mulberry trees.' The Japanese plates, however, give here the female mulberry tree. L. 7. The *keih* is the shrike or butcher bird, commonly called 伯勞. As the oriole gave notice of the time to take the silkworms in hand, so

the note of the shrike was the signal to set about spinning. L. 8. 績 is the term appropriate to the twisting of hemp. L. 9 describes the dyeing operations on both the woven silk and the cloth. 玄 denotes a black colour with a flush of red in it. L. 10. 陽 = 明, 'bright.'

St. 5. *Hunting;—to supplement the provision of clothes.* L. 1. Both Maou and Choo simply say of 葽 that it is 'the name of a grass.' Others describe it as like hemp, with flowers of a yellowish red, and a sharp-pointed leaf. Among other names given to it is that of 細草 'the small grass.' In the Japanese plates, it is the *polygala Japonica.* 秀 is said to be used of 'a plant that seeds without having put forth flowers.' L. 2. 蜩 is the cicada or broad locust. L. 3. The reaping here must be of the earlier crops.

此室處。婦子。曰爲改歲。入鼠。塞向墐戶。嗟我八我牀下。穹窒熏月在戶。十月蟋蟀在野。八月在宇。九月莎雞振羽。七月五月斯螽動股。六獻豣于公。續武功。言私其豵。

And proceed to keep up the exercises of war.
The boars of one year are for themselves;
Those of three years are for our prince.

5　In the fifth month, the locust moves its legs;
In the sixth month, the spinner sounds its wings.
In the seventh month, in the fields;
In the eighth month, under the eaves;
In the ninth month, about the doors;
In the tenth month, the cricket
Enters under our beds.
Chinks are filled up, and rats are smoked out;
The windows that face [the north] are stopped up;
And the doors are plastered.
'Ah! our wives and children,
'Changing the year requires this;
Enter here and dwell.'

L. 4. 隕—落, 'to fall.' 蘀,—as in vii. XII.
L. 5. 于,—as in st. 1, l. 7. 貉—as in Ana.
IX. xxvi. It appears to be the same with the
huan of ix. VI. 1. L. 6. We often take 狐貍
together, as signifying a fox. The characters
denote different animals, however. The 貍 is
a sort of wild-cat. Yen Ts'an supposes that the
badgers' skins were for the hunters themselves,
and only the others for the princes. L. 8. 其
同 indicates a great hunting, when the chiefs
all went forth, and which was intended as a
preparation for the business of war. L. 9.
載 is the particle. 續,—'to continue,' or 'to
keep up.'
L. 10. 豵,—as in ii. XIV. 2. L. 11. 豣
denotes a boar three years old, i. e., full-grown.

Down to this point the ode tells of the arrangements in Pin to provide a sufficiency of raiment
against the cold.
St. 5. *Further provision made by the people
against the cold of winter.* Choo supposes that
sze-chung, so-ke, and suh-suh are only different
names for the same insect,—the cricket. But I
do not see why they should be thus identified.
Sze-chung is the same as *chung-sze* in i. V. The
so-ke appears to be, likewise, a kind of locust,
called 紡績娘, 'the spinner,' from the
sound which it makes with its wings. Ll. 3—5
may be assigned to the cricket. 宇,—'the sides
of a roof,' 'the eaves.' L. 8. Maou explains
穹 by 竆, 'entirely,' 'thoroughly.' I prefer
Choo's account of the term, as meaning 'chinks.'
窒—塞, 'to shut, or stuff, up.' L. 9. 向 is
to be understood of windows, or openings in the

六月食鬱及薁。
七月亨葵及菽。
八月剝棗。十月
穫稻。爲此春酒。
以介眉壽。七月
食瓜。八月斷壺。
九月叔苴。采荼
薪樗。食我農夫
九月築場圃。十
月納禾稼。黍稷

6 In the sixth month they eat the sparrow-plums and grapes;
In the seventh, they cook the k'wei and pulse;
In the eighth, they knock down the dates;
In the tenth, they reap the rice,
And make the spirits for the spring,
For the benefit of the bushy eyebrows.
In the seventh month, they eat the melons;
In the eighth, they cut down the bottle-gourds;
In the ninth, they gather the hemp-seed;
They gather the sowthistle and make firewood of the Fetid tree;
To feed our husbandmen.

7 In the ninth month, they prepare the vegetable gardens for their stacks,
And in the tenth they convey the sheaves to them;

wall, looking towards the north. 墐=塗, 'to plaster.' The doors of the houses of the people were made of wicker-work. In l. 10, 日 is not the verb 'to say,' but the particle; 爲 is that now in the 3d tone,—'because of.' The measures just detailed were all taken, because of the extreme cold which was at hand. Stress is not to be laid on the use of the terms 改歲, as if there were an indication in the employment of them after the 10th month, that the people did not use among themselves the calendar of Hëa.

St. 6. *Various articles of food; the richer for the old, and the others for the husbandmen.* L. 1. The 鬱 is a kind of plum. The tree grows to the height of 5 or 6 cubits, and produces a large red fruit. One of its names is 雀李, which I have adopted. The 薁 is called also 蘡薁; and must be a sort of vine. Williams calls it 'a wild grape, or a plant like it.' 'The fruit,' it is said, 'is like a grape, small and round, with a sour taste, and purplish.' L. 2. Choo simply says that 葵 is the name of a vegetable. One

name of it is *chung kwei*, which Medhurst says is alsine, or pimpernel; but the name *k'wei*, with various adjuncts, is given to a multitude of plants. L. 3. 剝=擊, 'to strike,' 'knock down.' LL. 4—6. The spirits distilled from the rice cut down in the 10th month would be ready for use in the spring. But in those days the use of spirits was restricted to the aged, who need their exhilaration. L. 6 is literally, 'to help the longevity of the eyebrows;' Maou explains 眉壽 by 豪眉, 'bristly eyebrows.' L. 7. 瓜 is the general name for gourds melons, &c. L. 8. 壺,—i.q. 瓠. L. 9. 叔=拾, 'to gather.' 苴=麻子, 'hemp-seed.' L. 10. 荼,—as in iii. X. 2. The 樗 is like the varnish tree 'with fetid leaves. It is good for nothing but to be used as fuel. It is commonly called 'the fetid tree (臭樹).' Another name is 'imps' eyes (鬼目).'

St. 7. *Harvesting; and repairs of houses, to be ready for the work of the spring.* L. 1. 築場圃—築場於圃, 'They form the areas

重穋。禾麻菽麥。嗟
我農夫。我稼既同。
土八執宮功。晝爾
于茅。宵爾索綯。亟爾
其乘屋。其始播百
穀。二之日鑿冰沖沖。
三之日納于凌陰。
四之日其蚤。獻羔
祭韭。九月肅霜十

The millets, both the early sown and the late,
With other grain, the hemp, the pulse, and the wheat.
'O my husbandmen,
Our harvest is all collected.
Let us go to the town, and be at work on our houses.
In the day time collect the grass,
And at night twist it into ropes;
Then get up quickly on our roofs:—
We shall have to recommence our sowing.'

8   In the days of [our] second month, they hew out the ice with
      harmonious blows;
      And in those of [our] third month, they convey it to the ice-
      houses,
      [Which they open] in those of the fourth, early in the morning,
      Having offered in sacrifice a lamb with scallions.
      In the ninth month, it is cold, with frost;

for stacks in the kitchen gardens.' Williams translates the words incorrectly, 'to form a kitchen garden.' Ground was valuable. In the early part of the year, this space was cultivated for the growth of vegetables. When the harvest of the fields was ready, they beat the same space into a hard area, to place in it the produce of the fields. L. 2. Choo says that 禾 denotes the grain and the stalk together; and 稼 the same as being in the fields. L. 3. 重 denotes what is first sown, and ripens last; 穋, the opposite of this. L. 4. 禾 is a general name for rice and all the grains mentioned. L. 6. 同=聚, 'to be collected. L. 7. 宮 denotes the houses of the people in their towns or villages where they lived in the end of autumn and in winter, when their labours in the field were completed. These were to them, compared with their huts in the fields, as the capital

to the other towns in a State; hence the use of 上, 'to go up to.' Some, however, take 宮 of the palace and other public buildings of the State; but this is very unnatural. L. 8. 于, —as in st. 1. 茅,—as in ii. XII. L. 9. 綯— 絞, 'to twist.' 綯=索, 'ropes.' L. 10. 乘 —升, 'to get upon.'

St. 8. *Preparation of ice against the summer heat; the harvest feast.* L. 1. The ice was dug out of deep recesses in the hills. 沖沖— 和, 'harmoniously,' or 'with harmonious blows.' L. 2. 凌陰=冰室, 'an ice-house,' LL.3,4, This sacrifice was in connection with the opening of the ice houses, and henceforward ice could be taken from them as it was required. It was offered to 'the Ruler of the cold (司寒).'

月滌場。朋酒斯饗。曰殺羔羊。躋彼公堂。稱彼兕觥。萬壽無疆。

In the tenth month, they sweep clean their stack-sites.
The two bottles of spirits are enjoyed,
And they say, 'Let us kill our lambs and sheep,
And go to the hall of our prince,
There raise the cup of rhinoceros horn,
And wish him long life,—that he may live for ever.'

II. *Ch'e-hëaou.*

鴟鴞

一章

鴟鴞。鴟鴞。既取我子。無毀我室。恩斯勤斯。鬻子

1 O owl, O owl,
You have taken my young ones;—
Do not [also] destroy my nest.
With love and with toil
I nourished them.—I am to be pitied.

The collecting and depositing of ice, and the solemn opening of the ice-house, as here described, was appropriate, I suppose, only to great Families; but there would be something analogous to it in the customs of the people also.

The remaining lines belong to the customs of the people, and show the sympathy there was between them and their rulers. L. 6. This cleansing of the farm-yards was after the harvest had all been brought into them. L. 7. 朋,—'two bottles of spirits' were so denominated. L. 8. The lambs and sheep would be an offering, I suppose, to the ruler. L. 9. 躋—升, 'to ascend to.' L. 10. 稱—舉, 'to raise up.' The last lines give the words in which they would drink their ruler's health.

[While I have accepted the ordinary view of this ode, as descriptive of the ways of Pin in the olden time, and explained it accordingly, I must state my own disbelief that the tribe in Pin had attained to anything like the civilization here described, in the time of Kung-lëw, or for centuries after.]

The rhymes are—in st. 1, 火., 衣, cat. 15, t. 2 (but 衣 is more commonly t. 1); 發, 烈, 褐, 歲, cat. 15, t. 3; 耜, 趾, 子, 畝., 喜, cat. 1, t. 2: in 2, 火., 衣; 陽, 庚., 筐, 行., 桑, cat. 10; 遲, 祁, 悲, 歸, cat 15, t. 1: in 3, 火., 葦, cat. 15, t. 2; 桑, 斨, 揚, 桑, 黃, 陽, 裳, cat. 10; 鵙, 績, cat. 16, t. 3: in 4, 葽, 蜩, cat. 2, but 蜩 prop. belongs to cat. 3, acc. to the analogy of 周; 穫, 蘀, 貉, cat. 5, t. 3; 貍, 裘., cat. 1, t. 1; 同, 功, 豵, 公, cat. 9: in 5, 股, 羽, 野., 宇, 戶, 下., 鼠, 戶, 處, cat. 5, t. 2: in 6, 薁, 菽, cat. 3, t. 3; 棗., 稻., 酒, 壽, cat. 3, t. 2; 瓜., 壺, 苴, 樗, 夫, cat. 5, t. 1: in 7, 圃, 稼., cat. 5, t. 2; 穋 (prop. cat. 3), 麥., cat. 1, t. 3; 同, 功, cat. 9; 茅., 綯., cat. 3, t. 1; 屋, 穀, cat. 3, t. 3: in 8, 沖, 陰 (prop. cat. 7), cat. 9; 蚤., 韭, cat. 3, t. 2; 霜, 場, 饗, 羊, 堂, 觥., 疆, cat. 10.

Ode 2. Metaphorical. THE DUKE OF CHOW, IN THE CHARACTER OF A BIRD, WHOSE YOUNG ONES HAVE BEEN DESTROYED BY AN OWL, VINDICATES THE DECISIVE COURSE HE HAD TAKEN WITH REBELLION. We have an account of the composition of this piece in the Shoo, V. vi. 15.

之鴟斯。

迨天之未陰雨。

徹彼桑土綢繆

牖戶今女下民。

或敢侮予

予手拮据

將荼予所蓄租

予口卒瘏曰予

未有室家。

2　Before the sky was dark with rain,
　I gathered the roots of the mulberry tree,
　And bound round and round my window and door.
　Now ye people below,
　Dare any of you despise my house?

3　With my claws I tore and held,
　Through the rushes which I gathered,
　And all the materials I collected,
　My mouth was all sore;—
　I said to myself, 'I have not yet got my house complete.'

Two of his brothers, who had been associated with the son of the dethroned king of Shang in the charge of the territory which had been left to him by king Woo, joined him in rebellion, having first spread a rumour impeaching the fidelity of the duke to his nephew, the young king Ching. He took the field against them, put to death Woo-kăng and one of his own brothers, dealing also with the other according to the measure of his guilt. It is supposed that some suspicions of him still remained in the mind of the king, and he therefore made this ode to show how he had loved his brothers, notwithstanding he had punished them, and that his conduct was in consequence of his solicitude for the consolidation of the dynasty of his family.

St. 1. _Ch'e-heaou_,—see on xii. VI. 3. It is generally supposed that by the owl Woo-kăng was intended. I should refer it rather to rebellion generally. The 子, 'young ones' is referred to the duke's brothers. 'My house,' the bird's nest, denotes the infant dynasty of Chow, the fortunes of his family, and involving the welfare of king Ching himself. The last two lines are difficult and perplexing, though Choo's view of them, which I have followed, is preferable to any other. The 斯, as pointed out by Wang Yin-che, is merely a final particle. 恩斯 鬻斯, both qualify 鬻子,—as in the translation. Of the 之 I can make nothing, and can only regard it as a meaningless particle,

introduced for the sake of euphony. 鴟斯 tells how the duke was to be pitied in the circumstances. This exegesis is harsh; but, as I said, it is the best which any critic has devised.

St. 2 indicates how the duke of Chow had laid the foundations of their dynasty. 迨=及, 'while.' Followed by 未, the two characters =our 'before.' 陰雨,—as in xiv. IV. 4. 徹=取, 'to take away,' 'to gather.' 土 is here=根, 'roots.' Han Ying gives here 杜 for 土; and hence the meaning assigned to the term. 綢繆,—as in x. V. L. 4 is interrogative, and 或 which gives to it that force may further be translated by 'any.' See Confucius' eulogium of this stanza in Mencius, II. Pt. i. IV. 3.

St. 3 is to the same effect as the preceding. Choo, after the Shwoh-wăn and Han Ying, says that 拮据 denotes 'the app. of hands and mouth working together.' But in that case they would not appear as a predicate of 手 alone. They describe the intense action of the bird's legs and claws in gathering the materials of its nest. 將=取, 'to take.' 荼 is here the same as that in vii. XIX. 2. 蓄,—'to accumulate.' 租 —'to collect.' 卒=盡, 'all,' 'entirely.'

曉。維漂風室儵譙。子^四
音搖。雨翹翛子羽譙
曉子所翹。子尾譙

4 My wings are all-injured;
　My tail is all-broken;
　My house is in a perilous condition;
　It is tossed about in the wind and rain:—
　I can but cry out with this note of alarm.

III. *Tung shan.*

制心曰濛。零來不山。我^一東
彼西歸。我雨自歸。慆徂山
裳悲。我東其東。我慆東

1 We went to the hills of the east,
　And long were we there without returning,
　When we came from the east,
　Down came the rain drizzlingly.
　When we were in the east, and it was said we should return,
　Our hearts were in the west and sad;
　But there were they preparing our clothes for us,

渚,—as in l. III. 4. 曰 may be taken as I have done. The 5th line gives the reason of all the laborious toil in the preceding ones.

St. 4 gives the reason of the vehement feeling in the ode. 譙譙 describes the appearance of the wings, frayed and injured. Maou and Choo explain it by 殺, 'to clip,' 'to pare.' 翛 翛=做, 'broken,' 'worn' (Medhurst has strangely erred in his account of this character). 翹 翹=危, 'perilous.' 漂搖=動, 'to move,' 'to shake.' 嘵嘵 is intended to indicate a note or cry of alarm.

The rhymes are—in st. 1, 子 (prop. cat. 1), 室, cat. 12, t. 3; 斯 斯, cat. 16, t. 1: in 2, 雨 土, 戶, 予, cat. 5, t 2: in 8, 摧 茶 租 渚, 家, cat. 5, t. 1: in 4, 譙 (prop. cat. 8), 翛 翹 搖 嘵, cat. 2.

Ode 3. Narrative. THE DUKE OF CHOW TELLS OF THE TOILS OF HIS SOLDIERS IN THE EXPEDITION TO THE EAST AND ON THEIR RETURN, OF THEIR APPREHENSIONS, AND THEIR JOY AT THE LAST. The piece nowhere says that it was made by the duke of Chow; but I agree with Choo and the critics generally, who assign to him the composition of it as a sort of compliment to his men.

Ll.1—4, in all the stt. The expedition here referred to was that mentioned in the notes on the last ode,—undertaken by the duke of Chow against the son of the last king of Shang, and his own rebellious brothers. The seat of the rebellion was mainly in the north-eastern parts of the present Ho-nan, lying of course east from the capital of Chow: hence the expedition is spoken of as 'towards the hills of the east.' 徂.—as in v. IV. 4. 慆慆.—'for a long time.' 零=落, 'to fall.' The Shwoh-wǎn defines 濛 by 微雨, 'small rain;' 其濛.—'drizzlingly.'

在伊之零不我在野蜎衣。
尸。威實雨歸祖車敦者勿
町在亦其我東下。彼蠋。士
畽室。施濛。來山。獨烝行
睡蟏于果自慆宿。在枚。
鹿蛸宇。臝東慆亦桑蜎
場。蛸　　　　　　　

As to serve no more in the ranks with the gags.
Creeping about were the caterpillars,
All over the mulberry grounds;
And quietly and solitarily did we pass the night,
Under our carriages.

2　We went to the hills of the east,
　And long were we there without returning.
　When we came back from the east,
　Down came the rain drizzlingly.
　The fruit of the heavenly gourd
　Would be hanging about our eaves;
　The sowbug would be in our chambers;
　The spiders' webs would be in our doors;
　Our paddocks would be deer-fields;

St. 1. Ll. 5—12. I take the 日 in l. 5 of what was said about the soldiers—of the orders for their return to the west. Ll. 7—12 are descriptive of the preparations being made by the wives and families of the soldiers to receive them on their return, and of their thoughts about them during their march. For this I am indebted to Këang Ping-chang (此制裳衣是室家初聞捷音，喜而預待), and it is much preferable to the usual construction which assigns them to the soldiers themselves. All critics take 裳衣 of the unmilitary, ordinary dress; why should the soldiers set about making this for themselves, when they were commencing their march? Choo says he does not understand l. 8; but he adopts the view of it given by Ch'ing, that 士一事, 'to do service;' 行一行陣, 'ranks;' and 枚 = 'gags.' 勿 is appropriate as the thought of their no more doing such service, in the minds of their families. 蜎蜎 = 動貌, 'the app. of creeping.' 蠋 is the name of a cater-

pillar like the silkworm, 'as large as a finger,' found on the mulberry trees. 烝 is to be taken as simply an initial particle; as is 亦 in l. 12. 敦 (tuy) is descriptive of the soldiers as 'lodging alone,' and 獨, of their 'solitariness,' away from their families. The sight of the caterpillars on the mulberry trees made their wives think of them thus under their carriages.

St. 2, 5—12. These lines describe the thoughts of the men on their journey home,—the foolish fancies which crowded into their minds. Medhurst calls the kwo-lo the papaya; but this is a creeper, not a tree. Another name for it is 栝樓. It is also called 天瓜,—as in the translation. The leaves come out, two and two, opposite to each other. A flour, beautifully white, is made from the root, and much used in medicine. The plant grows wild, and here the men see it encroaching on their houses In the Japanese plates it is the musk-melon. 施,—as in i. 11. 亦 is the initial particle. 伊威 (or with 虫 at the side of the characters) is the large sow-bug, or oniscus.

我^{四章}
祖
東
山。
慆
慆
不

不
見。
于
今
三
年。

苦。
烝
在
栗
薪。
自
我

我
征
聿
至。
有
敦
瓜

嘆
于
室。
洒
埽
穹
窒。

其
濛。
鶴
鳴
于
垤。

歸。
我^三
來
自
東。
零
雨。
婦

也。
伊
可
懷
也。

熠
燿
宵
行。
不
可
畏

The fitful light of the glow-worms would be all about.
These thoughts made us apprehensive,
And they occupied our breasts.

3   We went to the hills of the east,
    And long were we there without returning.
    On our way back from the east,
    Down came the rain drizzlingly.
    The cranes were crying on the ant-hills;
    Our wives were sighing in their rooms;
    They had sprinkled and swept, and stuffed up all the crevices.
    Suddenly we arrived from the expedition,
    And there were the bitter gourds hanging
    From the branches of the chestnut trees.
    Since we had seen such a sight,
    Three years were now elapsed.

4   We went to the hills of the east,
    And long were we there without returning.

The *ssaou-shaou* is a small spider. Maou wrongly explains *t'ing-t'wn* by 鹿迹 'deers' foot-prints.' The phrase means the vacant ground about the peasants' hamlets. The men fancy that through their absence the deer must have encroached upon it. Maou takes 熠燿 as the name of the fire-fly (螢火); but the error was pointed out by Ying-tah. These two characters denote 'the appearance of a bright but fitful light.' The name of the insect is 宵行, 'a glow-worm.' The 11th line is to be construed interrogatively, so that it is really affirmative. 伊=惟, 'only,' or 'but.'

St. 3 describes the experiences and feelings of the men immediately on their return, so different from the apprehensions they had felt. Ll. 5

—12. 鶴 is the white crane. 垤 is an anthill. When it is about to rain, the ants show themselves. The crane has in the meantime taken its place on their hill or mound, screaming with joy in anticipation of its feast. This 5th line serves to introduce the 6th and 7th. 穹窒, —see on I. 5. 聿=忽, 'suddenly.'—'we who had been on the expedition, suddenly arrive.' 瓜苦=苦瓜;—the characters are reversed for the sake of the rhyme. 敦,—as in st. 1, 'the app. of the gourds, hanging one by one, on the trees.' 烝,—also as in st. 1. 薪 —as in iii. VII. 2.

St. 4, ll. 5—12. These lines should be translated in the pres. tense. The men are now at home, and in their own joy at reunion with their

歸。我來自東。
零雨其濛。倉
庚于飛。熠耀
其羽。之子于
歸。皇駁其馬。
親結其縭。九
十其儀。其新
孔嘉。其舊如
之何。

On our way back from the east,
Down came the rain drizzlingly.
The oriole is flying about,
Now here, now there, are its wings.
Those young ladies are going to be married,
With their bay and red horses, flecked with white.
Their mothers have tied their sashes;
Complete are their equipments.
The new matches are admirable;—
How can the reunions of the old be expressed?

IV. *P'o foo.*

破斧
既破
我斧。
又缺
我斯。
周公
東征。
四國
是皇。
哀我

1 We broke our axes,
   And we splintered our hatchets;
   But the object of the duke of Chow, in marching to the east,
   Was to put the four States to rights.

families, sympathize with all of a joyful nature around them. 倉庚,—as in l. 2. 于 is the particle. 熠耀,—as in st. 2. L. 7 may be construed in the plural. 皇—'yellow, with white spots;' 駁—'red, with white spots.' 親 here —母, 'mother.' Williams' account of 縭 is— 'an ornamented girdle put on a bride by her mother.' 儀 denotes here the equipments, all the things sent with the brides. They are said to be 九十, 'nine or ten,' to indicate how numerous they were. Great as was the joy of the new couples, it was not equal to that of the husbands and wives, now reunited after so long a separation.

The rhymes are—in all the stt. 東濛, cat. 9: in st. 1, 歸歸悲衣枚, cat. 15, t. 1; 蜎宿, cat. 3, t. 3; 野。下。, cat. 5, t. 2: in 2, 宇戶, *ib.*; 罶寶, cat. 12, t. 3; 場行。, cat. 10; 畏懷, cat. 15, t. 1: in 3, 垤室窒至。, cat. 12, t. 3; 薪年, cat. 12, t. 1: in 4, 飛歸, cat. 15, t. 1; 羽馬。, cat. 5, t. 2; 縭儀。嘉何, cat. 17.

Ode 4. Narrative. RESPONSIVE TO THE LAST ODE.—HIS SOLDIERS PRAISE THE DUKE OF CHOW FOR HIS MAGNANIMITY AND SYMPATHY WITH THE PEOPLE. With both the old and the new school the praise of the duke of Chow is the subject of

人斯。亦孔之將。

既 二章 破我斧。又缺我

錡。周公東征。四國

是吪。哀我人斯。亦

孔之嘉。

既 三章 破我斧。又缺我

錸。周公東征。四國

是遒。哀我人斯。亦

孔之休。

His compassion for us people
Is very great.

2　We broke our axes,
And splintered our chisels;
But the object of the duke of Chow, in marching to the east,
Was to reform the four States.
His compassion for us people
Is very admirable.

3　We broke our axes;
And splintered our clubs.
But the object of the duke of Chow, in marching to the east,
Was to save the alliance of the four States.
His compassion for us people
Is very excellent.

this piece. The Preface, however, refers its composition to some great officer; Choo, much better, to the soldiers of the duke.

Ll. 1, 2, in all the stt. 破 and 缺 are evidently synonymous. The latter term properly denotes 'a cracked or broken vessel.' I take it here as meaning 'to splinter.' 斧 and 斯,—see on I.

3. Both Choo and Maou take 錡 here as 'a sort of chisel.' Han Ying made it some wooden instrument. The last thought that 錸 was 'a kind of chisel,' whereas the other two critics say it was a club (木屬). Yen Ts'an is struck with the specification of such implements instead of the ordinary weapons of war; and infers from it that the duke of Chow had accomplished the object of his expedition without any fighting.

Ll. 3-6. 四國 does not here, as sometimes, denote all the States of the four quarters, but what had been the royal domain of Shang,

and which had been assigned in four portions to Woo-kāng, and three of the duke of Chow's brothers. It was there where the rebellion had been. See the Shoo, V. xiv. 21, and xviii. 2. 皇 is taken as—匡 'to rectify;'—such, moreover was the reading in the Ts'e recension of the poems. 吪—化, 'to reform' or rather 'to transform.' 遒 is 'to collect and make firm,' 'to consolidate.' L. 5. The duke's compassion for the people was seen in the object he had in view in his operations against the rebellious States, and the way in which he reduced them to order with little effusion of blood. In l. 6, 亦 is the initial particle, and 之 is a mere expletive. 將,—'great.' 休—美, 'excellent.'

The rhymes are—in st. 2, 斯, 皇, 將, cat. 10: in 2, 錡, 吪, 嘉, cat. 17: in 3, 錸, 遒, 休, cat. 3, t. 1.

V. *Fah ko.*

伐柯

伐柯如何_{一章}
匪斧不克。

取妻如何。
匪媒不得。

伐柯伐柯_{二章}
其則不遠。

我覯之子。
籩豆有踐。

1 In hewing [the wood for] an axe-handle, how do you proceed?
Without [another] axe it cannot be done.
In taking a wife, how do you proceed?
Without a go-between it cannot be done.

2 In hewing an axe-handle, in hewing an axe-handle,
The pattern is not far off.
I see the lady,
And forthwith the vessels are arranged in rows.

Ode 5. Metaphorical. IN PRAISE OF THE DUKE OF CHOW. So say the old critics and the new, and I say with them, hardly knowing why, but having nothing better to say. On the different interpretations of the piece, see at the end of the notes.

St. 1. Comp. viii. VI. 4. 柯=斧柄 'the handle of an axe.' It is interesting to find the go-between existing as an institution in those early times. Such an agent was thought to be necessary, and helpful to the modesty of both the families interested in the proposed marriage. Originally, the go-between was an arranger of marriages only; now he or she is often a purveyor of them.

St. 2. 則=法, 'pattern.' 'The pattern is not far off;' i.e., the handle in the hand is the model of that which is to be made. I cannot do other than understand 之子 of the lady, with whom the marriage has been arranged. The last two lines of this stanza must surely be connected with the last two of the preceding. Choo, with his correct, critical discrimination, thus understands the characters. Maou and his school refer them to the duke of Chow. The *pow* were vessels of bamboo, and the *tow* vessels of wood, of the same size, lackered within, and with stands rather more than a foot high. They were used at feasts and sacrifices, to contain fruits, dried meat, vegetables, sauces, &c. 踐 denotes 'the app. of rows,'—the way in which those vessels were arranged. The meaning seems to be that when the go-between had done his work, all subsequent arrangements were easy, and the marriage-feast might forthwith be celebrated.

THE INTERPRETATION. The Preface says that the piece is in praise of the duke of Chow, and was made by some great officer to condemn the court for not acknowledging the worth of the great statesman. 'There is a way,' says one of the great Ch'ings, 'to hew an axe-handle, and a way to get a wife; and so, if the duke of Chow was to be brought back to court, there was a way to do it.' Is not this mere trifling with the text? Then the second stanza is interpreted.—'The axe in the hand is the pattern of that which is to be made. If you would bring the duke home, you have only to arrange a feast, and receive him with the distinction which is his due.' This is trifling, and moreover, as I have observed in the notes, 之子 cannot be referred to the duke of Chow. Choo He, seeing that the old interpretation was untenable, assigned the piece to the people of the east, whose feelings towards the duke it expresses. St. 1, acc. to him, intimates how they had longed to see the hero, and their difficulty to get a sight of him; st. 2, how delighted they were, when they could now see him with ease. But neither can I get for myself this meaning out of the lines.

A most important principle is derived by Confucius from the first two lines of st. 2 in the 'Doctrine of the Mean,' xiii. 2,—that the rule for man's way of life is in himself. There is, probably, no reference at all to the duke of Chow in the ode. May not its meaning be that *while there is a necessary and proper way for every thing, men need not go far to find out what it is?*

The rhymes are—in st. 1, 何, 何, cat. 17; 克, 得, cat. 1, t. 3: in 2, 遠, 踐, cat. 15.

VI. *Këw yih.*

九罭之魚。鱒魴。
我覯之子。衮衣繡裳。
鴻飛遵渚。公歸無所。於女信處。
鴻飛遵陸。公歸不復。於女信宿。

1 In the net with its nine bags
  Are rud and bream.
  We see this prince
  With his grand-ducal robe and embroidered skirt.

2 The wild geese fly [only] about the ialets.
  The duke is returning;—is it not to his proper place?
  He was stopping with you [and me] but for a couple of nights.

3 The wild geese fly about the land.
  The duke is returning, and will not come back here?
  He was lodging with you [and me] but for a couple of nights.

Ode 6. Allusive and narrative. THE PEOPLE OF THE EAST EXPRESS THEIR ADMIRATION OF THE DUKE OF CHOW, AND SORROW AT HIS RETURNING TO THE WEST. On better grounds than in the case of the last ode, Choo He assigns this to the people of the east, sorry that the duke of Chow was now being recalled to court. The Preface on the other hand gives the same argument of this ode as of the other, and assigns it to some officer of Chow, who wished to expose the error of the court in not acknowledging the merits of the great man. The K'ang-he editors seem to think that other differences of view are unimportant, while there is an agreement in finding in the piece the praise of the duke of Chow.

St. 1. The Shwoh-wǎn explains *yih* as meaning 'a fish-net;' but the Urh-ya gives that definition for *këw yih* together. The net in question was, no doubt, composed somehow of nine bags or compartments. Medhurst says that 鱒 is the roach; Williams says, 'a fish like the roach.' It has 'red eyes,' and must be the rud or red-eye (*leuciscus erythrophthalmus*). Both this and the bream are good fish; and the writer therefore passes on from them to speak of the duke of Chow. The other stanzas make it plain that he is the 之子 of l. 3. 衮衣 is explained in the dict. as 天子服, 'the dress of the Son of Heaven.' But a 'high duke,' one of the three *kung* of the Chow dyn. (Shoo, V. xx. 5), had also the right to wear it, with a small difference in the blazonry of the upper robe. The emblematic figures of rank (Shoo, II. iv. 4) were all depicted on the robes of both, but whereas on the royal robe there were two dragons 'one ascending and one descending,' on that of a grand-duke there was only the descending dragon. The same four figures were embroidered on the skirts of both. It was only the 'high,' or grand duke, whose dress approximated so nearly to that of the king.

St. 2. 鴻—as in iii. XVIII. 3. 渚,—as in ii. XI. 2. The 2d line is understood interrogatively.—公歸登無所乎。 The connection between the first line and this seems to be:—'The geese come here among the islands, but it is only for a time. We know they will soon leave us. We should have known, that the duke was only temporarily among us.' 信,—'to rest two nights in the same place is called *sin*.' The 於女, 'among you,' is a difficulty in the way of Choo's view, that the piece should be assigned to the people of the east. He meets it by saying that the people of the east in speaking to each other would naturally say 'you;' so that 'among you' is really equivalent to 'among us.'

St. 3. 陸 is often used of the land in distinction from the water. Here the speaker has reference, probably, to the departure of the geese for the dry, northern regions; yet it might have occurred to him that they would be back among the islands in the next season. 宿 is here—the 處 in st. 2.

是以有衰衣兮。無以我公歸兮。無使我心悲兮。 （四章）

4 Thus have we had the grand-ducal robe among us.
Do not take our duke back [to the west];
Do not cause us such sorrow of heart.

VII. *Lang poh.*

狼跋
狼跋其胡。載疐其尾。公孫碩膚。赤烏几几。
狼疐其尾。載跋其胡。公孫碩膚。德音不瑕。

1 The wolf springs forward on his dewlap,
Or trips back on his tail.
The duke was humble, and greatly admirable,
Self-composed in his red slippers.

2 The wolf springs forward on his dewlap,
Or trips back on his tail.
The duke was humble, and greatly admirable;
There is no flaw in his virtuous fame.

St. 4 is all narrative, and must be taken as an address to the people of the west, complaining of the recall of the duke to the court. 無—毋, imperative.

The rhymes are—in st. 1, 衮, 裳, cat. 10: in 2, 渚, 所, 處, cat. 5, t. 2: in 3, 陸, 復, 宿, cat. 3, t. 3: in 4, 衣, 歸, 悲, cat. 15, t. 1.

Ode 7. Allusive. THE PRAISE OF THE DUKE OF CHOW, THE MORE DISTINGUISHED THROUGH HIS TRIALS. Choo again assigns this piece to the people of the east, while the Preface and Maou's school assign it, like the two odes that precede, to some officer of Chow. In other points they agree.

Both stanzas. The wolf in the text is supposed to be an old wolf, in which the dewlap (胡) and tail have grown to a very large size. He is further supposed to be taken in a pit, and to be making frantic efforts to escape,—all in vain, for his own dewlap and tail are in his way. The duke of Chow, under suspicion of disloyalty, and because of his dealing with his brothers. might have been expected to fret and rage; but his mind was too good and great to admit such passions into it. 跋 —蹇, 'to jump,' 'to spring forward.' 疐— 'to be hindered,'—跲, 'to trip or stumble.' 載—則. It is here equivalent to our 'or.' 孫—遜 or 讓, 'complaisant,' 'yielding;' with reference to the meekness with which the duke bore his trials. 膚—美, 'admirable.' The 'red slippers' were worn both by the king and the princes of States. 几几 denotes 'the app. of quiet composure.' Wang Gan-shih observes, '几 is used by men to lean and rest themselves on; hence 几几 means *quiet*.' 德音—as in vii. IX. 2, et al. 瑕—疵病, 'a blemish,' 'a flaw.'—It is astonishing with what lengthened eloquence the critics dilate here on the marvellous virtues of the duke of Chow

The rhymes are—in st. 1, 胡, 膚, cat. 5, t. 1; 尾, 几, cat. 15, t. 2: in 2, 胡, 膚, 瑕, cat. 5, t. 1.

CONCLUDING NOTE UPON THE BOOK. The last three of the pieces are of a trifling character;

but the 1st and 3d, as they are longer than the other odes in this 1st part of the She, so they are of a superior character. The 1st, could we give entire credit to it, would be a valuable record of the manners of an early time, with touches of real poetry interspersed; and the 3d has also much poetical merit. Various speculations, into which we need not enter, have been indulged as to the place given to the odes of Pin at the very end of these Lessons from the States.

With regard to the order of the odes themselves, there is also a difference of opinion; and I transfer here what Këang Ping-chang has said upon it, especially as it illustrates what the critics have to say about the 'deep plans' of Confucius in the arrangement of the Books and of the odes:— ' Heu K'ëen, in his scheme of the order of the pieces in the odes of Pin (豳風

大序圖), places the Fah ko, the Lang poh, the Ch'e-heaou and the Kew yih immediately after the Ts'ih yueh, and makes the Tung shan and the P'o foo the last odes; but I venture to think that he thus misses the idea of the Master in arranging the odes as he did. The Ts'ih yueh, the Ch'e-heaou, and the Tung shan, were all made by the duke of Chow himself. They are placed first; and all the particulars of the rumours against the duke, his residence in the east, his return to the capital, and his expedition to the east, become quite plain. The P'o foo, and the three odes that follow, were all made by others in the duke's praise. The P'o foo fol-

lows the Tung shan, because they are on kindred themes. The other three pieces were all made by the people of the east, and we are not to think that the Master had no meaning in placing the Lang poh last. The duke's assumption of the regency looked too great a stretch of power; his vesting such authority as he did in his two brothers seemed like a want of wisdom; his residing in the east seemed to betoken a fear of misfortune; the Ch'e-heaou seemed to express resentment; his expedition to the east seemed to show impetuous anger; and his putting Kwang-shuh to death seemed to indicate cruelty:—all these things might be said to be blemishes in his character. The master, therefore, puts forth that line,—

" There is no flaw in his virtuous fame,"

as comprising the substance of the odes of Pin, and to show that the duke of Chow was what he thus was through the union in him of heavenly principle, and human feelings, without the least admixture of selfishness. His purity in his own day was like the brightness of the sun or moon, and it was not to be permitted that any traitorous and perverse people in subsequent times should be able to fill their mouths with his example. Thus though the author of the Lang poh had no thought of mirroring in it the duke's whole career, yet the Master, in his arrangement of the odes, comprehended the whole life of the great sage.'

Made in the USA
Las Vegas, NV
20 January 2024

84665023R00260